Drafting Trusts and Will Trusts in Northern Ireland

Drafting Trusts and Will Trusts in Northern Ireland

James Kessler QC

Barrister, of Lincoln's Inn, and of the Bar of Northern Ireland

Sheena Grattan

Senior Lecturer, School of Law, Queen's University of Belfast
Barrister, Northern Ireland

Print on Demand Edition

Tottel
publishing

Published by
Tottel Publishing Ltd
Maxwelton House
41-43 Boltro Road
Haywards Heath
West Sussex
RH16 1BJ

Tottel Publishing Ltd
Fitzwarren Business Centre
26 Upper Pembroke Street
Dublin 2
Ireland

ISBN 13: 978-1-84592-391-4
ISBN 10: 1-84592-391-X

Formerly published by LexisNexis Butterworths

Reprinted by Tottel Publishing Ltd 2007

British Library Cataloguing-in-Publication Data
A catalogue record for this book is available from the British Library

Printed and bound in Great Britain by
CPI Antony Rowe Limited, Chippenham, Wiltshire

Preface

Trust drafting is a professional skill. Trust drafting needs trust law, succession law, a considerable amount of tax law (and time and energy to keep up to date); some property law; and a dash of insolvency and family law. That is not all. Many laymen's wishes are unformulated beyond a general desire to put their affairs in order; conversely, some clients have firm ideas as to the disposition of their property which are far from suited to their circumstances. To deal with this calls for empathy and an ability to communicate.

The aim of this work is to aid the drafter by discussing all the issues which arise in drafting settlements and will trusts, and to provide precedents.

The precedents are accompanied with an explanation of why the text is there and the choices that have to be made. The explanation is of the essence; the adoption of a precedent without understanding it fully is a recipe for trouble. The precedents in this book adopt a drafting style which reads simply and naturally.

We also discuss many standard forms and questions which the reader of settlements in common use will often meet. This book will also serve as a guide to the interpretation of trust documentation. Obfuscatory formulae, which spring so lightly from the pen of the experienced practitioner, will baffle the less experienced. Here is some guidance for those who wish to understand their origin, meaning and effect, if any.

Although this book contains many precedents, we hope to persuade the reader to regard standard drafts with an independent eye; as a suggestion and not a solution. The solicitor does not serve his client well if he produces to him for execution any standard draft without consideration of individual circumstances.

It is unusual for a single work to discuss both settlements and will trusts. These topics are usually considered in isolation. More care is normally lavished on lifetime settlements than will trusts; this can be measured by the prolixity of a typical settlement, and the brevity of a typical will. But there are few differences of principle between them. If the will drafter took as much care as the trust drafter, then wills (if longer) would be better documents, and beneficiaries better provided for.

This is a practical book but it tries to address the hard questions which do arise in practice. Topics of trust and tax law are discussed so far as they impinge upon trust drafting. General questions of tax and tax planning are not developed here; the topic of drafting requires a book to itself. Drafting suffers if it is regarded as a mere afterthought to the more serious matter of tax planning. But some of the questions which arise are so interesting that this policy is adopted with regret, with the occasional lapse, and only by the exercise of considerable restraint.

Artificial tax avoidance schemes are beyond the scope of this book. When such arrangements are possible, this has sometimes been indicated. In such cases it would be necessary in any event to obtain specialist advice.

The Northern Ireland trust practitioner has traditionally had little option but to adapt precedents found in English texts. We hope that this book will remedy that unfortunate state of affairs. It is essentially the sixth edition of James Kessler's *Drafting Trusts and Wills Trusts* adapted in its entirety to take account of Northern Ireland law (although the opportunity has been taken where appropriate to include revisions which will appear in the next edition of the English version). The most important differences between the two jurisdictions relate to the accumulation period (permitting much greater brevity and simplicity in Northern Ireland) and the treatment of trusts of land (where the law in Northern Ireland is long overdue reform) but there are many other differences which can be significant in practice.

At the time of going to press the Northern Ireland version of the STEP Standard Provisions, which is reproduced in Appendix 1, is still only in draft form. Notification of the final approved form will be posted on James Kessler's website (www.kessler.co.uk).

We are indebted to the many friends and colleagues who have commented on the text, both of this book and of the original English version on which it is based. We would like to thank in particular Alan Hewitt of L'Estrange and Brett and Alastair Rankin of Cleaver Fulton Rankin. As always, the project would never have reached finality without the patience and support of our respective spouses, Jane and George.

Responsibility for errors is, of course, our own. As to responsibility for errors in a document which draws on this book, see paragraph 30.2 (Use and misuse of precedents). We have enjoyed writing this book and will be happy if any readers enjoy reading it.

This book attempts to state the law as at 31 October 2003 except that we have anticipated the Stamp Duty Land Tax reforms due to take effect on 1 December 2003.

JRK

24 Old Buildings
Lincoln's Inn
London WC2

kessler@kessler.co.uk

www.kessler.co.uk

SG

School of Law
The Queen's University of Belfast and

The Bar Library
Chichester Street
Belfast

Trusts Discussion Forum

Readers are invited to join the Trusts Discussion Forum, an internet discussion group dedicated to discussion of trust and will drafting and related private client topics, moderated by James Kessler QC in association with STEP and the Chancery Bar Association.

To subscribe: email majordomo@webwright-uk.com

The subject does not matter; the body of the message should read:

subscribe trustsdiscussionforum

For further information on the forum visit www.trustsdiscussionforum.co.uk

There is no charge.

A note to the lay reader

Our advice is not to draft your own trust or will, but find a competent solicitor to advise you. Self-help guides extol 'the benefit of bypassing expensive lawyers'; but the bypass may prove the more expensive route in the long run.

This book is not intended as a self-help guide, and is addressed to professional practitioners, but it is readable for a lay person. If you wish to research this subject in depth, and so take more control of your own legal affairs, read on.

Contents

Chapter 2

Chapter 3

Chapter 19

Will trusts 285

Chapter 20

Administrative provisions 301

Table of abbreviations

Legislation

Northern Ireland

AEA(NI) 1955	Administration of Estates Act (NI) 1955
PA(NI) 1966	Perpetuities Act (NI) 1966
TA(NI) 1958	Trustee Act (NI) 1958
TA(NI) 2001	Trustee Act (NI) 2001
WAP(NI)O 1994	Wills and Administration Proceedings (NI) Order 1994

United Kingdom and England

AEA:	Administration of Estates Act 1925
AJA:	Administration of Justice Act
CJJA 1982	Civil Jurisdiction and Judgments Act 1982
FA:	Finance Act
ICTA:	Income and Corporation Taxes Act 1988
IHTA:	Inheritance Tax Act 1984
LPA:	Law of Property Act 1925
PAA:	Perpetuities and Accumulations Act 1964
SLA:	Settled Land Act 1925
TA:	Trustee Act
TCGA:	Taxation of Chargeable Gains Act 1992
TLATA:	Trusts of Land and Appointment of Trustees Act 1996
VATA 1994	Value Added Tax Act 1994

Periodicals

BTR:	British Tax Review
LQR:	Law Quarterly Review
NILQ:	Northern Ireland Legal Quarterly
OITR:	Offshore & International Taxation Review (formerly OTPR)
OTPR:	Offshore Tax Planning Review[1]
PCB:	Private Client Business
PTPR:	Personal Tax Planning Review
TLI:	Trust Law International
WTLR:	Wills and Trusts Law Reports

Other

A&M:	Accumulation and Maintenance
CGT:	Capital Gains Tax
CTO:	Capital Taxes Office (reorganised into IR (Capital Taxes) in 2001)
IHT:	Inheritance Tax
IP:	Interest in Possession
PET:	Potentially Exempt Transfer
SP:	Statement of Practice

An italic font is used to set out forms discussed but not adopted as precedents in this book; ordinary print is used for forms approved and adopted as precedents.

Trust terminology

Settlement

In general usage the word 'settlement' describes the situation in which property is held in trust for a succession of interests, or the disposition creating that situation.[2]

In the Income Tax Settlement Provisions (and other provisions which copy them), the term 'settlement' is given an artificial meaning and includes any 'arrangement'. It is unfortunate that the Parliamentary Counsel used the word 'settlement' as a label for this concept. The word 'settlement' does not bear this wide meaning unless otherwise indicated.[3]

'Trust' and 'settlement'

In general contemporary usage the term 'trust' is used with exactly the same meaning as 'settlement.'[4]

1 Renamed 'Offshore Taxation Review' in 1997 and renamed (again) as OITR in 1999.

2 The statutory definitions of TCGA 1992, s 69 and IHTA 1984, s 43 correspond closely to this general sense. The word 'settlement' is not a term of art, with one specific and precise meaning. Its meaning depends on the context in which it is being used; *Brooks v Brooks* [1996] AC 375 at 391. However this is also true of virtually all terminology relating to the law of trusts or anything else.

3 ICTA 1988, s 660G. The criticism made by Lord Upjohn in relation to ICTA 1988, s 709 definitions applies here also: 'They cannot possible be described as definition clauses; they are 'artificial inclusion' clauses. I say 'artificial' because the draftsman has paid no attention to the proper use of language' *IRC v Cleary* (1965) 44 TC 399 at 428.

4 Eg TCGA 1992, s 69 where the usage varies between sub-ss (1) and (2). An even more striking example was TCGA 1992, s 5(2) (repealed) ('a trust is an accumulation or discretionary settlement where ...').

Two doubtful linguistic distinctions

Sometimes a distinction is drawn under which the term 'Settlement' is used to refer to a settlement for the purposes of the (obsolescent) Settled Land Act 1925; anything else is referred to as a 'trust'.[5] But the distinction is 'one sided': while a Settled Land Act settlement is properly called a 'settlement' (not a 'trust')[6] the word 'settlement' is used indiscriminately, and refers to all settlements whether or not governed by the Settled Land Act. Therefore, if one needs to draw a distinction between the two, some more specific expression should be used.

Sometimes a distinction is drawn under which the term 'trust' is used to refer to Will Trusts; and 'Settlement' refers to lifetime settlements. But this distinction is not firmly established and is not recommended.

Bare trust and substantive trust

A bare trust is one where the trustees hold property on trust for another absolutely.[7] Here, the term 'settlement' is not an apt term. A trust which is not a bare trust is described as a 'substantive' trust.

'Trust' and 'estate of deceased person'

The legal and equitable interest in the estate of a deceased person vests in the Executors until the estate is administered and so an unadministered estate is not a 'trust' if 'trust' is understood to mean a situation where there is a separation of legal and equitable interests.[8] See *Comr of Stamp Duties (Queensland) v Livingston* [1965] AC 694. Executors are nevertheless often said to hold property on 'trust' and the word 'trust' is often used to refer to the way in which executors hold

---

The word 'settlement' in the 1925 legislation means a settled land act settlement, not any other kind of trust. But this is by virtue of a statutory definition of 'settlement' so one cannot on that basis infer that the general usage is incorrect.

In some offshore jurisdictions, the word 'trust' seems to be preferred to the exclusion of the word 'settlement.' This trend seems to be adopted in modern statutory drafting, such as the Trustee Act 2000.

5 Eg the headnote of the English TLATA 1996, s 2 (abolishing SLA Settlements) reads: 'Trusts in place of Settlements'.

6 Because this is the usage of the SLA 1925 itself.

7 The statutory definition in TCGA 1992, s 60 represents the only contemporary meaning of 'bare trust'. (In the past the expression was used in a variety of senses. The old cases are assembled in *Re Blandy Jenkins* [1917] 1 Ch. 46 but this is now of historic interest only.)

8 There is a debate between Lord Nicholls and Lord Millett whether the situation where legal and equitable interests are separated should always be described as a trust: see Millett, 'Restitution and Constructive Trusts' (1998) 114 LQR 399. But happily the private client lawyer can leave that issue to the commercial lawyers.

property in an estate. This usage is so common both in statutes[9] and in law reports[10] it cannot be described as improper or even loose language; it might perhaps be described as a non-technical usage.

Other usage of 'trust'

'Trust' is also used as a synonym of 'duty'. This usage is confusing and best avoided.[11]

The term was in the past used to describe an equitable interest, but this usage is now archaic.[12]

The expression 'trusts' is sometimes used simply to mean all the provisions of a settlement.

Types of trusts

Most family trusts fall into one of three categories:[13]

Interest in possession trust. An interest in possession trust is one where trust income must be paid to a particular beneficiary ('the life tenant').

Discretionary trust. In common parlance (and in this book) the expression 'discretionary trust' is applied where trust income and capital may be paid to one or more of a class of beneficiaries, as the trustees think fit ('at their discretion'), without significant restrictions.[14] If it is desired to identify this type of trust more precisely, it may be called a 'conventional discretionary trust'[15] or 'a common form discretionary trust'. The property of such trusts is the commonest example

9 In England, AEA 1925, s 33 provides that on the death of a person intestate, his personal representatives hold his estate 'upon trust' (in the original wording) and 'in trust' (as amended by the TLATA 1996). Another example can be found in the English Statutory Will Forms 1925, Form 8. Thus where necessary statute provides that personal representatives are not trustees: eg ICTA 1988, s 686(6).

Failure to understand this has led to comical misunderstandings, such as the view that IHTA 1984, s 143 does not apply to unadministered estates. But this is not a drafting issue.

10 See eg *Stamp Duties Comr (Queensland) v Livingston* [1965] AC 694 at 707.

11 Para 6.2 (Duties and Powers distinguished).

12 It was found in s 9 of the Statute of Frauds 1677 ('all grants and assignments of any trust or confidence shall be in writing…'). The usage survives in the successor to that section: LPA 1925, s 53(1)(c) ('a disposition of an equitable interest or trust … must be in writing').

13 This is a loose categorisation. There is infinite potential for variety within each category. Settlements will change from one form to another through exercise of trustees' powers or change in the circumstances of the beneficiaries. A settlement may take partly one form and partly another.

14 The Schedule to the IHT (Double Charges Relief) Regulations 1987 contains examples of this usage.

15 The first recorded usage of this expression in the law reports is in [1974] Ch 324, reflecting the rising popularity of this form in the 1960s.

of 'relevant property' for IHT purposes and subject to what is popularly called the 'discretionary trust regime' of 10-year charges and exit charges.[16]

In contexts other than IHT, the expression 'discretionary trust' is used to mean any settlement in which the trustees (or others) have powers ('discretions') over trust income, whether the property is or is not relevant property for IHT purposes. In this sense A&M Trusts are 'discretionary', the trustees having some discretion over trust income.[17]

In the strictest and most literal sense the expression 'discretionary trust' is taken to mean any trust in which the trustees (or others) have powers ('discretions') over trust income or trust capital. In this strict sense almost all trusts are 'discretionary', since trustees will at least have the power over capital conferred by the Trustee Act 1925, s 32. This usage is rare, confusing, and best avoided.[18]

Accumulation and maintenance trust. An A&M trust is one which satisfies the conditions set out in s 71 of the Inheritance Tax Act 1984. This will generally be a settlement for the benefit of persons under 25.

Other terminology

The following are not full definitions but brief explanations and, inevitably, over simplifications. So 'except where the context otherwise requires …':

Accumulation and maintenance settlement: see 14.1.

Administrative power: power to deal with the administration of a trust; such as a power to invest trust property. As opposed to dispositive power.

Advancement: see 'power of advancement'.

Appointment: see 'power of appointment'.

Capital condition: term used in this book to describe one of the conditions which must be satisfied by an A&M Settlement.

Closed class: a fixed class of beneficiaries; contrast 'open class'.

16 The heading to IHTA 1984, Chapter III, Part III refers, more accurately, to 'settlements without interests in possession' rather than 'discretionary settlements', because non-discretionary settlements may fall within the scope of these provisions.
17 There are examples of this usage in TCGA 1992, s 5 (repealed); and in the sidenote to ICTA 1988, s 686.
18 The sidenote to ICTA 1988, s 689, was an example of this usage. The expression 'discretionary trust' is employed in the Income Support (General) Regulations (NI) 1987 in a manner which suggests that the drafter was not entirely familiar with trust terminology. It is thought that the term there is used in this wide sense.

Cross-generation settlement: term used in this book to describe an A&M settlement where the principal beneficiaries do not satisfy the 'single generation' test.

Default clause: provision in settlement directing who should become entitled to the trust property if all the other beneficiaries should die or the trusts fail.

Default beneficiary: beneficiary entitled under a default clause.

Disabled trust: trust satisfying conditions for IHT or CGT reliefs for disabled beneficiaries: see 4.8 (Mentally handicapped beneficiaries).

Discretionary trust: see 17.1.

Discretionary trust regime: code of Inheritance Tax charges on discretionary trusts: exit charges and 10-year charges.

Dispositive: See 18.1 (Administrative, dispositive, beneficial: terminology).

Duties and powers, distinguished: see 6.2.

Exit charge: IHT charge imposed under the Inheritance Tax Act 1984, s 65 where property ceases to be held on discretionary trusts.

Hold-over relief: relief from CGT charge (which arises in principle on lifetime gifts and on the termination of a settlement): see Taxation of Chargeable Gains Act 1992, ss 165 and 260.

Income condition: term used in this book to describe one of the conditions which must be satisfied by an A&M trust.

Interest in possession trust: see 13.1.

Interest in possession: the right to the income from trust property.

Life tenant: person entitled to income of trust property.

Nil rate band: amount of chargeable transfer permitted before IHT becomes payable.

Open class: a class of beneficiaries which might increase (eg 'the Children of the Settlor' is an open class while the settlor is alive and capable of having more children). Contrast 'closed class'.

Overriding powers: term used in this book to refer to:

(i) power of appointment;

(ii) power to transfer property to a new settlement;
(iii) power of advancement.

Power of advancement: power to give a beneficiary trust capital or to apply it for his benefit: see 10.8 (Power of advancement).

Power of appointment: power to create new trusts for the benefit of beneficiaries.

Protection clause: clause to restrict a trust to ensure it satisfies the relevant tax conditions: see 18.17 (Protection clauses).

Protector: name given to a person who oversees trustees with power of consent and dismissal.

Settlement provisions: rules which apply (in short) where a settlor or spouse has an interest in a settlement. See ICTA 1988, Pt XV of the Income Tax Settlement Provisions; Taxation of Chargeable Gains Act 1992, s 77 (CGT Settlement Provisions).

Single generation settlement: term coined in this book to describe an accumulation and maintenance trust where the principal beneficiaries satisfy the 'single generation' test.

Substantive trust: term used in this book to describe a trust other than a bare trust.

Synonymy: The use of strings of synonyms in a blunderbuss, rather than a discriminatory fashion (Garner).

Ten-year charge: Inheritance tax charge on the 10-year anniversary of a discretionary settlement. See IHTA 1984, s 64.

Other forms of settlement

It would not be possible to specify all the fanciful terminology sometimes used in connection with trusts.

Inheritance trust is a term propagated in marketed IHT avoidance arrangements. The expression has no settled meaning; indeed it has virtually no meaning. It generally involves insurance policies settled on some form of trust.

Asset protection trust is one in which the avoidance of insolvency legislation is a primary motive. The term (perhaps understandably) originates from America.

Marriage settlement. A settlement made in consideration of marriage or in contemplation of an intended marriage. The old form was: a life interest for husband

and wife; with remainder to such of their issue as they might appoint; and in default of appointment for their children in equal shares. These forms are now obsolete[19] but any modern form of settlement may be a 'marriage settlement'. Marriage settlements enjoy two tax advantages of trivial importance:[20] no practitioner will waste much time on them.

19 But financial negotiations prior to marriage, not dissimilar to those described in dusty textbooks on marriage settlements, may yet return in the guise of pre-nuptial agreements.

20 1. An IHT exemption for gifts to the settlement: IHTA 1984, s 22. The conditions for the relief are of a complexity quite out of proportion to the size of the relief, only £5,000 for a parent and £2,500 for a grandparent. An absolute gift is the only sensible way to take advantage of the relief.
2. A minor exemption from the Settlement Provisions: ICTA 1988, s 660A(4)(c).

Table of statutes

References in the right-hand column are to paragraph number. Paragraph references printed in **bold** type indicate where the Act is set out in part or in full.

Table of statutory instruments

References in the right-hand column are to paragraph number. Paragraph references printed in **bold** type indicate where the Statutory Instrument is set out in part or in full.

Table of cases

PARA

A

B

PARA

D

E

F

PARA

PARA

PARA

N

O

P

PARA

R

CHAPTER 1

First principles

Duty to the client

1.1

The purpose of drafting a settlement or will is to carry out the wishes of the settlor or testator. The professional adviser will do more than this: his duty is to advise, ascertain and carry out his client's wishes. This is a matter of explanation and common sense. Suggestions from solicitors or textbook writers are often brushed aside by those wary or suspicious of them. It is easy to let a client do what he wants; or what he thinks he wants. Their families will pay the resulting bills in due course, probably without complaint; almost certainly without redress. But the responsibility of the adviser is to help his client whose basic wish will be to benefit his family in the most appropriate way. Empathy and an ability to communicate are called for; a little persuasion or cajolery may not be amiss.

A docile client may sign anything put in front of him. The professional adviser does not serve that client well if he simply places before him the firm's standard draft – even if settled by counsel – for execution without discussion and explanation.

Consultation with the client comes at two stages. First, the general strategy; at this stage consideration can be given to the nature of the trust property, the tax position, the class of beneficiaries and the choice of trustees or executors. Later, when the draft is completed, it should itself be explained to the settlor clause by clause. A modern style of drafting renders this task much easier. The execution of a document which the client does not understand is a recipe for disaster.

Where the settlor is a trustee or a beneficiary – especially if he is both – the solicitor has the difficult duty of explaining to the settlor the nature of his rights and duties under the trust. Legal and equitable ownership are subtle concepts. The client must not be left with the impression that the trust fund is simply 'his fund'. The trustee acting on that assumption will inevitably act in breach of trust; disabused of his illusions the client may blame his advisers; alternatively the trust deed may be dismissed as a sham.[1]

Elderly or ill client

1.2

> 'In the case of an aged testator or a testator who has suffered a serious illness, there is one golden rule which should always be observed, however straightforward matters may appear, and however difficult or tactless it maybe to suggest that precautions be taken: the making of a will by such a testator ought to be witnessed or approved by a medical practitioner who satisfies himself of the capacity and understanding of the testator, and records and preserves his examination and findings.
>
> There are other precautions which should be taken. If the testator has made an earlier will this should be considered by the legal and medical advisers of the testator and, if appropriate, discussed with the testator. The instructions of the testator should be taken in the absence of anyone who may stand to benefit, or who may have influence over the testator.
>
> These are not counsels of perfection. If proper precautions are not taken injustice may result or be imagined, and great expense and misery may be unnecessarily caused'.[2]

The same applies of course to a lifetime settlement made by such a client.

Does drafting matter?

1.3

Lord Reid said that the courts do not penalise the client for his lawyer's slovenly drafting.[3] It would be more accurate to say that the courts *try* not to penalise the client for bad drafting. If the meaning is clear, the court will 'adopt methods of construction appropriate for documents *inter rusticos*'. For instance when a drafter uses the word 'assent' when he means 'convey' or says 'Bishop of Westminster' instead of 'Archbishop' the intended meaning will be understood.[4] But slovenly

1 Kessler, 'What is (and what is not) a Sham' (1999) The Offshore & International Taxation Review, vol 9, p 125, accessible on www.kessler.co.uk.

2 BMA, *Assessment of Mental Capacity, Guidance for Doctors and Lawyers* (1995); *Re Simpson* (1977) 121 Sol Jo 224 (Templeman J).

3 *Whishaw v Stephens* [1970] AC 508 at 517.

4 The examples are from *Re Stirrup* [1961] 1 WLR 449 and *Re Hetherington* [1989] 2 All ER 129. Many illuminating and amusing examples can be found in Lewison *Interpretation of Contracts* (2nd edn, 1997) ch 8.

drafting leads to ambiguity and sometimes invalidity. To ascertain the meaning of a badly drafted document can be a matter of great difficulty. Some apparently trivial drafting errors have disastrous tax consequences.[5] Drafting *does* matter.

Flexibility

1.4

A trust needs to be flexible. This means that trustees require overriding powers to enable them to rewrite the terms of the trust as seems appropriate. Beneficiaries' circumstances change in ways that are not possible to foresee. Trustees need to adapt to tax changes which are wholly unpredictable. 'The major distinguishing feature of the British tax system is its instability'.[6]

Simplicity

1.5

This book strives for simplicity of *style* and simplicity of *concept*. Simplicity of style is self-explanatory: a preference for the shorter formula over the longer; the use of aids to the reader such as punctuation and clause headings; and the rejection of material which is archaic or superfluous.

Simplicity of concept calls for the broad structure of a trust to be simple and comprehensible. Provisions should be set out in a logical sequence. Vastly complicated settlements should not be employed where simpler provisions would be satisfactory.

Dense and obscure drafting carries a heavier price than may be realised. The more complex a draft, the more professional time must be spent studying it in order to ascertain the meaning, and the greater the chance of error escaping observation.

5 Although the courts may not penalise the client for his lawyer's slovenly drafting, the Revenue (quite rightly) has no such scruple. A classic example is the *Vandervell* litigation ([1971] AC 912). A modern example would be the inclusion of a power which might destroy an interest in possession.

6 Sven Steinmo *Taxation and Democracy* (1993) Yale University Press, p 44. This was written in the light of the budgets of 1986, 1987, 1988, 1989 and 1992 which all contained fundamental changes; this under the administration of a single stable Conservative administration! The Labour administration brought in a new dividend regime in 1999, which is unlikely to endure, and CGT taper relief in 1998 substantially amended in the Finance Acts 2000, 2001 and 2002.

Sources for drafting

1.6

The aim of the drafter is to keep so far as possible to familiar paths; to be unoriginal. He is happy to use well-worn phrases of established meaning and fearful to use novel forms. To this end the drafter may draw on many sources. Of course such sources should be used as a guide and not a crib. The wide variety of forms and styles employed in statute and published precedents force the drafter to some form of selection. Innovation is constantly required to meet changes in tax and trust law, circumstances of beneficiaries and wishes of settlors.

(1) Statute

1.7

Statute (and statutory instrument) should be the drafter's starting point: wording which the parliamentary drafter thought adequate can rarely be criticised as defective. This applies not only to the precedents thoughtfully set out by the parliamentary drafter for the benefit of the profession,[7] but to the vast body of statutory material. Many different styles of drafting are to be found in statutory precedent. This is hardly surprising when one bears in mind that many different hands may have been at work even in a single Act. English property legislation offers clearer sources of precedent than any precedent book. The precedents in this book have drawn whenever possible on statutory precedent.[8] Reference may also usefully be made to foreign trust laws.

(2) Law reports

1.8

In the law reports an immense number of precedents are discussed and analysed, and the adoption of a clause or formula which has the benefit of judicial consideration and approval may be attractive. Conversely, where the court has disapproved of a form, the drafter should take careful note.

7 Eg SLA 1925, Sch 1; LPA 1925, Schs 3, 4 and 5. Of course neither of these extended to NI. There has been no culture of statutory precedents for the conveyancer in NI – a consequence of the absence of twentieth century legislation.

8 This book specifies the statutory provisions which are used as the basis of its precedents. Also noted in footnotes are any other provisions which may also have served as precedents for the clause under discussion. This may serve as a starting point for research for the drafter creating a specific draft, or for a practitioner construing a particular clause in a document before him. It also illustrates the endless variety of formulae which may properly be used to achieve the same end and the different drafting styles used. Where possible a NI provision has been used. English legislation is used where there is no NI counterpart.

(3) Company law

1.9

Precedents from a company law context may assist the trust drafter. This book makes occasional use of standard company articles in Table A form,[9] the Companies (NI) Order 1986 and the Insolvency (NI) Order 1989.

(4) Legal literature and precedent books

1.10

There is a large body of published precedents of varying age and authority. (For a selection, see the bibliography.) The authors of these works have naturally drawn from similar sources and each other. The forms proposed have a great deal in common; a review of any indenture from an earlier century will reveal phrases or entire clauses still familiar today. At the same time, copyright considerations may have led to an unnatural multiplicity in published precedents.

Formal qualifications for the drafter

1.11

Drafting requires formal qualifications. The general rule is that drafting must be done by a solicitor or barrister. The non-solicitor, who, for a fee, 'draws or prepares an instrument relating to real or personal estate' commits an offence.[10]

The expression 'an instrument relating to real or personal estate' clearly covers the drafting of any trust. It is a criminal offence for a firm of accountants or a trust corporation to draft a trust. This is so even if the work is done by an employee of the firm who is a solicitor; for it is the firm which supplies the service and receives the reward. The drafting of other trust documentation, such as an appointment of new trustees, is also forbidden.

Interesting questions arise where the law is broken. Suppose the unqualified firm drafts a trust. Could it sue for its fees? Obviously not. Suppose the document was negligently drafted and the firm was sued for negligence. Would the firm be covered by its professional indemnity insurance? That would depend on the terms of the insurance cover. If the firm is supervised by an SRO, what would be the attitude

9 Table A is found in the Companies (A to F) Regulations 1986 (SR 1986/264).

10 Solicitors (NI) Order 1976, art 23. There are minor exceptions for certain employees and others: art 23(2).

of the regulatory body? Clearly, the penalty for breaking the solicitor's monopoly may extend further than the maximum statutory penalty, a fine at level three on the standard scale.

The restriction does not apply to:
(1) a will;
(2) an agreement not intended to be executed as a deed;
(3) a transfer of stock containing no trust;
(4) acts not done for a reward.[11]

In both England and Scotland, there is a similar monopoly.[12] the drafting of documentation relating to property in England must be done by those qualified under English law and that relating to property in Scotland is restricted to those qualified under Scots law. Thus an offshore trust company may prepare a trust, in local form, if the initial trust property is local property. The trust company could also draft a transfer of United Kingdom stock to the trustees; it should not prepare a transfer of land to the trustees if the land is situated in the United Kingdom.

Money laundering[13]

1.12

Recent legislation which extends to Northern Ireland, namely the Proceeds of Crime Act 2002 and the Money Laundering Regulations 2003, makes it imperative for the trust drafter to be alert to his possible involvement in money laundering.

The following is not a full discussion of the law, which goes beyond the scope of a book on trust drafting, but a summary in the nature of a checklist.

- Does the drafter suspect that the trust fund represents proceeds of criminal conduct? If so, drafting the trust may be an offence. In a prosecution the onus rests on the drafter to prove that he did not know or suspect that the arrangement related to criminal conduct.[14]
- Does the drafter know the client and any person on whose behalf the client is acting? If not, the identification procedures required by the Money Laundering Regulations 2003 must be applied. These regulations apply regardless of

11 Solicitors (NI) Order 1976, art 23(1) and (3).

12 Solicitors Act 1974, ss 22, 90(4); Solicitors (Scotland) Act 1980, s 32.

13 On this topic see the guidance published by the Law Society of Northern Ireland (available from Law Society House). See also the English Law Society's 'Money Laundering legislation: Guidance for Solicitors', accessible on www.lawsociety.org.uk.

14 Proceeds of Crime Act 2002. The maximum sentence is 14 years' imprisonment. In July 2002 Jonathan Duff, an English solicitor, was sentenced to six months' imprisonment, being the first solicitor to be convicted of offences of failing to disclose knowledge or suspicious circumstances of money laundering. 'Criminal conduct' as defined will include UK tax evasion but not the evasion of exchange control or forced heirship. Whether it includes the evasion of foreign taxes is controversial.

whether the drafter has any suspicion of criminal conduct. Failure to do so may be an offence.

The Law Society of England and Wales advise:

> 'Cause for concern is likely to arise where ... a transaction is proposed but it transpires that the client is not the person you are dealing with ie they wish you to act for their niece/parents/elderly grandfather who you have not met nor have they given you instructions'.[15]

The problems in such a case go beyond money laundering. The drafter needs to meet the client to advise properly, and to be satisfied there is no undue influence, etc.

Example

S is the mother of a young child. The father (to whom S is not married) is prepared to make a trust for the benefit of the child, on terms that his identity is not revealed to anyone including the solicitors. S instructs solicitors to prepare the anonymous trust.

Comment: On these facts the drafter has no cause to suspect that the trust fund represents the proceeds of criminal conduct. But S is acting on behalf of an undisclosed principal, and the drafter cannot act on those instructions.[16]

Civil claims against the drafter

1.13

A drafter may of course incur civil liabilities. In this work we need only mention the main heads of liability:

(1) in contract or negligence, to the client;
(2) in negligence, to beneficiaries or trustees;
(3) for dishonestly assisting a breach of trust even though the funds never pass into the drafter's hands.
(4) as constructive trustee for breach of trust, if the trust funds do pass through the drafter's hands as trustee or nominee (ie funds paid to a client account);
(5) in due course, if the drafter becomes trustee, for actual breach of trust.

15 'Money Laundering legislation: Guidance for Solicitors' (2nd edn) Annex H.

16 The question whether S is acting 'on behalf of' the settlor may be arguable; but since the drafter faces personal criminal liability (the maximum sentence being two years' imprisonment) there is no question of acting in cases of doubt.

CHAPTER 2

Style

2.1

The drafting style established in earlier centuries should be adapted to contemporary usage. The need for this is unquestionable. The drafter's aim should be to satisfy his client's wishes; and the general public wish to see plain English.[1]

To subject old precedents to critical review is not to disparage them. The old forms offer harmonious cadences which ravish the ear and intellect of the conveyancer; but they make little concession to the natural breaks and lucidities of the English tongue. There is nothing praiseworthy in practising the errors of one's forefathers.

This has for some years now been the establishment view. Lord Nicholls, then Vice-Chancellor, was asked at the annual conference of the Law Society of England and Wales in October 1993 what single change he would most like to see in the system of justice. He replied:

> If I could make one change, I would have the White Book rules rewritten in English, in a form that anyone can understand.[2] I would have orders drafted in a form that people can understand and recognise as being in English. That would make an improvement in the administration of justice but also in the impression that the consumer gets. Instead of thinking he's going into some strange world where people use language in documents and sometimes orally that people never use, he would actually be able to understand what was going on.

1 This can hardly be doubted; but see the Consumer Council report 'Plain Language, Plain Law', (1990) or the diatribe in *The Times* leader, 30 November 1990: 'The Solicitors' word processors spew forth an ever-increasing flood of garbage. A clearer case of a profession 'conspiring against the public' is hard to imagine.'

2 This comment can now be seen as a precursor of some of the Woolf reforms which have since been effected in England and Wales. Perhaps the fact that Northern Ireland has yet to implement comparable reforms contributes to the fact that the movement for promoting plain English in drafting is at a less advanced stage.

This comment drew spontaneous applause from the audience.

The modern drafting style adopted in this book, once revolutionary, is the present orthodoxy – at least in England. It would seem that old habits die harder in Northern Ireland. In Great Britain the old controversy – whether mistakes are likely to be introduced by the adoption of a modern drafting style – is over.[3] Scarcely any law reform proposal nowadays fails to include 'plain legal English' as one plank of its reforms.[4] The Clinton Memorandum on Plain Language shows how far the movement has reached in the United States.[5] It is interesting to speculate as to the reason for this perceptible change of mood which can be dated to the early 1990s though its roots lie far earlier.[6] It is probably connected with

3 In this debate it was not always appreciated just how far the most 'traditionalist' drafting style has advanced. For instance the modern practice of using separate clauses is innovatory: nineteenth-century documents contained no paragraph breaks and different sections were marked only by the use of capitalised words. Virtually no practitioner still adopts this style in mainland Britain. However, an examination of the wills proved in Belfast in the course of 1997 would suggest that it is still used relatively frequently in Northern Ireland, at least for wills.

4 Three examples will suffice:

1. Goode Report on Pension Law Reform Com 2342 (1993), pp 192-194:

   > 'The skilled draftsman produces text which is almost wholly unintelligible...it is of course very easy to criticise drafting and very difficult to do it. ...What concerns us is not particular infelicities of drafting, which are unavoidable, but a sense that clarity is not seen as important. Little thought seems to be given to the need of the user to be able to understand, at least in a broad sense, what it is that Parliament is saying. This results in professionals having to spend much more time than should be necessary trying to understand what the legislation is saying...of course the paramount consideration must always be to produce the required legal effect; communication of that effect necessarily takes second place in the order of priorities. But the two are not incompatible. In recent years government departments had made substantial progress towards simplifying official forms and reducing the numbers in use. This has been widely welcome. We strongly urge a similar approach towards statutory and other rules affecting pension schemes.'

2. *Woolf Report on Access to Justice* (1996) proposed the new Civil Procedure Rules for England and Wales.. One of the objects of the new rules was 'to remove verbiage and adopt a simpler and plainer style of drafting.' (*Access to Justice*, chap 20). A similar rationale underlies the Civil Justice Reform Report in Northern Ireland: see D Capper, 'Keeping Woolf From the Door: Reform of Civil Procedure in Northern Ireland' (1999) 50 NILQ 434.
3. The most extraordinarily ambitious project arising out of this trend is the current re-write of UK tax legislation in plain English.

A striking reflection of the current mood can be found in a Hansard debate of 26 June 1996 accessible on www.kessler.co.uk.

5 Accessible on http://www.faa.gov/avr/arm/plmemo.htm and www.kessler.co.uk.

6 An early statutory example is Common Law Procedure Amendment (Ireland) Act 1853, s 56 ('Pleadings shall state all facts which constitute the Ground of the Defence or Reply in ordinary Language, and without Repetition, and as concisely as is possible consistent with Clearness'). Fierce dissatisfaction with legal drafting can be traced back at least to the Enlightenment:

> 'Lawyers ... charge exorbitant fees for piling up heaps of turgid documents couched in arcane terminology purposely incomprehensible to non-lawyers, rendering the public helpless victims of their wiles, a conceited, grasping clique, who, instead of serving the common good, cunningly exploit their supposed expertise to generate wealth and

the loss of respect for the professions generally and the assumption that they 'know better' than the layman; the commercial advantages offered by 'plain English' in a competitive market[7]; that lawyers now learn no Latin in their childhood (or learn it to a low level and forget it); but ultimately it is because the arguments in favour of 'plain legal English' are convincing.

In some areas plain English drafting is required by law. The Unfair Terms in Consumer Contracts Regulations 1999, only one example, requires consumer contracts to be in 'plain, intelligible language'.

In the past, the style of drafting in the field of trusts and conveyancing fell behind the style of drafting in other areas of law; but this too is changing; as witness the Charity Commissioners' model charitable trust,[8] or the STEP[9] Standard Provisions. There are still many who draft without punctuation, etc, but they are somewhat behind the curve.

2.2

A last point on style: it is not a subject on which one should devote too much time and attention. Most questions of style are merely matters of taste and discretion, and do not admit of confutation. To say 'hereinafter called' or to avoid that expression; the choice between 'witnesseth' and 'witnesses'; abhorrence of or reliance on the word 'shall'; these and a myriad of like issues are of no fundamental importance. Yet although literary style does not matter – in theory – wherever style is poor, more serious errors are often found.

---

bogus status for themselves.' (Adriaen Koerbagh (1664) cited in Jonathan Israel, *Radical Enlightenment*, (OUP, 2001).)

The development of drafting styles can be traced to some extent in the drafting of Acts of Parliament which occasionally contain precedents. For instance, the precedents in the Conveyancing and Law of Property Act 1881, Schs 3 and 4 are not divided into clauses; the only punctuation is a full stop at the end of the precedent. By the time of the LPA 1925, clauses are used, and, though sparingly, punctuation: see Sch 5.

7 Thus insurance companies, banks and others boast in their advertising that their legal documentation, including trust documentation, is framed in plain English.

8 Many Northern Ireland practitioners adapt the Charity Commissioners' draft documentation for use in this jurisdiction. The precedents can generally be downloaded from the Commission's website. See Appendix 3.

9 The Society of Trust and Estate Practitioners. The Society was founded in 1992 with the aim of bringing together senior practitioners who are involved in the planning, creation, management of and accounting for trusts and estates, executorship administration and related taxes . STEP currently has over 7000 members worldwide For further information, including how to become a member see the Society's website www.step.org. One of the major contributions which STEP has made to trusts practice has been the publication of its Standard Administrative Provisions (see further 20.19). The Draft Standard Administrative Provisions adapted for use in Northern Ireland are found in Appendix 1. At the time of going to press these had not been finally approved by STEP.

Punctuation

2.3

Punctuation was traditionally omitted in legal documents. Many trust drafters still use no punctuation. If it is used, a sense of guilt or unease or tradition causes drafters (like children) to use it sparingly and in a manner quite distinct from ordinary English composition.[10]

The traditional practice rests on a precedent both ancient and authoritative. The Bible itself, in the original Hebrew, lacks punctuation and even paragraph breaks are rare; though the absence of punctuation adds little ease to its reading or interpretation.

Fortunately the old order has changed and punctuation has begun to appear in trust drafting. The parliamentary drafter led the way. Precedents in the Conveyancing Act 1881 have full stops at the end of them, though no other punctuation. This seems to have been the first concession to the rules of grammar as understood by the non-legal world. Precedents in the English Law of Property Act 1925-which, of course, does not extend to Northern Ireland – use commas in addition, though sparingly. The Statutory Will Forms 1925[11] use punctuation in the manner of ordinary English prose. So do the Law Society's Standard Conditions of Sale – in Northern Ireland[12] as well as England. That is the approach adopted in this book.

Punctuation serves two functions: it will make a document easier to read; and it may convey meaning, showing which of two possible readings is correct. In the precedents in this book, punctuation is used only in the first of these ways. So the precedents would have the same meaning even if the punctuation were diligently abstracted by a drafter in time honoured tradition. However, this self restraint is quite unnecessary: the courts will have proper regard to punctuation in the construction of a document. Thus Lord Shaw:

10 Thus one sees underlining or absurd spaces to avoid the ordinary use of commas:

> *This Deed is made by John Adam   Peter Jones and Adam West ...*
>
> *This Deed is made by <u>John Adam</u> <u>Peter Jones</u> and <u>Adam West</u> ...*

This is at least better than the older form:

> This Deed is made by John Adam Peter Jones and Adam West ...

where it is not even clear how many parties there are to the deed.

11 There is no equivalent to the English Statutory Will Forms in Northern Ireland. The Lord Chief Justice is given power by virtue of s 42 of the Administration of Estates Act (NI) 1955 to prescribe forms, reference to which would automatically include them into a will, but no such regulations have ever been made. Perhaps the fact that the Parliamentary Draftsman for Northern Ireland did not have the same opportunities to produce statutory precedents as his English counterpart has contributed to the fact that the campaign for plain English is at a less advanced stage in this jurisdiction..

12 In Northern Ireland they are known as the General Conditions of Sale.

> Punctuation is a rational part of English composition ... I see no reason of depriving legal documents of such significance as attaches to punctuation in other writings.[13]

As Lord Shaw suggests, punctuation is an aid, and no more than an aid, towards revealing the meaning of a text. Punctuation is the servant and not the master of substance and meaning. Excessive reliance on punctuation to convey meaning is also contrary to good prose style.[14] For all these reservations, it remains plain that proper use of punctuation makes a document easier to read and understand and this is sufficient justification for its use in legal documents.

Use of capitals

2.4

In lieu of punctuation and paragraph breaks, the traditional style capitalised certain expressions to aid the reader to find his place. The few large letters offered, in Dickens' words: 'a resting place in the immense desert of law hand and parchment, to break the awful monotony and save the traveller from despair.' The main expressions put in capitals were as follows:

> the opening words: THIS SETTLEMENT
>
> the names of parties;
>
> the introduction to the body of the deed: NOW THIS DEED WITNESSETH ...
>
> words of action: DECLARE, APPOINT
>
> that the trustees hold ... UPON TRUST ...
>
> the first words of the 'parcels' clause: ALL THAT ...

13 *Houston v Burns* [1918] AC 337 at 348. Scots lawyers never adopted the English custom of drafting without punctuation. It is therefore significant that Lord Shaw was a Scot. However the principle is now firmly established in English law. The same rule applies for Acts of Parliament: *Hanlon v Law Society* [1981] AC 124 at 197-198; *Marshall v Cottingham* [1981] 3 All ER 8 at 12 where Megarry VC sets out, with customary wit, the view which he expressed 20 years earlier: 'Statutory Interpretation' (1959) 75 LQR 29.

14 *Fowler's Modern English Usage*: 'Ambiguities may sometimes be removed by punctuation, but an attempt to correct a faulty sentence by inserting stops usually portrays itself as a slovenly and ineffective way of avoiding the trouble of re-writing. It may almost be said that what reads wrongly when the stops are removed is radically bad; stops are not to alter meaning but merely to show it up.' But Fowler does not mean to say that one should try to write without meaningful use of punctuation. This is a feat difficult to achieve and quite contrary to English usage. One need only contrast *Don't Stop!* and *Don't! Stop!!*

provisos: SUBJECT TO ... PROVIDED THAT ...

and finally: IN WITNESS ...

Some drafters capitalise the first word or two of every paragraph.

Now all this has lost its purpose with the introduction of paragraph breaks and numbering. The old practice is still common, perhaps because it is thought to give a pleasing legal feel to a document.[15]

One sometimes sees:

the Trustees hold ... Upon Trust .... .

Wavering between legal usage (fully capitalised) and ordinary usage (uncapitalised) the drafter sought a compromise and capitalised the first letter only.

The precedents set out in the 1925 property legislation do not adopt an entirely consistent practice. They have virtually abandoned the practice of full capitalisation.[16] They waver inconsistently between conventional usage and capitalisation of first letters. Thus in successive forms one sees ' ... supplemental to a legal charge ...' and ' ... Supplemental to a Legal Charge ...'. The drafter clearly gave little thought to the matter.

The initial letters of defined words should be capitalised. In other cases it is submitted that ordinary English usage should be adopted, and this is the practice adopted in this book.

Sentence length

2.5

It is better to use a number of short sentences in preference to a single lengthy sentence. Short clauses help to produce a document which is easy to understand. The lengthy clause easily hides ambiguity or error. This has long been recognised.[17] A good example of the problems of an over-extended clause is to be found in the

15 The pleasure may not be shared by non-lawyers. 'The mutual massaging of the whole profession's ego. Give us capital letters and raise our status.' See *Outrageous Fortune*, an autobiography by Terence Frisby, 1998; (recommended holiday reading for any lawyer.) Frisby is unconsciously repeating criticism already made three centuries earlier: see n 6.

16 A stray 'WITNESSETH' is found in the LPA 1925, Sch 3, Form 1.

17 'I have never understood why some conveyancers should regard it as beneath their dignity to employ sub-paragraphs in a clause so as to make their meaning plain': *Whishaw v Stephens* [1970] AC 508 at 526 (Lord Donovan).

Finance Act 1984, Sch 13, para 10(2). Here the drafter failed to understand his own creation and omitted the word 'not'! Parliament later inserted the word in the provision. That convenient remedy is not open to the trust drafter (except in accordance with an express power to vary, or under the expensive and embarrassing procedure of rectification).

One could give countless examples of ambiguity arising from over-long clauses. But even when there is no ambiguity an over-loaded clause is best avoided. Take a clause such as this:

> The Trustees shall stand possessed of the trust fund on trust to sell call in or convert into money such part of the trust fund as shall not consist of money with power to postpone such sale calling in or conversion for so long as the trustees shall in their absolute discretion think fit without being responsible for loss and shall at the like discretion invest the monies produced thereby in the names or under the legal control of the trustees in or upon any investments hereinafter authorised with power at such discretion as aforesaid to vary or transpose any investment for or into others of any nature hereby authorised.

In this standard but tortuous provision are four elements: a trust for sale; a duty to invest trust money; a power to vary investments; and a power to use nominees. They could more clearly be contained in separate clauses. The drafter might then turn his mind to expressing the same thoughts more concisely; he might further consider where the provisions should most logically come; and even whether the provisions are needed at all.

Another example:

> The trustees shall stand possessed of the trust fund UPON TRUST to pay the income thereof to X during her lifetime Provided that the Trustees may at any time or times in their absolute discretion transfer the trust fund to X absolutely free and discharged from the trusts hereof ...

This should be dealt with in two clauses: one conferring X's right to income, and the other dealing with the trustees' power to transfer capital.

Must every clause be a single sentence?

2.6

Normally each clause is a single sentence. This should not be regarded as an absolute rule. Standard Table A Company Articles set a good example here. It is sometimes convenient to divide a single clause into two paragraphs. This may be simpler than dividing the material into subclauses, and beginning the second 'In the above subclause. ... 'There is statutory authority for this practice.[18]

Indentation

2.7

The parliamentary drafter is quite prepared to use indentation:
(1) to break up text into smaller pieces; and
(2) to carry meaning.

In England the 1925 property legislation makes considerable use of indentation and even introduces it when re-enacting older provisions where it was not found.[19] The courts take account of indentation to ascertain meaning.[20]

General comment

2.8

The guiding principle is simplicity and clarity. Ordinary English usage is the guideline. Double negatives and worse[21] should be avoided.

Some say that the active tense should be preferred to the passive, on the grounds that readers will stumble over sentences in the passive. In relation to readers of trust deeds, this seems a little far fetched.

Brevity is a merit, but not a central aim. Lord Reid deplored 'the modern drafting practice' of compressing to the point of obscurity provisions which would not be difficult to understand if written out at rather greater length.[22] But in the authors' experience the professional trust drafter is hardly ever guilty of causing obscurity by an excess of brevity.

18 Examples are too numerous to compile a complete list; but see the English SLA 1925, ss 29(1) and 105(1) (which both contain three paragraphs); TA 1925, s 41 (note, however, that the Parliamentary Draftsman in NI declined to follow this practice, using instead separate sub-clauses, s 40(1) and (2) of TA (NI) 1958); Insolvency(NI) Order 1989, art 377.

19 See eg TA 1925, s 31 re-enacting material from Conveyancing and Law of Property Act 1881, s 43(1). The same approach was taken in NI with TA (NI) 1958, s 32. This process of introducing indentation and modern punctuation when re-enacting old legislation offers the opportunity is still continuing: see eg FA 1999, Sch 13, para 7, re-enacting Stamp Act 1891, s 59(1). (Contrast again the Hebrew bible where the now familiar punctuation was introduced into MSS as recently as the 10th century.)

20 *Macarthur v Greycoat Estates Mayfair* (1995) 67 TC 598 at 613.

21 Parliament sets a poor example: Value Added Tax Act 1994, s 89(2) is a simple triple negative; the proviso to Income and Corporation Taxes Act 1988, s 660G(4) (where the word 'not' is used six times) is a quadruple negative; IHTA 1984, s 102A (inserted by the FA 1999) is another.

22 *Anisminic Ltd v Foreign Compensation Commission* [1969] 2 AC 147 at 171.

Generally, rules of style should be regarded as no more than guidelines. Fowler has discredited many silly schoolmaster's rules of style (such as that no sentence should begin with *and* or *but*). It would be a pity to replace them with new ones (such as that one should never use the word 'shall' or the passive verb).

Miscellaneous points

Numbers: words or figures?

2.9

The authors endorse the recommendation of Garner, to spell out numbers up to ten and to use numerals for numbers 11 and above. But numerals are used even for numbers below ten in the context of calculations, before units of measure, or if the numbers are frequent throughout the text.[23]

The use of figures alone is certainly a defensible practice. This has long been the case in court documents.[24]

To set out words and figures is an act of supererogation and in Garner's words 'a noxious practice'.[25]

Style of clause numbering

2.10

The choice lies between:
(1) the style used in statutes and
(2) decimal numbering (so-called 'legal numbering').

The choice does not much matter. The latter though more cumbersome is gaining ground, and has the support of International Standard 1502145-1978.[26] This is

23 *Dictionary of Modern Legal Usage* (2nd ed, OUP, 1995), entry under *numerals*. This was the usage of the parliamentary drafter, until the regrettable change in the TCGA 1992; now the word *two* has become 2, etc. Perhaps this is an attempt to make the legislation appear shorter?

24 See, eg, RSC Ord 41, r (1) 7 (all numbers in affidavits to be expressed in figures). In pleadings the use of figures goes back to the Supreme Court of Judicature Act 1875, Sch 1, Ord 19, r 4.

25 There have been many cases where words and numbers failed to correspond. The mistake is easy enough to make in all conscience. The authors have seen such errors in practice. Thus a drafting technique presumably intended to prevent ambiguity actually gives rise to new and quite unnecessary difficulties. For the construction of documents where numbers and figures conflict, see Lewison, *The Interpretation of Contracts* (2nd ed, 1997), para 8.11. The parliamentary drafter has never, so far as the author s areis aware, used both words and figures.

26 Accessible on www.kessler.co.uk.

used in the precedents in this book; though not quite consistently, as cross-references within a clause are easier to arrange with the other system.

Dates

2.11

The form '1st February 1991' is recommended.[27]

The form '*The first day of February 1991*' is unwieldy and '*The first day of February one thousand nine hundred and ninety one*' should certainly be avoided.

Addresses

2.12

Parties to a deed are identified by name and address:

> John Smith of 5 High Street, Belfast, BT1 3FF[28].

or

> X Limited of [address][29] ...

Two individuals with the same address

Where two individuals share the same address one could set it out twice in full, though this appears slightly clumsy. The traditional form was to abbreviate using the word 'aforesaid'; eg:

> This Deed is made [date] between
>
> John Smith of 21 High St, Belfast, BT1 3FF and
>
> Lucy Smith of 21 High St *aforesaid*

27 The form: '1/2/1991' is acceptable, but may confuse Americans (who put the month before the day).

28 It is sensible to use the conventional form of address with which the Post Office would be familiar rather than the archaic 'in the county of Derby'.

29 Alternatively, 'whose registered office is at ...'; but that is unnecessary. The address is after all only for identification.

This should be modernised: the following sets out formulae to suit all occasions. Where the two individuals are joint parties to a deed one can simply set out the single address; eg:

> John Smith and Jane Smith both of 21 High Street, Belfast, BT1 3FF ('the Trustees')

Where the two individuals are separate parties say:

> This Deed is made [date] between
>
> John Smith of 21 High St, Belfast, BT1 3FF ('the Settlor') of the one part and
>
> Lucy Smith also of 21 High St, Belfast[30] ('the Trustee') of the other part.

In the case of husband and wife it is more elegant to state the relationship and omit the address of the second party mentioned. An address is included for purposes of identification and having stated the relationship nothing more is needed; thus:

> This Deed is made [date] between:
> (1) John Smith of 21 High St, Belfast, BT1 3FF ('the Settlor') of the one part and
> (2) the Settlor and Lucy Smith the wife of the Settlor ('the Trustees') of the other part.

Age

2.13

It is sufficient to say 'the age of 25', not 'the age of twenty-five years'. There is statutory authority for the omission of the word 'years'.[31] No one will think it means months, lunar or solar.

30 Give the first part of the address only; alternatively one could say: *of the same address.*

31 IHTA 1984, s 71 ('a specified age not exceeding twenty-five'); TCGA 1992, s 163 ('the age of 50').

Singular and plural

2.14

The singular includes the plural.[32] So do not say 'person or persons',[33] 'by deed or deeds', 'Trustee or Trustees',[34] 'beneficiary or beneficiaries', 'other or others'.

Male and female

2.15

There are three ways to deal with the problem of gender:

(1) The drafter may seek circumlocutions appropriate to both genders. It is tiresome to have to avoid the convenient words 'his' and 'her'. The cost is some inelegance of phrase:

> The Trustees shall pay the income to the Principal Beneficiary during the life of the Principal Beneficiary and thereafter to the surviving spouse of the Principal Beneficiary during the life of that spouse.

(2) The traditional approach is to use the masculine, which may be taken to include the feminine:

> The Trustees shall pay the income to the Principal Beneficiary during his life and thereafter to his widow during her life.

(3) Where the drafter knows the identity of the person referred to, he may select his/her; widow/widower as required:

> The Trustees shall pay the income to Jane during her life and thereafter to her widower during his life.

In the authors' view the choice is a matter of style and one should not be dogmatic.[35] The authors' practice is to adopt form (3) where possible. It is not too much trouble: every trust must be revised to some extent to the circumstances of the

32 In England there is direct statutory authority for this in LPA 1925, s 61 which applies to all deeds, contracts, wills and other instruments. In NI there is no equivalent provision dealing with instruments. However, the principle that the singular includes the plural is enshrined for statute in both Interpretation Acts (the Interpretation Act (NI) 1954 which governs all NI legislation, and the Interpretation Act 1978 which applies to Westminster legislation).

33 Or worse, 'person or persons or corporation or corporations' since the word 'person' includes a corporation.

34 Unfortunately the TA (NI) 1958 does not set a good example and often says 'trustees or trustee', eg TA (NI) 1958, *s* 35(1).

35 It must be added that some do not see this as a question of style but as an issue of sexual politics on which views may be highly dogmatic. For an introduction to this fraught topic see Garner, *Modern Legal Usage* (2nd ed, 1995), entry under 'Sexism'. The second edition is more politically correct than the first edition (1987).

case. Where that is not possible then this book adopts form (2) for the sake of simplicity.

And/provided that/but

2.16

There is nothing wrong with the word 'and'. There is no harm in a proviso (a clause beginning 'provided that ...') if used in moderation; but a separate sentence or clause would usually be clearer.

'And/or' generates strong feelings ('that bastard expression'[36]) and should be avoided.[37]

Deemed/treated as

2.17

The proper use of 'deem' is to assume something to be a fact which is not, or may not be the case: to create a legal fiction. A piquant example is the rule, now abolished, that the income of a married woman living with her husband was:

> *deemed* for income tax purposes to be his income and not to be her income.[38]

The expression 'treated as' is a modern equivalent of 'deemed to be'.[39]

Thankfully, deeming provisions are rarely if ever needed in trust drafting and the word 'deemed' is not used in this book.

'Deemed' is sometimes employed as a verbose equivalent of the simple present tense. If the reader sees the word 'deemed' in trust drafting he will almost always find it misused this way. The sort of sloppy usage one finds is:

> Section 33 Trustee Act (NI) 1958 shall be *deemed* to apply as if the provisos had been omitted.

> 'X' shall be *deemed* to mean ...

36 *Bonitto v Fuerst Bros & Co Ltd* [1944] AC 75 at 82 (Viscount Simon).
37 For a discussion see Garner, *Modern Legal Usage* (2nd ed, 1995), entry under 'and/or'.
38 ICTA 1988, s 279. The rule survives in other jurisdictions, such as Jersey.
39 Eg s 4(4) of the English PAA 1964, which the Law Commission propose in their report (Law Comm. No 251) to re-enact as clause 8(2) of the draft Perpetuities and Accumulations Bill. The drafter has taken the opportunity to replace 'deemed to be' with 'treated as'.

These should read:

> Section 33 Trustee Act (NI) 1958 shall apply as if, *etc* ...
>
> 'X' means ...

The otiose 'deemed' is used here merely to give a spurious legal feel to the text and should be omitted.[40] The parliamentary drafter adopts this approach.

Archaic and prolix expressions

2.18

Here are some archaic or prolix forms which can clutter legal documentation. It is not suggested that these forms should never be used: in normal circumstances, however, they add nothing and are best avoided. The list is not and cannot be comprehensive.

Archaic or prolix form	**Suggested form**
accretion eg holds as an accretion to	add to
as the case may be	[omit]
as the trustees shall/may think fit	as the trustees think fit
deemed	[generally, omit][41]
desirous of	desires to; wishes to[42]

40 Of course where the word 'deemed' is misused the context should govern the meaning. Thus the literal reading of 'deemed' in FA 1894, s 2 accepted in *Earl Cowley v IRC* [1899] AC 198 was rejected in the striking judgment of Viscount Simmons in *Public Trustee v IRC* [1960] AC 398 at 415. The language deserves to be remembered even though Estate Duty is now obsolete: 'Observations so patently wrong (may I be forgiven for saying so) that they leave only a sense of wonderment – unnecessary to the decision, for, as Lord Davey pointed out, the same result could be reached by another route – by Lord Davey himself accepted and dissented from in the same breath – flatly contradicted in 1924 by Lord Haldane who in 1914 had adopted them – the source of endless doubt and confusion to all who have been concerned in the examination or administration of this branch of law...'

41 Para 2.17 (Deemed/treated as).

42 The 1925 English property legislation uses 'is desirous of' and 'desires to' interchangeably and in about equal measure. Modern Parliamentary drafting in both England and Northern Ireland generally adopts the advice of Garner's *Modern Legal Usage* (2nd ed, 1995), see eg s 35(1) of TA (NI) 1958.

Archaic or prolix form	**Suggested form**
even date eg of even date herewith	at the same time as this settlement
hereby	[omit]
hereof eg clause 1 hereof clause 10 hereof the date hereof the trustees hereof	clause 1 above clause 10 below the date of this deed the trustees of this settlement
hereto eg the first schedule hereto	the first schedule below
irrevocably witnesses	witnesses[43]
infant	minor[44]
instrument	document
issue	descendant
it is hereby declared that	[omit]
it shall be lawful for the trustees to	the trustees may
The Laws of England	English law *or* the law of England[45]
moiety	half
moneys	money
notwithstanding any rule of law or equity to the contrary	[omit]

43 Para 9.26 (Testatum)

44 'Infant' has been archaic since the Age of Majority Act (NI) 1969, s 7: 'A person who is not of full age may be described as a minor instead of an infant...'. The modern practice of the parliamentary drafter in the context of property law is to adopt the term 'minor' – see eg the English TLATA 1996, s 7(5), re-enacting LPA 1925, s 28(4). The Children (NI) Order 1995 (and other legislation outside the property law context (eg The Civil Procedures Rules 1998) prefer the term 'child'. But in a settlement the term child will be used in the definition of Beneficiaries, so 'minor' is retained here to refer to a person under 18.

45 The plural form has scarcely been used by the Parliamentary Drafter since the 19th century. William Twining delightfully construes the plural *laws* as an affirmation of legal positivism: *Blackstone's Tower: The English Law School* (1994) p 68. But we may leave that to the dons as it would neither occur to, nor trouble, anyone else.

Archaic or prolix form	**Suggested form**
notwithstanding that	even though; whether or not
or other the ...	or
presents eg these presents	this deed
provided always that	provided that; but
said	[omit]
stand possessed	hold
subject as aforesaid	subject to that
testatrix	testator[46]
the following, that is to say:	the following:
the trustees shall have power to/the right to	the trustees may
upon the trusts and with and subject to the powers and conditions of	on the terms of ...
the trust fund and the income thereof[47]	the trust fund
on trust as to both capital and income	on trust
will or codicil	will[48]

46 Para 19.2 (Will trusts and lifetime trusts: drafting differences).

47 This form is quite common, following the example of the Statutory Will Forms, accessible on www.kessler.co.uk. But in *Re Geering* [1964] Ch 136, concerning a deferred gift of 'the trust fund and the income thereof', Cross J. held that (in the absence of a special context) no inference could be drawn from these words. In particular, the form did not shed any light on the question of whether the gift carried the intermediate income. So the words are plainly otiose.

48 The word 'will' (subject to context) is taken to include a codicil. This was accepted without argument in *Re Meredith* [1924] 2 Ch 552.

Clause headings

2.19

Clause headings are widely used, and rightly so, since they greatly assist the reader of a document. In wills they are less frequent; that only reflects the sad truth that less attention is lavished on a will. Nevertheless they are still regarded with suspicion. It is common to see a provision to the effect that:

> The clause headings are for convenience of reference only and shall not affect the construction hereof.

This is unnecessary. In a well-drafted document there will be no real conflict between the clause headings and the clauses. Moreover the courts would not construe a clause heading so as to override any express provision in a clause. The clause heading at most would be an aid to the construction of a clause.[49] Why should a court be denied that aid? The parliamentary drafter does not use such a clause.[50]

It is sometimes appropriate to give clause headings to sub-clauses.

Incorporation by reference

2.20

As a general rule it is better to set text out in full and not to incorporate text by reference. Rather than say:

> the Trustees shall have the powers of appropriation and other incidental powers conferred on personal representatives by section 37 of the Administration of Estates Act (NI) 1955 ...

it is better to set out a power of appropriation in full. Not everyone is familiar with the terms of s 37 of the Administration of Estates Act (NI) 1955.

To the general rule exceptions may be made of convenience or necessity. The majority of trust deeds incorporate s 33 of the Trustee Act (NI) 1958 by reference with slight amendment. In this book this is unnecessary, but no criticism could be

49 'The road north leads northwards even when the signpost has been turned round in the opposite direction', *Trow v Ind Coope (West Midlands) Ltd* [1967] 2 QB 899, at 929 (Salmon LJ). *DPP v Schildkamp* [1971] AC 1 at p 28: 'A side-note is a very brief precis of the section and therefore forms a most unsure guide to the construction...' (Lord Upjohn). See further Lewison, *The Interpretation of Contracts* (2nd ed, 1997).

50 There are sporadic exceptions, eg Value Added Tax Act 1994, s 96(10). But the normal statutory practice is to omit this form.

fairly made of this drafting technique. Statute sometimes requires the incorporation by reference of s 32 of the Trustee Act (NI) 1958 (maintenance and accumulation). On a convenient short form of trustees' powers using the technique of incorporation by reference see paragraph 20.20 (STEP Standard Provisions). Wills in this book make gifts of personal chattels 'as defined in section 45, Administration of Estates Act (NI) 1955'. This statutory definition broadly corresponds to the ordinary meaning of the expression.

Artificial rules of construction

2.21

Some drafters like to take advantage of artificial rules of construction. There are two which are commonly used in trust drafting. They are best avoided.

The class closing rule

2.22

The class closing rule is also known as the rule in *Andrews v Partington*.[51] For instance: a gift is made to 'such of my children as shall attain 21 absolutely.' Once the first child has attained 21, the class closes so a child born later will not take a share in the gift. The trust lawyer should understand this. However, a document which does not spell out exactly what it means is confusing for the less experienced reader; the drafter should avoid such usage on principle.

The rule in Lassence v Tierney or Hancock v Watson

2.23

This rule is sometimes applied in drafting accumulation and maintenance (A&M) trusts: see 15.8 (Division into shares).

Cross-references

2.24

It is tempting when drafting one clause to refer to another; for instance:

51 (1791) 3 Bro CC 401.

> subject to the overriding powers conferred by clause ... hereof ...

The authors avoids cross-reference by paragraph number. Any amendment to the draft will require consequent amendment to the clause references. Errors easily slip in. Where there are cross-references it is helpful to add in brackets a short explanation of the provision referred to, eg 'subject to clause 4 (overriding powers)...'

Obsolete forms

Coverture

2.25

> *The trustees shall pay the income to Mrs X during her life without power of anticipation during coverture.*[52]

This form prevented a married woman from disposing of her right to income. These restraints have long been abolished, and do not now take effect.[53]

'For her separate use'

2.26

> The trustees shall pay the income to Mrs X during her life for her separate use.

This form protected a married woman's property from her husband. It has been unnecessary since 1882. The concept of 'separate' property was abolished in 193.[54]

52 'During coverture' means 'during marriage'. Sometimes the same point is made in a general clause (usually placed at the end of a Will or Trust) along these lines:

> 'In every case in which any interest whether absolute or limited and whether in possession or remainder or in expectancy is given to or in trust for any female she shall not during any coverture have power to dispose of or charge the same or any part thereof by way of anticipation.'

53 The Married Women (Restraint Upon Anticipation) Act (NI) 1952. In England this law reform led to a blimpian diatribe in *Key & Elphinstone* (14th ed) concluding with an (with hindsight) unfortunate recommendation for the use of protective trusts.

54 Married Women's Property Act 1882; see now Law Reform (Miscellaneous Provisions) Act (NI) 1937.

Entails

2.27

Although entails may in theory still be created in Northern Ireland they have been effectively obsolete for many years.[55] In England they have been formally abolished by the Trusts of Land and Appointment of Trustees Act 1996, and similar recommendations have been made for Northern Ireland by the Land Law Working Group.[56]

Otiose forms: a general comment

2.28

Drafters are constantly adding to their drafts, but rarely deleting. The inclusion of additional material, it is thought, does no harm whereas (who knows?) any omission might be unfortunate. In this way much material is introduced where it serves no purpose. This book attempts to step back from that process. Whenever common forms are omitted, an attempt is made to give the basis and justification why such forms or expressions are considered to be unnecessary or otiose. Few questions are so difficult to prove as those to which the answer is obvious; sometimes the reasoning must end in an appeal to self-evidence.

55 The Land Law Working Group estimated that there were fewer than 10 entails in existence in Northern Ireland in the early 1990s.

56 Final Report (HMSO, 1990), vol 1, para 2.1.28.

CHAPTER 3

Principles of interpreting trust documents

Introduction

3.1

This subject is difficult and it is helpful at the start to say why. Any short formulation of the principles of construction [1] can only be expressed at a high level of generality which makes their application difficult and their immediate usefulness to the practitioner questionable. There is no single principle of construction, but a cluster of overlapping principles, with sub principles or sub-rules. Construction issues which arise in practice are generally complex and cases cannot be briefly summarised or neatly categorised. The principles upon which decided cases are based are often assumed or not clearly expressed. Cases are not consistent: different judges have applied different principles, or the same principles in different ways; or any principle available as a post hoc rationalisation to justify a preconceived desired result. Even now some important aspects are hotly debated. The total case law relating to construction of documents or statutes is so vast that no-one can draw it all together into a coherent body of law. In short, as Voltaire observed, language is difficult to put into words. Nevertheless it is worth persevering because there are some useful results to be found for a trust practitioner.

'The old intellectual baggage'

3.2

The starting point should be Lord Hoffmann's fine speech in *Investors Compensation Scheme v West Bromwich Building Society*. [2]

1 The terms 'Construction' and 'interpretation' are synonymous.

2 [1998] 1 WLR 896 reaffirmed *BCCI v Ali* [2002] 1 AC 251. There are similar trends in Canada: see SM Waddams *The Law of Contracts* (4th ed, Canada Law Book, 1999).

> I think I should preface my explanation of my reasons with some general remarks about the principles by which contractual documents are nowadays construed. I do not think that the fundamental change which has overtaken this branch of the law ... is always sufficiently appreciated. The result has been, subject to one important exception, to assimilate the way in which such documents are interpreted by judges to the common sense principles by which any serious utterance would be interpreted in ordinary life. *Almost all the old intellectual baggage of 'legal' interpretation has been discarded.* (Emphasis added)

Lord Hoffmann wisely did not try to identify the 'baggage' which has been discarded, but the context shows that he had in mind any rule which conflicts with 'the common sense principles by which any serious utterance would be interpreted in ordinary life.' In this category one can identify several distinct (though overlapping) rules derived from:

(1) application of the 'natural' ('ordinary' or 'dictionary') or 'legal' meaning of words; [3]
(2) application of precedents; [4]
(3) application of rules of construction [5] such as
   (a) ejusdem generis
   (b) noscitur a sociis
   (the Latin tags themselves redolent of a past age).

These rules are useful in their spheres indeed they arise out of 'common sense principles': it is their rigid or insensitive application (or misapplication) which Lord Hoffmann intended to reject. They mean us to use them as signposts and are not to blame if, in our weakness, we mistake the signpost for the destination.

It is not possible to identify a precise date or single author of this 'fundamental change.' In the field of contracts, the 1970s decisions of Lord Wilberforce in England (to which Lord Hoffmann refers) were an important development. But like many important changes, the roots of change in lawyers attitudes to construction can be traced much earlier:

> It is difficult to measure what success the courts have achieved in attempting to give effect to the intentions of testators. One Chancery judge is reputed to have said 'I shudder to think that in the hereafter I shall have to met those testators whose wishes on earth have been frustrated by my judgments.' [6] This dictum seems to have been in the mind of Lord Atkin when, in a case which did much to free the courts from some rather technical rules of

[3] See 3.5 (Words v document).
[4] See 3.6 (Precedent v document).
[5] Not discussed in this book; but see bibliography.
[6] Attributed to Eve J, (1941) 60 Law Notes 26.

construction [7], he said 'I anticipate with satisfaction that henceforth the group of ghosts of dissatisfied testators who, according to a late Chancery judge, wait on the other bank of the Styx to receive the judicial personages who have misconstrued their wills, may be considerably diminished'. [8]

General principle

3.3

Lord Hoffmann posits:

> (1) Interpretation is the ascertainment of the meaning which the document would convey to a reasonable person having all the background knowledge which would reasonably have been available to the parties in the situation in which they were at the time of the contract.

We return to this formulation later.

Factual background/previous negotiations

3.4

Lord Hoffmann continues:

> (2) The background was famously referred to by Lord Wilberforce as the 'matrix of fact', but this phrase is, if anything, an understated description of what the background may include. Subject to the requirement that it should have been reasonably available to the parties and to the exception to be mentioned next, it includes absolutely anything which would have affected the way in which the language of the document would have been understood by a reasonable man.
>
> (3) The law excludes from the admissible background
> [a] the previous negotiations of the parties and
> [b] their declarations of subjective intent.
> They are admissible only in an action for rectification. The law makes this distinction for reasons of practical policy and, in this respect only, legal interpretation differs from the way we would interpret utterances in ordinary

7 *Perrin v Morgan* [1943] AC 399 at 415. *Pepper v Hart* [1993] AC 593 can be understood as reflecting the trend to search slightly harder for intention at the cost of convenience (though subsequent experience has shown the cost/benefit ratio to be so low that the Courts are now resiling from it).

8 Megarry's wonderful *Miscellany at Law* (1955), p 162.

> life.[9] The boundaries of this exception are in some respects unclear. But this is not the occasion on which to explore them.

We have here one rule of inclusion: the Court must consider what Lord Hoffmann terms 'background'; and two exclusions – the Court will not consider previous negotiations or declarations of intention. There are (as Lord Hoffmann suggests) a number of tensions in these three principles. Some commentators advocate extending admissibility to include previous negotiations; others wish to restrict admissibility of evidence relating to background.[10] If one ignores those dissidents and adopts the rules in the form Lord Hoffmann proposes, the distinction between background (admissible) and previous negotiations (inadmissible) is still troublesome since previous negotiations will contain factual background.

Separate from the question of what background the Court must 'consider' is the question of what effect this considering should have on construction[11]. This takes us to Lord Hoffmann's next point:

Meaning of words v meaning of document

3.5

Lord Hoffmann continued:

> (4) The meaning which a document (or any other utterance) would convey to a reasonable man is not the same thing as the meaning of its words. The meaning of words is a matter of dictionaries[12] and grammars; the meaning of the document is what the parties using those words against the relevant background would reasonably have been understood to mean. The

9 Literary criticism (or at least one school of it) adopts the same approach so legal interpretation is not unique as Lord Hoffmann perhaps implies. See Wimsatt and Beardsley's essay, 'The Intentional Fallacy' (reprinted in *The Verbal Icon*, 1954):

> 'The intention of the author is neither available nor desirable as a standard for judging the success of a work of literary art ... Critical enquiries are not settled by consulting the oracle [the author].'

10 There seems to be a academic/practitioner divide on this issue. Professor McMeel advocates extending admissibility of in his excellent article [2003] LQR 272 'Prior negotiations and subsequent conduct – the next step forward for contractual interpretation?' Sir Christopher Staughton calls for restrictions: 'It is hard to imagine a ruling more calculated to perpetuate the vast cost of commercial litigation.' See [1999] CLJ 303. Few advocate admissibility of simple declarations of intent by the parties (but even if officially excluded they may slip in under the guise of background fact). Subsequent conduct raises similar problems: the general view is that it is not relevant to construction but some advocate that it should be.

11 The questions overlap of course because it can only be right to consider background which may have an effect on the construction of a document.

12 Lawyers are not the only ones who have misused dictionaries. Cf the definition of 'Dictionary' in Bierce's *Enlarged Devils Dictionary*: 'A malevolent literary device for cramping the growth of a language and making it hard and inelastic.'

> background may not merely enable the reasonable man to choose between the possible meanings of words which are ambiguous but even (as occasionally happens in ordinary life) to conclude that the parties must, for whatever reason, have used the wrong words or syntax: see *Mannai Investments v Eagle Star Life Assurance* [1997] AC 749.
>
> (5) The 'rule' that words should be given their 'natural and ordinary meaning' reflects the common sense proposition that we do not easily accept that people have made linguistic mistakes, particularly in formal documents. On the other hand, if one would nevertheless conclude from the background that something must have gone wrong with the language, the law does not require judges to attribute to the parties an intention which they plainly could not have had.
>
> ... Leggatt LJ said that the judge's construction was not an 'available meaning' of the words. If this means that judges cannot, short of rectification, decide that the parties must have made mistakes of meaning or syntax, I respectfully think he was wrong. The proposition is not, I would suggest, borne out by his citation from *Through the Looking-Glass*. Alice and Humpty-Dumpty were agreed that the word 'glory' did not mean 'a nice knock-down argument.' Anyone with a dictionary could see that. Humpty-Dumpty's point was that 'a nice knock-down argument' was what he meant by using the word 'glory.' He very fairly acknowledged that Alice, as a reasonable young woman, could not have realised this until he told her, but once he had told her, or if, without being expressly told, she could have inferred it from the background, she would have had no difficulty in understanding what he meant.

Lord Hoffmann draws a distinction between:

(1) the meaning of words[13] and
(2) the meaning which a document conveys.[14]

13 Of course this begs the question of how one ascertains the meaning of a word (isolated from background or context). The conceptual problem is not clarified but rather made even more obscure, by adding the epithet 'natural', and seeking a 'natural' meaning. Lord Hoffmann again:

> 'I think that in some cases the notion of words having a natural meaning is not a very helpful one. Because the meaning of words is so sensitive to syntax and context, the natural meaning of words in one sentence may be quite unnatural in another. Thus a statement that words have a particular natural meaning may mean no more than that in many contexts they will have that meaning. In other contexts their meaning will be different but no less natural.' (*Charter Reinsurance Co Ltd v Fagan* [1997] AC 313 at 391.)

One sees how philosophers are drawn to the (apparently paradoxical) view that a word in isolation has no meaning (eg Karl Popper). If an exaggeration, this is at least a healthy reaction against over-emphasis on dictionary meaning.

14 Of course this begs the question of how one ascertains 'the meaning which a document conveys'.

It is obvious that such a conflict may exist. It may arise in three different circumstances:

(1) The conflict may arise having regard only to the words of the document ('document context'). No-one has ever doubted that words must be construed with regard to document context.

(2) It may arise having regard to such background not stated in the document but which would be known to the parties and known to any reader (including a judge) without need for evidence. We refer to this as 'intuitive context'. In such cases it is almost self evident that one should prefer the meaning of the document (if one can find it) to the meaning of the words. Lord Hoffmann is only expressing more clearly and with more enthusiasm a principle which has for some time been observed by lawyers[15] and others[16].

    The hard question in cases (1) and (2) is not *whether* either kind of context can overturn the meaning of words but how easily or in what circumstances. In other words, how *does* one ascertain the meaning of a document?

(3) The conflict may arise only when one has regard to evidence of background fact that would be known to the parties but not known to a judge (or others) unless additional evidence was provided . Lord Hoffmann's approach which envisages that this kind of background may be used to a greater degree than before in deciding issues of construction is controversial because (1) it may be unfair to assignees of rights under the document who would not be aware of that background; (2) it adds to the cost of litigation. It is still unclear to what extent such evidence may be used. This problem does not so often arise in construction of trusts and wills.

Precedent not the solution

3.6

Precedent is not the solution to problems of construction:

15 For example, see *Re Doland* [1970] Ch 267 at 272:

> 'The point may be reached at which apparent caprice does become a warning signal that something may have gone awry with the testator's true expression of his intention. An error in drafting is sometimes clearly apparent from a grammatical defect, when for instance some word or words have been obviously omitted by accident. Or it may be manifest from the context that a testator has at a particular point used a mistaken word or a wrong name. In such cases if the court is clear about the true intention, it will, as an exercise of interpretation, give effect to that intention and for that purpose will remould the testator's language. Similarly, if the consequence of the language used by a testator, read in its primary and natural sense, is to produce a disposition or a series of dispositions which is so capricious as to be really irrational, the court may, in my judgment, be justified in concluding that the testator has failed to express himself adequately, and in such a case if, but only if, it can discern the true intention of the testator, it will give effect to it.'

16 Eg CS Lewis *Studies in Words* (1960) Chap 1, Pt IV distinguishes 'word's meaning' and 'speaker's (or writer's) meaning'. Wittgenstein *Tractatus Logico-philosophicus* 5.4732: 'we cannot give a sign a wrong sense'. The battle between words and documents also extends to biblical interpretation; see James Barr *The Semantics of Biblical Language* (OUP, 1961).

> I think it is the duty of a Judge to ascertain the construction of the instrument before him, and not to refer to the construction put by another judge upon an instrument, perhaps similar, but not the same. The only result of referring to authorities for that purpose is confusion and error, in this way, that if you look at a similar instrument, and say that a certain construction was put upon it, and that it differs only to such a slight degree from the document before you, that you do not think the difference sufficient to alter the construction, you miss the real point of the case, which is to ascertain the meaning of the instrument before you. It may be quite true that in your opinion the difference between the two instruments is not sufficient to alter the construction, but at the same time the Judge who decided on that other instrument may have thought that that very difference would be sufficient to alter the interpretation of that instrument. You have in fact no guide whatever, and the result especially in some cases of wills has been remarkable. There is, first document A, and a Judge formed an opinion as to its construction. Then came document B, and some other Judge has said that it differs very little from document A – not sufficiently to alter the construction – therefore he construes it in the same way. Then comes document C, and the Judge there compares it with document B, and says it differs very little, and therefore he shall construe it in the same way. And so the construction has gone on until we find a document which is in totally different terms from the first, and which no human being would think of construing in the same manner, but which has by this process come to be construed in the same manner.[17]

We set this out at length (it deserves to be set out in stone) because it has not always been observed by judges. But the idea that precedent can solve problems of construction has been tried and failed, as it was bound to. It is part of the old legal baggage: the approach is inconsistent with the 'common sense principles by which any serious utterance would be interpreted in ordinary life.' The point is summed up succinctly by Lord Hoffmann:

> No case on the construction of one document is the authority on the construction of another, even if the words are very similar.[18]

17 *Aspden v Seddon* (1875) 10 Ch App 394 at 398, approved by the Court of Appeal in *Equity and Law Life Assurance v Bodfield* (1987) 281 Estates Gazette 1448. Likewise *Pedlar v Road Block Gold Mines of India Ltd* [1905] 2 Ch 427 'I remember hearing Sir George Jessel say that he should not regard himself as bound by the decision of a previous judge on the construction of the identical document and the identical passage of the document which he had to construe.' (Warrington J). The authorities are discussed in Lewison *The Interpretation of Contracts* (2nd ed, 1997), para 3.05.

18 *Deeny v Gooda Walker* [1996] STC 299 at 306. This is also the position in Canada: *Re Burke* [1960] OR 26 at 30, 20 DLR (2d) 396 at 398.

Objective v subjective intention

3.7

We return to the question of how one finds the meaning of a document. The old style of legal interpretation approached this problem with a sharp distinction between:

(1) subjective intention, ie the intention in the mind of the author, the psychological data; and
(2) objective intention, the (supposedly) objective meaning of the words used.

Having drawn this distinction, the solution to the problem of construction was seen to lie in ignoring the former in favour of the latter:

> The question is not so much what was the intention, as what, in the contemplation of the law, must be presumed to have been the intention.[19]

This is here called 'the objective principle.'

Arguments for the objective principle

The objective principle is said to be a logical consequence of the rule of inadmissibility of pre-contract negotiations and declarations of intent.[20] This does not follow at all. There is a distinction between the aim of interpretation and the materials the Court has to achieve that aim. It is consistent to say that the law *does* seek subjective intention where possible but for good reason imposes certain restraints on how it sets about to do so (and so sometimes will fail to find the subjective intention which may actually exist.).[21]

19 *Miller v Farmer* (1815) 1 Merrivale 55 at 80 (Lord Eldon), merely an example. The expression 'what in the contemplation of the law is presumed to be the intention' might give the comforting but misleading impression that the law was seeking to find the intention; which is at best only partly the case. Oliver Wendell Holmes, speaking extra-judicially, put the point more strongly: 'We don't care a damn for the meaning of the writer, the only question is the meaning of the words'. Holmes-Pollock letters (9 December 1898).

Some say that the author's intention *is* or *means* the interpretation of the author's words: see Stanley Fish *Doing What Comes Naturally* (1989), p 116 (a stimulating surprisingly readable *Derrida* inspired text). But (1) that is not the way the word 'intention' is normally used (2) this usage makes all discussion of the subjective/objective aspects of intention impossible and (3) this usage is a sleight of hand giving the comforting impression that the reader or judge was seeking to find the true subjective intention; which is at best only partly the case.

20 'If actual intent were the criterion, no reason can be given against admitting proof that the testator used every word in the language in a non-natural sense peculiar to himself. Short of that, we can only fall back on the objectively reasonable meaning of what the testator has said.' (Holmes Pollock letters, 22 Feb 1899.)

21 Contrast a trial which is generally and properly regarded as a search for truth even though relevant evidence is excluded (so sometimes the court will reach a wrong conclusion).

The objective principle is said to be a logical consequence of those situations where a Court cannot find a subjective intention because none exists. There are circumstances where there is no subjective intention. One case is where the issue never came to the mind of the author. This can happen with wills and trusts, though it is more common in wider ranging documents (typically statutes). A second case is in a multilateral document where different parties may have agreed a form of words with different subjective intentions. A third case is in a statute where so many minds are involved (or half involved) that the concept 'the intention of Parliament' is best regarded as a metaphor or legal fiction which may fall more distant from the subjective intentions of all of those who had a hand in the process of passing the act.[22] However, it does not follow from these cases that the law cannot or should not seek subjective intention *at all*. It merely follows that the law cannot always find a subjective intention.

Arguments against the objective principle

There are good reasons why a court should aim to find the subjective intention of the parties where possible. Objective intention is pernicious, because it leads away from subjective intention where such intention does exist. Construction disassociated from the fetter of seeking subjective intention may become very distant from it.

Objective interpretation is also naive because it assumes that documents have an objective meaning, independent of the subjective mind of the author and reader, but that is not the case. Admittedly, one cannot ascertain subjective intention with certainty from the materials available to the Court. But one can generally aim to find it, and in practice reach near it *if one tries*. How one ascertains objective intention (as distinct from seeking the subjective intention of the author) is more problematic (and more subjective ie dependant on the mind of the reader) than proponents of the objective principle may realise[23].

In practice the concept of an 'objective' reading is often taken to be synonymous with a literal or semantic as opposed to a less literal (purposive or intentionalist[24]) approach. Of course the difference between these approaches is a matter of degree rather than clear distinction. Even the most ardent supporter of a literal or objective reading would agree that, say, a gift to the Royal Society for the Promotion of Cruelty to Children should take effect as a gift to the Royal Society for the Prevention of Cruelty to Children. But as soon as that is conceded, the extreme position that construction should *only* have regard to the plain meaning of words is lost.

22 *Cross on Statutory Interpretation* (3rd ed, 1995), Chap 2.
23 Hence construction is often described by judges as 'a matter of impression'.
24 Intentionalist is the term used in *Hawkins on the construction of Wills* (5th ed, 2000).

The current law

The modern approach (extension of reliance on (and admissibility of) background fact, rejection of 'old intellectual baggage' and recognition of less literal readings) are large steps away from the false god of objective interpretation and towards seeking the true subjective intention: they require judges to try harder to put themselves in the shoes of the author(s) and the result is that they are more likely to find the subjective intention.

The harder question is not *whether* one seeks the subjective intention of the author but *how hard* one tries to find it and *what materials* one uses in the search. These are questions of degree. In the exceptional cases where there is (or appears to be) no subjective intention one should try to construe the document sympathetically, as if there were one (and of course one will not normally *know* that there is no subjective intention, that too requires one to look into the mind of the author).

In summary, the aim of construction is neither wholly subjective nor objective intention: it is a subjective aspiration ascertained as best one can from limited information available, and departed from on occasions when there is practical necessity to do so. On reflection that is exactly what the test ought to be.

The modern Canadian position is the same: 'the Court should attempt to ascertain, if possible, the testator's actual or subjective intent, as opposed to an objective intent presumed by law'.[25]

Lord Hoffmann's statement of general principle set out above sidesteps the problems of 'intention' (objective or subjective). He refers to 'meaning which a document would convey to a reasonable person'. However, a reasonable person looks for subjective intention of the author where possible so it comes to the same thing.

We have not finally answered the question of how one does ascertain the meaning of a document/ the subjective (or even objective) intention of the author. The tone of this chapter has been predominantly negative. The construction of a document is *not* determined by the meaning of the words; by the decided cases; or by rules of construction. One has regard to background but that is not conclusive. How does one decide? The truth of the matter is that there is no simple formula; it is a matter of judgment and balancing conflicting factors. The modern tendency favours a purposive construction,[26] and *Investors Compensation Scheme* may be taken as supporting this or encouraging this further. At the end of the day, interpretation

25 *Feeney's Canadian Law of Wills* (4th ed), para 10.1.

26 Some unreported cases are discussed in John Child, 'Purposive Construction in the Law of Trusts' [2000] PCB 238 accessible on www.kessler.co.uk. For the background of linguistics and philosophy of language see Adam Kramer's 'Common Sense Principles of Contract Interpretation' [2003] Oxford Journal of Legal Studies 173.

requires 'the exercise of common sense, rather than the brute application of verbal formulae'.[27]

Are principles of construction of wills and trusts the same as contracts and statutes?

3.8

One difference between wills and trusts on one hand, and contracts (and even more so, statutes) on the other, is that there are fewer occasions where there is any practical necessary to abandon the search for subjective intention. That is, there is more often a subjective intention to be found, at least if one looks for it sympathetically. The principles are essentially the same[28] but with that different nuance. 'A Will is a soliloquy, while the language of a contract is addressed to another'.[29] Because a will or a trust is normally a unilateral document,[30] it is more often possible to seek to find the subjective intention of the author. In a contract one must assume that the parties are of one mind (which may not be the case) and seek a common intention.

A second difference is that, in the past, Chancery judges were generally more inclined to a literal rather than a purposive approach, and more inclined to follow precedents, but both these approaches are now rightly out of favour.

'Construction not restricted by technical rules'

One sometimes sees this form:

> These powers shall not be restricted by any technical rules of interpretation. They shall operate according to the widest generality of which they are capable.

The point that this clause is probably trying to make is to echo or seek to apply Lord Hoffmann's sentiment, that the interpretation of the document should not be governed by the 'old intellectual baggage of legal interpretation'. Since this is what the Courts are now supposed to do, the clause has no effect[31].

27 *Zim Properties Ltd v Procter* (1984) 58 TC 371 at 392 (Warner J).

28 *Investors Compensation Scheme* principles were applied by the Court of Appeal to the trust in *IRC* v *Botnar* [1999] STC 711.

29 *Skelton v Younghouse* [1942] AC 571 at 579.

30 In the case of a trust, there will usually be two parties but the intention of the trustees is to carry out the intention of the settlor, they generally have no independent intentions.

31 A further reason why the clause has no effect in practice is that a trust with such a clause almost always confers very wide powers.

Further, the wording that the clause employs in order to make its point is not very happy. One's first thought reading this clause is to ask: Which rules of interpretation are 'technical'? For example, suppose trustees have powers 'of a beneficial owner'. It is nevertheless a clear inference the powers are fiduciary[32]. Can trustees argue[33] that this is a 'technical' rule of construction which should not restrict the power when this form is used? The word 'technical' used (as here) pejoratively is hopelessly imprecise. A construction which gives a result one does not like can usually be castigated as 'technical.'[34] 'Technical' (in this sense) is not a technical term!

So this form is not used in this book. Nor are the authors able to offer any better wording. The difficulty the drafter faces here is he is attempting to prescribe a principle of interpretation which acts at such a high level of generality that it is impossible to reduce it to a formula which assists when any hard, stubborn, practical issue of interpretation arises. For a more modest form which achieves all that this form could hope to achieve see (Ancillary powers).

32 Para 5.19 ('Absolute owner' 'beneficial owner' clauses).

33 Or is it the trustees' argument which is the 'technical' one?

34 In *Marshall v Kerr* (1994) 67 TC 56 Lord Templeman famously said: 'Your Lordships were invited to accept a *narrow and technical* argument in order to produce a result which Parliament could not have intended and to favour a minority of United Kingdom residents to the detriment of the majority. This is an invitation which is not difficult to resist.' (Emphasis added). Substitute for 'technical argument' the expression 'an argument whose results would seem odd to a layman.' The sense is not much altered if at all; but the reasoning is nakedly exposed: (1) A layman using common sense would think the consequences of the argument odd (2) therefore the argument is 'technical' (3) therefore the argument is wrong.

CHAPTER 4

Beneficiaries

Too much money

4.1

It is generally agreed, among adults of mature age, that young people should be settled in life before they receive an income sufficient to make them independent of the need to work. 'Many a child has been ruined by being given too much.'[1]

No difficulty should arise here, no matter how large the trust fund. There are many possible strategies. Until the beneficiaries reach the age of 25 or so, the terms of the trust may allow trustees to accumulate income rather than paying it to the beneficiaries. The trustees may reduce the amount of income by investing trust funds in investment products which yield little or no income (such as an insurance bond, capital growth unit trust or OEIC) or (if the tax considerations permit) by acquiring a company themselves for this purpose and arranging that trust income accrues to it. The trustees should have appropriate powers[2] to revoke a child's interest and so to reduce the child's income or capital receipts to an appropriate amount.[3]

A related concern is that the beneficiaries should be encouraged to take an active interest in their own affairs and should not be passive recipients of trust income. The solution here may be to appoint the beneficiary trustee, so as to give him a direct interest in his financial affairs.

1 *Re Weston* [1969] 1 Ch 223 at 245 (Lord Denning in good form).

2 In desperate cases a power of advancement will suffice: see para 10.11 (Power of advancement used to create new trusts).

3 Another response to this problem is not to inform the beneficiary of his right to the income! Instead the trustees apply the income for his benefit or retain and invest it. There may be a duty of disclosure, but the duty is not accompanied by any sanction: see generally *Hawkesley v May* [1956] 1 QB 304. This does not work in theory though it may work in practice. Complete concealment may (indeed should) be difficult. The adult beneficiary will need to sign his tax return which must disclose the trust income. In some circumstances concealment may be evidence of a sham, on which see para 1.1 (Duty to the client). A solution may be to invite the beneficiary voluntarily to consent, or even covenant, to allow surplus income to be retained by the trustees on his behalf or resettled; (watch undue influence).

Profligacy

4.2

The financially irresponsible beneficiary, do what he may, cannot squander the trust fund of a well drafted trust. This is one of the great advantages of trusts.

Where a trust has infant beneficiaries – which is virtually all trusts – it is wise to bear in mind that a child may turn out to be insufficiently mature to handle capital; at the age of 18 or 25 or 40 or at all. Conceivably the receipt of a large sum of money may be most unwelcome to him, eg on insolvency.

How should the trust be drafted so as to secure against a beneficiary's profligacy or insolvency?

The following methods will not give complete protection:

(1) *The trustees shall stand possessed of the trust fund upon trust for X on attaining the age of 25.*
This confers little protection. As soon as X attains the age of 18 he can sell his contingent interest. Alternatively, if he became insolvent, the interest would be transferred to his trustee in bankruptcy.

(2) *The trustees shall hold the trust fund upon trust for X if he attains the age of 40 absolutely.*
This is little better. X may only become absolutely entitled to the trust property at the age of 40; but were he so minded, he could sell his contingent interest at the age of 18. Again, if he became insolvent, the interest would be transferred to his trustee in bankruptcy.

(3) *The trustees shall stand possessed of the trust fund upon trust to pay the income to X during his life with remainder to such of his children as shall attain the age of 21. …*
This gives X a life interest; he might sell that life interest for a capital sum. Again, on his insolvency the interest would become transferred to his trustee in bankruptcy and the income would accrue for the benefit of his creditors.

A protective trust?

4.3

The old-fashioned solution is a protective trust.[4] This is a particular form of interest in possession trust. Trustees are directed to pay income to the life tenant, but if he should sell his right to trust income or become insolvent then his interest

4 Where the settlor was intended to be the principal beneficiary, this was not possible and the standard form was a discretionary trust during the life of the settlor, with gifts over to his children and issue.

ceases and the income becomes held on discretionary trusts for the beneficiary and his family.

The laudable purpose of a protective trust is to prevent a prodigal beneficiary selling his income interest for a lump sum which might be dissipated, and to protect the trust fund from his creditors.

The terms of the protective trust may be written out in full in the trust deed, but the usual form is to provide that:

> The income of the Trust Fund shall be held on protective trusts for the benefit of X for his life.

This shorthand form incorporates by reference the standard provisions of s 34 of TA(NI) 1958.[5]

The standard form protective trust has significant disadvantages. There may sometimes be doubts whether the life tenant's interest has been forfeit. More significantly, under the standard form, the discretionary trust arises automatically if the beneficiary tries to dispose of his interest. A life tenant may have good reasons to dispose of his interest (for instance IHT planning) but the 'protection' makes this difficult. In the 1940s and 1950s protective trusts were created as a matter of routine; they caused such difficulties that the statutory Variation of Trusts Act 1958 was required to allow the protection to be overridden, though at considerable trouble and expense. The necessity of the Variation of Trusts Act 1958 and its Northern Ireland counterpart, s 57 of the TA(NI) 1958, reflects a failure of vision of that generation of drafters; or a failure of the then state of trust law or trust draftsmanship to provide them with appropriate tools for their work. Special provisions govern the taxation of protective trusts but overall they do not enjoy tax advantages of any value.[6]

A better solution

4.4

What, then, is the answer to the problem of the profligate beneficiary? The best solution is also a simple one: the beneficiary's interest should be *terminable at the*

5 The equivalent English provision, which is similar but not identical, is s 33 of the TA 1925. If the drafter is minded to use protective trusts, it is advisable to provide that acts done with consent of the trustees do not cause a forfeiture. Underhill and Hayton *The Law Relating to Trusts and Trustees* (16th edn, 2003) p 213 also criticise the standard form and suggest amendments if a protective trust is to be used.

6 IHTA 1984, s 88. On the cessation of the principal beneficiary's interest, he is treated for IHT purposes as if his interest continued. The trust thus faces a tax charge on his death without the usual CGT uplift applicable to an interest in possession trust.

trustees' discretion. The interest of the beneficiary is then transferable but unsaleable. No purchaser would pay a penny for it: it could be terminated by the trustees the next day. If the beneficiary became insolvent the interest could be terminated and the trust fund applied for his benefit in the most appropriate way.[7] Wherever a trust contains overriding powers in the form of this book, the beneficiary's interest will be terminable, and the problem is solved.

Insolvency of a beneficiary

4.5

Let us look ahead to the time when a beneficiary (who is, let us assume, the life tenant of a trust but not the settlor) has become insolvent. A bankruptcy order will shortly be made. The trustees have the usual overriding powers. What steps can they take? The trustees have two problems. The first is to prevent the property becoming available to the creditors. We shall call this 'the insolvency problem.' The second is to minimise the tax costs. We shall call this 'the tax problem'.

The trustees have available to them a number of solutions to the insolvency problem. The reader will not be surprised to find that these all have different tax consequences; and the task for the trustees is to select the most attractive of them. One must consider IHT, CGT and income tax.

Before or after the bankruptcy order is made

4.6

(1) The trustees may use the overriding power to create a discretionary trust for a class including the insolvent life tenant. Thereafter trust assets can be used for the benefit of the insolvent beneficiary.[8] Tax consequences:

(a) *IHT.* There will be a chargeable transfer. This may or may not rule out this option. That will depend on the value of the trust property, and whether or not it qualifies for any relief.

(b) *Income tax.* The income may continue to be taxed effectively as income of the insolvent life tenant, though the trustees have the tiresome administration of a discretionary trust and additional problems for dividend income.

7 For an example see *Skyparks Group plc v Marks* [2001] EWCA Civ 319, [2001] WTLR 607 (judgment debt against beneficiary with revocable life interest; no charging order against trust land).

8 Capital receipts from a trust may be after-acquired property: a beneficiary who is an undischarged bankrupt must declare them and the trustee in bankruptcy may claim them: Insolvency (NI) Order 1989, art 280. This applies to a loan from trustees: *Hardy v Buchler* [1997] PIR 643. Income receipts may fall within Insolvency (NI) Order 1989, art 283 (Income Payment Orders).

(2) The trustees may use the overriding powers to create an interest in possession trust for another beneficiary, who is prepared to help out the insolvent. Let us say the other beneficiary is a relative of the insolvent. The relative will in due course receive trust income, but can to some extent use it for the benefit of the insolvent. This route depends on the co-operation of another beneficiary, which may or may not be forthcoming. Tax consequences:

(a) *IHT.* There will be a PET. This will sometimes be more attractive than route (1) above.

(b) *Income tax.* The income will be taxed as the income of the relative.

Before the bankruptcy order is made

4.7

The trustees may convert the life tenant's interest into a protective trust (subject to the further exercise of the overriding powers). That will be tax neutral. Then on the making of the bankruptcy order, the life tenant's interest will cease, and the discretionary trusts of the TA(NI) 1958, s 34(1)(b)(ii), take effect. Tax consequences:

(a) *IHT.* There is no transfer of value. The bankrupt is deemed still to have an interest in possession.[9] For this reason, this route will sometimes be more attractive than routes (1) or (2) above.

(b) *Income tax.* The trust income (except dividends) may continue to be taxed effectively as income of the insolvent life tenant, which may be helpful.

(c) *CGT.* There will be no tax-free uplift on the death of the life tenant, even though there will be an IHT charge at that time.[10]

It is easy to envisage the different circumstances in which any of these routes would be best.

This route requires action before the bankruptcy order is made, but the trustees should have time to consider the position before the order is made.

As far as the drafting is concerned, the important point which arises from the discussion is that there will be no need to put any particular provision in a draft in normal circumstances. The problems can be dealt with when they arise.

9 IHTA 1984, s 88.

10 The rule that the life tenant is treated as having an interest in possession in the fund applies for IHT only. Here, as so often in the tax code, Parliament has failed to carry the implications of a policy through the various taxes that apply. (Contrast deeds of variation, which apply for IHT, in part for CGT, and not at all for income tax.) This is not the result of policy, but chance and legislative neglect. It would be possible to overcome this difficulty by giving a new life interest to the life tenant. This requires the consent of the trustee in bankruptcy, but the trustee in bankruptcy could not reasonably refuse.

Anti-creditor clauses

4.8

These raise problems similar to anti-alimony clauses: see para 4.15 (Anti-alimony forms).

Divorce of beneficiaries

4.9

This is a common concern of settlors and a very real one: that the beneficiary's spouse, the son-in-law or daughter-in-law of the settlor, might claim trust property in the event of divorce. What steps can be taken to prevent that?

Where a divorcing spouse is a beneficiary under a trust the court has three possible courses:

(1) the court may deal with an equitable interest as property of the spouse;
(2) the court may regard the trust as a financial resource;
(3) the court may vary the terms of a nuptial settlement.

(1) Dealing with beneficiary's equitable interest

4.10

In the event of a divorce the court may divest the beneficiary of his property, including an interest under a trust. In the precedents used in this book, that interest will be of no value. The beneficiary's interest will be subject to an overriding power of appointment. A court order to transfer any revocable interest is impractical: the trustees would exercise their power to revoke the interest. In practice such an order would not be made.

(2) Interest under the trust as a financial resource

4.11

In making financial provision the court has regard to the 'financial resources' of a spouse.[11] Any interest under a trust may be a financial resource even an interest under a discretionary trust, or an interest subject to an overriding power.

11 Matrimonial Causes (NI) Order 1978, art 27.

In assessing such a 'resource', the court will ask what the beneficiary may reasonably expect to receive from the trust.[12] Where the beneficiary has a fixed interest, this may be easy enough to determine. With flexible trusts like those in this book the position is not so straightforward. A life interest would be revocable; a beneficiary may only be the object of discretion, so that has only the hope that the trustees might exercise their powers in his favour. In such cases the courts will 'look at the reality'. Where history shows that a beneficiary has had 'immediate access' to funds in a discretionary trust, the court may treat the beneficiary as if the funds were his own.

Once the court has assessed this 'financial resource' it can proceed to make a financial provision order. The consequence of the trust is that a beneficiary will face a greater lump sum order or greater maintenance payments than would have been the case in the absence of the trust.

In theory the trustees might exercise their powers so that the beneficiary no longer receives anything from the trust. In practice the trustees can hardly reduce the beneficiary to penury. The courts may commit the spouse to prison for non-payment of funds. This puts such pressure on the trustees that there is little alternative but to fund the spouse's liabilities.[13]

Despite all these powers, the bargaining position of a beneficiary under a trust is perhaps somewhat stronger than if the beneficiary had owned the trust property absolutely. Is there anything the drafter can do to improve the situation? The reader will not expect to find a simple drafting solution and there is none. The courts are less concerned with the drafting than with the actual use to which the settled funds have been put.

If a divorce is foreseen, the best solution is not to make trusts of any kind, but simply to make loans of cash, or allow free use of assets; but this is a course of despair.[14]

12 *J v J* [1989] 1 All ER 1121.

13 *J v J* [1989] 1 All ER 1121; *Browne v Browne* [1989] 1 FLR 291, accessible on www.kessler.co.uk. The Court of Appeal described the trust in such loose layman's language that the report is distressing for a trust lawyer to read. For instance, we are told that the spouse was the 'sole beneficiary' of the trust. The lesson to be drawn is that in a family law context courts not only refuse to be bound by technicalities of trust law; they may not recognise their existence. The approach is described by those who approve of it as 'robust'. This may be regarded as analogous to the company law concept of 'lifting the corporate veil'. There is, however, an important distinction. A company belongs to its shareholders and to regard a company's assets as belonging to its shareholders does not ignore the rights of any third parties. Trust property belongs to all the beneficiaries and to regard it as belonging to *one* beneficiary is to ignore and override the rights of the others. (The position is if course different if there is a sham in the true sense.)

14 The courts may regard gifts and loans from a parent as a financial resource; but plainly only very limited weight can be given to that 'resource'. The courts will not blackmail a parent in the way that they blackmailed the trustees in *Browne v Browne* [1989] 1 FLR 291. See n 19 below.

(3) Variation of marriage settlements

4.12

The court may vary any marriage settlement for the benefit of the parties or the children of the family. The court may also reduce or extinguish the interest of either of the parties to the marriage under such a settlement.[15] This is different from treating the settlement as a financial resource: here the court order does not only affect the spouse's own property, it amounts to expropriation of property of third parties (other beneficiaries).

The jurisdiction of the court to vary settlements was formerly of the greatest importance, and attracted a substantial case law. The court then acquired broader powers to order financial provision, and the power to vary settlements ceased to be much used. There is no need to vary a settlement if the spouses have property of their own for the court to share out between the parties to the marriage. Now the position is changing again. There has been a re-emergence of orders made under the power to vary settlements, perhaps because such settlements (with a view to avoiding claims for financial provision, or for tax reasons) have become more prevalent.

Fortunately the courts cannot vary every settlement of which a divorcing spouse is a beneficiary. The jurisdiction is limited to marriage settlements, defined as:

> any ante-nuptial or post-nuptial settlement (including such a settlement made by will or codicil) made on the parties to the marriage.

4.13

The terminology originates from the Matrimonial Causes Act 1858, s 5. At that time a settlement on marriage was a standard procedure taking a standard form, and no one would have had much difficulty in classifying a settlement as a marriage settlement. Now social conditions and drafting styles have changed and the marriage settlement is a matter of history. The term has lost its original reference[16] and the courts have had to do the best they can to invent a new one.

Some test must be framed to decide if a settlement is a marriage settlement. A measure of guidance can be drawn from the old case law; but the cases need careful evaluation, as times have changed, and the text of the statutory provision has also changed.

15 Matrimonial Causes (NI) Order 1978, art 26(1)(c) and (d). A marriage settlement may also be varied under the Inheritance Provision for Family and Dependants (NI) Order 1979, art 4(1)(f).

16 Contrast Frege's distinction between sense and reference adopted by *Hawkins* discussed in Appendix 2 (Annotated Bibliography).

Often the test is said to be whether the settlement is 'upon the husband in the character of husband or upon the wife in the character of wife, or upon both in the character of husband and wife;' or whether it benefits them 'with reference to their married state' or whether the settlement is made 'in respect of the marriage'.[17] These three formulae (which seem to be three ways of expressing the same test) made sense in relation to the old marriage settlements in which the parties to the marriage were described as 'the Husband' and 'the Wife'. It is submitted that this test is not now of much practical use. How does one decide if a settlement in a modern form is made on the husband in his own character or in the character of husband?[18]

Sometimes the test is said to be whether the settlement has a 'nuptial element' and this, it is submitted, offers a more satisfactory approach. A variety of factors will be relevant in determining whether a settlement has the requisite nuptial element:

(1) the existence of a marriage or proposed marriage at the time the settlement is made. A settlement made for the principal benefit of a beneficiary who is neither married nor contemplating marriage at the time of the settlement is not a marriage settlement.[19] Conversely 'a settlement made on the parties to a marriage during the marriage' is almost bound to be a marriage settlement;
(2) the terms of the settlement. The settlement must be 'on the parties'. So, broadly stated, the disposition must be one which makes some form of continuing provision for both or either of the parties to a marriage, with or without provision for their children.[20] A discretionary settlement may be caught.[21] A settlement genuinely for the benefit of parties to more than one marriage is not, it is submitted, a marriage settlement. Presumably a settlement for the children of the marriage, from which the parents are excluded, is not a marriage settlement;
(3) the nature of the trust property. A settlement holding the matrimonial home is almost bound to be a marriage settlement.

Some general points can be made.

The substance matters more than the form. So the addition of potential beneficiaries not intended to benefit at all (or only intended to benefit as fall back beneficiaries

17 *Prinsep v Prinsep* [1929] P 225. The test goes back to *Worsley v Worsley* (1869) LR 1 P & D 648 and has often been cited since.

18 One is reminded of the test for Sch E, whether funds are received by a person 'in his capacity as employee': a test easy to state, but often impossible to apply.

19 *Hargreaves v Hargreaves* [1926] P 42 is an example. A settlement not made in contemplation of marriage was held not to be a nuptial settlement, even though the beneficiary had powers of appointment in favour of a future spouse. (The finding of fact in this case, that the settlement was not made in anticipation of marriage, was surprising: the settlement was made 28 April 1914, and the marriage was agreed before 25 May! But that cannot affect the authority of the case.) See also *Brooks v Brooks* [1996] AC 375.

20 *Brooks v Brooks* [1996] AC 375 at 391.

21 *E v E* [1990] 2 FLR 233. Here it was conceded that the settlement was a marriage settlement, and the court held that the concession was 'plainly right.'

if the husband and wife die childless) would not preclude 'marriage settlement' status. A declaration that the settlement is not a marriage settlement will not carry any weight.[22]

It is submitted that the question whether a settlement is a marriage settlement is normally to be determined when the settlement is made. So where there is an existing settlement, and a subsequent appointment is made for the benefit of parties to a marriage, the appointment cannot turn the settlement into a marriage settlement. This is so whether the appointment deals with all the property or only part.[23]

Special considerations apply to will trusts. The original legislation referred simply to 'ante-nuptial or post-nuptial settlements' without reference to wills. It was held that will trusts were not within its scope. Then the statute was amended in a curious way: it now says that 'marriage settlements' means an ante- or post-nuptial settlement (including one made by will). The settlement made by will can only be varied if it is a nuptial settlement; but marriage settlements in the old sense were never made by will and settlements made by will were not nuptial settlements. The present position is probably that will trusts can be marriage settlements if they contain the requisite 'nuptial element'; but it is less likely that they will do so.

A settlement with a foreign governing law may be a marriage settlement.[24]

Divorce of beneficiaries: conclusions

4.14

What conclusions can be drawn from this discussion? The first is that it may not much matter whether or not a settlement is a marriage settlement. For even if the drafter succeeds in creating a non-marriage settlement, so the court could not vary the settlement, the settlement may remain a 'financial resource': see para 4.11 (Interest under the settlement as a financial resource). Nevertheless a settlor will often not wish to create a marriage settlement if it is possible to create a non-marriage settlement. The best time to provide for one's family is well before a marriage. Settlements made when the marriage is contemplated, or made after the marriage, for the benefit of the parties of the marriage, are the ones at risk. One

22 In *Prescott v Fellowes* [1958] P 260 a document which described itself as 'settlement on marriage' was held not to be a marriage settlement.

23 *Hargreaves v Hargreaves* [1926] P 42 might be taken as authority to the contrary. There an appointment under a non-nuptial settlement created an annuity which was a nuptial settlement. But the annuity was regarded as a separate settlement.

24 In *T v T* [1996] 2 FLR 357 foreign trustees were joined as parties to English matrimonial proceedings.

can avoid or reduce the risk of a settlement being varied by the court by making it as 'un-nuptial' as circumstances allow. For instance consider a settlor with two married children. He may create two separate settlements for each family. Those might each be 'a marriage settlement'. He may alternatively create a single trust for the benefit of his whole family, and others whom he wishes to benefit. The settlement could not so easily be described as a marriage settlement.

Anti-alimony forms

4.15

One sometimes sees (particularly in offshore trusts) a provision that trustees' powers are not exercisable in favour of a beneficiary if sums paid to him would substantially accrue to satisfy the claims of a divorcing spouse. This form ('an anti-alimony form') raises significant practical difficulties and is not recommended.

If the form is used, how would it work in practice? The following general comments are subject to the point that much in any particular case would depend on the precise circumstances and especially the drafting. It is assumed that H is regarded by the trustees as the principal beneficiary, and W is not.

Suppose H has assets of £5m in his own estate, and a trust fund of £5m. Plainly the court could order him to transfer his own £5m to W. Could the Trustees subsequently appoint the trust fund to H? Obviously, yes. In other words, the court may regard H's interest under the trust as a financial resource and the anti-alimony form cannot prevent that.

Suppose now that H has no significant assets in his estate at all, but £10m in the trust fund. Assuming that the court would order half of whatever H receives from the fund to be transferred to W, the form read literally may seem to say that nothing can ever be paid to H at all! In result it could be that it would be a breach of trust to transfer funds to a beneficiary at a time when access to funds is needed. Probably, the anti-alimony form would be construed as imposing no more than the usual rules relating to fraud on a power. In that case the apparently disastrous effect of the anti-alimony form is avoided, but the form achieves nothing.

If the settlement is a marriage settlement, another approach for W is to seek to vary the settlement by deleting the anti-alimony clause.

One may say of course that the anti-alimony form will help the negotiating position of H in the divorce proceedings; but it may require the trustees to seek the guidance of the court in order to be secure from possible claims later of breach of trust.

Similar points arise on anti-creditor clauses.

Foreign domiciled beneficiary

4.16

A United Kingdom domiciled settlor may wish to make a trust for persons who are not domiciled in the jurisdiction. In particular, a settlor domiciled in Northern Ireland will often wish to include beneficiaries who are domiciled in the Republic of Ireland. Special consideration must then be given to United Kingdom tax law and any restrictions imposed by the law of the beneficiary's home country. These questions are beyond the scope of this book.[25]

Marriage under 18

4.17

A traditional form is:

> In trust for [my children] who being male attain the age of 21 years or being female attain that age or marry ... [26]

This is not a point of much importance; marriage under 21 is relatively uncommon. However, clauses of this kind are not recommended.

Definition of 'Beneficiaries'

4.18

Anyone interested in a trust may be called a 'beneficiary'.[27] However, the term 'Beneficiaries'[28] is used in a defined sense in the precedents in this book. The

25 Kessler, *Taxation of Foreign Domiciliaries* (2nd edn, 2003) Key Haven Publications, for details, see www.kessler.co.uk.

26 It should be remembered that in Northern Ireland minors who are entitled under the intestacy rules found in Part II of the AEA(NI) 1955 have an absolute interest. This is in contrast to the position in England where an intestate's estate is held in trust for children [the children] who attain the age of 18 years or marry under that age: AEA 1925, s 47(1)(i); TA 1925, s 31(2)(i).

27 The word 'beneficiary' is not a term of art. In common parlance it means:
1. a person with an equitable interest under a settlement; and
2. an object of trustees' powers over income or capital.

Views may differ on whether a person who the trustees may add to the class of objects is to be described as a beneficiary in the general sense of the word or merely a potential beneficiary. The distinction may be a wholly formal one in circumstances where there is no realistic prospect of a beneficiary who is an object of trustees powers receiving anything; and every prospect of a person later being added and receiving something. In practice where it matters the word is usually defined, eg TLATA 1996, s 22; ICTA 1988, s 118G(6); FA 1995, s 128(6); TCGA 1992, Sch 5, para 9(10C). Without a definition there is ambiguity, eg in the ill thought out TCGA 1992, Sch 5B, para 17.

28 The term 'Principal Beneficiaries' is used in A&M trusts and the definition of that term is discussed in para 15.1 (A&M trusts: income clauses).

term is used in this book in the power of appointment, and other overriding powers; and also in discretionary trusts:

> *The Trustees may appoint that they hold the Trust Fund for the benefit of any* Beneficiaries *on such terms as the Trustees think fit.*
>
> The Trustees may pay the income of the Trust Fund to such of the Beneficiaries as they think fit.

Other terms are sometimes used in such clauses, such as:

> 'Appointed Class'
>
> 'Appointable Class'
>
> 'Specified Class'
>
> 'Wider Class'
>
> 'Discretionary Class'
>
> 'Discretionary Beneficiaries'[29]

However the term 'Beneficiaries' seems quite apt.

4.19

The definition of the term 'Beneficiaries' is an important issue in the drafting of a trust. The definition should set out in full in the definition clause (not relegated to a schedule, forcing every reader to leaf through many pages to find the meat).

The draft must try to reconcile two contradictory considerations. On the one hand, it is desirable to compile a list of everyone who it might in any circumstances be desired to benefit from the trust fund; not just the persons *expected* to benefit. On the other hand, a wide class will enable the trustees to benefit those whom the settlor would not normally wish to benefit, and the settlor may be unhappy with that result even allowing for the comfort of a statement of wishes. This can be dealt with by drafting techniques of fall-back beneficiaries, and powers to add beneficiaries subject to safeguards.

The starting point is usually the family of the settlor:

> 'The Beneficiaries' means:
> (i) The children and descendants of the Settlor

[29] This appears to be a novel coinage of the 1997 edition of the *Encyclopaedia of Forms and Precedents*, and has a great deal to be said for it.

(ii) The spouses, widows and widowers (whether or not remarried) of (i) above and
(iii) The widow (whether or not remarried) of the Settlor.[30]

Children and descendants

4.20

There are of course a number of ways to describe children and descendants. Statutory precedents include:

> ... children or more remote issue ...[31]

> ... children or remoter descendants ...[32]

> ... the issue, whether children or remoter descendants ...[33]

The terms 'issue' and 'descendants' are in this context synonymous. The term 'descendants' is here preferred as it is in common usage. It would be sufficient to say 'the descendants of the Settlor'; the term 'descendants' connotes descendants of any degree. The form 'children and descendants' is used in the precedents in this book as the more readily understood. It is plainly unnecessary to refer to 'children or *remoter* descendants'.[34]

'Children of X and Y'

4.21

The clause used in this book would include all the children of the settlor, including children of a re-marriage. It is not usually desired to restrict the trust to children of an individual and his present spouse. If such a case does arise the recommended form is:

30 Some add: 'and "Beneficiary" has a corresponding meaning.' This only expresses an inference which would be made in any event. The use of the word 'Beneficiary' with a capital 'B' is sufficient indication that the word is used in its defined sense. Some restrict the class to beneficiaries born before the end of the Trust Period. This is not necessary. All that matters is that the power of appointment is properly restricted: see para 8.6 (Remaining within the perpetuity period).

31 TA(NI) 1958, s 34.

32 WAP(NI)O 1994, art 22. This modernised the wording of the provision which it replaced, s 33 of the Wills Act 1837 ('children and other issue').

33 The English Statutory Will Forms 1925, Form 9, accessible on www.kessler.co.uk.

34 The word 'remoter' should only be used where it adds to the meaning. For instance 'grandchildren and remoter descendants of the Settlor' where the word 'remoter' is apt as the children of the Settlor are excluded.

The children of X born to Y.

or: The children of the marriage between X and Y.

or: The children of X who are also children of Y.

The form '*the children of X and Y*' is not suitable. This seemingly innocuous form hides three ambiguities. It may mean:

(1) the children whose parents are both X and Y.
(2) the children whose parents include either X or Y.
(3) the children of X, and Y himself (not Y's children.)[35]

Illegitimate beneficiaries

4.22

Illegitimacy raises a question of principle and a technical point of drafting. Should illegitimate descendants of the settlor be included as beneficiaries under the trust? This is a matter for the settlor. If the drafter may offer tentative advice, the authors' preference is to include the illegitimate children, not to exclude them. This is not based on moral judgment, nor an assessment of the spirit of the times,[36] but a matter of practical advantage. Parents are under a legal obligation to maintain their children legitimate or not. A family trust is a natural source of funds for the purpose, and the exclusion of illegitimate children from the trust may cause inconvenience. Trustees should not be deterred by the fear that unknown illegitimate beneficiaries might later emerge with claims against them; appropriate protection can be given by the trust deed.[37]

If it is desired to include the illegitimate beneficiaries then nothing need be done. The words 'child', 'descendant' and so forth are understood to include illegitimate children and descendants.[38]

If it is desired to exclude illegitimate children then what form of words should the drafter use to achieve that end? A traditional formula is as follows:

> In this settlement references to family relationships shall be construed as if the Family Law Reform (NI) Order 1977 had not been enacted.

35 The ambiguous form has often been used and has given rise to considerable litigation. *Williams on Wills* (8th edn, 2002) p 720 cites no less than a dozen authorities. The ambiguity is exploited in a parody reprinted in Megarry's wonderful *Miscellany at Law* (1955) Stevens & Sons, pp 298-301 (Bequest of 'all my black and white horses'. Did this include the pied horses?) A traditional form somewhat archaic is 'the children of X by Y'.

36 Yet it is striking that the illegitimacy rate is currently approximately one-third of births in Northern Ireland.

37 Paragraph 5.27 (Excluding claims by unknown illegitimate beneficiaries).

38 The Family Law Reform (NI) Order 1977, art 4(1).

The Family Law Reform (NI) Order 1977 reversed the common law rule, that reference to relationships did not include the illegitimate. The effect of this provision is thus to restore the former position. The form of wording used has the advantage of seemliness; avoiding the word 'illegitimate' let alone any more offensive synonym. But the wording is unintelligible to the layman and indeed to a lawyer or accountant unfamiliar with finer points of trust law. There is then scope for misunderstanding and the form is not recommended.[39]

The obscurity may be a virtue in a case where a settlor wished to exclude his illegitimate children from the trust without openly admitting their existence: an example of Talleyrand's epigram that *la parole a été donnée à l'homme pour déguiser sa pensée.*[40] But that is exceptional. The authors propose a more explicit clause for general use:

> (1) 'Children' does not include illegitimate children
> (2) References (however expressed) to any relationship between two persons does not include anything traced through an illegitimate relationship.[41]

A fair but complex set of rules takes effect to determine whether a person is legitimate, but need only be considered in the rare cases where legitimacy matters.[42] The authors have occasionally seen trusts taking a middle way between excluding and including illegitimate beneficiaries:

(1) illegitimate beneficiaries are *prima facie* excluded from benefit; but trustees are given powers to add them in as beneficiaries; or
(2) illegitimate beneficiaries are included as a fall back if and only if there are no legitimate ones.

These are rather complex solutions but they might appeal to some settlors.[43]

39 A minor disadvantage with this form is the need to keep the statutory references up to date. Sooner or later the current legislation will be repealed and replaced by new legislation and the form will need amending. Fortunately it will not usually matter if out of date forms are used (for instance a form referring to the 1977 Order which omits to refer to the 1995 Order): Interpretation Act (NI) 1954, s 29(1).

40 Franz Rosenzweig makes a similar point in language which could serve as an epigram for this book: 'Words are bridges over chasms. One usually walks across without looking down. If one looks down one is liable to feel giddy. Words are also boards laid over a shaft, concealing it. To be a philosopher [or, the authors add, a lawyer] is to look into abysses, climb down shafts.'

41 The drafting is loosely derived from the Interpretation Act 1978, Sch 1.

42 See Grattan *Succession Law in Northern Ireland* (1996) para 6.34. The English provisions, which are identical in substance, are considered in detail in Barlow, 'Children and Issue: Some Lingering Growing Pains' (1993) PCB 99, accessible on www.kessler.co.uk. These rules could of course be amended in a particular case; but it is suggested that in normal cases they should be regarded as quite satisfactory.

43 Particular care will be needed in drafting A&M trusts with these kinds of provision.

Adopted beneficiaries

4.23

When a child is adopted by a married couple, he is treated as the child of the couple.[44] A child adopted by a single person is treated as a legitimate child of the person. No settlor would wish to provide otherwise. Complicated provisions apply to ascertain the age of the adopted child for the purpose of the trust.[45]

Stepchildren

4.24

The term 'children' would not include stepchildren (unless the context of the definition showed otherwise). This rule could be reversed by the drafter if the settlor so desired. In practice most settlors wish to benefit their own children to the exclusion of their stepchildren. Accordingly, unless the settlor so requests, there should not be any general form to the effect that 'children' include 'stepchildren' or that relationships include step relationships.[46] If, later, it is in fact desired to benefit stepchildren, this could in principle be done by using the power to add beneficiaries.

Artificial fertilisation

4.25

If an embryo or egg is placed in a woman the position (simplifying slightly) is as follows:

(1) the woman is regarded as the mother;

(2) the woman's husband is regarded as the father if he consented to the treatment, and (in some circumstances) the same applies to an unmarried partner.

References to relationships in a trust are construed accordingly.[47] While these rules could be reversed by the drafter, it is not thought that a settlor would usually wish to provide otherwise.

44 The Adoption (NI) Order 1987, art 40. A full account of this legislation and its predecessors, which will still govern trusts made while they were in force, is found in Grattan *Succession Law in Northern Ireland* (1996) para 6.26.

45 The Adoption (NI) Order 1987, art 43. The rules could in theory give rise to difficulty, but problems in practice are rare. See again, on the identical English provisions, Barlow, 'Children and Issue: Some Lingering Growing Pains' [1993] PCB 99, accessible on www.kessler.co.uk.

46 The word 'stepchild' is never defined when used by the parliamentary drafter. However, its meaning is not always clear: see *IRC v Russell* (1955) 36 TC 83; *Mander v O'Toole* [1948] NZLR 909, [1948] GLR 445, accessible at www.kessler.co.uk. An express definition would be desirable if the term is used in trust documentation.

47 For full details see the Human Fertilisation and Embryology Act 1990, ss 27-29.

Children by surrogacy

4.26

There are two types of surrogacy. In host surrogacy, which dates from 1989, the surrogate mother carries an embryo derived from the egg and sperm of an infertile couple. The surrogate has no genetic relationship with the baby but acts as a host for the pregnancy. In traditional surrogacy, the egg is derived from the surrogate mother while the sperm is from the male partner of the infertile woman. In either case, s 30 of the Human Fertilisation and Embryology Act 1990 allows for fast-track adoption of a surrogate baby. However, until a court order is obtained, the child is regarded as the child of the surrogate and not of the genetic parents. In some cases it might be appropriate to provide a definition of 'children' specifically to include children by surrogacy even before a parental order is made. The drafting should copy the language of the 1990 Act.

Spouses of settlor's children and descendants

4.27

The class of beneficiaries should normally include the spouses of the settlor's children and descendants. This is done for two reasons. First, there is a practical advantage. It may be desired to benefit a spouse: a beneficiary might die and leave an impecunious widow. Secondly, there is the immediate prospect of substantial tax advantages. Married women are taxed separately from their husbands. It will then be desirable to arrange that they receive an independent income so they can use their personal relief and lower rates of tax. The trust is a convenient source of income for this purpose. Further, in the case of an interest in possession trust, inheritance tax may be avoided or deferred by arranging for a beneficiary's interest in possession to be followed by a short term interest in possession for his spouse or widow.[48] It may still be possible to salvage some of these advantages where the spouse is not a beneficiary.[49] On settlors who object to including spouses of beneficiaries see para 13.6 ('Subject to that to his widow ...').

Spouses of beneficiaries: drafting points

4.28

The form used in this book is as follows:

48 IHTA 1984, s 18. Note the exemption does not apply if the spouse is not UK domiciled for IHT purposes. Some settlors with domicile in Northern Ireland have spouses with domicile in the Republic of Ireland.

49 Either by appointing a beneficiary an interest for more than his life, which he may leave by will to a surviving spouse or by exercise of power of advancement, see para 11.11 (Example resolution of advancement).

> **'The Beneficiaries'** means:
> (a) The children and descendants of the Settlor.
> (b) The spouses, widows and widowers (whether or not remarried) of (a) above.

An alternative form is:

> **'The Beneficiaries'** means:
> (a) The children and descendants of the Settlor.
> *(b) The spouses and former spouses of (a) above.*

The alternative form is wider as it includes not only a widow[50] but also the divorced spouse of a beneficiary. But under the form used in this book the 'former spouse' can be added as a beneficiary. The difference between the two forms is little more than one of style, or at most, one of emphasis. The form used in this book (a change from the fourth edition) reflects what is understood to be the more common preference or perception of settlors.

An interesting question arises with the form used here. Suppose trustees appoint a life interest to a spouse within limb (b) of the definition (eg a spouse of a child of the settlor). Suppose the spouse subsequently divorces and ceases to be a Beneficiary. Does the life interest automatically terminate on the divorce? The answer is, no. Provided that the spouse is a Beneficiary at the time the appointment is made, the life interest continues after a divorce.[51]

Settlor and spouse as beneficiaries

4.29

It is usual to exclude the settlor and spouse from benefit under their trust:

50 Is it possible that 'former spouse' might be construed to refer to a divorced spouse but not a widow or widower? Since a widow is someone who was formerly a spouse, it is considered that the expression 'former spouse' can only reasonably be taken to refer to widows and widowers as well as divorcees. In the context any other interpretation would be perverse.
The alternative form is not wide enough to cover the situation where:
1. a beneficiary ('A') marries a person ('B');
2. the marriage comes to an end;
3. B marries a third person ('C').

Even though B is a beneficiary, C is not. This may be tax-inefficient; but one has to stop somewhere. C will be very far from the benevolent intentions of the settlor. This unusual case may be dealt with by the use of the power to add beneficiaries, if appropriate.

51 At first sight this seems doubtful: the ex-spouse has ceased to be a 'Beneficiary', so how can she continue to receive income from the trust? The paradox resolves when one recalls that the term 'Beneficiary' here is used in a defined sense. It means objects of the power of appointment. Thus it is quite consistent to say that: (i) the ex-spouse is not a 'Beneficiary' in the defined sense, being no longer an object of the power of appointment; but at the same time; (ii) the ex-spouse is a beneficiary in the general sense of that word, having a beneficial life interest.

(1) settlor and spouse will not be included in the class of beneficiaries (which is the subject of this section); and
(2) a settlor exclusion clause will expressly exclude settlor and spouse from benefit; see para 12.1 (Excluding settlor and spouse).

If this is not done, then trust income and capital gains may be taxed at the settlor's rate[52] and the settlor may be subject to IHT on the settled property as if he had never given it away.

This is not necessary for a will trust; a testator cannot benefit under his own will.

Exceptions and avoidance

4.30

The income tax and CGT Settlement Provisions have six exceptions, the IHT Gifts with Reservation rule, ten. In particular, it is possible to arrange that trust property should revert to the settlor on the bankruptcy of a beneficiary, or, in some cases, on the death of beneficiaries. It is not thought worthwhile to take advantage of these in a standard draft. But where a settlor wishes specifically to be able to recover the trust property in the event that her children should die before her, that can be done.

There is also some scope for tax avoidance, ie, giving away property and retaining rights to enjoy it. This can lead to inheritance tax, CGT and income tax savings. But this is a matter for specialist advice.

Meaning of 'spouse' of settlor

4.31

The exclusion of the 'Settlor' is relatively straightforward.[53]

Statute gives a partial definition to the term 'spouse' for the purposes of the Settlement Provisions rules which require settlor and 'spouse' to be excluded. Three categories of person are stated not to be 'spouses' for this purpose:

52 ICTA 1988, s 660A; TCGA 1992, s 77; FA 1986, s 102 (gifts with reservation).
53 For the position where a trust is made by joint settlors see para 9.11 (Form where trust made by joint settlors). For indirect or contributory settlors, see para 12.13 (Exclusion of contributory and indirect settlors).

(1) the widow or widower of the settlor does not count as a 'spouse'. This merely codifies the long established rule, that the word 'spouse' in its natural sense does not include a widow;[54]
(2) a potential spouse[55] does not count as a spouse. This appears to be otiose: no one could contend that a potential spouse is a 'spouse';[56]
(3) a separated spouse[57] does not count as a 'spouse'.

The practical consequence of this definition for trust drafting is that it is possible to include in the class of beneficiaries:
(1) the widow or widower of the settlor; and
(2) a separated spouse.

Widow of settlor as beneficiary of a lifetime trust

4.32

It is recommended that the widow of the settlor should be included in the class of beneficiaries as a matter of course in a lifetime trust. The intended beneficiaries of the trust may be children and descendants of the settlor; there may be no intention to use the funds to benefit the settlor's widow. Nevertheless, there are advantages in including her in the class of beneficiaries. It is to be stressed that we are not concerned with any actual benefit for the widow, but to retain the opportunity of benefiting her. It is conceivable that a widow might find herself in need after the death of the settlor. More significantly, the existence of the power to benefit her may be a comfort to her; and specifically it may enable her to make lifetime gifts to her family, confident in the knowledge that the trust fund is there to fall back on in case of unforeseen need. The inclusion of the widow of the settlor in the class of beneficiaries may therefore be an important aid to long-term IHT planning.

54 ICTA 1988, s 660A(4). The House of Lords held that the term 'spouse' did not include a widow or widower: *Vestey v IRC* 31 TC 1, reversing *IRC v Gaunt* (1941) 24 TC 69. *Gaunt*, though obsolete, deserves a mention in a footnote as an exemplar of judicial mentality. Reversing the decision of the High Court, Goddard LJ said the point was 'clear'. Clausen LJ thought it was 'perfectly clear'. Scott LJ thought it was 'obvious'. Yet only six years later, the House of Lords held their view to be wrong.

55 In the words of the statute, 'a person to whom the settlor is not for the time being married but may later marry'. See too *Unmarried Settlor* v *IRC* [2003] STC (SCD) 274.

56 In the Revenue's view this reverses the decision in *IRC v Tennant* (1942) 24 TC 215: see CGT Manual 34753. This might be doubted but that is not a drafting issue.

57 In the words of the statute, 'a spouse from whom the settlor is separated under an order of a court, or under a separation agreement or in such circumstances that the separation is likely to be permanent'. As a matter of general law, a marriage continues until dissolved by decree absolute. Until decree absolute, therefore, the parties to a marriage are still 'spouses', except where the word is given an artificial definition. Authority is not needed as this proposition is obvious; but see *Aspden v Hildesley* (1982) 55 TC 609.

Widow of testator as beneficiary of a will

4.33

A married testator will normally include his wife[58] in the class of beneficiaries under his will as a matter of course. The will of an unmarried testator should not include any reference to a wife since: (1) if the testator does not marry, there will be no wife; and (2) if he does marry the will is revoked by the marriage! So the reference to 'wife' in the will of an unmarried testator can never take effect and may cause confusion. A will expressed to be in contemplation of marriage may include in the class 'my intended wife [*Jane*].'

Separated spouse of settlor as beneficiary

4.34

The next question is whether a typical settlor will want to include his separated spouse as a beneficiary. The answer, in general, is that he will not; so it is suggested that it is not appropriate in a standard draft to include the separated spouse expressly as a beneficiary. (If the settlor exclusion clause permits, it may be possible later to add the spouse as a beneficiary after separation or at least after divorce.)

Charities as beneficiaries

4.35

No drafting problem should arise if the settlor wishes to include specific charities by name. The charity should be identified by name, address, and, if an English charity which has been registered with the Charity Commissioners, its charity registration number. It is the duty of the drafter to check that:
(1) the name given by the client is correct,
(2) the body is still in existence when the will or trust is made.[59]

58 It makes no difference whether one refers to 'wife', 'spouse' or 'widow'. The term 'wife' is preferred in this book since (at the time when the will is written) it is more apt than 'widow' as well as being more cheerful.

59 *Re Recher* [1972] Ch 526. One should not need to emphasise this 'most elementary' duty but in the authors' experience this is sometimes overlooked (a fault perhaps attributable to cut price will drafting). Recent research into charitable bequests made in the wills proved in Northern Ireland in 1997, disclosed numerous examples of mis-described charities. Two very obvious ones, involving the same organisation, the Chest, Heart and Stroke Association, were: 'Heart Chest and Throat Association' and 'The Chest and Hart [!] Association' – Dawson, Grattan and Lundy, *Dying to Give, A Study of Charitable Giving by Will* (2003) HMSO. It is not sufficient to check in published reference books. In *Recher* the drafter was

In Northern Ireland the absence of registration makes this more difficult than it is in England where practitioners may readily access the register of charities is accessible on www.charity-commission.gov.uk. Some help may be obtained from the Northern Ireland Council for Voluntary Action (NICVA)[60] which maintains an informal database of many Northern Ireland voluntary associations (not just charities).[61] However, the database (known as SectorNet) is not comprehensive. There is no enforceable obligation for charities to file annual reports and no requirement to notify that a charity has been wound up so entries are often out of date. NICVA staff are pleased to take telephone enquiries from solicitors who are seeking current information about charities within the jurisdiction.

If a settlor has set up a private charitable trust then that trust may conveniently be named as one of the class of beneficiaries.

If it is desired to benefit any charity, define 'Beneficiaries' to include:

> *any company, body or trust established for charitable purposes only.*

The wording is derived from statutory precedent.[62]

'Any charity' would be sufficiently precise[63] but the common practice is to define the term.

Some English precedents use the definition 'any institution which is a charity for the purposes of the Charities Act 1993' but this is inappropriate for use in Northern Ireland as it would exclude charities governed by Northern Ireland law, as well as those governed by Scottish or foreign laws.

---

criticised for drafting a will which made a gift to an association less than six months after the association was wound up. A phone call would have identified the problem but most reference books would have been out of date. Fortunately well advised bodies do not disband on a reorganisation or merger: they continue a dormant existence in order to receive future legacies.

60 NICVA promotes good practice among voluntary organisations and assists them to become formally established within an appropriate legal framework. It provides a Charity Advice Service which makes available information on matters such as drawing up a Constitution and claiming tax exemption. It has no regulatory responsibilities. NICVA's telephone number is 028 9087 7777.

61 It includes non-charitable voluntary groups and purely contemplative religious groups which would fail the public benefit test.

62 ICTA 1988, s 506(1); Charities Act 1993, s 96 (which, of course, does not extend to NI). The expression 'company, body or trust' is preferred to the statutory phrase 'body of persons' with its archaic Taxes Act definition; or 'undertaking', the (deliberately wide) Charities Act expression. It is obviously unnecessary to say that 'charitable' means 'charitable according to Northern Ireland law'; see para 27.1 (The governing law). It is equally unnecessary to say that charitable means 'exclusively charitable'. The court would not give the word any other meaning unless the context so required; in which case something has gone very wrong with the drafting. For an example see *George Drexler Ofrex Foundation v IRC* (1965) 42 TC 524.

63 In the CGT and VAT legislation, the statute contentedly uses the word 'charity' without definition; likewise the Enduring Powers of Attorney (NI) Order 1987, art 5(5)(b); Companies (NI) Order 1986, art 257A(2), and the Law Commission of England and Wales draft Perpetuities Bill.

Where a trust wishes to make a gift to charity, it will usually be more tax efficient in practice to transfer funds to a beneficiary who (independently) makes a donation to charity which qualifies for income tax relief.[64]

Non-charitable companies as beneficiaries

4.36

No difficulty arises where non-charitable companies (eg campaigning organisations such as the National Anti-Vivisection Society) are to be beneficiaries. The drafter should check that the name given by the client is correct and that the body is still in existence when the will or trust is made, and that a non charitable institution is not mis-described in the documentation as a charity. The drafting should not create a trust for the purposes of the institution, but simply a gift to the company.[65]

Subject to the same checks, no problem should arise with a gift to an unincorporated non-charitable body.

Foreign charities as beneficiaries

4.37

Foreign charities are not 'charities' for either UK tax or Northern Ireland charity law purposes.[66] In particular the drafter should be alert to this issue when the settlor wishes to benefit Irish charities with an all-island dimension.[67]

Foreign charitable trusts may nevertheless be beneficiaries of a Northern Ireland law trust. While Northern Ireland law would not recognise a non-charitable purpose trust as valid, it will recognise a power or duty for trustees to transfer property to foreign trustees to hold on the terms of foreign trust law. This does not breach the Northern Ireland law rule which is based on propositions that a trust must be enforceable by beneficiaries: the foreign trustees are the 'beneficiaries' for this purpose.

64 *Venables and Kessler on the Taxation of Charities* (4th edn, 2003). For charities as default beneficiaries see para 12.20 (Default clause).

65 A gift to the company is not regarded as a trust for the purposes of the company: *Re Recher* [1972] Ch 526.

66 See *Venables and Kessler on the Taxation of Charities* (4th edn, 2003) ch 1.

67 It appears that the Revenue considers a number of factors when deciding whether or not a charity is 'established' in the UK (although there is no published Statement of Practice). It would seem that when dealing with an Irish charity which has a branch in Northern Ireland the key factor is whether that branch has a sufficiently independent administration.

Power to add beneficiaries

4.38

A settlor who specifies even a very wide class of beneficiaries may later regret that the trustees cannot benefit some other persons. Hence the popularity of powers to add beneficiaries, which arm the trustees with a weapon which will enable them to consider all developments and respond to all future mishaps and disasters. It is a convenient way to provide for unmarried cohabitees of beneficiaries. The power can simplify the drafting of a trust: it may become unnecessary to include some classes of beneficiaries 'just in case'. The power to add beneficiaries could, however, be used to frustrate the wishes of the settlor. The authors would not confer a power to add beneficiaries unless it is subject to constraints to prevent abuse. The obvious restraint is to require the consent of the settlor during his life. That is straightforward, but what should be done after his death? One does not want the power to lapse. The proposed solution is to require the consent of two beneficiaries after the death of the settlor. It is unlikely that two beneficiaries and the trustees should all conspire to defeat the intentions of the settlor. It may occasionally happen that there is only one adult beneficiary; the power to add beneficiaries would then be suspended until such time as there are two adult beneficiaries available.

The High Court has consistently upheld as valid a power for trustees to select almost anyone in the world and add them to the class of beneficiaries.[68] The view has been expressed that a power to add any beneficiaries may be struck down by the higher courts. The objection is that this power is too wide to be exercised in a fiduciary manner. But the law on this point should not be regarded as settled.[69]

The problem can and should be avoided. The settlor, protector, or beneficiaries of the trust should be given power to propose additional beneficiaries. This would not be a fiduciary power and so could not be void as too wide. Then the trustees are to be given a power to accept as the beneficiaries any nominees proposed to them: that is a power in favour of a limited class, and so clearly valid.

The power to add beneficiaries may be treated either as a separate power in a clause of its own; or it may be included in the definition of 'Beneficiaries.' The latter course is adopted in this book, since the form used is short and concise.

The form adopted in this book is therefore to say that 'the Beneficiaries' include:

68 *Re Manisty* [1974] Ch 17; *Re Hay* [1982] 1 WLR 202. These supply convincing reasoning for not following the dicta of the Court of Appeal to the contrary in *Blausten v IRC* [1972] Ch 256. The same applies to will trusts: *Re Beatty* [1990] 3 All ER 844.

69 Underhill and Hayton *The Law Relating to Trusts and Trustees* (16th edn, 2003) pp 96–97). But *Lewin on Trusts* curtly dismisses this view: (17th edn) p 85. Many trusts, drafted not unreasonably in reliance on the High Court decisions, would be disastrously affected.

> any person[70] or class of persons nominated to the Trustees by:
> (i) the Settlor, or
> (ii) two Beneficiaries (after the death of the Settlor)
> and whose nomination is accepted in writing by the Trustees.

If there is a Protector, one can simplify this form and say that 'the Beneficiaries' include:

> Any person or class of persons nominated to the Trustees by a Beneficiary whose nomination is accepted in writing by the Trustees with the consent in writing of the Protector.

Power to exclude beneficiaries

4.39

This is not needed as the overriding powers can be used to exclude any beneficiary if desired.

Other possible beneficiaries

4.40

In drafting any trust, the drafter should as a matter of course ask the settlor whether it is desired to include any other particular beneficiaries. There may be other specific individuals or members of his family whom he wishes to keep in mind; and there are certain categories of beneficiaries to which we can now turn. These are not for inclusion in a standard draft.

Dependants

4.41

It is certainly possible to include in the class of beneficiaries the dependants of any person. It is a matter of fact and degree what constitutes 'dependence' but the courts have held the concept to be sufficiently certain for trust law requirements.[71] The inclusion of dependants may be desirable for both practical and tax reasons.

70 This term would include charitable trusts and charitable purposes generally: *Re Triffitt* [1958] Ch 852 at 862.

71 *Re Baden (No 2)* [1973] Ch 9. IHTA 1984, s 86(1)(b) is also drafted on the basis that 'dependancy' is sufficiently certain to satisfy trust law requirements, and the law on this point must be regarded as settled.

The precedents in the book do not include dependants in a standard form as the power to add beneficiaries ought to be sufficient.

Although it would be satisfactory to use the bare term 'Dependants', the authors would prefer to use the wording from art 3(1)(e) of the Inheritance (Provision for Family and Dependants) (NI) Order 1979. This is slightly more precise and has the benefit of some discussion in the case law. The class of dependants of a testator would be defined in these terms:

> Any person who immediately before the death of the testator was being maintained, either wholly or partly, by the testator. For this purpose a person shall be treated as being maintained, either wholly or partly, by the testator if the testator otherwise than for full valuable consideration, was making a substantial contribution in money or money's worth towards the reasonable needs of that person.

It is better practice where possible to name specific dependants as beneficiaries, and not to leave them to qualify under this clause. That saves the trustees from having to satisfy themselves that such persons qualify as dependants.

Employees of beneficiaries

4.42

It may be convenient to include employees in the class of beneficiaries, especially where employees may live on trust property. This also offers the prospect of substantial tax savings, conceivably for income tax, CGT, and IHT. The employee could be added by name. Otherwise the following form is proposed:

> **'The Beneficiaries'** means ... [children, etc]; and (iv) any employee or former employee of the above.

Employees of family company

4.43

Where the trust property is shares in a family company it should be considered whether employees of that company might be added to the class of beneficiaries. This gives the trustees flexibility to convert the trust, or any part of it, into an employee trust enjoying significant IHT advantages.[72]

72 IHTA 1984, s 86.

'Fall back' beneficiaries

4.44

A settlor will generally want his trust fund to be used in the first instance for his children and their families. They may all die: what should happen to the fund then? This issue arises under any form of trust: interest in possession, A&M, or discretionary.

This is of course a matter for the settlor to decide: the drafter should seek instructions.

Charity as 'fall back' beneficiary

4.45

The settlor may wish the trust fund to pass to charity absolutely. This is straightforward and can be dealt with in the default clause. The settlor may wish the trust fund to pass either to charity or (at the discretion of the trustees) to some other beneficiaries. Careful drafting is needed to ensure that, if the gift to charity takes effect, the IHT charity exemption applies.[73]

Distant relatives as 'fall back' beneficiaries

4.46

The common and understandable wish is that if the settlor's own family die out, the fund should pass to the nearest surviving family: brothers or sisters and their families; or nephews and nieces and their families. (For the purpose of this discussion we shall refer to 'direct family' and 'distant relatives'.) How is the drafter to achieve this?

4.47

Use of default clause. It is possible to name some distant relatives in the default clause. Then on the death of the direct family, the trust fund passes to the named relative; if he is dead, the fund passes with his estate, on the terms of his will. This is a crude and unsatisfactory solution. The default clause is too inflexible. Who is to be specified? At the time the trust is made, the only practical course may be to name (say) the brothers or sisters of the settlor; but by the time of the death of the

73 See *Venables and Kessler on the Taxation of Charities* (4th edn, 2003) Key Haven Publications, ch 21.

direct family, it may be desired to pass the fund not to the siblings of the settlor, but to their children or grandchildren.

4.48

Simple addition to the class of beneficiaries. A better course is to expand the class of Beneficiaries, the objects of the overriding powers of appointment, to include the distant relatives as well as the direct family. Thus:

> '**The Beneficiaries**' means
> (a) The children and descendants of the Settlor;
> (b) The spouses, widows and widowers (whether or not remarried) of (a) above; and
> (c) The children and descendants of [name and address] and their spouses, widows and widowers (whether or not remarried).

This is superior to the first course considered above, the use of a default clause. On the failure of the direct family, the trustees have the discretion they need to benefit the more distant relatives in the most appropriate way.

This clause does give the trustees an unnecessarily wide discretion. They could use their overriding powers to cut out the settlor's direct family in order to benefit the distant relatives. That does not matter too much, since the trustees will not in practice behave in such an irrational manner. However, the settlor may not want the trustees to possess such a power at all.

A general power to add beneficiaries could also be used to solve this problem, but should not be regarded as satisfactory: something more specific is needed.[74]

4.49

Limited extension of the class of beneficiaries. The intention of the settlor in this sort of case is that the distant relatives become beneficiaries on the death of all the direct descendants of the settlor. While the form is slightly more complicated, there is no reason why this should not be expressed in the trust. The following is proposed:

> '**The Beneficiaries**' means:
> (a) The children and descendants of the Settlor;
> (b) The spouses, widows and widowers (whether or not remarried) of (a) above; and
> (c) At any time during which there are no Beneficiaries within (a) above:

74 The power to add beneficiaries in the form used in this book would not be exercisable unless the settlor or two adult beneficiaries were living and willing to give consent to the exercise of the power.

(i) the children and descendants of [name and address] and
(ii) the spouses, widows and widowers (whether or not remarried) of (i) above.

Tax and the class of beneficiaries

4.50

Apart from the exclusion of the settlor and spouse, are there any other exclusions from the class of beneficiaries which are needed for tax reasons? The following matters are mentioned here for completeness:

Offshore trusts. The exclusion of 'defined persons' from the class of Beneficiaries may avoid the application of the CGT offshore settlor rules.[75] Non-resident trusts do not qualify for the income tax relief for excluded income if there are 'relevant beneficiaries'.[76]

Re-investment relief. There are (somewhat curious) restrictions on beneficiaries in certain cases where trustees wish to claim CGT re-investment relief.[77] All that matters however is that the relevant conditions are satisfied when the trustees realise a gain on which they want to claim the relief. Accordingly, the drafter need not be concerned with this at the time he makes the trust. If need be, beneficiaries can be excluded at some later time, so as to qualify for the relief.

CGT taper relief. The class of beneficiaries may enable trust property to qualify as business assets for CGT taper relief.[78]

75 TCGA 1992, s 86; on this topic see Robert Venables QC *Non-Resident Trusts* (8th edn, 2000).

76 FA 1995, s 128. The expression 'relevant beneficiaries' is widely defined but construed more narrowly by the Revenue in practice.

77 TCGA 1992, Sch 5B, para 17.

78 TCGA 1992, Sch A1, para 6.

CHAPTER 5

Trustees

Number of trustees

5.1

The minimum number of trustees is one.[1] In Northern Ireland, in contrast to England,[2] there is no restriction on the number of trustees (or indeed the number of personal representatives)[3] that may be appointed. However, having more than four trustees is unwieldy and ought to be avoided.[4]

Our recommendation is that there should normally be two trustees:

(1) A professional trustee who should be a partner in a firm of solicitors or accountants. This gives slightly more security than a sole practitioner.
(2) The settlor, or a friend or member of the family.

In older precedents one occasionally sees requirements that there should be at least two or even three trustees at all times. This seems unnecessary and has rightly fallen out of favour.

1 A sole trustee is competent in every respect with the following exceptions:
(1) A sole trustee cannot give a valid receipt for capital sums derived from settled land: SLA 1882, s 39, or trusts for sale: TA(NI) 1958, s 14.
(2) Two trustees are needed to discharge a retiring trustee under the statutory power.
(3) A sole professional trustee cannot charge under the statutory power: TA (NI) 2001, s 28.

These rules are excluded in the precedents in this book; see para 5.34 (Requirement of two continuing trustees on retirement of trustees); para 20.55 (Trustee remuneration). These restrictions do not apply to a trust corporation.

(4) The drafter may require that two trustees are required to exercise certain powers: see para 6.14 (Two-trustee rule).

2 In England s 34(2) of TA 1925 as amended by the TLATA 1996 limits the number of trustees to four in the case of dispositions creating trusts of land.

3 In England the maximum number of personal representatives is also four: Supreme Court Act 1981, s 114(1).

4 It may also give rise to minor complications. For example, under standard company articles the directors may refuse to register the transfer of shares to more than four transferees: see Table A, art 24. But if necessary the shares could be vested in nominees for the trustees.

Choice of trustees

Settlor and spouse as trustees

5.2

The settlor may be a trustee and so may his spouse. The appointment of the settlor (or spouse) as trustee does not have any tax drawback.[5] The prejudice sometimes met against the settlor-trustee probably reflects a distant memory of Estate Duty provisions which discouraged the appointment of a settlor as trustee.[6] On the settlor as sole trustee see paragraph 6.27 (Settlor as sole trustee?).

Beneficiaries as trustees

5.3

Old precedents sometimes direct that a beneficiary may not be appointed trustee. This is entirely the wrong approach.[7] The appointment of a beneficiary as trustee gives him a direct interest and involvement in his or her family's financial affairs, and may be highly advantageous.

The appointment of a beneficiary as trustee does, however, give rise to a possible conflict of interest. There are various ways to minimise the problems which may arise. First, of course, no one will appoint a beneficiary trustee unless confident that he will act properly. Secondly, the beneficiary will not be the sole trustee. There will be a professional trustee to hold the balance. A settlor creating a trust for his two children and their respective families might appoint each child trustee to safeguard each family interest. Thirdly, the trust will provide that a beneficiary who is a trustee cannot exercise powers in his own favour without the concurrence of an independent trustee. See paragraph 5.12 (Conflicts of interest).

In short it is thought that the conflict of interest will be manageable and should not be a serious objection to the appointment of a beneficiary as trustee. There are

5 A settlor may be a trustee (or the sole trustee) without transgressing FA 1986, s 102 (gifts with reservation): *Perpetual Executors and Trustees Association of Australia Ltd v Commonwealth of Australia Taxation Comr* [1954] AC 114. The Revenue accept this: CTO Advanced Instruction Manual D.75. On trustee remuneration, where the settlor is trustee see para 20.62 (Trustee remuneration clause: dispositive or administrative?) and para 20.64 (Can the Settlor charge if he is a trustee?)

6 FA 1940, ss 40, 58(5). There is no equivalent in current tax legislation.

7 This may in the past have been done for Estate Duty reasons doubtful then and now obsolete. See 12.15 (Extending the settlor exclusion clause to exclude trustees). Where an existing trust has this or any other inappropriate prohibition on the choice of trustees, it would be possible to override it, if there was a good reason, by an application to the Court.

many cases where the law accepts an element of conflict of interest.[8] Given the advantages of a beneficiary acting as trustee, the rigorous exclusion of the possibility of conflicts of interest carries too high a price.

Professional trustees

5.4

The aim in combining family and professional trustees is that the trust should be administered both with technical expertise and an understanding of the needs of the beneficiaries.

Professional trustees will be reluctant to act if they may incur personal liabilities unless indemnified. Trustees may incur liabilities to third parties (eg loans to acquire trust property or leases with onerous covenants). Here, with care, it should be possible to arrange that the professional trustees are not personally liable beyond the extent of any trust property. This, therefore, should not cause the trust to be deprived of the benefit of a professional trustee. Tax liabilities (and liability for breach of trust) are inescapably joint and several liabilities of trustees. These may be liabilities for which trustees cannot be suitably indemnified. The solution may be for a professional trustee to retire in favour of a family trustee before any liability accrues.[9]

A trustee who is a member of a partnership is safer than a sole practitioner – as the trust has more protection in the event of fraudulent breach of trust.

Corporate trustees

5.5

There is a choice between professional individuals, and trust companies. Trust companies will neither die nor retire. On the other hand, if a trust corporation is appointed trustee, the personnel actually managing the trust may change from time to time without the consent of the settlor.

8 The concept of a trustee-beneficiary is, of course, enshrined in the Settled Land Act scheme, under which many trustee powers are given to the tenant for life. For further cases where a sensible conflict of interest is accepted see EPA (NI) O 1987, art 5(4); TLATA 1996, s 9; the Companies (Tables A to F) Regulations 1986, Table A, art 85.

9 However, a retirement in order to facilitate a breach of trust may itself be a breach of trust.

Accountants as trustees

5.6

An accountant may be unable to act as trustee if his firm also audits a company held by the trust. See ICAEW Code of Conduct paras 4.42–4.47.[10] In brief, either the trust holds more than 10% of a company or the company is more than 10% of the trust fund. This rule does not apply to unlisted companies but the trustee should not be responsible for the audit.

Director of listed company as trustee

5.7

If a director of a listed company acts as trustee, disposals of a trust's shareholding in that company must be in accordance with the Stock Exchange Listing Rules.[11]

Insider dealing and trusteeship

5.8

Similarly, any person who may obtain inside information relating to trust property may be constrained by the Insider Dealing legislation and unable to deal with trust property. Such a person may be unsuitable to act as trustee.[12]

Foreign trustees

5.9

If it is desired to appoint non-resident trustees the choice is generally restricted to professional trustees.[13] The disadvantages of non-resident trustees in terms of additional expense and inconvenience is one factor to be balanced against the tax advantages; the tax advantages were reduced but by no means eliminated by the reforms in the Finance Acts 1991 and 1998.

If offshore trustees are appointed it is recommended that the settlor (i) should find a firm with professional liability insurance and (ii) should insist that there is

10 Accessible on www.icaew.co.uk.

11 Chapter 16 of the Listing Rules. The restrictions may apply in any event, if the director or his minor children are beneficiaries, in which case the appointment of the director as trustee may make no practical difference.

12 *Wight v Olswang* [1998] NPC 111 accessible on www.kessler.co.uk illustrates these difficulties.

13 For a discussion on non-resident trusts see Venables *Non-Resident Trusts* (8th ed, 2000).

no wide indemnity clause. An anxious settlor who cannot satisfy his concerns might set up his own offshore trustee company.

Order of trustees' names

5.10

The order in which the trustees' names appear is of little significance. The idea that the first named trustee is in a special position is a fallacy. This misconception is based on a confusion with the company law rule that, in the case of joint shareholders, the company has regard to the vote of the first named on the register.[14] There is no reason why the first name on the register should be the first named trustee. Moreover, while the company will only regard the first named on the register, the first so named may only act with the concurrence of his co-trustees, and he may be restrained by them from acting without their consent.[15]

Flee clauses

5.11

The purpose of 'flee clauses' is to facilitate the appointment of new trustees if, where the old trustees reside, there is a breakdown of law and order, or a change of tax regime. These are only of importance to offshore trusts and fall outside the scope of this book.

Conflicts of interest

5.12

The general rule is that a trustee cannot enter into any transaction which might conflict with his duty as trustee. Trustees cannot purchase trust property,[16] or sell property to the trust, nor can property be sold between trusts which share a trustee. Trustees cannot take a lease of property which was formerly let to the trust.[17] A trustee-landlord cannot consent to the assignment of the lease of his land to a property company of which he is director.[18] The prohibition is not absolute: such

14 Table A of the Companies (Tables A to F) Regulations 1986, art 55.

15 *IRC v Lithgows Ltd* (1960) 39 TC 270. Although a Scottish case, the same principles will apply in England. The order of trustees may matter for tax (eg *IRC* v *Barclays Bank* [1961] AC 509) but in practice that will only exceptionally be the case.

16 See generally *Holder* v *Holder* [1968] Ch 353.

17 *Keech v Sandford* (1726) Sel Cas Ch 61.

18 *Re Thompson* [1986] Ch 99.

acts may be carried out with the consent of the court, or may be authorised in the trust deed.

The aim of the rule is the prevention of fraud; but the rule is too strict: one independent person would be sufficient to safeguard the interests of the trust.[19] That is the aim of this clause:

> (1) In this paragraph:
> (a) **'A Fiduciary'** means a Trustee or other Person[20] subject to fiduciary duties under the Settlement.
> (b) **'An Independent Trustee',** in relation to a Person, means a Trustee who is not:
> (i) a brother, sister, ancestor, descendant or dependent of the Person;
> (ii) a spouse of (i) above or of the Person;
> (iii) a company controlled by one or more of the above.
>
> (2) Subject to sub-clause (3) below a Fiduciary may:
> (a) enter into a transaction with the Trustees, or
> (b) be interested in an arrangement in which the Trustees are or might have been interested, or
> (c) act (or not act) in any other circumstances;
> even though his fiduciary duty under the Settlement conflicts with other duties or with his personal interest.
>
> (3) Sub-clause (2) above only applies if:
> (a) the Fiduciary first discloses to the Trustees the nature and extent of any material interest conflicting with his fiduciary duties, and
> (b) there is an Independent Trustee in respect of whom there is no conflict of interest, and he considers that the transaction arrangement or action is not contrary to the general interest of the Settlement.

5.13

This draft is loosely based on statutory precedent.[21] It is sometimes said that clauses of this type should be strictly construed. But it is submitted that these clauses should be construed fairly and naturally, according to their terms, like any other clause.[22]

19 This is the view of Millett LJ as he then was:

> 'The rule has been thought in modern times to operate harshly where one of several trustees purchases the trust property at a fair price properly negotiated with his co-trustees.' (*Ingram v IRC* [1997] STC 1234 at p 1260.)

20 The expression 'person' is defined in the precedents in this book to include any person in the world, and to include a trustee.

21 SLA 1925, s 68; Companies (Tables A to F) Regulations 1986, Table A, art 85; Intestates' Estates Act 1952, Sch 2, para 5(1).

22 This was the approach of the Court of Appeal in *Sargeant v National Westminster Bank plc* (1990) 61 P & CR 518 accessible on www.kessler.co.uk.

The aim is to cover all eventualities. This has led to a fairly complex draft; though not so complex, it is hoped, that it needs reading more than once to be understood. The clause is in three respects more widely drawn than many others in use.

(1) The clause authorises a wide range of transactions. A common form which simply authorises trustees to purchase trust property would not solve many difficulties which arise in practice.[23]

(2) The clause defines in detail the qualifications of an independent trustee. The definition is not wholly comprehensive; there may be occasions where it is doubtful whether there is a 'conflict of interest' or what is meant by 'control of a company.' This should not matter in practice, where there will generally be a professional trustee of undoubted independence. Further refinements (such as defining 'control') are thought unnecessary. The short-cut of incorporating statutory rules[24] is rejected. The statutory rules are too cumbersome, and the trust may need to be read and understood many years after those provisions have become obsolete.

(3) The clause applies to trustees and other persons subject to fiduciary duties. If it applied only to trustees then others (eg former trustees and the protector if there is one) might remain subject to the self-dealing rule.

The clause specifies that the transaction is only to proceed if the trustees consider it to accord with the general interest of the settlement. This phrase 'the general interest of the settlement' now has statutory authority in England.[25] It would be possible simply to require the independent trustee's 'consent'; but it seems better to spell out the circumstances in which consent is to be granted.

Distinguishing personal and fiduciary conflicts

5.14

Some drafters distinguish between:

(1) *Fiduciary* conflicts of interest, for instance, where it is desired to sell assets from one trust to another, and the same persons are trustees of both trusts.

(2) *Personal* conflicts of interest, for instance, where a trustee wishes to purchase property himself from a trust of which he is a trustee.

23 For instance, such a limited form would not have helped the trustees in *Re Thompson* [1986] Ch 99, where a trustee breached the self-dealing rule when he consented (in his capacity as trustee) to the assignment of a lease to a company of which he was a director. Nor would the limited form help the trustees in *Keech v Sandford* (1726) Sel Cas Ch 61, where the trustees took a new lease of property after an earlier lease to the trustees had expired. Nor would the limited form help where trust property is to be sold from one trust to another, and the same person was trustee of both trusts.

24 Such as the Pensions (NI) Order 1995, art 23 (independent trustee) or tax provisions defining 'control'.

25 TLATA 1996, s 11.

The distinction is a real one and, strictly, rather more protection is needed in the case of a personal conflict of interest. This school of drafting therefore sets out different rules to govern the dealings of trustees in the two situations. For instance, trustees may be authorised to act in all situations where there is merely a fiduciary conflict of interest; and an independent trustee is required only in cases of personal conflict. In our view the matter is not of sufficient practical importance to be worth taking the trouble to make these distinctions in a standard draft.

Trustee – beneficiaries: sub-clause (3)

5.15

> The powers of the Trustees may be used to benefit a Trustee (to the same extent as if he were not a Trustee) provided that there is an Independent Trustee in respect of whom there is no conflict of interest.

This deals with the entirely different problems which may arise where a beneficiary is a trustee, and wishes to, say, appoint property to himself.

The course adopted here is to say that this can be done with the approval of an independent trustee.[26]

Another possible course is to provide that the beneficiary could appoint property to himself even if there is no independent trustee, provided there is at least a second trustee in respect of whom there is no conflict of interest. This would be more appropriate where a settlor wanted all the trustees to be members of the family, so there would be no independent trustee (as defined).

Another course is to provide that the beneficiary could appoint property to himself even if he is sole trustee. This raises a number of trust law difficulties, and is not recommended.[27]

What is the position in the absence of such a provision: can a trustee use a power of appointment to benefit himself? This is a matter of construction of each individual trust and the answer may not be entirely clear.[28]

26 For a statutory precedent see Pensions (NI) Order 1995, art 39.

27 *Drexel Burnham Lambert UK Pension Plan,* discussed in the following footnote; *Re Penrose* [1933] Ch 793 discussed below.

28 The issue had arisen in the context of pension funds; here the High Court ruled that a trustee-beneficiary cannot exercise powers in his own favour (unless with the consent of the Court) *Re Drexel Burnham Lambert UK Pension Plan* [1995] 1 WLR 32, but the Court of Appeal has said the opposite: *Edge v Pensions Ombudsman* [2000] Ch 602 at 621-2. For private trusts, it would be sensible to draw a distinction between original trustees (where the settlor should be taken to intend the trustees to be able to exercise the power in their own favour) and others; the issues have yet to be full discussed in the Courts, but *Cooper v Public Trustee* [2001] WTLR 901 contains a useful clarification. See John Mowbray 'Choosing Among the Beneficiaries of Discretionary Trusts' [1998] PCB 239 accessible on www.kessler.co.uk. Review

Alternative form where there is a 'protector'

Where there is a protector, he is an ideal person to authorise a breach of the self-dealing rule. This allows the form to be simplified:

> (1) In this paragraph **'a Fiduciary'** means a Trustee, or other person subject to fiduciary duties under this Settlement, but not the Protector.
>
> (2) Subject to (3) below a Fiduciary may:
> (a) enter into a transaction with the Trustees, or
> (b) be interested in an arrangement in which the Trustees are or might have been interested, or
> (c) act (or not act) in any other circumstances;
> even though his fiduciary duty under the Settlement conflicts with other duties or with his personal interest.
>
> (3) Sub-clause (2) above only has effect if:
> (a) the Fiduciary first discloses to the Protector the nature and extent of any material interest conflicting with his fiduciary duties, and
> (b) the Protector considers that the transaction arrangement or action is not contrary to the general interest of the Settlement.
>
> (4) The powers of the Trustees may be used to benefit a Beneficiary who is a Trustee (to the same extent as if he were not a Trustee) with the consent in writing of the Protector.

Trustee exemption clauses[29]

Construction of exemption clauses

5.16

This section considers the meaning of the wide range of expressions used in exemption clauses.

'Actual fraud'

The leading case *Armitage v Nurse*[30] discussed the following clause:

29 A note on terminology. The terms 'exemption clause' 'exoneration clause' 'exclusion clause' 'exculpation clause' and 'indemnity clause' are all used interchangeably. 'Indemnity clause' is less apposite (to be pedantic) as the clauses considered here prevent liability rather than providing an indemnity for an extant liability.

30 [1998] Ch 241.

> No Trustee shall be liable for any loss or damage which may happen to the Trust Fund or any part thereof or the income thereof at any time or from any cause whatsoever unless such loss or damage shall be caused by his own actual fraud.

It was held that the expression 'actual fraud' means dishonesty.[31] 'Dishonesty' connotes action by the trustee:

(1) knowing that it is contrary to the interests of the beneficiaries (in the discussion below, 'knowing dishonesty'); or
(2) recklessly indifferent whether it is contrary to their interests or not ('reckless indifference'); or
(3) with the honest belief that it is proper, but which is objectively so unreasonable that no reasonable solicitor-trustee could have thought it for the benefit of beneficiaries. This category may not apply to non-professional trustees.[32]

'Wilful fraud or dishonesty'

This has the same meaning as 'actual fraud'.[33]

'Wilful default'

Some exemption clauses exclude liability for loss unless due to the 'wilful default' of the trustee.[34] The expression 'wilful default' has two meanings. It sometimes means want of ordinary prudence (*ie* negligence); or any breach of fiduciary duty (for instance in the phrase 'liable to account on the footing of wilful default'). In the context of a trustee exemption clause, however, wilful default means fraud: knowing dishonesty or reckless indifference[35].

31 The word 'actual' excluded an extended meaning of 'fraud' (known as 'constructive fraud' or 'equitable fraud') with the vague definition (or non-definition) of 'a breach of duty, falling short of deceit, to which equity attached its sanction.'

32 *Walker v Stones* [2000] 4 All ER 412. A layman using ordinary language would not describe category (2) or (3) as 'dishonesty', so 'dishonesty' is being used in an artificial, technical sense. This is unfortunate but understandable. The court's regrettable ruling that exclusion clauses are effective (except for dishonesty) causes injustice which the court mitigates by giving an unnaturally wide meaning to 'dishonesty'. The concept of dishonesty in categories (1) and (2) is denied from *Armitage* v *Nurse*. This concept of dishonesty is consistent with the definition of 'fraud' for the purposes of the tort of deceit (fraudulent misrepresentation). See *Derry v Peek* (1889) 14 App Cas 337; the headnote reads: 'In an action of deceit the Plaintiff must prove actual fraud. Fraud is proved when it is shown that a false representation has been made knowingly, or without belief in its truth, or recklessly, without caring whether it be true or false.' *Walker* v *Stones* [2001] QB 902 at 937 adds category (3). A layman using ordinary language would not describe category (2) or (3) as 'dishonesty', so 'dishonesty' is being used in an artificial, technical sense. This is unfortunate but understandable. The court's regrettable ruling that exclusion clauses are effective (except for dishonesty) causes injustice which the court mitigates by giving an unnaturally wide meaning to 'dishonesty'.

33 *Walker v Stones* [2000] 4 All ER 412.

34 TA (NI) 1958, s 31(1) (repealed) was the pattern for such clauses.

35 *Armitage v Nurse* [1998] Ch 241 at 711, approving *Re Vickery* [1931] 1 Ch 572. This view of 'wilful default' seems well grounded in the natural sense of the expression, and settled in law, despite severe academic disapproval illustrated, for instance, by the *Trust Law Committee Consultation Paper on Trustee Exemption Clauses*, para 3.10 ff accessible on www.kcl.ac.uk/depsta/law/tlc.

It is submitted that 'wilful misconduct' has the same meaning.

'Conscious wrongdoing'

Some exemption clauses exclude liability for loss unless due to 'conscious wrongdoing' on the part of the trustee. It is suggested that 'conscious wrongdoing' is best construed to mean the same as 'actual fraud', that is, both knowing dishonesty and reckless indifference[36].

'Free from responsibility for loss'

5.17

A clause discussed in *Armitage v Nurse* provided:

> The Trustees may carry on the business of farming *and the Trustees shall be free from all responsibility and be fully indemnified out of the Trust Fund in respect of any loss arising in relation to the business.*

Millett LJ commented:

> In the absence of the clause, the trustees would have no power to carry on a farming business. If they did so, however prudently, they would commit a breach of trust. The concluding words of the clause confer upon the trustees a consequential exemption from liability for trading losses incurred in the carrying on of the farming business. It does not exonerate them from liability for imprudently investing in a farming business yielding poor returns or from failing to ensure that the business is properly managed.

On this construction the words in italics (which appear at first sight to be an exemption clause) are not an exemption clause at all: they simply spell out the implications of the power to carry on the business of farming; the words must in fact be completely otiose. This should be regarded as an application of the principle of construction that exemption clauses are to be narrowly construed[37] (overriding the weaker principle of construction that words in a document should not be regarded as otiose).[38]

It would be better drafting not to use this form of words.

36 Millett LJ in *Armitage v Nurse* [1998] Ch 241 at 712 referred to both 'Knowing Dishonesty' and 'Reckless Indifference' as 'conscious and wilful misconduct.' He also expressed the view that the prolix exemption clause in *Key & Elphinstone* (15th ed, 1953), vol 2, p 695 had the same meaning as an exemption clause referring to actual fraud. The *Key & Elphinstone* clause referred to 'personal conscious bad faith of the trustee sought to be made liable.'

37 *Wight v Olswang* [1998] NPC 111 accessible on www.kessler.co.uk; cf *Walker* v *Stones* [2001] QB 902 at 941; exclusion clauses to be construed 'no more widely than a fair reading requires.'.

38 'There is no canon of construction which denies to a testator the privilege of indulging, to some extent, in tautology': *Re Ward* [1941] Ch 308 at 318 (Luxmore J).

'In the professed execution of the trusts and powers hereof.'

These words add nothing.[39]

'No liability for loss resulting from exercise of powers'

5.18

Wight v Olswang (No 1)[40] considered the following common form:

(1) Every discretion or power hereby conferred on the trustees shall be an absolute and uncontrolled discretion or power and

(2) no trustee shall be held liable for any loss or damage accruing as a result of his concurring or refusing or failing to concur in any exercise of any such discretion or power.[41]

The second part seems like an exemption clause, but it is not. The Court of Appeal correctly held that its purpose was 'to make clear that the trustee would not be liable for exercising or not exercising a discretion or power merely because the court considered the trustees' grounds unreasonable or merely because the court would not have exercised the discretion or power in the same way:'

> Whilst on its face exempting every trustee from liability it does so only in relation to loss or damage accruing as a result of the trustees concurring or failing to concur in the exercise of the absolute and uncontrolled discretion or power. It is significant that there is no reference to, for example, a breach of trust or other impropriety in the exercise or non-exercise of the power ... the loss or damage, liability for which is exempted, is that which accrues merely as a result of the trustee concurring or failing to concur.

It follows that the words in the second part of the clause are not only otiose, but misleading (since there could be no liability in any event in the absence of a breach of trust). Forms of this kind should generally not be used. It may be appropriate if the drafter wishes to authorise some exercise of a power that could cause a loss and which might (in the absence of these words) be regarded as an improper exercise of the power. The wording must describe the act quite specifically, not in general terms.

39 *Walker* v *Stones* [2001] QB 902 at 935.

40 [1998] NPC 111 accessible on www.kessler.co.uk.

41 Needless to say, sub-paragraphing added for clarity by the authors. The first part of the clause is discussed briefly in *Re Locker* [1977] 1 WLR 1323. The parliamentary drafter used similar forms: AEA 1925, ss 33, 47(1)(iii).

'Absolute owner' 'beneficial owner' clauses

5.19

In *Bartlett v Barclays Trust Co Ltd* Brightman J considered the following clause:

> The Trustees may act in relation to the Bartlett Trust Ltd or any other company and the shares securities and properties thereof in such way as it shall think best calculated to benefit the trust premises and *as if it was the absolute owner* of such shares, securities and property.

This was rightly held merely to confer on the trustee power to engage in a transaction which might otherwise be outside the scope of its authority; it was not an exemption clause protecting the trustee against liability for breach of trust (on authorising a transaction that a prudent man of business would have eschewed). The power was fiduciary.[42]

Validity of exemption clauses

5.20

It is now settled, at all levels below the House of Lords, that one can exclude liability except for fraud, in the wide sense of 'knowing dishonesty' and 'reckless indifference'.[43]

Plainly one cannot exclude liability for 'knowing dishonesty'. That is inconsistent with any trust at all.

Can one accept liability for 'knowing dishonesty', but at least exclude liability for mere 'reckless indifference'? Millett LJ said:

> There is an irreducible core of obligations owed by the trustees to the beneficiaries and enforceable by them which is fundamental to the concept of a trust. If the beneficiaries have no rights enforceable against the trustees there are no trusts. But I do not accept that these core obligations include

42 [1980] Ch 515 at 536. The same applies if the reference is to a 'beneficial' owner (the form used in TA(NI) 1958, s 10). Some even say: 'absolute beneficial owner' (synonymy). These words 'as absolute owner' mean no more or less than the expression 'as the trustees think fit'. Cf the cases cited in 20.22 (Power of investment).

It might be said that if a power is fiduciary, and so restricted, it is not the power of an absolute owner, so the terms of the clause are misleading. But then a power to invest 'as the trustees think fit' is equally misleading. There are a number of occasions where the parliamentary drafter uses the expression 'as absolute owner' to confer wide fiduciary powers: see, eg TA (NI) 2001, s 1, TLATA 1996, s 6.

43 In conformity with the common law approach, the new statutory duty of care is subject to contrary intent: TA (NI) 2001, Sch 1, para 7.

> the duties of skill and care, prudence and diligence. The duty of the trustees to perform the trusts honestly and in good faith for the benefit of the beneficiaries is the minimum necessary to give substance to the trusts, but in my opinion it is sufficient.

Since honesty is a 'core obligation' and reckless indifference is regarded as a form of dishonesty, the natural reading of the passage is that one cannot exclude liability for reckless indifference; and this is considered to be the law. Nor can one exclude liability for an act which no reasonable solicitor/trustee could have thought proper – another category of 'dishonesty'.[44]

A clause purporting to exclude liability for reckless indifference would be wholly void, unless its invalidity could be severed so the clause could be taken as void so far as it purported to exclude liability for reckless indifference, but nevertheless valid so far as it deals with other matters (eg excluding negligence).

The Court of Appeal, surprisingly, have rejected an argument that an exemption clause in a will may be invalid on the grounds that:

(1) the clause was inserted by a drafter who, in a conflict of interest, acted for the testator and was a trustee (or partner of a trustee); or
(2) the clause was not expressly brought to the testator's attention.[45]

Should the drafter insert an exemption clause?

5.21

Exemption for trustees' negligence is wrong in principle. It would directly contravene the wishes of the settlor, if he were fairly asked; which he certainly never is. It should not need saying, but if it does it should be shouted from the rooftops: *The duty of the drafter is to advise, ascertain and carry out the wishes of his client the settlor.* The blanket exemption clause has no place in a standard draft.

The most respected textbooks all take this view. Prideaux states 'the form should only be used in special circumstances'. Hallett advises that the relieving clause should only be used for unpaid trustees. The *Encyclopedia of Forms & Precedents* adopts the same approach: the proposed exemption clause does not apply to professional trustees and a note properly adds: It is essential that the settlor is made fully aware of how the clause operates and agrees to its inclusion.[46] Some

44 This view is supported by comments on the meaning of 'dishonesty' in other cases, discussed in Simon Gardner 'Knowing Assistance and Knowing Receipt: Taking Stock' (1996) 112 LQR 56 accessible on www.kessler.co.uk.

45 *Bogg v Raper* [1998] CLY 4592. The failure of law reports to report this decision may be taken as an indication of silent disapproval.

46 Prideaux, *Forms and Precedents in Conveyancing* (25th ed, 1959), Vol 3, p 158; Hallett, *Conveyancing Precedents* (1965), p 801, n 30; 40 *Encyclopedia of Forms & Precedents* (5th ed), p 512.

firms are unwilling to listen to that note of caution, and insert the widest possible trustee exemption clauses for the benefit of themselves as professional trustees. Others, to their credit, do not, and a fair indication of a firm of integrity is that they do not take that course.

Suppose there are non-professional, unpaid trustees. Certainly less can reasonably be expected of them. The law already recognises this; or, more positively, it may be said that more is expected of the professional trustee.[47] Moreover, in the usual case, where there are professional and family trustees, the professional (and his firm) will act for the trustees as a whole; so in the event of professional incompetence, the professional will carry the liability. The settlor may sometimes want to authorise lay trustees to be negligent. However, it should not be assumed that he will do so in the absence of express instructions, and a wide exemption clause, even for the unpaid trustee, should not be a standard form.

The reason sometimes put forward is that trustees refuse to act where there is no exemption clause. This is true only in exceptional cases: most trustees will not so lightly turn way good business.

There are circumstances where a wide exemption clause may properly be inserted by the drafter. For example:[48]

1. Where the settlor (or spouse or other family members) are trustees. Here the settlor may indeed wish for a low standard of duty to rest on the trustees, because he may like the trustees more than he likes the beneficiaries. It is suggested that an exemption clause in such a case should be limited to unpaid trustees.
2. Where the drafter is acting for the trustees and is not acting for the settlor. The clause is in the interest of the drafter's client. It would be good practice to require the settlor to be separately advised.

Where a broad exemption clause is used, the effect of the clause should be fully and fairly explained to the settlor.[49] A full and fair explanation is that, in Lord Millett's words, the clause 'exempts the trustee from liability for loss or damage to the trust property no matter how indolent, imprudent, lacking in diligence, negligent or wilful he may have been, so long as he has not acted dishonestly'.

It is difficult to see how a drafter can properly include such a clause when he is acting for the settlor and the drafter (or a partner in the same firm) will be a

47 *Bartlett v Barclays Trust Co Ltd* [1980] Ch 515.

48 This is nt a comprehensive list. Another example may be artificial tax avoidance schemes, under which the client may not mind (or may even (dangerously) prefer) that trustees are not diligent in carrying out their functions as trustees.

49 Even *Bogg v Raper* [1998] CLY 4592 recognises at para 53 that an exclusion clause is not effective 'if the draftsman inserted the provision without calling the settlor's intention to it and knowing that the settlor did not realise its effect'.

trustee. There is a conflict of interest here, and professional conduct implications for solicitors who draft wills or trusts if the same firm is to act as trustee.[50]

Drafting an exemption clause

5.22

There are many statutory precedents, but in drafting it would be best now to use a form based on that approved in *Armitage v Nurse*.

Commentary: should exemption clauses be allowed?

5.23

In *Armitage v Nurse*, Millett LJ said:

> The view is widely held that these clauses have gone too far, and that trustees who charge for their services ... should not be able to rely on a trustee exemption clause excluding liability for gross negligence.

Such clauses are outlawed in both Northern Ireland and England for directors (whose position is analogous to trustees) in some investor protection legislation[51]; and in many foreign jurisdictions.[52] Yet if settlors genuinely wish their trustees to

[50] In England, *The Guide to the Professional Conduct of Solicitors* accessible on www.guide-on-line.lawsociety.org.uk (which does not extend to NI) does not specifically address the question of exemption clauses in trusts or wills. It is, however, relevant to note para 12.11: 'There is no objection as a matter of conduct to solicitors seeking to limit their liability provided that such limitation is not below the minimum level of cover required by the Solicitors Indemnity Rules. The cover currently required is £1m. Any limitation must be brought clearly to the attention of the client and be understood and accepted by him or her. It is preferable that the clients acceptance of the limitation should be evidenced in or confirmed by writing'. This comment, however, relates to an exemption clause in direct contractual relationships between solicitor and client; it does not concern the relationship between solicitor and potential settlor (though there is no good reason to draw any distinction between the two). So the inconspicuous inclusion of an exemption clause would not appear to be a breach of the code of conduct, although in our view it is in normal circumstances a plain failure of what ought to be the drafter's duty to advise, ascertain and carry out the settlor's wishes. These difficulties were brushed aside in *Bogg v Raper*. In Northern Ireland the Solicitors (NI) Order 1976 provides that any attempt by a solicitor when agreeing remuneration in writing with a client in relation to non-contentious business to exclude liability for negligence shall be wholly void. While this provision is of relatively limited scope, it is submitted that the spirit of it is clearly that *Armitage* v *Nurse* style exemption clauses (and exclusion of the statutory duty of care) should be avoided when a solicitor is to be appointed as a trustee. In Northern Ireland, the basic cover under the Law Society of Northern Ireland Master Policy is £2m per claim.

[51] Companies (NI) Order 1986, art 201 and art 318; Financial Services Act 1986, s 84; Pensions (NI) Order 1995, art 33.

[52] Foreign jurisdictions use the full gamut of solutions. Some prohibit exclusion of liability for negligence or failure to act with reasonable care: s 9 Trust of Property Control Act 1988 (South Africa). The position is similar in the Turks and Caicos Islands. Others, eg Jersey,

have the benefit of an exemption clause, it is hard to see why they should not be allowed to do so. In its recent report the English Law Commission[53] has recommended that professional trustees should not be permitted to exclude liability for negligence and if this recommendation is implemented it is likely that Northern Ireland will follow suit. However Moreover statutory reform may bring additional problems and complications to the law. For instance, if reform prohibited exclusion of liability for gross negligence, the courts would have to identify what is or is not 'gross' negligence. It will not be easy to frame legislation in a manner which a careful drafter cannot evade, and yet which does not outlaw reasonable, targeted, exemption clauses such as those mentioned below.

Further, in most cases the firm of the trustee/solicitor will have acted for the trust (and submitted invoices accordingly). So the trustees (or beneficiaries) will have a right to sue the firm in negligence, and no exclusion clause will affect that.

The problem with exemption clauses, it is submitted, is not one of trust law but of trust draftsmanship. The solution is not law reform, but a drafting solution; to require appropriate use of such clauses in trust drafting. A strengthening of the rules of professional conduct – or a greater recognition of the implications of existing rules – would be the best solution to the problem.

What standard of care rests on trustees

5.24

The form used in this book is as follows:

> The duty of reasonable care (set out in s.1, Trustee Act (NI) 2001) applies to all the functions of the Trustees.

The duty is expressed at length in the statute but amounts effectively to 'reasonable care'.

This applies to powers relating to investment, acquisition of land, agents, nominees and custodians and insurance. It is submitted that case law imposes the same duty in the exercise of trustee functions generally but it is best to say so expressly.[54]

---

more tentatively, prohibit exclusion of liability for gross negligence (so the Jersey Trustee may act negligently, so long as he takes care not to be grossly negligent). Belize prohibits exclusion of liability for fraud or wilful misconduct; a provision which merely codifies the common law rule. Also see the Trust Law Committee's Consultation Paper accessible on www.kcl.ac.uk/depsta/law/tlc.

53 Law Com 171.

54 Although some commentators have questioned whether there is authority in the case law for the subjective element (a higher standard expected of those who claim to be trust specialists) of the statutory duty – Reed and Wilson, *The Trustee Act 2000 – A Practical Guide* (2001), p 27.

Excluding strict liability

5.25

Trustees have the benefit of what may be regarded as a statutory exemption clause. They are not liable if they have acted honestly and reasonably and ought fairly to be excused for any breach of trust.[55] Do they need any more than this? It is considered some slight tinkering is desirable to get the fairest balance between the needs of trustees and beneficiaries.

The first concerns no-fault liability. Trust law may impose liabilities for innocent and non-negligent errors[56]. In this book liability is restricted to acts of negligence:

> A Trustee shall not be liable for a loss to the Trust Fund unless that loss was caused by his own actual fraud or negligence.

Trustees may object that the duty of care is so vague that they may always feel at risk; no matter how carefully they act it is easy with hindsight to allege an innocent error was negligent. The higher standard of care may increase the costs of running the trust. The answer to this, it is suggested, is that money spent on careful (ie non-negligent) administration of a trust is not wasted. While one certainly wishes to make the administration of the trust as easy and as cheap as possible, this must be balanced against the hazards of authorising sloppy practice. Solicitors and accountants are generally subject to a duty of care for their work in contract or in negligence. There is no reason why trust administration should be different.

Moreover the professional trustee will be insured. So the effect of the trustee exemption clause is to lighten the burden on the trustees' insurer.

There is a respectable argument that trustee liability should be limited to the amounts for which the trustees can reasonably obtain insurance cover. The drafting would be tricky. This course is not pursued in practice.

Excluding claims by unknown illegitimate beneficiaries

5.26

There is a fear that unknown illegitimate beneficiaries may emerge with claims against the trustees, who (unaware of their existence) may have distributed the trust fund on the wrong basis.

55 TA (NI) 1958, s 61. See also WAP(NI)O 1994, art 29(3).

56 It is submitted that the law ought to develop in this direction and impose the simply stated duty of reasonable care in relation to all trustee liability. The rules of Breach of Trust should in many respects be assimilated with those of professional negligence. TA (NI) 2001, s 1 is a step in this direction.

When the Family Law Reform (NI) Order 1977 first extended the rights of illegitimate beneficiaries, special protection was provided by statute: art 6 of the 1977 Order. Unfortunately for trustees, the statutory protection was repealed by para 3 of Sch 6 to the Children (NI) Order 1995. The trustees may already have the protection of the general clause above, and statute provides some general protection, especially s 28 of the Trustee Act (NI) 1958 (Protection by means of advertisements)[57]; but something specific is probably appropriate.

The following is based on the original statutory wording:

> The Trustees may distribute Trust Property or income in accordance with this Settlement but without having ascertained that there is no person who is or may be entitled to any interest therein by virtue of an illegitimate relationship. The Trustees shall not be liable to such a person unless they have notice of his claim at the time of the distribution. This clause does not prejudice the right of any person to follow property or income into the hands of any person, other than a purchaser in good faith, who may have received it.

Relying on counsel's advice

Counsel's advice generally

5.27

The relevant principles of professional negligence are as follows[58]:

(1) In general, a solicitor is entitled to rely upon the advice of counsel properly instructed.
(2) For a solicitor without specialist experience in a particular field to rely on counsel's advice is to make normal and proper use of the Bar.
(3) He must not do so blindly but must exercise his own independent judgment. If he reasonably thinks counsel's advice is obviously or glaringly wrong, it is his duty to reject it. The more specialist the nature of the advice, the more reasonable it is likely to be to follow it.

It is submitted that exactly the same rules should apply to trustees who rely on counsel even in the absence of anything dealing with the matter in the trust deed; and *a fortiori* if there is a clause (as in this book) restricting trustees' liability to cases of negligence.

57 But advertising is hardly appropriate in small cases.

58 *Locke v Camberwell Health Authority* [1991] 2 Med LR 249 at 254 accessible at www.kessler.co.uk. See *Cordery on Solicitors*, looseleaf, J553 citing nearly a dozen more cases.

However, dicta in some antique cases[59] might be taken to suggest that trustees who (acting reasonably) rely on counsel may nevertheless be liable for breach of trust in some circumstances. It is best for an express clause to make the position clear. An express clause may save the costs of cautious trustees who might otherwise seek directions from the court.

Counsel's advice on litigation

Where trustees propose to be involved in litigation, they should (under the general trust law) apply to the court for prior approval.[60] In 1893 it was said to be a matter of ease and comparatively small expense for trustees to obtain the opinion of a judge of the Chancery Division on the question whether an action should be brought or defended at the expense of the trust.[61] Nowadays the procedure is slow and far too expensive and in these cases it is suggested that the opinion of counsel is as much protection for the trust as can reasonably be provided. Counsel owes a duty of care to the trust and could be sued if negligent. This is the background to the following clause:

> (1) A Trustee shall not be liable for acting in accordance with the advice of counsel, of at least ten years' standing, with respect to the settlement. The Trustees may in particular conduct legal proceedings in accordance with such advice without obtaining a Court Order. A Trustee may recover from the Trust Fund any expenses where he has acted in accordance with such advice.
>
> (2) The above paragraph does not apply:
>
> (a) if the Trustee knows or has reasonable cause to suspect that the advice was given in ignorance of material facts;
>
> (b) if proceedings are pending to obtain the decision of the court on the matter;
>
> (c) in relation to a Trustee who has a personal interest in the subject matter of the advice; or
>
> (d) in relation to a Trustee who has committed a breach of trust relating to the subject matter of the advice.

59 'The advice of counsel is not an absolute indemnity to trustees in bringing an action, though it may go a long way towards it': *Stott v Milne* (1884) 25 Ch D 710 at 714, approved *Re Beddoe* [1893] 1 Ch 547 at 558. Relying on a solicitor (as opposed to Counsel) was thought no excuse for a breach of trust in *Re Dive* [1909] 1 Ch 328 at 342: 'Although no doubt it seems hard to hold a trustee liable where he has followed the advice of his solicitor, I do not think I can allow the trustee to be excused where, if he had with reasonable care considered the authority under which he was acting, he would have found that it did not authorize that which he was doing.'

60 Failure to do so may result in the trustees being personally liable for the costs: *Re Beddoe* [1893] 1 Ch 547. Hence the application is called a *Beddoe* application.

61 *Re Beddoe* [1893] 1 Ch 547 at 558. Jessel MR considered 'It very often is cheaper to take the opinion of the Court than even the opinion of counsel'; *Sharp v Lush* (1879) 10 Ch D 468 at 471. One can only conclude that the operation of the Courts and the legal profession as recently as the late 19th century was amazingly different from today. It is important to bear this in mind in considering the relevance of these antique cases to the law today.

This follows the precedent of s 29 of the English Charities Act 1993 (which provides that charity trustees are not liable if they follow the advice of the charity commissioners).[62] The clause does not state expressly that the trustee should refuse to follow counsel's advice if 'glaringly wrong'. However, this must be implied, as no exclusion clause will relieve a trustee for reckless indifference.

'Ten years' standing' would mean ten years since call to the Bar.[63] Younger practitioners may feel that five years is sufficient.[64]

Excluding duty to supervise family companies

5.28

Where the trust property includes a controlling shareholding in a family company it is the duty of trustees under the general law to keep a close eye on the company's activities. A trustee may run the business himself; or become a non-executive director; or appoint a nominee on the board to report to him. Alternatively the trustee may be able to oversee the company's affairs by studying the agenda and minutes of board meetings if regularly held, or management accounts, or quarterly reports. A trustee should not sit back and allow the company to be run by its directors, receiving no more than statutory accounts. If he does so, he is at risk if things go wrong.[65] The same principle applies where the trustees hold a substantial minority interest, if their holding gives them effective power to interfere in the company's business.

Now, where the trust property is shares in the family company, the last thing that the settlor wants is his professional trustees on the board; or interfering in any way with his management of his company. Professional trustees – not by training or

62 A further statutory precedent is found in WAP(NI)O 1994, art 33. The form used in this book may be contrasted with that in *IRC v Botnar* [1999] STC 711:

> 'The Trustees may take the opinion of counsel locally or where appropriate elsewhere concerning any difference arising under this Settlement or any matter in any way relating to the Trust or to their duties in connection with the trusts hereof and in all matters may act in the accordance with the opinion of such counsel.'

The form in this book merely saves trustees from personal liability: the *Botnar* form is wider as it authorises trustees to act in a manner which would bind the beneficiaries. In *Botnar* the trustees had been advised that they may use the trust fund to benefit the settlor (the unusually drafted settlor exclusion clause was somewhat ambiguous). It was stated (*obiter*, but rightly) that the settlor had an interest in the settlement, regardless of the true construction of the settlor exclusion clause, because of the effect of the *Botnar* form combined with the advice the trustees had received. However, it is unlikely that there will be many, if any, cases like *Botnar*.

63 Parliamentary counsel often use this phrase (eg Taxes Management Act 1970, s 4) and it is not necessary to be more specific.

64 That was the view of the STEP Standard Provisions (1st ed). Parliament thought 10 years appropriate: WAP(NI)O 1994, art 33 (action taken in reliance on Counsel's Opinion).

65 *Re Lucking* [1968] 1 WLR 866; *Bartlett v Barclays Trust Co Ltd* [1980] Ch 515 at 533.

temperament qualified to run a business[66] – will not want to undertake this duty of oversight. Here, then, is a case where too much is expected of trustees, under the general law, and some relaxation may be thought appropriate.

The proposed form is:

> The Trustees are under no duty to enquire into the conduct of a company in which they are interested, unless they have knowledge[67] of circumstances which call for enquiry.

This clause does not prevent trustees from interfering in the company's business; but it allows them to do very little; this they will normally prefer. A common form allows trustees to do nothing until they have notice of acts of dishonesty: under the suggested clause, the trustees should interfere if they have knowledge of directors' negligence or incompetence; and they may do so even if they do not. This is thought to strike a fair balance.

Excluding duty to supervise parents and guardians

5.29

The proposed form is:

> The Trustees are under no duty to enquire into the use of income paid to a parent or guardian on behalf of a minor, unless they have knowledge[68] of circumstances which call for enquiry.

Where a payment is made to a parent for the benefit of a beneficiary, trustees are obliged to take reasonable care to ensure that that sum is properly applied for the beneficiary's benefit, not misappropriated by the parent or misapplied by the beneficiary.[69]

The common practice is to exclude this duty. Is this advisable? On one hand, it eases the burden of the trustees, and reduces administrative costs of the trust. On the other hand, the wider power would permit negligent trustees to dissipate trust funds.

66 This accords with the principle that a solicitor's duty 'is to advise on matters of law and the solicitor is under no duty to advise on matters of business, unless he specifically agrees to do so' (*Cordery on Solicitors*, J354).

67 On the concept of 'knowledge' (to be contrasted with 'notice') see an illuminating article by Simon Gardner, 'Knowing Assistance and Knowing Receipt; Taking Stock' (1996) 112 LQR 56 accessible on www.kessler.co.uk.

68 See above footnote.

69 *Re Pauling* [1964] Ch 303.

This clause confers a carefully circumscribed freedom on the trustees. They may make regular payments of income to the parents. If they are dealing with capital – the sums will usually be greater - they must take proper care. Moreover, if their suspicions are aroused at any time, the trustees are expected to investigate. It is thought that this is as much relief as reasonably diligent trustees would ask for.

Appointment of new trustees

5.30

The Trustee Act (NI) 1958 provides a detailed code of rules to regulate the appointment and retirement of trustees. The usual practice is to adopt the statutory rules with slight amendments. The approach in this book is to specify in the main part of the deed the person who has power to appoint new trustees; that is an important matter. Points of detail are placed in the Schedule.

Who appoints trustees?

5.31

The form used in this book is as follows:

> The power of appointing trustees[70] is exercisable by the Settlor during his life and by will.

This form is self-explanatory.[71]

Obviously the settlor will want the power of appointment of new trustees during his life. (Under the forms in this book he can release or delegate the power if desired.) It is less clear who should have the power to appoint new trustees after the settlor's death.

70 The small 't' is appropriate here: see 9.35 (Definitions).

71 Three minor variants of wording may be noted here:

(1) Some drafters refer to 'the *statutory* power of appointing new trustees ...' but the clause can hardly be read as referring to anything else.

(2) Some refer to a power to appoint 'new *or additional* trustees'. TA(NI) 1958, s 35(1) confers a power to appoint a 'new' trustee in place of a retiring trustee; s 35(6) confers power to appoint 'one or more other persons ... to be an additional trustee or trustees.' There is statutory authority for the phrase 'new or additional trustees': TA(NI) 1958, ss 64(2) and 67; but elsewhere statute is content to use the shorter form: see, eg SLA 1925, s 30(3); and the precedents in Forms Nos 1 and 2 of Sch 1 to SLA 1925.

(3) Some refer to the power as 'vested in' the Settlor; 'exercisable by' the Settlor seems more lucid.

It is not necessary to say: 'will or codicil': see 2.18 (Archaic or prolix expressions).

The position in the absence of anything in the trust is that the power will vest in the continuing trustees. This is the most satisfactory general solution and it is adopted in the precedents in this book. Where this course is adopted, it does not seem necessary to spell the position out in full.[72] Occasionally the surviving spouse of the settlor is given the power; that is:

> The power of appointing trustees is exercisable by the Settlor during his life, *and after his death by his widow during her life.*

Is this desirable? In an age where one third of marriages end in divorce – the proportion may still be rising – it is quite possible that the widow of the settlor will not be the mother of the main beneficiaries, the settlor's children. In such cases this form might be a recipe for trouble.

If the settlor wants to decide trustees in the event of his death, he should have an express power to appoint new trustees by will.[73] It is suggested that most settlors would like this power so it should be a standard form. (A more complex solution is to provide that a 'protector' should appoint new trustees. The settlor can appoint his wife, or child, or whoever, to be protector and can have power to revoke that appointment and appoint a different protector. The advantage of this course is that the protector's powers continue after the death of the settlor. The protector can (if desired) appoint his own successor in due course. See paragraph 6.29 (Protectors).)

Where there are two settlors see paragraph 9.11 (Form where trust made by joint settlors).

Appointment of foreign trustees

5.32

> A person may be appointed trustee of the Settlement even though he has no connection with the United Kingdom.

Is it possible to use the statutory power to appoint foreign trustees? A cryptic passage in *Re Whitehead* states that this is not generally 'right or proper'.[74] If that were right, it would be a serious deficiency in the statutory power. No-one seriously

72 If the drafter does wish to set the position out in full, it would be best to set out the relevant parts of the TA(NI) 1958, s 35(1) and (6) more or less in full. This of course is not impractical, but the form becomes a little complicated.

73 The position in the absence of an express power is unclear. *Re Parker* [1894] 1 Ch 707 decided that (what in NI is now TA(NI) 1958, s 35(1)(b)) did not permit an appointment of new trustees by will. It is arguable that TA(NI) 1958, s 35(1)(a) or s 35(6) would authorise such an appointment.

74 [1971] 1 WLR 833. The *Whitehead* principle did not apply where (a rare case) the beneficiaries have themselves become resident in a foreign jurisdiction.

thinks that the *obiter dicta* in *Re Whitehead* represent the law[75], but still, the drafter can and should avoid the issue: the form in this book therefore sets out an express power to appoint foreign trustees. This is generally desirable even if the appointment of foreign trustees is not contemplated; one can never anticipate the future needs of beneficiaries.

There is no reported case in which a clause of this kind has been considered. The drafter has no judicial guidance as to what form of words is required. It would be sufficient to give power to appoint trustees 'not resident in the United Kingdom' or 'anywhere in the world.' This precedent adopts a slightly wider formula.

The clause does not affect the duty to consider the suitability of any new trustees before making an appointment. This may be especially important when foreign trustees are to be appointed.

The statutory power allows a trustee to be replaced if he remains out of the United Kingdom for more than a year. It is fairly standard practice, where the appointment of foreign trustees is permitted, to amend this rule so that:

> remaining out of the United Kingdom shall not be a ground for the replacement or removal of a trustee.

However, there is something to be said for retaining what is effectively a power of dismissal over foreign trustees. This can do no harm: the non-resident trustee does not have to be replaced so in this book the statutory rule is not amended in this way. Of course, the statutory power to replace non-resident trustees is nugatory if the power of appointing new trustees is vested in trustees who are all non-resident.

[75] For the following reasons:

(1) *Whitehead* gives insufficient weight to the tax advantages which may be enjoyed by beneficiaries of offshore trusts. If the duty of trustees is to secure the maximum benefit for beneficiaries, then in some cases it should be a breach of trust *not* to retire in favour of non-resident trustees.
(2) There is little cause for indiscriminate jurisdictional chauvinism: in some jurisdictions professional trustees are at least as well regulated as in the United Kingdom.
(3) The law is influenced by the practice of the profession. *Whitehead* is ignored in practice: non-resident trustees are regularly appointed under the statutory power.
(4) The case was not followed in two cases in 1987: *Richard v Mackay* and *Re Beatty (No 2)*, belatedly reported in *Trust Law International*, Vol 11, (1997) pp 23 and 77 accessible on www.kessler.co.uk.

If *Whitehead* were correct, interesting questions would arise as to the consequences of an 'improper' appointment. The fourth edition of Kessler *Drafting Trusts and Will Trusts* touches on these; but the discussion is wholly theoretical, except so far as it supplies further reasons why *Whitehead* cannot be good law. On this topic see Paul Matthews' thorough *Migration and Change of Proper Law* (Key Haven Publications, 1997).

Retirement of trustees

5.33

> A Trustee who has reached the age of 65 shall retire if:
> (a) he is requested to do so by his co-trustees, or by a Person interested in Trust Property; and
> (b) he is effectually indemnified against liabilities properly incurred as Trustee.
> On that retirement a new Trustee shall be appointed if necessary to ensure that there will be at least two trustees. This sub-paragraph does not apply to a Trustee who is the Settlor or the spouse or widow of the Settlor.

A retirement date is set for virtually every public office and private employment. Company law directs that a director of a public company must offer himself for retirement at the age of 70.[76] However, trust law does not impose a retirement date on a trustee and difficulties occasionally arise.

The clause therefore requires that a trustee can be replaced on attaining retirement age. The use of this clause may also avoid the doubts which can sometime arise as to whether an elderly unsatisfactory trustee is (in the words of s 35(1) of the Trustee Act (NI) 1958) 'unfit' or 'incapable' or 'refusing' to act. The rule is not applied to the settlor, his spouse, or beneficiaries who are trustees; on balance that would be as likely to cause problems as to offer solutions. Contrast the STEP standard provision which is more restrictive still and provides that only a 'professional trustee' as defined is required to retire at 65.

The form does not say how the retirement is to be carried out. The usual statutory rules will apply, so that retirement will take place under the Trustee Act (NI) 1958, ss 35-38. This needs a deed with the signature of the retiring trustee. This procedure is the most satisfactory for two reasons. (1) It will always be plain whether or not a trustee has retired. (2) A trustee is protected so that he cannot be dismissed unless he (or the court) is satisfied that he is effectually indemnified.[77]

Could this form lead to abuse: a trustee may be retired in order to allow the other trustees to commit a breach of trust? There is little cause for concern. The point is not so much that such cases would be surpassing rare; but rather, the retiring trustee will always have the right to apply to the court to seek directions. In particular, he can raise the question whether he should hand over the trust property to the new trustees. If he is acting in good faith, the costs are borne by the trust fund.

76 Companies (NI) Order 1986, art 301.
77 TA(NI)2001, s 34 adopts the same procedure.

Requirement of two continuing trustees on retirement of trustees

5.34

Section 36(1)(c) of the Trustee Act (NI) 1958 provides that a retiring trustee is not discharged from the trust unless there remain two individuals to act as trustees, or a trust corporation.[78]

Thus if a foreign trust company[79] is appointed to be trustee in place of United Kingdom trustees, the United Kingdom trustees would not generally be discharged, unless the trust provided otherwise.

In 1993 it was confirmed that the English equivalent of this provision could be modified.[80] It is unlikely that a Northern Ireland court would take a different approach. The rule now offers little protection to the trust.[81] It is considered that the provision serves no real purpose, and for ease of trust administration it should be excluded:

> A Trustee may be discharged even though there is neither a trust corporation nor two individuals to act as trustees provided that there remains at least one trustee.

This form resolves a somewhat theoretical doubt whether a single trustee can be appointed in place of more than one trustee without satisfying the conditions of s 38 Trustee Act (NI) 1958.

Further provisions concerning appointment of additional trustees?

5.35

In practice, new trustees are usually needed to replace trustees who have died or wish to retire. Under the statutory code a new trustee may also be appointed to

78 Similar rules apply where a trustee retires without the appointment of a new trustee – TA(NI) 1958, s 38. In England the counterpart of s 36(1) is s 37(1)(c) of TA 1925 as amended by the TLATA 1996, Sch 3. The 1996 Act changed the requirement of two individuals to two persons.

79 A foreign trust company is not generally a 'trust corporation' as defined, see para 6.14 (Requirement of two trustees or trust corporation to exercise powers).

80 *London Regional Transport Pension Fund Trustee Co Ltd v Hatt* [1993] PLR 227. This was followed without discussion in *Adam v Theodore Goddard* [2000] WTLR 349 where the issue was whether a particular clause had the effect of reversing the normal rule. (Both cases are accessible on www.kessler.co.uk). Prior to 1993 it was unclear whether the rule could be amended. Accordingly the STEP provisions (1st ed, 1992) did not deal with this point. Failure to exclude the rule matters less in England after the TLATA 1996 reforms.

81 The second company to act as trustee may be a subsidiary of the first, with nominal share capital. See para 6.14 (Two trustee rule).

boost the number of trustees, without a retirement. In Northern Ireland the statutory power contained in s 35(6) of the Trustee Act (NI) 1958 is wider than the counterpart English provision, s 36(6) of the Trustee Act 1925. In contrast to the position in England the appointor may appoint himself[82] and there is no limit on the number of trustees that may be appointed.[83] In Northern Ireland the drafter has no reason to alter the statutory code.

Trustees' right to resign

5.36

Trustees are sometimes given a right to resign. The statutory provision, under which a trustee can retire with the consent of his co-trustees, is generally thought to be sufficient. In the case of a charity, where there may be a large number of unpaid trustees, a right to resign without the consent of fellow trustees would be appropriate. The following form is suggested:[84]

> A Trustee may resign by giving notice in writing to the other Trustees. On receipt of such notice the retiring Trustee shall cease to be a Trustee provided that there shall be remaining at least two persons to act as Trustees or a Trust Corporation (within the meaning of the Trustee Act (NI) 1958ct 1925). The retiring Trustee shall do any act necessary or desirable to vest the Trust Fund in or under the control of the Trustees.

Sections 34 and 35 of the Trustee Act (NI) 2001

5.37

Sections 34 and 35 of the TA(NI) 2001, which correspond to sections 19 and 20 of the English Trusts of Land and Appointment of Trustees Act TLATA 1996, give beneficiaries powers to dismiss trustees where beneficiaries are all adult and absolutely entitled to trust property. In our view, it is not appropriate to exclude these sections in a standard form for two reasons:

(1) It is relatively rare that all the beneficiaries will be of full age and (taken together) absolutely entitled to the trust property. In particular, that would not be the case in any of the precedents in this book.

82 Although some commentators argue that the changes made to s 36(6) of TA 1925 by TLATA 1996 have removed this restriction there also.

83 In England one cannot add trustees so as to increase the number beyond four trustees, even if the general law permits more than four trustees (eg because the trust does not hold land or is a charity).

84 For a statutory precedent see Trusts (Jersey) Law 1984, art 15. For a case (of construction) where a right to retire was inferred from exiguous wording see *Davis v Wallington* [1990] 1 WLR 1511 at 1528.

(2) In the simple case where the beneficiaries are so entitled, the power conferred by sections 34 and 35 is appropriate. The beneficiaries could in any event direct the trustees to transfer the trust property to other trustees, by virtue of the rule in *Saunders v Vautier*.[85] Sections 34 and 35 only allow them to achieve the same result without a possible capital gains tax difficulty.

Power to dismiss trustees

5.38

On this topic see paragraph 6.30 (Power to dismiss trustees).

Short form

5.39

In short forms (eg a declaration of trust for an insurance policy) it would be simplest to adopt the statutory rules without amendment. In that case the trustees will have the power to appoint their successor. When that is done, nothing need be put into the trust deed at all. It is quite unnecessary to say (as one sometimes sees) that:

> The statutory power of appointing new trustees shall apply hereto.

85 (1841) 4 Beav 115.

CHAPTER 6

Trustees' powers

6.1

This chapter considers some general questions relating to powers of trustees: the drafting of specific powers is considered at paragraph 10.1 (Overriding powers) and 20.1 (Administrative provisions).

Duties and powers distinguished

6.2

Trust law distinguishes between:
(i) A power conferred on trustees, which permits them to act.
(ii) A duty imposed on trustees, which obliges them to act.

There is also a hybrid between the ordinary power and a duty, a form such as:

> The trustees shall pay the income to A, B, or C.

Here trustees have a duty to act – to pay the income to somebody – but a choice as to which of A, B or C is to receive it. In this book this is referred to as a 'discretionary duty' or a 'discretionary trust of income'.

Duties or powers: does it matter?

6.3

The distinction between a duty and a power seems crucial. If one reads 'The trustees *shall* pay the income to X' then X will receive the income. If one reads that 'The trustees *may* pay the income to X' then he may or may not do so.

However, when duties and powers are combined together, the formal distinction loses most of its significance. Contrast:

(i) The trustees may accumulate any income and shall pay the remainder to X.
(ii) The trustees may pay any income to X and shall accumulate the remainder.
(iii) The trustees shall either accumulate the income or pay it to X.

The first of these clauses confers a power to accumulate income, with a duty to pay unaccumulated income to X. The second confers a power to pay income to X, with a duty to accumulate the remainder. The third imposes a discretionary duty to do one or the other. The practical differences between them all are very small and only rarely is the distinction important.[1] The drafter will not usually mind which form is used but there should be no ambiguity. The drafter should be aware whether he is creating a duty or a power.

Powers and duties: terminology

6.4

Terminology in this area is something of a headache.

Terms to describe 'duties'

The modern approach – much to be encouraged – is to use the word 'duty'[2]. The traditional term for this was the word 'trust'. That usage was unfortunate. Nowadays the word 'trust' is more commonly used as a synonym of 'settlement' – except in a few stylised phrases, such as 'trust for sale' (meaning a duty to sell).[3]

Terms to describe powers

The words 'power' and 'discretion' are used indiscriminately to refer to both true powers and discretionary duties.[4] The usage is understandable and (it is submitted)

1 There are different results if the trustees cannot agree about the exercise of the power; or if they delay before its exercise. The clauses would have different results in the event of a breach of the rule against accumulations. The distinction also affects income accruing but not paid on the death of X or on an assignment of X's interest: *IRC v Berrill* [1981] 1 WLR 1449. The distinction may remain of some significance for the rule relating to 'administrative workability' of a trust. These differences savour more of academic than practical interest and need not concern the trust drafter.

2 An early statutory example was in the Trustee Investments Act 1961, s 2(4) ('the exercise of any power or duty of a trustee'). There are many examples in the updating provisions of Trusts of Land and Appointment of Trustees Act 1996, Sch 3, where the word 'trust' in the old legislation is replaced by the word 'duty'.

3 Also see the discussion of *trust* in *Terminology*.

4 On use of 'power' in this wide sense, see for instance, *Re Wellsted* [1949] Ch 296 at 308 (where Lord Greene said the word power could 'properly' be used to describe an obligation to

acceptable. 'True powers' and 'discretionary duties' are best regarded as two types of power.[5] Where (as is almost always the case) the difference does not matter, it is not realistic to expect any precision in normal use.

Statute and drafters often use the phrase 'powers and discretions.'[6] Here it could be that 'power' refers to true powers; and 'discretions' refers to discretionary duties; but in view of the vagaries of usage, the better view must be that the two terms are used as synonyms.

The phrase is sometimes expanded to 'powers, authorities and discretions'.[7] This is mere synonymy: the word 'authorities' adds style but contributes nothing to the sense. Thoughtful drafters in the modern style need not use this expression.

The best and modern term to describe duties, powers and discretionary duties of trustees is 'functions'.[8]

Drafting duties and powers

6.5

The best approach is to adopt the well settled rule that the word 'may' confers a power: the word 'shall' imposes a duty.[9] Thus we simply say as required.

---

choose between a number of objects, ie a discretionary trust). Statutory examples of this usage are: TA (NI) 1958, ss 18, 31(2) (repealed), 32, 68(2) and ICTA 1988, s 674.

Statutory examples of 'discretion' in this wide sense are: ICTA 1988, s 686, s 698(3).

5 *Mettoy Pension Trustees Ltd v Evans* [1991] 2 All ER 513 at 545. Something should be done on those occasions (rare outside textbooks) when one does need to distinguish between true powers and discretionary duties. One must use some special phrase but at present there is no agreed terminology. One sometimes finds 'mere powers' or 'powers in the strict sense' to describe powers; and 'imperative trusts' 'trust powers' or a whole variety of other expressions to describe discretionary duties. Perhaps one day a decision of the higher courts will prescribe some terminology. We need better descriptive labels than those adopted by Warner J in Mettoy: 'Categories 1, 2, 3 & 4.'

6 For instance, TA (NI) 1958, s 26 as amended and ICTA 1988, s 664(1)(a).

7 For instance, TA (NI) 1958, s 35(7).

8 Eg TA 1925, s 36(9) (which dates from 1959) – although note that the term 'functions' does not appear in the counterpart NI provision, TA(NI) 1958, s 35(9). An early triumph of the term 'functions' in modern statutory usage is illustrated by Financial Services Act 1986, s 84 (which makes void certain exclusion clauses). Here the parliamentary drafter had before him the precedent of Companies (NI) Order 1986, art 201; but he substituted the word 'functions' for the traditional phrase 'powers, authorities or discretions'. The term is ubiquitous in the TLATA 1996. In *Hazell v Hammersmith and Fulham London Borough Council* [1992] 2 AC 1 at p 29 the House of Lords held that the word 'functions' in Local Authority legislation 'embraces all the duties and powers of a Local Authority, the sum total of the activities Parliament has entrusted to it'. The word is (rightly) undefined in the TLATA 1996 though (unnecessarily) given a partial definition in both the TA 2000 and the TA(NI) 2001.

9 Of course the context may show that the word 'may' or 'shall' has been used wrongly, and the context governs the sense; this is self-evident but for an example see *Grunwick Processing Laboratories Ltd v ACAS* [1978] AC 655 at 698: 'Prima facie the word 'shall' suggests that it is mandatory but that word has often been rightly construed as being directory. Everything turns upon the context in which it is used – the subject matter, the purpose and effect of the section in which it appears.' (Lord Salmon.)

the trustees may ... *or* the trustees shall ... .

The alternative methods of imposing duties and powers are innumerable. For duties:

The Trustees shall hold the trust property on trust to ...

It shall be the duty of the Trustees to ...

The Trustees shall be bound to ...

The Trustees must ...

For powers:

The Trustees shall have full power to ...

The Trustees shall have the right to ...

It shall be lawful for the Trustees to ...

The Trustees shall be entitled and are hereby authorised to ...

The Trustees shall be at liberty to ...

I empower my Trustees to ...

The Trustees shall... if they think fit ...[10]

It is better to use a simple and consistent form.

10 Thus (as in *Pearson v IRC* [1980] STC 318) a direction that:

> 'the trustees shall accumulate so much of the income of the Trust Fund as they shall think fit'

confers a power to accumulate income. Likewise, in a normal context, (as in *Breadner v Granville – Grossman* [2001] Ch 523 a provision that:

> 'The Trustees shall stand possessed of the Trust Fund and the income thereof upon trust for the Principal Beneficiaries or any one or more of them exclusive of the other or others in such shares as the Trustees shall from time to time by deed appoint'

confers a power of appointment (not a discretionary duty). See 6.10 ('Absolute discretion and as the trustees think fit').

Other usage of 'shall' and 'may'

6.6

A draft should be composed in the simple present tense. Unless one is conferring a duty or a power, it is best not to use the modal auxiliaries 'may' or 'shall'. Thus for:

> ...as the Trustees **may** think fit; or

> ...as the Trustees **shall** think fit;

Read:

> ... as the Trustees think fit

Again, for:

> 'The Trust Fund' **shall** mean ...

Read:

> 'The Trust Fund' means ...

Some stylists or grammarians advise that the word 'shall' should be used in legal drafting only in this mandatory sense of imposing a duty, others say the word should not be used at all.[11] A blanket application of either rule is contrary to ordinary English usage and common legal usage. While no doubt it would always be possible to paraphrase, the word 'shall' does in some contexts serve as well as any other. So this approach has not been completely adopted in this book.

Provisions about how often and when powers are exercised

Should true powers have time limits?

6.7

Consider a simple power such as:

> the Trustees may pay the income of the trust fund to X.

11 *Garner's Modern Legal Usage* (2nd ed, 1995) entry under Words of Authority contains a good discussion of the possible ambiguities of the word 'shall'.

Such powers have to be exercised within a reasonable time. If it is not exercised within a reasonable time, the power will lapse. What is a 'reasonable time' is uncertain and will vary according to the circumstances. Some drafters would specify a time limit (typically 12 months). This avoids the uncertainty, which might otherwise arise: in the event of some delay trustees may not know whether their power remains exercisable or has lapsed. This book does not impose any time limit. The 'reasonable time' period raises little difficulty in practice; a fixed and inflexible time limit may cause greater difficulty. In this we follow the example of the statutory power of maintenance; indeed there is no statutory trustee power for which a fixed time limit is imposed.

Should discretionary duties have time limits?

6.8

Suppose trustees hold income on discretionary trusts:

> the Trustees shall pay the income to any Beneficiaries as the Trustees think fit.

The trustees should, within a reasonable time, decide who to pay the income to. The drafter could if he wished specify some time limit. There seems little point in doing this. The discretionary duty will never lapse.[12]

Powers exercisable 'at any time' and 'from time to time'

6.9

A common formula provides that trustees' powers may be exercised 'at any time'. The purpose of this must be to make it clear that the power will not lapse during the life of the trust.

A related and equally common formula is to direct that the power may be exercised 'at any time or times', or 'at any time and from time to time ...'. This emphasises that the power can be exercised more than once. Another form to the same effect is to say that the trustees may exercise a power 'by deed or deeds'.

These forms are not usually necessary. In most cases it is obvious from the nature of the power concerned whether any sort of time limit is implied. It is also obvious

12 *MacPhail v Doulton* [1971] AC 424; *Re Locker* [1977] 1 WLR 1323. For completeness it should be said that the time limit does have one consequence. Suppose the trustees failed to distribute the income, in breach of trust. The beneficiaries could take action (i) after the fixed time, if there was a fixed time; but (ii) only after a 'reasonable time' if no time was fixed. But this is not important in practice.

whether the power may be exercised more than once. The forms are considered undesirable. To specify on every occasion that powers are exercisable 'at any time and from time to time' would be inordinately repetitive; to scatter the phrase here and there might give an entirely misleading impression that the omission of the phrase in other contexts is significant.

The solution adopted in this book is to set out a general provision that trustees' powers in general may be exercised 'from time to time as occasion requires.' It is then unnecessary to say anywhere else in the document that the trustees' powers are exercisable 'from time to time' or 'at any time or times'. This is in fact the approach adopted by the parliamentary drafter as long ago as 1882.[13] A drafter seeking brevity could safely omit the clause.

The provision is included in the absolute discretion clause, to which we can now turn.

'Absolute discretion' and 'as the trustees think fit'[14]

6.10

In general it should be the trustees – and no one else – who decide how their powers should be exercised. The 'absolute discretion' clause is intended to make this clear:

> The trustees may ... in such manner as they may *in their absolute discretion think fit*.

It is reasonably clear that the absolute discretion clause has no effect whatsoever. If trustees act improperly they may be restrained even if their powers are said to be 'uncontrollable'.[15] Conversely beneficiaries cannot control trustees acting

13 SLA 1882, s 55(1) provided that: 'Powers and authorities conferred by this Act ... are exercisable from time to time.' Then the Interpretation Act 1889 introduced a general principle, now found in Interpretation Act 1978, s 12 (and in s 17 of the Interpretation Act (NI) 1954, which governs NI legislation). Where any Act confers a power or imposes a duty then (subject to contrary intention): 'the power may be exercised, or the duty is to be performed, from time to time as occasion requires'. So when the SLA 1882 was recast in England as the SLA 1925 the drafter was able to jettison SLA 1882, s 55(1); its work was done by the Interpretation Act provision. (Inconsistently, the form 'at any time or times' surfaces in TA 1925, s 32 (and in s 33 of the TA(NI) 1958); and the form 'from time to time' is in SLA 1925, s 102(3). The words must be considered otiose as the context could hardly supply the contrary intention.) The clause in this book is of course modelled on the Interpretation Act 1978, s 12. It is unnecessary to refer to duties.

14 A note on terminology. The authors have seen the term 'Gisborne clause' used to describe what is here called an 'absolute discretion' clause; but the more transparent term is to be preferred.

15 *Whishaw v Stephens* [1970] AC 508; *Harris v Lord Shuttleworth* [1994] I.C.R. 991. For a discussion see *Thomas on Powers* (1st ed, 1998).

properly. This is so even in the absence of an 'absolute discretion' clause. Trustees' freedom of action is not increased by including an 'absolute discretion' provision, and not decreased by its omission.[16] The clause can be justified as for the avoidance of doubt or as a statement of what might not be obvious to the layman. For these rather marginal reasons, the precedents in this book include an absolute discretion clause.

6.11

Parliamentary drafters have used a variety of formulae:

> The trustees may
> ... as they shall in their absolute discretion think fit
> ... as the trustees in their absolute discretion, without being liable to account for the exercise of such discretion, think fit.
> ... at their sole discretion ...
> ... if and as they think fit ...
> The power shall be exercised according to the discretion of the trustees.[17]

These expressions are all equally efficacious; the drafter may take his choice.

What, then, is the drafter to do? One could specify whenever trustees are given a power that such power is to be 'absolute'; that would be inordinately repetitive. The usual approach is to scatter a variety of 'absolute discretion' formulae intermittently throughout a trust.[18] This is not an attractive course; it sets in defiance the usual principle of interpretation which would suggest that where the words were omitted, trustees' powers were intended to be less than absolute.[19]

The authors' preferred approach is to insert in the trust a general provision, expressed to apply to every power of the trustees:

> Powers of the Trustees are exercisable at their absolute discretion.

16 In the leading case *Gisborne v Gisborne* (1877) 2 App Cas 300, the Court refused to interfere with the trustees' decisions even though they would have exercised the power differently. The House of Lords drew some comfort from the use of the word 'uncontrollable' in the trust concerned, but see Parry, 'Control of Trustee Discretions' [1989] *The Conveyancer* 244 accessible on www.kessler.co.uk; Underhill & Hayton, *The Law Relating to Trusts and Trustees*, (16th ed, 2003) p 702.

17 The examples are from TA (NI) 1958, ss 3, 15, 32, 33, 34. The authors have even seen the form 'fullest, widest and most unfettered discretion'.

18 The favourite place for 'absolute discretion' formulae is in discretionary trusts of income and trust for sale clauses; perhaps this shows the influence of the statutory precedents: TA (NI) 1958, s 34(1)(b)(ii) (discretionary trust of income), and in England; LPA 1925, s 25(2)(now repealed) and; AEA 1925, s 33 (trusts for sale).

19 An argument of this kind was rejected in *Julius v Lord Bishop of Oxford* (1880) 5 App Cas 214. Here the words 'if he shall think fit' qualified one power but not another. The House of Lords refused to draw any inference from this; the words were 'mere surplusage'. The litigation would have been unnecessary had the words been omitted.

It is then unnecessary to provide anywhere else that trustees' powers are 'uncontrollable' or exercisable at the trustees' 'absolute discretion', or 'exercisable at any time or times.'

The clause may be omitted where brevity is desired.

The clause should be amended where trustees' powers are made subject to the consent of a 'protector.' The following is proposed:[20]

> Subject to obtaining the consent of the Protector when necessary, the powers of the Trustees may be exercised:
> (a) at their absolute discretion and
> (b) from time to time as occasion requires

Guidance and control of trustees

6.12

This section is concerned with methods of controlling trustees. First, however, a short note on how trustees make decisions in the absence of any form of control in the trust deed.

Majority decisions

6.13

Trustees' decisions must be unanimous unless the trust directs otherwise. The usual practice is to leave the rule of unanimity to apply and this is the course taken in the forms in this book.[21]

If majority rule is desired the drafting is simple enough:

> The functions of the Trustees may be exercised by a majority of them.[22]

20 But it would not matter if there was no reference to the Protector.

21 Where two or more family members are to be trustees, and their relationship may be inharmonious a majority clause may be an effective solution so long as there is a third trustee to hold the balance. But a better course may be the creation of two or more separate trusts, one for each member of the family; or to use professional trustees alone. Majority rule applies in the case of charitable trusts.

22 The draft is loosely based on that approved in *Re Butlin* [1976] Ch 251. A variant sometimes used is that the power may be exercised by a majority so long as a Professional Trustee is one of the majority. There should be a consequential amendment in the conflict of interest clause, so that where a trustee was under a conflict of interest, his vote could not override his co-trustee.

Some drafters add that the trustees in the minority must join in the execution of documents in accordance with the decision of the majority but that is plainly implied.

Two-trustee rule

6.14

A sole trustee can generally exercise all the powers of the trustees.[23] It is quite common to specify that powers of appointment should only be exercised by two trustees or a trust corporation.[24]

This restriction may formerly have been imposed for estate duty reasons which are long obsolete. The requirement does impose some restraint on wayward acts of a sole trustee but only a limited restraint. One point may be made in particular. Generally a sole trustee has (after the death of the settlor) the power to appoint additional trustees. So a sole trustee can side-step the restriction by the simple means of appointing a like-minded co-trustee, if he can find one[25]. For what it is worth, however, the restriction is applied to the overriding powers in this book.

If the trustee is a substantial trust company the requirement of a second trustee is not necessary and may be inconvenient. Accordingly the precedents in this book provide that the requirement of two trustees does not apply if the trustee is a company carrying on a business which consists of or includes the management of trusts.[26] A simpler course, which would work in practice, would be for the draft just to say that the requirement of two trustees does not apply if the trustee is a company.

Another course would be for the draft to say that the requirement of two trustees does not apply if the trustee is a *trust corporation* and to define that expression to have the same meaning as in art 9 of the Administration of Estates (NI) Order 1979. This could be inconvenient if a foreign trust company is appointed trustee as it would not normally be a trust corporation within this definition. (This inconvenience is avoided by widening the definition but the drafting becomes more complicated.)

23 Subject to minor exceptions: see n 1 above.

24 The Parliamentary drafter has occasionally adopted this approach: see n 1 above. A more drastic version of the same idea is to require at least two (or even three) trustees at all times.

25 An individual could not avoid a two-trustee rule simply by appointing as a second trustee an 'off the shelf' company, of which he was sole director. In *Gilford Motor Co v Horne* [1933] Ch 935 (as explained in *Yukong Lines Ltd v Rendsburg Investments Corp (No 2)* [1998] 1 WLR 294 at 307) a one man company was held to be ineffective as a device to avoid a restraint of trade clause. It is suggested that similar reasoning applies in the case of a one man company used as a device to avoid a two-trustee rule.

26 The wording is derived from s 69(2) TCGA 1992.

A course to avoid is for the draft to say that the requirement of two trustees does not apply if the trustee is a *trust corporation* and to leave that expression undefined. When the parliamentary drafter uses the expression he always takes care to define it.[27] Without a definition it is ambiguous.[28] The drafter is best advised to avoid the expression *trust corporation* altogether.

Statement of wishes

6.15

Where trustees have wide powers, it is always desirable to record the settlor's wishes as to how they should be exercised. The settlor's wishes were conventionally recorded in a document addressed to the trustees and called a 'letter'. Perhaps the epithet 'letter' was adopted to emphasise the informal and non-binding nature of the statement of wishes but an epistolatory form is artificial. The document should more aptly be titled: 'statement of wishes' or perhaps 'memorandum of wishes'.

27 'Trust Corporation' as defined by the Administration of Estates (NI) Order 1979 means (a) a corporation appointed by the High Court in any particular case to be a trustee; or (b) a corporation which (i) is constituted under the law of the UK or any part of it, or under the law of any other Member State of the EU or any part of it; and; (ii) is empowered by its constitution to undertake in NI the business of acting as trustee under wills and settlements and as executor and administrator; and (iii) has one or more places of business in the UK; or (iv) is (aa) a company incorporated by special Act or Royal Charter, or (bb) a company registered (with or without limited liability) in the UK or in another EU Member State and having a capital in stock or shares for the time being of not less than £250 000 (or its equivalent) of which not less than £100,000 (or its equivalent) has been paid up in cash, or (cc) a company which is registered without limited liability in the UK or in another EU Member State and of which one of the members is a corporation within any of the previous provisions; or (c) a corporation which is constituted under the law of the UK or any part of it, or under the law of any other EU State and which satisfies the Lord Chief Justice (i) that it undertakes the administration of any charitable, ecclesiastical or public trust without remuneration, or (ii) that by its constitution it is required to apply the whole of its net income for charitable, ecclesiastical or public purposes and is prohibited from distributing, directly or otherwise, any part thereof by way of profit, and which is authorised by the Lord Chief Justice to act in relation to any charitable, ecclesiastical or public trust (as the case may be) as a trust corporation.

28 There are three possible meanings:

1. A definition may be implied from the statutory definitions. (An objection to this solution is that there are various statutory definitions but the one in the 1979 Order is the one which will immediately come to the mind of a trust lawyer.)
2. *Trust corporation* may mean any company carrying on trust business.
3. *Trust corporation* may mean any company which is a trustee.

The better view is that the expression (if written in lower case letters and assuming no guidance from the context) should be taken to have the second of these meanings but in practice one should proceed on the most cautious view.

Drafting the statement of wishes

6.16

The statement of wishes may be put in a recital or in the body of the trust itself, but it is more appropriately put in a separate document. This also makes changes to the wishes less obvious. On rights of beneficiaries to see the statement of wishes see 28.3 (Beneficiaries' right to information).

The important drafting point is to state that the wishes are not binding on the trustees, so the status of the memorandum of wishes is clear. A statement of wishes expressed in imperative terms may be construed to be binding and override the terms of the trust instrument.[29]

This is the sort of precedent one might use:

> Joan Smith Will Trust: Statement of Wishes
>
> This note sets out my wishes for my will trust. I express these wishes only for the guidance of the trustees. It is not intended to bind them. They must use their own discretion. They should also have regard to any change in circumstances of my family and of course to any wishes which I may record for their guidance in the future.
>
> My wishes are as follows:
> (1) My Trustees should ensure that my husband is reasonably provided for.
> (2) Subject to that, I would like my trustees to regard my children (and if the fund is not distributed, their families in due course) as the principal beneficiaries of the residuary estate.
> (3) Subject to that I would like my trustees to regard my nephews and nieces as the principal beneficiaries per stirpes [or per capita].

The statement of wishes must not be peremptory but can, if appropriate, be strongly worded. This is not always appreciated and may be helpful for settlors reluctant to create wide powers or trusts of long duration. Some examples:

> I wish to express my firm desire (without binding the trustees) that they should transfer the Trust Fund to my son Adam absolutely, on attaining the age of 25, unless there are overpowering reasons for not doing so.

29 For an example see *Chen v Ling* (High Court of the Hong Kong Special Administration Region, 7 November 2000) accessible on www.kessler.co.uk.
A statement of wishes (however expressed) could not override the terms of a will, unless executed in accordance with the formalities required for a will, but it could form the basis of an application to rectify the will.

> I have accepted the advice of my solicitors that the most tax efficient form of will is a discretionary will trust, but (tax apart) I would rather have made an absolute gift to my son Adam. I request the trustees (without binding them) to give weight to Adam's wishes accordingly.
>
> I wish to express my desire (without binding my Trustees) that the Trustees should regard my son Adam as the principal beneficiary of the Trust Fund.

The statement of wishes should give reasons (if not obvious). It should be reviewed periodically to review statements relating to existing trusts and best practice would be for the trustees to seek confirmation that the wishes are unaltered every few years as appropriate.

The settlor's signature is normally witnessed, as a matter of good practice, and this is desirable though not strictly essential.

Some drafters put into the trust a clause requesting the trustees to have regard to any statement of wishes, but this is plainly unnecessary and best omitted.

When should the statement of wishes be executed?

Some commentators advise that the statement of wishes should not be executed at the time of the trust. The reason is to make the non-binding nature of the statement even clearer. Of course, this will not help if the facts are that the settlor gives binding oral directions to trustees at the time of the settlement, and merely delays putting them into writing to avoid giving the *appearance* of a sham. Conversely, if the statement of wishes is non-binding, as it should be, there is absolutely no need to wait after executing the trust. It is suggested that the better practice is that the statement of wishes should be executed at the same time as the trust. In practice the settlor *will* indicate his wishes to the trustees (no other course is really practical) and formal legal documentation should accord with the reality.

Power of appointment of new trustees

6.17

The power of appointment of new trustees gives considerable power to the appointor. In particular if trustees propose to do something of which the appointor disapproves, he can frustrate their intention by appointing a trustee opposed to the idea. The consent of existing trustees is not required for that appointment.

Duty of consultation with beneficiaries

6.18

Should the drafter impose a duty on trustees to consult with beneficiaries? This has become a matter of some significance in recent times for the English trust practitioner following the enactment of the Trusts of Land and Appointment of Trustees Act 1996. Prior to this legislation no-one ever thought of imposing any duties of consultation on trustees. However the Act now provides:

> The trustees of land shall in the exercise of any function relating to land subject to the trust-
> (a) so far as practicable, consult the beneficiaries of full age and beneficially entitled to an interest in possession in the land, and
> (b) so far as consistent with the general interest of the trust, give effect to the wishes of those beneficiaries, or (in the case of dispute) of the majority (according to the value of their combined interests).[30]

Has the Northern Ireland trust practitioner any lessons to learn from the inclusion of this provision? A duty of consultation by itself is plainly unnecessary. Trustees should where practical consult with beneficiaries without express provision.[31] In the rare case where the relationship between trustees and beneficiaries has broken down, a formal duty of consultation will not make a great deal of difference: after a formality of consultation the trustees will make up their own minds anyway.[32]

A duty of consultation could be bolstered with a requirement that the trustees give effect to the wishes of a majority of the beneficiaries, so far as consistent with the general interest of the trust. In the following discussion this is called 'a re-inforced duty of consultation'. A re-inforced duty of consultation is an unhappy compromise between the two practical options of (i) giving powers to trustees and (ii) giving powers to beneficiaries. It is almost entirely ineffective, since, in practice, if the trustees did not want to adopt the beneficiaries wishes, they would maintain that this was contrary to the 'interests of the trust.' It also introduces uncertainty into the administration of the trust.[33] In England the statutory provision contained in the Trusts of Land and Appointment of Trustees Act 1996, s 11 is invariably expressly excluded by the drafter.

30 TLATA 1996, s 11 replacing LPA 1925, s 26(3) (which imposed a reinforced duty of consultation only where the trust instrument expressly so directed, so in practice it could be ignored). The only other comparable statutory precedent is Form 6, the English Statutory Will Forms 1925 (notice of intended appropriation) accessible on www.kessler.co.uk.

31 This proposition is self-evident, but if authority is needed: see *X v A* [2000] 1 All ER 490.

32 Contrast the Government's phoney consultation exercise leading to the introduction of CGT taper relief in the FA 1998.

33 It is debatable what is 'the best interest of the trust.' In the event of a dispute, it is unclear who decides what is in the best interest of the trust. Would the court accept the trustees' view, unless no reasonable body of trustees would reach that view? Or would the court form its own view?

The powers of the Trustees may be exercised ... at their absolute discretion ...[34]

This form of words, though devised before the TLATA, is apt to exclude the duty to give effect to a beneficiary's wishes; though not the duty of consultation itself. This is the basis of the precedent now used in this book, which is as follows:-

> The Trustees are not under any duty to consult with any Beneficiaries or to give effect to the wishes of any Beneficiaries. The powers of the Trustees may be exercised at their absolute discretion.

Control of trustees

6.19

Most settlors will be content to select trustees whom they trust and to guide them if necessary with a statement of wishes. In the precedents in this book the only important controls are the restraints on adding beneficiaries, the power to dismiss a trustee after retirement age, and the conflict of interest clause.[35]

Human nature being what it is, some settlors seek further methods of controlling their trustees. This is particularly common where shares in the settlor's family company are held in a trust.

It is no answer to say that the settlor should find trustees in whom he has complete faith.[36]

Of course it is possible as a matter of trust law to provide a variety of checks on trustees' powers. Three related sets of questions arise here: (i) what powers of trustees should be subject to control; (ii) what methods of control should be applied; (iii) to whom should these powers of control be given?

What powers of trustees need to be subject to control?

6.20

A list of important powers can easily be drawn up.

(1) The most important are the overriding powers of appointment, resettlement and advancement.

34 STEP Standard Provision 10. A draft version of the Provisions, adapted for use in NI, are in Appendix 1. At the time of going to press these had not been approved by STEP.

35 Para 4.36 (Power to Add beneficiaries); para 6.30 (Power to Dismiss Trustees); para 5.12 (Conflicts of interest).

36 '*... There is no art/to find the mind's construction in the face ...*' (Macbeth) .

(2) Power to lend interest-free to a beneficiary. Money lent to a beneficiary is rarely repaid.
(3) Power to allow beneficiaries to use trust property, and power to charge trust property for their benefit and power to apply capital as if it is income. These may have a similar effect to a power of appointment.
(4) Power to release powers and power to change the governing law may be used to change the effect of a trust.

In the discussion below we shall refer for the sake of brevity to restrictions on 'the power of appointment, etc'.

What sorts of checks can be made on trustees' powers and who exercises them?

6.21

The sorts of checks which may be made on trustees are as follows:
(1) powers of consent: so the trustees cannot exercise powers of appointment, etc, without consent;
(2) giving powers of appointment, etc, to other persons instead of the trustees;
(3) power to dismiss trustees.

These powers may be given to:
(1) beneficiaries
(2) the settlor
(3) a protector.

We will discuss in turn the possible role of beneficiaries, settlors and protectors. The power to dismiss trustees is in a category of its own and will be considered separately. One general comment may be made at this point. Of course whoever is given these powers of control may act wrongly. This is not a problem of trust law or drafting, but an aspect of the human condition: at some point someone must be trusted.

Giving powers of appointment to beneficiaries personally

6.22

A traditional approach is to give powers of appointment, etc, to a beneficiary, rather than to the trustees. It is still common to see trusts for a beneficiary for life, with remainder to such of his issue as *he* may appoint, and in default of appointment, for the beneficiary's children at 21.[37]

[37] This form was so common that a precedent was provided in the English Statutory Will Forms 1925: see Forms 7 and 9 accessible on www.kessler.co.uk. The form formerly had some advantages for the rule against perpetuity. This has not been the case since the reforms of the PA (NI) 1966, s 33.

This sort of provision may be thought of not so much as controlling the trustees, but conferring rights on the beneficiary for his own benefit, making his position slightly closer to beneficial ownership. This is why such powers are classified in the authors' terminology as semi-fiduciary. See 6.33 (Nature of powers of consent and appointment).

The use of personal powers of appointment remains an acceptable drafting technique. However it has a few disadvantages.

The personal power would, in absence of specific provision, lapse on the death of the beneficiary. The exercise of the power in the course of winding up a trust may sometimes be frustrated by the doctrine of a fraud on a power.[38] There are further complications if the beneficiary could appoint the property to himself.[39]

These problems may be solved if the drafter confers overlapping powers, ie a beneficiary has a personal power of appointment and the trustees have a second (usually wider) fiduciary power of appointment. This is quite often seen. There can be no harm in this practice beyond the complications of drafting. Yet there is no obvious advantage to be gained from it. (Possibly, it might be thought to give the beneficiary greater involvement in the devolution of his trust fund? But that is little more than cosmetic.)

Personal powers might be supported on the grounds that a beneficiary is the best qualified person to have the powers. Who better to decide how to appoint property to his children? The argument is wrong. Some beneficiaries may not have the best understanding of their financial affairs. The trustees will in practice consult the beneficiary and the beneficiary may be appointed trustee.

In conclusion, the authors see little merit in personal powers of appointment, and they are not used in the forms in this book.

Giving powers of consent to beneficiaries[41]

6.23

The next possibility is to direct that the trustees can only exercise a power of appointment with the consent of a particular beneficiary (typically the life tenant).[42]

38 *Re Brook* [1968] 1 WLR 1661. See *Thomas on Powers* (1st ed.), para 9-53.

39-40 Such a power may not be a fiduciary power: *Re Penrose* [1933] Ch 793. See also Insolvency (NI) Order 1989, arts 11(4). It can, however, be argued that there was no reason in principle to support the dictum in *Penrose* that a power cannot be fiduciary if the donee is an object. On the contrary, such a power may be fiduciary or not: it is a matter of construction. A full discussion, which would require a review of many authorities and statutory provisions, falls outside the scope of this book; see John Mowbray QC, 'Choosing Among the Beneficiaries of Discretionary Trusts' (1998) PCB 239 accessible on www.kessler.co.uk.

41 *Thomas on Powers* (1st ed), ch 5 has a good general discussion on consents to powers.

42 For statutory examples see TA(NI) 1958, s 33(1)(c) (power of advancement), AEA(NI) 1955, s 37 (power of appropriation).

If the power of consent is a wholly personal one,[43] this route raises some intriguing tax questions.[44] If the reader uses the forms in this book the questions do not arise (but of course the questions do arise with less carefully drafted trusts).

Giving powers of consent to the settlor

6.24

A common and practical course is to provide that powers of appointment, etc, should only be exercisable with the consent of the settlor. This normally[45] raises no tax problems thought the simpler course in these cases would be to make the settlor a trustee. The drafting is straightforward:

> The Trustees may (*with the consent in writing of the Settlor during his life*) and afterwards at their discretion ...

This echoes a statutory precedent.[46] The need for written consent is obvious. Some say 'with the *prior* written consent ...'; but 'prior' in this context is unnecessary.[47]

A power exercisable 'with the consent of the settlor' lapses after the death; but a power exercisable 'with the consent of the settlor *during his life*' will be exercisable after the death of the settlor without any consent.

Giving powers of appointment to a settlor

6.25

This is a possible course, but not often adopted in practice. Plainly, some provision would be needed to ensure that the power does not lapse at the death of the settlor, and the benefits would not justify the drafting complications.

Better methods of controlling trustees

6.26

Imposing the requirement for settlor consent is a practical step, as far as it goes. It is of course a limited control on trustees. The settlor can prevent the trustees

43 On this terminology see para 6.33 (nature of powers of consent and appointment).
44 See James Kessler, *Taxation of Foreign Domiciliaries* (2001, Key Haven Publications), para 25.12 (Consent to exercise of trustees' powers).
45 A CGT problem might arise in the case of a non-resident trust.
46 TA (NI) 1958, s 33(1)(c).
47 The statutory powers of consent mentioned above do not use the word 'prior'.

taking some step of which he disapproves but cannot require them to take any action when he wishes. What, then, can be done for a settlor who wishes to possess effective control over his trust fund?

Settlor as one of the trustees. If the settlor is one of the trustees, he will in principle have a power of veto, for (in the absence of contrary provision) trustees' powers must be exercised unanimously. This may be sufficient for most settlors.

Settlor (and spouse) as sole trustees?

6.27

One obvious suggestion is that the settlor should be the sole trustee. As a matter of trust law there is little difficulty.[48] Alternatively the settlor and his spouse may wish to be the only trustees. This is particularly common when the trust property is the family company, and the settlor is not prepared to contemplate the possibility of interference. However, the authors do not favour the settlor (or spouse) acting as sole trustees. A trust will benefit in practice from having a professional trustee to keep an eye on administration and the exigencies of tax planning from time to time. Yet although undesirable in principle, this may be done. The professional adviser should stress the need to seek regular professional advice and the difficulties which may arise if this is not done. Alternative possibilities to this are to be preferred where possible.

For those who want a greater measure of control, there are two recommended solutions. The first is the use of a weighted majority clause. The second is the use of a protector.

Weighted majority clause

6.28

Under this route, the settlor will be a trustee, jointly with a single professional trustee. In addition there will be a clause providing that trustees' decisions are made by a majority; *and in the case of equality of votes, the settlor should have a second and casting vote.*

So provided that there are only two trustees, the settlor's wishes must prevail. The settlor should be advised that he will not own the trust property. He must act in good faith in the best interest of the trust and its beneficiaries.[49] Nevertheless for many practical purposes the settlor will have the control which he desires.

48 See 5.1 (Number of trustees). If the settlor is a beneficiary, problems may arise if he wishes to appoint trust property to himself: see para 5.15 (Trustee-beneficiaries).

49 In addition, if the settlor is a beneficiary, he may require the consent of his co-trustee to appoint the fund in his own favour: see para 5.16 (Trustee beneficiaries).

A precedent is:

> The functions of the Trustees shall be exercisable by a majority of them, each trustee to have one vote. In the case of an equality of votes, the Settlor (if a trustee) shall have a casting vote in addition to his first vote.[50]

This draws on familiar company law precedent.[51]

Sometimes the settlor may wish control to pass to some other person on his death. The easiest solution here is to use a protector.

Protectors[52]

6.29

The solution of a weighted majority vote only works if the settlor can be a trustee. That is not possible where non-resident trustees are to be appointed. The now traditional solution is to create an office of 'protector'.

In practice protectors are used principally for offshore trusts. They may have a useful role for United Kingdom trusts.

The word 'protector', as a term of property law, was first used in the Fines and Recoveries Act 1833, in relation to entails. That area of law is effectively obsolete, but its nomenclature of 'protector' survives to the modern law of trusts.

The protector is commonly given the following powers:

(1) The protector's consent is required to the exercise of powers of appointment, etc, by the trustees.
(2) The protector is given power to appoint new trustees; to dismiss trustees; and to authorise breach of the self-dealing rule.

The following precedent is proposed as a definition of 'protector' where the settlor is the initial protector.[53]

50 There should be a consequential amendment in the conflict of interest clause, so that where there was a conflict of interest, a settlor could not override his co-trustee.

51 Companies (NI) Order 1986, Table A, para 50.

52 On this topic, see Deborah Hartnett and William Norris, 'The Protector's Position' (1995) PCB 109 accessible on www.kessler.co.uk; John Mowbray QC, 'Protectors' OTPR, Vol 5, p 151 accessible on www.kessler.co.uk; Antony Duckworth, 'Protectors – Fish or Fowl?' (1996) PCB 169 accessible on www.kessler.co.uk; and ch 4, *Contemporary Trends in Trust Law* (Oakley ed, OUP, 1996).

53 It is clear that the Settlor may be a protector; this is acknowledged in the Law Commission Consultation Paper No. 171, Trustee Exemption Clauses, para 4.8. The appointment of settlor as protector is possible but less than ideal where the settlor is also the principal beneficiary. See Kessler, 'What is (and what is not) a Sham' (2000) The Offshore & International Taxation Review, Vol 9, p 125 accessible on www.kessler.co.uk.

The Protector

(1) The Settlor shall be the first Protector.

(2) [The widow of the Settlor][54] shall be the next Protector.

(3) The Protector for the time being may appoint one or more persons to be protector for such period as the Protector shall specify. All the powers of the Protector (including this power of appointment) shall be vested in the new Protector accordingly. The appointment shall be made by will or by deed. The appointment may be revocable or irrevocable. The appointment has priority to sub-clause (2) above.

(4) A Person ceases to be Protector in the event of the following:
(a) death;
(b) execution by the Protector of a deed of retirement;
(c) refusal or incapacity to act.

(5) If at any time there is no Protector able or willing to act, the Trustees shall appoint a new Protector.

(6) A Protector shall not be appointed trustee. A Trustee shall not be appointed Protector.

A slight variation is needed where the settlor is not the first protector:

The Protector

(1) [Name and address] shall be the first Protector.

(2) [Name and address] shall be the next Protector.

(3) [As (3) above]

(4) [As (4) above]

(5) If at any time there is no Protector able or willing to act:
(a) The Settlor if able and willing to act, and subject to that
(b) the Trustees
shall appoint a new Protector.

(6) [As (6) above]

54 The trust will name here the person provisionally intended to be protector after the death of the Settlor. This need not be the widow of the Settlor: it might for instance be a child of the Settlor.

The draft should make provision for the death of the first protector. The usual form is to provide that the protector may select his successor. A provisional successor is named in this draft. This is more convenient than an immediate exercise of the power of appointment (or the risk that the protector may die without having appointed a successor). The protector may alter the position later if desired.

The drafter must cater for the possibility that there is no protector. One course is to allow all the trustees' powers which require the protector's consent to lapse permanently. That could be most unsatisfactory. The course adopted here is to rely on the trustees to appoint their new protector. The only objection is that the checks intended to restrict the trustees will not at that moment be fully operative. It might be best to say that the power to add beneficiaries should lapse or become further restricted.

One could add further precautions to try to ensure a suitable person is chosen as a new protector. For instance, one could direct the trustees to appoint a new protector being a solicitor of, say, ten years' standing and nominated by two beneficiaries or by the President of the Law Society of Northern Ireland. The form adopted here is slightly simpler; and is not likely to give rise to any problems in practice.

Occasionally a grander precedent is seen where the protector is not an individual but a committee.[55] The charging clause should if appropriate be extended to allow a protector to charge. It is not necessary to make the protector a party to the trust deed.[56]

Nature of protector's powers and duties

It is a question of construction of any particular trust to determine the nature of a protector's powers and duties. If the trust does not contain anything to answer the question expressly, the gap must be filled by a legal presumption or principle of construction. In the absence of anything unusual in the trust, the protector's powers will be understood to be fiduciary and not personal powers.[57]

One could provide that the powers conferred on the protector are personal and not fiduciary. The typical settlor would want the protector to exercise the powers in the interest of the trust, and not in his own interest.

55 For an example see *IRC v Schroder* (1983) 57 TC 94. But *quaere* whether a committee is likely to reach wiser decisions than an individual.

56 Para 145 (Who should be parties).

57 This follows from *Von Knieriem v Bermuda Trust Co Ltd (Star Trusts)* [1994] 1 Offshore Cases and Materials 116. (Supreme Court of Bermuda). It also follows from English authorities such as *Re Skeats* (1889) 42 Ch D 522, which was cited in the Bermudan case; and *IRC v Schroder* (1983) 57 TC 94.

The description of the powers as 'fiduciary' does not answer all the questions which may arise. In particular:

(1) Suppose a protector has a power to dismiss trustees. Is the protector obliged to review the trust regularly, to satisfy himself that the trustees are doing a good job, and should not be removed? Or may he wait until something comes to his attention to suggest that action is needed?

(2) Suppose the protector has power to consent to appointments by the trustees. Is this subject only to the requirements of honesty and proper motive (summarised as 'good faith'); or must the protector consider whether the proposed appointment is desirable?

The question, in the authors' terminology, is whether the protector's duties are fully fiduciary, or semi-fiduciary.[58] It is best to deal with these matters expressly:

> **Duties of Protector**
>
> (1) The powers of the Protector are fiduciary in nature.
>
> (2) The Protector is under no duty to enquire into or interfere with the management or conduct of this Trust, unless he has actual knowledge of circumstances which call for enquiry.
>
> (3) The Protector shall consider the appropriateness of any act before exercising his powers.[59]

It is unnecessary to provide any further indemnity for a protector, or provision for access to trust documents. If trustees refuse to supply documents the protector would exercise his power to remove them.

Where trustees have power subject to consent of the protector it is implicit that the protector cannot be a trustee. It is desirable to say this expressly so that the position is made clear.

Protectors: tax implications

James Kessler has considered this topic in detail elsewhere[60] and concluded that the use of a protector has no significant tax implications. In particular:

58 On this terminology see para 6.33 (Nature of powers of consent).

59 What would the position be in the absence of express provision? This is a matter of construction of each individual trust. In the absence of any indication in the trust, it is submitted that the protector's power of consent is (in the authors' terminology) semi-fiduciary only. The protector is not usually expected to involve himself actively in the affairs of the trust. This view is based on the expectation of the profession, a relevant matter in construction.

60 James Kessler, *Taxation of Foreign Domiciliaries* (2nd edn, 2003, Key Haven Publications).

1. A protector cannot be treated as a trustee for tax purposes.
2. A trust with a United Kingdom resident protector may nonetheless be non-UK resident for CGT purposes. The most that can be said is that where there is a United Kingdom protector, particular care may be needed to ensure that the general administration of the trusts takes place outside the United Kingdom.

The position could be different if the protector was given unusually wide powers.

Power to dismiss trustees

6.30

It is increasingly common to see powers to remove trustees. Such powers are valid as a matter of trust law.[61] It is considered that a will cannot confer a power to appoint or dismiss executors.

It is considered that a power to dismiss trustees is not normally appropriate for United Kingdom trusts and should not be a standard form. The appointment of the settlor as trustee, backed with a weighted majority clause is sufficient. The following discussion is therefore principally of importance for offshore trusts. It is also relevant to trustees in the United Kingdom or elsewhere considering whether to accept an appointment to a trust containing a power of dismissal.

A power of removal does not operate retrospectively. If the trustees have done an act of which the settlor disapproves, the subsequent dismissal of trustees may come too late. The power to dismiss trustees should therefore be seen as ancillary to the other controls on trustees' powers.

The power of removal would be a fiduciary power. It could not be used for the private benefit of the settlor. Suppose the trustees refused to transfer trust funds to the settlor; and the settlor then dismissed them and appointed more amenable trustees. This would probably be an invalid exercise of the power.[62] The power to dismiss trustees may, for this reason, fail when the settlor wants to use it. The drafter should warn the settlor of the problem; or he may seriously misunderstand his rights under the trust. For all this, the power does seem to offer a solution to settlor's fears that trustees may refuse to resign or will resign only on unacceptable terms.

Who will exercise the power? A trust with power to dismiss trustees will generally have a protector who will be given the power.

61 The power was accepted as valid in *London and County Banking Co v Goddard* [1897] 1 Ch 642; and in *Davis v Richards and Wallington Industries Ltd* [1990] 1 WLR 1511 the power was held to be exercised by mere implication. See also *Chelleram v Chelleram* [1985] Ch 409 at 432. The validity of the power is assumed in TA (NI) 1958, s 35(2).

62 *IRC v Schroder* [1983] STC 480 at 500.

Dealing with the former trustee

6.31

It is not enough to dismiss a recalcitrant trustee. One must also recover the trust property which was vested in him. Suppose the trustee refused to part with it; which, in the context of a dispute, is likely to happen. Obviously the new trustees could take proceedings; but is there some short cut which might avoid that process?

There are three methods of extracting trust property from an ex-trustee without his consent:

(1) Use of Trustee Act (NI) 1958, s 39

Suppose that on the dismissal of the ex-trustee a new trustee is appointed by deed. This automatically vests many types of property in the new trustees without any need for a conveyance or assignment. The dismissed trustee does not need to be a party to the deed.

Section 39 does not apply to certain types of property, of which the most important category is company shares; and such property cannot be dealt with in this way.

(2) Use of power of attorney

A trustee on his appointment might give the protector an irrevocable power of attorney authorising the protector to execute a transfer of the trust property. Appropriate provision would be needed in the trust deed and in every appointment of new trustees. While possible in theory, this is a somewhat impractical solution.[63]

(3) Use of nominees

Suppose at the time of the dismissal the trust fund is vested in nominees. In that case our problem does not arise at all. After the dismissal of the ex-trustee, the nominees will hold the fund for the new trustees. In anticipation of such problems, it would be possible to provide in the trust deed that the trust fund should at all times be held by nominees on terms approved by the protector.

6.32

So it is possible, by one method or another, to arrange that trust property can be wrested from an ex-trustee without his co-operation. However, there is a difficulty. These methods allow the protector to override what may be reasonable needs of the trustees. Trustees may incur substantial liabilities – particularly tax liabilities – to which they will generally remain liable even if they are later removed from

63 The power would have to satisfy the conditions of the Powers of Attorney Act (NI) 1971, s 3, if it is to be irrevocable. A related idea is to have the trustees execute blank transfers of the trust property and hand them to the protector or settlor. Besides the obvious problem that the trust property may change, the trustees might counteract this by a transfer of trust property to a nominee prior to their dismissal.

their trust. Trustees need recourse to the trust fund to meet those liabilities and while they may have other remedies, they may not so easily be enforced.

The problem here is not the mechanisms of trust or property law. It is more fundamental: the drafter must find a fair balance between the conflicting interests of trustees on the one hand, and beneficiaries on the other. It is submitted that there is no objection to powers to dismiss trustees. However, the more extreme routes, which allow the protector to divest ex-trustees of the trust property, do not find the right balance. They should not form part of a standard draft or standard administrative procedures. Otherwise careful trustees will refuse to act without an appropriate indemnity.

The approach of this book is to have the power of dismissal only where there are foreign trustees, and when trustees have reached retirement age. Provision is made to provide fair protection for trustees.

Case law offers some precedents of far-reaching powers to dismiss trustees and recover trust property.[64]

Nature of powers of consent and appointment

6.33

Where a person has a power of consent under a trust, what rights and duties does this impose on him? This is a question of construction of the trust concerned. In general, however, the trust will not contain anything which expressly answers the question, so the gap must be filled by legal presumptions or principles of construction.

There are three broad categories of power of appointment. There is general agreement as to their characteristics, but no agreed terminology. In this area 'a great deal of inaccurate argument arises from expressions undeveloped and not explained which may bear two senses.'[65] In particular the expressions 'fiduciary' or 'as trustee' in isolation are unhelpful, as they are applied to many quite different types of powers. If a power is not 'fiduciary' that is an end of the matter. But if the power is 'fiduciary', that is only the beginning of the enquiry: one has to go on and ask what are the duties which attach to it. The authors proposes the following terminology:

64 *London and County Banking Co v Goddard* [1897] 1 Ch 642 and *London County and Westminster Bank v Tompkins* [1918] 1 KB 515. For an English statutory precedent see LPA 1925, s 109(5).

65 *Palmer v Locke* (1880) 15 Ch D 294 at 303.

(1) *Completely Beneficial* Powers of Appointment. Here the appointor is not subject to any legal restraint in the motive or purpose for which the power is exercised. The appointor may exercise the power (or refuse to exercise it) for his own benefit. The classic example is an unrestricted power to appoint to anyone in the world, including the appointor: a general power.

(2) *Semi-Fiduciary* Powers of Appointment. Here the appointor is not under any obligation to exercise the power; but if he exercises it, he is subject to requirements of good faith and proper motive known as 'fraud on a power'. That is, 'the appointor under the power, shall, for any purpose for which it is used, act with good faith and sincerity, and with an entire and single view to the real purpose and object of the power, and not for the purpose of accomplishing or carrying into effect any bye or sinister object (sinister in the sense of its being beyond the purpose and intent of the power) which he may desire to effect in the exercise of the power'. In the same leading case, Lord St Leonards observed: 'A party having a power like this must fairly and honestly execute it without having any ulterior object to be accomplished. He cannot carry into execution any indirect object, or acquire any benefit for himself, directly or indirectly. It may be subject to limitations and directions, but it must be a pure, straightforward, honest dedication of the property, as property, to the person to whom he affects, or attempts, to give it in that character.'[66] The classic example is a power of appointment exercisable by a beneficiary in favour of his issue.

(3) *Wholly Fiduciary* Powers of Appointment: powers where the appointor is under an obligation to consider whether or not to exercise the power. The classic example is a common form power of appointment exercisable by the trustees.

It is submitted that the same framework should be applied to powers of consent. There are then three categories of powers of consent:

(1) *Wholly Personal* Powers of Consent. An example is the power under s 33 of the Trustee Act (NI) 1958 to consent to the exercise of the power of advancement. Another example is a will trust, letting the widow live in the matrimonial home, the trustees to sell only with the consent of the widow. Obviously, the person with this power may consult his own interests: that is what the power of consent is for. Another example is the protector's power of consent under the (obsolete) law of entails.[67]

(2) *Semi-Fiduciary* Powers of Consent. Here the consenter has a power of veto, which he may exercise or not subject only to the requirements of good faith and proper motive (summarised as 'fraud on a power').

(3) *Wholly Fiduciary* Powers of Consent. Here the consenter must consider whether the proposed appointment is desirable.

The question of which category any particular power falls in can only be a question of construction. In principle, it is submitted:

66 *Portland v Topham* (1864) 11 HL Cas 32, 54 accessible on www.kessler.co.uk.

67 Fines and Recoveries Act 1833, s 36 (a useful precedent for a draft to make a power of consent a wholly personal one).

(1) Trustees' powers of consent should prima facie be considered to be wholly fiduciary.
(2) Beneficiaries' powers of consent which do not affect their own interests should prima facie be considered to be semi-fiduciary.
(3) Beneficiaries' powers of consent which do affect their own interests should be considered to be wholly personal.

This is consistent with powers of appointment.

Does it matter which category a power falls into? The distinction between wholly personal and fiduciary powers is obviously important. The distinction between semi and wholly fiduciary powers is not important in practice. What does it matter if a person is not obliged to consider whether an appointment to which he consents is suitable? In practice, he will surely do so.

The distinction does not matter for other trust law purposes.[68]

Unfortunately the authorities in this area are extremely difficult.

First, they treat the question as one to be decided by authority. The better view should be that it is a question of construction, in which authority offers relatively little guidance. See paragraph 10.5 (The problem of narrow powers of appointment).

The law got off to the right start in *Eland v Baker.*[69] Trustees' power of consent were held to be, in the authors' terminology, wholly fiduciary. Trustees were required to consider the interests of beneficiaries affected by the appointment.

The next case is *Re Dilke.*[70] A power of appointment was subject to trustees' consent. The appointor appointed that the trust fund should be held on such trusts as he appointed. This was (rightly) held to be valid; for the trustees could properly consent to such an appointment, if they thought it appropriate.

The law took a wrong turn, it is submitted, with *Re Phillips.*[71] Here, it was deduced from *Dilke* the remarkable proposition that trustees had no duty to the persons appointed. The better view of that case was that the trustees did have a duty, but exercised it. As often happens to wrongly decided cases, *Phillips* was subsequently distinguished on wholly illusory grounds: *Re Watts.*[72] The nakedness of the

68 It does not matter for the rule against perpetuity: *Re Churston* [1954] Ch 334, as explained in *Estate and Succession Duties Comr v Bowring* [1962] AC 171. *Re Phillips* [1931] 1 Ch 347, if correctly decided, is an exceptional case. (Unfortunately, a full discussion is beyond the scope of this book.)
69 (1861) 29 Beav 137; 54 ER 579
70 [1921] 1 Ch 34
71 [1931] 1 Ch 347.
72 [1931] 2 Ch 302.

attempted distinctions was cruelly exposed in *Re Churlston.*[73] But both those cases concerned a different point – the rule against perpetuities – and did not have to decide the point now being discussed. Conversely, it must be admitted, *Phillips* obtained *obiter dicta* support in other cases.[74]

For all practical purposes, however, the drafter may simply impose a power of consent, and need not concern himself with the nature of the power.

73 [1954] Ch 334 at 342 'I cannot think why ... With all respect, I cannot agree... Again, I cannot appreciate the bearing of that.' (Roxburgh J)

74 *Re Triffit* [1958] Ch 852; *Estate and Succession Duties Comr v Bowring* [1962] AC 171, PC.

CHAPTER 7

Trust property

Particular assets

7.1

Special considerations arise where the trust property takes the form of certain assets.

(1) Shares in a private company

7.2

The normal procedure is to transfer the shares from the settlor to the trustees. It must be checked that the company's articles and any shareholder agreement permits the settlor to do this. The consent of the settlor's co-shareholders may be needed. Where company articles do not permit a transfer of the shares, it may be possible for the shareholder to create a trust by declaring himself sole trustee or nominee for the trustees. This involves no transfer of the legal title to the shares. This would need careful consideration in the light of the individual case. Where the company is in liquidation, the liquidator must sanction the transfer.[1]

(2) Unlisted securities

Similar considerations and restrictions may apply to unlisted securities, debentures or loan notes.

1 Insolvency (NI) Order 1989, art 74.

(3) Leasehold property

7.3

Similarly, if the trust property is a lease it may be necessary to obtain the landlord's consent to any transfer to trustees.

(4) Land subject to mortgage

7.4

If land subject to mortgage is to become settled property, the consent of the mortgagee will usually be required: standard mortgage deeds prohibit disposals of the mortgaged property without consent. A reasonable lender should readily grant consent, as his position is not prejudiced by the making of the trust.

There are further questions to be addressed. Are the donees – the trustees – to assume liability for the mortgage debt, or are they not? Whichever is decided there should be an agreement between the trustees and the settlor so the position is clear. If the trustees assume liability to pay the mortgage debt, they will need to satisfy themselves that the property is worth more than the mortgage; and that they have sufficient funds (and if necessary indemnities) to pay interest and capital. There are tax complications which cannot be fully discussed here.[2]

(5) Life insurance policies and pension benefits

7.5

See 22.1 (Trusts of Life Insurance Policies) and 23.1 (Trusts of Pension Death Benefits).

(6) Chattels

7.6

Trusts in this book are drafted with a view to holding land or investments. Further consideration may be needed where the trust property will consist of chattels.

2 Where the donees (the trustees) assume the mortgage debt, a charge to stamp duty and capital gains tax may arise as the gift may be treated like a sale for consideration. Where the trustees do not assume liability for the mortgage debt that problem is avoided but others arise. How will interest on the debt be paid? If it is paid by the trustees, one must ensure that the terms of the trust permit this. The capital gains tax position is interesting: what is the trustees' base cost? Is there a reservation of benefit problem for inheritance tax? Will the interest qualify for income tax relief?

Form 3 of the English Statutory Will Forms 1925 (text available on www.kessler.co.uk) will provide some ideas.

(7) Property qualifying for IHT business/agricultural property relief

7.7

Note one problem if such property is transferred to an A&M trust. If a beneficiary of the trust dies within two years of attaining an interest in possession, the property will not qualify for any relief. A discretionary trust is probably a better form for property qualifying for 100% business property relief or agricultural property relief.

On will drafting for an estate containing business or agricultural property, see paragraph 19.15 (Best form of will for married testator with business or agricultural property).

Consider IHT problems of IHTA 1984, ss 113A and 124A if the property may be sold by the donees. Also consider the problem of loss of CGT taper relief.

(8) Property situate outside Northern Ireland

7.8

Where property is situate outside the United Kingdom the tax and other requirements of the domestic law will need consideration. When property is situate outside Northern Ireland but in other parts of the United Kingdom non-tax aspects of the domestic law might still need consideration.

CHAPTER 8

The rule against perpetuities

8.1

The rule against perpetuities is designed to prevent a trust from lasting indefinitely.

In outline,[1] the rule prescribes a maximum period within which the interest of a beneficiary is required to vest. This period is:

(1) the period of the lifetimes of one or more persons living when the trust is created, and 21 years; or
(2) a fixed period of up to 80 years.

The fixed period only applies if specified in the trust.[2]

A simple trust may satisfy the perpetuity rule without any express provisions. The terms of the trust may be such that no beneficiary has an interest which could possibly vest outside the permitted period.[3] In practice such simple trusts are unduly restrictive. The drafter must therefore:

(1) direct that an appropriate perpetuity period applies to his trust; and
(2) take care to arrange that all beneficiaries' interests do vest within that period.

In 1998 the Law Commission for England and Wales published a report which contained proposals to simplify the law against perpetuities. As yet these proposals have not been implemented. If they are implemented it remains to be seen whether Northern Ireland will decide to follow the English lead.

1 See further, Wylie, *Irish Land Law* (3rd ed, 1997), ch 5.

2 PA (NI) 1966, s 1.

3 For instance:
(1) For A for life with remainder to such of his children as attain the age of 21.
(2) For A for life, with the remainder to such of A's issue as A should appoint, and in default of appointment, to such of his children as attain 21.

Which perpetuity period?

8.2

Until 1966 the perpetuity period could only be defined by reference to lifetimes of persons alive when the trust was made. Often use was made of the 'Royal lives' clause; this would specify as a perpetuity period:

> The period ending 21 years after the death of the last survivor of the issue living on the date of this Settlement of his late Majesty King George V.

It is now possible to specify a fixed period of up to 80 years and this is far preferable. The Royal Lives clause, which is still used by some practitioners, may allow a perpetuity period exceeding 80 years, but the period is uncertain. How are trustees to keep track of all those royal lives? If there is a fixed period the trustees will know exactly where they stand.

It is suggested that the drafter should specify the maximum possible fixed period, which is 80 years. Statute permits shorter periods (one occasionally sees 60 years selected) but it must be best to take advantage of the longest possible period. The trust can of course end sooner if desired.

The 80-year period cannot be used in non-charitable purpose trusts, so the drafter is limited to a period of 21 years.[4] Non-charitable purpose trusts are relatively rare in practice, although it would seem that there are a healthy crop of trusts for the upkeep of graves drafted annually in Northern Ireland, especially in rural areas.[5] Often the drafter omits to limit the trust to the perpetuity period with the consequence that the trust is void.[6]

4 PA(NI) 1966, s 16(4).

5 Recent research into wills proved in the jurisdiction in the year 1997 showed that approximately 5 per cent of the wills made some provision in relation to the upkeep of the testator's or another family grave – Dawson, Grattan and Lundy *Dying to Give* (HMSO, 2003). In about one-half of the cases money was (sensibly) left to a beneficiary (invariably a church) coupled with a mere request that the grave be maintained. The others were purpose trusts ('of imperfect obligation'). This interest in graves is not restricted to the Northern Ireland testator. Upkeep of grave clauses were so common in the Republic of Ireland that s 50 of the Charities Act 1961 was enacted. This provides that gifts for the maintenance or improvement of a 'tomb, vault, grave or tombstone' are deemed to be charitable gifts insofar as they do not exceed £60 a year in the case of income and £1,000 in any other case. There seems no similar culture of grave maintenance in Great Britain.

6 *Re Compton* [1946] 1 All ER 117. Often the amounts involved are modest (£1000 is the average) and the executors, either out of ignorance or because they choose to turn a blind eye, proceed to pay it to the trustee (often a church).

Drafting

8.3

It is helpful for the draft to coin a term to describe the perpetuity period or the day on which it ends. This term will be used later in the trust. The following terms are commonly used:

The Trust Period; The Trust Date

The Perpetuity Period; the Perpetuity Date; the Perpetuity Day

The Vesting Date; the Vesting Day

The following are also seen:

The Specified Period

The Distribution Date; The Termination Date[7]

The Ultimate Date[8]

The choice hardly matters and the term used in this book is 'the Trust Period'. The form is simple:

> **'The Trust Period'** means the period of 80 years beginning with the date of this Deed. That is the perpetuity period applicable to this settlement under the rule against perpetuities.

This clause does two things:

(1) The first sentence defines the expression 'trust period', which is used elsewhere in the settlement: powers are restricted so they must be exercised in that period; contingent interests are drafted so they will vest in that period.

(2) The second sentence specifies the perpetuity period which applies for the rule against perpetuities, in words modelled on the statute.[9]

7 These two terms are appropriate to trusts under laws like that of Jersey and Guernsey where the trust comes to an end on the expiry of the perpetuity period. They are strictly less appropriate to English trusts which do not, or at least need not, come to an end on the expiry of the perpetuity period. The rule is that interests must vest within that period.

8 This apocalyptic term seems to be a novel coinage in the *Encyclopedia of Forms & Precedents* (5th ed); the 4th ed used the more usual term 'perpetuity period'.

9 PA(NI) 1966, s 1. Some add 'instead of being of any other duration,' echoing the section exactly. This is clearly unnecessary; if there could be any doubt, *Re Green* [1985] 3 All ER 455 confirms the point. One could delete the words 'under the rule against perpetuities' but they do help to explain the effect of the clause to the general reader. One could delete the second sentence altogether as a trust may validly specify a perpetuity period by implication. However, it is better to specify the period expressly.

Normally one would deal with two such separate matters in separate clauses or sub-clauses and purists do so here. A combined clause is adopted in this book in deference to the more common practice and the reader's expectations; of course no difficulty can arise either way.

Confusion over dates

8.4

The manner of specifying the perpetuity period has given rise to some confusion; this is caused by applying (or misapplying) two rules of law:

(1) The law may ignore parts of a day. Suppose a trust is executed on 1 January 1992. The perpetuity period would expire on 31 December 2081. It would not matter what time on 1 January, the trust was made; the law does not usually take notice of fractions of a day.

(2) The word 'from' may be understood to be exclusive of the *terminus a quo*.[10]

Consider a trust executed 1 January 2000, using this form:

> The Perpetuity Period applicable to this settlement is the period of 80 years from the date of this deed.

In this case, it might perhaps be argued that the perpetuity period began on 2 January continuing until 1 January 2080, or even continuing to 2 January. If so, the perpetuity period would exceed 80 years, which is not permitted. That view does not survive examination. The true meaning would obviously be that the period begins on the day of the trust and ends on the last moment of 31 December. It must be intended that the perpetuity period begins as soon as the trust begins. This may however have been the fear which led some drafters to direct the perpetuity period to be a day or two less than 80 years.[11]

In this book the perpetuity period is expressed to 'begin with' the day of the trust, so it is plain that the perpetuity period includes the day of the trust, and the problem does not arise.

10 See the fine discussion on this point in Elizabeth Cooke, 'Touching the time of the beginning of a lease for years' [1993] The Conveyancer 206 accessible on www.kessler.co.uk.

11 The form is not much used now, but survives in some older trusts. In the early years of the PA (NI) 1966 some drafters apparently believed that the perpetuity period must be a whole number of years. (This is difficult to fathom. A fraction is a 'number'.) Hence (perhaps) the occasional use of a 79-year period.

Power to curtail the trust period

8.5

One sometimes sees this form:

> (1) The perpetuity period applicable to this settlement is the period of 80 years from the date of this deed.
>
> (2) 'The Trust Period' means the period ending on the earlier of
> (a) the perpetuity period or
> (b) such date as the Trustees by deed determine (not being earlier than the date of the deed).

This distinguishes between the perpetuity period (which applies for the purpose of the rule against perpetuities) and 'the Trust Period'. It gives the trustees power to curtail the 'Trust Period'.[12] The power is valid as a matter of trust law.[13] However, this power is not needed. The conventional overriding powers can be used to the same effect. Accordingly the power is not used in this book.

Jersey and Guernsey Trusts, especially those drafted before the Trusts (Jersey) Law 1984 or the Trusts (Guernsey) Law 1989 quite often define the expression 'trust period' with a meaning which is different, shorter, than the actual perpetuity period which applies for the purposes of the rule limiting the duration of a Jersey or Guernsey trust. In such a case it would perhaps be clearer if the defined expression used was some other term such as 'the Specified Period'.

Remaining within the perpetuity period

(1) Dispositive powers

8.6

All dispositive powers must be restricted so that they can only be exercised in the perpetuity period. Thus in the case of a power of appointment, it is necessary to say:

12 The precise significance of curtailing the trust period the power would depend on how the term 'Trust Period' was used in the trust. Generally the ending of the 'Trust Period' will bring forward the end of the trust.

13 A power to alter the perpetuity period (for the purposes of the rule against perpetuities) may arguably be invalid. One argument is based on PA(N I) 1966, s 1 which requires that the perpetuity period must be 'specified' in the trust. That argument is not convincing as a matter of linguistics alone, but the general scheme of the rule against perpetuities does not fit comfortably with a power to shorten the perpetuity period. However, the matter is academic. The objection does not apply to the type of power set out in the text. Here the perpetuity period (for the purposes of the law against perpetuities) remains fixed. All that is varied is the 'Trust Period', a term specific to the trust, to which the drafter is free to give any kind of definition. Perhaps the expression 'Specified Period' would be a more accurate label.

> The Trustees shall hold the Trust Fund on such trusts as they may during the Trust Period appoint.

In the case of a discretionary trust or power over income:

> During the Trust Period the Trustees may pay the income of the Trust Fund to such of the Beneficiaries as they think fit.

Administrative powers are not affected by the rule against perpetuities and do not need such restrictions.[14]

Powers of appointment and resettlement must of course be *exercised* in a manner which complies with the rule against perpetuities. This is not, however, a matter for the drafter of the trust itself.

(2) Beneficiaries' interests

8.7

> The Trustees shall hold the Trust Fund on trust for the Beneficiary during his life.

The position here depends entirely on the definition of 'the Beneficiary'. If the beneficiary is born before the expiry of the trust period there will be no difficulty. It may be that 'Beneficiary' is a defined term, under which a 'Beneficiary' may be born after the trust period expires, then there is a potential difficulty. So to avoid the problem the drafter must either restrict the definition of 'Beneficiary' to exclude beneficiaries born after the trust period expires; or else put the limitation in the clause giving an interest to the beneficiaries.[15]

Effect of failure to remain within perpetuity period

8.8

If the drafter does not follow these guidelines the trust he produces will confer interests which might vest outside the perpetuity period. This may not matter too much since the trust remains valid during a lengthy 'Wait and See' period.[16] Nevertheless it is better for the drafter not to rely on the 'Wait and See' rule. There are some uncertainties as to how it operates; and a trust where the 'Wait and See' rule applies may mislead the reader: it will not take effect according to its tenor.

14 PA(NI) 1966, s 8.
15 See 13.9 (A perpetuity problem) for an illustration of this technique.
16 PA(NI) 1966, s 3.

CHAPTER 9

General provisions of a trust

Order of provisions

9.1

Blackstone introduces our subject:

> The matter written must be legally and orderly set forth. ... It is not absolutely necessary in law to have all the formal parts that are usually drawn out in deeds, so long as there are sufficient words to declare legally the party's meaning. But, as these formal and orderly parts are calculated to convey that meaning in the clearest, distinctest, most effectual manner, and have been well considered and settled by the wisdom of successive ages, it is prudent not to depart from them without good reason or urgent necessity... .[1]

The following order is fairly standard:

1. Title, date and parties: 'This settlement is made ...'
2. Recitals: 'Whereas ...'
3. Testatum: 'Now this deed witnesses ...'
4. Definitions
5. Beneficial provisions
6. Overriding Powers[2]
7. Appointment of new trustees[3]
8. Incorporation of schedule (administrative provisions)
9. Settlor exclusion clause[4]
10. Default Clause[5]
11. Irrevocability clause
12. Testimonium clause: 'In witness ...'
13. Schedule: Administrative Provisions

These forms are discussed in this chapter except where footnotes give another reference.

1 *Commentaries* Book II (1st ed, 1766) p 297.
2 Para 10.1 (Drafting overriding powers).
3 Para 5.30 (Appointment of new trustees).
4 Para 12.8 (Settlor exclusion clause),
5 Para 12.20 (Default clause).

A lengthy document results: it is helpful to furnish it with a contents page.[6]

Declaration of trust or transfer to trustees?

9.2

There are two ways to create a settlement:

(1) A settlor may declare himself trustee (acting as sole trustee unless and until another trustee is appointed).

(2) The settlor may:-

  (a) transfer trust property to trustees;

  (b) direct the trustees to hold on the appropriate trusts.

The second is the normal route and adopted in the precedents in this book. The first route, the declaration of trust, may be convenient if for any reason it is difficult to transfer property to trustees. For instance, in the case of shares, if there are restrictions on transfers; or foreign land (especially if there is no time to seek local advice;) or certain pension policies (see 23.6 (Creation of the trusts of the pension death benefit)).

Of course, a declaration of trust may also be used for the different reason that the settlor wants to be sole trustee.

See also 9.11 (Form where settlor is sole trustee).

On the consequential amendment of the definition of 'the trustees': see paragraph 7-038 (*Definition of 'the trustees'*). Either in the body of the trust or in a separate document there will need to be a declaration of trust by which the settlor declares that he holds the intended trust property on the terms of the trust.[7]

Title

9.3

> This settlement is made ...

The title is self-explanatory.[8]

6 Some drafters subdivide their settlement into 'parts' like a statute. The precedents in this book are simple enough to render this unnecessary.

7 If the latter, the document might begin 'This Declaration of Trust is made ...'. However the term 'settlement' is just as apt. The authors prefers to retain it for the sake of uniformity.

8 The traditional custom was to begin all deeds with the words 'this Indenture' (if more than one party) or 'this Deed Poll' (if only one party). In England LPA 1925, s 57 put an end to that unhelpful practice (any deed whether an Indenture or not may be described as a deed

Date

9.4

A document should be dated, though the absence of a date or even a wrong date does not invalidate it.[9] It only means that there may be doubts as to when it was made. For the style of writing a date, see paragraph 2.11 (Dates).

On what date does a trust take effect?

9.5

The date is important for tax and property law purposes (eg if the settlor wishes to resile from his gift). The position is complex, because several distinct sets of rules interact:-

(1) Rules as to when a transfer of assets to a trustee takes effect. As every student learns, a trust cannot take effect until the trust property is vested in the trustee, or the settlor has done all he can to transfer it.

(2) Rules as to when a settlor becomes bound by a deed he has executed, but which other parties have not.[10]

(3) Rules as to when a deed signed by a settlor binds him: the law of 'delivery' (a confusing and unfortunate term) and escrow.[11]

Backdating

9.6

'Even the gods cannot alter the past.'[12] The same principle holds in English law: a document cannot be back-dated. If it is back-dated it does not alter anything that has happened in the past; the document can only take effect from the date of

---

simply or otherwise according to the nature of the transaction), but its demise in Northern Ireland has been slower. There is no reason why it should be. By virtue of the Real Property Act 1845 a deed purporting to be an indenture has the effect of an indenture though not actually indented or expressed to be an indenture.

9 Lewison discusses dates in *Interpretation of Contracts* (2nd ed) 9.02 – 9.03. Law Commission Report No 253, Cm 4026, 1998, *The Execution of Deeds and Documents by or on behalf of Bodies Corporate*, accessible at www.lawcom.gov.uk, also has a discussion at para 6.6.

10 Perhaps surprisingly, a settlor is in principle bound by a settlement which he has executed, even if the trustees are parties and have not executed it: *Lady Naas v Westminster Bank* [1940] AC 366.

11 *Emmet on Title* is a good starting point for research on this. See also the comprehensive account of the current law in Northern Ireland contained in the recent Discussion Paper on Deeds and Escrows issued by the Law Reform Advisory Committee for Northern Ireland (Discussion Paper No 7).

12 Agathon, *cit* Aristotle, *Nicomachean Ethics*, Vol 6, chap 2.

execution.[13] In this the law only reflects the human condition, inconvenient though it may sometimes be.[14] And yet the clear spring of principle is muddied by many real or apparent exceptions.[15] In view of the exceptions it is not surprising that the general principle itself is occasionally overlooked. So it should be well noted that the execution of a back-dated document with a view to mislead may involve criminal offences, *inter alia,* forgery and fraud on the Revenue. That a surprising

[13] Countless cases could be cited for this basic principle. For examples of private agreements failing to alter the past see *Waddington v O'Callaghan* (1931) 16 TC 187; *Bradshaw v Pawley* [1980] 1 WLR 10.

[14] Thus the non-judicial dictum of Edward Fitzgerald: 'The moving finger writes; and, having writ/ Moves on: nor all thy piety and wit/ Shall lure it back to cancel half a line/ Nor all thy tears wash out a word of it.' The inconvenience extends beyond the law. 'Reminded of the President's previous statements that the White House was not involved in the Watergate affair, Ziegler [government spokesman] said that Mr Nixon's latest statement is the Operative White House Position ... and all previous statements are inoperative.' (Cited in the *Oxford Dictionary of Quotations* (4th ed).)

[15] There are seven categories of exception:

(1) Parliament can enact retrospective legislation.

(2) Parliament sometimes empowers private persons to make arrangements which are wholly or partly retrospective. (Retrospectivity is not all or nothing, but a matter of degree.) One example is IHTA 1984, s 142 (deeds of variation). A deed of variation which purports to vary past dispositions does not do so for the general purposes of the law, but is treated for some tax purposes as if it had that effect. Again, an election for hold-over relief and indeed most tax elections have some retrospective fiscal effect.

(3) The Courts sometimes have power to make orders which are wholly or partly retrospective. For instance, the statutory powers to set aside transactions under insolvency or matrimonial legislation. There are dicta suggesting that the jurisdiction for rectification is in this category. There is a better argument of principle that rectification ought to fall in category (5) below. The issue will probably never be resolved.

(4) The Courts have no general inherent jurisdiction to change the past: *Morley-Clarke v Jones* 59 TC 567. But some judgments are effectively backdated: eg in *Spence v IRC* (1941) 24 TC 311 where a party to a contract exercised his right to set it aside for fraud. The *restitutio in integrum* represented by the court order obtained some years later did not reconstruct history: it recognised and declared that which had been the legal position before the judgment, although until the order the parties were in a state of some uncertainty as to what their rights were. So the court order in this case was not retrospective in the strict sense; but the distinction requires a legal microscope. Likewise new judge-made law, such as the *Ramsay* principle, is harshly retrospective in reality, if not in legal theory.

(5) A few legal acts or events have some retrospective effect at common law. Examples include disclaimers, assents escrows (said to 'relate back'); the exercise of a right to render a voidable disposition void will sometimes make it void *ab initio*. Whether these acts are retrospective for fiscal purposes has been decided on an ad hoc basis. A disclaimer was held not to have retrospective fiscal effect: *Re Stratton* [1958] Ch 42. In *Spence v IRC* (1941) 24 TC 311, T sold shares under a contract completed in 1933. T set aside the contract (for fraudulent misrepresentation) in 1936. The House of Lords ordered the fraudulent purchaser to transfer the shares back to T in 1939. It was held that T was rightly assessed on dividends from the shares for the years 1936 to 1939. That was obviously correct: see (4) above. More interestingly, it was said that the effect of the exercise of T's right of rescission was retrospective (for income tax) back to the date of contract. (But this was perhaps obiter since dividends were only assessed from after the date of the rescission.)

(6) Private persons may agree between themselves that a document should have effect from an earlier date. But this is not true retrospectivity, and only parties to the agreement are affected. For instance, the Revenue will not be bound.

(7) Samuel Butler observed that although God cannot alter the past, historians can. Accountants-financial historians-enjoy some similar licence.

number of practitioners do not realise that backdating is a crime will not much avail anyone in the Courts.

Parties

9.7

This settlement is made [date] between
(1) X of [address] ('the Settlor') of the one part and
(2) (a) Y of [address] and
(b) Z of [address]
('the Trustees') of the other part

The form is so standard that it is rare to stop to consider whether these words are all necessary or indeed what they may mean. In fact the words 'of the one part' and 'of the other part' have no significance in the context of a deed of settlement.

Who should be parties?

9.8

It is not strictly necessary that the trustees should be parties to the trust deed. All that matters is that the trust property is vested in the trustees.[16] The only significance of making trustees a party is that (1) they cannot disclaim trusteeship; and (2) they cannot deny that they have notice of the trust deed. It is, however, the standard practice to include them. The practice in will drafting is a striking contrast: trustees of a will trust are not made a party to the will. Likewise it is not necessary that a Protector should be a party to the trust deed, and it is better practice that he should not be a party, though no harm is done if he is a party. The same applies to a beneficiary (of a bare trust or otherwise). All the parties should execute the deed (and if they do not they should not be parties).

Describing the parties

9.9

Full names and addresses should be given so that there can be no doubt as to identity. For the style of writing the address, see paragraph 2.12 (Addresses). Further details should be given in unusual situations where ambiguity may still

16 *Re Chrimes* [1917] 1 Ch 30. If trustees are made parties, it does not matter if they do not sign the trust deed: see 9.5 (On what date does a trust take effect?).

remain (eg where an individual uses two names; or two individuals in the same family share the same name).

The traditional practice was to specify the occupation and (for women only) marital status of each party. This usually is (and should be) omitted as unnecessary and (to some) offensive. It would be convenient to give former names, if a person is referred to in an earlier relevant document by different name, as this avoids confusion.

Each name should begin on a separate line.

Form where settlor is one of the trustees

9.10

The settlor is commonly one of the trustees. The use of a definition conveniently shortens the text:

> This Deed is made the ..... day of ..... between
> 1. John Smith of [address] ('the Settlor') of the one part and
> 2. (a) The Settlor and
>   (b) Peter Smith of [address]
>
> ('the Trustees') of the other part.

It was formerly the practice for the person to sign twice, once in each capacity, but this is not necessary and not recommended.

Form where trust made by joint settlors

9.11

It happens occasionally that two settlors (usually husband and wife) contribute funds to a single trust. (Two separate trusts may be advantageous for tax,[17] but the administrative convenience of a single trust may outweigh any tax considerations.)

The form hardly needs to be spelt out:

> This Settlement is made [date] between
> 1. John Smith and Jane Smith both of [address] 'the Settlors', etc.

Note that consequential amendments must be made elsewhere in the trust. Amendments are usually needed for the following:

17 Two separate trusts will qualify for two separate CGT annual exemptions.

(1) The definition of Beneficiaries.
(2) The power to appoint new trustees.
(3) The settlor exclusion clause.

This seems, and indeed is, obvious; but it is easy to forget and therefore not infrequently overlooked in practice.[18]

Form where settlor is sole trustee

9.12

The form is self-explanatory:-

> This Settlement is made [date] by [name] ('the Settlor').
>
> Whereas...

It is wrong to say:

> This Settlement is made [date] between
> (1) John Smith of [address] ('the Settlor') of the one part and
> (2) John Smith ('the Original Trustee') of the other part

But no harm is done (save as to reputation) if this uncouth form is used.

No named settlor

9.13

It is possible for a settlor to convey his property to trustees and for the trustees then to declare appropriate trusts at his direction[19]: there then is no need to name the settlor in the trust deed. This may be done for confidentiality which may be desired for reasons proper or improper. Bearing in mind the risk that an uncharitable or cynical court may infer that the reasons are improper, it seems a wiser policy to name the settlor in the trust deed. This is, however, a better course than to use a nominee settlor.

18 Interesting questions can arise where this mistake is made. For instance: suppose there are two settlors, Mr and Mrs X. The Beneficiaries are defined as 'the children of the Settlor'. Y is the child of Mr X but not of Mrs X. Is Y a beneficiary?

19 A written and signed direction is of course needed in NI (Statute of Frauds 1695, s 6) and also in England (LPA 1925, s 53(1)(c)).

Nominee settlor

9.14

It is the custom in some offshore jurisdictions to arrange for a lawyer or trust company to settle an initial nominal trust fund. This may be referred to as a nominee settlor; though others may use pejorative terms such as dummy, puppet or stooge. The real settlor then adds the substantial trust fund. It goes without saying that the person who provides trust property directly or indirectly will be the 'settlor' for tax purposes[20] and likewise for insolvency and matrimonial law purposes. This style of drafting may have the pernicious result of leading a court to infer an intention to mislead the reader into thinking that the nominee settlor is the only and real settlor. (Though the true explanation may be that the parties are seeking lawful confidentiality and mistakenly believe that every trust deed ought to specify a named settlor; or the drafter had adopted a form he has seen elsewhere without any thought on the subject at all.)

Recitals

9.15

Before the operative part of the deed there are traditionally inserted a series of statements known as 'recitals.' Their function – in a trust context – is to assist the reader of the deed by explaining its background and purpose. They are not intended to have legal effect and do not normally have any.[21] The use of recitals to instruct or entertain has fallen into sad decline.[22]

Recitals are traditionally introduced by the word 'whereas'. A radical drafter might replace this with the word 'Background' which describes precisely the place and function of the recitals.

20 See James Kessler, *Taxation of Foreign Domiciliaries* (2nd edn, 2003, Key Haven Publications Plc), ch 30 ('Who is the Settlor').

21 Recitals occasionally serve a legal function, operating to supply evidence or to form an estoppel. None of these are normally relevant to a deed of trust. In addition, of course, recitals will have a legal effect if the context shows that that is the intention. The correct practice is to put such material into the body of the deed. For a couple of examples of erroneous recitals disregarded, see 11.8 (Drafting resolutions of advancement).

22 But note the preamble to AP Herbert's Spring (Arrangements) Bill (which did not pass into the statute book):

> 'Whereas on every lawn and bed
> The plucky crocus lifts his head,
> And to and fro the sweet birds go,
> The names of which we do not know ...'

(Cited in the biography by R Pround, Michael Joseph, 1976).

A glance at different trusts encountered in practice or in precedent books show that a wide variety of recitals are used. The authors's approach is to include recitals which will be of assistance to the reader or user of the deed. These are as follows:

Recital 1: A list of the principal beneficiaries of the trust

9.16

The Settlor has two children, namely:
(i) Adam Smith, who was born on [date] and
(ii) Daniel Smith, who was born on [date]

The names and dates of birth will be convenient to later users of the deed. The layout – each name on a separate line – adds greatly to the clarity of the precedent. Dates of birth may be omitted if irrelevant to the trust; this will usually be the case where the beneficiaries are adult.

Recital 2: Name of trust

9.17

This settlement shall be known as the John Smith 1997 Settlement.

A trust needs a name, if only for the purposes of Revenue correspondence: the first question asked in form 41G (Trusts) is: 'Full Title of the Trust.'

It seems appropriate for the drafter to supply the name in the draft (though no harm can arise if this is not done; the trust will be named in due course).

It is suggested that the name belongs logically in the recitals. The body of the trust should contain the provisions which have legal effect.

The choice of name hardly matters. It is usually taken from the name of the settlor and the year. Where the settlor creates a number of trusts in one year, they may be distinguished by number, or by the type of trust ('John Smith Grandchildren Settlement 1994'). Sometimes a trust is named after the principal beneficiary, or the trust property ('the Green Farm Trust').

Will trusts (which lack recitals) are not usually given a name in the will; the trust will no doubt be called 'the John Smith Will Trust' without the benefit of an express name clause. If a will creates two separate trusts (not a course adopted in this book), the drafter should provide two names.

Power to change name of trust

9.18

The authors have seen trusts conferring a power to change (by deed!) the name of a trust; this is based on a misconception. A name is only a label and trustees may name and rename a trust at their pleasure. Power to do so derives not from the terms of the trust, but from the nature of human language. Individuals commonly change their name by deed poll, but the deed is merely evidence of the intention to change a name.[23]

Recital 3: Foreign domicile of settlor

9.19

It may be helpful to state in a recital where the settlor is domiciled (if not in the United Kingdom).[24]

Useless recitals

9.20

Recitals are strictly unnecessary: they have no legal effect. The will drafter manages without them. The justification for the recitals included in our standard precedents is that they assist the reader. Others serve no purpose whatsoever, in normal circumstances, and should be omitted. This includes some quite common recitals. The following list is not exhaustive.

(1) Statement of purpose of the trust

9.21

> The Settlor wishes to provide for his family and others.

This is innocuous; but it must be admitted to be completely unnecessary[25]. At any rate, this form would be preferable to grandiloquent forms such as:

23 35 *Halsbury's Laws of England* (1994), para 1279. The authors have also seen the form:

> '*For the purposes of identification* this settlement shall be known as ...'

One wonders what purposes a name can serve other than identification.

24 For precedents, see 19.18 (Best form of will for foreign domiciled testator).

25 The vacuity of this recital is illustrated by *IRC v Botnar* [1998] STC 38 at 61. This records a submission that a recital in this form was relevant to the construction of a power to transfer to a new trust. The submission (rightly) raised no ripple of response before the Special Commissioners or on appeal.

> The Settlor is desirous of making such provision as hereinafter appears for the benefit of the persons hereinafter specified ...

(2) Transfer of trust property to trustees

9.22

It is common to recite that the settlor has transferred the trust property to the trustees. Thus:

> The Settlor has transferred the property specified in the first schedule below to the Original Trustees.

This may conceivably serve as a useful reminder to ensure that the trust property is in fact transferred to the trustees.[26] But would advisors who need the reminder read or act on the recital? One frequently turns to the schedule and finds a reference to a nominal sum. No harm is done if the recital is omitted, and it is not used in this book.

There is certainly no point in elaborations; such as:

> The Settlor has paid or caused to be transferred to or otherwise caused to be vested in the joint names of the Original Trustees the investments and other property specified in the schedule hereto to be held on the trusts declared by this deed and for the purposes hereinafter appearing ...

(3) Intention to transfer additional property to trustees

9.23

> It is apprehended that further moneys, property or investments may from time to time be assigned delivered transferred to or otherwise vested in the name or control of the trustees to be held on the trusts declared by this deed.

If the initial trust fund is a nominal sum this is obvious. If the trust fund is substantial, and it is *actually* intended to increase the trust fund, then the recital may serve some purpose. The recital serves no purpose in standard precedents.

26 See para 30.8 (Transfers of trust property to trustees).

(4) Consent of trustees

9.24

The trustees have consented to act as trustees of this settlement.

Would the trustees execute the deed if they did not consent?

(5) Irrevocability

9.25

On this see 9.50 (Irrevocability).

Testatum

9.26

Now this deed[27] witnesses as follows:

This introduces the body of the deed. It serves as a marker, and has no other purpose. The radical would omit the phrase altogether, as meaning no more than 'this document says what it says.' Others modernise the language and say 'this deed therefore provides as follows...' or use the heading 'Operative Provisions'. There is a lot to be said for this. At any rate, the drafter should avoid embellishment such as:

Now in consideration of the premises[28] *this deed witnesseth ...;*

Now this deed made in pursuance of the said desire[29] *witnesseth ...*

Now this deed witnesseth and it is hereby declared as follows ...

The additional words add nothing. If the drafter is tempted to add words to the testatum, he should consider whether they should better be placed in recitals or in the body of the deed.

Witnesseth is dying a surprisingly gradual death, but is becoming rarer.

27 Some say: 'this *settlement* witnesses. ...'. The word 'deed' is preferable: it is the document which is doing the 'witnessing'.

28 'Premises' is an archaic term referring to the body of the deed before the 'habendum'. The reference is to a recital that the settlor intends to benefit his family.

29 This refers to the recited desire of the settlor to create the settlement.

'*Irrevocably* witnesses' is a neologism based on a twofold misunderstanding of the need to state that a deed is irrevocable, and the nature of a witness, whose testimony can never be revoked (though it might be contradicted). The form should not be used.

Definitions

9.27

For this topic see paragraph 9.35 (Definitions).

Trust for sale

9.28

In Northern Ireland land held in trust for the benefit of successive owners is still governed by the antiquated provisions of the Settled Land Acts 1882-1890. In England there have been two major reforms in the interim: the 1925 property legislation and the Trusts of Land and Appointment of Trustees Act 1996. Readers who practise in Northern Ireland will be all too familiar with the fact that the law relating to trusts of land in this jurisdiction is long overdue a radical overhaul. The source of this current unsatisfactory state of affairs was the extension of the Settled Land Act 1882 to trusts for sale as well as strict settlements (seemingly because of an oversight on the part of the reformers). The unfortunate consequence was that trustees for sale were deprived of their power of sale – unless they obtained the consent of the tenant for life. The very rationale of the trust for sale had been vitiated. In the wake of the outcry which followed the 1882 Act, an ill-advised legislature sought to rectify the situation by hastily enacting ss 6 and 7 of the Settled Land Act 1884. Section 6 effectively gave the life tenant's power of sale back to the trustees where there was a trust for sale, but only so long as the tenant for life had not obtained a court order under s 7. If the tenant for life had successfully obtained such an order the power of sale reverted to him. And so the position remains.

It almost beggars belief that these confusing provisions still determine who has the power to sell land in Northern Ireland which is held in trust in the twenty-first century. After 1925 the English trust drafter could at least guarantee that the inclusion of a trust for sale would avoid vesting administrative powers in the tenant for life. His Northern Ireland counterpart can only hope that the tenant for life does not apply to the court for an order under s 7. Nothing can be done to prevent or even discourage him doing so, as attempts to do so would be void. However, two points should be made to place the threat in perspective. The first is that very few applications have ever been made under s 7, so in practice it is not of any real significance.[30] The second is that where the trustees really do not wish the tenant for life to exercise the power of sale (and presumably relationships will already have broken down completely if an application is being made to the court) they can (in the trusts in this book) as a last resort exercise their overriding powers and revoke his life interest.

It follows that the trust for sale is an essential provision. Land held on trusts which are not 'Trusts for Sale' is generally 'settled land'. The provisions of the Settled Land Acts 1882-1890 apply. Enough has been said to show how highly complex these provisions are. The trust for sale is the means of escape from the Settled Land Act (even if in Northern Ireland that escape is not quite so watertight as it was in England after 1925). The more logical solution of directing that 'the provisions of the Settled Land Act will not apply' is not available as such a clause would be void.

Drafting the trust for sale

There are a number of statutory precedents, generally from the English 1925 property reforms.[31] The English Statutory Will Forms provide another form:

> '(1) The Property shall be held -
> (a) as to the real property, if any, including chattels real, upon trust to sell the same, and
> (b) as to the personal property, if any, upon trust to call in, sell and convert into money such part thereof as may not consist of money.
>
> (2) The trustees shall have power to postpone such sale and conversion for such a period as they, without being liable to account, may think proper...
>
> (3) The trustees may invest in their names or under their control, the residue of the said money, or so much thereof as may not have been distributed, in any authorised investments, with power, at their discretion, to vary such investments for others of a like nature.'[32]

The essence of a trust for sale clause is a direction that the trustees shall hold property 'on trust to sell the same.' The common form of the clause is stylised and elaborate and matters are exacerbated by adding the trust for sale itself (i) a direction to invest the proceeds of sale; and (ii) a power to vary investments. In

30 The authors inquired of a number of experienced NI practitioners and none could recall being involved in a transaction in which s 7 was an issue. And, of course, even if an application is made there is no guarantee that the tenant for life will be successful – see Wylie, *Irish Land Law* (3rd ed, 1997) at p 483.

31 Eg Administration of Estates Act 1925, s 33.

32 English Statutory Will Forms 1925, form 8.

the English Statutory Will Forms these extraneous provisions are sensibly divided into distinct sub-clauses.

In drafting the trust for sale clause it is necessary to abandon the usual aim, to find a form which a layman will understand: the best that can be done is to keep the form short and inconspicuous. Provisions which are not directly to do with the trust for sale are placed elsewhere. This results in a form of pleasing concision.

Land held on trust for sale

> The Trustees shall hold land on Trust for Sale with power to postpone sale

The common form trust for sale clause applies not only to land. Recognising that some forms of property may not normally be sold (eg a debt) the trustees are directed not just to sell the trust fund, but to 'sell, call in or convert into money'. But a trust for sale is only required for land; it serves little purpose for other property. There may be cases where trustees are really intended to convert the trust property into money, in which case the wide form of trust for sale clause is entirely appropriate.

In England it was unnecessary to provide that trustees should have power to postpone a sale of the land as this was implied by statute after 1925.[33] The absence of equivalent statutory provisions in Northern Ireland makes it desirable to expressly include a power to postpone. In England it was also expressly provided by statute that trustees should not be liable for postponing a sale in the exercise of their discretion; or that a purchaser need not be concerned with the timing of the sale.[34] A provision exonerating trustees from liability has not been included as part of the standard form here: this is adequately dealt with by the ordinary rules relating to trustee liability discussed in Chapter 5 of this book. Nor has express provision been made in relation to the duties of a prospective purchaser in relation to a postponement. Some practitioners may wish to add the provision:

> A purchaser of the legal estate shall not be concerned in any way with any directions respecting the postponement of a sale.

The common form is concerned not only with a sale, but with the application of the proceeds of sale. The trustees are directed to reinvest and given power to vary investments. Since trustees will have power to invest trust property, the direction here to reinvest is unnecessary. The power to vary investments is a separate matter from the trust for sale, though logically connected to it; if it is needed at all it is better placed with the other administrative provisions.

33 LPA 1925, s 25(2).
34 LPA 1925, s 25(2).

Sometimes the trust for sale clause makes specific provision for deduction of expenses which must be paid out of the rent of the land or out of the proceeds of its sale. Thus trustees are required to hold property on trust for sale, and the trustees are to hold:

> 'The net proceeds of sale, after payment of costs, and the net rents and profits until sale after payment of rates, taxes, costs of insurance, repairs and other outgoings'

on the appropriate trusts.[35]

This expanded wording recognises that in reality the trustees will deduct costs of sale from the proceeds of sale; and rates, etc from the rents before sale. But so long as the trustees are given power to do this elsewhere there is no necessity to spell the matter out in the trust for sale clause.

The short form has in fact been adopted by the parliamentary draftsman on a number of occasions,[36] so the drafter may use it with confidence.

Position of trust for sale clause

The Trust for Sale clause is often placed at the beginning of a settlement, immediately after the definitions clause and before the beneficial provisions. But the clause is no less effective if it is relegated to a schedule; and since the clause is essentially a technicality that course has been adopted in this book.

Direction to retain or to sell

Some difficulties have been caused in England where trustees were directed to hold land on trust 'either to sell or to retain it'. Is this a trust for sale?[37] In Northern Ireland the position is even less clear and this form should be avoided.

Beneficial provisions

9.29

Clauses appropriate to IP trusts, discretionary trusts, and A&M trusts are discussed in the chapters on these topics.

35 See the statutory precedent of LPA 1925, s 35.

36 LPA 1925, ss 3 (1)(b)(ii), 25(4), 28(1)(4), 31, 36(1).

37 In England s 25 (4) of the Law of Property Act 1925 has resolved the conundrum; this form is to be construed as a trust for sale.

It is common to preface the beneficial provisions with a general declaration of trust such as this:

> The Trustees shall hold the Trust Fund upon the trusts and with and subject to the powers and provisions hereinafter declared concerning the same.

Sometimes this is followed by a direction that property added is held on the same trusts.[38]

This is the drafter clearing his throat. He is politely requesting his reader's attention to what follows. The formula is omitted from the precedents in this book.

In our precedents the beneficial provisions are normally contained within three clauses:
(1) Trust Income
(2) Overriding Powers
(3) Default Clause

This division provides conceptual simplicity. It is better style not to mix income and capital powers in one single clause such as:

> The Trustees shall pay the income of the Trust Fund to X during her life but with power to pay or apply the capital thereof to or for her benefit during her life.

Testimonium clause

9.30

> Signed sealed and delivered by ...
>
> Witness ...

The practice is to make a lifetime trust by deed. There is no legal requirement to use a deed: any signed document would have the same effect; a trust (except of land) can even be made orally. The formalities associated with a deed[39] (signing,

38 Section 20.6 (Power to accept additional funds).

39 In Northern Ireland a deed must generally still be sealed and delivered. The common law rule that it is not essential that a deed be signed still prevails although it is the regular practice for a person executing a deed to sign the same near the place where his seal is affixed. Apart from statute (Registration of Deeds Act (NI) 1970 and the Land Registry Rules (NI)) it is not necessary for the validity of a deed that its execution shall be attested by witnesses. Nevertheless witnessing of all deeds has become standard practice. See the Law Reform Advisory Committee for NI Discussion Paper 7, Deeds and Escrows. In England the formalities of a deed (signature, witness, delivery as a deed) have been modernised by the Law of Property (Miscellaneous Provisions) Act 1989, s 1.

sealing and delivery together with witnessing) – though unnecessary – are appropriate; a deed being, in Blackstone's words, 'the most solemn and authentic act that a man can possibly perform with relation to the disposal of his property.'[40]

Every party should execute the deed.

Schedule of initial trust property

9.31

It was conventional to set out a list of the original trust property in a schedule to the trust deed. The authors suggests that there is little point in this: the relevant information will be provided in the trust accounts.

The old practice was to create an initial trust with a nominal sum of cash, formerly £5 and nowadays £100, and to transfer the real settled property to the trust immediately afterwards. The good reason for this curious arrangement was the avoidance of stamp duty on gifts. Stamp duty on gifts was abolished in 1985, and this practice should now be abandoned.

Schedule of administrative provisions

9.32

The form used in this book is:

> The provisions set out in the schedule shall have effect[41]

The practice of placing administrative provisions in a schedule at the end of a trust is a modern innovation and a welcome one. These provisions are of some length, but are of secondary importance. This may assist the client who will wish to understand the beneficial provisions, but who may be content to rely on his advisers to supply a suitable collection of administrative provisions. The schedule allows the matters which are of no interest to the lay client to be tucked away in decent obscurity; and has become established practice. This book adopts a fairly rigorous policy here: all routine provisions are excluded from the body of the trust. The credit for this innovation appears to belong to Potter and Monroe. The draft is based on standard statutory precedent.

40 *Commentaries* Book II (1st ed, 1766) p 297.
41 Eg FA 1989, s 51.

Schedule of beneficiaries?

9.33

In some foreign jurisdictions drafters have the tiresome habit of defining 'Beneficiaries' as the persons listed in the third or fourth schedule, so the reader has to stop and locate the schedule, only to find a few lines of text which would be more conveniently placed in the definitions clause.

Unnecessary provisions

'No conflict' clauses

9.34

These are not recommended forms, see paragraph 18.21 ('No conflict' clause).

Definitions

9.35

Definitions are used in various ways. A definition may serve to identify the status of an individual ('the Settlor', 'the Trustees', 'the Principal Beneficiary'). It may be used simply to avoid repeating a full name ('Adam' or 'Mr Smith' instead of 'Adam Philip Newbury Smith'). A definition may serve as a label for the complex concept (eg 'the Beneficiaries'). It is a useful tool for dividing text into pieces of manageable size. The use of a definition may ease the adoption of a standard precedent to its specific circumstances. The first letter of defined terms should be capitalised whenever used in the defined sense: 'the Trustees'; 'the Trust Fund'. This reminds the reader that the term is defined.[42] This practice is generally adopted in lifetime trusts but often ignored in wills; the distinction is not justifiable and only reflects the lower quality of will drafting.[43]

A modish fad is to italicise or even capitalise every letter of defined expressions wherever used. The result is rather messy typography.

42 This rule of construction was adopted without comment in *Beautiland Co Ltd v IRC* [1991] STC 467 PC Lord Keith, at 471, said: 'The context of the reference to 'the properties' (with a small '*p*') ... makes it clear that the definition of 'the Properties' is not imported.'

43 In drafting statutes, defined terms are not capitalised. But there the reader should be alert to the use of definitions; and to capitalise every defined expression (there are so many) would irritate rather than aid the reader. Moreover the reader will find editions of the statutes which will direct his attention to the defined terms at the end of each section. The reader of a private trust will not have that aid.

A defined expression should only be used in its defined sense. Occasionally it may be convenient to breach this rule. The drafter should signal this by using a small initial letter instead of the usual capital letter. There is only one example of such latitude in this book. The expression 'the Trustees' is defined to mean the trustees of the trust for the time being. This book nevertheless refers to:

> a former trustee
>
> a new trustee
>
> the trustees of another settlement

in each case the small 't' is appropriate.

The words 'said' or 'aforesaid' are not used in this book. If they are used, be it noted that they are not appropriate where an expression has been defined. It is a solecism to say:

> Hereinafter called 'the said trustees.'

It is generally undesirable to incorporate substantive provisions in a definition clause, but this is a rule of style and not inflexible.

How to make definitions

9.36

There are two common ways to make definitions. The first, one might call 'define as you go'; the second uses a formal definition clause.

'Define as you go'

9.37

This is established practice in the introductory paragraph of a trust. The modern practice – sanctioned by Parliament[44] – is to signify the definition by use of quotation marks and brackets alone. Thus:

> This Settlement is made on the 6th April 1991 between Mr John Smith ('the Settlor') ...

The traditional formula was grander:

44 Eg ICTA 1988, s 343.

Jack Spratt (hereinafter called 'the Settlor')

or the plural form:

> *Adam Smith and Barry Jones (hereinafter together*[45] *called the 'Trustees')*

'Hereinafter' is unattractive legalese. One could say:

> 'here called. ...'
>
> 'in this Deed called ...'

It seems safe enough to omit the tiresome word altogether. Indeed, the time may come when even the quotation marks are abandoned.[46]

A definition clause

9.38

Except for the parties to a settlement (where the above form is well established) it is helpful to assemble the principal definitions in a definition clause at the beginning[47] of the trust. A definition clause in a trust is a fairly recent innovation though now standard practice.

The drafter has a variety of statutory precedents to choose from. The form used in the English 1925 property legislation is:

> In this Act unless the context otherwise requires, the following expressions have the meanings hereby assigned to them respectively, that is to say:

This wordy form is an abbreviation of even lengthier nineteenth-century forms.[48] It has been shortened to:

> In this Act, except where the context otherwise requires:[49]

Or concisely:

> 'In this Act ...'[50]

45 Of course it would not matter if the word 'together' is omitted, as the sense is clear enough.
46 For a statutory example, see FA 1991, s 71.
47 Curiously the general practice in drafting Acts of Parliament (though not statutory instruments or in Schedules to an Act) is to place the definitions at the end. Each practice, now established, is best adhered to; the experienced reader will know where to turn.
48 Wills Act 1837, s 1.
49 IHTA 1984, s 272.
50 PA(NI) 1966, s 16; VATA 1994, s 96.

The form used in this book follows this:

> In this Settlement,[51] **'the Trustees'** means ...

It is kind on the eye to print the expression being defined in bold type. There is, however, no need to embolden the word where used throughout the document.

'Means' and 'includes'

9.39

Means is the appropriate word for an exhaustive definition. *Includes* is the appropriate word for an inclusive, non-comprehensive definition.[52] An inclusive definition is usually imprecise and not generally appropriate in trust drafting because a comprehensive definition is possible. To say 'X means and includes Y' is a contradiction in terms.[53] Of course where the wrong word is used the courts will allow the context to govern the sense.[54]

The practice in this book is to say:

> X means ...

not:

> X shall mean ...

This is more in accordance with English usage; and it is also the more standard practice of the parliamentary drafter.[55]

Grammarians may debate whether the singular or plural verb is appropriate where the term being defined is in the plural. Does one say **'the Trustees'** *means* ... or **'the Trustees'** *mean* ... ? The 1925 English property legislation employs the

51 'In this *Deed*' would do just as well but the word 'settlement' is better as the same form can be used without amendment in lifetime settlements and will trusts. One occasionally sees the archaic form, 'in these presents ...'.

52 Four cases on different nuances of 'include' are summarised in *Dunstan v Young Austen Young* [1987] STC 709 at 721.

53 It can be proper usage to say:

> X means 'a' *but* includes 'b'; or
>
> X means 'a' *and* includes 'b'.

54 No authority is needed for this self-evident proposition, but the point is made in *Dilworth v Stamps Comr* [1899] AC 99 at p 105. For an example see *Gibson v South American Stores (Gath and Chaves) Ltd* [1950] Ch 177 at 184: 'the class of beneficiaries shall include ...' held to form a comprehensive definition.

55 Para 6.6 (Other usage of 'shall' and 'may').

plural verb (with a slip in the Law of Property Act 1925, s 205(1)(xii)). Since one is defining a single expression, the singular seems more correct; this is now the practice in modern statutory and trust drafting.

The word 'comprises' is best avoided in a definition clause.

Unnecessary forms in a definition clause

9.40

The traditional form provides that definitions apply 'except where the context otherwise requires' or (more tentatively) 'where the context so permits'.[56] A well-drafted trust will use defined terms in their defined meanings. The form was included perhaps to cover the exceptional case, or to allow for drafting oversights. In either case the words are unnecessary: the context will always govern the meaning. In the first edition of this book these words were retained 'to serve as a ritual confession of the drafter's fallibility' but the value of ritual confessions is perhaps open to question. So the authors now follows the example of more concise drafters[57] and omits these words altogether.

It is plainly unnecessary to say: 'the following terms have the following meanings'. The heading 'Definitions' is sufficient indication of what is to come.

Some standard definitions

9.41

'The Settlor' should be defined by name. The authors have seen this form:

> 'The Settlor' means the Original Settlor and any person who shall make any addition to the trust fund.

The consequence is that the settlor exclusion clause will exclude not only the original settlor but all the contributor settlors. The authors do not favour this form.

56 In *Melville v IRC* [2000] STC 628 at 634, Lightman J recognises the difference in nuance between the two formulas; while linguistically this seems right, it is difficult in practice to conceive (1) that any drafter ever ponders carefully on the choice between the two wordings; or (2) that any case of construction is ever so finely balanced as to turn upon this distinction. The authors have even seen the form 'where the context so permits or requires'; a bad example of syllogism.

57 The parliamentary drafter occasionally omits this form in a definition clause governing an entire Act. In providing definitions for a Schedule or a particular section, on the other hand, the form 'unless the context otherwise requires' is almost invariably omitted.

'The Original Trustees' are also defined by name.

Definitions of 'Beneficiaries', 'Charities', 'Interest in Possession' and 'Trust Period' are considered elsewhere.[58] If the term 'Trust Corporation' is used it should be defined.[59] We here consider other commonly defined expressions.

Definition of 'the trustees'

9.42

> ***'The Trustees'** means the Original Trustees or other the trustees or trustee*[60] *for the time being of this Settlement.*[61]

Until quite recently this appeared to be an almost universally adopted form; so common, perhaps, that few drafters pause to ponder its significance or syntax. The purpose may be twofold: (i) to confirm the appointment of the 'Original Trustees' (defined by name) as the trustees of the trust; (ii) to confirm that the trustees' powers are given to them *ex officio*, and pass on to succeeding trustees. The clause is not strictly necessary: both inferences would be made quite naturally in the absence of indications to the contrary.[62] The archaism in the traditional formula, 'other the trustees' is a particularly unhappy one: the expression is dismissed by laymen as a typographical error.

In will drafting, a different formula is generally used to make these two points:

> *I appoint X and Y to be the executors and trustees of my will (hereinafter called 'my*[63] *trustees' which expression includes the trustees for the time being).*

Some lifetime trusts use this approach too.[64]

Statute provides two precedents:

58 Para 4.18 (Definition of beneficiaries); para 4.35 (Charities); para 18.19 (IP protection clause); para 8.2 (Perpetuity period).

59 Para 6.14 (Two-trustees rule).

60 Note the use of the small '*t*' is appropriate.

61 More traditionally 'hereof' stood for 'of this settlement'; or even, wrongly, 'of this deed'.

62 *Re Smith* [1904] 1 Ch 139; see also TA (NI) 1958, s 35(7). *London Regional Transport Pension Trustees Co Ltd v Hatt* [1993] PLR 227 at 257 is a further authority that 'the Trustees' will be taken to mean, the Trustees for the time being. Wolstenholme and Cherry, *Conveyancing Statutes* (13th ed, 1972) Vol 4, p 6 goes so far as to say that the definition is undesirable; though it does not seem to do any harm.

63 It is a curious custom that the form '*my* trustees' is used in a will, while the form '*the* trustees' is used in a lifetime trust. It is convenient to use the form 'the trustees' generally.

64 Eg Potter and Monroe, *Tax Planning with Precedents* (11th ed), contrast the 10th ed; *Kelly's Draftsman*.

> **'The Trustees'** means the trustees appointed by the Testator ... and the persons who by appointment by the court or otherwise become the trustees.[65]

> The provisions of this Act referring to the trustees of a settlement apply to the surviving or continuing trustees or trustee of the settlement for the time being.[66]

This is the basis for the definition used in this book:

> 'The Trustees' means[67] the Original Trustees or the trustees of the settlement for the time being.

The best approach would possibly be to abandon the definition altogether, as Prideaux did a generation ago;[68] though it would be a bolder drafter than the authors who is prepared to step this far out of line with conveyancing practice.

The draft needs amendment where the Settlor is the sole Trustee. The term 'Original Trustees' will not have been used. Thus:

> **'The Trustees'** means the Settlor or the trustees of this Settlement for the time being.

Definition of 'the trust fund'

9.43

A common form is:

> *'The Trust Fund' means:*
> (i) the property specified in the First Schedule hereto; and
> *(ii) all accretions thereto by way of further settlement, accumulation of income or otherwise,*[69] *and*
> (iii) all property from time to time representing the above.

This is another standard and self-evident definition. In this book, a simplified version is proposed:

65 The English Statutory Will Forms 1925, para 3(1)(iii) accessible on www.kessler.co.uk. Extraneous material has been omitted.

66 SLA 1925, s 94.

67 'includes' is not the appropriate word here (it is occasionally used by confusion with the form used in wills, set out above, where 'includes' is the appropriate word.)

68 *Prideaux's Forms and Precedents in Conveyancing* (25th ed, 1959)

69 This is about as common as the grander form with the same meaning: *'all other property investments or money* [as if investments or money were not 'property'!] *hereinafter transferred or paid to, or under the control of the Trustees as additions to the Trust Property.'* This is plainly unnecessary – see para 20.6 (Power to accept added property).

> 'The Trust Fund' means:
> (i) property transferred to the Trustees to hold on the terms of this Settlement[70]; and
> (ii) all property representing the above.

This definition is not necessary[71] but it is universal practice to include this form, and the authors include it in deference to the reader's expectation.

It is plainly not necessary to say that the trust fund includes property which shall be added to the trust fund. If property is subsequently transferred to the trustees to the intent that it should be added to the trust fund, then the trustees can hardly be heard to say the added property is not held on the terms of the original trust. It is not necessary to refer to accumulated income here, since the provision dealing with accumulation states it is to be added to the trust fund.[72]

9.44

A further definition is also introduced here:

> **'Trust Property'** means any property comprised in the Trust Fund.

The additional definition of 'Trust Property' facilitates drafting the trustees' administrative powers, where references to 'property comprised in the trust fund' are otherwise very frequent.

Unnecessary definitions

9.45

> 'This Settlement' means the Settlement created by this Deed.
>
> 'The settlor', and 'the trustees' have the respective meanings hereinbefore assigned to these expressions.

70 This form avoids the unnecessary chore of specifying the trust property in a Schedule: see para 9.31.

71 This proposition is self-evident but support for it can be found if needed in statutory drafting practice and case law. The Parliamentary drafter uses the terms 'trust funds', 'trust property' and 'trust money' without any definition: see, eg TA(NI) 1958, ss 1, 11, 15(1)(b), 37. In *Hume v Lopes* [1892] AC 112 at p 115 Lord Watson said: ' the expression 'trust funds' ... signifies funds belonging to the trust, including money invested on security or otherwise, as well as uninvested cash. I do not doubt that such is the ordinary and natural meaning of the words.' (When s 1 TA 1925 was re-enacted as s 1 of the Trustee Investments Act 1961 (now repealed) the Parliamentary drafter preferred the word 'property' to 'trust funds' but that is a stylistic change only.)

72 Para 15.6 (Drafting the accumulation limb).

Comment seems unnecessary. Enthusiasm for definitions can be taken to excess and the authors, having already included two redundant definitions in their text, are reluctant to admit more.

Where a word is used once or twice, a definition may be more trouble than it is worth. Thus, in a straightforward trust for a named beneficiary on attaining the age of 40, there is little advantage in providing that the trust fund is held on trust for 'the principal beneficiary' on attaining the 'specified age', and then separately defining these expressions to be the beneficiary concerned and the age of 40 years.

Definitions implied by law

9.46

In England the following definitions are implied by statute into every document[73]:
(1) 'Month' means calendar month.
(2) 'Person' includes a corporation.
(3) The singular includes the plural and vice versa.
(4) The masculine includes the feminine and vice versa.

Unfortunately there is no Northern Ireland equivalent and the absence of such statutory authority might persuade more cautious drafters to repeat these definitions in every document. All of them, however, are now established beyond doubt by way of the Interpretation Acts and case law. It is submitted that the Northern Ireland practitioner may also safely omit their constant repetition.

There is no need to introduce the anatomical curiosity that 'references to one gender include all genders'; the court will not infer from the use of the masculine word 'he' or 'his' that the reference is intended to exclude a company (even though a company is referred to by the neuter 'it' or 'its').[74]

Definitions to break up text

9.47

A definition may be used to break up text into manageable parts. In this context a defined term may be used once only, and it may be more convenient to define the term where used, rather than to place the definition in the definition clause.[75]

73 LPA 1925, s 61. See also para 2.14 (Singular and plural); and para 2.15 (Male and female).

74 In *Re Carnarvon* [1927] 1 Ch 138 a company was held to be entitled to powers conferred by SLA 1925, s 20 on a person 'of full age'. The argument that the words 'of full age' excluded companies was rejected. A similar argument based on the words *he* or *his* must be rejected *a fortiori*.

75 Para 2.6 (Must every clause be a single sentence?).

Drafting successive interests

9.48

The practice in this book is to employ a chain of clauses linked with the words 'subject to that'. Thus:

> (1) The Trustees shall pay the income of the Trust Fund to John during his life.
> (2) **Subject to that** the Trustees shall pay the income to John's widow during her life.

An alternative approach is to specify the starting point of each sub-clause more precisely:

> (1) The Trustees shall pay the income of the Trust Fund to John during his life.
> (2) On the death of John, the Trustees shall pay the income to his widow during her life.

This is considered to be an inferior approach. Using the phrase 'subject to that', each sub-clause forms, as it were, a slat which rests firmly on that which has gone before. The structure will be sound: there can be no gaps. If, however, each sub-clause stands independently, there is a risk of an omission. What happens, for instance, in the example above, if John should surrender or disclaim his interest? Who is then entitled to the income during John's life?[76]

9.49

'Subject to that' is adopted in this book as synonymous for the more archaic 'subject as aforesaid'. The form has the sanction of Parliamentary usage.[77] It is common to find grander forms with the same meaning, for instance, following a power of appointment:

> *in default of and until and subject to any such appointment ...*[78]

or in a Default Clause:

> in default of and subject to the trusts and powers hereinbefore declared and to the extent that the same shall not extend or take effect. ...

But the modest phrase 'subject to that' is equal to them all.

[76] The answer is supplied by the presumptions of the doctrine of acceleration; like all the artificial rules of construction this involves some difficult case law.

[77] IHTA 1984, s 204(8).

[78] This form is used in the English Statutory Will Forms 1925, Form 9 accessible on www.kessler.co.uk.

Irrevocability

9.50

> This settlement is irrevocable.

In the middle of the nineteenth century a power of revocation was standard form. (Of course the powers caused no tax problems in those days.) If the power was, exceptionally, omitted, the court might set aside or rectify a settlement unless the settlor had 'distinctly repudiated and refused to have a power of revocation.'[79] This explains the origin of the recital that:-

> The Settlor has been advised that unless a power of revocation is reserved the Settlement will be irrevocable but well understanding such advice he had decided to reserve no power of revocation whatsoever and the settlement is irrevocable.

This is sometimes shortened to a recital that: –

> It is intended by the Settlor that this settlement shall be irrevocable.

This approach was reversed in the 1880s and the omission of a power of revocation ceased to be a reason for setting aside a trust.[80] Nowadays a UK trust hardly ever has a power of revocation. A trust will therefore be irrevocable unless it actually reserves a power of revocation.[81]

Irrevocability forms have accordingly been unnecessary in English law for more than a century. They were not used in James Kessler's *Drafting Trusts and Will Trusts* until the 6th edition. However, the new American Uniform Trust Code[82] provides that American trusts are revocable unless stated to be irrevocable. So it now seems (just) worthwhile to state the point expressly, not because there would otherwise be any doubt, but because American readers unfamiliar with English law principles might possibly misunderstand the position.

The appropriate place to put this form is in the body of the deed, not a recital.

79 Many cases could be cited, but since they are now obsolete it is sufficient to refer to *Hall v Hall* (1871) LR 14 Eq 365; *James v Couchman* (1885) 29 Ch D 212; *Coutts v Acworth* (1869) LR 8 Eq 558; *Wollaston v Tribe* (1869) LR 9 Eq. 44.

80 *Henry v Armstrong* (1881) 18 Ch D 668; *Dutton v Thompson* (1883) 23 Ch D 278; *Tucker v Bennett* (1887) 38 Ch D 1.

81 No authority is needed for this self-evident proposition (which is of course the basis on which the cases in the two footnotes above were decided). See however, *Farwell on Powers* (3rd ed, 1916), p 306: 'A deed once executed cannot be revoked unless it reserves a power of revocation'.

82 Section 602; accessible on www.law.upenn.edu/bll/ulc/uta/2001final.pdf.

CHAPTER 10

Drafting and understanding overriding powers (appointment, re-settlement and advancement)

10.1

The fundamental desire of the settlor, in creating his trust, is this: to benefit the beneficiaries of his trust in the most appropriate way. It is impossible for settlor or drafter to anticipate in advance exactly what that will be. Drafts in this book are based on the premise that the trustees should be trusted – as their name suggests – and they may be given wide powers to achieve the settlor's intention. This is the principal function of the overriding powers.

There is a further advantage: the existence of the overriding powers effectively prevents a profligate beneficiary from selling his interest in a trust. He will not find a purchaser for an interest subject to the overriding power: the interest could and probably would be revoked the day after the sale. This, in turn, has an incidental tax advantage. Any tax charge based on the market value of the equitable interest is effectively avoided. These powers raise questions of principle. The flexibility intended to satisfy the wishes of the settlor may be used to frustrate them. The question of who should exercise the powers, and with what constraints, is discussed at paragraph 6.12 (Guidance and control of trustees). This chapter is devoted to the technical drafting issues.

Overriding powers may be divided into three categories.

- *Power of appointment*: Power to create new trusts for the beneficiaries.
- *Power of resettlement*: Power to transfer funds to a new settlement for the beneficiaries.
- *Power of advancement*: Power to apply capital for the benefit of a beneficiary.

Power of appointment

10.2

The power of appointment may take the form of a true power to terminate existing provisions and create new ones; or it may take the form of a discretionary duty, the trustees being (in theory) required to appoint new provisions. The distinction is of little importance.[1] In this book the form used is a true power: this corresponds more closely to the reality.

The clause must, obviously, specify the form of the new trusts which may be created and the objects who may benefit. In this book the objects are simply described as 'the Beneficiaries' and the definition of the term is considered at paragraph 4.18 (Definition of 'beneficiaries').

The parliamentary drafter provides one influential precedent:

> The capital and income of the trust fund shall be held in trust for all or any one or more exclusively of the other or others of the Beneficiaries, and if more than one in such shares, with such provisions for maintenance, education, advancement and otherwise, at the discretion of any person or persons, and with such gifts over, and generally in such manner, for the benefit of such beneficiaries, or some or one of them, as the Trustees shall, by deed, revocable or irrevocable, or by will appoint.[2]

This precedent will be known to anyone familiar with trust deeds. Old style precedents take this material, delete the punctuation, and expand it in a single clause of extraordinary length. The single clause has become unwieldy: Hallett led the way and divided the power into separate clauses, with a view to greater comprehensibility. The clause used in our precedents is a simpler version of the statutory precedent:

> During the Perpetuity Period, the Trustees shall have the following powers:
>
> (1) Power of Appointment
> (a) The Trustees may appoint[3] that they shall hold the Trust Fund for the benefit of any Beneficiaries, on such terms as the Trustees think fit.
> (b) An appointment may create any provisions and in particular
> (i) discretionary trusts
> (ii) dispositive or administrative powers
> exercisable by the Trustees or any other person.
> (c) An appointment shall be made by deed and may be revocable or irrevocable.

The draft refers to 'such terms as the Trustees think fit', which covers all the various terms used in the Statutory Will Forms precedent.

1 Para 6.2 (Duties and powers distinguished).
2 The English Statutory Will Forms 1925, Forms 7 and 9, (here slightly amended to stand in isolation) accessible on www.kessler.co.uk.
3 The words 'appointment' and 'appoint' are the appropriate technical term. Plain English enthusiasts may prefer to call the power of appointment, a 'power of variation' and substitute 'direct' or 'declare' or 'appoint'. Some old precedents use the formula 'direct and appoint'. The authors have seen 'appoint direct and declare'; meaningless synonymy.

It is usual to require an appointment to be made by deed. This is not essential, but a deed is appropriate since an appointment is a formal legal document. There is no particular reason why trustees need make revocable appointments when they have a wide flexible power, but it may be convenient to do this.

The power of appointment can be used to alter administrative provisions as well as beneficial provisions.[4]

Sub-clause (b) is essential. A stumbling block for older powers of appointment was the court's view that a power of appointment was (in the absence of clear words) a power to create fixed interests and could not be used to create dispositive trusts and powers. This clause makes the position clear. The position in the absence of such a clause is discussed in an excursus at paragraph 10.5 (The problem of narrow powers of appointment). It is normal to state that the appointment may be revocable or irrevocable, though strictly any donee of a power is in principle entitled to make a revocable appointment within the time that the power itself may be exercised.

Unnecessary provisions in the power of appointment

10.3

Some drafters refer not just to 'the Beneficiaries' but to

> ... all or any one or more exclusively of the other or others of the Beneficiaries

This has been unnecessary since 1874.[5]

Some drafters do not refer to trusts for the benefit of the beneficiaries, but to:

> Such trusts *in favour or* for the benefit of the Beneficiaries

It is submitted that the extra words have no meaning. The expression 'favour or benefit' is a mere synonymy.[6]

Occasionally drafters use the word 'respective' thus:

> The Trustees shall hold the trust fund on trust for the Beneficiaries ... with such trusts for their *respective* benefit ... as the Trustees shall appoint.

4 In the standard overriding powers in this book, this is stated expressly, though it will normally be implied: *Re Rank* [1979] 1 WLR 1242. In consequence, a power to add administrative powers is unnecessary: see para 20.5 (Power to add powers).

5 The Powers of Appointment Act 1874. See *Re Hughes* [1921] 2 Ch 208 and para 2.14 (Singular and plural).

6 In PA(NI) 1966, s 3(5) the expression used is 'a power of appointment exercisable in favour of members of a class' (without the word 'benefit').

In one case it was held that this word 'respective' suggested that the creation of discretionary trusts was not permitted.[7] In practice the trustees will expressly be permitted to create such trusts. So the word 'respective' is either erroneous (if Cross's comments in *Hunter* are correct) or superfluous (if they are not.) Plainly no one who cares about accurate language will use the word here.

It is common to add a requirement that any appointment must observe the rules against accumulation and perpetuities. This has no legal effect, and may be omitted. (The form might conceivably serve as a reminder to the person who drafts the deed of appointment; but a person who needs that reminder is unlikely to be capable of drafting the necessary deed in any event.)[8]

Some drafters add a provision saying that to the extent that the power of appointment is not exercised, the original trusts continue to apply. This is implied in any case, and is omitted.[9]

Some drafters add a provision that the power of appointment cannot be operated retrospectively. For instance:

> No exercise of this power shall reduce the amount of any accrued benefit to which a beneficiary shall have become entitled under this settlement.
>
> No appointment shall affect income payable to the Trustees before the date of that appointment.

A provision of that type will be understood by necessary implication and is therefore unnecessary.[10]

10.4

Hallet[11] adds two further provisions not generally found in modern powers of appointment, but which should be mentioned for completeness. The Hallett precedent directs that the power of appointment may be used to:

7 Cross J said that a discretionary trust is not for the respective benefit of the beneficiaries: it is a trust for the *collective* benefit of all of them under which none has any separate benefit: *Re Hunter* [1963] Ch 372. Is this convincing? To the authors, the word 'respective' is vacuous in this context. It does not carry the inference which Cross J. put upon it. But this makes no practical difference. Either the power of appointment will expressly permit the creation of discretionary trusts; or else it will be silent and (as the authorities now stand) discretionary trusts will not be permitted in any event. See the excursus at para 10.5.

8 See 8.6 (Remaining within the perpetuity period). The authors have seen a trust (perhaps drafted for an economically minded settlor) in which the overriding power was subject to 'the rules against excessive accumulations and gratuities.'

9 *Re Hastings-Bass* [1975] Ch 25; *Re Master* [1911] 1 Ch 321 followed in *Re Sharp* [1973] Ch 331.

10 This was accepted without argument in *Pearson v IRC* [1981] AC 753 (confirming the view taken in the Revenue Press Release of 12 February 1976). It is apparent that the power of appointment in that case contained no such proviso: see the judgment of Fox J, at first instance [1980] Ch 1. This view is also supported by *Re Delamere* [1984] 1 WLR 813 and *Re Master* [1911] 1 Ch 321.

11 Hallett's *Conveyancing Precedents* (1st ed, 1965), p 772.

> provide for the appointment or remuneration of trustees on any terms and conditions whatever.

There is no need to make an express provision here for remuneration of trustees, since the normal trustee remuneration clause is sufficient.[12]

The Hallett precedent provides that the power of appointment may be used to:

> direct that the Trust Fund shall be transferred or paid to and held by any persons as trustees ...

The power of appointment (as drafted in this book or in any common form) cannot itself be used to transfer the fund to new trustees.[13] However there is the usual power to appoint new trustees, power to appoint separate trustees of separate funds[14] and (in precedents in this book) a separate express power of re-settlement. That seems comprehensive enough.

The problem of narrow powers of appointment[15]

10.5

Modern powers of appointment are generally widely drawn and give rise to no difficulty, but there are many older trusts with powers more narrowly drawn. It is worth considering these in some detail. The reader who is not familiar with the case law may go wrong here: If the old cases are still good law, these powers of appointment do not have the effect which a simple reading would suggest.

Let us start with an example. In *Re Joicey*,[16] property was held on trust for the beneficiaries:

> for such interests in such proportions and in such manner in all respects as the appointor should appoint.

12 For good measure, the overriding power in the precedents in this book could be used to make further provision for remunerating trustees. Such provision is an administrative provision. Of course this could only be done if (i) this was for the benefit of the beneficiaries and (ii) there was an independent trustee who did not benefit from the new remuneration clause. See para 5.12 (Conflicts of interest). It seems unlikely that this would ever need to be done.

13 This proposition is self-evident, but if authority is needed, see *Re Mackenzie* [1916] 1 Ch 125. Happily there is a solution to problems when such powers are lacking. A power of appointment in common form will generally be wide enough to confer upon trustees a power of resettlement.

14 TA (NI) 1958, s 36(1)(b).

15 See generally Richard Oerton *Trusts and Estates* (1994), pp 317 and 402.

16 [1915] 2 Ch 115. This is just an early example of a long line of cases, of which the most recent is *Re Hay* [1982] 1 WLR 202. Here Megarry J took the principle to a new height of absurdity by holding that the trustees had wrongly delegated their discretions to themselves.

Appointments were made for children who attained a certain age. Trustees were given power to transfer the capital to them under that age (a dispositive power). The appointment was void. This was said to follow from the rule against delegation.

In the following discussion powers of appointment which allow the appointor to create dispositive powers are described as wider powers; and powers which do not are called narrower powers. The effect of *Joicey* therefore, is to hold that the sort of power used in that case was a narrower and not a wider power.

It is submitted that the law has taken a wrong turning here.

An issue of delegation. First, this line of cases has treated the matter as one of delegation. It need not and (it is submitted) should not be put that way. The trustees are not delegating their existing power of appointment: they are exercising the power so as to create new dispositive powers.[17]

A matter of construction. The question whether a power of appointment is narrower or wider is a question of construction. That is not in dispute. The correct question to ask is not whether the power contains within it a right to delegate, but whether it was to be construed widely enough to permit the creation of new dispositive powers. The difference is one of nuance, but it is a significant nuance.

Let us return to the *Joicey* sort of power, and consider whether it should be construed as wider or narrower. Property was held on trust for the beneficiaries:

> for such interests in such proportions and in such manner in all respects as the appointor should appoint.

The answer obviously depends on the meaning of 'interests'. The word may be used to mean only fixed equitable interests; it may also mean interests under true powers or trust powers.[18] In the nineteenth century the courts would naturally give it the former, limited meaning; for discretionary trusts were then hardly known. In the present time, a natural reading would apply the wider meaning; for discretionary trusts are common; it is most unlikely that the settlor intended the power to be so limited.

What has happened is that the courts have followed the nineteenth century authorities – summed up in *Joicey* – to the present day. This is why such powers are given such a limited meaning. This is a misuse of precedent, which should not be regarded as binding in matters of construction. Unfortunately the Court of Appeal missed the opportunity to correct these errors in *Re Morris*.[19] Evershed MR preferred to follow the old authorities, more or less conceding that they were

17 The point was accepted in *Re Wills* [1964] Ch 219 at 237 and in *Re Weightman* [1915] 2 Ch 205 (a power of revocation 'in no sense' a delegation of a power of appointment).
18 *Leedale v Lewis* (1982) 56 TC 501.
19 [1951] 2 All ER 528.

wrong, than to construe the document according to its plain language. The complaint about the state of the law was repeated by Cross J in *Re Hunter*.[20] If the matter came to be reviewed by the courts, it is submitted that principle should be given priority over precedent. This, indeed, is what precedent requires.[21] Of course, for the time being, one should act on the cautious view that the decided cases might represent the law.

Happily, there is a solution to the problems presented by these narrow powers of appointment. Such powers can in principle be used to confer on the trustees a power of advancement, being either the statutory power (which is exercisable over half the trust fund) or a power of advancement extended over the entire trust fund[22]. Once that is done, of course, the trustees can use their power of advancement to achieve results beyond the scope of their narrow power of appointment: see paragraph 10.8 (Power of advancement).

Power of resettlement

10.6

The form used in this book is as follows:

(1) The Trustees may by deed declare that they hold any Trust Property on trust to transfer it to trustees of another settlement, wherever established, to hold on the terms of that settlement, freed and released from the terms of this Settlement.

(2) The Trustees shall only exercise this power if:-

20 [1963] Ch 372.

21 See 3.4 (precedent v meaning of document).

22 In *Re Mewburn* [1934] Ch 112 the Court approved of the exercise of a power of appointment (in relatively narrow form) to create a power of advancement exercisable over one half the trust fund. The judge noted that a power of advancement would nowadays be implied in any event by the English equivalent of s 33 of the Trustee Act (NI) 1958. The case was approved by the Court of Appeal in *Re Morris* [1951] 2 All ER 528 at 533 where the principle was held to apply

> '... at all events where the instrument creating the power [of appointment] enables any appointment to be made 'in such manner and form in every respect' or 'generally in such manner for the benefit of' the objects of the power, as the donee of the power may appoint.'

If it is possible to create a power over one half the trust fund, it must logically be possible to create a power over the whole, especially since the extension of s 33 to cover the whole is a standard form. The opposite conclusion was apparently reached in *Re Joicey* [1915] 2 Ch 115. There an appointor tried unsuccessfully to use a narrow power of appointment to create a power which (at first sight) appears an ordinary power of advancement. But this case no longer represents the law. That decision was based on the view that the (to modern eyes unexceptional) power which the appointor had attempted to create was *not* an ordinary power of advancement. That view could not now be sustained in the light of (i) s 33 and (ii) current drafting practice and (iii) the comments in *Re Pauling* [1964] Ch 303 at 333 (which contradict the view of the power taken at [1915] 2 Ch 123).

(a) every Person who may benefit is (or would if living be) a Beneficiary; or
(b) with the consent of
    (i) the Settlor, or
    (ii) two Beneficiaries (after the death of the Settlor).

The wording makes it clear that the new settlement will be a separate trust from the existing trust, as intended. The reported cases indicate what is needed. The phrase 'freed and released from the terms of this settlement' could be omitted, but it spells out the effect of the transfer clearly, and has judicial approval.[23]

Trustees are sometimes given power to transfer the trust fund to any trust if only one beneficiary of the present trust happens also to be a beneficiary of the new trust. That is equivalent to authorising trustees to add beneficiaries; a serious proposition if the power is exercisable without restraint. The form used here brings in the same safeguards as the power to add beneficiaries; see 4.36 (Power to add beneficiaries).

Power of resettlement and power of appointment compared

10.7

A power of appointment can vary the terms of a trust. The power of resettlement may effectively achieve the same result, but will also result in trust property being held by a different trust (perhaps, but not necessarily, different trustees and a different governing law). As a matter of trust law there may not be much difference between altering the terms of an existing trust (in a power of appointment) and transfers to a new trust (by a power of re-settlement). There are, however, important differences for tax purposes:

(1) The transfer to another trust is a disposal for CGT purposes; an exercise of a power of appointment does not normally involve a disposal.[24]
(2) If only part of the trust fund is transferred to a new trust, the result is two separate trusts. The trustees of one trust are not subject to liabilities of the second, and that may obviously be more convenient when different branches of a family wish to go separate ways. It would then be possible to appoint foreign trustees for one trust but not for the other.
(3) Many tax planning arrangements require transfers of funds to new trusts. A discussion of such planning is beyond the scope of this book: sufficient to say

23 *Hart v Briscoe* (1977) 52 TC 53. The leading cases are *Roome v Edwards* (1979) 54 TC 359; and *Bond v Pickford* [1983] STC 517.
24 TCGA 1992, s 71. This may be undesirable if a CGT charge would arise. For this reason trustees will generally prefer the power of appointment to the power of resettlement if the aim is only to vary the terms of the trust. However there will be occasions when trustees want a disposal of trust property; for instance, to restart the CGT taper relief 'clock' or to realise losses.

that a well drafted trust should give scope to make such arrangements in case it becomes appropriate.

Tax aside, this power may also be useful to combine trusts with similar terms, so as to reduce administrative costs; or to split up one trust with several sub-funds into separate trusts with separate classes of beneficiary.

Power of advancement

10.8

The term 'power of advancement' is used to describe a power to transfer trust property to a person, or apply it for his 'advancement or benefit.'[25] The person for whose benefit the trust property may be applied (or to whom the property may be transferred) is called the 'object' of the power.

Trustees have a power of advancement by statute. The statutory power is however subject to three important restrictions[26]:

(1) Only a beneficiary with some interest in trust capital is an object of the power. Thus a life tenant is not an object of the power.
(2) The power only extends over one-half of the object's share in the trust fund.[27]
(3) The trustees can only exercise the statutory power with the consent of any beneficiary with a prior interest.

These restrictions are in line with the cautious approach of English trust law, that trustees are not to have wide powers.

It is standard practice to override the second of these restrictions, by a form such as:

> *Section 33 of TA (NI) 1958 (Power of Advancement) shall apply with the following modification: the words 'one-half of' in section 33(1)(a) shall be deleted.*[28]

25 This is the usage of the Parliamentary drafter, who describes the power conferred by s 32, TA 1925 as 'the statutory power of advancement'; eg AEA 1925, s 47(1)(ii); likewise FA 1950, s 44(2) (an estate duty provision).

26 And for completeness three minor restrictions:
(1) The power does not apply to Settled Land Act settlements (TA (NI) 1958, s 33(2)).
(2) The power does not apply where there is an expression of contrary intent; it seems that a very shadowy one will suffice (TA (NI) 1958, s 68(2)).
(3) Where the beneficiary is to become entitled to a share (and not the whole) of the trust property, any advance is to be brought into account as part of that share (the hotchpot rule) (TA (NI) 1958, s 33(1)(b)).

27 It is possible (if expensive) to apply to the Court under s 57 of the TA (NI) 1958 to extend this power to the entire trust property.

28 This is the STEP standard provision. Some use the form:

This book adopts a different approach. The form used in this book is:

> The Trustees may pay or apply Trust Property for the advancement or benefit of any Beneficiary.

None of the restrictions which inhibit the statutory power of advancement apply:-
(1) All beneficiaries are objects of the power.
(2) The entire trust fund may be advanced.
(3) Consents of beneficiaries are not needed.

This is in line with the approach of this book, that trustees should be trusted with wide powers and that beneficiaries' consents are not desirable.[29] The restrictions which apply to the statutory power raise some difficult questions of trust law.[30] An advantage of our approach is that none of these difficulties can arise.

The form adopts unabridged the statutory phrases 'pay or apply', and 'advancement or benefit.' The full form is used to display the clause's parentage, s 33 of Trustee Act (NI) 1958, so as to suggest that the valuable case law giving a wide meaning to 'benefit' should apply.

It is intended that trustees should be able to use their power of advancement informally, so no deed or written document is required. This rather simplifies the administration of the trust. The statutory power takes the same approach.

Where there is a wide power of advancement, as in our draft, there is clearly no call for the statutory power. In the drafts in this book it is therefore not necessary to provide that the statutory power should apply (with or without amendment).

Other forms in powers of advancement

The statutory power of advancement is a power to pay or apply capital *money*. However, the power nevertheless applies to trust funds not in the form of money.[31]

S 33 TA (NI) 1958 shall apply with the deletion of proviso (a) thereof.

Note that this is arguably wider than the STEP form. For example consider a trust for A and B contingently upon attaining the age of 21 in equal shares. The statutory power of advancement allows one quarter of the trust fund to be used for the benefit of A and one-quarter for the benefit of B. The STEP form allows one-half to be used for A and one-half for B. The form set out in this footnote arguably allows the *entire* fund to be used for A or B.

29 See 6.23 (Giving powers of consent to beneficiaries).

30 How is the fraction of one-half to be calculated? What is a 'prior' interest? (A question 'of great difficulty' according to Clausen J in *Re Spencer* [1935] Ch 533; in *IRC v Bernstein* (1960) 39 TC 391 at 403 Lord Evershed MR was 'glad' to follow authority which refrained from expressing a view on the question. Such authorities are of more assistance to the Bench than to practitioners.) The hotchpot rule does not work well since no account is taken of inflation.

31 *Pilkington v IRC* [1964] AC 612 at 639.

In drafting a power of advancement it is more apt to refer to trust property than to 'money'.

Older trust precedents often give trustees power to *raise* and pay or apply trust property for the advancement or benefit of a beneficiary. However, the word 'raise' adds nothing[32] (which is presumably why it was omitted from both s 32 of the Trustee Act 1925 and s 33 of the Trustee Act (NI) 1958). The word 'raise' should not be used in modern drafting.

Power to pay or transfer to beneficiary

10.9

A common form in older trusts is that:

> The Trustees may pay or transfer trust funds to [a Beneficiary] for his own use and benefit absolutely.

This power is narrower than the common form power of advancement, since it does not allow funds to be applied for the benefit of the beneficiary but only to be paid or transferred to him absolutely.[33] The power is unnecessary where (as in the drafts in this book) there is a wide power of advancement.

32 It has been said that *raise* has 'a broad sense' and means no more than identify or set aside for the purpose of the exercise of the power: *Re Wills* [1959] Ch 1 at 14. This does however give the word a sense which it does not normally have. When one talks in ordinary usage of 'raising funds', 'raising' means obtaining money, either by loan, or by issuing shares for cash, or by any other method, (as in charity 'fundraising'). So the authors suggests another interpretation. The power of advancement should be read with a comma after the word 'pay' so it empowers trustees to do one of two things:
(1) 'Raise' trust capital (i.e. raise money, by borrowing, or by mortgage, or by sale of trust assets) and pay the money to or for the benefit of beneficiaries; or
(2) apply trust capital *in specie* (without 'raising' money) for the benefit of beneficiaries.
Whichever is the right approach does not in practice matter: the trustees can exercise a power of advancement without troubling themselves about any requirement of 'raising ' capital.

33 The words 'pay or transfer *to*' do not in their normal sense mean 'pay to or apply *for the benefit of*'. Of course the context may show that an extended sense is meant: for examples see para 14.7 (Does a beneficiary become 'entitled to' property if it is applied for his benefit?). But here the words 'for his own use and benefit absolutely' require the object becomes absolutely and beneficially entitled to the property paid or transferred to him. If appropriate, the Court may extend a narrow power to 'pay or transfer' into a wider power to 'apply for the benefit' under TA (NI) 1958, s 56; this may solve the problem of the narrow power. Another solution is to transfer to the beneficiary and let the beneficiary re-settle; but of course that has possible tax and property law problems.

Power of appointment used to make advance to beneficiary

10.10

The power of appointment (or indeed the power of resettlement) may be used so as to transfer trust capital to a beneficiary. But it may be easier to use the power of advancement for this purpose, since no formal deed is required. Trust money can simply be transferred by cheque.

Power of advancement used to create new trusts

10.11

The power of advancement in a trust may be used:

(1) to transfer trust property to a new trust where it may be held on terms wholly[34] or partly[35] different from the original trust;
(2) to alter the terms of the existing trust so as to create new beneficial interests which may wholly or partly replace the existing beneficial interests;[36]
(3) to alter administrative provisions.[37]

Thus the power of advancement may be used broadly to the same effect as powers of appointment or resettlement.

This is particularly important where a trust is drafted badly, or inflexibly, because even badly drafted trusts generally contain a full power of advancement, which should allow terms of the trust to be altered where necessary.

In the following discussion:

(1) It is assumed that under a trust ('the Original Settlement') trustees have power to apply capital for the benefit of an object, 'O'.
(2) The exercise of the power of advancement which results in a settlement of the funds advanced is called a 'settled advancement' and the trusts created are called 'advanced trusts'.
(3) The beneficiaries of the trusts created by the settled advancement are called 'Advanced Beneficiaries.'

34 As in *Re Clore* [1966] 1 WLR 955 (transfer to charity). In the leading case of *Pilkington v IRC* (1959) 40 TC 416 the new trusts were nearly, but not quite, exhaustive.

35 In *Re Hastings Bass* the trustees transferred trust property to a new trust but created only a limited beneficial interest in income and no exhaustive beneficial trust of capital of the funds advanced. The new trustees held on the terms of the old trusts, which remained in effect to the extent that the new trusts were not comprehensive. See [1975] Ch 25 at 42.

36 In *Re Hampden* the new trusts were nearly but not quite exhaustive. This important case is reported in [1977] TR 177 and also, belatedly, reported in [2001] WTLR 195 and accessible at www.kessler.co.uk.

37 *Howell v Rozenbroek* (14 December 1999, unreported).

A typical case is where trustees, having power of advancement for the benefit of O, exercise that power by a settled advancement, in such a way that the trust fund is held on trust for O for life, with remainder over to O's family.

The starting point is to note that the Advanced Beneficiaries include persons other than the object, O – in this example, his family. The advance must be for the benefit of O; but it is easy to see that this Settled Advancement may be an application of the trust fund for the benefit of O, since it will usually be for O's benefit that there should be funds to maintain his family after his death. It is not in the least relevant whether or not O's family are beneficiaries under the original settlement. They may be or they may not be; but the reason they become Advanced Beneficiaries is because this is for the benefit of O, and not because of their status under the original settlement. O himself need not be an Advanced Beneficiary at all. All that matters is that the Settled Advancement is for the benefit of O.[38]

A settled advancement can only create new trusts in a manner which is specifically for the benefit (albeit 'benefit' in the wide sense) of the object, O.[39] If there is a power to advance for the benefit of O, one cannot normally create new[40] trusts giving trustees a wide power of appointment in favour of O's siblings, or cousins, or more remote family, as that will not normally be for the benefit of O. The test is whether the trustees have O's interest and O's interest only, in mind. By contrast, the normal power of appointment can be used to create any type of trusts so long as the beneficiaries of the created trusts are objects of the power of appointment.[41] Where it is not obvious that a proposed advance is for the benefit of the object, a possible course may be to exercise the power of advancement so as to confer powers of appointment which are exercisable by the object or which are exercisable with his consent or for his benefit. This brings out more clearly the benefit for the object. The next chapter sets out some precedents.

The commonest examples are a settled advance:
(1) to make provision for O's family; or
(2) to prevent O from becoming absolutely entitled to trust capital because:-

38 Striking examples are *Re Clore* [1966] 1 WLR 955 – transfer to charity favoured by object of power of advancement; *Re Hampden* [1977] TR 177, also belatedly reported in [2001] WTLR 195, accessible at www.kessler.co.uk: transfer to trust for benefit of children of object of power of advancement.

39 'Under such a power the trustees can deal with capital in any way which, viewed objectively, can fairly be regarded as being to the benefit of the object of the power, and subjectively they believe to be so.' *Re Hampden, supra.*

40 It is different if such trusts already exist and the exercise of the power of advancement merely preserves them.

41 This is all that Upjohn J. meant in *Re Wills* [1959] Ch 1 at 14: 'Trustees cannot under the guise of making an advancement create new trusts merely because they think that they can devise better trusts than those which the settlor has chosen to declare. They must honestly have in mind some particular circumstances making it right to apply funds for the benefit of an object or objects of the power.'

(a) O is immature and irresponsible as regards money so it is a benefit to retain the capital in the trusts;[42] or

(b) this avoids a tax charge on O becoming entitled to the trust fund;

(3) to transfer to another trust for the reasons discussed at para 10.7.

It is considered that similar principles govern a common form power of *appointment*. For instance, a power of appointment for the benefit of the children of the settlor may be used to create trusts for the children for life with remainder to the grandchildren (not objects of the power, but assuming the provision for the grandchildren is regarded as a benefit to the children who are objects).[43]

42 This was grudgingly accepted in *Re T* [1964] Ch 158 'only because a strong case on the facts is made out for protection of this nature'. In Jersey, on the other hand:

> 'It is not in our judgment generally in the interests of young persons to come into possession of large sums of money which might discourage them from achieving qualifications and from leading settled and industrious lives to the benefit of themselves and of the community.'

See *Re Gates* (7 July 2000, unreported) but accessible on www.jerseylegalinfo.ie. This view would surely be accepted now in both England and Northern Ireland.

43 The word 'benefit' has two distinct meanings, a narrow meaning and a wide meaning:

(1) *Direct Financial Advantage only* In the narrow sense, 'benefit' means only a direct pecuniary benefit. In this sense it is not a 'benefit', say, to a father to pay his children's school fees.

(2) *Intangible Non-financial Benefit also* In the wide sense, 'benefit' includes not only direct financial advantage, but also intangible non-pecuniary advantages including mental satisfaction. In this sense (only) it is for the benefit of a person:
   (a) to pay his children's school fees (assuming the person wishes to see his children privately educated); or
   (b) to provide a fund for their use (assuming the person wishes to see his children financially secure); or
   (c) to make a contribution to a charity which that person wishes to support.

A similar distinction is made in the law relating to a fraud on a power. An appointment with the motive of securing a financial benefit to the appointor is void: but an appointment satisfying an appointor's *moral* obligation is valid. See *Palmer v Locke* (1880) 15 Ch D 294 at 303.

Confusion can be caused by failing to ask which of these meanings applies. The context must decide which meaning is intended.

In general fiscal legislation the narrow meaning is normal and the wide meaning is exceptional. For instance, the word 'benefit' in the context of the income tax or CGT settlement provisions or the IHT gifts with reservation provisions has the narrow meaning and refers to direct financial benefits only. No-one has ever suggested that a payment to a person's minor children is a 'benefit' to the parent, so as to bring those sections into application.

In the context of a power of advancement, a power to apply for the advancement or 'benefit' of O, the word 'benefit' bears the wide meaning and includes any intangible non-financial advantage. This construction is perhaps suggested by the phrase 'advancement or benefit' showing that a wider sense of 'benefit' is intended; but in any event it is long settled by the authorities cited above.

In the context of a common form power of appointment, a power to appoint on trusts for the 'benefit' of O, it is suggested that the word 'benefit' has the same wide sense. (The contrary view is arguable. That construction is conceivably supported by the context which is '*trusts* for the benefit of the Beneficiaries.' One is looking at benefits conferred by trusts: direct entitlements conferred by property law.) The position is exactly the same if the power of appointment refers to 'trusts *in favour* or for the benefit of the Beneficiaries', i.e. the words 'in favour of' are mere synonymy and do not extend the width of the power.

In the context of a common form power to apply income for the benefit of a beneficiary, it is again suggested that the word 'benefit' has the same wide sense. A little support for this

Under the statutory power of advancement the trustees need the consent of a beneficiary with a prior interest. The consent of O is not needed however,[44] though in practice trustees should take his views into account and circumstances where the trustees can properly act contrary to O's views (if adult) will be rare.

O is not the settlor of the advanced trusts for any tax purposes.

The statutory power of advancement can only be used for the benefit of an object or objects individually, and not for the benefit of two or more objects as a class.[45]

The statutory power of advancement can only be used in favour of living beneficiaries, and not in favour of unborn beneficiaries.[46]

There has been some debate whether, under the statutory power of advancement, the terms of the Advanced Trusts can include any dispositive powers for the trustees or others. That is said by some to amount to a delegation of the power of advancement, and so prima facie not permitted. After some disagreement in the lower courts, this view has been rejected by the House of Lords and does not represent the law. Such at least is the authors' view.[47] In the precedents in this

---

view might be gained from the old case of *Allen v Coster* (1839) 1 Beav 202, accessible on *www.kessler.co.uk*. In this remarkable case a fund of £6,000 was held (in short) for the benefit of two minors. The parents 'were in a state of great indigence, and kept from the parish by a person who charitably allowed them 10*s*. a week'. Lord Langdale said: 'I think this is a case in which the Court can increase the maintenance of the children for the support of their parents ... I may give to the infants the benefit of the property, so as to assist the parents: To do so is evidently for the benefit of the infants themselves.'

In any particular case, regard must be given to the exact wording of the power concerned.

44 'It is no bar to the exercise of the power of advancement that the primary object neither requested nor consented to it'; *Re Cameron* [1999] Ch 386 at p 415; *Pilkington v IRC* (1959) 40 TC 416 at p 439.

45 Suppose a trust fund is held on trust for A and B contingently upon attaining the age of 25 in equal shares; and the trustees have the statutory power to apply capital for the benefit of 'any person contingently entitled to the capital'. They can apply half the trust fund for the benefit of A; and they can apply the other half for the benefit of B separately. They cannot create discretionary trusts for the class of A and B; or create a trust of the whole fund for A for life with power to appoint to B. This is an application of capital for the benefit of A and B, collectively, as a class. Even applying the Interpretation Act principle that the singular includes the plural, it does not seem correct to construe the section to mean that this is permissible.

The authors are inclined to think that the wide power of advancement in the form in this book could be exercised in favour of a class of Beneficiaries.

46 In relation to the statutory power this is clear. An unborn beneficiary cannot be said to be 'entitled' to trust property, even contingently, and so is not an object of the statutory power. The authors are inclined to think that the wide power of advancement in the form used in this book could be exercised in favour of unborn beneficiaries.

47 The view that the power of advancement is restricted in this way was championed by Lord Upjohn. He expressed this view in *Re Wills* [1959] Ch 1. The view was criticised in strong language by Dankwerts J in *Pilkington v IRC* ('I am not quite sure what the learned Judge had in his mind ...') but repeated by Upjohn in *Pilkington* in the Court of Appeal. The law was definitively settled by the House of Lords in *Pilkington* (1964) 40 TC 416. For the terms of the advanced trusts approved by the House of Lords included protective trusts, ie they

book, however, the question does not arise since trustees have a wide power of delegation.

The advanced trusts are governed by the perpetuity and accumulation rules as they apply to the original trust. However, where a common law perpetuity period applies, the advanced trusts can include an appropriate 'Royal Lives' period.

One conclusion to draw from all this is that the drafter should include in a trust all three overriding powers: powers of appointment, resettlement and advancement. He should not rely on one to do the work of the others.

A narrowly drafted trust will generally include a power of advancement but no power of appointment or resettlement. In such a case the trustees still have some scope to alter the terms of the trust, or to transfer to a new trust, by use of the power of advancement. This is a matter of considerable practical importance.

included discretionary trusts. This is absolutely right in principle, it is respectfully submitted, because any powers exercised by the trustees of a new trust are not the powers of advancement, delegated; they are new powers created by the exercise of the powers of advancement. See para 10.5 (The problem of narrow powers of appointment). Many of the other cases also authorised settled advances with dispositive powers of some kind. Lewis on Trusts now agrees: 17th ed, para 32-18. The contrary view must necessarily involve the conclusion that the decision of the House of Lords was *per incuriam*.

CHAPTER 11

Exercising overriding powers

Who should draft deeds of appointment?

11.1

The drafting of deeds of appointment (and other documentation supplemental to existing trusts) is more difficult than drafting a new trust. Save for more straightforward deeds, such as absolute appointments to a beneficiary, or appointments of new trustees, the practitioner who does not have considerable experience of trust documentation should delegate the work to a suitably qualified specialist. The same applies to the drafting of new trusts in non-standard form. A fair test of competence is whether the drafter has a working knowledge of *Thomas on Powers.*[1] In the words of a leading member of the English Chancery Bar:

> The reality is that the use of defective or inadequate trust instruments produces far more work for the specialist Bar, when things go wrong (or, rather, when it is appreciated that they are going wrong) than if a suitable trust instrument had been settled in the first place.[2]

Drafting is deceptively difficult: an inexpert drafter skates on thin ice, the more innocent of danger, the more at risk.

How to instruct counsel

11.2

Where counsel is instructed it is normally best to send the relevant information and instruct counsel to prepare the draft. It is more time-consuming, more costly and ultimately less satisfactory for counsel to settle another person's draft than to start afresh.

1 1st ed, 1998.
2 Robert Venables QC, *Non-Resident Trusts* (8th ed, 2000), para 3.1.1. A list of English Specialist Counsel can be obtained from the Chancery Bar Association www.chba.org.uk.

Drafting deeds of appointment

11.3

Parties The trustees jointly form one party to the deed. The drafting may need to distinguish between (1) the trustees who make the appointment and (2) the trustees from time to time (ie, including future trustees). The author's' practice is to refer to the former as 'the Present Trustees'. The more cumbersome title is 'the Appointors'. There will not usually be any other party to the deed except where a consent is needed to the appointment.

If a Deed of Appointment has only one party it is said to be made 'by' that party. If two or more, it is said to be made 'between' the parties. It is a solecism to say:

> This appointment is made [date] between A, B and C ('the Trustees')...

Useful recitals The authors' practice is to give recitals setting out the following:
(1) The appointment is supplemental to:
  (a) the settlement (or the will and relevant codicils);
  (b) relevant deeds of appointment (but not irrelevant ones such as those which have been revoked or absolute appointments of capital).

The form is as follows:-

> This deed is supplemental to the following:
> (1) The settlement ('the Settlement') made [date] between (1) ... and (2)(a) ... (b) ...
> (2) The Deed of Appointment ('the 1994 Appointment')[3] made [date] between, *etc.*

(Add the numbering for ease of reading and avoid the words 'one part' 'other part'). When there are a large number of supplemental deeds, it is easiest to set out the list in a schedule.
(2) The power being exercised. This saves later readers from looking back, concentrates the drafter's mind on what he is doing and satisfies the requirement of showing intention to exercise the power.[4]
(3) The identity of the trustees. The authors' practice is not to recite all the deeds of appointment of new trustees.

Useless recitals Do not bother to say:

3 It is a matter of style whether to describe earlier deeds as 'the 1994 Appointment', etc, or 'the First Appointment', etc.

4 Of course 'An express reference to the power, though much to be preferred, is not essential, provided that an intention to exercise that power is manifested in substance'; *Thomas on Powers* (1st ed, 1998), pp 236-8.

The Trustees wish to exercise the power of appointment in the following manner.

It is not usually necessary or useful to set out a schedule of the assets of the trust fund. (In complex cases it is not unknown to miss some asset out, raising an obvious question of the extent of the appointed fund.)

The deed is not subject to stamp duty.[5]

Appointment creating royal lives clause

11.4

A full discussion of perpetuities is outside the scope of this book. One common question arises where a power of appointment or advancement is exercised under a settlement governed by the common law rule against perpetuities (either a pre-1966 settlement or a post-1966 settlement which does not specify a fixed perpetuity period). It is sometimes desired to create a new perpetuity period consisting of 'royal lives' in being at the date of the original settlement. This is plainly permissible.[6]

Some points to watch in drafting deeds of appointment

11.5

These include:

(1) time limits imposed by the trust;[7]
(2) the rules against perpetuities and accumulations;
(3) in discretionary will trusts, appointment within three months of death;[8]

5 See 29.7 (Deed of appointment)

6 (1) The common law rule is that every interest must vest within 21 years after the determination of lives in being at the date of the trust. The 'royal lives' will satisfy this because they were in being at that time. It is not the case that the lives in being must be specified at the date of the trust and an appointment or advancement could not bring in other lives in being. That is often done with other lives and 'royal lives' can be no different. See, generally, Maudsley, *The Modern Law of Perpetuities* (1979), p 94ff. (2) Even if that were wrong, the appointment or advancement is valid under the so-called 'second look' principle: See *Thomas on Powers* (1st edn), para 4.31. (3) This is the general practice of conveyancers. See, eg *Re Wills* [1964] Ch 219 where a 'royal lives' clause was inserted without criticism from the judge.

We add for completeness that the Law Commission Report No 251 (Rules against Perpetuities and Excessive Accumulations) para 4.30 does describe this issue as never having been 'finally settled'. However that is only because no-one has ever seriously argued the contrary view.

7 Is this unnecessary to say? It is not. A time limit was overlooked with the consequence of invalidity despite ingenious arguments in *Breadner v Granville-Grossman* [2001] Ch 523.

8 See para 19.6 (Best form of will for married testator).

(4) self-dealing rule, if appointment may benefit the trustee;
(5) fraud on a power, if a non-beneficiary may benefit directly or indirectly;
(6) the width of the power: see para 10.5 (The problem of narrow powers of appointment), check there are no unexpected restrictions tucked away, eg in a settlor exclusion clause[9] or conflict of interest clause;[10]
(7) Inheritance tax:
   (a) the burden and incidence of IHT on any transfer of value made by the appointment; loss of life tenant's nil rate band;
   (b) insurance against IHT;
   (c) a notice under IHTA 1984, s 57(3) (to use transferor's annual IHT exemptions);[11]
   (d) if the trust holds business or agricultural property, the effect of IHTA 1984, ss113A and 124A on earlier transfers of value within the last seven years.
(8) CGT: possible charge under TCGA 1992, s 71; possibility of hold-over relief; loss of taper relief;
(9) trustee liabilities:
   (a) if the appointment transfers assets to a beneficiary absolutely, consider the need for (i) expressly preserving a trustee lien; (ii) an indemnity from the beneficiary and (iii) perhaps, security for that indemnity;[12]
   (b) if the appointment creates separate sub-funds, and the trustees have existing liabilities, consider how the separate funds are to share the burden of the liabilities; this arises especially in appointments in the course of administration of an estate of a deceased person;
(10) if a living person has made a gift to the trust by will, a codicil to the will is needed: see 19.20 (Gifts by will to existing trust).

9 See para 12.13 (Exclusion of contributory and indirect settlors), para 12.15 (Extending the settlor exclusion clause to exclude trustees).

10 See 5.12 (Conflicts of interest). If the STEP Standard Provisions apply, note the conflict of interest rules in clause 9.

11 The Revenue practice is set out in the CTO Advanced Instruction Manual M.60:

> 'The form for giving the notice is form 222. This does not have to be sent to this office, but the trustees are instructed on the form to retain it 'in case it is subsequently required by the CTO.' You should not ask for the notice unless you suspect abuse – eg where the annual exemption is claimed twice for the same year. Although the notice should be given within six months of the transaction, you need not check this. You should not disallow the exemption solely for the reason that it was given out of time.'

Accordingly, it is safe in practice not to complete this form in straightforward cases.

12 See the Trust Law Committee Consultation Paper 'The proper protection by liens, indemnities or otherwise of those who cease to be trustees' (December 1999) accessible on www.kcl.ac.uk/depsta/law/tlc.

Example deed of appointment

11.6

This is an example of an appointment which:
(1) divides a trust fund into two shares;
  (a) one share is held on IP trusts;
  (b) one share is held on A&M trusts;
(2) the trust retains a wide power of appointment (subject, in the case of the A&M share, to the A&M restrictions).[13]

It is assumed the power of appointment is wide, as in the forms in this book. The drafting at least aims at relative comprehensibility. It illustrates how these deeds tend to become complex as children and grandchildren are born, and different branches of the family have different needs. The IP and A&M forms are those from this book (but note the necessary modifications in relation to the A&M form).

This deed of appointment is made [date] by
(1) [Name] of [address] ('the Settlor')[14] and
(2) [Name] of [address]
(together called 'the Present Trustees').

WHEREAS:-
(A) This deed is supplemental to the following:
  (1) A settlement ('the Settlement') made [date] between (1) the Settlor and (2)(a) the Settlor (b) [name of other original trustee].
  (2) An appointment ('the First Deed of Appointment') made [date] by the Present Trustees.
(B) Clause ... of the Settlement confers on the Trustees the following power ('the Power of Appointment'):
[set out power]
(C) The Present Trustees are the present trustees of the Settlement.

Now this deed witnesses as follows:
1. In this deed:
  (1) '**Gillian**' means [name] of [address].
  (2) '**Giles**' means [name] of [address].
  (3) '**Giles' Children**' means:

13 See para 14.16 (A&M restrictions on overriding powers) and para 13.12 (IP forms for two life tenants).

14 It is assumed in this draft that the settlor is one of the two trustees: the definition of settlor is used in recital A(1) (contrast the next draft where the settlor is not one of the trustees, and the following draft which concerns a will trust).

(a) [name] born [date].
(b) [name] born [date].
(c) any other child of Giles born:
(i) at a time when any of Giles' Children is under the age of 25 and
(ii) during the Trust Period.

(4) Words defined in the Settlement have the same meaning in this deed.

2. In exercise of the Power of Appointment[15] the Present Trustees irrevocably appoint[16] that they hold the Trust Fund on the following terms.

3. Subject to the Overriding Powers conferred below the Trustees shall divide the Trust Fund into two equal shares ('Gillian's Fund' and 'Giles' Fund').

4. **Gillian's Fund**

Subject to the overriding powers conferred below:-

(1) The Trustees shall pay the income of Gillian's Fund to Gillian during her life.
(2) Subject to that, if Gillian dies during the Trust Period, the Trustees shall pay the income of her fund to her widower during his life.
(3) Subject to that, during the Trust Period, the Trustees shall pay or apply the income of Gillian's Fund to or for the benefit of any Beneficiaries as the Trustees think fit.

5. **Giles' Fund**

Subject to the Overriding Powers conferred below:

(1) Giles' Fund shall be divided into equal shares ('the Shares') so that there shall be one Share for each of Giles' Children and each of Giles' Children is in this clause called a 'Principal Beneficiary'.
(2) So long as a Principal Beneficiary is living and under the age of 25:
(a) The Trustees may apply the income of his Share for the maintenance, education or benefit of any of the Principal Beneficiaries who have not attained the age of 25.
(b) Subject to that, the Trustees shall accumulate the income of the Share during the Trust Period. That income shall be added to Giles' Fund.
(3) The Trustees shall pay the income of the Share to the Principal Beneficiary during his life if he attains the age of 25.
(4) Subject to that, if the Principal Beneficiary dies during the Trust Period, the Trustees shall pay the income of the Share to the widow of the Principal Beneficiary during her life.

15 Do not add: *...or any other power enabling them...* . The trustees should usually know which power they are exercising! Where there is doubt these words may be appropriate, but a power will in appropriate circumstances be taken to be exercised by implication, so even then it makes no difference whether these words are added or not; see eg *Re Pennant* [1970] Ch 75.

16 Do not say: '... appoint *and declare*'; or '... appoint *and direct*', this is pointless synonymy.

(5) Subject to that, the Trustees shall during the Trust Period pay or apply the income of the Share to or for the benefit of any Beneficiaries, as the Trustees think fit.

6. **Overriding Powers**
[set out the standard overriding powers in this book]

7. **Restrictions on Overriding Powers**

The Overriding Powers may only be exercised over Property in Giles' Fund in the following circumstances:

(1) If a Beneficiary has or has had an Interest in Possession in the Property after the date of this deed.

(2) If there is no Principal Beneficiary in relation to the Property under the age of 25.

(3) If on the exercise of the power a Principal Beneficiary in relation to the Property under the age of 25 becomes entitled to the Property or to an Interest in Possession in it.

(4) If, after the exercise of the power:

(a) one or more Qualifying Beneficiaries will on or before attaining a specified age not exceeding 25 become beneficially entitled to the Property or to an Interest in Possession in it; and

(b) no Interest in Possession subsists in the Property and the income from it is to be accumulated so far as not applied for the maintenance, education or benefit of such Qualifying Beneficiaries.

'Qualifying Beneficiaries' here means:

(i) Principal Beneficiaries in relation to the Property and

(ii) the children and widow of a Principal Beneficiary in relation to the Property who died before the age of 25.

8. This appointment shall carry all the income payable after the date of this deed and no apportionment shall be made.[17]

9. Subject to that the Settlement as amended by the First Deed of Appointment shall stand.[18]

In witness *etc*

Points to watch in drafting transfers to another settlement

11.7

The points at paragraph 11.3 (deeds of appointment) apply here, but in addition:

(1) It may be necessary first to alter the terms of the transferor or transferee settlement to ensure that there is no breach of the rules against perpetuities

[17] This clause is not strictly necessary if the trust excludes the statutory apportionment rule, which is usually the case: para 20.54 (Statutory apportionment) but the authors prefer to make it plain.

[18] This would of course be implied, but the authors prefers to make it plain.

and accumulations, to satisfy the settlor exclusion clause of the transferor settlement, and to satisfy any restrictions on the power of transfer (see the draft below for an example).

(2) Especially for pre-1978 Settlements, watch out for illegitimate beneficiaries[19] who may not be 'beneficiaries' under the old settlement and may easily and unexpectedly be 'beneficiaries' under the transferee settlement.

(3) The transfer will govern trust capital (including accumulated income) but some income of A&M or discretionary trusts may be received and not yet distributed or accumulated. There are two ways to deal with such income:-
   (a) The trustees may resolve to accumulate the income just before executing the transfer (so the accumulated income passes with the rest of the trust capital).
   (b) The income may be distributed (before or after the execution of the transfer) under the terms of the old settlement.

Example exercise of power to transfer to another settlement

11.8

This deed illustrates a transfer of funds from one settlement (most conveniently defined in the draft as 'the Old Settlement') to another.

This deed is made [date] between
(1) [name] of [address] ('the Settlor') of the one part and
(2) (a) the Settlor and
    (b) [name] of [address]

('the Trustees') of the other part.

WHEREAS:-
(A) This deed is supplemental to a Settlement ('the Old Settlement') made *etc*
(B) The Trustees are the trustees of the Old Settlement.
(C) Under clause 1.6 of the Old Settlement 'the Beneficiaries' includes:
'1.6.4 Any Person or class of Persons nominated to the Trustees by:
1.6.4.1 the Settlor or
1.6.4.2 two Beneficiaries (after the death of the Settlor)
and whose nomination is accepted in writing by the Trustees.'
(D) Clause 3.2 of the Old Settlement confers on the Trustees the following power ('the Power of Resettlement'):

[19] The rules of construction changed in relation to adoptive children in 1950: the Adoption of Children Act (NI) 1950, s 9(3).

> 'The Trustees may by deed declare that they hold any Trust Property on trust to transfer it to trustees of a Qualifying Settlement, to hold on the terms of that Qualifying Settlement, freed and released from the terms of this Settlement.
>
> 'A Qualifying Settlement' here means any settlement, wherever established, under which every Person who may benefit is (or would if living be) a Beneficiary of this Settlement.'[20]

Now this deed witnesses as follows:

1. In this deed
   (1) Words defined in the Old Settlement have the same meaning in this deed.
   (2) **'The 1996 Settlement'** means the settlement made *etc*
2. In exercise of the power conferred by clause 1.6 of the Old Settlement the Settlor nominates and the Trustees accept as Beneficiaries the class of beneficiaries of the 1996 Settlement (so far as not already Beneficiaries).
3. In exercise of the Power of Resettlement the Trustees declare that they hold the Trust Fund on trust to transfer it to the trustees of the 1996 Settlement, to hold on the terms of the 1996 Settlement as one fund for all purposes, freed and released from the terms of the Old Settlement.

In witness *etc*

Who should draft settled advances?

11.9

The point made at 11.1 (Who should draft deeds of appointment?) applies even more to the drafting of settled advances:

> It cannot be sufficiently stressed that this is highly technical work which requires the advice of a trusts and tax expert. The penalty for failing to take such advice could well be nullity.[21]

The authors respectfully agree but add that the heavier penalty is likely to be a fiscal one.

20 This is the form used in the first five editions of Kessler *Drafting Trusts and Will Trusts*. The form in the 6th edition is slightly wider.

21 Robert Venables QC, *Non-Resident Trusts* (8th ed, 2000), para 10.6.3.

Drafting resolutions of advancement

11.10

The exercise of a standard form of power of advancement does not need a deed. In the case of a simple advance of capital, all that is needed is a cheque (or transfer of an asset). In the case of a settled advance, a trustee resolution is the appropriate form. The content will be similar to a deed of appointment.

It is good practice to say for whose benefit the power is being exercised.[22]

Example resolution of advancement used to create new trusts

11.11

The following example was drafted for a trust under which a share was held for John for life, with remainder to his children absolutely. This poor form would leave John's widow unprovided for, incur an IHT charge on his death which could be deferred or avoided if he left a widow, and give the children absolute interests at too young an age. There was fortunately a power of advancement for the benefit of John which is used here to give John power to create more appropriate trusts.

The form illustrates the slight variants appropriate to a will trust.

> This Trustee Resolution is made [date] by
> (1) [Name] of [address] and
> (2) [Name] of [address]
>
> ('The Present Trustees').
>
> Whereas:
> (A) This Resolution is supplemental to the will ('the Will') made [date] by [name] ('the Testator').
> (B) The Testator died on [date] and probate was granted on [date] by the [name] registry.
> (C) The Present Trustees are the present trustees of the Settlement constituted by the Will.

22 In *Re Hampden* [1977] TR 177 also belatedly reported in [2001] WTLR 195 accessible on www.kessler.co.uk the advance contained a 'slightly unfortunate' recital stating that the trustees intended to benefit A. In fact they were solely motivated by the desire to benefit A's father. The Judge accepted affidavit evidence to this effect and (correctly) disregarded the erroneous recital. For another example see *Osborne v Steel Barrel Co Ltd* (1942) 24 TC 293 at p 305 'As between the Crown and the Appellant company neither is bound by an untrue recital'.

(D) Clause 6(6) of the Will confers on the Trustees the following power ('the Power of Advancement'):

> 'The Trustees may in their uncontrolled discretion from time to time during the lifetime of the Life Tenant by mortgage or sale of the share or any part thereof or assets comprised therein raise any monies (up to the total value of the share) and pay or apply the same to or for the benefit of the Life Tenant in such manner as the Trustees shall think fit'.

(E) The Present Trustees now wish to exercise the Power of Advancement by applying John's Share for the benefit of the Life Tenant so as to enable John to make the most appropriate provision for John's family.

The Present Trustees hereby resolve as follows:

1. In this Resolution:
   (1) Terms defined in the Will have the same meaning in this Resolution.
   (2) '**John**' means [full name]
   (3) '**The Family of John**' means
      (a) the children and remoter issue of John.
      (b) the spouses and former spouses (whether or not remarried) of (a) above and
      (c) the widow of John.
   (4) '**John's Share**' means the share of the Trust Fund to which John is entitled under the terms of clause 6 of the Will.
2. In exercise of the Power of Advancement, the Present Trustees apply John's Share for the benefit of John by declaring that they hold John's Share in their capacity as the Trustees upon the terms of the Settlement, but as if clause 6(2) of the Will provided as follows:

> 'From and after the death of John the capital and income of the said share or so much thereof respectively as shall not have become vested or been paid or applied under any trust or power affecting the same shall be held upon trust for all or any one or more of the Family of John at such time and if more than one in such shares with such provision for maintenance education advancement and otherwise at the discretion of the Trustees or any persons and with such gifts over and generally in such manner for the benefit of the Family of John or some or one of them as John shall by deed or deeds revocable during the Trust Period or irrevocable or by will or codicil taking effect during the Trust Period appoint and it is declared for the avoidance of doubt that this power extends to the creation of discretionary trusts and powers for the benefit of the Family of John and in default of and subject to any such appointment upon trust for all or any the children of John born within the Trust Period who shall attain the age of twenty one or

who (without attaining that age) shall be living at the expiration of the Trust Period if more than one in equal shares.'

[*This is emphatically not the 'plain English' form which the authors would have preferred. It is however the wording used elsewhere in the documentation of this trust, and it is probably better in supplemental documentation to use consistent forms throughout.*]

3. Subject to that, the Will shall stand.

Signed by the Present Trustees

....

....

[date]

Example Resolution of Advancement used to transfer property to two separate settlements

11.12

This resolution illustrates a power of advancement used to transfer separate funds to two separate settlements. The terms of the new settlement would need careful consideration to ensure that the transfer was for the benefit of the objects of the power of appointment.

This Trustee Resolution is made [*date*] by
(1) [Name] of [*address*] and
(2) [Name] of [*address*]

('**the Present Trustees**')

Whereas
(A) This Resolution is supplemental to a Settlement (**'the Old Settlement'**) made [date] between (1) [name of settlor] and (2) [name of trustees].
(B) Clause 6 of the Old Settlement confers on the Trustees the following power ('the Power of Advancement'):
'NOTWITHSTANDING anything to the contrary hereinbefore contained the Trustees may at any time in their absolute discretion apply for the benefit of any Beneficiary the whole or any part of the capital of his or her share (and any accumulations added thereto) freed and discharged from the provisions of this DeedY'

(C) The Trustees now wish to exercise the Power of Advancement by applying each Beneficiary's share for his benefit by transferring that share to a settlement in which that Beneficiary shall be entitled to an interest in possession.

The trustees hereby resolve as follows:

1. **Definitions**

   In this Resolution:

   1.1 Terms defined in the Old Settlement have the same meaning in this Resolution.

   1.2 '**Danny**' means [full name].

   1.3 '**Adam**' means [full name].

   1.4 **'The Adam Smith Settlement 2004'** means the settlement of that name made the same date as this resolution by [parties].

   1.5 **'The Danny Smith Settlement 2004'** means the settlement of that name made the same date as this resolution by [parties].

2. **Advancement**

   2.1 In exercise of the Power of Advancement the Trustees resolve to apply Adam's Share for the benefit of Adam by declaring that they hold the same on trust to transfer it to the Trustees of the Adam Smith Settlement 2004 on the terms of that Settlement as an accretion to the Trust Fund of that Settlement freed and discharged from the terms of the Old Settlement.

   2.2 In exercise of the Power of Advancement the Trustees resolve to apply Danny's Share for the benefit of Danny by declaring that they hold the same on trust to transfer it to the Trustees of the Danny Smith Settlement 2004 on the terms of that Settlement as an accretion to the Trust Fund of that Settlement freed and discharged from the terms of the Old Settlement.

Signed by the Trustees [*etc*]

Example Resolution of Advancement used to transfer property from one settlement to another

11.13

The difference between this form and the above is that the trust funds become held on separate sub funds of a single new settlement.

2 **Advancement**

   2.1 In exercise of the Power of Advancement the Trustees resolve to apply the capital of Adam's Share for the benefit of Adam by declaring that they hold the same on trust to transfer it to the Trustees of the William Smith Grandchildren Settlement 2004 to hold as an accretion to the share of Adam under that Settlement freed and discharged from the terms of the Old Settlement.

2.2 In exercise of the Power of Advancement the Trustees resolve to apply the capital of Danny's Share for the benefit of Danny by declaring that they hold the same on trust to transfer it to the Trustees of the William Smith Grandchildren Settlement 2004 to hold as an accretion to the share of Danny under that Settlement freed and discharged from the terms of the Old Settlement.

Chapter 12

Settlor exclusion clause and default clause

Excluding settlor and spouse

12.1

It is usual to exclude the settlor and spouse from benefit under their trust.[1] If this is not done, then trust income and capital gains may be taxed at the settlor's rates. Further, the settlor may be subject to IHT on the settled property as if he had never given it away.

This is not necessary for a will trust; a testator cannot benefit under his own will. The exclusion of the settlor and spouse is not as straightforward as one might have thought. There are five ways by which a settlor may benefit under his trust; each requires separate means to counteract it.

(1) Direct benefit

12.2

The trust may make express provision for his benefit. This should be easy enough to avoid. The following should be noted.

Trustees to pay the costs of setting up the trust. This is not permitted. These costs will usually be liabilities of the settlor; a provision of this kind operates for the benefit of the settlor. Until the costs are paid, income tax, CGT and IHT anti-avoidance provisions may apply.

12.3

Trustees to pay tax on gift to trust. A gift to an IP trust or an A&M trust is a PET and so an IHT charge may arise if the donor does not survive seven years. This tax

1 Paragraph 4.29 (Settlor and spouse as beneficiaries).

charge is primarily the liability of the trustees.[2] Accordingly it is unnecessary to say that the trustees shall pay the tax. The same applies to the additional IHT payable on a chargeable transfer (such as a gift to a discretionary trust) which may arise if the donor dies within seven years of the gift.[3]

A provision that the trustees *may* pay the IHT if the donor dies within seven years raises a number of difficulties and is not recommended.

The trustees should not be directed or empowered to pay CGT arising on the transfer to the trust; the Revenue takes the view that this allows the settlor to benefit from his trust.

(2) Resulting trust

12.4

The settlor may benefit under a resulting trust. This is prevented by an effective default clause: see para 12.20 (Default clause).

(3) Power to benefit settlor

12.5

The settlor may benefit if the trustees have any powers which may be used to benefit him. It does not matter whether the power is in fact exercised so as to benefit the settlor; the mere possibility of benefit is disastrous. This possibility is averted by a Settlor Exclusion Clause: see para 12.8.

(4) Actual benefit

12.6

The settlor may benefit directly or indirectly from trust property, despite everything in the trust, by the consent of beneficiaries or through breach of trust. No feat of draftsmanship can prevent this: this problem must be dealt with through careful trust administration.

2 See para 30.10 (Arrangements for payment of IHT on death within seven years).

3 The position is more complicated for IHT immediately payable on a gift to a discretionary trust (which is a chargeable transfer). This is discussed in the first edition of this book at para 4-071. However, the point is fairly academic: in practice a well advised settlor will not normally make gifts which give rise to an immediate charge to IHT.

(5) Reciprocal arrangements

12.7

The settlor may be excluded from his own trust, but may benefit from another trust under a reciprocal arrangement. The solution of this problem does not lie in the trust drafting; but in the careful avoidance of arrangements which have an element of reciprocity.

It sometimes happens that husband and wife (or other members of one family) make trusts at the same time, and each settlor may benefit under the other's trust. It is considered that these are not (normally) 'reciprocal settlements' because (normally) one trust is not made in return for the other.[4]

Settlor exclusion clause

12.8

> Notwithstanding anything else in this settlement, no power conferred by this settlement shall be exercisable, and no provision shall operate so as to allow Trust Property or its income to become payable to or applicable for the benefit of the Settlor or the spouse of the Settlor in any circumstances whatsoever.

This 'settlor exclusion clause' is a convenient drafting technique to help to ensure that the requirements of the settlement provisions are satisfied:

(1) trustees may have some powers which could be used to benefit the settlor (or spouse) as well as others. If all the powers are made subject to the settlor exclusion clause, it is unnecessary to exclude the settlor (or spouse) from benefit specifically under each individual power;

(2) if by some error any clause in a settlement directs a benefit be provided to the settlor (or spouse), the settlor exclusion clause should prevent the erroneous clause from taking effect.[5]

[4] There is an interesting discussion of the concept of reciprocity from a sociological perspective in Zygmunt Bauman *Postmodern Ethics* (1993) pp 56–58, accessible on www.kessler.co.uk. There is no discussion in the cases, but it is suggested that Bauman is right that the essential element of reciprocity is that it affects motive. The distinction is between disinterested generosity on the one hand and conduct inspired by considerations of self interest on the other. Reciprocity (like so much in life) offers delicate shades of grey, which the tax system must treat a matter of fact and degree, and resolve into black or white.

[5] At least if it is clear which clause is erroneous: see para 12.9 (When is a settlor exclusion clause appropriate?).

When is a settlor exclusion clause appropriate?

12.9

A settlor exclusion clause is needed whether the settlor is married or single; it is of course unnecessary in a will trust. Where, exceptionally, the settlor or his spouse are intended to benefit under a trust it is essential to amend or omit the settlor exclusion clause as appropriate.[6]

What a settlor exclusion clause does not cover

12.10

The words of the common form settlor exclusion clause 'are so wide that everyone agrees there must be some limitation placed upon them'.[7] There are a number of situations where it has been held that they do not apply.

An obvious case is where the benefit to the settlor is 'a mere voluntary application of income by a beneficiary to the settlor, outside the provisions of the trust itself'.[8] For the same reason, the clause does not prevent trustees paying capital to a child of the settlor who is a minor, even though the settlor would benefit on the intestacy of the child (and of course the child could not make a will preventing the settlor from so benefiting).

The clause does not exclude the settlor's right to reimbursement for tax paid by him on trust income or gains, under the settlement provisions.[9] This is because

6 It happens occasionally that the settlor exclusion clause is accidentally retained in a trust intended for the principal benefit of the settlor; so in one clause the trustees are directed to pay the income to the settlor; and in another clause they are prohibited from doing so. Which clause prevails? Applying a literal construction the answer would be the settlor exclusion clause, which is stated to apply 'notwithstanding anything else in the Settlement'. It is suggested that a literal construction should not be applied. On the principle of construction, see para 3.3 (Meaning of words v meaning of document). A similar argument was accepted in *Padmore v IRC (No 2)* [2001] STC 280. Here it was rightly held that the context showed that one provision overrode a second, even though the second provision was stated to apply 'notwithstanding anything in any enactment'. Rectification may be available to put matters right, if construction cannot do so.

7 *Glyn v IRC* (1948) 30 TC 321 at 329.

8 *Glyn v IRC* (1948) 30 TC 321 at 329. The Revenue accepts this. Helpsheet IR270 for 2000/01 provides:

> 'Because the words "in any circumstances whatsoever" are so wide there are certain circumstances in which you will not be treated as having an interest even though you may have. [!] These are
>
> - where you give money to another person absolutely (in other words, you give up any rights or control over the money). That person could decide of their own accord to give the money back to you. You will not be regarded as having an interest because the person has complete freedom to do what they want with the money.'

9 The Revenue accepts this: SP5/92, paras 8-10.

that right does not arise under the settlement: it arises under the statute. The settlement cannot exclude a right which does not arise under the settlement. (Suppose, for instance, that the trustees owed money to a creditor, and the creditor assigned the right to that debt to the settlor. No one could possibly suggest that a settlor could not (as a matter of property law) enforce the debt, just because there was a settlor exclusion clause). It may also fairly be said that reimbursement is not a 'benefit' for the settlor because (looking at the matter broadly) the settlor has gained no advantage.[10] Likewise the clause does not exclude the right of a settlor-trustee to reimbursement for out of pocket expenses under TA(NI) 2001, s 31. For similar reasons it is considered that the clause does not exclude the settlor's right to trustee remuneration.[11]

The clause does not prevent trustees making a payment to maintain or pay school fees for a settlor's children. One reason is that such a payment is generally merely an intangible, non-financial benefit to the settlor, not a 'benefit' within the sense of the clause, which means, a direct financial benefit.[12] But the same applies where the settlor is under a direct legal obligation to maintain and pay school fees for his children (such as may arise on a divorce or in other family law proceedings). Here, there is a benefit to the settlor but the benefit is not prohibited by a standard form settlor exclusion clause because it is unintended, merely incidental.[13] Likewise the clause does not prevent trustees making a payment to a divorced spouse of the settlor, even though an incidental and unintended effect may be to increase the settlor's claim for financial relief in divorce proceedings. In these cases special consideration must be given to the doctrine of fraud on a power.

Drafting the settlor exclusion clause

12.11

The draft echoes the relevant statutory provisions.[14] The words 'notwithstanding anything else in this settlement' are traditional, though unnecessary; Potter and Monroe's *Tax Planning with Precedents* (looseleaf) omits them.

10 See (if authority is needed) *IRC v Lactogol Ltd* (1954) 35 TC 230. A third reason for reaching this conclusion is that the payment is merely administrative and the settlor exclusion clause applies only to dispositive matters: see para 18.2 (Significance of administrative/dispositive distinction).

11 Paragraph 20.64 (Can the settlor charge if he is a trustee but there is a settlor exclusion clause?).

12 On this distinction see para 10.11 (Power of advancement used to create new trusts).

13 *Fuller v Evans* [2000] WTLR 5, accessible on www.kessler.co.uk. It is interesting (and relevant, because some have doubted the correctness of *Fuller v Evans*) to note that the courts reached exactly the same conclusion two centuries ago in relation to comparable wording in the English Mortmain Acts: *A-G v Munby* (1816) 1 Mer 327, accessible on www.kessler.co.uk.

14 For an example of a (perhaps deliberately) botched settlor exclusion clause see *IRC v Botnar* [1999] STC 711. This case turns on the trust's unusually worded settlor exclusion clause and has no general importance but it illustrates the danger of not following the wording of a statutory provision, where it is intended to satisfy that statutory provision.

Joint settlors

12.12

Where a trust is made by joint settlors (most commonly husband and wife), each must be excluded, together with their spouses. See para 9.11 (Form where trust made by joint settlors).

Exclusion of contributory and indirect settlors

12.13

Our draft assumes the term 'the Settlor' is defined elsewhere in the trust, and excludes only the person so defined.

However, for the purposes of the income tax and CGT settlement provisions, any person who provides funds for the purposes of a settlement is a 'settlor'. To avoid these provisions every such 'settlor' must be excluded from benefit under the settlement. Some drafters therefore extend the settlor exclusion clause so as to exclude not only the settlor named in the trust, but also any other person who provides any funds, directly or indirectly, and their spouses. This has the attraction of possibly[15] defeating Revenue arguments that a beneficiary has provided property indirectly for the trust and is taxed under the income tax or CGT settlement provisions.

The drawbacks, however, are considerable. There may be uncertainty as to whether a person has 'provided funds' for the purposes of the settlement. The concept of 'providing funds' is difficult and has generated a substantial case law.[16] Perhaps it is necessary to use vague language in anti-avoidance provisions. The trust drafter should hesitate to follow that lead. There are other difficulties. There may be substantial tax charges and disastrous practical consequences if any funds were inadvertently 'provided' by a beneficiary or spouse. Paying trustees' fees, or some minor expenditure on trust property, may suffice. So might working at an undervalue for a company owned by the trust. An interesting (one hopes theoretical) question arises if the default beneficiary provides funds for the trust. Does the default trust then fail, and if so, is there a resulting trust to the settlor or *bona vacantia*?[17]

This book does not use an extended settlor exclusion clause. If such a clause is used, it is recommended that each settlor is only excluded from the property he

[15] Whether or not this argument will be valid depends on the circumstances. The point is too near to academic to justify a full discussion here, but the conclusions of any detailed analysis must be that in many, if not most, cases an extended settlor exclusion clause would not avail the taxpayer.

[16] See Kessler, *Taxation of Foreign Domiciliaries* (2nd edn, 2003) Key Haven Publications, ch 30 ('Who is the Settlor?').

[17] Paragraph 12.19 ('No resulting trust for the settlor').

actually provides. Otherwise a trivial provision of property to the trust may have drastic repercussions. The drafting becomes complex and is rarely attempted.

Reference to 'spouse' in settlor exclusion clause

12.14

It is necessary to say 'spouse of the Settlor' in the settlor exclusion clause and wrong to identify the spouse by name. This is for two reasons. First, so that after the death of the settlor, the widow, no longer a 'spouse', falls outside the clause. The widow may then benefit under the trust.[18] Secondly, in case the settlor should divorce and remarry: it is necessary to exclude future spouses.

The standard settlor exclusion clause before the Finance Act 1995 provided simply that the trust property should not be used to benefit:

> The settlor or the spouse of the settlor.

This form was apt to exclude the settlor's wife or husband. It did not exclude the settlor's widow or widower, since a widow or widower was not a spouse.[19] Nor did it exclude a divorcee.

Since the Finance Act 1995, the term 'spouse' in the settlement provisions is defined: see paragraph 4.30 (Meaning of 'spouse' of settlor) This will not affect the construction of the standard form settlor exclusion clause because the statutory definition will not apply for the purposes of the trust.

One could adopt the statutory definition and draft the settlor exclusion clause to say that a separated spouse is not excluded. The question is whether a typical settlor would want to include his separated spouse as a beneficiary. The answer, in general, is that he will not; so this would not be appropriate as a standard form.

Unnecessary provisions in settlor exclusion clause

Extending the settlor exclusion clause to exclude trustees

12.15

In the days of estate duty some practitioners extended the settlor exclusion clause to exclude trustees, but even then this was 'unnecessary and overly restrictive'.[20] See para 5.3 (Beneficiaries as trustees).

18 Paragraph 4.32 (Widow of settlor as beneficiary).

19 *Vestey v IRC* (1947) 31 TC 1.

20 *Tankel v Tankel* [1999] 1 FLR 676, [1999] Fam Law 93, accessible on www.kessler.co.uk. In this amusing (except to those concerned) case the clause excluding trustee-beneficiaries

No reservation of benefit

12.16

Some drafters provide that:

> The Trust Fund shall be possessed and enjoyed to the entire exclusion of the Settlor and of any benefit to him by contract or otherwise.

This echoes the IHT gift with reservation provision.[21] There is no advantage in this form: the drafting cannot alter one way or the other the question of whether the settlor actually enjoys any direct or indirect benefit from the trust fund. The conventional form, excluding entitlement to benefit, does all that documentation can achieve. This particular form does not even accurately reproduce the IHT rules (unless a further clause is put in to incorporate the rules in FA 1986, Sch 20, para 6 but the authors have never seen that done).

12.17

The effect of the standard settlor exclusion clause is to prohibit the trustees making a loan to the settlor (or spouse) on beneficial or favourable terms. In the drafts in this book, it remains possible for trustees to lend money to the settlor on commercial terms as an investment. Some drafters prohibit this. This course is not taken here: the existence of the power to make the loan has no adverse tax consequences, (though tax problems may arise if such a loan is actually made).[22]

12.18

One occasionally sees this form:

> If any person who enjoys any benefit hereunder or under any exercise of any power conferred by this settlement should marry the Settlor then this settlement and any appointment made pursuant to any power hereby conferred shall upon such marriage take effect as if such person were dead.

It is considered that the standard settlor exclusion clause would in principle exclude any beneficiary who married the settlor. So a provision of this kind is not necessary to satisfy the tax requirements. Moreover the possibility that the settlor should

---

from benefit was later overlooked and subsequent appointments were void. An attempt to rectify the clause rightly failed on the facts.

21 FA 1986, s 102. This is a different rule than that adopted by the income tax settlement provisions. The CGT settlement provision is different again.

22 In brief:
(1) if the trust has 'undistributed income': ICTA 1988, ss 677 and 678;
(2) if the trust is non-resident: ICTA 1988, s 739(3);
(3) the loan may not be deductible from the settlor's estate for IHT: FA 1986, s 103.

marry a person who enjoys some benefit under the trust seems exceedingly remote. Accordingly this provision is unnecessary.

'No resulting trust for the settlor'

12.19

Some drafters provide in the settlor exclusion clause that:

> *There shall be no resulting trust to the Settlor;* or
>
> Under no circumstances shall any interest be taken under this deed by the Settlor.

The correct way to avoid a resulting trust is to use an effective default clause; see para 12.20 (Default clause). If this is done there can be no resulting trust, and it is neither necessary or appropriate to exclude one. Accordingly, this form is not used in this book.

If a badly drafted trust does have not have a proper default clause, and does exclude resulting trusts with a form like the above, what (to the extent that the validly declared trusts do not take effect) is the result? Some say that there is nonetheless a resulting trust and a form of words simply purporting to prevent a resulting trust do not take effect. So the form is totally ineffective.[23] Another view is that the clause takes effect as it says, and the trust property becomes property of the Crown as *bona vacantia*.[24] That might or might not suit the settlor, depending on the attitude of the Crown, the value of the property forgone, and the tax position. The authors tentatively suggest that neither extreme view should be adopted, but the question should be regarded as one of construction, turning like all questions of construction, on the circumstances of the individual case.[25]

23 This is the view taken by Robert Chambers *Resulting Trusts* (1997) pp 64–66; and supported by *Air Jamaica Ltd v Charlton* [1999] 1 WLR 1399.

24 *Davis v Richards and Wallington Industries Ltd* [1990] 1 WLR 1511 at 1538; *Westdeutsche Landesbank Girozentrale v Islington London Borough Council* [1996] AC 669 at 708.

25 Faced with inconsistent case law, it is helpful to stand back and ask what the law should be (as opposed to what it actually is).

It is suggested that the answer to this question is as follows:

(1) The law ought to permit a person to abandon property if he wishes. 'Abandonment' meaning that the property passes to the Crown as *bona vacantia*. After all, any person can give his property to the Crown (subject of course to a disclaimer). It would be foolish to draw a distinction which gives effect to words of assignment and not to words of abandonment.

(2) *A fortiori* the law ought to permit a settlor to abandon an interest under a resulting trust.

(3) Effect should only be given to a desire to abandon property if expressed in clear words. One does not lightly abandon. The words must be especially clear if the property abandoned is of considerable value, and if the settlor would not have appreciated the value of what he is said to have abandoned.

It is further suggested that this sensible position is more consonant with the authorities than either extreme; but a full discussion is beyond the scope of this book.

Default clause

12.20

The clause used in this book is as follows:

> Subject to that, the Trust Fund shall be held on trust for
>
> [a named living individual] absolutely.
>
> **or** [two or more named living individuals] in equal shares[26] absolutely.
>
> **or** [a named charity] absolutely.
>
> **or** such charities as the Trustees shall determine.[27]

The default clause (sometimes called a 'longstop provision') has a general purpose and a specific tax function.

The general purpose is to specify who should become entitled to the trust property, should the other terms of the trust fail (eg if all beneficiaries die). The trust should state how the trust property should pass in that event. (Even though it is unlikely or almost inconceivable that the default clause will ever come into effect.)

The tax function relates to the settlement provisions. In the absence of a default clause, on the death of all the beneficiaries, the trust fund would revert to the settlor under a resulting trust. It is usually desired to exclude the settlor from all benefit under the trust to avoid the settlement provisions. The drafter must provide that the trust property will have a clear destination in all circumstances, so the trust fund cannot revert to the settlor. (The tax function does not apply to a will trust, but the authors prefer to have a default clause even in a will trust, if only for tidiness, to avoid a remote possibility of a partial intestacy.)

Drafting the default clause

12.21

The usual practice is to direct that the property should pass to named children or grandchildren of the settlor or more distant relatives. If these have died, the trust

26 The words 'in equal shares' are significant: they ensure that the individuals hold as tenants in common and not as joint tenants (so there is no right of survivorship).

27 This trust could not fail since it would be administered by the court in default of the performance of the trustees' duty to select objects. Authority is scarcely needed but see the Special Commissioners' decision in *IRC v Schroder* [1983] STC 480 at 489; the Crown quite rightly did not appeal on that point. A definition of 'charity' is usual but not strictly necessary: see para 4.33 (Charities as beneficiaries).

property will then pass according to the terms of their wills or intestacies.[28] An alternative is that the trust property should pass to charity or a more distant relative. The person who receives the trust property in these circumstances is sometimes called 'the Default Beneficiary.'

The following clauses fail to satisfy the tax requirement:

> Subject as aforesaid the trust property shall be held on trust for X if he is then living.

This fails to satisfy the tax function: X may not then be 'then' living; so the trust fund may revert to the settlor.

> *Subject to that, the Trust Fund shall be held upon trust absolutely for such of them the Beneficiaries*[29] *as shall then be living.*

This is no better. It is possible that none of the 'Beneficiaries' may then be living.

> Subject as aforesaid the trust property shall be held on the trusts of [another] settlement.

This is only satisfactory if the second trust has an adequate default clause, and entirely excludes the settlor and spouse. Where the second trust is made later than the first, care must be taken that the arrangement does not breach the rules against accumulation or perpetuity.

Unnecessary provisions in a default clause

12.22

It is unnecessary to say that the trust fund should be held on trust for:

> [a named individual] *or his estate or assigns* absolutely.
>
> **or** [a named individual] *or his personal representatives* absolutely.[30]

28 It is then possible that the property will revert to the settlor, under the will or intestacy of the default beneficiary. That does not matter for the purposes of the settlement provisions. This has never been judicially decided, but only because it has never been challenged: see *Barr's Trustees v IRC* (1943) 25 TC 72 (where this was assumed without argument) and the dicta of Singleton J in *Glyn v IRC* (1948) 30 TC 321 at 329.

29 Assume this is a defined term.

30 Authority is not needed for this proposition, but see *Stamp Comr Duties v Bone* [1976] STC 145. For an example of a case where this was held to be the correct construction, see *Barclays Bank v McDougall* [2001] WTLR 23.

The clause is sometimes expanded to read:

> Subject to that, *and if and so far as not wholly disposed of by the above provisions the capital and income* of the Trust Fund shall be held on trust for X absolutely.

The italicised addition is harmless but plainly unnecessary.

Correcting errors in a default clause

12.23

Where a default clause is not exhaustive, it is possible to set the matter right for the future. The settlor may assign his interest to some other person or the trustees may exercise their overriding powers.

An unnecessary default clause

12.24

Where the provisions of a trust are exhaustive, which may happen in a relatively simple case, a default clause is not strictly needed; but if the clause is included, no harm is done (save as to the reputation of the drafter). In *Barclays Bank v McDougall*[31] Rimer J rightly rejected a fanciful construction intended to give effect to an obviously redundant default clause.

[31] [2001] WTLR 23.

CHAPTER 13

Interest in possession trusts

13.1

The IP trust is one where trustees are to pay trust income to a particular beneficiary. In the discussion below that beneficiary is called 'the life tenant'; in the drafting he is usually identified by name or given the title of 'the Principal Beneficiary'.

Why use interest in possession trusts?[1]

13.2

The reason may simply be that it is desired to pay all the income to the life tenant: but the following outline tax points may also be noted here.

IHT Advantages. A lifetime gift to an IP trust is a potentially exempt transfer: the gift will not give rise to IHT if the donor survives his gift by seven years. (A&M trusts also enjoy this treatment.)

The property is treated for IHT purposes as if it belonged to the life tenant: it will be subject to tax on his death, unless the value of the estate is within the nil-rate band, or an exemption (eg the spouse exemption) applies. This may be more or less attractive than the IHT discretionary trust regime.

CGT Advantages. There is a tax-free uplift on death. The important benefit of paying CGT at the basic rate only has been abolished by the Finance Act 1998.

Income Tax Advantages. Under other forms of trust, income may be accumulated and enjoy a slightly lower rate of tax. However, this will cease from 2004/5. The administration of an IP trust is much easier and unless the amounts involved are large this should be a significant factor. IP trusts are also more tax-efficient for

1 See also para 14.2 (Why use A&M trusts?); para 17.2 (Why use discretionary trusts?); para 21.2 (Why use bare trusts?). The existence of an interest in possession is relevant for some minor trust law purposes, eg TA(NI) 1958, s 35(9); but these will not concern the drafter.

beneficiaries who pay tax at the basic rate when the trust receives Schedule F income.[2]

Interest in possession income clause

13.3

The income clause of an IP trust must give the life tenant the right to trust income as it arises.

Drafting the income clause seems a straightforward matter. Statutory precedents provide a choice of forms:

> The trustees shall stand possessed of the trust fund upon trust to pay the income thereof ...
>
> ... to X during his life[3]
>
> ... to X for life[4]
>
> The trust fund shall be held on trust for X during his life.[5]

The form adopted in this book is:

> The Trustees shall pay the income of the Trust Fund to X during his life.[6]

The drafter must also omit provisions inconsistent with an interest in possession: see para 18.1 (Provisions inconsistent with IP, A&M and discretionary trusts).

Structure of standard interest in possession trust

13.4

The form proposed in this book is straightforward:
(1) income is paid to the life tenant for life;
(2) income is then paid to his widow for life;
(3) there is then a discretionary trust over income;
(4) the trustees have the standard overriding powers which may override any of the above;

2 See Appendix 5 of Kessler, *Drafting Trusts and Will Trusts* (5th edn, 2000).
3 The English Statutory Will Forms 1925, Form 7, accessible on www.kessler.co.uk.
4 The English Statutory Will Forms 1925, Form 9, accessible on www.kessler.co.uk.
5 AEA 1925, s 46(2) (this has no NI counterpart as the surviving spouse does not take a life interest on an intestate death).
6 The form is loosely derived from TA(NI) 1958, s 32.

(5) lastly there is a standard default clause.

These five limbs are contained in three clauses. The first deals with trust income. The second contains the overriding powers. The third is the default clause.

1. Trust Income

Subject to the overriding powers below:

(1) The Trustees shall pay the income of the Trust Fund to the Principal Beneficiary[7] during his life.

(2) Subject to that, if the Principal Beneficiary dies during the Trust Period, the Trustees shall pay the income of the Trust Fund to his widow during her life.

(3) Subject to that, during the Trust Period, the Trustees shall pay or apply the income of the Trust Fund to or for the benefit of any Beneficiaries as the Trustees think fit.

2. Overriding Powers

[Here set out the standard Overriding Powers of this book.]

3. Default Trusts

Subject to that, the Trust Fund shall be held on trust for the Principal Beneficiary absolutely.

(1) Income to the principal beneficiary for his life

13.5

The settlor may prefer that the beneficiary should become absolutely entitled to the trust property on attaining the age of (say) 25, 30, 40; as to which see para 13.17 (Variant: life tenant to become absolutely entitled at specified age).

(2) Subject to that ... to his widow during her life

13.6

What should happen after the principal beneficiary dies? It is best to give a life interest to his widow. Whatever the settlor thinks of his daughter-in-law, it is rarely sensible to exclude her. If the life tenant relies on the income from the trust

7 The 'Principal Beneficiary' will be defined in the definition clause. Where the Principal Beneficiary is female, it is good practice to replace 'his' with 'her'; 'her' with 'his', and 'widow' with 'widower' as appropriate in this clause.

for his living expenditure, or resides in trust property, then his widow must usually have a similar interest after his death; otherwise she will face some financial difficulty. Secondly, this course allows inheritance tax to be deferred until her death, and possibly avoided.[8]

The spouse's interest in the trust fund is actually a precarious one. It need confer no real or valuable rights on the spouse as it may be revoked at any time before or after the death of the original life tenant, the principal beneficiary. The trustees can respond to the beneficiaries' needs and changes in tax law. In particular, they can revoke the spouse's interests as soon as the IHT advantage is secured.

An alternative: beneficiary's power to appoint to widow

13.7

There is an alternative course which is quite common in practice. This is to give the principal beneficiary a power to confer (technically 'to appoint') a life interest on his widow. This is well enough in theory. The principal beneficiary can review the position and give the interest, or refrain from doing so, as he thinks best. This solution is less satisfactory in practice. The power is as likely as not to be overlooked. Assuming it is not overlooked the power will in most cases be exercised with concomitant expense. It is easier all round to start off as one means to go on: give the reversionary interest to the principal beneficiary's widow and not merely empower the principal beneficiary to do so. This alternative course might be adopted when a particular settlor has a rooted objection to giving the spouse an interest directly under the trust.[9]

It is said that this power gives the beneficiary a measure of power over his or her spouse. So it does; but just how conducive that may be to matrimonial harmony must be open to question.

Describing the widow

13.8

> [Subject to the Principal Beneficiary's life interest] the Trustees shall pay the income of the Trust Fund to his widow during her life.

8 IHTA 1984, s 18. Note the exemption is not available if the life tenant is, but his spouse is not domiciled in the UK; IHTA 1984, s 18(2). The tax position then is discussed in James Kessler, *Taxation of Foreign Domiciliaries* (2nd edn, 2003) Key Haven Publications, ch 27. On the question of using the principal beneficiary's nil-rate band, see the discussion on disclaimers at para 20.53 (Power to disclaim).

9 For a precedent see English Statutory Will Forms 1925, Form 7(6), accessible on www.kessler.co.uk.

The word 'widow' is chosen deliberately. In the event of divorce, the divorced wife will not take any interest under this clause. The person who is married to the principal beneficiary at the time of his death will continue to receive the income even if she remarries.

Three bad forms

The drafter should not identify the wife of the principal beneficiary by name, saying:

> [Subject to Mr Jones' interest] the trustees shall pay the income of the Trust Fund to *Mrs Pauline Jones* during her life.

For then, if Mr Jones (the principal beneficiary) should divorce and remarry, the first Mrs Jones will still receive a life interest after his death; which will not at all be the intended result.

The use of the word 'wife' rather than 'widow' can introduce an element of doubt where the beneficiary remarries. Consider:

> [Subject to the Principal Beneficiary's life interest] the trustees shall pay the income to his *wife* during her life.

It may be doubtful whether a first or second wife is intended to benefit.[10]

What is the position if the drafter combines the two forms above, and says:

> [Subject to Mr Jones' life interest] the trustees shall pay the income to his *wife Mrs Pauline Jones* during her life.

If the Principal Beneficiary should divorce and remarry and then dies, there are three theoretical possibilities:

(1) Mrs Pauline Jones, the first wife, receives the income: since she is expressly named in the clause.
(2) The second wife receives the income, since she is the 'wife' at the time of the Principal Beneficiary's death.
(3) The clause does not take effect, since there is no person who satisfies the description 'his wife Mrs Pauline Jones' at the time of the death of the Principal Beneficiary.

There are rules of construction which can resolve such questions, but it is better that the drafter should not require beneficiaries (and their lawyers) to consider them.

10 For a case where such confusion arose, see *Re Drew* [1899] 1 Ch 336.

A perpetuity problem

13.9

The widow's reversionary life interest also causes a perpetuity difficulty.[11] Assume the 80 year perpetuity period is selected. One cannot simply say:

> [Subject to A's life interest] the trustees shall pay the income to A's widow during her life.

The objection is that if A dies after the expiry of the 80 year perpetuity period, then the gift to his widow will breach the rule against perpetuities.

Where A is married at the time the trust is made, one could avoid this difficulty by naming his wife expressly:

> [Subject to A's life interest,] the trustees shall pay the income to Mrs A during her life. ...

But this is unsatisfactory for the reason already mentioned: A may divorce.

What, then, can be done? There are various possibilities. The solution adopted here is to say:

> ... **If A dies during the Trust Period,** the trustees shall pay the income of the trust fund to the widow of A during her life.

The widow's interest must vest within the perpetuity period. Note that it is not appropriate to say:

> During the trust period:
> (1) The trustees shall pay the income of the trust fund to A during his life.
> (2) Subject to that, the trustees shall pay the income of the trust fund to the widow of A during her life.

This form would terminate both interests on the expiry of the perpetuity period, which is unnecessary: the requirement is that the interests must vest (begin) within that period.

Alternatively one could select a different perpetuity period. It would be permissible to choose a perpetuity period of the lifetime of the principal beneficiary, A, and 21 years.[12] This solves the problem. A must die within the perpetuity period; so his widow's interest must vest in that time. The cost is the introduction of artificiality into the trust; so this is not adopted in this work.

11 For a general discussion of the perpetuity rule, see ch 8 (The rule against perpetuities).

12 There could be a longer period, being the lifetimes of the principal beneficiary and 'royal lives', and 21 years.

The drafter searching for simplicity may be very tempted to ignore the problem. If A is aged 30 at the time the trust is made, it is inconceivable that he should still be living in 80 years' time when the perpetuity period ends; he would then be 110! So it is tempting to ignore the problem and say:

> [Subject to A's life interest,] the trustees shall pay the income from the trust fund to the widow of A during her life.

The authors are not content with that approach. The fear is not so much that the life tenant will outlive the perpetuity date; though who knows what life expectancies will be in the future; but rather the reliance on the 'wait and see' rule; this is not entirely certain or satisfactory in its operation. The drafter should not leave this problem for the next generation to sort out.

Position after death of widow

13.10

The drafter must lastly make appropriate provision for the time after the death of the principal beneficiary and spouse. This is to look far into the future; it is difficult to decide what form the trust should best take. The choices are:

(1) A&M trusts under which:
   - (a) the children become absolutely entitled at (say) 25; or
   - (b) the children become entitled to an interest in possession at the age of 25; or

(2) discretionary trusts under which:
   - (a) the children become entitled to an interest in possession at 25; or
   - (b) the trusts may remain discretionary for the whole trust period.

It might be desirable to create A&M trusts for the children (or grandchildren) of the life tenant, but the variety of potential circumstances is so wide that it is impossible to cater for them all. The attempt to do so leads to endless complexity, from which the drafter will not emerge completely satisfied. This route is rarely taken in practice.

A traditional solution is to direct the trust property to pass absolutely to the children of the principal beneficiary who attain 21. That course is too inflexible; it should be rejected out of hand. A refinement, which allows some flexibility, is to give the principal beneficiary power, during his lifetime, to appoint appropriate trusts for his children and remoter issue. But this course would vest an important power in the beneficiary which is considered undesirable.[13]

[13] Paragraph 6.22 (Giving powers of appointment to beneficiaries). If for some specific reason such a form is desired, the following form is proposed (to be inserted after the sub-clause giving the life tenant his interest and before the sub-clause giving his widow a reversionary life interest:

A discretionary trust over income offers the best solution by far. This – combined with the overriding powers in the trust – gives the trustees complete flexibility to do what seems best at the time. The drafting is pleasingly simple.

The tax consequences of the discretionary trust under current law are satisfactory. The death of the spouse of the 'Principal Beneficiary' will give rise to an IHT charge on trust property in which she has an interest in possession. No additional charge is caused by creating a discretionary trust. To avoid charges under the discretionary trust regime, the trustees may wish to convert the trust into interest in possession form or accumulation and maintenance form: the overriding powers allow them to do this. This may give rise to an exit charge, but the amounts involved will be nil or trivial if the trustees act reasonably promptly after the death of the life tenant.

It is possible – indeed likely – that the tax treatment of discretionary trusts will change; perhaps even a short-term discretionary trust may become fiscally unattractive. But the trustees can amend the terms of the trust at any time, even during the lifetime of the original beneficiary or his spouse. By use of the overriding power of appointment, they can create any form of trust that may be desired.

Alternatively the trust may provide that after the death of the life tenant and his spouse, the trust property is held on trust for the children who reach the age of (say) 18, absolutely, but subject to the trustees' overriding power of appointment. This is likely to be perfectly satisfactory, at least for smaller funds. It may be easier for clients to accept than the discretionary trusts preferred here.

Future accumulation of income

13.11

While the trust is interest in possession in form, income will not of course be accumulated. However, the form of the trust may change, after which the trustees may wish to accumulate.

Here the Northern Ireland drafter has considerable advantages over his English counterpart as income may be accumulated throughout the Trust Period. In England it is recommended that the period of 21 years from the date of the trust be selected.[14]

---

(1) subject to that, the Principal Beneficiary may appoint that the Trustees shall hold the Trust Fund for the benefit of any Beneficiaries other than the Principal Beneficiary, on such terms as the Principal Beneficiary thinks fit;

(2) an appointment may create any provisions and in particular:
  (a) discretionary trusts;
  (b) dispositive or administrative powers;
  exercisable by any Person;

(3) an appointment shall be made by deed during the Trust Period and may be revocable or irrevocable.

[14] See further Kessler *Drafting Trusts and Will Trusts* (6th edn, 2000) p 178.

IP forms for two life tenants

13.12

The settlor may wish to make an interest in possession trust for the benefit of two or more life tenants. One course is to create a separate trust, one for each; but it may be more convenient to create one trust for all the life tenants.

A straightforward and flexible form

The following is the structure of a straightforward and flexible form of trust:
(1) trust fund to be divided into shares;
(2) income of each share to be paid:
  (a) to each life tenant for life,
  (b) subject to that, to his widow for life,
  (c) subject to that, there are discretionary trusts over income;
(3) the trustees have the standard overriding powers which may override any of the above.

The central parts of the draft are as follows. The two life tenants are here called Adam and Danny.

1. Subject to the overriding powers below the Trustees shall divide the Trust Fund into two equal shares 'Adam's Share' and 'Danny's Share'.
2. **Adam's Share**
   Subject to the overriding powers below:
   (1) The Trustees shall pay the income of Adam's Share to Adam during his life.
   (2) Subject to that, if Adam dies during the Trust Period, the Trustees shall pay the income of Adam's Share to his widow during her life.
   (3) Subject to that, during the Trust Period, the Trustees shall pay or apply the income of Adam's Share to or for the benefit of any of *the Beneficiaries* as the Trustees think fit.
3. **Danny's Share**
   Subject to the overriding powers below:
   (1) The Trustees shall pay the income of Danny's Share to Danny during his life.
   (2) Subject to that, if Danny dies during the Trust Period, the Trustees shall pay the income of Danny's Share to his widow during her life.
   (3) Subject to that, during the Trust Period, the Trustees shall pay or apply the income of Danny's Share to or for the benefit of any of *the Beneficiaries* as the Trustees think fit.
4. **Overriding Powers**
   [Here come the overriding powers in this book: see para 10.1 (Overriding powers). The objects of the Overriding Powers will be Adam *and* Danny and their families.]

Commentary on straightforward flexible form

13.13

In the following discussion the two life tenants are called A and B.

Under the straightforward flexible form, as the italicised words make clear, A's share could be used (if the trustees think fit) to benefit B and his family; and vice versa. This may happen by exercise of the overriding powers, or after the death of a life tenant and spouse, when the discretionary trusts of income take effect. This is the position under a standard form A&M trust, after the A&M beneficiaries have reached the age of 25. It may be the intention of the settlor that the trustees should have this flexibility. If not, a letter of wishes will guide the trustees against that course; but the wishes do not bind the trustees. This is a theoretical rather than a practical problem. In practice, trustees may be expected to act in accordance with the settlor's wishes so far as it is appropriate to do so. If that is thought to be insufficient then A's family and B's family may be represented as trustees, or a protector may be used.

An inflexible form

13.14

An alternative approach is to provide that A's share cannot be used for the benefit of B and his family, and vice versa. The drafting is rather more complicated and the authors prefer the flexible form set out above. But it can be done. The central parts of the draft are as follows:

1 **Definitions**

In clauses [2] to [5] below

(1) '**Adam's Fund**' means:

(a) Adam's Share and

(b) All property from time to time representing the above.

(2) '**Trust Property**' means any property comprised in Adam's Fund.

(3) '**Adam's Family**' means:

(a) Adam and his children and descendants;

(b) The spouses and former spouses of (a) above;

(c) Any Person or class of Persons nominated to the Trustees by:

(i) Adam, or

(ii) two members of Adam's Family (after the death of Adam)

and whose nomination is accepted in writing by the Trustees.

(d) At any time during which there are no members of Adam's Family within (a) above:

(i) Danny and his children and descendants;

(ii) the spouses and former spouses of (i) above; and

(iii) any company body or trust established for charitable purposes only.

(4) **'Adam'** means [full name].

(5) **'Danny'** means [full name].

(6) **'Person'** includes a person anywhere in the world and includes a Trustee.

2 Division of Trust Fund into Shares

The Trustees shall divide the Trust Fund into two equal shares ('Adam's Share' and 'Danny's Share').

3 Trust Income

Subject to the Overriding Powers below:

(1) The Trustees shall pay the income of Adam's Fund to Adam during his life.

(2) Subject to that, if Adam dies during the Trust Period, the Trustees shall pay the income of Adam's Fund to Adam's widow during her life.

(3) Subject to that, during the Trust Period, the Trustees shall pay or apply the income of Adam's Fund to or for the benefit of any of Adam's Family as the Trustees think fit.

4 Overriding Powers

[Here set out the standard overriding powers.]

5 Default Clause

Subject to that, Adam's Fund shall be held on trust for Adam absolutely.

6 Danny's Fund[15]

Clauses [1] to [5] shall apply to Danny's Share with the following modifications:

(1) 'Danny' shall replace 'Adam' wherever it occurs except in clause [1(4)] (definition of 'Adam')

(2) 'Adam' shall replace 'Danny' wherever it occurs except in clause [1(5)] (definition of 'Danny')

[or – much better but not done here for reasons of space – set out clauses in full.]

15 There are three ways to deal with the drafting of trusts containing multiple funds for different primary beneficiaries; (1) one can set out each fund at length. That is best if the total length is not too great to bear; (2) one can use a substitution clause like the clause set out in the text. That becomes complicated if the beneficiaries are of both genders as 'his' or 'her' becomes messy; (3) one can set out a single standard anonymised form like that used in the A&M trusts in this book, ie:

1. the Primary Beneficiaries means [specify];
2. the Trust Fund shall be divided into one share for each Primary Beneficiary;
3. subject to the Overriding Powers below:
   (1) the Trustees shall pay the income of the share of the Primary Beneficiary to the Primary

Beneficiary during his life, *etc.*

Objection to simple accruer clause

13.15

A common form where there are two life tenants is to provide:
(1) A's share to be held on trust for A for life, then A's widow for life, then for A's issue;
(2) B's share to be held on trust for B for life, then B's widow for life, then for B's issue;
(3) *In default each share will accrue to the other share.*

A form along these lines could easily lead to multiple IHT charges.[16] Far better to have a simple discretionary trust on the death of the spouse of A and B. Appropriate trusts can then be appointed, either before or after the time of the deaths, in the light of the then circumstances.

Variant: life tenant to become absolutely entitled at specified age

13.16

A trust should usually be drafted so that it may continue for as long as possible. It is far preferable to arrange that beneficiaries need not become absolutely entitled to the trust property. This offers many advantages. Trust property is safe in the trust. It should be secure from creditors in the event of insolvency; and secure from a spouse in the event of divorce. The trust property may be better administered by the trustees than by the beneficiary, were he to become absolutely entitled. There are substantial tax advantages. Conversely the termination of a trust will often lead to tax difficulties.[17]

On this point the views of the client may be far from those of his professional adviser. The client may prefer his children or grandchildren to become absolutely entitled to the trust property on attaining the age of 25, or 35 or 40. It should be pointed out that the trustees may transfer the trust fund to the beneficiaries at the desired age. There are many methods of controlling trustees to comfort a nervous or reluctant settlor. See paragraph 6.12 (Guidance and control of trustees). If that course is not acceptable to the settlor, one may resort to the following precedent.

16 For instance:
(a) if B dies childless and A dies shortly thereafter;
(b) if B dies, and is survived only for a short period by his only child.
IHTA 1984, s 141 (successive charges) provides only a limited relief.

17 The main problem is the CGT disposal on the termination of the trust: TCGA 1992, s 71(1). Hold-over relief is not always available; but even if it is, CGT taper relief, which is very important, will be lost. Also, if income has been accumulated, termination of the trust may lose a valuable 'tax pool' of credit which could be utilised under ICTA 1988, s 687.

1. **Trust Income**
   Subject to the following clauses:
   (1) The Trustees shall pay the income of the Trust Fund to the Principal Beneficiary[18] until he attains the age of 40.
   (2) Subject to that, if the Principal Beneficiary dies before attaining the age of 40, the Trustees shall pay the income of the Trust Fund to his widow during her life.
   (3) Subject to that, during the Trust Period, the Trustees shall pay or apply the income of the Trust Fund to or for the benefit of any Beneficiaries[19] as the Trustees think fit.
2. [Here come the standard overriding powers of this book as in para 10.1.]
3. **Principal Beneficiary to receive Trust Fund at 40**
   Subject to any prior exercise of the overriding powers, the Trustees shall transfer the Trust Fund to the Principal Beneficiary when he attains the age of 40 free from the terms of this settlement.
4. **Default Trusts**
   Subject to that, the Trust Fund shall be held on trust for the Principal Beneficiary [OR: specify default trusts as appropriate] absolutely.

The purpose of this form is that the trustees can review the position before the principal beneficiary attains the age of 40. If they consider that tax or other considerations make it desirable to do so, they can take action to prevent him becoming entitled by exercising their overriding power.

Variant: life tenant a minor

13.17

For child beneficiaries, the normal course is to use A&M (or discretionary) trusts, ie, to direct that the income may be accumulated or applied for the child's benefit. So the minor will not usually have an interest in possession. However, it is often[20] advantageous to give a minor an interest in possession. The trustees then avoid the tiresome and expensive administrative chore of paying income tax at the discretionary trust rate, then reclaiming that tax on behalf of the beneficiaries. The income is simply that of the beneficiary, and the straightforward procedure of IP trusts can be used. This also avoids the unfair Schedule F rules.

18 The 'Principal Beneficiary' will be defined in the definition clause. Where the principal beneficiary is female, it is good practice to replace 'his' with 'her'; 'her' with 'his', and 'widow' with 'widower' as appropriate in clause 1.

19 The term 'Beneficiaries' would of course be defined.

20 Where the trust produces a very substantial income, this may be unwise for practical (non-tax) reasons: any income not applied for the child's benefit will be retained and paid to him on his 18th birthday; that may not be a satisfactory state of affairs. In the normal case the annual trust income will be consumed on the child's education and maintenance; so this difficulty does not arise.

To give a minor an interest in possession, the following form is proposed:

> The Trustees shall pay the income of the Trust Fund to or for the benefit of [Georgina] during her life.[21] Section 32 of the Trustee Act (Northern Ireland) 1958 shall not apply to this Settlement.[22]

No other amendment is needed to the standard IP form.

Variant: interest in possession for settlor

13.18

There are various reasons why a settlor may transfer his assets to a trust under which he has an interest in possession, rather than retaining them in his absolute ownership:

(1) in anticipation of mental incapacity of a settlor (avoiding the need to invoke the Office of Care and Protection or the rather more restricted regime under the Enduring Powers of Attorney (NI) Order 1987);
(2) for those who plan well ahead, the trust allows the ability in the future to make a gift without CGT or loss of CGT taper relief;
(3) avoidance of the Inheritance (Provision for Family and Dependants) (NI) Order 1979.

In practice the main use nowadays is for foreign domiciled settlors[23] and in other contexts these settlements are very rare.

The trust will take the form set out above; appropriate amendments will be made in the definition of 'the Beneficiaries', and the settlor exclusion clause.[24]

21 This clause confers on a minor beneficiary an interest in possession for income tax and IHT purposes because income applied for the benefit of a beneficiary is regarded as income of the beneficiary: *Gascoigne v IRC* 13 TC 573; *Stanley* v *IRC* (1944) 26 TC 12 and *Stevenson* v *Wishart* (1986) 59 TC 740 at 757. The Revenue quite rightly accepts this: see (for income tax) Tax Bulletin 26 ('Trusts – liability at the rate applicable to trusts'); (for IHT) Press Notice of 12/2/1976, reprinted in Revenue Booklet IHT 16. See also para 20.51 (Power to retain income of child).

22 The second sentence is not strictly necessary, in the authors' view, since the first sentence by implication excludes the operation of TA(NI) 1958, s 32. It should, however, be included for the avoidance of doubt. 'The draftsman may be well advised out of caution either expressly to provide that s 32 is to apply, or expressly to exclude its application altogether': *Re Delamere* [1984] 1 WLR 813 at 823.

23 See Kessler, *Taxation of Foreign Domiciliaries* (2nd edn, 2003) Key Haven Publications.

24 Paragraph 12.8 (Settlor exclusion clause).

Impeachment for waste

13.19

In Northern Ireland it is still the case that a tenant for life is liable for voluntary waste unless the settlement exempts him expressly. This is why the interest of a life tenant is sometimes expressed to be 'without impeachment for waste'. If this formula is used the life tenant becomes entitled to

(1) all (rather than three quarters) of the profits of timber ripe for cutting;[25]

(2) three quarters (rather than one quarter) of mining rents (the rest is trust capital)[26]

Most practitioners now omit these words and they are not included in the standard forms in this book. A beneficiary's rights to mining rents and timber profits will not often be of concern. In England the form is obsolete since the enactment of the TLATA 1996.

Trust for sale

13.20

The trust for sale was discussed at para 9.28. It is imperative that IP trusts include this device in order to avoid (as best as one can in Northern Ireland) the undesirable effects of the Settled Land Acts.

25 SLA 1882, s 35.

26 SLA 1882, s 11. Although the trustees may be empowered to treat all rents as income.

CHAPTER 14

Accumulation and maintenance trusts: general comments

Introduction

14.1

The accumulation and maintenance trust is a child of capital transfer tax: the trust is one which satisfies a set of rules concocted in 1975, and now found in s 71 of the IHTA 1984.

In this book the cumbersome expression 'accumulation and maintenance' is abbreviated to A&M. While a trust satisfies the A&M conditions it is described as having 'A&M status'. The period during which the trust satisfies those conditions is called the 'A&M period'.

The material has been divided into three chapters. This chapter deals with the general questions raised by A&M trusts. The next chapter (A&M trusts: income clauses) deals with the drafting of income clauses: clauses dealing with the income of A&M trusts. The following chapter then deals with the appropriate provisions on the death of an A&M beneficiary.

Why use A&M trusts?[1]

14.2

The A&M trust is not ancient but modern. A&M forms offer certain tax advantages, but there is little else to commend them. A&M forms were not known before the introduction of capital transfer tax; they will be forgotten and unlamented if its successor, IHT, is repealed.

Three tax advantages are on offer if the trust will comply with the necessary conditions:

1 See also para 13.2 (Why use interest in possession trusts?); para 17.2 (Why use discretionary trusts?); para 21.2 (Why use bare trusts?).

Potentially exempt transfer on gift to trust

A lifetime gift to an A&M trust is a PET: the gift will not give rise to IHT if the donor survives his gift by seven years. IP trusts also enjoy this treatment.

IHT holiday during A&M period

An A&M trust should not suffer an IHT charge during the A&M period: there is no 10-year charge, no exit charge, and no charge on the death of a beneficiary. This tax advantage is unique to A&M trusts. In this book this is described as the 'IHT holiday'. This may not be the most important of the tax advantages, but as will be seen, it is the one which will cause the drafter the most trouble to preserve.

CGT hold-over relief on exit from trust

Hold-over relief may be available to defer the CGT charge on the termination of an A&M trust. This is not as significant as may at first appear. So long as the trust endures there is no need for hold-over relief. However, it may be desired to transfer capital to a beneficiary or to transfer funds from one trust to another so the relief may be important. The beneficiary's qualifying holding period (for CGT taper relief) starts from nil, thus losing valuable CGT taper relief.

Using A&M forms unnecessarily

The A&M is a trust for the benefit of children; but it must be remembered that discretionary, IP and bare trusts can be used for that purpose and would often be more suitable. A full discussion belongs to a book on tax planning but two points should be noted:

(1) where the value of the trust property will fall well within the nil-rate band, there is generally little point in using an A&M trust. Discretionary trusts are to be preferred;

(2) where trust income is all used for the benefit of beneficiaries, IP trusts are much easier to administrate. They are also much more tax efficient where the trust receives Schedule F income.[2]

[2] See Appendix 5 of the fifth edition of James Kessler *Drafting Trusts and Will Trusts*.

Using unsuitable A&M precedents

A common failure is over-complexity. In England it is not yet[3] possible to achieve 'plain intelligible language'[4]; but even there it is never necessary to use a form whose meaning can only be disentangled by an experienced trust practitioner with a morning's leisure to bestow upon it. The Northern Ireland practitioner has no excuse for not producing an instrument which satisfies the 'plain intelligible language' test.

The 'income' and 'capital' conditions

14.3

The two principal conditions are set out in IHTA 1984, s 71(1):
(a) one or more persons ('beneficiaries') will, on or before attaining a specified age not exceeding 25, become beneficially entitled to the settled property or to an interest in possession in it; and
(b) no interest in possession subsists in the settled property and the income from it is to be accumulated so far as not applied for the maintenance, education or benefit of a beneficiary.

In this book, condition (a) is referred to as 'the Capital Condition', and condition (b) as 'the Income Condition'.

'A&M beneficiaries'

14.4

The capital condition refers to 'beneficiaries' and the income condition refers to 'a beneficiary'. This is a source of confusion, because 'beneficiaries' is used in the statute in a special sense. The word is normally used to refer to any person who may benefit under a trust. Here:
(1) 'beneficiaries' means the persons who will become entitled to the trust property (or an interest in possession in it); and
(2) 'a beneficiary' means any of those persons (for whose benefit only the income may in the meantime be applied).

The trust will usually have many beneficiaries (in a general sense) who are not 'beneficiaries' (in the A&M sense).

3 This will be possible when Parliament finds time to enact the recommendation of the Law Commission to repeal the rule against accumulations.

4 The standard set by the Unfair Terms in Consumer Contracts Regulations 1999, SI 1999/2083.

In the discussion below, we refer to:
(i) 'A&M beneficiaries' who satisfy the two conditions above; and
(ii) beneficiaries 'who are not A&M beneficiaries'.

The distinction is essential and fundamental.[5] The A&M beneficiaries may broadly be regarded as the principal beneficiaries of the trust.

There must be at least one living A&M beneficiary when the A&M trust is created.[6]

The capital condition

14.5

The capital condition is:

> The A&M Beneficiaries will, on or before attaining a specified age not exceeding 25, become beneficially entitled to the settled property or to an interest in possession in it.[7]

Entitlement to interest in possession: at what age?

Once the beneficiary becomes entitled to an interest in possession, there are two consequences:
(1) the trust (or his share in it) loses A&M status: there will in principle be an IHT charge on the death of the beneficiary. However, since the beneficiary will only be 25 this will not usually be a matter of much concern;
(2) transfers out of the trust (or the beneficiary's share of it) will cease to qualify for CGT hold-over relief. The trustees should therefore review the position before the beneficiary attains an interest in possession to consider whether they wish to transfer capital to him with the benefit of this relief.

Obviously, the best course for drafting is to set the latest possible age, which is normally 25 years.

Should A&M beneficiaries become entitled to trust property or just to an interest in possession in it?

14.6

The better course in principle is that the A&M beneficiaries should only become entitled to an interest in possession. In this way the trust does not come to an end

5 It is unfortunate that the statute did not supply a clearer terminology; contrast TA(NI) 1958, s 34 where the draftsman thoughtfully used the transparent term 'principal beneficiary.'
6 IHTA 1984, s 71(7). See n 22 below for a possible solution if this causes a problem.
7 The words 'or to an interest in possession in it' are otiose; see IHTA 1984, s 49(1). They must have been inserted simply to spell out the implications of the clause.

when the beneficiary attains 25. It merely becomes an IP trust. This offers many advantages. Trust property is safe in the trust. It should be secure from creditors in the event of insolvency; and secure from a spouse in the event of divorce. The trust property may be better administered by the trustees than by the beneficiary, were he to become absolutely entitled. There are substantial tax advantages. Conversely the termination of a trust may lead to tax difficulties and may also affect state benefits.[8]

On this point the views of the client may be far from those of his professional adviser. The client may prefer his children or grandchildren to become absolutely entitled to the trust property on attaining the age of 25, or 35 or 40. It should be pointed out that the trustees may transfer the trust fund to the beneficiaries at the desired age. There are methods of controlling trustees to comfort a nervous or reluctant settlor. See para 6.12 (Guidance and control of trustees).

In what shares should the A&M beneficiaries become entitled, if there are more than one?

This is a matter for the settlor. Equality between all the A&M beneficiaries is the usual form. This is the solution taken in precedents in this book. Note that grandchildren of an accumulation and maintenance trust would then take equal shares *per capita* and not *per stirpes.*

Flexibility

Fortunately it is not necessary to determine these matters irrevocably at the time the trust is made. The trustees may be given power:

(1) To direct that a beneficiary becomes entitled to an interest in possession at any age under the age of 25.[9]

8 The main problem is the capital gains tax disposal on the termination of the trust: TCGA 1992, s 71(1). Careful drafting would be needed to ensure that hold-over relief is available to UK resident beneficiaries; but even then, CGT taper relief, which is very important, will be lost. Also, if income has been accumulated, termination of the trust may lose a valuable 'tax pool' of credit which could be utilised under ICTA 1988, s 687. For a possible solution where trusts of this kind have been made see para 10.11 (Power of advancement used to create new trusts).

9 It may be objected that this is not permissible since the capital condition refers to 'a *specified* age not exceeding 25'. On one view ('the narrow view') the use of the word 'specified' requires that the precise age be specified in the trust deed. On this view, a trust with power to give beneficiaries an early interest in possession would not be an A&M trust; it would breach the capital condition. The alternative view ('the wide view') is that the age need not be 'specified' in the sense of being stated, fixed and immutable, in the trust deed; it is sufficient that an A&M beneficiary will in fact become entitled to the settled property (or to an interest in possession in it) by the age of 25.

The Revenue believe the narrow view to be the law, but by concession they adopt the wide view. See ESC F8.

It is submitted that the wide view is unquestionably correct in law, and the 'concession' merely represents the law. For while the word 'specified' could be read either way, only the wide view leads to a sensible result. The narrow view leads to the absurd result that a common form power of advancement would be incompatible with the capital condition.

(2) To direct that the beneficiary becomes entitled to the trust property (not merely an interest in possession) at any time.
(3) To vary the size of the shares to which (or to an interest in possession in which) the A&M beneficiaries will become entitled by the age of 25.[10] The power to vary shares before the A&M beneficiaries attain interests in possession is important. This is because the variation is not a transfer of value for IHT purposes. Contrast the position if the beneficiary attains an interest in possession, and that interest is later revoked, when the revocation will normally be a PET or a chargeable transfer.

The drafting of these powers is considered below.

Does a beneficiary become 'entitled to' property which is applied for his benefit?

14.7

The requirement that a beneficiary becomes 'entitled to' property may be satisfied by applying that property for his benefit, eg paying his school fees or debts. This is even though the beneficiary does not (in a narrow literal sense) become 'entitled to' the money applied in this way. See *Inglewood v IRC* [1983] STC 133 at 139:

> The statutory power of advancement is so commonly incorporated in trusts that [s 71] must be read so as to accommodate that and not so as to withdraw the benefit of the [section] from a trust containing such a power. We would not regard the much used extension of the statutory power from a moiety to the whole as being in any different position.

White v Whitcher (1928) 13 TC 202 is cited in favour of the narrow view. That case concerned a similar phrase in another statute; reported cases should not be used as a sort of legal dictionary, applied regardless of meaning or context. Such reasoning was brushed aside in *Re Green* [1985] 3 All ER 455, which supports the wide view. It would follow that the word 'specified' is otiose; but that is not a serious objection: other words in the capital condition are unquestionably otiose, see n 6 above.

In the precedents in this book it is happily an academic question whether the wide or narrow view is correct in law. No difficulty will arise in practice. The issue could arise where (unlike in this book) a wide accumulation and maintenance protection clause is used. It could also arise in exceptional cases where A&M status was not fiscally advantageous. For instance, in order to avoid a charge under IHTA 1984, s 71(3) or to claim hold-over relief under TCGA 1992, s 260(2)(a), a taxpayer with chutzpah may argue that the Revenue should assess tax on the basis of the narrow view!

10 The Revenue quite rightly accepts this. SP E1 provides that: 'It is not necessary for the interests of individual beneficiaries to be defined. They can for instance be subject to powers of appointment. ... It is considered that settled property would meet the [capital] condition if at the relevant time it must vest for an interest in possession in some member of an existing class of potential beneficiaries on or before that member attains 25 ... Also, a trust which otherwise satisfies the [capital condition] would not be disqualified by the existence of a power to vary or determine the respective shares of members of the class (even to the extent of excluding some members altogether) provided the power is exercisable only in favour of a person under 25 who is a member of the class.'

Although this passage is *obiter*, it is authoritative.[11] The Revenue accepts it as correct.[12]

11 It is instructive (though for the purposes of s 71 academic) to consider the reasoning which lends to this conclusion. Two independent reasons emerge from the judgment.

The first reason rests on the construction of the word 'entitled'. It was held that the expression 'entitled to' property is (in a wider, perhaps less literal, sense) capable of extending to a case where the property is applied for one's benefit:

> 'The words "to a beneficiary" cannot be construed literally. They must include, for example, payment of a minor's school fees or payment of his debts.' (*Inglewood* at 139).

The same approach is found in the context of ICTA 1988, s 687(1). This section applies if: (i) trustees make a payment *to* any person; and (ii) the payment is income of the person *to whom* the payment is made.

> 'Literally construed s [687] does not apply to the case where trustees of a conventional discretionary trust exercise their discretion in favour of a beneficiary by applying income for his benefit, for instance by paying rates on property which he occupies. The sum paid does not become the income "of the person to whom it is paid" but becomes the income of the person for whose benefit it was paid. But s [687] must clearly have been intended to apply to such a case ... .'

IRC v Berrill (1981) 58 TC 429 at 455. The same approach is found in the rule that income applied for the benefit of a person is regarded as income of that person: see para 13.17 (Minor life tenant).

What is striking is that *exactly* the opposite conclusion was reached in the age of Lord Simonds: *Potts v IRC* (1950) 32 TC 211. Here the House of Lords held that the payment of tax owed by T was not a payment 'to' T for the purposes of the predecessor to ICTA 1988, s 677. But that reflects the high tide of literality to the construction of taxing statutes, an approach long since abandoned.

The second reason given in *Inglewood* is an application of the rule that administrative provisions are ignored for determining whether tax conditions (such as the A&M capital condition) are satisfied. See para 18.2 (Significance of administrative/dispositive distinction). It was held that the power of advancement is 'similar to an administrative power'. At first sight this seems wrong, since the power of advancement is plainly dispositive (authority is hardly needed, but see *Re Batty* [1952] Ch 280 where the power was described as 'confiscatory').

But the point being made, correctly if tersely, is this. Although generally dispositive, the power of advancement may also be used in a purely administrative manner. Call the object of the power of advancement 'O'.

(1) Where the power is used to override the interests of beneficiaries other than O (eg to convert O's contingent interest into an absolute interest) this is dispositive.

(2) By contrast, suppose a bare trust: O has an absolute entitlement; and the power is used so O's property is applied for his benefit (eg payment of school fees, debts, or even to create a new trust). This is merely administrative.

The consequence that even if (on the exercise of the power of advancement) O may not be 'entitled' to trust property (applying a narrow literal sense of this word) that is a consequence of a merely administrative aspect of the exercise of the power of advancement. So far as O is concerned, the difference between:

(1) a transfer or payment to O; and

(2) an application for the benefit of O

is merely administrative and should therefore be ignored for the purpose of s 71(1) and (4).

12 Statement of Practice E2 (Power of Advancement) stated this in 1975, long before *Inglewood*. This statement was withdrawn from the published list of statements of practice in 1994. Presumably the Revenue thought it was unnecessary and there could be no doubt as to the law. But the CIOT had doubts (one sometimes wonders if there is any proposition of tax law which is plain beyond doubt), so the Revenue confirmed that their view was unchanged in correspondence: *Taxation Practitioner* (Nov 1995) [1996] PCB 76, accessible on www.kessler.co.uk.

It is therefore permitted to have a power of advancement in favour of an A&M beneficiary. One way to do this is to incorporate the power by reference to s 33 of the TA(NI) 1958. In this book the power is set out expressly, and it is made exercisable in favour of any A&M beneficiary.

Some drafters restrict the power of advancement, incorporating express restrictions drawn from s 71 of the IHTA 1984. This is certainly unnecessary. On such clauses see para 18.17 (Protection clauses).

It follows from this that the exercise of a power of advancement in a manner creating a settled advance, or transferring funds to a charity favoured by an object, does not give rise to an IHT charge under s 71(3) as the exemption in s 71(4) will apply.

The income condition

14.8

This condition has two parts:
(i) no interest in possession subsists in the settled property; and
(ii) the income from it is to be accumulated so far as not applied for the maintenance, education or benefit of an A&M beneficiary.

Property which does not produce income

14.9

Some forms of property (for instance, an insurance policy) produce no income and cannot be enjoyed in kind. One would not say that such property cannot satisfy the income condition; that leads to absurdities. Such property can satisfy the A&M condition; all that is necessary is to provide that, if there were income from the property, it would be held on terms which satisfy the income condition.[13]

On property which produces no income but is be enjoyed in kind, see para 18.15 (Power to permit beneficiary to use or occupy trust property rent free).

13 *Dymond's Inheritance Tax* agrees: para 11.310.

Duties and powers

14.10

The wording of the income condition is somewhat untechnical. The drafter must somehow adapt it into the traditional categories of trust law: duties and powers.[14] The natural reading of the income condition suggests that:

(1) the trustees should have a power to apply trust income for the maintenance, education and benefit of beneficiaries; and
(2) the trustees should be directed to accumulate the rest of the income (here called 'surplus income'), ie there is a duty to accumulate surplus income.

Suppose that under the terms of a trust the trustees were given a duty to apply trust income for the benefit of beneficiaries with *power* to accumulate surplus income: would the income condition be satisfied then? The better view is that this makes no difference: this form would also satisfy the income condition.[15] However, in the drafting the safe course is to provide a power to apply income for maintenance, coupled with a duty to accumulate surplus income. That is the form used in this book.

The distribution trust

14.11

Suppose under the terms of a trust the trustees are given a duty to apply *all* the trust income for the benefit of A&M beneficiaries. No income is 'to be accumulated.' It is useful in the discussion below to coin a word to describe such a trust: we shall call it 'a distribution trust.' The distribution trust will normally satisfy the first limb of the income condition: no beneficiary will have an interest in possession in the trust fund.[16] Can the distribution trust satisfy the second limb of the income condition? Can one say that the income is truly:

> 'to be accumulated' so far as not used for the beneficiary's benefit?

14 For the distinction between duties and powers, see para 6.5.

15 *IRC v Berrill* (1981) 58 TC 429 has been cited against this view. There the words 'to be accumulated' were held to be 'apt to describe only income which the trustees are under a positive duty to accumulate'; (at 439). But words take their meaning from their context: it is fallacious to say that the meaning of a passage in one statute must be the same in any other statute.

16 If there is more than one A&M beneficiary, then none of them will have an interest in possession in the trust fund. The same will apply if there is only one A&M beneficiary but the class of A&M beneficiaries may be increased by the birth of further children: *Re Trafford* [1984] STC 236.

If there is a single A&M beneficiary (and no possibility of more being born), that beneficiary will have an interest in possession in the fund; the income can only be applied for his benefit. Then the distribution trust will not be an A&M trust.

In fact the income is *all* to be distributed, and nothing will be accumulated. Few practitioners have any doubt as to the right answer: the distribution trust can satisfy the income condition.[17]

The point which causes unease, and on which professional views differ, is one's degree of confidence in this answer. Is it right beyond all doubt? Is there any risk that the alternative view would be upheld?

The question is of great importance. Once a trust reaches a certain age, the trustees will cease to be entitled to accumulate income because of the rule against accumulation.

What should happen then? The drafter faces a dilemma. He would like, if only it were possible, to direct that the trust take the form of a distribution trust: the trustees to distribute all the income among the A&M beneficiaries until they reach the age of 25. But is this safe? Perhaps the Revenue will argue that the distribution trust did not satisfy the A&M condition. If that is correct, a catastrophic tax charge would result.[18] Adherents of the school of caution avoid the risk: they draft their trusts so that as soon as the trustees can no longer accumulate income, the beneficiaries are given interests in possession. Caution has its price. The premature ending of the A&M period cuts short the 'IHT holiday' which is one of the principal attractions of the A&M trust. The drafting is made more complex.

Faced with this quandary, James Kessler wrote to the Capital Taxes Office and asked them for their views. The official view, here repeated with the kind permission of the Revenue, is this:

> A trust to apply all the income for the education, maintenance and benefit of beneficiaries (beneficiaries being defined in the terms of Section 71(1)(a)

17 This view leads to a more sensible result and it accords more closely with the statutory language. It is supported by the following *reductio ad absurdum*. Suppose a valid trust to accumulate were essential. The first limb of the income condition (which requires that there be no interest in possession in the trust property) would then be otiose. For no interest in possession would subsist in the property in any event. Those words do make sense on the supposition that the distribution trust is capable of satisfying the income condition. They are directed to the situation where the trust income is all to be applied for the benefit of a single beneficiary, so as to prevent such a trust (which satisfies the second but not the first limb of the income condition) from qualifying as an A&M trust.

A consideration of Scots law reinforces this view. Scots law has no equivalent of the rule in LPA 1925, s 165. After the permitted accumulation period, it is never possible to accumulate income in Scotland. Thus if the preferred view is wrong, then few Scots settlements more than 21 years old could satisfy the A&M conditions; it is thought that the courts would prefer a view of the law which did not entail that result.

An entirely different objection is sometimes raised. The distribution trust requires the trustees to distribute all the trust income for the benefit of a beneficiary. Suppose a wealthy beneficiary does not need any sums paid for his benefit? The argument is weak: however rich the beneficiary, it is still for his benefit to pay money to him.

18 IHTA 1984, s 71(3) imposes a tax charge at a penal rate when an A&M trust ceases to satisfy the A&M conditions in these circumstances.

of IHTA 1984) will satisfy Section 71(1)(b) of IHTA 1984. The essential thing is that the possibility of any income going for the benefit of a person not within the definition of beneficiary should be excluded.

This helpful pronouncement was made subject to a proviso which detracts from its force: 'that the implications in terms of inheritance tax of an event will need to be finally determined in the light of the law as it is then understood to be.' One can hardly criticise the Board for this cautionary note. *Dymond* also records the 'Official View' that a distribution trust can qualify for relief.[19]

Now, where does that leave the more cautious drafter? In the authors' view, both law and practice are clear. This book therefore proceeds on the basis that the distribution trust can qualify as an A&M trust.

The time limit

14.12

No private trust can last forever, of course, and an A&M trust will not normally last until the end of its perpetuity period. When the A&M beneficiary becomes entitled to the settled property, or to an interest in possession in it – as he must, for the capital condition requires it – the trust will lose A&M status. Yet it would often be possible to create a trust which satisfied both capital and income conditions for a very long time. In 1975, such trusts were created. The time limit, introduced in 1976, sets slightly more restricted bounds to the duration of the A&M period.[20] There are two distinct tests: an A&M trust need only satisfy one of them. One test is that:

Not more than 25 years have elapsed since the commencement of the settlement or, if it was later, since the time (or latest time) when the income and capital conditions became satisfied.

We refer to this as the 25-year condition.

The alternative test is more complicated:

All the persons who are or have been beneficiaries [that is, A&M beneficiaries] are or were either:

19 *Dymond's Inheritance Tax*, para 21.327. It is unlikely that the Revenue would or could resile from this in a matter affecting existing A&M trusts: *R v IRC, ex p Unilever* (1996) 68 TC 205.

20 IHTA 1984, s 71(2). The time limit took effect in 1976, so from the year 2001 cross-generation A&M settlements began to fail the 25-year test. The greatest risk is for A&M settlements created before 15 April 1976. The 25-year limit was introduced, unfairly, with a considerable degree of retrospective effect, and affects many pre-FA 1976 Trusts. A&M trusts created after Budget Day 1976, will only break the 25-year condition if badly drafted.

(i) children of a common grandparent; or
(ii) children, widows or widowers of such grandchildren who were themselves A&M beneficiaries but died before the time when, had they survived, they would have become entitled to the trust property or an interest in possession in it.

It is convenient (if slightly inaccurate) to call this the 'common grandparent' condition; and A&M trusts which satisfy this test are called 'common grandparent settlements.' Trusts which do not satisfy the common grandparent condition may be called 'cross-generation trusts'.

A trust where the A&M beneficiaries are all living at the time the trust was made will automatically satisfy the 25-year condition. The drafter need not concern himself with the time limit any further.

'Common grandparent' v 'cross-generation' trusts

14.13

The time limit is an important consideration where (as is generally the case) the class of A&M beneficiaries is to include unborn beneficiaries. There are two categories of A&M trusts.

(1) *Common grandparent A&M trusts.* These restrict the class of A&M beneficiaries to a single generation. The class will usually be the children[21] or grandchildren of the settlor.[22] This trust will satisfy the common grandparent condition.[23]
(2) *Cross-generation A&M trusts.* These widen the class of A&M beneficiaries so that it includes more than one generation, normally children, grandchildren or great-grandchildren of the settlor.[24]

On the 25th anniversary of the trust, at the latest, it should become interest in possession in form.[25] The usual drafting technique is to define the term

21 'Children' has a wider meaning than usual and includes step-children. So a settlor may if he wishes create a single A&M trust for his children and step-children. IHTA 1984, s 71(8). (See para 4.24, Stepchildren).

22 The class could alternatively be the children, nephews and nieces of the settlor (grandchildren of the parent of the settlor) or A&M children or grandchildren of a person other than the settlor but in practice that is rare.

23 The drafter may adopt the class of beneficiaries set out above, and add that if a member of that class should die under 25, his children and widow (if any) can be included. Thus in this exceptional case a trust for children and grandchildren (or grandchildren and great-grandchildren) may satisfy the common grandparent test. This extension is limited. It only applies if the A&M beneficiary dies after the trust is made. It only applies once, eg if the child of a deceased A&M beneficiary also dies under the age of 25, the trust would not satisfy the common grandparent condition if the widow or children of that child were included in the class of A&M beneficiaries.

24 Alternatively, the A&M beneficiaries could of course be children of the settlor and children of some more distant relative or friend; or unrelated children.

25 Otherwise the trust will breach the 25-year condition and become subject to a tax charge under IHTA 1984, s 71(3).

'Closing Date' to mean 25 years from the time the trust is created and then to provide that all the A&M beneficiaries are given interests in possession on the Closing Date.

Which form should the drafter choose? In general, the common grandparent trust is to be preferred to the cross-generation trust and should be regarded as a standard form. The common grandparent trust offers two advantages: it may retain A&M status for more than 25 years and the drafting is simpler. There is rarely any inconvenience in restricting the class of A&M beneficiaries to satisfy the common grandparent condition. A settlor may wish to benefit two generations, his children and grandchildren. He should then create two separate common grandparent A&M trusts,[26] one for each generation.

The cross-generation trust should be seen as a form appropriate only in rather special circumstances. One such situation is where the settlor wishes to create a trust for his family, and his children are young adults. He might create a conventional (common grandparent) trust for his children; this would soon become an IP trust. Suppose grandchildren are born in the next few years. The trust may be converted into an A&M trust for grandchildren. There would be a transfer of value. (That would not matter much under present law, but it would have mattered considerably under the CTT regime, and such a tax may be restored.) Here a cross-generation settlement for the children and future-born grandchildren would be advantageous. If grandchildren are born before the children (or the youngest of them) attains 25, it will be possible to turn the trust into a grandchildren trust without this transfer of value.[27]

Common grandparent trust with power to cross the generations

14.14

The Revenue says:

> '... after the relevant period of 25 years has elapsed a settlement will only qualify under S71 of the Inheritance Tax Act 1984 so long as all beneficiaries are grandchildren of a common grandparent (or are a surviving spouse or child of such a grandchild.
>
> We have been asked whether the mere existence of a power to appoint (which does not offend the conditions of S 71(1)(a)) in favour of beneficiaries who

26 Or one trust with two separate sub-funds.

27 Another very exceptional case is where the settlor wishes immediately to create a trust for the benefit of his future-born children, but no child has yet been born. In these circumstances the solution may be to create a trust for the benefit of the settlor's future-born children and some existing children (sometimes known as 'borrowed beneficiaries').

are not grandchildren of a common grandparent will take the settlement outside the common grandparent rule. We have said that in our opinion the mere existence of such a power, as opposed to its actual exercise, does not take a trust outside the common grandparent category.'[28]

This considers a trust which is different in form from a simple common grandparent or cross-generation A&M trust. It is one which starts off as a common grandparent trust but confers on the trustees the power to switch to a cross-generation trust. The Revenue apparently accepts that the 'cross-generation' beneficiaries are not persons who 'are or have been beneficiaries' for the purposes of the 25-year condition so long as the trustees merely have power to benefit them but do not actually benefit them. This seems doubtful.[29]

One could, nevertheless, draft an A&M trust with potential to switch to a cross-generation trust. However, complexity is considerable. The advantages of tax and flexibility depend wholly on the Revenue Statement which seems doubtful, and which is at risk of withdrawal. The authors therefore will generally prefer to stick to the simple common grandparent settlement (or the cross-generation settlement where appropriate) and will not use this complex hybrid form.

Trustees' dispositive powers

14.15

The A&M conditions allow the trustees to have some considerable dispositive power over the trust fund. Four powers are commonly found.

During the A&M period:

1. power of advancement; (power to transfer trust capital to an A&M beneficiary or to apply capital for his benefit);
2. power to give an A&M beneficiary an interest in possession before 25 (when he would otherwise receive that interest);
3. power to vary the shares to which the beneficiaries will become entitled.

After the A&M period:

4. the trust now takes interest in possession form, and the trustees usually have the wide overriding powers common under IP trusts.

28 Tax Bulletin 55 (December 2001).

29 In the type of trust envisaged, the A&M beneficiaries are not merely the grandchildren of the common grandparent because one cannot say that they 'will' become entitled to the trust property or an interest in possession in it. The A&M beneficiaries are the totality of the persons who must between them become entitled to the trust property (or an interest in possession).

Trustees should have all the powers set out above; one often sees them contained in four separate provisions. An easier way to proceed is to provide one standard set of overriding powers; these powers are then restricted so as to satisfy the A&M conditions. The standard overriding powers (see paragraph 10.1 (Overriding powers)) are appropriate. They are then restricted so as to be exercisable:

(1) after the trust has ceased to be A&M in form;
(2) so as to bring the A&M period to an end in conformity with the capital condition; eg by giving an A&M beneficiary the trust property or an interest in possession in it;
(3) in such a way that the trust continues to satisfy the A&M conditions.

A&M restrictions on overriding powers

14.16

The forms used in this book are as follows:

(1) Exercise of Overriding Powers where the trust has ceased to be A&M in form:

> The Overriding Powers may be exercised over Trust Property if:
> (a) a Beneficiary has or has had an Interest in Possession in the Property, or
> (b) there is no living Principal Beneficiary under the age of 25.

A common form is to direct that the overriding power becomes exercisable after the A&M beneficiary has attained 25 (ie at the age when he acquires an interest in possession). It is usual to direct that he must retain his interest for a period. The fear is that if the interest may be terminated very soon after the beneficiary reaches the relevant age, his interest might be illusory, and not an interest in possession. Thus one sees overriding powers exercisable once an A&M beneficiary attains such curious ages as 25¼, 25½, or even 26. That is unnecessary.[30] Under the above form, this problem does not arise.

(2) Exercise of Overriding Powers so as to bring the A&M period to an end.

> The Overriding Powers may be exercised over Trust Property if immediately after the exercise of the power, a Principal Beneficiary under the age of 25

[30] This proposition is really self-evident but some support can be found if needed from estate duty cases. In *Scott v Scott* [1916] 2 Ch 268 the question was whether chattels had been 'enjoyed in kind' (within the meaning of FA 1896, s 20) by a legatee who had sold the chattels before they were transferred to her. Neville J held that the chattels had been 'enjoyed in kind' albeit only for a moment. 'It seems to me that you cannot draw any distinction between enjoyment for a moment and enjoyment for 50 years ...'. In *A-G v Watson* [1917] 2 KB 427 an unfortunate annuitant acquired her interest two days before she died. No one argued that this affected the estate duty charge.

> becomes beneficially[31] entitled to the Property or to an Interest in Possession in it.

It is considered that this form allows property to be applied for the benefit of a beneficiary.[32]

(3) Exercise of overriding powers so that the trust continues to satisfy the A&M conditions.

This is a little more complicated as it is necessary to set out the A&M conditions in full. The form used in this book is:

> The Overriding Powers may be exercised over Trust Property if after the exercise of the power:
> (a) one or more Qualifying Beneficiaries will on or before attaining a specified age not exceeding 25 become beneficially entitled to the Property or to an Interest in Possession in it; and
> (b) no Interest in Possession subsists in the Property and the income from it is to be accumulated so far as not applied for the maintenance, education or benefit of such Qualifying Beneficiaries.
> 'Qualifying Beneficiaries' here means:
> (i) the Principal Beneficiaries and
> (ii) the children and widow of a Principal Beneficiary who died before the age of 25.

This would in particular allow the trustees to vary shares of A&M beneficiaries before they acquire interests in possession in the trust property. The definition of 'qualifying beneficiaries' is introduced to keep the trust within the 'common grandparent' condition. This rather complex form might be better omitted in smaller trusts.

31 The word 'beneficially' is not necessary but it is wise to echo the statutory language.

32 The words would be construed in accordance with the *Inglewood* decision (see para 14.7).

CHAPTER 15

A&M trusts: income clauses

Three-part structure of the income clause

15.1

This chapter is concerned with the income clause of the A&M trust.

The income clause will usually have two distinct parts to deal with the trust income while the beneficiary is under 25:

(1) one part allowing trustees to use the income for the maintenance, education or benefit of the beneficiaries: 'the distribution limb';

(2) a part dealing with the accumulation of the income: 'the accumulation limb'.

These two parts are very much bound together. They are often to be found in the same clause; but in the interest of clarity they should be placed in separate clauses.

The next part of the income clause must provide that the trust income is to be paid to the beneficiary when he attains 25.

Who is allowed to benefit from trust income?

15.2

The income condition requires that income which is not accumulated must be applied for the benefit of 'a beneficiary' (as defined). That is, a person who is one of the A&M beneficiaries, one of the persons who:

> '... will, on or before attaining a specified age not exceeding twenty-five, become beneficially entitled to [the trust property] or to an interest in possession in it.'

Under the standard form of income clause, income can be used to benefit any of the A&M beneficiaries.

Where there are a number of A&M beneficiaries, and trustees have a power of appointment or power to vary shares, there is a theoretical difficulty. Who are the persons who 'will' become entitled to an interest in possession? One or more of the class of A&M beneficiaries will certainly become entitled, but one cannot tell which individuals will do so. The section must be read as permitting income to be applied for the benefit of any of this class of A&M Beneficiaries; the income condition is satisfied if income is used to benefit A, even if the trustees later use their powers to exclude him and give the trust fund to B. Statement of Practice E1 shows that the Revenue accepts this.

It is also permissible for the income clause to provide that income can be used to benefit some of a class of A&M beneficiaries but not others.

A power to pay income for the benefit of a person who is not a member of the class of A&M beneficiaries (ie who cannot in any circumstances become entitled to an interest in possession in the trust property) is not permitted – even if that person is under the age of 25.

Three types of A&M trust

15.3

We shall consider three types of A&M trust:

(1) a trust for a single A&M beneficiary;
(2) a trust for a fixed number of A&M beneficiaries who are all living at the time the trust is made;
(3) a trust for a class of A&M beneficiaries which is to include children born after the trust is made.

Income clause for a single beneficiary

15.4

The income clause for a single beneficiary is fairly straightforward.

The drafter must find a short term to describe the beneficiary as it is cumbrous to use his full name more than once. One may either refer to him as the 'Principal Beneficiary', or some such term, or else by his first name ('John'). In either case the definition clause will supply the full name. The second, more personal, solution is preferred in this book.

The distribution limb

15.5

There is a statutory precedent for the clause. For the distribution limb of the clause this provides:

> During the infancy of [the Principal Beneficiary] the trustees may, at their sole discretion, pay to his parent or guardian, if any, or otherwise apply for or towards his maintenance, education, or benefit, the whole or such part, if any, of the income of that property as may, in all the circumstances, be reasonable, whether or not there is:
> (a) any other fund applicable to the same purpose, or
> (b) any person bound by law to provide for his maintenance or education.[1]

The form used in this book is as follows:

> While the Principal Beneficiary is living and under the age of 25:
> (1) The Trustees may apply the income of the Trust Fund for the maintenance, education or benefit[2] of the Principal Beneficiary ...

This form echoes the language of the income condition itself: it is a considerable simplification of the statutory precedent.

The power to pay to parents and guardians has been deleted: that is more conveniently dealt with in the schedule of administrative provisions.

The statutory precedent provides that the power of maintenance is exercisable whether or not there is another fund or person to provide for the maintenance. This would be implied in any event. It is standard practice to omit it.

Drafting the accumulation limb

15.6

How should one draft the second part of the income clause, dealing with accumulation? Again, statutory precedent is the best starting point:

1 TA(NI) 1958, s 32(2). The drafter of the IHTA 1984, s 71 almost certainly had the English equivalent of this precedent in mind.

2 The words 'maintenance' and 'education' are strictly otiose: the word *benefit* should include them. The words are retained here as it seems better practice to copy the statutory words faithfully. (Why were they included then in TA 1925, s 31? Perhaps the drafter thought that education may not be a 'benefit'; as witness Caliban's (non-judicial) dictum: *'You have taught me language/and my profit on't is, I know how to curse'.)* On the wide meaning of 'benefit' in this context, see para 10.11 (Power of advancement used to create new trusts).

> 'The trustees shall accumulate all the residue of the income [by investing it and any profits of so investing it][3] from time to time in authorised investments, and shall hold those accumulations ... as an accretion to the capital of the [trust fund], and as one fund with such capital for all purposes, ... but the trustees may, at any time ... apply those accumulations, or any part thereof, as if they were income arising in the then current year.'[4]

This is often adopted verbatim (but with the punctuation deleted!). That it is not necessary to do so can be seen by comparing another statutory precedent:

> The Trustees shall ... accumulate the profits from the capital money by investing them and the resulting profits under the general power of investment in section 3 of the TA 2000 and shall add the accumulations to capital.[5]

The form used in this book is as follows:

> The Trustees shall accumulate the income of the Trust Fund. That income shall be added to the Trust Fund.

This draws on the statutory language, but considerably simplifies it. It is, of course, unnecessary to direct the trustees to invest the accumulated income: the trustees will have a power of investment, and no one expects that they will place accumulated income in a current account.[6] The power to deal with accumulated income as income is important; but it is best relegated to the schedule of trustees' powers.

The basic A&M clause for a single beneficiary will therefore run as follows:

(1) While A is living and under the age of 25:
   (a) The Trustees may apply the income of the Trust Fund for his maintenance, education or benefit.
   (b) Subject to that, the Trustees shall accumulate the income of the Trust Fund. That income shall be added to the Trust Fund.
(2) Subject to that, the Trustees shall pay the income of the Trust Fund to A during his life.

In England this basic form must be reviewed in the light of the rule against accumulations.[7]. In Northern Ireland the drafter's task is much more straightforward as income may be accumulated throughout the perpetuity period (ie the Trust Period).[8] The basic form is therefore all that is required.

3 Words inserted by the TA 2000 (and by TA(NI) 2001) to replace '*in the way of compound interest by investing the same and the resulting income thereof*'. The only purpose of the change seems to be to modernise the language. The old words will remain familiar as they are found in many precedents.
4 TA(NI) 1958, s 32(3).
5 SLA 1925, s 39(2) as amended by the TA 2000.
6 This was recognised by the drafter of Trusts (Jersey) Law 1984, art 34.
7 See Kessler, *Drafting Trusts and Will Trusts* (6th edn, 2002) ch 15.
8 This includes the fixed period of 80 years introduced by PA(NI) 1966. The common law rule against accumulations is that income may be accumulated throughout the perpetuity period.

Income clause for several beneficiaries

15.7

We can now turn to consider the position where there are a number of A&M beneficiaries.

The drafter's first task is to coin a term to describe the class of beneficiaries. A variety of terms are in common use:

> 'The Specified Class'
>
> 'The Specified Beneficiaries'
>
> 'The Beneficiaries' (where some other term is used to describe the wider class of beneficiaries; such as 'the appointed class').

The term used in this chapter is 'the Principal Beneficiaries'. This gives some flavour of their status under the trust. Where the beneficiaries are the grandchildren of the settlor it is more helpful to call them 'the Grandchildren'. Where the beneficiaries are the children of the settlor, it is tempting to call them 'the Children'; but that is best avoided. The term 'child' is used elsewhere in the trust in its natural meaning; and the result is confusion.

Division into shares

15.8

Where the A&M trust has a class of beneficiaries, it is convenient to divide the trust fund into shares, one for each 'Principal Beneficiary'. This is achieved by saying what is intended: the following form is used in this book:

> The Trust Fund shall be divided into equal[9] shares ('the Shares') so that there shall be one Share for each Principal Beneficiary.

Having defined the shares, one can deal with the income of each share.

The same result is often achieved by adopting the form usually called *Lassence v Tierney* form (sometimes called the *Hancock v Watson* form).[10] The essence of this

---

Since the enactment of the 1966 Act the settlor may elect for a fixed period not exceeding 80 years. While the rule against accumulations is not mentioned in PA(NI) 1966, it is surely beyond argument that the 80-year period, if elected, now governs also the accumulation of income.

9 It is strictly unnecessary to say 'equal' as that must be implied.

10 *Lassence v Tierney* (1849) 1 Mac & G 551, 41 ER 1379; *Hancock v Watson* [1902] AC 14. For a discussion of this form see *Watson v Holland* [1984] STC 372.

form is to confer shares which first appear to be absolute entitlements; and then (inconsistently) to provide that the shares do not belong to the beneficiary absolutely, but are held on trust. Thus:

(1) The Trust Fund shall be held on trust for such of the Principal Beneficiaries as shall attain the age of 25 and if more than one in equal shares.
(2) On the Principal Beneficiary attaining the age of 25 his share shall be held on the following trusts ...

This is unnecessary and confusing, at least to the reader who is not a trust practitioner.

The distribution limb

15.9

We can now consider the distribution limb of the income clause. In the discussion below, it is assumed there are three A&M beneficiaries, A, B, and C.

What is to be done with the income of each beneficiary's share? There are two approaches to this question: these may be called 'share-by-share approach' and 'the global approach'.

(1) The *share-by-share* approach is to direct that:
    (a) the income of A's share may be applied for the benefit of A;
    (b) likewise the income of B's share may be applied for the benefit of B; and likewise for C's share.
(2) The *global* approach is to direct that:
    (a) the income of A's share may be applied for the benefit of A or B or C (while under 25);
    (b) likewise, B's share and C's share may be applied for the benefit of A or B or C (while under 25).

The Revenue accepts that this 'global' approach is permitted in the distribution limb of an A&M income clause.[11] Which is the better form? There is no doubt: the global approach. The trustees may need the flexibility: there may be strong reasons for preferring one beneficiary over another. The form used in this book is as follows:

11 SP E2A. An interesting question is whether this statement of practice represents the true state of the law, or a concession. If the statement of practice is correct in law the consequence is this: income may be applied for the benefit of one beneficiary ('A') whereas another beneficiary ('B') may later receive an interest in possession in the trust fund. For the trustees will usually have power to vary the shares in favour of B, depriving A. This is just arguably inconsistent with the capital condition, IHTA 1984, s 71(1)(a). The statement of practice might therefore represent an extra-statutory concession. That question would only be significant if a wide A&M protection clause were used. See para 18.17 (Protection clauses).

(1) While the Principal Beneficiary is living and under the age of 25:
  (a) The Trustees may apply the income of the share of the Principal Beneficiary for the maintenance, education or benefit of any of the Principal Beneficiaries who are under the age of 25.

The accumulation limb

15.10

The existence of several beneficiaries raises a further problem for the accumulation limb of the income clause. Income not spent on the beneficiaries must be accumulated. The trust fund will be divided into shares, one for each of the beneficiaries. The question is, to which shares should the accumulated income be added? Let us take the example again of the A&M trust for three beneficiaries: A, B and C.

The two possibilities may again be described as the share-by-share approach and the global approach.

(1) The *share-by-share* approach is to direct that:
  (a) the surplus income of A's share must be added to A's share;
  (b) likewise the surplus income of B's share must be added to B's share; and likewise for C's share.

(2) The *global* approach is to direct that:
  (a) the surplus income of A's share is to be added to the trust fund as a whole;
  (b) likewise, the surplus income of B's and C's share is to be added to the trust fund as a whole.

The global approach is without question the superior one. The share-by-share approach would be extremely inconvenient for trust administration. Inevitably income will be accumulated and added to one share, and no (or less) income will be accumulated and added to the other shares. So the shares will become of different sizes. The trustees must then keep separate sets of investments representing the shares' accumulated income; or at least they must keep records so as to identify each share, and the income of each share (as the income of each share would be treated differently). The work (and cost) is out of proportion to the amounts involved. Sensibly, it is often ignored in practice.

Do the A&M conditions permit the global approach to be adopted for accumulation of income? The relevant condition is the income condition: IHTA 1984, s 71(1)(b):

> No interest in possession subsists in [the settled property] and the income from it is to be accumulated so far as not applied for the maintenance, education or benefit of a beneficiary.

This condition requires surplus income to be accumulated. Adopting the global approach, the income is certainly 'accumulated' in the general sense of the word.

So the question is whether there is an additional requirement that the accumulated income must be held on:

(1) the identical A&M trust from which it arose; or
(2) other trusts which satisfy the conditions of s 71 of the IHTA 1984.[12]

There is nothing which imposes this additional requirement expressly and there is nothing which imposes it by implication. Accordingly the global approach satisfies the conditions for A&M status.[13]

An alternative view?

Of course the courts are nowadays sometimes prepared to ignore the natural construction and add a gloss to the terms of a statutory provision in order to fit the scheme of the legislation, or (which comes to the same) to avoid anomalies. One must consider whether s 71(1)(b) should be subject to a gloss that the accumulated income is:

(1) to be added to the share of the beneficiary from which it accrued; or
(2) to be added to that part of the capital of the trust fund which is held on A&M trusts.

The gloss could be expressed in different ways, with different practical results. That is one argument against making the gloss. There is, however, a more fundamental difficulty.

The argument in favour of any such gloss must be based on anomaly. What is the anomaly here? Perhaps it is this:

(1) income which is added to the share of A&M beneficiaries forms part of the estate of the A&M beneficiaries. It could then only leave their estate in principle by a transfer of value: IHTA 1984, s 50;
(2) by contrast, if the accumulated income can be added to a part of the Trust Fund held on other terms, then this income may pass to any other estate free of IHT.

Can that be described as an anomaly having regard to the scheme of the IHTA? It cannot, for section 21 of the IHTA 1984 provides a comparable rule in relation to an individual's own income.[14] So the scheme of the Act is consistent with the

12 One sometimes sees the following form, which is a compromise between the global and share-by-share approaches:

> *The Trustees shall accumulate the income of the trust fund and shall hold those accumulations as an accretion to the shares of the beneficiaries who have not reached the age of 25.*

13 This is the view adopted in the only inheritance tax textbook to address the point: *Foster's Inheritance Tax* (looseleaf) LexisNexis UK, at para 5.12.

14 'Normal expenditure out of income

natural construction of s 71(1)(a). For 'surplus income' is income which could in principle fall within s 21(1) if it were income of an individual. In the normal case surplus income will only be accumulated if the maintenance needs of A&M Beneficiaries are already properly provided for. (It is true that the analogy is not a perfect one; one could imagine hypothetical cases where s 21 would not apply to an individual but surplus income could be disposed of without IHT; but nevertheless, s 21 is sufficiently close to dispose of any argument based on 'anomalies'.)

On the contrary, a construction of the income condition which would in every case require trustees to account separately for (typically) small amounts of surplus income and (typically) tiny amounts of income derived therefrom could itself be derided as a construction which leads to absurdities.

Conclusion and summary

The conclusion is that the global approach does comply with the conditions of section 71 of the Inheritance Tax Act 1984, and is better from a practical view point than any alternative.

In summary of the discussion so far: the basic A&M income clause for a number of beneficiaries (in our drafts called 'Principal Beneficiaries') runs as follows:

(1) while a Principal Beneficiary is living and under the age of 25:
  (a) the Trustees may apply the income of his share for the maintenance, education or benefit of any of the Principal Beneficiaries who are under the age of 25;
  (b) subject to that, the Trustees shall accumulate the income of the Share. That income shall be added to the Trust Fund.

(2) Subject to that, the Trustees shall pay the income of the Share to the Principal Beneficiary during his life.

In England this basic form must be reviewed in the light of the rule against accumulations. Life for the Northern Ireland practitioner is so much simpler as income may be accumulated throughout the perpetuity period (the Trust Period). No amendment of the basic form is needed.

---

(1) A transfer of value is an exempt transfer if, or to the extent that, it is shown:
  (a) that it was made as part of the normal expenditure of the transferor, and
  (b) that (taking one year with another) it was made out of his income, and
  (c) that, after allowing for all transfers of value forming part of his normal expenditure, the transferor was left with sufficient income to maintain his usual standard of living.'

Income clause for class of beneficiaries including unborns

15.11

In England the rule against accumulations poses a serious problem for the A&M trust which is to cater for unborn beneficiaries. The tortuous solution is to provide for accumulation under Trustee Act 1925, s 31 (the equivalent of TA(NI) 1958, s 32) since accumulation under the statutory provision is permitted even after the usual 21-year accumulation period has expired.[15] The Northern Ireland practitioner can avoid these complexities: income may be accumulated throughout the perpetuity period (the Trust Period).

The form used in this book is as follows:

> (1) While a Principal Beneficiary is living and under the age of 25:
> (a) The Trustees may apply the income of his Share for the maintenance, education or benefit of any of the Principal Beneficiaries who have not attained the age of 25.
> (b) Subject to that, the Trustees shall accumulate the income of the Share. That income shall be added to the Trust Fund.
>
> (2) The Trustees shall pay the income of the Share to the Principal Beneficiary during his life if he attains the age of 25.

15 See further Kessler *Drafting Trusts and Will Trusts* (6th edn, 2002) ch 15.

CHAPTER 16

Providing for death of an A&M beneficiary

Death of A&M beneficiaries

16.1

If the beneficiary dies over the age of 25, no difficulty arises. By then the trust has interest in possession form; and the position is as discussed in para 13.1 (Interest in possession trusts).

Death pays no regard to the convenience of the drafter; beneficiaries may die under the age of 25. How should this be dealt with? There are three distinct possibilities, which need to be considered separately:

(1) *An A&M beneficiary may die under 25 leaving children, or a spouse, or both.* The drafter should direct that his share in the trust fund should pass to a trust which includes them at least as possible beneficiaries. It is clearly wrong in principle to exclude the widow, as some drafters do.

(2) *An A&M beneficiary may die under 25 without children or spouse, but leaving other A&M beneficiaries.* Here it is common to provide that his share should pass to the other shares. This will usually be the most desirable course, but not necessarily so.

(3) *The A&M beneficiary may die under 25 without children or spouse, leaving no other A&M beneficiaries.* Some drafters direct in these circumstances that:
   (a) income should be accumulated for as long as possible (which in Northern Ireland means for the entire trust period), and
   (b) if another A&M beneficiary is born, then he will become the A&M beneficiary for the trust.

If another child is born relatively soon all would be well. However, if no child is born then the trust fund will be subject to a pointless accumulation. In the meantime, the family of the deceased beneficiary may go unprovided for. Later, on the expiry of the trust period, there could be a substantial tax charge.[1]

1 IHTA 1984, s 71(3). The tax charge applies on the assumption that the trust remains an A&M trust during the period of accumulation, where there is no beneficiary, but ceases to be an A&M trust on the expiry of the accumulation period. The contrary view is perhaps arguable.

A crystal ball is not to be found in the drafter's toolkit. The best course will be to leave the trustees at the time to determine what trusts would be most suitable. On the death of an A&M beneficiary, the trust fund (or his share of it) should become held on discretionary trusts. The discretionary trust opens a window of opportunity: the trustees can create the form of trust which seems best. A further advantage of this approach is that the drafting is relatively simple; whereas clauses substituting the children of the deceased beneficiary become immensely complicated; the result is never completely satisfactory.

The tax consequences of the discretionary trust under current law are satisfactory. The death of an A&M beneficiary does not give rise to an IHT charge. No additional charge is caused by creating a discretionary trust. To avoid a succession of 10 year charges, the trustees may wish to convert the trust into IP form or A&M form: the overriding powers allow them to do this. This may give rise to an exit charge, but the amounts involved will be nil or trivial if the trustees act reasonably promptly after the death.

It is possible – perhaps, likely – that the tax treatment of discretionary trusts will change; perhaps even a short-term discretionary trust may become fiscally unattractive. But the trustees can amend the terms of the trust at any time. By use of the overriding power of appointment, they can create any form of trust that may be desired.

Three types of A&M trust

16.2

We shall consider three types of A&M trust:

(i) trusts for a single A&M beneficiary;
(ii) trusts for a number of A&M beneficiaries who are all living at the time the trust is made;
(iii) trusts for a class of A&M beneficiaries which is to include children born after the trust is made.

The life of every A&M trust falls into two parts:

(i) The A&M period, during which the trust must satisfy the A&M conditions.
(ii) After the A&M period. The trust first takes the form of an IP trust. Thereafter there are no restrictions. The trusts in this book adopt the forms discussed in para 13.1 (Interest in possession trusts) above. The reader is referred back to that chapter.

This is the structure of all the A&M trusts in this book:

1 while the A&M beneficiaries are under 25, the trustees may use income for their benefit; the remainder of the income to be accumulated; thereafter all the income to be distributed for the benefit of A&M beneficiaries.

2 income then to be paid to the beneficiaries for life; then to the spouse for life; then on discretionary trusts for their issue.
3 the trustees have a power of appointment restricted to satisfy the A&M conditions.
4 there is a default trust.

This is contained in four clauses.

The first deals with trust income (1 and 2 above). The drafting of 1 above requires a chapter to itself, and is discussed in para 15.1 (A&M trusts: income clauses). The drafting of 2 above follows the form of the IP trusts, discussed in para 13.1 (Interest in possession trusts).

The second clause contains the overriding powers. These are provisions standard to all the trusts in this book: see para 10.1.

The third clause restricts the overriding powers to satisfy the A&M conditions: see para 14.16.

The fourth contains the default clause, which is relatively simple: see para 12.20.

A&M trust for a single beneficiary

16.3

This is the standard precedent of an A&M trust where there is a single A&M beneficiary (here called 'the Principal Beneficiary').

1. **Trust Income**
   Subject to the overriding powers below:
   (1) While the Principal Beneficiary is living and under the age of 25:
      (a) The Trustees may apply the income of the Trust Fund for his maintenance, education or benefit.
      (b) Subject to that, the Trustees shall accumulate the income of the Trust Fund. That income shall be added to the Trust Fund.
   (2) Subject to that, the Trustees shall pay the income of the Trust Fund to the Principal Beneficiary during his life.
   (3) Subject to that, if the Principal Beneficiary dies during the Trust Period, the Trustees shall pay the income of the Trust Fund to his widow during her life.
   (4) Subject to that, during the Trust Period, the Trustees shall pay or apply the income of the Trust Fund to or for the benefit of any Beneficiaries, as the Trustees think fit.
2. **Overriding Powers**
   Subject to the following clause, during the Trust Period, the Trustees shall have the following powers ('Overriding Powers'):

[There follow the standard form Overriding Powers.]

3. **Restrictions on Overriding Powers**
The Overriding Powers may only be exercised over Trust Property in the following circumstances:
(1) If the Principal Beneficiary has or has had an Interest in Possession in the Property.
(2) If the Principal Beneficiary has died.
(3) If, on the exercise of the power, the Principal Beneficiary becomes beneficially entitled to the property, or to an Interest in Possession in it.
[This is the simpler form; contrast the trusts below for the fuller form. The main use of the more complex form is to vary shares of A&M beneficiaries; this does not arise where there is a single A&M beneficiary.]
4. **Default Clause**
Subject to that, the Trust Fund shall be held on trust for the Principal Beneficiary [or: specify default beneficiary as appropriate] absolutely.

Death of principal beneficiary

16.4

If the principal beneficiary dies under the age of 25, the position under this draft is as follows:

(i) if he leaves a widow, she will receive an interest in possession in the trust fund;
(ii) otherwise there will be a discretionary trust for the 'Beneficiaries' (as defined in the trust).

In either case, the trustees will be able to exercise their overriding power (or if appropriate the widow may disclaim her interest) so as to create the form of trust most appropriate in the circumstances actually existing at the time of the death.

The temptation to adopt more complex forms is avoided.

A&M trust for a number of living A&M beneficiaries

16.5

We can now turn to consider an A&M trust form where there are to be a number of A&M beneficiaries all of whom are living at the time the trust is made.

In this chapter the class of beneficiaries is described as 'the Principal Beneficiaries.'

(An alternative approach is to deal with each beneficiary by name. This produces a longer draft, and is harder to adapt to the individual case. Perhaps the end result is clearer and more elegant if there are only two A&M beneficiaries; if there are more the balance of convenience favours the generic approach.)

In the following trust, it is assumed that the term 'the Principal Beneficiaries' has been defined by naming those referred to, eg 'the Principal Beneficiaries' means John Smith, Peter Smith and Joanna Smith, the grandchildren of the settlor.

1. **Trust Income**
   Subject to the overriding powers conferred below:
   (1) The Trust Fund shall be divided into equal shares ('the Shares') so that there shall be one Share for each Principal Beneficiary.
   (2) While a Principal Beneficiary is living and under the age of 25:
      (a) The Trustees may apply the income of his Share for the maintenance, education or benefit of any of the Principal Beneficiaries who have not attained the age of 25.
      (b) Subject to that, the Trustees shall accumulate the income of the Share. That income shall be added to the Share.
   (3) Subject to that, the Trustees shall pay the income of the Share to the Principal Beneficiary during his life.
   (4) Subject to that, if the Principal Beneficiary dies during the Trust Period, the Trustees shall pay the income of the Share to the widow of the Principal Beneficiary during her life.
   (5) Subject to that, during the Trust Period, the Trustees shall pay or apply the income of the Share to or for the benefit of any one or more of the Beneficiaries, as they think fit.
2. **Overriding Powers**
   Subject to the following clause, during the Trust Period, the Trustees shall have the following powers ('Overriding Powers'):
   [There follow the standard form Overriding Powers.]
3. **Restrictions on Overriding Powers**
   The Overriding Powers may only be exercised over Trust Property in the following circumstances:
   (1) if a Beneficiary has or has had an Interest in Possession in the Property;
   (2) if there is no living Principal Beneficiary under the age of 25;
   (3) If, on the exercise of the power, a Principal Beneficiary under the age of 25 becomes beneficially entitled to the Property, or to an Interest in Possession in it; or
   (4) if, after the exercise of the power:
      (a) one or more Qualifying Beneficiaries will on or before attaining a specified age not exceeding 25 become beneficially entitled to the Property or to an Interest in Possession in it; and
      (b) no Interest in Possession subsists in the Property and the income from it is to be accumulated so far as not applied for the maintenance, education or benefit of such Qualifying Beneficiaries.

   '**Qualifying Beneficiaries**' here means

(i) the Principal Beneficiaries and future [grand]children[2] of the Settlor

(ii) the children and widow of a Principal Beneficiary who dies before the age of 25.

4. **Default Clause**
Subject to that, the Trust Fund shall be held on trust for the Principal Beneficiaries in equal shares absolutely.

Death of an A&M beneficiary

16.6

If an A&M beneficiary dies under the age of 25, the position under this draft is that:

(i) if he leaves a widow, the widow will receive an interest in possession in his share of the trust fund; or

(ii) otherwise his share will be held on discretionary trusts for the 'Beneficiaries' (as defined in the trust).

In either case, the trustees will be able to exercise their overriding power (or if appropriate the widow may disclaim her interest) so as to create the form of trust most appropriate in the circumstances actually existing at the time of the death. The temptation to adopt more complex forms is avoided.

However, in this form, there is another possibility. The trustees are given a power to alter the terms of the trust for the benefit of qualifying beneficiaries (defined within the terms of the single generation test). Thus, if trustees fear that a beneficiary may die under 25, they may take steps before the death as well as after.

A&M trust for class of A&M beneficiaries including unborns

16.7

We can now turn to a trust where the class of A&M beneficiaries includes future born children. This raises various problems which do not afflict the simpler trusts. Many of these concern the Income Clause, for which see para 15.1 (A&M trusts: income clauses).

A further problem is that each newborn child may reduce the share of existing children in the trust fund. This is best illustrated by example. Consider a trust for present and future grandchildren of the settlor:

2 In the case of a children's trust, this will refer to the children of the settlor; in the case of a grandchildren's trust, this will refer to his grandchildren.

(1) suppose at the time the trust is made, the settlor has two grandchildren; A and B. Each will (subject to the birth of further children) become entitled to an interest in possession in one-half of the trust fund, on attaining the age of 25;
(2) suppose a new child, C, is born while A and B are under 25. Each child now stands to become entitled to a one-third share. That causes no tax problems;
(3) suppose further that the oldest, A, attains the age of 25 and becomes entitled to an interest in possession in his one-third share of the fund. What would happen if a fourth child, D, is born then? Each child's share in the fund might automatically be reduced to one-fourth. This is the fairest result. The problem is that since the oldest child, A, has an interest in possession in the trust fund, the reduction of his share (from one-third to one-quarter) is a transfer of value. A tax charge may arise.[3] Like biblical patriarchs, the inheritance of the younger child would prejudice the older.

16.8

Two solutions to this problem are commonly proposed:

1 *Exclude the newborn infant.* That is, once the first child, A, has attained 25, any children born thereafter are excluded. Many drafters adopt this route. The policy of exclusion is a complete solution to the problem, but it is not a very satisfactory one.[4]
2 *Protect the adult beneficiary.* It is possible to allow the newborn child to share in the trust fund, with special protection for the beneficiary who has attained an interest in possession. The share of the child who has attained an interest in possession will not be automatically reduced if a new child is born. Instead the new child takes a share in the fund in which no interest in possession has yet vested. Thus, in the example considered above, where D is born after A has reached the age of 25: A's share remains fixed at one-third and B, C and D take the remaining two-thirds share between them, ie two-ninths each. Under this route, both the drafting and administration of the trust will be made rather complicated.[5]

Neither solution is wholly satisfactory. The authors propose something simpler. The problem is more theoretical than real. It is unusual in the course of nature for an A&M beneficiary to be born after another A&M beneficiary has attained 25. As the law now stands, the transfer of value on the birth of the new beneficiary will be a PET, almost certainly a matter of no significance. Moreover, the amounts involved will usually be small.[6] The problem now detaining us is one which only affects

3 IHTA 1984, s 52. The transfer of value is, under current law, a potentially exempt transfer, but that may not be the case in the future when 'D' is born.
4 The trust may lose A&M status, once the class of beneficiaries closes, see para 15.23.
5 Under either solution, the position could be restored to equality by exercise of the trustees' overriding powers.
6 In the example above, the transfer of value would only amount to one-twelfth of the value of the trust fund. Unless the trust fund was well in excess of £2m, it will fall within the nil-rate band. Where the trust property qualifies for business property relief, or agricultural property relief, the problem is even less significant.

trusts of very considerable size, in the event of a change in the law and an unlikely sequence of births.

Now the drafter would still go to some trouble to avoid the problem if there were no other way to deal with it. But there is: children are not born without notice. In the very exceptional case where it is necessary to exclude the newborn beneficiary from the trust before his birth, the period of gestation is sufficient time for the trustees to make an appropriate appointment to achieve this.

The technique used in this book is therefore not to exclude the future unborn beneficiary. Only where all the A&M beneficiaries have attained the age of 25 is it best to exclude future born A&M beneficiaries. If any are born after that time (which is most unlikely) they can benefit from the trust by exercise of the trustees' overriding powers.

16.9

The definition of 'the Principal Beneficiaries' in the trust will be as follows:

> 'The Principal Beneficiaries' **means [specify existing beneficiaries] and any other child [or grandchild] of the Settlor born:**
> (a) at a time when a Principal Beneficiary is under the age of 25 and
> (b) during the Trust Period.

The trust takes the following now familiar form:

1. **Trust Income**
   Subject to the Overriding Powers conferred below:
   (1) The Trust Fund shall be divided into equal shares ('the Shares') so that there shall be one Share for each Principal Beneficiary.
   (2) While a Principal Beneficiary is living and under the age of 25:
      (a) The Trustees may apply the income of his Share for the maintenance, education or benefit of any of the Principal Beneficiaries who have not attained the age of 25.
      (b) Subject to that, the Trustees shall accumulate the income of the Share. That income shall be added to the Trust Fund.
   (3) The Trustees shall pay the income of the Share to the Principal Beneficiary during his life if he attains the age of 25.
   (4) Subject to that, if the Principal Beneficiary dies during the Trust Period, the Trustees shall pay the income of the Share to the widow of the Principal Beneficiary during her life.
   (5) Subject to that, during the Trust Period, the Trustees shall pay or apply the income of the Share to or for the benefit of any one or more of the Beneficiaries, as they think fit.

2. **Overriding Powers**
   Subject to the following clause, during the Trust Period, the Trustees shall have the following powers ('Overriding Powers'):
   [There follow the standard form Overriding Powers.]
3. **Restrictions on Overriding Powers**
   The Overriding Powers may only be exercised over Trust Property in the following circumstances:
   (1) If a Beneficiary has or has had an Interest in Possession in the Property; or
   (2) If there is no Principal Beneficiary under the age of 25; or
   (3) If on the exercise of the power a Principal Beneficiary under the age of 25 becomes beneficially entitled to the Property or to an Interest in Possession in it; or
   (4) If after, the exercise of the power:
      (a) One or more Qualifying Beneficiaries will on or before attaining a specified age not exceeding 25 become beneficially entitled to the Property or to an Interest in Possession in it; and
      (b) No Interest in Possession subsists in the Property and the income from it is to be accumulated so far as not applied for the maintenance, education or benefit of such Qualifying Beneficiaries.

      '**Qualifying Beneficiaries**' here means:
      (i) the Principal Beneficiaries and
      (ii) the children and widow of a Principal Beneficiary who dies before the age of 25.
4. **Default Clause**
   Subject to that, the Trust Fund shall be held on trust for the Principal Beneficiaries living at the date of this settlement in equal shares [or specify default beneficiary as appropriate] absolutely.

Which form?

16.10

At the outset of this chapter it was noted that there were three types of A&M trust, depending on the class of beneficiaries. There may be:
(1) a single living beneficiary under 25;
(2) a class of beneficiaries who are all living and under 25;
(3) a class of beneficiaries under 25, including unborn beneficiaries.

In practice the third of these forms, for present and future born children, is generally to be preferred. This is because a settlor will not usually wish to make a trust for the benefit of a single beneficiary or for living beneficiaries only. He will wish to make a trust for the benefit of present and future children (or grandchildren). It is possible that more beneficiaries will be born. Future born children could be accommodated by using the overriding powers, but it is easier to create a trust for present and future born children.[7]

Moreover, in Northern Ireland the drafting of trusts which cater for future born beneficiaries is relatively simple (compared to the task faced by an English practitioner who has to navigate the rule against accumulations). However, there may be cases where the settlor intends to benefit a particular beneficiary (perhaps setting up separate trusts for others) in which case the narrower form will be preferred.

7 In England where accumulation is effectively limited to 21 years the narrower form also poses a minor problem if any beneficiary is less than four years old when the trust is made. The trust ceases to be A&M in form at the expiry of the accumulation period, when the beneficiary is still under 25. Under the wider form, for present and future children, the trust continues to be A&M in form until the youngest beneficiary reaches 25.

CHAPTER 17

Discretionary trusts

17.1

The discretionary trust is one where trust income and capital may be paid to one or more of a class of beneficiaries, as the trustees think fit.[1] The discretionary trust is simple in concept and there are no exacting tax requirements to satisfy. The drafting is relatively easy.

Why use discretionary trusts?[2]

17.2

The simple reason may be that it is desired to give trustees the flexibility to pay income to different beneficiaries (or accumulate it). In practice tax considerations are often paramount. The following outline tax points may also be noted here:

IHT advantages There is no tax charge on the death of any beneficiary. Instead the trust will be subject to the IHT discretionary trust regime; for small trusts (in particular those under the nil rate band) this is not harsh.

CGT advantages Gifts to the trust will usually qualify for CGT hold-over relief.

Income Tax The appalling reforms of Schedule F taxation in the Finance (No 2) Act 1997 make it unattractive to use discretionary trusts to receive and distribute Schedule F income to basic rate taxpayers; IP trusts are preferable.[3]

1 See Trust Terminology for a fuller discussion of this term.
2 See also 13.2 (Why use interest in possession trusts?); 14.2 (Why use accumulation and maintenance trusts?); 21.2 (Why use bare trusts?).
3 See Appendix 5 of James Kessler, *Drafting Trusts and Will Trusts* (5th ed, 2000).

Discretionary trust: income clause

17.3

In the discretionary trust the trustees may have power either to distribute income to any beneficiaries, or to retain and accumulate it.[4]

Income clauses in discretionary trusts therefore contain two limbs: distribution and accumulation. These are very much bound together, and are often to be found in the same clause. In this book, they are placed in two separate sub-clauses. We shall discuss the distribution limb before turning to the question of accumulation.

Distribution limb

17.4

Distribution of income under a discretionary trust is simple. There is a statutory precedent:

> The income shall be held upon trust for the application thereof for the maintenance or support, or otherwise for the benefit of, all or any one or more exclusively of the other or others of the [Beneficiaries].[5]

The form used in this book says the same more simply:

> The Trustees shall pay or apply the income of the Trust Fund to or for the benefit[6] of any Beneficiaries.

A traditional form prefers:

> ...such one or more of the Beneficiary or Beneficiaries exclusive of the others or other of them.

That clumsy syntax has been unnecessary since 1874.[7]

It is not necessary to add, 'as the Trustees think fit', see paragraph 6.10 ('Absolute discretion' and 'as the trustees think fit').

4 There are, strictly, three possibilities: (i) a power to distribute the income with a duty to accumulate any undistributed income (ii) a power to accumulate and a duty to distribute unaccumulated income (iii) a duty either to distribute or to accumulate. There is little practical difference. See para 6.2 (Duties and powers distinguished).

5 TA (NI) 1958, s 34(1)(b)(ii).

6 On the wide meaning of 'benefit', in this context, see 10.11 (Power of advancement used to create new trusts).

7 Powers of Appointment Act 1874.

Accumulation limb

17.5

The Northern Ireland drafter does not have to worry about the rule against accumulations as income may be accumulated during the entire perpetuity period (the Trust Period). This leads to another very simple form.

> The Trustees may accumulate the whole or part of the income of the Trust Fund during the Trust Period. That income shall be added to the Trust Fund.[8]

In contrast English practitioners must define an 'Accumulation Period' and invariably select the period of 21 years beginning with the date of the settlement.[9]

Structure of discretionary trust

17.6

This is a structure of the discretionary trusts in this book:

(1) there is the income clause already discussed: the trustees have a power to accumulate income during the full perpetuity period and the trustees are directed to pay income to any beneficiaries they wish;
(2) the trustees have the standard overriding powers which may override the above;
(3) lastly, there is a standard default clause.

This is contained in three clauses. The first deals with trust income. The second contains the overriding powers. The third is the default clause. The draft is as follows:

> **1. Trust Income**
> (1) The Trustees may accumulate the whole or part of the income of the Trust Fund during the Trust Period. That income shall be added to the Trust Fund.
> (2) The Trustees shall pay or apply the remainder of the income to or for the benefit of any Beneficiaries, as the Trustees think fit, during the Trust Period.
>
> **2. Overriding Powers**[10]
> [Here follow the standard overriding powers in this book.]

8 For the derivation of this form, see 15.6.
9 This is the period selected in James Kessler, *Drafting Trusts and Will Trusts*.
10 For a discussion of this clause see 10.1 (Overriding powers).

3. Default Clause[11]
Subject to that, the Trust Fund shall be held on trust for [specify name] absolutely.

'Beneficiaries'

17.7

For the definition of 'Beneficiaries', see 4.18.

Some discretionary trusts specify two classes of beneficiaries: a narrow class to whom income is to be distributed: and a wider class who may benefit under the overriding power.[12] There was once a good reason for this. To satisfy the requirement of certainty, it was once thought that the objects of the discretionary trust over trust income had to be a narrow class: a class of whom a complete list could be drawn up. The object of a power of appointment (over capital) could be a wider class. It was worth having two classes, a narrow one for the discretionary trust of income, and a wide one for the power of appointment over trust capital. In 1970 the House of Lords decided that the broader test applied to discretionary trusts as well as to powers.[13] Accordingly, it has long been unnecessary to create two separate classes of beneficiaries.

Powers of discretionary trusts

17.8

There is no restriction on the powers of discretionary trusts. One may include powers not permitted in IP trusts, or A&M trusts. The additional powers include the following:

Power to pay insurance premiums out of income

The following form is used in this book:

> The Trustees may pay premiums of any insurance policy out of income.

11 For a discussion of this clause see 12.20 (Default clause).
12 These might be called 'the Beneficiaries' and 'the Appointed Class.'
13 *McPhail v Doulton* [1971] AC 424. Another solution to this trust law difficulty would have been to confer on trustees a mere power over trust income, not a discretionary trust in the strict sense. (On the distinction see 6.2 (Duties and powers distinguished).) But this was not possible for estate duty reasons.

Waiver of income

The following form is used in this book:

> The Trustees may waive the payment of income before it becomes due.

There may from time to time be situations where it would be convenient or tax efficient for trustees to waive the payment of rent, interest or dividends. In the case of the discretionary trust, this could only be possible if the trustees were expressly authorised.

CHAPTER 18

Provisions inconsistent with IP, A&M and discretionary trusts

Administrative, dispositive, beneficial: terminology

18.1

The provisions of a settlement may be classified as:
(1) 'administrative' (sometimes called 'managerial');
(2) 'dispositive' (sometimes called 'beneficial'[1]).

The distinction is broadly as these labels suggest: administrative provisions relate to trust administration; beneficial provisions deal with beneficial ownership.

Significance of administrative/dispositive distinction

18.2

The administrative/dispositive distinction arises for a number of purposes of trust law.[2] These are interesting, but only rarely of concern to the trust practitioner.

1 The word 'beneficial' when applied to powers is ambiguous and may mean:
(1) the power is dispositive (not merely administrative); or
(2) the power is neither fiduciary nor semi-fiduciary (on this terminology see para 6.33 (Nature of powers of consent)) so the appointor is not subject to any legal restraint in the motive or purpose for which the power is exercised, and may exercise the power to suit himself.

Accordingly it is best not to describe powers as 'beneficial' but to use some more precise description. For an example of ambiguity arising from this see *Von Brockdorff v Malcolm* (1885) 30 Ch D 172. 'All the real and personal estate ... over which at the time of my decease, I shall have any *beneficial disposing power* by this my will' – held in context to include a power of appointment which the testator could not exercise for the benefit of himself or his estate.

2 This common thread is slightly disguised as different statutory provisions use different forms of words to describe the administrative/dispositive distinction (although the underlying concept is the same or substantially the same in each case).
(1) *Perpetuities.* The rule against perpetuities does not affect a power to do any act in the administration (as opposed to the distribution) of any trust property: PA(NI) 1966, s 8. (The same distinction should apply in deciding whether any provision offends against the rule against accumulations; but see para 20.28 (Power to pay capital expenses out of income).)

The distinction is of considerable importance for tax purposes, and especially for the drafting of IP and A&M Trusts.

Existence of interest in possession. A beneficiary has an 'interest in possession' where (in short) he is entitled to trust income as it arises. Yet it is rare for a beneficiary to receive all the income of a trust. Some is spent on 'administration', for instance, trustees' and accountancy fees. The fact that income may in fact be withheld from a beneficiary by virtue of administrative provisions is ignored in deciding whether an interest in possession exists.[3]

A&M conditions. The income condition of an A&M trust requires that income must be applied for A&M beneficiaries or accumulated. Again, it is rare that all the trust income is so applied. Income may be spent on 'administration' for instance, trustees' and accountancy fees. Such income is not necessarily spent for the benefit of the A&M beneficiaries and is certainly not accumulated. These matters of administration are ignored in deciding whether the income condition is satisfied. The capital condition of an A&M trust requires that the A&M beneficiaries must become entitled to the trust property or an interest in possession in it. Here too administrative powers are ignored in deciding whether this condition is satisfied. A striking example, which has no Northern Ireland counterpart, is the old statutory power to transfer some trust land to charity.[4] If this power is used, the beneficiaries will not become entitled to all the trust property (or an interest in possession). The Court of Appeal have said that this power does not breach the capital condition because it is administrative.[5]

Tax rules generally. These are only two instances of a broader principle. Tax law lays down rules or exemptions which apply if income or capital are treated in a

(2) *Jurisdiction of court.* The inherent jurisdiction of the court to secure the proper administration of the trust fund is said to allow the court to deal with administrative matters, but not to deal with beneficial interests: *Re Duke of Norfolk* [1982] Ch 61. Likewise the jurisdiction under TA(NI) 1958, s 56 applies only to 'management and administration'.

(3) WAP(NI)O 1994, art 8. A 'beneficial interest' given to a witness of a will (or his spouse) is (generally) void.

(4) *Power of delegation.* Trustees do not have power to delegate 'any function relating to whether or in what way any assets of the trust should be distributed'; TA(NI) 2001, s 11(2)(a).

(5) *Insolvent estates.* Funeral, testamentary and administration expenses have priority over other debts: Administration of Insolvent Estates of Deceased Persons Order (NI) 1991.

(6) *Construction of particular trust.* If any particular trust document refers to administrative or dispositive powers, it then becomes necessary for the purpose of understanding that document to decide which is which. Such clauses are unnecessary and slightly imprecise.

3 *Pearson v IRC* [1980] STC 318; *IRC v Lloyds Private Banking* [1998] STC 559.

4 The power was formerly conferred by SLA 1925, s 55. (Since the TLATA 1996 the power is not expressly conferred on trusts of land, but the authors suggests it can be spelt out of TA 2000, s 8(3). That point is largely theoretical as the power is rarely wanted but this does not spoil the force of the example.)

5 See n 7 below. For a subtle example of this principle in application, see para 14.7 (Does a beneficiary become 'entitled to' property which is applied for his benefit?).

particular way under a trust. In general, one should ignore 'merely' administrative provisions in deciding whether these rules or exemptions apply.[6]

When is a provision administrative or dispositive?

18.3

The administrative/dispositive question arises most commonly in connection with trustees' powers, but it may also be applied to other provisions of the trust.

In general it is clear whether a provision is dispositive or administrative. For example:

(1) A direction to pay income to a beneficiary is a dispositive provision; a power to accumulate income is a dispositive power.

(2) A provision that trustees are not required to supervise companies is an administrative provision; a power of investment is an administrative power.

Yet there are borderline cases. Provisions may be administrative in character even though they impinge on or affect beneficial interests.[7] In such cases it is not obvious whether the provision should be regarded as administrative or not. 'The

6 The administrative/dispositive distinction arises in many tax contexts. Sometimes the statute sets out rules which expressly depend on whether an expense is administrative. There are too many to give a complete list, but for example, see: ICTA 1988, s 686 (referring to 'expenses'); IHTA 1984, s 65(5) ('costs or expenses'); TCGA 1992, Sch, 5, para 9(3) ('expenses relating to administration and taxation'). Often the rule to ignore merely administrative matters is left to be implied. For instance for the purpose of:

(1) ICTA 1988, s 686: income which is retained under an administrative provision is not subject to the tax charge on income which is 'accumulated'. This (it is submitted) is the basis of the Revenue practice that income from mineral rents and timber crops, capitalised under the SLA 1882, is not regarded as 'accumulated' for the purposes of ICTA 1988, s 686.

(2) IHT exemptions: a gift of a residuary estate by will qualifies for the IHT charity or spouse exemption in whole, even though part of the estate is spent on administration and never reaches the spouse or charity.

(3) TCGA 1992, s 225 (private residence relief): 'If trustees allow a beneficiary to occupy a trust property, by the use of their discretionary [ie dispositive] power, private residence relief may be due ... If the trustees allow any third party to occupy trust property, by exercise of their managerial [i.e. administrative] powers, the relief is not due.' (CGT Manual 65454.)

7 *Inglewood v IRC* [1983] STC 133 at 139:

> 'Some administrative powers (eg the power conferred by s 55 of the SLA 1925 to give away small parts of the trust land for public purposes or a power to trustees to apply income for capital purposes) do affect beneficial interests but they are not truly dispositive in nature.'

Russell v IRC [1988] STC 195 at 203:

> '... a power of appropriation is only ancillary and administrative although its exercise can, in times of fluctuating values, have a considerable impact on beneficiaries' rights inter se.'

boundary between administrative action and rewriting the trusts ... is incapable of precise definition'.[8] The approach of the courts may be summed up as pragmatic.

In general, the same line is drawn in all the areas where the distinction is relevant. A provision which is administrative for the purposes of the perpetuity rule is administrative for the purposes of deciding whether a beneficiary has an interest in possession. However, this is not invariably the case, and provisions may be classified as administrative for one purpose and not for another. So they should: different policy considerations may apply in the different cases.[9] A provision for trustee remuneration is in this special category.[10]

In a borderline case, how does one categorise a provision as administrative or dispositive? It has been said that 'what is decisive is the substance of the provision and not the clothes or label which it wears'.[11] That observation, while undoubtedly true, does not take us very far.

There is no single test to determine the question; but a number of relevant factors. One relevant consideration is whether a power which could consume all the income – no matter how much income there is; if so it is a dispositive power. Provisions which can only affect limited amounts of income are likely to be administrative. On this basis the following are all to be considered as administrative.

Power to pay capital expenses out of income

18.4

This is an administrative power permitted in IP and A&M trusts.[12] This power is a very useful one. Trustees often find that they cannot easily realise trust capital to pay capital expenses. (In practice trust income is often used for the purpose, in conscious or unconscious breach of trust.) Trustees can and should be given power to pay capital expenses out of income.

8 *Re Blackwell* [1952] 2 All ER 647. This part of the judgment was approved on appeal in *Re Downshire Settled Estates* [1953] Ch 218.

9 Further, of course, the terms of the relevant statutory provisions are all slightly different. In the same way, the question whether a power is to be classified as 'general' or 'special' may be answered differently for different trust law purposes.

10 Paragraph 20.62 (Trustee remuneration clause: dispositive or administrative?).

11 *IRC v Lloyds Private Banking Ltd* [1998] STC 559. Lord Templeman made the same point in *Street v Mountford* [1985] AC 809 at 819: 'The manufacture of a five-pronged implement for manual digging results in a fork even if the manufacturer, unfamiliar with the English language, insists that he intended to make and has made a spade.'

12 *Pearson v IRC* [1980] STC 318. The Revenue accepts that this is right: ICEAW Guidance Note, 14 December 1992. See para 20.29 (Power to apply trust capital as income).

Retention of income to provide for liabilities or depreciation of a capital asset

18.5

This rather less important power is administrative and so permitted in IP and A&M trusts.[13]

18.6

On the other hand the following powers are not merely administrative: Power to:

- apply income in the purchase or subscription of partly paid shares ...
- use income to pay life assurance premiums ...
- apply income in purchasing any annuity ...
- apply income to improve or develop trust property.

Capital/income and apportionment provisions

18.7

A second general point: trust law lays down various prima facie assumptions – sometimes somewhat arbitrary – which regulate the thorny question of whether a receipt is income or capital; or whether it accrues at one moment of time or another. These assumptions take effect subject to contrary provisions in the trust. Such provisions are administrative, not dispositive, if the drafter has merely adopted a different definition of the amorphous concept 'income' (or 'accrual'), which in principle is as legitimate as the general trust law definition. Here are common examples. Exclusion of the statutory apportionment rules is a matter of administration.[14] This is an important provision and should not be omitted out of a super-abundance of caution. The exclusion of the equitable apportionment rules is also an administrative provision.[15] A provision that a dividend in the course of an exempt demerger is capital is likewise an administrative provision.[16]

13 *Miller v IRC* [1987] STC 108; the Revenue accepts this: see n 3 above.

14 The arguments to this effect, which are overwhelming, are set out in detail in Kessler *The Personal Tax Planning Review* (Vol 2) p 171, accessible on www.kessler.co.uk. This view was evidently shared by the drafter of Form 8 of the Statutory Will Forms 1925, accessible on www.kessler.co.uk who described such forms as '*administration trusts*'. For the drafting of the provision, see para 20.54 (Statutory apportionment).

15 Paragraph 20.32 (Equitable apportionment).

16 See para 20.34 (Demergers).

Power of appropriation

18.8

It is suggested that the power of appropriation should be regarded as administrative, but the position is unclear.[17] Fortunately it rarely matters.[18]

IP trusts: 'departure' v 'disqualifying' powers

18.9

Any administrative provision can be included in an IP trust. We can now turn to consider what non-administrative powers may safely be included in IP trusts. Non-administrative (ie dispositive) powers must themselves be divided into two categories:[19]

(1) trustees may have some power which allows them to withhold trust income from the beneficiary as it arises. The beneficiary cannot then have an interest in possession. This is here called a *Disqualifying Power*. An example is a common form power of accumulation;

(2) trustees may have some power which may allow them to withhold trust income from the beneficiary at some time in the future. The beneficiary has an interest in possession until that time comes. For the beneficiary is in the meantime entitled to trust income as it arises. This is here called a *Departure Power*. Standard form powers of appointment, advancement and resettlement are clear examples of departure powers. Such powers are consistent with an interest in possession: the life tenant is entitled to all income until the power is exercised.[20]

17 It has been held to be administrative for the purposes of TA 1925, s 57 (the English equivalent of TA(NI) 1958, s 56): *Re Thomas* [1930] 1 Ch 194. Likewise *Russell v IRC* [1988] STC 195 at 203. (The Court of Appeal took the opposite view in *Re Freeston* [1978] 1 WLR 741, but this appears to be *obiter*, lacking any discussion or citation of authority, and overlooking the principle that a provision which may affect beneficial interests can nonetheless qualify as 'administrative'. So the decision in *Re Thomas* is to be preferred.)

18 The question arises where one beneficiary becomes entitled to a share of a trust fund, (the other shares being held on continuing substantive trust). According to the Revenue CGT Manual 37530, there is in principle no CGT disposal, under TCGA 1992, s 71, if the trustees have a power of appropriation. The commonest case is an A&M trust for a class of beneficiaries absolutely at 25; and one beneficiary reaches 25, but others are younger. If the Revenue view is right it is best regarded as an exceptional case where the power of appropriation, an administrative provision, has substantial tax consequences; (or else perhaps the power is not merely administrative: see the above footnote). If the Revenue view is right, it will very often prevent a claim for hold-over relief under TCGA 1992, s 260. Is the Revenue view right? The authors respectfully think it is, though the arguments are finely balanced, and despite the terms of the Manual, the Revenue does not seem to take that view in practice. The issue does not arise for precedents of this book: see para 14.6 (Should the A&M beneficiaries become entitled to the property or just to an interest in possession in it?)

19 This important distinction was first clearly drawn in Richard Oerton, 'Safety Net Clauses' (1992) Trusts & Estates 66 and the authors gratefully adopt Oerton's terminology here.

20 See para 10.3 (Unnecessary provisions in the power of appointment).

Thus an IP trust may include departure powers. It may not include disqualifying powers. Whether a power is a disqualifying power or a departure power is sometimes difficult to discuss in the abstract: a great deal depends on the words used in each case.

Powers to pay insurance premiums out of income

18.10

There are two types of policy. *Administrative* policies (authors' terminology). For instance:

(a) a term policy;
(b) a policy used as a sinking fund against a wasting asset.

Power to pay premiums on an administrative policy out of income is administrative.

Other policies (essentially investments). A power to pay premiums on such policies out of income is a dispositive power. This power may be framed as a departure power, or a disqualifying power, depending on the words used. The actual effect of old common form clauses is uncertain.[21] The drafter should avoid these problems by ensuring that the interest in possession trust does not contain a wide power to pay life insurance premiums out of income.

Power to permit beneficiary to occupy or use trust property rent free

18.11

The power to allow a beneficiary to reside in trust property rent free is obviously a dispositive power. It is a departure power rather than a disqualifying power. Its

21 Older trusts often provided that:

> 'The trustees may pay life assurance premiums out of trust income.'

What is the effect of this if included in an ordinary interest in possession trust? At least three views are possible:

(1) the power is exercisable at any time. In this case, the power is a disqualifying power and the beneficiary does not have an interest in possession;
(2) the power is only exercisable if the trustees hold a life assurance policy, and only to the extent that there are premiums payable under the policy. In this case, the beneficiary has an interest in possession until the trustees acquire a life assurance policy. Thereafter his interest in possession will be restricted in part or in whole;
(3) the power is only exercisable if the trustees hold a life assurance policy, and only in respect of income arising after the trustees have resolved to make payments out of income. In this case, the beneficiary has an interest in possession until the trustees resolve to use the power.

The point is not covered by authority. In practice, the Revenue officially takes view (2) but might be persuaded not to take the point: see Inland Revenue Manuals E.61ff. This will normally benefit the taxpayer and so it will not often be challenged.

mere existence does not stop a person from having an interest in possession, though its exercise may do so, and may indeed confer an interest in possession on the new occupier.[22]

The best course, in drafting an IP trust, is to restrict the power so only the life tenant can be allowed rent free occupation in trust property. Then no difficult questions arise.

The same considerations apply to powers to allow beneficiaries to enjoy chattels or other trust property *in specie*.

Power to lend money interest free

18.12

A power to lend money interest free is not a disqualifying power. It is probably a departure power and arguably may be exercised so as to confer an interest in possession on the borrower. The best course in drafting an IP trust is to restrict the trustees' powers so that they can only lend interest free to the life tenant. Then no difficult questions can arise.

Power to waive income

18.13

Trustees sometimes have power to waive income before that income falls due. Such a power is arguably consistent with an interest in possession. It is not a power to withhold income: it is a power to prevent income arising. However, the position is far from clear. For safety's sake, it is thought that such a power should not be included in an IP trust. The omission should not cause difficulties. The trustees could always waive the income with the consent of the life tenant.

A&M trusts

18.14

Any administrative power may be included in an A&M trust. We can now turn to consider what non-administrative (ie dispositive) powers may safely be included in A&M trusts.

22 SP 10/79. The authors' tentative view is that this is a possible result, but everything depends on the precise circumstances. A written direction entitling a beneficiary to rent free occupation confers an interest in possession. The issue in *IRC v Lloyds Private Banking Ltd* [1998] STC 559 was one of construction, whether the words used in the will had the effect of such a direction.

'Departure' v 'disqualifying' powers

The same terminology can be used: dispositive powers in an A&M trust can be divided into two categories:

(1) a departure power is one which, if exercised, will cause the trust to cease satisfying any A&M conditions;
(2) a disqualifying power is one the existence of which, whether or not actually exercised, prevents the trust from satisfying any A&M conditions.

Power to permit beneficiary to occupy or use trust property rent free

18.15

We have already noted that a power to permit beneficiaries to use or occupy trust property is dispositive. The power raises difficulties under both the income and the capital conditions.

The income condition[23] requires that the income of the settled property is applied for the benefit of A&M beneficiaries (or accumulated). So long as trust property is enjoyed in kind, it will not produce income. How does the income condition operate then? It is suggested that the word 'income' in the income condition should be taken to refer to the use or enjoyment of trust property rent free; for such use and enjoyment is analogous to income.[24] If this is correct, the effect of the income condition is that trust property may only be enjoyed in kind by A&M beneficiaries. A power to allow beneficiaries who are not A&M beneficiaries to enjoy trust property on beneficial terms is a disqualifying power and breaches the income condition.

The capital condition raises a similar difficulty. A power of this kind may in principle be used to confer an interest in possession. If it can be used to benefit beneficiaries who are not A&M beneficiaries, the trust breaches the capital condition. It seems to be current Revenue practice not to take this point, but it is possible that they will do so in the future; so caution here is essential.

An A&M trust should therefore direct that only A&M beneficiaries can have free use of trust property: if other persons are to use the property, they must pay a market rent for it.

23 Paragraph 14.3 (The 'income' and 'capital' conditions).

24 As Lord Oliver said in *City of London Building Society v Flegg* [1988] AC 54 at 83: 'The beneficiary's possession or occupation is no more than a method of enjoying in specie the rents and profits pending sale in which he is entitled to share' (in relation to a beneficiary under a trust for sale). An economist would regard the right to occupation as 'income': Kay and King *The British Tax System* (5th edn, 1990), p 80, accessible on www.kessler.co.uk. While of course legal and economic concepts of income do differ, it is suggested that the law may have regard to the economists in this situation at least.

Similar considerations apply to powers to allow beneficiaries to use chattels, and powers to make interest-free loans; and to a power to charge property as security for debts and liabilities of beneficiaries.

Power to use income to pay life insurance premiums

18.16

Suppose trustees have power to pay life insurance premiums out of income. Textbooks record a theoretical argument that this power may breach the income condition but nobody believes it.[25] The slightly greater concern is the argument that the power may be inconsistent with an interest in possession, so that it breaches the capital condition (requiring that a beneficiary will become entitled to an interest in possession).[26] The practical solution is that trustees should not be given power to pay life insurance premiums out of income. The absence of this power is not significant in practice.[27]

25 The argument is that:
(1) the payment of a life insurance premium out of income will not (usually) be the application of income for the exclusive benefit of A&M beneficiaries; and
(2) the payment of a life insurance premium does not amount to the 'accumulation' of income.

Support for this view could be drawn from *Bassil v Lister* (1851) 9 Hare 177, 68 ER 464 discussed in *Carver v Duncan* (1983) 59 TC at 166, but it is not convincing. The Revenue agrees: CTO Advanced Instruction Manual E.64.

26 See para 18.10 (Power to pay insurance premiums out of income). CTO Manual E.64 is intriguing:

> 'In the light of this, and of the judgement of the Court of Appeal in *Inglewood v IRC* [1983] 1 WLR 366 the **mere existence** of a power to pay life policy premiums out of income **may** prevent a trust from satisfying the condition in IHTA 1984, s 71(1)(a), because it renders it uncertain whether the beneficiary will acquire an interest in possession on or before attaining the specified age.
>
> The text at this point has been withdrawn under the Code of Practice on Access to Government Information.
>
> **E.65. Practice (England and Wales)**
>
> You may concede, however, that IHTA 1984 s 71 is satisfied in cases where:
> (i) the parties agree that in the circumstances of the particular case, the power can be exercised only for **purely administrative purposes** of the sort illustrated above or
> (ii) they accept that the application of the rules against excessive accumulations precludes the exercise of the power after the beneficiary has attained 25 or
> (iii) the powers of the trustees are subject to a general restriction if their exercise would infringe the conditions for relief.'

(Emphasis in original.)

What is it that the Revenue does not want us to know? I guess it is an instruction not to take the point unless the taxpayer is arguing inconsistently for the benefit of an interest in possession when it suits him but not when it does not.

27 The same result can generally be achieved by first accumulating the income, turning it into capital, and then investing the capital in the insurance policy.

Protection clauses

18.17

In an ideal world a drafter would know exactly what sort of provisions were permitted in a trust which was intended to qualify as an IP trust, or A&M trust. In practice there are inevitably a few doubtful areas. This has led to 'protection clauses' (or 'safety net' clauses) intended to restrict the terms of a trust so as to satisfy the relevant tax conditions. These clauses have become common since the introduction of capital transfer tax in 1975.

It goes without saying that a protection clause is no substitute for analysing the statutory provisions and framing the trust accordingly. A protection clause is not an essential drafting technique. In the drafts in this book the clauses are not relied upon: their omission would not affect the operation of any of the trusts. However, there is perhaps a possibility that the Revenue might argue that some provision (which the drafter had judged to be satisfactory) breached the relevant conditions. The authors' practice is to include the clause in all types of trusts except standard discretionary trusts.[28]

Drafting and construction of protection clauses

18.18

One sometimes sees in practice a wide protection clause which if literally construed has an extremely restrictive effect which was certainly unintended by the drafter. The question whether such clauses should be literally construed is therefore one of general importance – though of course in any particular case, much will depend on the exact wording. As an example, consider this clause:

> None of the trusts, powers and discretions conferred upon or vested in the Trustees shall be capable of exercise in any way such as will or may directly or indirectly prevent Section 71 of the Inheritance Tax Act 1984 from applying or continuing to apply to the Trust Fund.

Literally construed, this prevents trustees exercising their power of advancement to transfer trust property to the A&M beneficiaries![29] It is submitted that clauses of this type should not be so literally construed. Otherwise the express power of advancement (typically found elsewhere in the trust) is rendered virtually otiose. This construction makes more sense in the context of the scheme of s 71 of the Inheritance Tax Act 1984.

28 In a discretionary trust there are no uncertain conditions to be satisfied.

29 Since s 71 ceases to apply to property so advanced.

The moral is that one should take care not to make protection clauses unduly wide. The approach in this book is to apply the restrictions of the protection clause only to what are intended to be the administrative powers of the trust. The safety net clause is there in case unintended dispositive powers have found their way in. No advantage can be seen in imposing any restriction on the beneficial provisions. In the case of a simple IP trust, this is plainly unnecessary. In the case of an A&M trust, which is a more complex matter, the imposition of a protection clause on the beneficial provision may lead to uncertainty.[30]

We have already mentioned the distinction between disqualifying and departure powers. Richard Oerton[31] rightly points out that there is no need for a protection clause to restrict departure powers. Unfortunately the drafting of the clause distinguishing between the two types of power is somewhat cumbersome.[32] The form in this book does not discriminate and applies to both sorts of power. Our protection clause is therefore wider than it strictly need be. This does not matter since the clause – restricted as it is to administrative provisions – is only for the avoidance of doubt and has no discernable practical effect.

Interest in possession protection clause

18.19

The form used in this book is as follows:

> The powers conferred by this schedule[33] shall not be exercisable so as to prevent a Beneficiary from being entitled to an interest in possession in Trust Property (within the meaning of the Inheritance Tax Act 1984).

30 In particular, if the Revenue view of the capital condition is correct, a wide A&M protection clause would render invalid the most important power to give a beneficiary trust property (or an interest in possession in it) before the age of 25! See para 14.6, n 8. The Revenue may apply the concession to the construction of the trust deed; but the beneficiaries would not be bound by this: what are the trustees then to do?

A similar point arises when drafting an employee trust, (satisfying the conditions of IHTA 1984, s 86); or a disabled trust (satisfying the conditions of IHTA 1984, s 89, or TCGA 1992, Sch 1, para 1). It is tempting to introduce a wide protection clause: so that nothing in the trust can cause the trust to lose the benefit of the relevant statutory conditions. If the statutory conditions are not entirely free from doubt, the drafter should hesitate before introducing the uncertain statutory provisions into the heart of the trust. The result is a trust deed the meaning of which is unclear: fiscal certainty may be purchased at too high a price.

31 Richard Oerton, 'Safety Net Clauses' Trusts & Estates 66 (1992).

32 The Oerton form is in outline:

> 'If during any period the mere existence of any powers given to the Trustees in relation to this settlement would be enough (without their exercise) to prevent (and would be the only thing preventing) the conditions stated in section 71, IHTA 1984 from being satisfied in respect of the property comprised in the trust or some part of it then during that period those powers shall be restricted (in relation to that property or that part) so far as may be necessary to avoid that result.'

33 This will be the Schedule of administrative powers in the precedents used in this book.

It is not strictly necessary to define 'interest in possession' which is a familiar term in our law. But the IHTA 1984 gives a special meaning to the phrase,[34] so a referential definition is desirable.

It is not necessary to say: 'the IHTA 1984 *or any modification or re-enactment thereof*' as those words are implied.[35]

A&M protection clause

18.20

The form used in this book is as follows:

> The provisions of this Schedule shall not have effect:
> (a) so as to prevent a Beneficiary from being entitled to an interest in possession in Trust Property (within the meaning of the Inheritance Tax Act 1984); or
> (b) so as to prevent the conditions of Section 71(1) of the Inheritance Tax Act 1984 from applying to Trust Property.

It is submitted that the provisions of the trust dealing with beneficial interests should not be subject to any A&M protection clause.

'No conflict' clause

18.21

One sometimes sees forms like this:

> The provisions of the schedule below shall not take effect so as to conflict with the beneficial provisions of this settlement.

> Nothing in the schedule hereto shall authorise any of the Trust Fund or income to be dealt with in a manner inconsistent with the beneficial provisions applicable to the Trust Fund.

The effect of this 'no conflict' clause naturally depends on what is in 'the schedule' to which it refers. The provisions will be largely administrative in nature. 'Administrative' and 'beneficial' provisions are mutually exclusive categories. Administrative provisions aid beneficial provisions and do not conflict with them

34 IHTA 1984, s 50. The expression is used in the CGT legislation and in the 1925 property legislation without definition.
35 Interpretation Act 1978, ss 17, 23.

or destroy them. This is bolstered by a presumption, a rule of construction – which does not need to be stated expressly in a trust – that provisions contained in a section of a trust dealing with administration would be administrative and would not be construed to conflict with beneficial provisions.[36] In the authors' view, therefore, administrative provisions are not affected by the no conflict clause.[37] Dispositive provisions do conflict and would be restricted by the clause.

This form is intended to perform the same task as a protection clause. It is submitted that it should be construed to have this effect. In an IP trust, the form will prevent powers in the schedule from being exercised in a way which would prevent the life tenant from having an interest in possession. In an A&M trust, the form would prevent the powers from being exercised in such a way as to lose A&M status.[38]

Where there is a protection clause, as in the precedents in this book, there is no need for a no-conflict clause. The form is also too vague to be satisfactory and it is not used in this book.

CGT protection clause

18.22

> The powers conferred by this schedule shall not be exercisable so as to cause the settlement to be an accumulation or discretionary settlement (within the meaning of section 5 of the Taxation of Chargeable Gains Act 1992).

This clause is obsolete. It related to the foolish rule (introduced in 1988 and abolished 10 years later) that an accumulation or discretionary trust paid CGT at a higher rate than an IP trust. Where the form is still used no harm is done.

36 This presumption is supported by common sense, and authority: *Miller v IRC* [1987] STC 108 at 112; *Inglewood v IRC* [1983] STC 133 at 139.

37 But provisions properly classified as 'administrative' may nonetheless affect a beneficiary's entitlement very substantially; and in such cases some might argue that there is a 'conflict'. An esoteric example is the power conferred by SLA 1925, s 55, to give away small parts of the trust land for public purposes. This is an administrative power (per Fox LJ, *Inglewood v IRC* [1983] STC 133 at 139), but one which may be said to conflict with beneficial provisions. If so the effect of the 'no conflict' clause is to restrict the s 55 power.

38 For instance, suppose (i) a beneficial provision directs trustees to pay income to A; and (ii) a power in the Schedule (subject to the no conflict clause) permits trustees to allow A, B or C to reside in trust property. The power could not be used to allow B or C to reside, as that would conflict with the beneficial provisions: para 18.15 (Power to permit beneficiary to occupy or use trust property rent free).

Suppose (i) a beneficial provision directing trustees to hold trust property on trust for A contingently upon attaining 25; and (ii) the Schedule (subject to the no conflict clause) confers on the trustees the statutory power of advancement. It is suggested that the power of advancement could be used and that would not 'conflict' with the beneficial provisions. This is consistent with the comment of the Court of Appeal in *Inglewood v IRC* [1983] STC 133 that the power of advancement is 'like an administrative power'. But the contrary is arguable. Compare *Re Batty* [1952] Ch 280 where the power of advancement is described as 'confiscatory'.

CHAPTER 19

Will trusts

Overview

19.1

There are seven forms of will trust which will usually be the most satisfactory choices in any normal but reasonably substantial estate:

(1) *Discretionary will trust.* This is a suitable form for a testator who is not married.

(2) *Life interest for surviving spouse.* This form is simple and adequate for a married testator, but arrangements would have to be made after the death of the testator to use his nil-rate band. Forms (3) to (6), which include nil-rate band gifts, are better.

(3) *Life interest for surviving spouse; absolute gift of nil-rate band.* This form is simple and adequate for a married testator. However, it is only suitable where (1) the family assets are sufficiently large that the surviving spouse does not need access to the nil-rate band fund and (2) the children of the testator are adult and settled in life, so it is appropriate to give them the nil rate sum absolutely.

(4) *Life interest for surviving spouse; nil-rate band discretionary trust.* This is generally the best form for a married testator.

(5) *Nil-rate band discretionary trust; residue to surviving spouse absolutely.* An alternative to (4) more suited to a married testator with a smaller estate or who wants simplicity.

(6) *Nil-rate band discretionary trust; residue to surviving spouse absolutely or to discretionary trust (if no surviving spouse)*. Better than Form (5), though more complex, this provides appropriate flexibility if the spouse does not survive.

(7) Nil-rate band discretionary trust; residue to unmarried partner absolutely.

Will trusts and lifetime trusts: drafting differences

19.2

A will trust is, of course, a different matter from a lifetime trust. It takes effect in different circumstances – the testator *ex hypothesi* being dead at the time – and there are specific rules which apply only to wills. Tax considerations are different. These factors, however, do not cause many differences between the drafting of will trusts and lifetime settlements.

A handful of minor drafting points:

- one refers to the 'testator' rather than the settlor. ('Testator' will serve for both sexes and 'testatrix' should be best regarded as obsolete.[1]);
- the perpetuity period (which doubles as the accumulation period) runs from the date of the testator's death;
- the will has no settlor exclusion clause; for the settlor *ex hypothesi* will not benefit from his own will.;
- the will is traditionally drafted in the first person, so one refers to 'my trustees' instead of 'the trustees', 'my residuary estate', etc; a convention of no significance and not fully adopted in this book;
- there are conventionally no recitals in wills; these are unnecessary in a lifetime settlement, so their omission does not matter. It follows that there is no testatum ('now this deed witnesses ...') whose purpose is to indicate where the recitals end and the body of the document begins.

The great distinction in common practice is that a lifetime trust is generally a lengthy document, drawn up with some care; a will trust is too often a short document and drawn up without much thought. This is usually the explanation of deficiencies of wills met in practice, as well as the routine absence of good drafting techniques, such as a definition clause or the use of a schedule of administrative provisions.[2] This practice has been castigated[3] but still continues. The drafter's first duty is to produce a will that suits his client's needs. However, the drafter (and authors of drafting books) must recognise commercial reality and seek to devise forms of wills which are technically adequate and approach the simplicity that the client would like to see.

In this chapter it is assumed that the client has at least a reasonably substantial estate.

1 Following Garner *Modern Legal Usage* (2nd edn, 1995) (article under 'Testatrix').

2 Perhaps in the past the use of Schedules was discouraged by the rule that the will had to be signed at the 'foot or end thereof,' but that rule has been abolished, and it is now clear that a will may be signed either before or after the Schedule: WAP(NI)O 1994, art 5.

3 'Trusts appear in wills as well as in lifetime settlements, and of course they need to be drafted with as much skill and care in either place; yet by tradition, solicitors and public alike seem to treat settlements as being specialised and difficult and wills as being so easy that they can be drafted by almost anyone and given away with packets of cornflakes ...' (Richard Oerton, (1993) New Law Journal, 19 February, p 246.) Indeed, if anything, will trusts are harder to draft than lifetime settlements, as the drafter has to look ahead to the time of the death of the testator and cater for a much wider variety of circumstances.

Foreign trustees

19.3

In very large estates serious consideration should be given to the appointment by the will of non-resident trustees. (The executors may, if preferred, be UK residents.) This offers the possibility of substantial tax savings.

Best form of will for unmarried testator

19.4

The best form of will where a testator is not married, and wishes to benefit his family or other individuals, is generally a discretionary will trust of the entire residuary estate. This allows the decision of what to do with the property to be made after the death.[4] Then so long as IHTA 1984, s 144 remains in force, the testator need not in principle revise his will to take into account changes in circumstances or tax law. The drafting is straightforward: see Form 1 in the precedents.

A possibility for unmarried co-habitees is a nil-rate band discretionary trust with an absolute gift of residue to the testator's partner: see Form 7.[5]

Bad form of will for unmarried testator

19.5

A form of will which the authors consider unsuitable for substantial estates is one giving the estate to children absolutely at the age of 18 or 25. This ignores the needs of grandchildren and spouses of children and creates real tax difficulties.[6]

Best forms of will for married testator

19.6

Where the testator is married, a discretionary will trust of the residuary estate is firmly *not* the authors' preferred choice, as:

4 IHTA 1984, s 144.

5 This is the unmarried co-habitee's equivalent of Form 5. IHT is payable on the first death but this does avoid 'bunching' – the additional IHT payable on the second death which would arise if the first co-habitee gives everything by will to his partner. Of course the same result can be achieved by a simple discretionary will trust followed later by a deed of appointment.

6 The difficulties and a possible solution are discussed in para 14.6 (Should A&M beneficiaries become entitled to trust property or just to an interest in possession in it?).

(1) the process of obtaining probate is easier if the widow has an interest in possession in the entire estate apart from the nil-rate band;[7]
(2) IHT planning after the testator's death is made rather more difficult; and
(3) the almost inevitable execution of a deed of appointment involves additional legal work and expense.[8]

The most appropriate form of will for a married testator is in principle as follows:
(1) personal chattels pass to the surviving spouse absolutely;[9]
(2) gift or gifts to use the nil-rate band;
(3) residue to pass to will trust under which:
   (a) the surviving spouse has an interest in possession;
   (b) subject to that there are discretionary trusts.

In result there is no IHT on the death of the testator if his spouse survives him.[10] There is also scope for further IHT planning, eg, the will trustees may terminate the spouse's interest. The form is Form 3 or 4 in the precedents below. Form 3 makes absolute gifts of the nil-rate band, which is simpler. Form 4 creates a discretionary trust of the nil-rate band, which is more complicated but necessary if the widow may need access to the nil-rate fund or if the children cannot be trusted with that money.

7 IHT must be paid up front in order to obtain probate; and the tax is then reclaimed after execution of the appointment in favour of the spouse. Occasionally in practice the Inland Revenue Account is completed on the basis that an appointment in favour of a spouse will be made and IHT is not paid up front. It seems that this leads to no worse sanction than admonition: ('I trust you will take note of this for future cases' – see the curiously named *CTO General Examination Manual*, Vol 2, reference SL 64). But correct practice should be followed, since otherwise (i) the solicitor involved is submitting an incorrect return, which should never be done knowingly; and (ii) there remains a risk of penalties if the appointment is not made because (say) the surviving spouse unexpectedly dies.

The problem can in principle be avoided by an appropriate appointment executed (i) before obtaining probate; and (ii) after three months have elapsed from the death. (A deed within three months does not qualify for the relief. A literalist Court of Appeal in *Frankland v IRC* [1997] STC 1450 refused to read words into the statute to avoid this result which is plainly absurd and could not have been the intention of Parliament. Statutory reform on this point is overdue.)

8 These objections do not apply if the entire estate falls within the nil-rate band. In such a case the simple discretionary trust (Form 1) has the same effect as the more complex Forms 4-7. In many cases one will prefer the more complex Form as one cannot be confident that the value of the estate at the time of death will be within the nil-rate band.

9 This must be the most convenient course unless there are any particular valuable items in the personal chattels.

10 IHTA 1984, s 18 (spouse exemption). This exemption does not apply if a UK domiciled testator leaves a foreign domiciled spouse: s 18(2). Remember that this includes a spouse who is domiciled in the Republic of Ireland. See on foreign domiciliaries generally Kessler *Taxation of Foreign Domiciliaries* (2nd edn, 2003) Key Haven Publications.

Simpler forms of will for married testator

19.7

If the estate is relatively modest, an appropriate form is:
(1) nil-rate band discretionary trust; and
(2) residue to spouse absolutely.
Then there is only one settled fund, and not two. The form is Form 5 or 6 in the Precedents below.

There is another relatively simple form of will which the authors would regard as acceptable. This is to give the entire estate to a trust under which the spouse has an interest in possession. This is much simpler: there is no need for the nil rate formula, and the separate trusts of the nil rate sum. On the death of the testator, it is still possible to use his nil-rate band. The widow may disclaim her interest in the appropriate part of the testator's estate.[11] The authors' preference would be to make the nil rate gift in the will. The cost of the simple will is additional legal work at the time the will takes effect. But some clients may prefer the simpler will. A form along these lines is also appropriate for a married couple who wish their entire[12] estates to pass to charity on the death of the survivor. The form is Form 2 in the Precedents below.

Bad forms of will for married testator

19.8

A form of will which the authors consider unsuitable for substantial estates is one giving the estate to the spouse absolutely. Of course she could make a deed of variation after the death, so as to use the nil-rate band. The problems arising are foreseeable. For various reasons, the spouse may not make the necessary arrangements. A deed of variation is not effective for income tax or (arguably[13]) the CGT settlement provisions.

An even worse form of will for a married testator is one making chargeable gifts in excess of the nil-rate band (ie not to spouse or UK charities). The usual case is where the testator has remarried and makes substantial gifts to his children by his

11 Paragraph 20.53 (Power to disclaim). The disclaimer must be done before the widow takes any benefit under the will. Alternatively the same result can be achieved by a deed of variation. In neither case do the IHT gift with reservation rules apply.

12 Or the entire estates less gifts within the limit of one nil-rate band payable on the death of the survivor.

13 The interesting question of 'who is the settlor' of a settlement made by a deed of variation is discussed in Kessler *Taxation of Foreign Domiciliaries* (2nd edn, 2003) Key Haven Publications, ch 3.

first marriage. This gives rise to unnecessary IHT[14] on the death of the testator. There are two better ways to deal with this situation. The testator may give a short interest in possession to his spouse (eg to pay income to her for three months) and subject to that for (say) the children absolutely. Alternatively the testator could give a revocable life interest to the spouse and leave a letter of wishes requesting the trustees to make an appropriate appointment in favour of (say) the children. In either case there will be no IHT on the death of the testator if the spouse survives him. The spouse exemption will apply,[15] and the termination of the spouse's interest later will be a PET. Either of these two solutions is satisfactory and it does not matter much which are chosen. The authors suggests the former solution where smaller sums are involved and the latter where larger sums are involved because it gives more flexibility. That course does, however, require the testator to rely wholly on his executors.

Nil-rate band gifts

19.9

Basic IHT planning for husband and wife requires that each should make full use of the nil-rate band. The nil-rate band (2003/04) is £255,000 so use of nil-rate band may save tax of £102,000. Two steps are needed to achieve this saving. First, the spouses must equalise their estates, or at least put the equivalent of the nil-rate band into each, (including, ideally, a half share of the family home held as tenants in common.) Secondly, there should be a suitable will. (An unsuitable will can generally be put right by a deed of variation but it is better to draft a suitable will in the first place.)

The nil rate formula

It cannot be known what the nil-rate band will be at the time of the death; or how much of it will be available in the circumstances of the testator. Since testators cannot be asked to review their wills each year, normal practice is to give a legacy of a sum of money fixed by a formula to equal the available nil-rate band.

This is easy enough in principle:

> 'The Nil Rate Sum' means the maximum amount of cash which I can give on the terms of the Nil Rate Fund without incurring any liability to Inheritance Tax on my death.

14 If this bad form of will is made it is possible to put matters right by a deed of variation, but this may involve a good deal of legal work and expense.

15 IHTA 1984, s 143 will not override the spouse exemption: *Harding v IRC* [1997] STC (SCD) 321. The only complication is the loss of the spouse's nil-rate band if she dies within seven years of the PET: see para 30.11 (Arrangement for loss of nil-rate band).

Nil-rate band gifts are inappropriate unless the testator is married at the time of his death. It is possible that IHT may be abolished, in which case the form is not wanted. It is also worthwhile putting in a small minimum limit, to save executors having to deal with trivial amounts. All this is easy to provide for.

The difficulty with the use of a formula is its inherent uncertainty. The nil rate may be increased substantially: some lobbyists have called for a £500,000 limit.[16] It may be substantially reduced. So the will should be drafted so that it still works satisfactorily even if the amount of the nil rate sum turns out to be substantially more or less than expected. This is best achieved in the following manner:

(1) The nil rate gift should be given to *a discretionary trust for the benefit of the widow and the family of the testator*. Except perhaps in very substantial estates, where the widow would not need the nil rate sum, it should not be given to the children absolutely, or to a trust for the benefit of the family excluding the widow. Thus no member of the testator's family need be prejudiced by an unexpected increase in the nil-rate band.

(2) Other legacies in the will should be given priority to the nil rate sum. Thus other legatees will not be prejudiced by an unanticipated increase in the nil-rate band.[17]

The nil rate sum is therefore defined in the following manner:

> (1) 'The Nil Rate Sum' means the maximum amount of cash which I can give on the terms of the Nil Rate Fund without incurring any liability to Inheritance Tax on my death, but subject to the following clauses.
> (2) The Nil Rate Sum shall be nil if:
>   (a) Inheritance Tax has been abolished at the time of my death; or
>   (b) I am not married at the time of my death; or
>   (c) The amount of Nil Rate Sum would otherwise be less than £5,000.
> (3) Any other legacy given by my will or any codicil shall be paid in priority to the Nil Rate Sum.

Terms on which nil rate sum is held

19.10

There are two ways to give the nil rate sum to a discretionary trust:

(1) the nil rate sum may be given to a lifetime trust in existence at the time the will is made. In practice this normally involves creating a trust (known as 'a pilot trust') with a nominal trust fund;

16 In addition, the nil rate sum may effectively increase if the testator owns business or agricultural property at the time of his death, or if he has acquired a foreign domicile.

17 An alternative is to put a cap on the formula, so the amount given will not exceed a specified amount. This approach is adopted in Will Form 3.

(2) the nil rate sum may be held on terms set out in the will.[18]

It makes little difference which is chosen, from a trust or a tax viewpoint.[19] The forms in this book make the gift to a discretionary trust declared in the will, which seems much the easier course.

The will may also provide that the widow will have an interest in possession in the residuary estate. The drafter then has another choice:

(1) the will may create two separate trusts, a trust of the nil rate sum and a trust of the residuary estate;
(2) the will may create one single trust with two funds, a nil rate fund and a residuary fund.

It makes little difference from a trust or a tax viewpoint, and the balance of convenience favours a single trust with two funds (sometimes called 'sub-funds').

Loan and charge arrangements

19.11

Let us look ahead to the time where a will with a nil-rate band gift comes into effect. The executors will be required in principle to raise the nil rate sum, to hold on discretionary trusts. Alternatively they may appropriate assets to that value to the trust. A share in the family home should not be appropriated as the Revenue currently contends – though with diminishing enthusiasm – that a beneficiary occupying the property has an interest in possession in it.[20]

It will often be impractical to raise such sum or appropriate such assets. Even if practical, it will generally be more convenient to leave the money owed to the nil

18 A common form is:

> 'I give the nil rate Sum to the Trustees to hold on the terms set out below'

This is not needed. It goes back to before Part IV of the Local Registration of Title (Ir) Act 1891 and the Law Reform (Miscellaneous Provisions) Act (NI) 1937, together the equivalent of the English Land Transfer Act 1897. Then real property did not vest automatically in executors, so a testator had to devise it expressly to trustees, if he wanted to create a trust. So even for land the form has been unnecessary for more than 60 years. The meaning of the will is plain enough without it.

19 Note in particular that IHTA 1984, s 80 will apply to the fund in which the surviving spouse has an interest in possession. In consequence, briefly, that fund is treated as being comprised in a trust (i) made when the surviving spouse dies, or when her interest terminates, and (ii) which is treated as a separate trust from the nil-rate band trust.

20 There are very strong arguments against this view, which the Revenue have at least on some occasions accepted. A full discussion is outside the scope of this book: see 'Splitting Up the Family', *Taxation*, Vol 137 (1996) p 113, accessible on www.kessler.co.uk. In the absence of the TLATA 1996 in Northern Ireland an even stronger argument can be mounted against the Revenue view.

rate fund outstanding, as a loan from the surviving spouse or a charge on property passing to the surviving spouse. The advantages are:

(1) the nil rate fund will not produce income, and so it will not be necessary to pay additional rate tax (with associated administrative costs);
(2) it is not necessary to invest the nil rate fund separately, incurring additional investment management costs;
(3) it is not necessary to prepare separate accounts of the nil rate fund, incurring additional accountancy costs.

The loan or charge will often be an extremely attractive course.

This raises six sets of problems. First, the drafter must ensure that the loan or charge is within the powers of the trustees. (A family trustee may be prepared to make such loans in breach of trust; a professional trustee could not do so.) The will should pave the way for arrangements of this kind by including appropriate powers for the trustees, and these are contained in Forms 3–6. Secondly, the arrangement must not be a sham. Properly executed arrangements will not be a sham.[21] It would be different if (say) the widow were advised not to bother about the documentation as the funds were 'yours really'.

Secondly, the terms of the trust must not be such as to give the widow of the testator an interest in possession in the loan. Otherwise the entire advantage of the nil-rate band gift is lost. The circumstances in which an interest-free loan can give rise to an interest in possession have not been fully worked out by the courts.

The solution proposed here is that:

(1) (a) in a case where the widow has a life interest in the residuary estate (Will 5/6) there should be separate persons as trustees of the nil rate sum and trustees of the residuary estate;
    (b) in a case where the widow is absolutely entitled to the residuary estate the widow should not be sole executor or trustee of the nil rate trust;
(2) the loan is index linked.

If this is done, it is considered impossible for the Revenue to maintain that the widow has an interest in possession and harder to argue 'sham'.[22]

Thirdly, the arrangement must not fall within FA 1986, s 103 (which disallows certain liabilities for IHT). Fourthly, the debt must not become statute barred. Fifthly, the loan should not constitute a debt on a security for CGT purposes or a 'relevant discounted security' within FA 1996, Sch 13.

21 Kessler, 'What is (and what is not) a Sham' (1999) Offshore & International Taxation Review, Vol 9, p 125, accessible on www.kessler.co.uk.

22 An alternative is that the loan carries interest (though the trustees of the nil rate sum have power to waive the interest before it is paid). It should by no means be conceded that an interest in possession need exist in the absence of all these precautions. In practice the Revenue appear not to take the point.

Just explaining all this to an ordinary testator may be a considerable challenge.

Implementation of loan scheme

19.12

There is an important distinction between Wills 4 and 5-7 which impacts on the implementation of the loan scheme.

(1) in a Will 4 case the residue is retained by the executors in their capacity as the trustees, (who hold on trusts under which the widow has an interest in possession.)

(2) in a Wills 5/6 case the residue is transferred to the widow absolutely and the executors will eventually drop out of the picture.

This affects the way that the nil rate legacy ('NRL') is dealt with.

Implementation of loan scheme in a Will 5-7 case

In the Will 5-7 case there are two main ways of dealing with the NRL:

(1) the widow may promise to pay the NRL personally, so she gets the entire unencumbered residuary estate but has a debt which will be deductible under IHTA 1988, s 5(3).

(2) the NRL may be charged on the testator's interest in the home (so the widow does not have a debt; she does not get the entire unencumbered estate, and the assets she does acquire from the estate are reduced in value by the charge on the testator's interest in the home). This requires a formal charge and the documentation and implementation is rather more complicated.

Of these, (1) is easier except in cases where FA 1986, s 103 is a problem, in which case (2) is necessary.

Implementation of loan scheme in a Will 4 case

In the will 4 case there is a simpler solution. The NRL may simply be left unpaid. One does not need a loan agreement imposing a personal liability on the trustees of the residuary estate, or a formal charge. The NRL is a liability of the residuary estate by virtue of the will, and remains such by an agreement under clause 11 of Will 4.

Liability if the NRL becomes irrecoverable

In the Will 4 case, the trustees of the NRL could not possibly be liable for breach of trust if the NRL becomes unrecoverable (ie the loan is left outstanding and the residuary estate becomes insolvent.) The reason is that the beneficiaries interested in the capital of the NRL are the same as the beneficiaries interested in the capital of the residuary estate. Leaving the loan outstanding is an action which favours the capital beneficiaries of the residuary estate, so what they lose on one side they gain on the other.

Hence an exclusion clause such as in 8.4 or Will 5 (= 9.4 of Will 6) is not needed.

Wills 5-7 contain an exclusion clause to cover this case. It is not really needed; the power to lend is a dispositive power, it is intended to be used to benefit the widow.

Nil-rate band arrangements when the main asset is a family home

19.13

It often happens that a couple can only fully use the nil-rate band by dealing with the family home. This raises a number of difficulties. On one hand, it may be essential to give the surviving spouse security in his home. On the other hand, it is essential not to give him an interest in possession in the property (and a provision giving the surviving spouse the status of sole occupier would give an interest in possession).[23] This happy result is achievable in a number of ways.[24] Nil rate loans are probably the simplest. The Revenue currently does not challenge this, if properly carried out, although it seems that they are revisiting the matter. Another possibility is to arrange that the children have revocable interests in possession.[25] The execution of the arrangements after the death requires care, and this is a matter on which it may be desirable to seek specialist advice.

Commentary: let's abolish nil-rate band discretionary trusts

19.14

Nil-rate band trusts complicate drafting and increase administrative cost, though not out of proportion to the tax saving. There is a simple legislative reform which would make nil-rate band discretionary trusts unnecessary: a transferrable nil-rate band. That is, if H by his will gives his entire estate to W (not using his nil-

23 *IRC v Lloyds Private Banking Ltd* [1998] STC 559. Note that this includes the exclusive 'right of residence' which appears frequently in Northern Ireland wills, especially those of farming testators.

24 For an overview, see a three-part series in *Taxation Practitioner* (Nov 1990–Jan 1991) (James Kessler) accessible on www.kessler.co.uk; Matthew Hutton, 'Revocable Interests in Possession: Some Further Thoughts' 4 PTPR 55, accessible on www.kessler.co.uk.

25 Another possibility is the will gives the property to the children, who settled the property on trust for the widow in a manner which qualifies for the IHT reverter to settlor exemption on the death. In practice this is a more complicated solution (requiring consideration of the obscure FA 1986, ss 102A and 102B) and not often done.

rate band) W should on her death enjoy the unused nil-rate band of H in addition to her own.[26] This is in substance what the device of a nil-rate band discretionary trust achieves. The only objection to this reform can be the loss of tax paid by the estates of those unaware of (or who choose not to take advantage of) existing possibilities for tax planning. IHT payable on the nil-rate band of the first spouse to die may fairly be described as an irrational but voluntary tax. It almost certainly benefits professional advisers more than the Revenue, though to ascertain by how much would be worthwhile empirical research.

Best form of will for married testator with business or agricultural property

19.15

The difficulty with drafting a will of business or agricultural property is that the drafter can have no idea what IHT relief will apply to that property at the time of the testator's death. There is no reason to think that the present rules are destined to endure.

From an IHT viewpoint the ideal form of will for a married person, whose estate includes business or agricultural property, is as follows:

1 a discretionary trust consisting of:
  (1) all property qualifying for 100% business property relief;
  (2) property qualifying for less than 100% relief (up to the nil-rate band);
2 an interest in possession for the widow for the remainder.

Unfortunately the drafting is frightfully complicated because the draft must deal with: (i) assets qualifying for 100% relief; (ii) assets qualifying for 50% relief; (iii) restrictions on relief under section 112 of the IHTA 1984 (excepted assets). The result is not appropriate except for clients whose estates are sufficiently large to justify more than usual care. For ordinary estates, the better course is to use a discretionary will trust, which is simple and nearly as satisfactory. (Some practitioners avoid this course because of the risk that s 144 of the IHTA 1984 may be abolished. But in the authors' view the risk of this is remote; if it happened the worst that would follow would be that the testator has to make a new will.)

Bad form of will for testator with business or agricultural property

19.16

A testator with agricultural or business property should not make a nil-rate band gift in common form. A gift of 'the maximum amount of cash which I can give on

26 Compare the provisions for transfer of the old Married Man's Allowance.

the terms of the Ni Rate Fund without incurring any liability to inheritance tax on my death' will not have the expected effect because of the application of IHTA 1984, s 39A.

Best forms of will making substantial gifts to charity

19.17

Will drafting is straightforward if the entire estate (or the entire estate above the nil-rate band) passes to United Kingdom charities; but there are many difficult questions if the testator wishes to share his estate between charities and individuals who receive more than the nil-rate band. There is much scope for maximising the tax reliefs. Care is also needed for foreign charities. For these problems, and suggested solutions, see *Venables and Kessler on the Taxation of Charities*.[27]

Best form of will for foreign domiciled testator

19.18

A testator not domiciled in the United Kingdom with a substantial estate in the United Kingdom should make two wills:

1. A will governed by Northern Ireland (or English)[28] law to deal with property situate in the United Kingdom. This should be drafted by United Kingdom lawyers in the first instance but reviewed by lawyers in the country of the testator's domicile.
2. A will governed by the law of his domicile, to govern all other property. Such a will should be considered even if there is no such property.

While a single Northern Ireland or English will could be made which deals with United Kingdom and foreign property, there is a risk that problems may arise through ignorance of requirements of the law of domicile. Conversely a foreign will may deal with United Kingdom situate property[29] but the IHT complications are such that the foreign will must be reviewed by United Kingdom lawyers; and it is easier to have a separate Northern Ireland or English will made for the purpose.

The UK will, where the testator is married, should normally give an interest in possession to the spouse; and if appropriate a nil-rate band discretionary trust. In

27 (4th edn, 2003) Key Haven Publications: for details see www.kessler.co.uk.

28 For these purposes the law in the two jurisdictions is identical. Generally the will should be made in the country in which the property is situate.

29 The Wills Act 1963 – which extends to NI – was enacted to make this easier: *inter alia* a will executed in accordance with the law of domicile is treated as properly executed.

other cases, a simple discretionary will trust is probably the best form for the English will.[30]

The UK will should contain a governing law clause: see para 27.1 (Governing law, place of administration and jurisdiction clauses). Both wills should contain declarations of the testator's domicile.[31]

Best form of will for UK domiciled testator with foreign domiciled spouse

19.19

Where a UK domiciled testator has a foreign domiciled spouse – and remember that this includes one domiciled in the Republic of Ireland – the usual IHT spouse exemption will not apply. The choice lies between a discretionary will trust or an absolute gift to the foreign domiciled spouse. The latter is better from a UK tax viewpoint allowing scope for further tax planning. Of course, the impact of the law of the spouse's place of domicile would also need to be considered.[32]

30 For a full discussion of the IHT issues for wills with foreign domicilaries see Kessler *Taxation of Foreign Domicilaries* (2nd edn, 2003) ch 26 (Wills and Deeds of Variation).

31 The recital will be evidence, though not necessarily cogent evidence, of the testator's domicile. This is obvious on principle but if authority is needed, see *IRC v Bullock* 51 TC 522 at 540: 'The declaration as to domicile contained in the Appellant's will is also a matter to be taken into account, although the weight to be attributed to it must depend on the surrounding circumstances.' (Buckley LJ).

Rather than simply recite the foreign domicile, it would be preferable to set out the facts which justify that domicile. The recital should be drafted according to the individual's circumstances, and not taken from a standard precedent. Three examples:

> 'I declare that my domicile is and continues to be the Province of Nova Scotia, Canada, where I was born and brought up, to which Province I intend to return and remain permanently upon my wife's death.' (The form used in the *Bullock* case.)
>
> 'I declare that (i) although I have resided in England since [date] I do not have, and have never had the intention of residing there permanently, and (ii) it is my intention on my retirement to return to my home in Bermuda and to cease to reside in the United Kingdom; and I am domiciled in Bermuda accordingly.'
>
> 'I declare that:
> (1) I was born in and have a domicile of origin in England.
> (2) I have resided in The Bahamas since [date] and intend to reside there permanently.
> Accordingly I am and intend to remain domiciled in the Bahamas.'

32 See Kessler *Taxation of Foreign Domiciliaries* (2nd ed, 2003) Key Haven Publications.

Gifts by will to existing trust[33]

19.20

The will precedents in this book do not make gifts to existing trusts. However, such gifts are sometimes made. Some concern has been caused by the view expressed by one commentator, that one cannot make gifts by will to existing trusts. The following discussion may therefore be of interest.

The leading cases in this area are *Re Edwards*[34] and *Re Schintz*.[35] It is submitted that the rules of law which emerge from these cases are as follows:

(1) A testator cannot make a gift by will to trustees to hold on the terms of a trust made after the will.[36]

(2) A testator cannot make a gift by will to trustees to hold on the terms of a trust
   (a) made before the will, but
   (b) affected by an appointment made after the execution of the will (and before the testator's death).[37]

   Whether a particular gift is of this type is a matter of construction.[38] If a testator purports to make a gift of this type then the gift might be entirely void,[39] or else it may take effect as a gift to the trustees to hold on the terms which had effect at the time the will was made (ignoring the subsequent appointment). In that case the power of appointment may then remain exercisable after the death of the testator.

(3) A testator can make a gift by will to trustees to hold on the terms of a trust made before the will. That trust may confer powers of appointment exercisable (in relation to the estate of the testator) after the death of the testator. This is often done. If (while the testator is still alive) the trustees of a trust make an appointment altering the terms of the trust, it would be necessary to make a new will.[40] This is a trap easily overlooked.

33 See also para 20.6 (Power to accept additional funds).

34 [1948] Ch 440.

35 [1951] Ch 870.

36 This breaches WAP(NI)O 1994, art 5 (unless the trust is executed with the formalities of a will).

37 Unless the power of appointment is exercised in a way which satisfies the formalities for wills, which would require that the testator signed it in the presence of two witnesses. That is not, of course, the position for powers of appointment in common form. The reported cases concern powers of appointment exercisable by the testator. But in principle the same should apply to powers of appointment exercisable by trustees.

38 Suppose the gift is 'to the Trustees of the [name] trust, to hold on the terms of that trust'.
It is considered that this clause as worded will result in the gift being held by the trustees on the terms of the Trust as it stood at the time of the will. For while a will 'speaks and takes effect' from the time of the testator's death, as far as descriptions of property are concerned, it does not 'speak and take effect' from the time of death for other purposes: see art 17 of the WAP(NI) O 1994. Thus the reference in the will to 'the terms of the trust' should be taken to mean the terms of the trust at the time the will was made, so the gift is valid. The cases are reviewed in *Thomas on Powers* (1998) Sweet & Maxwell, 2-19 to 2-38.

39 As in *Re Jones* [1942] Ch 328.

40 Assuming the intention is that the property passing under the will should pass to the terms of the trust as affected by the appointment.

In the drafting, also watch out if the trust holds two or more funds on distinct terms: remember to specify to which fund the gift is made, or how it is shared between the funds.

CHAPTER 20

Administrative provisions

20.1

The administrative powers of trustees conferred by the general law are broadly but not wholly satisfactory. The Trustee Act (Northern Ireland) 2001 improved matters considerably, but the general law still imposes restrictions (sometimes complex and bureaucratic) intended to reduce the risk of mismanagement.[1] The statutory power of delegation is a good example. This approach is well intentioned but misguided. A more serious problem arises if land is held in Northern Ireland on trust for sale in that no powers of management are conferred on the trustees by the general law, a situation which has not been altered by either of the Trustee Acts. Where the general law of trusts fails, it falls to the drafter to ensure that the trust has the administrative provisions needed to allow trustees to manage the trust fund in the best way; and to find a fair balance between trustees and beneficiaries when their interests conflict.

It is convenient to place all the provisions dealing with the administration of the trust in a schedule.[2]

1 Law Com, Report No 260, para 2-19, (Trustees' Powers and Duties) accessible on www.lawcom.gov.uk:

> 'The law must aim to achieve a balance between two factors-
> (1) the desirability of conferring the widest possible investment powers, so that trustees may invest trust assets in whatever manner is appropriate for the trust; and
> (2) the need to ensure that trustees act prudently in safeguarding the capital of the trust.'

See also Powers and Duties of Trustees, Consultation Paper by the Northern Ireland Office of Law Reform (August 2000).

2 Para 9.32 (Schedule of administrative provisions).

Unnecessary provisions

Provisions duplicating the Trustee Acts

20.2

Where the general law already confers powers on trustees, no purpose is served in repeating the terms of the statute at length in the trust. This is often found in trust deeds: probably the drafter is following precedents unrevised since the enactment of the Trustee Act (Northern Ireland) 1958 or its nineteenth century predecessors. Common examples are the power to apportion blended funds[3] and power to ascertain and fix valuations.[4]

Power to insure

20.3

Trustees now have full power to insure trust property.[5]

It is quite common to provide that trustees should not be liable for any loss that may result from a failure to take out insurance. In this book a provision of this kind is intentionally omitted. In the authors' view trustees should be expected to give proper consideration to the question of whether or not to insure trust property. Proper reasons for not taking out insurance may include cost and difficulties of funding. They would not of course be liable for loss if, having considered the matter, they reasonably decided not to insure.[6]

Power to vary investments

20.4

> *The Trustees may vary or transpose the investments for or into others of any nature hereby authorised.*

Wherever trustees have a power to invest, they have by implication power to sell any trust property and invest or reinvest the proceeds.[7] This provision is still found in some precedents.. Perhaps it is thought worthwhile to express clearly what would otherwise only be implied; perhaps the form is retained under the

3 TA (NI) 1958, s 15(1)(b).
4 Para 20.46 (Power of appropriation).
5 TA (NI) 1958, s 19, substituted by TA (NI) 2001, s 37.
6 This is the view of the Law Commission: Law Com, Report No 260, *Trustees' Powers and Duties*, para 6-8, accessible on www.lawcom.gov.uk.
7 *Re Pope* [1911] 2 Ch 442.

influence of obsolete statutory precedent.[8] The provision is sometimes incorporated into the trust-for-sale clause, but it is certainly unnecessary; especially where there is a general power of management.

Power to add powers

20.5

Some trusts give trustees power to confer additional administrative powers. In the precedents in this book such a power is unnecessary. The powers conferred expressly are comprehensive. For good measure the power of appointment can be used to confer additional administrative powers.[9] The power to add powers would do no harm;[10] but the possibility of the power being usefully invoked is so remote that it merits no place in a standard draft.

Power to accept additional funds or onerous property

20.6

> *The Trustees may accept such additional money or investments or other property as may be paid or transferred to them upon the trusts hereof by the settlor or by any other person (including property of an onerous nature) the acceptance of which the Trustees consider to be in the interest of the beneficiaries.*

Trustees do not need express power to accept additions to the trust fund. (If anyone doubts this, let him ask: what remedy would there be for a breach of trust of this kind?)

The power as regards onerous property needs more consideration. The expression 'onerous property' suggests property which may give rise to a liability, such as a lease with tenants' covenant, or shares which are not fully paid up or contaminated land.[11] 'Accepting' such property suggests that on acquiring the property, the trustees become liable for leasehold covenants, calls on the shares, or subject to duties imposed on the owner of the land.

8 Trustee Investments Act 1961, s 1(1), extended to NI by the Trustee (Amendment) Act (NI) 1962 but repealed by TA(NI) 2001. The contemporary provisions in the TA (NI) 2001 have no equivalent.

9 Para 10.2 (Power of appointment).

10 It might be objected that the extent of the power is unclear: the borderline between administrative and dispositive powers is not a precise one. But the *existence* of the power would not give rise to difficulties; and questions of doubt should not arise in practice.

11 The expression 'onerous property' is not a term of art. Contrast the more elaborate definition of 'onerous property' in the Insolvency (NI) Order 1989, art 152.

The trustees could use trust funds to purchase such property. On what basis could it possibly be said that they were not entitled to accept such property if given to them? Possibly the onerous property may have no value or a negative value: it may (in common parlance) be a liability. In that case the trustees could not properly accept it as a gift (unless authorised in specific terms to accept onerous property to the benefit of the 'donee' and to the detriment of the trust fund). It is therefore considered that a general power to accept additional property is unnecessary in a standard draft.[12]

Powers relating to accounts and audits

20.7

For all practical purposes the powers in the Trustee Act (NI) 1958 are sufficient, and no special provision is required.[13]

Powers to deal with shares and debentures

20.8

Section 10(4) of the Trustee Act (NI) 1958 gave trustees a general power to deal with securities:

> Where any securities of a company are subject to a trust, the trustees may concur in any scheme or arrangement –
> (a) for the reconstruction of the company;
> (b) for the sale of all or any part of the property and undertaking of the company to another company;
> (bb) for the acquisition of the securities of the company, or of control thereof by another company;
> (c) for the amalgamation of the company with another company;
> (d) for the release, modification, or variation of any rights, privileges or liabilities attached to the securities or any of them; in like manner as if they were entitled to such securities beneficially ...

'Securities' here meant shares and stocks, but not, it seems, debentures.[14] Some drafters therefore set out at length in their drafts the terms of s 10(4) of the TA

12 The power may be useful in the context of tax avoidance arrangements where it may be particularly important that added property forms part of the trust to which it is added. This is not sufficiently common to merit a place in a standard draft. See also 19.20 (Gifts by will to existing trusts).

13 TA (NI) 1958, s 23(4) provides that trustees may arrange audited accounts every three years or more often if it is reasonable to do so. The power is wide enough to allow trustees to have accounts audited every year if they wish, or produce unaudited accounts, or for a dormant trust, not to produce any accounts at all.

14 TA (NI) 1958, s 67.

(NI) 1958 but with one extension: the term 'securities' is defined to include 'debentures.' This is here called 'the extended s 10(4) power.'

Is the extended s 10(4) power needed? It is thought not. The only reason for s 10(4) is that the proposed arrangements might cause the trustees to acquire new assets in place of their old securities. Those new assets might not be authorised investments. This is the problem which the s 10(4) power was intended to meet.[15]

It follows that where (as is now the case) the trustees have a wide power of investment they do not need the s 10(4) power at all; *a fortiori* they do not need any extension of the power to deal with debentures. This was recognised by the Trustee Act (NI) 2001 which repealed s 10 in its entirety. For good measure, the general power of management would cover this situation. In this book, therefore, the extended s 10(4) power is not adopted.

Unnecessary forms relating to administrative powers

'Powers not restricted by technical rules'

20.9

> *These powers shall not be restricted by any technical rules of interpretation. They shall operate according to the widest generality of which they are capable.*

This form is not desirable: see 3.6 (Construction not restricted by technical rules).

Restricting administrative powers to perpetuity period

20.10

Administrative powers are not subject to the rule against perpetuities and need not be restricted to the perpetuity period.[16]

The following form is therefore unnecessary (though occasionally seen):

> *Any powers set out in Schedule 1 [which contained the usual administrative powers] which are not powers to do acts in the administration of the Trust Fund for the purposes of section 8(1) of the Perpetuities Act (Northern Ireland) 1966 shall be exercisable only during the Trust Period*

15 Wolstenholme and Cherry, *Conveyancing Statutes* (13th ed, 1972) Vol 4, p 10.
16 PA(NI) 1966, s 8(1).

This is the trust drafter showing off; he is only stating what would in any case be the position.

'In addition to the statutory powers'

20.11

One sometimes sees a form that the powers of the trustees conferred by the trust shall be in addition to the powers conferred by statute or by law. This is unnecessary.[17]

Trustees entitled to expenses of exercising powers

20.12

The exercise of a power may involve expense. One sometimes sees an express provision authorising the trustees to incur that expense. Even the parliamentary drafter is not above this practice.[18] However, trustees have a general power to reimburse themselves for all expenses properly incurred when acting on behalf of the trust.[19] Individual 'charging' provisions are therefore unnecessary.

A further issue is whether the expenses should be paid out of income or capital. In the precedents in this book this is dealt with in a separate clause so it is not necessary to address this question in any individual power.

Trustees not liable for loss from exercising powers

This is otiose: see 5.17 (Trustee exemption clauses).

Other provisions

20.13

Some provisions are not permitted in trusts intended to qualify as IP or A&M trusts. Such powers must be avoided in trusts of the appropriate type; they may be included in discretionary trusts. See 18.1 (Provisions Inconsistent with IP A&M

17 TA (NI)1958, s 68(2) already provides that the powers conferred by statute shall be in addition to the powers conferred by the trust.

18 TA(NI) 1958, s 24(1) (repealed): 'Trustees ... may, instead of acting personally, employ and pay an agent ... *and shall be entitled to be allowed and paid all charges and expenses so incurred.* ...'.

19 TA (NI) 2001, s 31; *Dowse v Gorton* [1891] AC 190.

and Discretionary Trusts). For provisions authorising trustees to act negligently, see 5.12 (Conflicts of interest). For power to change the name of a trust, see 9.18. For power to change the perpetuity period, see 8.5 (Power to curtail the trust period).

Void powers

Power to decide between income and capital

20.14

The following power was held to be void as an attempt to oust the jurisdiction of the court[20] :

> The trustees may: –
> (1) determine what articles pass under any specific bequest
> (2) determine whether any moneys are to be considered as capital or income
> (3) determine all questions and matters of doubt arising in the execution of the trusts of my will
>
> and every such determination whether made upon a question actually raised or only implied in the acts or proceedings of the trustees shall be conclusive and binding upon all persons interested under my will.

Accordingly trustees were not entitled, despite the clear terms of this power, to decide whether the proceeds of a sale of timber constituted capital or income. Danckwerts J said:

> the insertion of a clause of this kind ... is not desirable, because it is likely to mislead equally trustees and beneficiaries as to their true position and rights; and, therefore, it would be far better if a clause of this kind was omitted.

So trustees should not be given power to decide whether a sum received by them is income or capital; or whether expenditure is of an income or capital nature. These questions must be decided by the courts; even though it has been said that the courts have not made a particularly good job of answering them.[21] This principle

20 *Re Wynn* [1952] Ch 271. The power set out below is a simplification of the actual form used in *Wynn*. Other parts of the clause (not set out here) repeat provisions of the TA 1925 and were otiose. The division into sub-clauses as set out in the text above is made by the authors and not in the original draft. If the drafter in *Wynn* had divided his long clause into subclauses it would have been easier for him to consider their implications.

21 JA Kay, *Is Complexity in Taxation Inevitable?* (IFS Working Paper 57) accessible on www.kessler.co.uk. Kay is an economist; but few lawyers would disagree. There is a good argument that *Wynn* should not be followed by a modern court, but the drafter should not proceed on that basis. A good study of the older cases is Gover, *A Concise Treatise on the Law of Capital and Income as Between Life Tenant and Remainderman* (sadly the most recent edition is 1933). But modern market practices have blurred the distinction still further.

does not prohibit powers which allow trustees to treat income as capital, or vice versa; see 20.27 (Provisions relating to the income/capital distinction).

Power to determine questions of fact or law or 'matters of doubt'

20.15

The general rule is that trustees should not be given power to determine questions of law. Plainly it is a mistake – though once a common form – to give trustees power to determine 'questions and matters of doubt.'

Trustees may in principle be given power to determine questions of fact. The classic example is a power to make valuations. There is a statutory precedent for this.[22]

In practice many questions are difficult to classify as 'fact' or 'law'. The drafter must tread warily in this area. To be safe, no-one should be given power to determine the meaning of expressions used in a trust. Nor, which is similar, should anyone have power to determine whether a condition of the trust is satisfied. But in special cases the courts will permit this.[23] If the point is likely to be important the general practitioner should seek specialist advice. This book does not employ any provisions using this technique.

Power to make determinations subject to jurisdiction of court

20.16

> The Trustees may (subject to the jurisdiction of the Court) determine whether receipts and liabilities are to be considered as capital or income, and whether expenses ought to be paid out of capital or income. The Trustees shall not be liable for any act done in pursuance of such determination (in the absence of fraud or negligence) even though it shall subsequently be held to have been wrongly made.

This is a power to determine doubtful capital/income issues, but only so far as the law allows. This is not objectionable, but it is of limited effect, so long as *Wynn* is

22 TA (NI) 1958, s 23(3). Trustee Investment Act 1961, s 5 (repealed) is another example.

23 Thus the Court brushed aside a provision that 'my trustees shall be the sole judges of what the term 'advancement in life' may signify': *Molyneux v Fletcher* [1898] 1 QB 648. But the Courts respected a provision that the question whether a person belonged to 'the Jewish Faith' be determined by the Chief Rabbi: *Re Tuck* [1978] Ch 49. The logical basis for this area of law has yet to be fully worked out. This is not the place to summarise the tentative solutions proposed in the cases. The practitioner is fortunate that this area has sparked considerable academic interest and a correspondingly large literature; perhaps equally fortunately, the point arises only rarely in practice.

good law. More importantly, there follows an exclusion of liability for trustees who make erroneous determinations. This may help trust administration.

Power exercisable with consent of court

20.17

The drafter should not direct that any power or provision in the trust should depend on the consent of the court. Such provisions are void.[24]

Which powers should the drafter include?

20.18

It is hard to predict exactly what powers trustees will need, because trustees in different circumstances need different powers. Trusts designed to hold investments, a residence, or shares in a family company each have different requirements.

When drafting administrative provisions two considerations lead the drafter to a policy of all-inclusion. First, circumstances may change. It is easy to see that trust property of one sort may be sold and other property acquired. So broad provisions should be included regardless of current needs. The second motive is the desire for a standard form of trustees' powers; so the drafter can run off his trusts and wills without *too* much consideration of individual circumstances. And since the client pays for the drafter's time and trouble, this consideration is neither selfish nor lazy.

What is the drafter to do? One course is to put every conceivable power in every trust. In the first edition of *Drafting Trusts and Will Trusts* (1992) James Kessler proposed a compromise solution: two standard forms of trustees' administrative powers; a longer form and a short form. The longer form would contain every power which might possibly be desired. In simpler trusts a shorter form would be preferred. One need not pack a wetsuit to cross the Sahara.

STEP Standard Provisions

20.19

A better course is now available in simple cases. This is to use the standard provisions promulgated by the Society of Trust and Estate Practitioners (STEP),

24 *Re Hooker* [1955] Ch 55.

which at the time of writing are being adapted for use in Northern Ireland.[25] A lengthy schedule may then be replaced by the words:

> The standard provisions of the Society of Trust and Estate Practitioners (Northern Ireland version, 1st ed) shall apply.

Standard forms of this type are not an innovation. Standard forms in conveyancing and company documentation are taken for granted. Standard precedents in trust and will drafting are not unknown.[26] The standard form shortens the length of a document; reduces the risk of unfortunate omissions or inclusions; and the lawyer familiar with the standard form will save a considerable amount of time.

On the other hand, if the provisions are set out at length, the material is immediately available for the reader; he need not turn to a separate document to find out the terms of the trust.

Where is the balance of advantage? One suggestion would be to use the STEP Provisions in simple matters, and to set out an express schedule of provisions in more substantial ones. In England the standard provisions are now very widely used in exactly this sort of situation. The course for which there is absolutely no justification is where the drafter failed to provide adequate provisions. This happened far too often in will drafting before the Trustee Act (NI) 2001. The typical will is only two pages long.[27] Now after the Trustee Act (NI) 2001 a trust governed by the general law is more or less adequate, save that a trustee for the sale of land is still devoid of statutory powers of management.[28] Nevertheless the lot of the beneficiaries under such wills would be improved if the wills included the STEP Provisions by reference.[29] This led Professor John Adams to describe the English provisions as 'quite the most exciting development for private client drafters for several decades;' and Ralph Ray to describe them as 'an enormous asset'.[30]

25 The text, set out in Appendix 1, is not final at the time of going to press but will be available on www.kessler.co.uk. The original English version is also published in booklet form (Sweet & Maxwell); *Precedents for the Conveyancer* (Looseleaf); *Wills, Probate and Administration Service* (Looseleaf); 40 (1) *Encyclopaedia of Forms and Precedents* (5th ed, 1997), p 249; and *Administration of Trusts* (looseleaf).

26 Eg TA (NI) 1958, s 34 (protective trusts); LPA 1925, s 179 and; the Statutory Will Forms 1925 (in NI the comparable power given to the Lord Chief Justice by s 42 of the Administration of Estates Act (NI) 1955 has never been exercised); Married Women's Property Act 1882, s 11; Law Society's Standard Conditions of Sale; the English Agricultural Holdings Act 1986, s 7.

27 This was confirmed by Sheena Grattan through a study of wills proved in Northern Ireland in 1997. The position in England is no different, as James Kessler has been informed by the Probate Registry.

28 See 20.1.

29 Such wills generally contain absolute gifts, rather than trusts; but trusts for minors may come about under the WAP(NI) O, art 22.

30 *Taxation*, Vol 138, p 348.

Standard administrative provisions

20.20

We can now turn to consider the standard administrative provisions.

Power of investment

20.21

In the absence of an express power of investment, trustees may now invest in any investment.[31] This is wider than the comparable power contained in the English Trustee Act 2000, which prohibits trustees investing in land outside the United Kingdom.[32] The narrower English approach was influenced by the potential dangers in trustees being allowed to buy land in foreign jurisdictions where the legal system was not geared to trusteeship and may include fixed entitlements on death. The restriction has generally been regarded as misguided and English precedents invariably extend the power of investment to permit trustees to invest in land in any part of the world.

In Northern Ireland it was felt that prohibiting the acquisition of land in the Republic of Ireland without express authorisation could not be justified and so a completely unrestricted power was adopted, leaving the statutory duty of care to control the trustees' decision how to exercise it.

The power of investment used in this book is as follows:

> (1) The Trustees may make any kind of investment that they could make if they were absolutely entitled to the Trust Fund. In particular the Trustees may invest in unsecured loans.
> (2) The Trustees are under no obligation to diversify the Trust Fund.
> (3) The Trustees may invest in speculative or hazardous investments but this power may only be exercised at the time when there are at least two Trustees, or the Trustee is a company carrying on a business which consists of or includes the management of trusts.

The opening sentence echoes the statutory power.[33] The specific extension to unsecured loans is only for the avoidance of doubt.[34] It is unlikely that trustees

31 On the meaning of 'investment' see Andrew Hicks, 'The TA 2000 and the modern meaning of "investment"' [2001] TLI 203, accessible on www.kessler.co.uk.

32 TA 2000, s 3.

33 A power to invest 'in such investments as the trustees think fit' was held to be unlimited without any additional words: *Re Harari* [1949] 1 All ER 430; *Re Peczenick* [1964] 2 All ER 339. For another statutory precedent see Pensions (NI) Order 1995, arts 34.

34 *Khoo Tek Keong v Ch'ng Joo Tuan Neoh* [1934] AC 529, PC The decision was based on the curious ground that a secured loan is, but an unsecured loan is not, an 'investment'. The

would ever want to invest in unsecured loans, but on balance it is preferable to give them clear power to do so if they wish.

There is no rule which requires trustees to diversify trust investments. The rule is that trustees must consider the need for diversification (so far as is appropriate to the circumstances of the trust). Sub-clause (2) is therefore not strictly necessary.[35] Some drafters exclude the duty to *consider* the need for diversification[36] but that is wrong in principle.

20.22

Although wide, the power of investment is restricted by the usual principles applying to fiduciary[37] powers (supplemented by statutory provisions which merely state what the general law would in any case have implied). Accordingly:

(1) Duty to maximise return. The trustees must aim to seek the best return for the beneficiaries, judged in relation to the risks of the investments in question. For instance, they should not invest merely to accommodate the wishes of the settlor.[38]

(2) Prudence. Trustees must in principle be prudent in their choice of investments. This does not mean they must avoid risk altogether, but no more than a 'prudent degree of risk' is acceptable. Trustees must avoid 'hazardous' or 'speculative' investments unless the trust deed confers express authority to do so.

Should the drafter alter this rule? In some cases the settlor or beneficiaries will be entrepreneurs and the trust fund will be invested in their business. In these cases a power to invest in hazardous or speculative investments will be necessary. In other cases the trust fund is a 'nest egg' for the beneficiaries and the settlor would not want the trustees to indulge in anything approaching speculation.

What is the drafter to do? The practice of the authors is to include a clause authorising speculative investments subject to a two-trustee safeguard, though to delete it in appropriate cases.[39]

(3) Duty to select suitable investments. The trustees must have regard to the suitability of the investment to the trust. See s 4(3)(a) of the Trustee Act (NI) 2001. Some

---

concept of 'investment' is much wider than it used to be, and this ground of the decision would not now be adopted in the UK.

35 TA (NI) 2001, s 4(3)(b).

36 TA (NI) 2001 does not state expressly that the duty can be excluded but this should be implied: cf 20.35 (Occupation and use of trust property).

37 On the fiduciary nature of a power despite the 'absolute owner' form , see 5.19 ('Absolute owner' 'beneficial owner' clauses).

38 *Cowan v Scargill* [1985] Ch 270.

39 It is best to resist the temptation to specify the circumstances in which hazardous investments may be made. Even if speculative investments are authorised, the trustees remain under a general duty to seek the best return for the beneficiaries, judged in relation to the risk involved.

drafters direct that this section should not apply, but that is not done here. Plainly, trustees should try to select suitable investments; where the power is expressly excluded the duty of the trustees could hardly be different.

(4) Duty to obtain and consider proper investment advice so far as necessary and appropriate.[40] This, again, does no more than spell out the implications of a fiduciary power in our era of investment sophistication and complexity, and it is not sensible to alter this rule.

Matters not belonging in an investment clause. An investment clause sometimes confers a power to acquire residential property, but this is not the logical place for that power. The acquisition of a residence for a beneficiary is not an 'investment.' The matter is more conveniently covered in a separate clause. Likewise questions of wasting assets, non-income producing assets and joint property are best dealt with in separate clauses. On power to vary investments see 20.4 (Power to vary investments). On the formula 'whether producing income or not': see 20.33 (Balance between income and capital). No express power is needed to acquire insurance policies as an investment.

Power of joint purchase

20.23

The form used in this book is as follows:

> The Trustees may acquire property jointly with any person and may blend Trust Property with other property.

Trustees may wish to acquire property jointly with others or to merge two trust funds together. It is considered that the general power of investment is wide enough to authorise this,[41] but the point is made expressly for the avoidance of doubt.

The clause refers to 'acquiring property' rather than 'investing in property.' The common case of joint property will be the purchase of a residence jointly by trustees and a beneficiary; such a purchase may not, strictly, amount to an 'investment.'

40 TA (NI) 2001, s 5.

41 This was the view of the Law Commission: Law Com, Report No 260, *Trustees' Powers and Duties*, para 2.28. For the position in the absence of such wide general powers, see *Webb v Jonas* (1888) 39 Ch D 660. In *Re Harvey* [1941] 3 All ER 284 the absence of such a power was solved by an application under TA 1925, s 57, the English equivalent to s 56 of the TA (NI) 1958. There is a power in TA (NI) 1958, s 15(1)(b) to apportion blended funds.

General power of management and disposition

20.24

The form used in this book is as follows:

> The Trustees may effect any transaction relating to the management or disposition of Trust Property as if they were absolutely entitled to it.[42]

This general power is still needed in Northern Ireland, both for land and personal property. Statute has conferred on trustees general powers in relation to land in England and Wales,[43] but one of the most unsatisfactory aspects of Northern Ireland trusts law remains the position of trusts of land. It will be recalled that although s 6 of the Settled Land Act 1884 reinstated the power of sale to trustees for sale, it did not confer any powers of management. This position remains unchanged following the enactment of both the Trustee Act (NI) 1958 and the more recent Trustee Act (NI) 2001. Management powers therefore have to be conferred expressly by the trust instrument.

One could attempt to specify and authorise every conceivable form of disposition. This leads to a thesaurus of legal terminology:

> The Trustees may retain or sell, exchange, convey, lease, mortgage, charge, pledge, licence, grant options over and otherwise conduct the management of any real or personal property comprised in the trust fund ...

Section 56 of the Trustee Act (NI) 1958 and s 64 of the English Settled Land Act 1925 are the basis for other precedents to the same effect.

Power to repair and maintain trust property

20.25

There is clear judicial authority that trustees have power to repair and maintain trust property.[44] It is not strictly necessary to make express provision. However, as Northern Ireland has no equivalent to s 6 of the Trusts of Land and Appointment of Trustees Act 1996 the trust practitioner probably prefers to do so. The form used in this book is as follows:

> The Trustees may repair and maintain Trust Property.

42 On the interpretation of these words see 5.20 ('absolute owner' 'beneficial owner' clauses).
43 TLATA 1996, s 6(1). The draft clause is loosely based on this section.
44 *Re Hotchkys* (1886) 32 Ch D 408 at 416-7. In England this principle has been codified for land in TLATA 1996, s 6.

Power to improve trust property

20.26

> The Trustees may develop or improve Trust Property in any way. None of the restrictions contained in sections 25-29 of the Settled Land Act 1882 or sections 13-15 of the Settled Land Act 1890 shall apply.

Trustees normally have power under the general law to make improvements to property other than land.[45] However, the statutory powers in relation to land contained in the Settled Land Acts 1882 and 1890 are rather limited and can cause many difficulties. First, only improvements listed in the Settled Land Acts are allowed. Secondly, they are allowed only if a scheme is approved by the trustees or the court. This form sets out to answer these difficulties by giving the trustees power to improve trust property in any way.

Improvements should be paid out of capital.[46]

It is quite common to find extended provision allowing the cost of improvement to be paid directly out of income:

> *The Trustees may apply capital* **or income** *of the Trust Fund in the improvement or development of Trust Property.*

This raises problems. The power to use income for improvements is dispositive in nature, and inconsistent with an interest in possession.[47] A clause of this kind is best avoided.

Provisions relating to the income/capital distinction

20.27

Under a trust it is frequently necessary to decide whether a receipt or an item of expenditure is one of income or capital. In principle this is a matter of law, to be

45 In that improvement expenditure is generally authorised as an 'investment' under the power of investment. In England trustees now have comprehensive powers to improve land under TLATA 1996, s 6(1).

46 Note that there is no NI equivalent to SLA 1925, s 84(2)(a) and (b) (which is considered to apply even after the TLATA 1996). This empowers trustees in some cases, and requires them in others, to recoup the cost of improvements gradually out of income, by instalments over a period of 25 years. English drafts (such as the STEP Standard Provisions) exclude this rule: 'Capital Expenses need not be paid out of income under s 84(2) of the Settled Land Act 1925, if the Trustees think fit.'

47 The question arises whether the power would be a 'departure' power or a 'disqualifying power'. This would depend on the words used, but in the absence of any clear indication in the wording, the latter is the better view. See 18.9 (IP trusts: 'departure' v 'disqualifying' powers).

decided by the courts if need be. A provision that the trustees can decide such questions is void as it ousts the jurisdiction of the court: see 20.15 (Power to decide between income and capital). This is a shame, as it cannot be said that the courts have made a particularly good job of elucidating this troublesome distinction. Fortunately there is another drafting technique which has the same effect and which does not 'oust the jurisdiction of the Court'. This is a provision which directs trustees (or empowers trustees at their discretion) to treat an income receipt as if it were capital, or to treat a capital receipt as if it were income. It is a question of construction whether a clause confers a power to determine whether a receipt is income or capital (void) or a power to treat income as capital (valid). In practice of course it is easy to devise a clause which is unambiguous and valid, if one bears these principles in mind.[48]

Power to pay capital expenses out of income

20.28

The form used in this book is:

> The Trustees may pay taxes and other expenses out of income although they would otherwise be paid out of capital.

This is an important power, for two reasons:

(1) It is sometimes unclear whether expenses should be paid out of capital or income;[49] using this power the trustees do not have to decide the point.
(2) It is sometimes convenient to pay out of income expenses which are strictly capital expenses.

The Trustee Act (Northern Ireland) 2001 has effected a significant change here. Formerly trustees had to pay capital expenses out of capital and income expenses out of income. Now in the authors' view they have a discretion.[50] The contrary view is arguable,[51] so it remains best to confer an express power.

48 This paragraph from James Kessler, *Drafting Trusts and Will Trusts* was cited with approval in *Morgan Trust Company of the Bahamas Limited v DIW,* Supreme Court of the Bahamas, Butterworths Offshore Service Cases, Vol 2, p 31.

49 The only modern case is *Carver v Duncan* [1985] STC 356. Here the House of Lords (*obiter*) took a very restrictive view of what constitutes an income expense. An expense is capital if it is incurred for the benefit of the estate as a whole. Annual investment management charges are on this test a capital expense!

50 To explain the law it is convenient to start with the power of insurance. The trustees have power to pay insurance premiums out of the 'trust funds'; this expression means any income or capital funds of the trust: see TA (NI) 1958, s 19(5) (as amended by TA (NI) 2001). (This overrides the natural meaning of 'Trust Funds', which is 'Trust Capital'.) Plainly, trustees can pay insurance premiums out of income or capital as they think fit. This is what the Law Commission intended: Law Comm Report 260, *Trustees' Powers and Duties*, para 6.6 accessible on www.lawcom.gov.uk.

This power is permitted for IP and A&M trusts, as it is administrative, see paragraph 18.4 (Power to pay capital expenses out of income).

Power to apply trust capital as income

20.29

The form in this book is as follows:

> The Trustees may apply Trust Property as if it were income arising in the current year. In particular, the Trustees may pay such income to an Income Beneficiary for the purpose of augmenting his income.
>
> **'Income Beneficiary'** here means a Beneficiary to whom income from that property is payable (as of right or at the discretion of the Trustees).

This power might be useful if trustees are unsure whether a receipt or an expense is one of income or capital. However it is also needed for basic tax planning purposes. Suppose trustees wish to transfer trust capital to a beneficiary. Under the trusts in this book there are two ways to achieve this:

(1) The trustees may use their overriding power to advance the capital to the beneficiary.
(2) The trustees may use this power to treat the capital as income; and then pay that 'income' to the beneficiary.[52]

From a practical, property law point of view there is no difference. Either way, the beneficiary simply receives the same property. There is, however, an important difference for tax. In the first case the receipt is one of capital;[53] in the other case

---

Now, TA (NI) 2001, s 31 authorises a trustee to be reimbursed out of 'trust funds' for any expenses properly incurred when acting on behalf of the trust. 'Trust funds' is likewise defined as 'income or capital funds of the trust': TA (NI) 2001, s 43(1). So the trustees must have the same discretion in relation to expenses generally.

It is surprising that this significant change was made without express discussion in the Law Commission paper; it appears to have been unintentional. However, it is the only natural construction. It is consistent with many other statutory provisions such as TA (NI) 1958, s 23(4). It is also a highly satisfactory result as the former law was complex, uncertain, unworkable, and ignored in practice. The old case law is still relevant as showing what is the position in the absence of an exercise of the trustees' powers. (*Carver v Duncan* (1983) 59 TC 125 would still be decided the same way, though slightly different reasoning is needed to reach the same conclusion.)

51 It is preferred by *Lewin on Trusts* (17thed, 2000), para 25-26B. The consequence of the authors' view is not as extreme as the horrified editors of Lewin suggest, because the power must be exercised in the context of the general duty on trustees to hold a fair balance between life tenant and remainderman.

52 It is assumed the Beneficiary is an 'Income Beneficiary' as defined in the clause.

53 *Stevenson v Wishart* (1986) 59 TC 740.

it is a receipt of income.[54] If it is income, the beneficiary will suffer income tax, so a capital receipt will normally be preferred. However, there will be circumstances where it is better to have an income receipt. The common case would be where the trustees have accumulated income and paid additional rate tax: an income receipt allows the beneficiary to reclaim that tax.[55]

In short, it will sometimes be better for a beneficiary to receive a sum as income; sometimes he should receive it as capital. It is desirable that the trustees should have power to achieve either result; so they can decide between income or capital as appropriate. The general law only allows this choice in restricted circumstances.[56]

The decision to apply trust funds as income should be documented by an appropriate trustee resolution.

Rent: income or capital receipt?

20.30

Under the general law rent is income. However under Settled Land Act settlements rent is partly income and partly capital in the case of mining leases granted under the statutory power. Section 11 of the Settled Land Act 1882 provides that unless a contrary intention is expressed in the settlement part of the rent should be set aside as capital money.[57] Section 11 is of little practical importance to professionally drafted trust in that it only applies to leases granted under the statutory power.[58] If trustees for sale are granting such leases it will be under their express power of management. Nevertheless the drafter may wish to make it clear beyond all doubt that the statutory rule does not apply:

> No part of any mining or other rent shall be set aside as capital;

It is unlikely that mining rents will be an issue in a standard draft. In England forms like this are now obsolete because the mining rent under a trust of land will in principle now be regarded as wholly income, not partly capital.[59]

54 That might not, exceptionally, be the case where the larger part of the trust fund is disposed of in this way. For the mere use of the label 'income' is not determinative: see *Jacksons Trustees v IRC* (1942) 25 TC 13.

55 ICTA 1988, s 687. (Assume the beneficiary does not pay tax at the higher rate.) There are also complex tax avoidance schemes which call for such powers. On the IHT position, see SP E6.

56 Income accumulated during a beneficiary's minority under the TA (NI) 1958, s 32 can be applied as income during the beneficiary's minority, so long as his interest continues. The power lapses when the beneficiary attains 18, or dies.

57 3/4 of the rent is to be set aside as capital where the tenant for life is impeachable for waste; 1/4 is to be set aside otherwise.

58 *Earl of Lonsdale* v *Lowther* [1900] 2 Ch 687; *Re Hall* [1916] 2 Ch 488.

59 According to Gover *Capital and Income* (3rd ed, 1937), this already was the position in England under a trust for sale, after 1925; until 1997 that was perhaps debatable; but since the repeal of LPA 1925, s 28, it is reasonably clear that SLA 1925, s 47 treatment does not apply to trusts of land.

The authors have seen a provision that:

> *No part of any mining or other rent shall be set aside as capital unless and until and except to such extent as the Trustees in each or any case may think fit so to set aside the same.*

Rather than this narrow form it would be better to have a general power to create a sinking fund (into which this power would be subsumed).

Sinking funds

20.31

It may occasionally be useful to have a general power to create a sinking fund:

> Income may be set aside and invested to answer any liabilities which in the opinion of the trustees ought to be borne out of income or to meet depreciation of the capital value of any Trust Property. In particular, income may be applied for a leasehold sinking fund policy.

This form would allow trustees to accumulate a sinking fund to replace wasting assets such as a lease. This is an administrative power, permitted in any form of trust.[60] The draft is based on statutory precedent.[61] If it is to be used with the provision about mining rents from the above section the two sub-clauses could be contained in the same clause.

Equitable apportionment

20.32

There are three cases where trustees must under the general law treat income as if it were capital, or capital as if it were income. These are sometimes called the rules of equitable apportionment[62]:

Disposal of unauthorised reversionary investment. Where trustees hold an unauthorised investment which produces little or no income, (eg a reversionary interest) they should generally sell it; the life tenant then receives some of the capital proceeds

60 Para 18.5 (Retention of income to provide for liabilities or depreciation of a capital asset).

61 *Re Hurlbatt* [1910] 2 Ch 553. Form 8(7)(b) of the Statutory Will Forms 1925 accessible at www.kessler.co.uk.

62 This name is unhelpful. The rules have nothing in common with the rules of apportionment under the Apportionment Act 1870, known as the statutory apportionment rule, discussed at 20.54 (Statutory apportionment).

of sale to compensate him for the income which he did not receive during the period that the trustees held the asset. This rule is known as the rule in *Howe v Earl of Dartmouth.*

Disposal of unauthorised wasting investment. Likewise, where trustees hold a wasting investment (eg a short lease) they should sell it; in the meantime some of the income is treated as capital to compensate the remainderman for the wasting nature of the asset concerned. This is known as the rule in *The Earl of Chesterfield's Trusts.*

Payment of debts. Where a testator leaves debts which are not paid immediately out of the estate, the life tenant may receive income from capital in fact required for payment of the debts. Part of that income should be treated as capital and used towards payment of the debts. This is known as the rule in *Allhusen v Whittell.*

The calculations involved are so complex that the costs and administrative difficulties are quite out of proportion to any advantage that arises. It is hardly surprising that the rules are excluded in all well drafted trusts, and if not excluded are more honoured in the breach than in the observance.[63]

There are two common methods of excluding the rules. The first is to exclude the rules by name:

> *The equitable rules of apportionment shall not apply to this Settlement;*

or:

> *The rule in Howe v The Earl of Dartmouth in all its branches shall not apply to this Settlement.*

The other technique is to say that income should be treated as income:

> *The income of the Trust Fund shall, however the property is invested, be treated and applied as income.*[64]

Now, under trusts in this book, the trustees have a wide power of investment which includes power to acquire wasting and non-income producing assets.[65] Such assets are therefore authorised investments. The rules in *Howe v Earl of Dartmouth* and *The Earl of Chesterfield's Trusts* cannot apply. It is unnecessary to exclude them.[66] Likewise, the rule in *Allhusen v Whittell* does not apply to lifetime

63 Law Reform Committee, 23rd Report, *The Powers and Duties of Trustees*, Cmnd 8733 (1982) paras 3.26 *et seq.*

64 This precedent is derived from Statutory Wills Forms 1925, Form 8.

65 See para 20.33 (The balance between income and capital). It is doubtful whether the rules apply at all after the TA(NI) 2001.

66 *Re Nicholson* [1909] 2 Ch 111; *Re Van Straubenzee* [1901] 2 Ch 779. But see Robert Mitchell, 'Trusts for Sale in Wills – Excess Baggage' [1999] The Conveyancer 84, for another view.

trusts, where trustees borrow under an express power. Accordingly, provisions of this type are unnecessary. However the rule in *Allhusen* v *Whittell* still applies to wills and should be excluded by the drafter.[67]

One sometimes sees a provision that it is for the trustees to decide whether or not to apply the rules. This is open to various objections. In particular, in trusts with wide powers of investment, of course, the clause is otiose or its effect is unclear.

The balance between income and capital

20.33

The following form is used in this book:

(1) The Trustees may acquire:
  (a) wasting assets
  (b) assets which yield little or no income
  for investment or any other purpose.[68]

(2) The Trustees are under no duty to procure distributions from a company in which they are interested.

(3) Generally, the Trustees are under no duty to hold a balance between conflicting interests of Beneficiaries.

It is a general principle that trustees should maintain a fair balance between beneficiaries interested in income and capital. Two consequences arise.

1. Investment policy

Trustees should invest trust funds so as to produce a reasonable amount of income and to protect capital values. It would be wrong to invest the entire trust fund in a non-income producing asset (eg an insurance policy) or in a building society account (leading to capital depreciation owing to inflation). *A fortiori* this precludes an investment of the entire trust fund in a wasting asset (such as a short lease).[69] The rule is flexible. For instance, where a life tenant is in special need of income, trustees might adopt an investment policy which will increase his income at some expense to capital.[70]

67 It has been suggested that following the enactment of the Trusts of Land and Appointment of Trustees Act 1996 the rule in *Allhusen* v *Whittell* has ceased to apply in England even to wills but this is doubtful and it is still desirable to exclude the rule in wills if only for the avoidance of doubt.

68 The words 'or any other purpose' are needed, for instance, to authorise the acquisition of a short lease for the residence of a beneficiary.

69 *Re Dick, Lopes-Hume v Dick* [1891] 1 Ch 423.

70 *Nestle v National Westminster Bank* [1993] 1 WLR 1260 at 1279.

This rule seems sensible enough; is it wise to exclude it? On balance, it is better to do so. There may be occasions where, for good reasons, trustees would like complete freedom either to invest in wasting assets B perhaps completely depriving the remainderman of his capital B or in non-income-producing assets B perhaps completely depriving the life tenant of his income. For instance, the life tenant may be in state residential accommodation and find that all her income is taken to pay the cost of her care.[71]

Decisions on these matters are better left to the good sense of the trustees rather than the general principles B however flexible B of trust law.

A standard form in old fashioned investment clauses authorises trustees to purchase investments 'whether producing income or not'. It is considered that this form does not affect the overriding duty to act fairly.[72] It addresses the (now rejected)[73] view that an asset not yielding income is not an 'investment' at all. Since it is clear that 'investments' does nowadays include assets not yielding income, this form serves no purpose and should not be used.

2. *Management of company held by trust*

The same principle governs the management of the trust fund. Where trustees exercise control over a company, they should adopt a dividend policy which is fair to all. The rule could be inconvenient, especially if the trust property consists of shares in a family company, and it seems best to exclude it.

Demergers

20.34

Where a company whose shares are held by a trust carries out an indirect demerger, the shares received are treated as trust capital, which is plainly right. Where there is a direct demerger, however, the demerged shares will be treated as income, which is equally plainly wrong.[74] This could be altered by appropriate drafting.[75]

71 Under the controversial National Assistance (Assessment of Resources) Regulations (NI) 1992.

72 *Lewin on Trusts* (17th ed, 2000), paras 35-152 inclines to the same view, though they describe this as 'a moot point', and offer other explanations of the purpose of the words.

73 *Marson v Morton* (1986) 59 TC 381.

74 'Direct' and 'indirect' demergers are transactions of the kind described by (a) and (b) respectively of ICTA 1988, s 213(3). See *Sinclair v Lee* [1993] Ch 497; the law is discussed in more detail in s 2 of the Trust Law Committee Consultative Paper on Capital and Income of Trusts (June 1999) accessible on www.kcl.ac.uk/depsta.law.tlc/.

75 *Bouch v Sproule* (1887) 12 App Cas 385.

Direct demergers are not uncommon.[76] It is easy to criticise the present rule but hard to frame a better one. Any fixed rule would be complex and to some extent arbitrary and unsatisfactory. One might say that a demerger specifically within s 213(3) of the Income and Corporation Taxes Act 1988 is to be a capital receipt. This would not work for foreign companies and a recasting of the tax rules (bound to happen sooner or later) could lead to unforeseeable results and uncertainties for the trust. A very wide discretion in the trustees might be thought to be dispositive rather than administrative. One might possibly give the trustees a narrow discretion, such as:

> A dividend from a company which in the opinion of the Trustees is a capital receipt in economic reality shall be treated as a capital receipt.

On balance, however, the authors prefer the drawbacks of the present law to the uncertainties raised by such a clause. Statutory law reform inspired by the Trust Law Committee may eventually solve the problem better than the drafter can. Specific provisions might be considered, however, for a trust in anticipation of a direct demerger which is of more than ordinary significance for the trust. This specific provision need refer only to the company concerned, and can in the authors' view be drafted so as to be an administrative provision for tax purposes.[77]

Occupation and use of trust property

20.35

The form used in this book is as follows:

> (1) The Trustees may acquire any interest in property anywhere in the world for occupation or use by an Income Beneficiary.
> (2) The Trustees may permit any Income Beneficiary to occupy or use Trust Property on such terms as they think fit.
> (3) **'Income Beneficiary'** here means a Beneficiary to whom income from that property is payable (as of right or at the discretion of the Trustees).

Trustees now have a statutory power to acquire land for a beneficiary's occupation.[78] In contrast to the equivalent English provision no restrictions are placed on the geographic location or legal nature or type of interest which is

76 They include the Courtaulds/Courtaulds Textiles and BAT/Wiggins Teape Appleton demergers (1990); Racal/Vodaphone and BAT/Argos (1991); Racal/Chubb (1992); and the Hanson demergers in 1995.

77 18.7 (Capital/income and apportionment provisions).

78 TA (NI) 2001, s 8(1)(b).

acquired.[79] Nevertheless there is no harm in retaining the express unrestricted power which it is preferable to use in England.

20.36

The draft clause covers both land and chattels; it seems unnecessary to deal with these in separate clauses. The clause rests loosely on statutory precedent.[80] Some precedents detail the terms on which the beneficiaries may use the property (eg 'on such terms as to payment of rent, repair, decoration, insurance, etc'). The formulae end with a general power ('and such terms generally as the trustees think fit') which must include all that has gone before; nothing is gained.

Some drafters follow the statutory precedent and add that trustees shall not be liable for loss. Presumably, the fear is that one beneficiary will drop the Ming vase; and another will sue the trustees. Now, if the trustees are acting properly and within their powers, it is hard to see that they are liable. And in any case, should not the vase have been insured? The matter is adequately dealt with by the general provision discussed at 5.17 (Trustee exemption clauses).

The restriction to 'Income Beneficiaries' reflects the requirements for A&M trusts.[81] In IP trusts it may be simplified by saying 'Income Beneficiary' means a beneficiary entitled to an interest in possession in the trust property; but a standard form for A&M and IP trusts makes life easier. In discretionary trusts the restriction may be omitted.

Loans to beneficiaries

20.37

The form used in this book is as follows:

> The Trustees may lend trust money to an Income Beneficiary. The loan may be interest free and unsecured, or on such terms as the Trustees think fit.

79 In England and Wales the statutory power only applies to freehold or leasehold land in the UK: TA 2000, s 8. On the wisdom of purchasing land outside the UK see 20.21 (Power of investment).

Re Power [1947] Ch 572 is sometimes cited as authority for the proposition that a common form power of investment never permits trustees to purchase a residence for a beneficiary because a residence is not an 'investment'. More accurately, the position is considered to be that the acquisition of a residence *may* not be an investment, and so may be outside the scope of a common form power of investment, but this depends on the circumstances of the acquisition. But after the TA (NI) 2001 the issue could only arise in unusual circumstances, eg if trustees wish to purchase property for occupation by a person who is not a beneficiary (at a rent or rent free with the consent of a life tenant).

80 TA (NI) 2001, s 8; AEA 1925, s 47(1)(iv) (there is no NI equivalent to this provision: under the intestacy scheme in NI infants take an absolute interest).

81 Para 18.14 (A&M trusts).

> 'Income Beneficiary' here means a Beneficiary to whom income of the money is payable (as of right or at the discretion of the Trustees).

Trustees should have power to make loans to beneficiaries on favourable terms. Such loans may be convenient in practice and tax efficient. This clause authorises trustees to do this. It is uncertain to what extent such loans would be proper in the absence of express authority.[82]

This power should be made subject to the consent of the protector where there is one.

20.38

Express mention is given in the draft to unsecured loans in view of the general suspicion of unsecured loans expressed in the context of trustees' power of investment.[83]

Some drafters provide that no loan should be made to the settlor. This is not necessary. The settlor exclusion clause will prohibit loans on favourable terms. No harm arises from the mere possibility that loans could be made on arm's length terms. The actual making of the loan may have severe tax consequences: but that is a matter for the trustees to consider at the time of the loan.

The restriction to income beneficiaries reflects the requirements for A&M trusts.[84] In IP trusts it may be simplified by saying

> 'Income Beneficiary' means a beneficiary entitled to an interest in possession in the trust property.

However, a standard clause for both forms of trust makes life easier. In discretionary trusts the restriction may be omitted.

Trust property as security for beneficiaries' liabilities

20.39

The form used in this book is as follows:

> The Trustees may charge Trust Property as security for any debts or obligations of an Income Beneficiary. 'Income Beneficiary' here means a Beneficiary to

82 The power of investment will authorise loans by way of investment. Loans on favourable terms raise more problems. In *Re Laing* [1899] 1 Ch 593 trustees had power to invest trust funds 'upon personal credit without security.' It was assumed that trustees, under this clause, could lend (presumably interest free) to the life tenant.

83 *Khoo Tek Keung v Ch'ng Joo Tuan Neoh* [1934] AC 529, PC.

84 Para 18.14 (A&M trusts).

> whom income of the Trust Property is payable (as of right or at the discretion of the Trustees).

An alternative to the trustees lending money to a beneficiary is for them to provide security so he can borrow more easily elsewhere. This requires express authorisation.

This power should be made subject to the consent of the protector where there is one.

The restriction to income beneficiaries reflects the requirements for A&M trusts.[85] In IP trusts it may be simplified by saying 'Income Beneficiary' means a beneficiary entitled to an interest in possession in the trust property. In discretionary trusts it may be omitted.

Power to trade

20.40

The form used in this book is as follows:

> The Trustees may carry on a trade, in any part of the world, alone or in partnership.

Trustees cannot properly carry on a trade without express power.[86]

In practice trustees rarely carry on a trade, though trading trusts offer some tax[87] and commercial[88] advantages. The inclusion of the power does no harm, whereas it is conceivable that its absence may be regretted. The standard practice is to include this power in all cases.

The draft is concise, self-explanatory and, it is thought, comprehensive. There is little trust law on the subject but there is a company law precedent.[89]

85 Para 18.14 (A&M trusts).

86 A standard form power of investment is wide but does not confer a power to 'invest' in a trade: *Re Berry* [1962] Ch 97.

87 It is a general feature of the IHT and CGT system that it favours trade over investment, a partial reversal of the 19th century aristocratic prejudice against trade. (Income tax is now heading the opposite way.) However, the distinction the law draws between trade and investment is (inevitably) a formal one, and often the same economic result can be achieved by an 'investment' or in a form which the law regards as a trade. For instance, trustees holding land used by a trader may arrange to trade in partnership with the occupier of the land so as to qualify for 100% IHT business property relief, or for CGT roll-over and business taper reliefs. This is easy if the land (often farmland) is occupied by a beneficiary, but may be possible even if the occupier is unconnected with the trust.

88 A trading trust with a corporate trustee enjoys an element of limited liability without public disclosure of trading accounts.

89 Companies (NI) Order 1986, art 14A.

Some drafters authorise the trustees to carry on a trade *or business.* The word 'business' is wider than the word 'trade.'[90] It is hard to see what this adds. If it is a business of making or holding investments, there is already ample authority for that in the power of investment. It is not necessary to give trustees an express indemnity against the trust fund for trading debts properly incurred by them.[91]

Power to borrow

20.41

The form used in this book is as follows:

> The Trustees may borrow money for investment or any other purpose. Money borrowed shall be treated as Trust Property.

The general law gives trustees power to borrow for some purposes.[92] Trustees do not have an unrestricted power to borrow, and, in particular, trustees may not borrow money for investment purposes.[93]

It is thought that trustees may be entrusted with unrestricted powers to borrow money, especially since loans made to trustees offer tax advantages.[94]

... *For investment or for any other purpose.* It is desirable specifically to override the case which held that trustees' statutory power to borrow does not allow trustees to borrow in order to invest.

The draft is drawn from s 71 of the English Settled Land Act 1925. Some drafters say that the trustees may borrow ... *On such terms as the trustees think fit.* These words (not found in statutory precedents) are strictly unnecessary: there is certainly no authority to suggest any need for lengthier formula such as 'on such terms and conditions relating to interest, capital' and so on.

In this book a power to give security is dealt with separately.[95]

90 *American Leaf Blending Co Sdn Bhd v Director-General of Inland Revenue* [1978] STC 561.

91 Para 20.12 (Trustees entitled to expenses of exercising powers).

92 SLA 1882, s 18; IHTA 1984, s 212; TA (NI) 1958, s 16(1); AEA (NI) 1955 s 40(4). The Law Commission suggest (Law Com Report No 260, *Trustees' Powers and Duties*, para 2-44) that TA 2000, s 8(1) (which is identical for these purposes to TA(NI) 2001, s 8(1)) authorises trustees to purchase land with the aid of a mortgage, but the contrary view is arguable.

93 *Re Suensen Taylor, Moores v Moores* [1974] 3 All ER 397, [1974] 1 WLR 1280.

94 An individual would not receive tax relief on interest paid unless the loan is eligible for relief under the restrictive conditions of ICTA 1988, Pt IX. Interest paid by trustees effectively enjoys higher rate tax relief; for a trustee does not pay higher rate tax, and a beneficiary would pay higher rate tax only on the net amount of income received from the trust (ie income after interest has been paid). *Murray v IRC* (1926) 11 TC 133; *Macfarlane v IRC* (1929) 14 TC 532. The settlement provisions counteract the tax advantages in some circumstances.

95 Para 20.45 (Power to give security for trustees' liabilities).

Delegation

20.42

The Trustee Act (NI) 2001 allows trustees to delegate to an agent, but imposes many restrictions, some understandable, others quixotic.[96] Four matters cannot be delegated:

(a) dispositive powers;[97]
(b) power to decide whether payments should be made out of income or capital;
(c) power of appointing new trustees;
(d) power of delegation, use of nominee.

A beneficiary cannot be appointed an agent.[98] This is in striking contrast to many other statutory regimes which recognise that it may be appropriate for a beneficiary to act as trustee.[99]

Trustees may not delegate the following matters unless it is 'reasonably necessary' to do so:

(a) power to sub-delegate;
(b) limitation of liability of agent;
(c) permitting agent to act in potential conflicts of interest.

There must be considerable doubt as to what constitutes 'reasonable necessity'.

Further restrictions apply to 'asset management functions'. Here we have the regulator's delight: written agreements and policy statements. Applied to trusts as a whole, will the benefit of all this paper outweigh the cost? The answer is by no means obvious; it might perhaps benefit from research but is probably unresearchable.[100]

In the absence of sound research the drafter must rely on intuition and it is submitted that trustees can be trusted with a general and unrestricted power of delegation. All these restrictions on the power of delegation are needless complications. Policy statements, for instance, may be regarded as good practice but should not be compulsory regardless of circumstances. If they are fit to be trustees they are fit to decide how to delegate.

96 TA (NI) 2001, s 11. Further rules apply to charitable trusts (not discussed here).
97 Para 18.2 (Significance of administrative/dispositive distinction).
98 The expression 'beneficiary' is undefined and in some cases it is unclear who is a 'beneficiary'. See 4.31 (Terminology).
99 See the references in 5.3 (Beneficiaries as trustees).
100 Written policy statements are however the spirit of the age, and it is likely that even trust practitioners will see more of them before the tide turns. In England the Charity Commission, for instance, now recommend charity trustees should 'develop a written policy' on how to deal with conflicts of interest relating to trustee remuneration (CC 11, Payment of Charity Trustees, Sept 2000), a charity reserves policy (RS3, 1993), a risks policy (Charities/Accounts and Reports) Regs 2000); etc.

The technical question then arises of whether these restrictions can be overridden by the drafting and, if so, what wording is required. The TA(NI) 2001 has used a variety of drafting techniques to impose the restrictions, which causes some unnecessary complexity and confusion.

The restriction that certain functions are not 'delegable' and the restriction on delegating to beneficiaries, apply only to the statutory power of delegation. These restrictions do not apply if the trust confers its own power of delegation, eg as in the STEP standard form ('a trustee may delegate ... any of his functions to any person'). It is reasonably clear that the same applies to the restriction relating to joint delegation and the three matters which can only be delegated if reasonably necessary.

This leaves the restrictions relating to asset management functions. In the authors' view the same applies. Trustee Act (NI) 2001, s 15 (Asset management functions: special restrictions) only imposes its restrictions on the statutory power of delegation. So if a trust confers an express power of delegation, whether before or after the Act, s 15 does not apply and there is no duty to prepare a policy statement. But the contrary view has been suggested.[101] However, even if (contrary to the authors' view) any of these restrictions apply at all to express powers of delegation, they only apply subject to contrary intent in the trust itself. The restrictions can be excluded by express words or by implication.[102]

Ideally one would set out at length exactly what is authorised, but the length of the clause would be out of proportion to the importance of the issue. Accordingly, the authors slightly reluctantly adopt the shorthand of an exclusion by reference to the specific statutory provisions. This leads to a simple form of draft:

> A Trustee or the Trustees jointly (or other person in a fiduciary position) may authorise any person to exercise all or any functions on such terms as to remuneration and other matters as they may think fit. None of the restrictions on delegation in ss 12 to 15 Trustee Act (NI) 2001 shall apply.

This draft is drawn from s 11 of the Trustee Act (NI) 2001. There are many other statutory precedents.[103] This clause applies to trustees and other fiduciaries. This

101 This view regards TA (NI) 2001, s 15 as a self standing section, not only applicable to the statutory power. But the context would seem to be against this.

102 Even this has been doubted, at least in the very early days of the TA (NI)2001, in relation to s 15 TA (NI) 2001! But the idea that Parliament should intend these petty restrictions on delegation to override the intention of the settlor is absurd. It is also contrary to the approach of the Court in *Re Turner* [1937] Ch 15 and *London Regional Transport Pension Trustees v Hatt* [1993] PLR 227 accessible www.kessler.co.uk in which apparently mandatory statutory words were held in context to apply subject to contrary intent.

103 TA (NI)1958, s 26; s 24(2) (repealed); LPA 1925, s 29, now replaced by the TLATA 1996, s 9; Powers of Attorney Act (NI) 1971, s 10; Enduring Powers of Attorney (NI) Order 1987, arts 5(3); Table A paras 71, 72. Contrast Trusts (Jersey) Law 1984, art 21.

would allow the settlor to delegate his power to appoint new trustees.[104] On the use of the words 'functions' as shorthand for 'trusts, powers and discretions' see 6.4 (Powers and duties: terminology). It is not necessary to add the words 'anywhere in the world'.[105]

Some drafters begin the clause with phrases such as:

> Notwithstanding any rule of law or equity to the contrary ...
>
> Notwithstanding the fiduciary nature of the Trustees' powers ...

What can be the purpose of this? It acknowledges that the general rule (that trustees may not delegate their powers) is overridden; but the general rule can be overridden by any clear words: no particular form is needed.[106] By this formula the drafter vaunts his superiority to the rule of equity; but the additional words add nothing of substance.[107]

Nominees and custodians

20.43

The form used in this book is as follows:

> (1) The Trustees may appoint a person to act as their nominee in relation to such of the assets of the trust as they may determine. They may take such steps as are necessary to secure that those assets are vested in the nominee.
> (2) The Trustees may appoint a person to act as custodian in relation to such of the assets of the trust as they may determine. The Trustees may give the custodian custody of the assets and any documents or records concerning the assets. The Trustees are not obliged to appoint a custodian of securities payable to bearer.
> (3) The Trustees may appoint a person to act as nominee or custodian on such terms as to remuneration and other matters as they may think fit.

It is often convenient to use a nominee or custodian. This can save time, paperwork and expense, especially on a change of trustees or on the sale of securities dealt with on the stock exchange. It also reduces the cost of investment management.

[104] The settlor could not delegate this power under any of the statutory powers of delegation applicable to trustees.

[105] See the discussion on similar wording in 5.32 (Appointment of new trustees).

[106] See (if authority is needed) *Pilkington v IRC* [1964] AC 612. Although TA (NI) 1958, s 26 uses this form, it is not found in other statutory powers of delegation, listed above.

[107] The authors have even seen a clause beginning: 'notwithstanding any rule of law or equity *or otherwise* ...'! One wonders what other rules the drafter had in mind.

In *Mason v Fairbrother*[108] Judge Blackett-Ord V-C. considered:

> a proviso about a nominee being a bank or something like that. But in my view that is an undesirable complication. I will simply authorise the trustees to appoint a nominee or nominees to hold any investment in the fund. That is a power that the trustees can exercise in proper circumstances and if they misuse it, they will be liable.

Quite so. All such attempts to safeguard trust property by fettering trustees' powers are misguided. This form (based on the statutory wording) overrides the elaborate restrictions on the statutory powers set out in the Trustee Act (NI) 2001, ss 16–20.

Power to give indemnities

20.44

The form used in this book is as follows:

> The Trustees may indemnify any Person for any liability relating to this Settlement.

Of course trustees may give indemnities without authorisation by the trust. The purpose of express authorisation is to permit the trustees:

(1) to reimburse themselves out of the trust fund if the indemnity is called upon; and
(2) to use their powers of mortgage and charge so as to secure the indemnity on the trust fund.

It is doubtful whether trustees would have power to do this in the absence of an express power.[109]

Power to give security for trustees' liabilities

20.45

The form used in this book is as follows:

> The Trustees may mortgage or charge Trust Property as security for any liability incurred by them as Trustees (and may grant a floating charge so far as the law allows).

108 [1983] 2 All ER 1078 at 1087. (This was an application for additional powers under TA 1925, s 57, the English equivalent of TA (NI) 1958, s 56.)

109 TA (NI) 1958, s 15(1)(f) would provide such a power in some cases: see Paul Matthews 'Indemnities for retiring trustees', OTPR (1990) Vol 1, Issue 2, p 27 accessible on www.kessler.co.uk.

The duty of trustees being to preserve trust property, they need express authority to mortgage it. The ability to mortgage trust property as security for trustees' liabilities is useful. The general law allows trustees to mortgage trust property for certain purposes only, but there seems no reason for any restrictions.

The drafter may append the power to mortgage trust property as an ancillary to various powers where security may be needed (power to borrow; power to give indemnities, etc). It is easier to put in a single self-standing paragraph to achieve this end. The concept of liabilities incurred 'as trustees' follows statutory precedent.[110]

A floating charge is possible under English law, except in relation to personal chattels.

Power of appropriation

20.46

The form used in this book is as follows:

> The Trustees may appropriate Trust Property to any person or class of persons in or towards the satisfaction of their interest in the Trust Fund.

Trustees need a power of appropriation to allow a division of the trust fund into separate shares, if desired. The powers conferred by the general law are inadequate, particularly in Northern Ireland.[111]

The draft is based on the statutory precedent.

110 TA 1925, s 26(1). Note that the NI equivalent, TA(NI) 1958, s 27(1) does not contain this phrase.

111

(1) AEA (NI) 1955, s 37 confers a power of appropriation on personal representatives, but not on trustees.

(2) TA (NI)1958, s 15(1)(b) confers power to apportion 'blended trust funds or property.' It is submitted that this gives trustees power to appropriate whenever trustees are directed to divide trust property into shares – so the power overlaps with (1) and (2) above. This is significant since this power (unlike the above) does not require any beneficiary to consent. But a narrower construction of s 15(1)(b) is arguable.

(3) The extent to which the common law allows appropriation is unclear. The old cases are discussed in *Kane v Radley-Kane* [1999] Ch 274.

An application could also be made under TA (NI) 1958, s 57 though perhaps not under TA (NI) 1958 s 56: see 18.8 (Power of appropriation).

The Law Reform Committee, 23rd Report, *The Powers and Duties of Trustees*, Cmnd. 8733 (1982) para 4.42 recommended that trustees should have a wide statutory power of appropriation and this would indeed be a desirable reform. It would simplify the law, shorten trust documents and help beneficiaries whose trusts are not well drafted. There is, however, no current prospect of reform.

This form authorises appropriation to a settled share, since the beneficiaries of the settled share are a 'class of persons'.

The statutory power of appropriation normally requires the consent of the beneficiary concerned. If the power is set out independently it is unnecessary, even for the avoidance of doubt, to say: 'without the consent of any person...'.

Where trustees have this power, they may ascertain the value of the property by qualified agents; and a valuation made by the trustees is binding on the beneficiaries. It is not necessary to say this expressly.[112]

Receipt by charities

20.47

The form used in this book is as follows:

> Where Trust Property is to be paid or transferred to a charity, the receipt of the treasurer or appropriate officer of the charity shall be a complete discharge to the Trustees.

This form solves a possible administrative difficulty where trust property is payable to a charitable trust, or an unincorporated charitable association. In such cases they would strictly need to investigate who could give them a valid receipt.

This is a provision of marginal significance. It is obviously unnecessary if the trust does not include charitable beneficiaries. It is unnecessary where trust property is to be transferred to a charitable company; most large charities are now incorporated. Omission of the clause is unlikely to matter: in the unlikely event that trust funds were accidentally paid to the wrong person, and then stolen, the trustees' own conduct would not usually cause them to be liable for breach of trust.

The draft is drawn loosely from statutory precedents.[113]

112 TA (NI) 1958, s 23(3).

113 TA (NI)1958, ss 14, 63(2); the English Statutory Will Forms 1925, Form 4 accessible on www.kessler.co.uk; SLA 1925, s 95. Some extend this form to apply not only to the 'treasurer or appropriate officer' of the charity, but any person 'appearing to be' treasurer or officer. It is difficult to see that this makes much difference in practice, particularly since trustees will generally have the defence to a breach of trust conferred by TA (NI) 1958, s 61 and (in the precedents in this book) a defence that they have not been negligent.

Release of rights and powers

20.48

The form used in this book is as follows:

> The Trustees (or other persons in a fiduciary position) may by deed release wholly or in part any of their rights or functions and (if applicable) so as to bind their successors.

This clause gives trustees power to release their powers.[114] It would also allow the settlor to release his power of appointing new trustees. This has become a standard provision in modern practice, though it is not strictly needed: the trustees' overriding powers could be exercised so as to have the same effect as a release.[115]

The power could be used to change the structure of the trust fundamentally. Where there is a protector the exercise of this power should require his consent.

The general question of when and which categories of power can be released under the general law has attracted a difficult case law, which is fortunately largely redundant. There is little in the cases relevant to drafting. The first limb of our draft clause is self-evident, and the second for the avoidance of doubt only. The words 'wholly or in part' would be implied in any case and could be omitted.[116] Some drafters authorise trustees to enter into a contract not to exercise their powers. This is implied in any event,[117] and it is hard to conceive of a case where such a power would be useful.

Some drafters begin the clause with phrases such as:

> Notwithstanding any rule of law or equity to the contrary ...

> Notwithstanding the fiduciary nature of the trustees' powers ...

This acknowledges that the general rule (that trustees may not release their powers) is to be overridden. But this general principle can be overridden by any clear form of words.[118]

114 Fiduciary powers cannot be released in the absence of an express power to release them: *Re Wills* [1964] Ch 219.
115 *Muir v IRC* [1966] 1 WLR 1269.
116 *Re Evered* [1910] 2 Ch 147.
117 *Ibid.*
118 See (if authority is needed) *Muir v IRC* [1966] 1 WLR 1269. See 20.42 (Delegation) where similar comments apply.

Ancillary powers

20.49

The form used in this book is as follows:

> The Trustees may do anything which is incidental or conducive to the exercise of their functions.

On a fair construction this form should never make any practical difference,[119] but it may dispel doubts raised by any arguments in favour of a narrow construction of trustees' powers. The form simplifies the drafting of the other administrative powers, since one need not scatter forms of this kind in all the other powers. There are trust and company law precedents.[120]

Provisions relating to minors

20.50

The form used in this book is:

> Where the Trustees may apply income for the benefit of a minor, they may do so by paying the income to the minor's parent or guardian on behalf of the minor, or to the minor if he has attained the age of 16. The Trustees are under no duty to enquire into the use of the income unless they have knowledge of circumstances which call for enquiry.

Payment of income to parent or guardian

Trustees may, under the general law, pay funds belonging to a child to the person who has parental responsibility for that child.[121] It is therefore not necessary to say that trustees may pay income to the parent or guardian of a child.[122] In the

119 The courts ought to apply to the construction of trustees' powers the principle well established in company law, that whatever may fairly be regarded as incidental to or consequent upon a company's objects ought not to be held *ultra vires*: *A-G v Great Eastern Railway Co* (1880) 5 App Cas 473 at 478.

120 Contrast TA (NI) 1958, s 15; Companies (NI) Order 1986, art 14A; Insolvency (NI) Order 1989, Sch 1, para 23; National Heritage Act 1983, s 33(5)(d); Local Government Act 1972, s 111. Case law records that local authorities have not had much success in trying to justify under this section acts (swaps, trading in land) not otherwise within their powers.

121 Children (NI) Order 1995, art 6(3). The Children Order 1995 sensibly changed the law. Previously, a guardian had power to give a receipt on behalf of a minor but a parent did not.

122 One often sees a clause which says that trustees may pay income to a parent of a minor. Presumably such drafts have not been revised since the Children Order came into force.
Incidentally, that clause is not entirely without effect. It would authorise trustees to make a payment to a parent who did not have parental responsibility for the child. This may happen, for instance, in the case of an illegitimate child. But the point is of trivial importance.

draft in this book, the important part of the clause is the second sentence. This deals with the question of what responsibility the trustees should have to ensure that income is properly used by the parent or guardian: this is discussed at 5.30 (Excluding duty to supervise parents and guardians).

Payment of income to child

In Northern Ireland a minor cannot give a receipt for trust money.[123] It might possibly be convenient to relax this rule though in practice the point is unlikely to be of much importance. This form does not give the child any right to demand payment: the trustees may choose whether or not to pay to him.[124]

Power to retain income of child

20.51

The form used in this book is:

> Where Trustees may apply income for the benefit of a minor, they may do so by resolving that they hold that income on trust for the minor absolutely and:
> (1) The Trustees may apply that income for the benefit of the minor during his minority.
> (2) The Trustees shall transfer the residue of that income to the minor on attaining the age of 18.
> (3) For investment and other administrative purposes that income shall be treated as Trust Property.

This power is intended to facilitate elementary income tax planning for children who are beneficiaries of A&M and discretionary trusts.

For income tax purposes one might like children to have an income of their own, so as to use their personal allowances. This offers a worthwhile annual tax saving. Where the beneficiaries are not children of the settlor, trustees can deal with trust income in the following ways.

(1) The trustees may accumulate it. The income will be subject to tax at the rates set out in s 686 of the Income and Corporation Taxes Act 1988.[125]

123 In England in the unlikely event that he or she is married, a minor can give a receipt for (1) trust income (LPA 1925, s 21); and (2) accumulated income payable to the minor under TA 1925, s 32(2)(i).

124 *Re Somech* [1957] Ch 165.

125 It may be possible to reclaim this tax by making income payments to the beneficiary in later years, but the beneficiary's personal allowance in the earlier years is lost.

(2) (a) The trustees may spend it for the benefit of the minor children.
(b) The trustees may retain the income on trust for the child by exercising this special power.[126]

In both these cases the income is effectively[127] taxed as the child's income (and up to the personal allowance, escapes tax altogether). The power to retain income for a child is therefore a useful means of obtaining the tax advantage without spending the income.

Where the beneficiary is an unmarried minor child of the settlor, s 660B of the Income and Corporation Taxes Act 1988 counteracts the tax advantage in situation (2). This is done by providing that the child's income should be treated as the income of the parent.[128]

Administrative provision for mentally handicapped beneficiaries

20.52

Where the terms of a trust require trustees to pay funds to a mentally handicapped beneficiary they should pay the funds to his receiver or to an attorney appointed under the Enduring Powers of Attorney (Northern Ireland) Order 1987. Where:

(1) it is not desired to appoint a receiver (because of the expense); and
(2) the beneficiary cannot appoint an attorney (because he does not have the necessary mental capacity),[129]

it is submitted that the trustees may properly retain the funds and invest them as nominee for the beneficiary, or apply the funds for the direct benefit of the beneficiary. However it is desirable to have an express power to confirm this. The form used in this book is self-explanatory:

126 The child might become entitled to quite a substantial sum at 18, a result the parents may not view with enthusiasm.

127 Since the trust is not IP in form (see 13.17 (Variant: life tenant a minor)) the tiresome additional rate procedures must be followed: (1) The trustees will pay tax at the rate set out in ICTA 1988, s 686. (2) On exercise of the power, the retained income becomes the beneficiary's income: *Stevenson v Wishart* [1987] STC 266; *Spens v IRC* (1970) 46 TC 276. (3) Tax is then reclaimed by the beneficiary under the credit system of ICTA 1988, s 687. (The exercise of the power to retain counts as a 'payment to a beneficiary' for the purposes of ICTA 1988, s 687. The word 'payment' in ICTA 1988, s 687 has a wide meaning: see *IRC v Berrill* (1981) 58 TC 429 at 444.) The position is less advantageous for Sch F (dividend) income.

128 It follows that a teenage marriage is an effective if drastic way round the anti-avoidance provision. The section applies in a more attenuated form where the trust was made before 8 March 1999 (for which see the fourth edition of James Kessler, *Drafting Trusts and Will Trusts*, para 15-055, accessible on www.kessler.co.uk).

129 The test for mental capacity is set out in *Re K* [1988] Ch 310.

> **Mentally Handicapped Beneficiary**
>
> Where income or capital is payable to a Beneficiary who does not have the mental capacity to appoint an attorney with an enduring general power, the Trustees may (subject to the directions of the Court or his Receiver) apply that income or capital for his benefit.

Where this form has not been used, trustees may be able to use a power of appointment or advancement to confer this power on themselves.

Power to disclaim[130]

20.53

The form used in this book is as follows:

> A Person may disclaim his interest in this Settlement wholly or in part.

This is another tax-motivated provision.

On the death of a life tenant, trust property will often pass to his widow: this will normally postpone an IHT charge.

There are circumstances where this would not be desirable. It may be better that some or all of the trust property should pass directly to the next generation, so as to take advantage of the life tenant's nil rate band. The difficulty is that the drafter cannot know at the time the trust is made whether this will be the case or not. In the case of non-settled property, issues of this kind can be resolved after death by means of a deed of variation; but deeds of variation are not available for settled property.[131]

The use of a disclaimer offers an answer to this problem. It allows the question of whether the spouse should take an interest in the trust property to be resolved after death. Inheritance Tax Act 1984, s 93 provides:

> Where a person becomes beneficially entitled to an interest in settled property but disclaims the interest, then, if the disclaimer is not made for a consideration in money or money's worth, the Inheritance Tax Act 1984 shall apply as if he had not become entitled to the interest.

130 On this topic see Oerton and Wood, *Capital Taxes News & Reports* (1989), p 17.

131 IHTA 1984, s 142(5). There is no good reason for this discrimination against settled property; but there is little prospect of law reform.

Thus if the widow becomes entitled to an interest in the settled property on the death of the life tenant, and it is desired to utilise the deceased's nil rate band, she simply may disclaim her interest.

The usual rule is that an individual must disclaim the entire interest in property given to him; he cannot disclaim part. That rule derives from a presumption that the donor so intended. It is therefore possible to authorise a beneficiary to disclaim an interest in part.[132] The IHT relief applies to a partial disclaimer as well as to a complete disclaimer.[133]

Statutory apportionment[134]

20.54

Under the general law, income is where possible treated as accruing from day to day as it is earned. It is not income of the day it happens to be received. This means that when there is any change of entitlement to income, the income may need to be apportioned and:

(1) one part treated as income received before the change would have been treated and
(2) the other part treated as income received after the change.

The implications of this are somewhat surprising and the matter is best illustrated by examples.

Example 1
Application of statutory apportionment rule on death of life tenant

Trustees hold a trust fund on trust for A for life, remainder to B. A dies on 30 April 1992. In 1993 trustees receive a dividend for the calendar year 1992.

(1) One-third of the dividend will be apportioned to the period before A's death (and so paid to A's estate).
(2) The remaining two-thirds is apportioned to the period after A's death and so paid to B.

132 *Guthrie v Walrond* (1883) 22 Ch D 573.

133 This appears to be the Revenue view; see SP E18 and Revenue correspondence published in *Tolley's Practical Tax*, 28 June 1989.

134 See 20.32 (Equitable apportionment) for the entirely distinct rules known unhelpfully as 'equitable apportionment'.

Example 2
Application of statutory apportionment rule on death of testator

The testator dies on 30 April 1992. By his will his residuary estate is held on trust for B for life with remainder over. In 1993 the executors receive a dividend for the calendar year 1992.

(1) One-third of the dividend is apportioned to the period before the testator's death, and is retained by the executors as trust capital (just as any sums actually received by the testator before his death would have become trust capital).
(2) B will be entitled to the remaining two-thirds.

Example 3
Application of statutory apportionment rule on A&M beneficiary attaining interest in possession

Trustees hold trust property on A&M trusts. On 30 April 1992 B reaches the age of 25 (and becomes entitled to an interest in possession). In 1993 trustees receive a dividend for the calendar year 1992.

(1) One-third of the dividend is apportioned to the period before B's birthday. It is held by the trustees on the A&M trusts which govern income which were in effect before B's birthday – that is, to apply for the benefit of any other A&M beneficiaries under 25 [135] or to accumulate it.
(2) B will be entitled to the remaining two-thirds.

The apportionment rule is intended to operate fairly between the different beneficiaries (or their estates). The rule produces a fairness which is expensive and inconvenient. The sums involved are usually small. Like motorists with the urban speed limit, trustees ignore the apportionment rule if they feel they can do so safely. So common is this practice that the rule is scarcely if ever observed. Where figures are large, and the rule has not been excluded by a trust, the question occasionally arises whether the application of the rule can be overridden by the appropriate exercise of a common form power of appointment: ie can a deed of appointment deal with income not yet payable, but which time apportioned would accrue before the date of the appointment? It is submitted that the answer is yes; but views may differ.

It is plainly desirable to avoid this pedantry and direct that the statutory apportionment rule should not apply. Instead income is treated as accruing when payable to the trustees: in the three examples above all the dividends would be paid to B. This is also the view of a very distinguished Law Reform Committee who recommended effective abolition of the rule.[136] Fortunately the apportionment

[135] Not B because he is now over 25! See *Re Joel* [1967] Ch 14.

[136] Law Reform Committee, 23rd Report, *The Powers and Duties of Trustees*, Cmnd 8733 (1982), para 3.39.

rule can be reversed without difficulty in trust law[137] or tax law.[138] The form used in this book is as follows:

> Income and expenditure shall be treated as arising when payable, and not from day to day, so that no apportionment shall take place.

The drafting echoes the language of the statute. It is not appropriate to say:

> This settlement shall be construed as if the Apportionment Act 1870 had not been enacted.

Interest was apportioned under the common law. The 1870 Act merely brings other types of income into line. It is unnecessary to refer to the 1870 Act or its predecessor the Apportionment Act 1834.[139]

Power for trustees to apply the apportionment rules?

Sometimes the trustees are given the power to decide for themselves whether or not to apply the apportionment rules. Thus in the three examples above the trustees would pay the dividends to B but with power:

(1) on the facts of Example 1, to pay one-third of the dividend to A's estate;
(2) on the facts of Example 2, to retain one-third of the dividend as capital; and
(3) on the facts of Example 3, to hold one-third of the dividend on the terms of the A&M trusts applicable to income arising before B attained 25.

It is possible to envisage circumstances where trustees might desire to do this, but in practice it would probably never happen. It is suggested that the form is not worth the trouble and accordingly it is not used in this book.[140]

Trustee remuneration

20.55

In the absence of any specific provision, the position is governed by rules set out in Part V of the Trustee Act (NI) 2001. For trusts other than charities a trust

137 Apportionment Act 1870, s 7 directs that the provisions of the section do not apply in any case where it is expressly stipulated that no apportionment shall take place.
138 Para 18.6
139 The 1834 Act was repealed in 1977, so forms referring to that Act are obsolete.
140 The authors have also been concerned about the tax implications of this power. On the facts of examples (1) (2) and (3) would one third of the dividend be within the scope of ICTA 1988, s 686 since it is income payable at the discretion of the trustees? The answer is probably no, since the power is merely administrative: see 18.2 (Significance of administrative/dispositive distinction).

corporation can always charge. A trustee acting in a professional capacity can also charge, but subject to the safeguard that he is not a sole trustee and each other trustee has agreed in writing. Should a professional trustee rely on this? It is submitted that an 'agreement' with the other trustees may be irrevocable (so that the professional trustee is not at risk if the other trustee later tries to change his mind). However, if the other trustee dies the surviving sole trustee could not charge until he has appointed a second trustee who will consent to his charges. Where two trustees are partners in the same partnership it is considered that one could consent to the charges of the other but the contrary is faintly arguable (because the trustee benefits from his own consent).[141] While little difficulty should arise in practice from the statutory rule, however, the form allowing trustees to charge without consent has long been used and few difficulties seem to have arisen. The precedents in this book therefore retain the traditional form. The drafting echoes the statutory wording[142].

(1) A trustee acting in a professional capacity is entitled to receive reasonable remuneration[143] out of the Trust Fund for any services that he provides to or on behalf of the Trust.
(2) For this purpose, a trustee acts in a professional capacity if he acts in the course of a profession or business which consists of or includes the provision of services in connection with
  (a) the management or administration of trusts generally or a particular kind of trust, or
  (b) any particular aspect of the management or administration of trusts generally or a particular kind of trust.

It is fair that lay trustees, such as members of the family of the settlor, should not charge for their services. If they do not want to do the work, they may appoint professional agents to do it for them. But this will need to be reconsidered in special cases. An old and traditional formula authorises charges to be made by:

> Any trustee being a solicitor or other person engaged in a profession or business ...

This is wider than the clause used in this book. There need be no connection between the trustee's business and the trust. Under this form, any self-employed person, carrying on a trade or profession, will be able to charge; the window cleaner just as well as the solicitor. A trustee who is a company director can charge for work done since he is engaged in the business of his company.[144] A trustee

141 It is even arguable that the same applies where there is a third trustee who also consents.
142 For other statutory precedents see TA (NI) 1958, s 41; School Standard and Framework Act 1998, Sch 11, para 6.
143 TA (NI) 2001, s 29(3) defines 'reasonable remuneration' but in such general terms as to add nothing to one's understanding, so it is not necessary or appropriate to set out the definition in the draft.
144 This natural reading is also supported by the reference to the 'business' of the directors in Table A, art 89.

who is an employee is likewise 'engaged' in the business of his employer or in the business of being an employee[145]. Even (say) a part time nanny is 'engaged' in the business of being a nanny. There is some sense in allowing a trustee to charge in all these cases. If the trustee were not involved in his duties as trustee, he would have more time to devote to, and might therefore expect more profit from, his other business. The test is to ask what the typical settlor or testator would want, and on this basis the traditional wording is thought to be rather wide as a standard form.

Standard charges and conditions

20.56

Another standard form provides:

> *A corporate trustee shall have the rights benefits and remuneration set out in its published terms and conditions for the time being ...*

As far as remuneration is concerned, it is suggested that the normal remuneration clause is quite sufficient. It will allow reasonable remuneration; if the corporate trustee cannot justify its charges as reasonable, the drafter should hesitate to provide a form which might allow them.

As far as the other 'conditions' are concerned, the drafter should himself deal with such matters and should not leave the matter to subsequent negotiation. Standard conditions drafted on behalf of corporate trustees will naturally give the trustees the most generous exemption clause.[146] Experience suggests that there will be no difficulty in finding corporate trustees prepared to act without these clauses.

Some commentators take the view that a reference to scale fees or conditions of a trust corporation in a will may be ineffective to incorporate a scale or conditions which are variable in the future.[147]

Commissions and bank charges

20.57

The form used in this book is:

145 This natural reading is also supported by *Ronbar Enterprises v Green* [1954] 2 All ER 266 (discussing comparable wording in a covenant in restraint of trade.)

146 See especially 5.16 (Trustee exemption clauses).

147 Williams, Mortimer and Sunnucks, *Executors, Administrators and Probate* (17th ed, 1993), p 309. Under the usual rules of incorporation by reference this is strictly correct. But the courts would probably not strike down what has become common conveyancing practice.

> A person may retain any reasonable commission or profit in respect of any transaction or service relating to this Settlement even though that was procured by an exercise of fiduciary powers (by that person or some other person) provided that:
> (a) The person would in the normal course of business receive and retain the commission on such transaction.
> (b) The receipt of the commission or profit shall be disclosed to the Trustees.

The form is self explanatory. On basic principles this could not be done without authorisation.[148] It could be omitted if the drafter is seeking to be concise.

Excursus: trustee charging clauses [149]

20.58

The burden of history rests heavily on the construction of trustee charging clauses. In earlier times there was a plenitude of persons with the leisure and resources to take on unremunerated trusteeships. In those days it was natural that the courts would regard charging clauses with suspicion, and construe them strictly. Of course times have changed. Professional trustees, who charge, have ceased to be the exception and have become the norm. On reading the older cases, this must be borne in mind: thoughtless citation of dicta from the old cases will give an entirely misleading impression.

Layman's work

20.59

A charging clause is taken (in the absence of contrary intent) to include charges for layman's work: Trustee Act (Northern Ireland) 2001, s 28(2).[150]

148 Authority is not needed for this proposition but see *Marley v Mutual Security Merchant Bank and Trust Co Ltd* [1995] CLC 261 and (belatedly) [2001] WTLR 483 accessible on www.kessler.co.uk.

149 The authors have seen a transcript B presumably prepared by a rueful litigant B which referred to a 'trustee chagrin clause'.

150 Some commentators expressed the view that before the TA (NI)2001 an express charging clause authorised charges for professional work but not layman's work unless this was expressly stated. In the author's' opinion this view was based on a misreading of some antique cases on the construction of specific charging clauses. The point is now academic but for a discussion see James Kessler, *Drafting Trusts and Will Trusts* (4th ed) at 15.062. Section 28(2) only applies where the trustee is a trust corporation or acting in a professional capacity. However, where lay trustees are authorised to charge, the rule excluding charges for layman's work cannot on any view be considered to apply. For charitable trusts see 24.8 (Remuneration of trustees).

Informing the client

20.60

The old cases laid down that a drafter should not include a charging clause of the kind used in this book except under express instructions given by the client himself with full knowledge of its effect.[151] This made sense at a time when the client would not expect trustees to charge. Nowadays no client of testamentary capacity will expect professional trustees to work for nothing. Further, charging clauses are generally implied by statute. Accordingly this rule has ceased to apply. Having said that, it is the solicitor's duty to explain the draft to the client, and an explanation of the charging clause would follow as part of that in any event.

Remuneration of corporate trustee

20.61

One commentator formerly expressed the view that a charging clause only authorised companies (as opposed to individuals) to charge if this was expressly authorised. In the authors' opinion this was based on a misreading of a case on the construction of a specific charging clause.[152] However, no-one could take this view now; the Trustee Act (NI) 2001 implied charging clauses for a trustee acting in a professional capacity plainly apply to companies and individuals.

Trustee remuneration clause: dispositive or administrative?

Status of remuneration clause for purposes of succession law

20.62

It was formerly the case that:

(1) The charging clause did not take effect in a will if the trustee B the 'beneficiary' of the charging clause (or his spouse) B was a witness. Likewise if the witness was a partner or the spouse of a partner of the trustee.
(2) The benefit of the clause would abate if the estate was insufficient for payment in full.

151 *Re Chapple* (1884) 27 Ch D 584; *Re Sykes* [1909] 2 Ch 241. There is no contemporary authority on the point, except the delphic comment of Vinelott J in *Re Orwell* [1982] 3 All ER 177 at 179: '*It has been said* that a wider form of charging clause entitling a solicitor trustee to charge ought not to be included except under express instructions given by the client himself with full knowledge of its effect.' (Emphasis added; the first four words are surely significant.)

152 The point is now academic but for a discussion see James Kessler, *Drafting Trusts and Will Trusts* (4th ed) at 15.064.

(3) The clause would not take effect if the estate was insolvent.

This was because the charging clause was a beneficial[153] provision for these purposes. Now these rules have been reversed in relation to professional trustees.[154]

Status of remuneration clause for other purposes

20.63

By contrast, a remuneration clause is administrative for the following purposes:

(1) The courts' jurisdiction to secure proper administration of a trust; so the court has inherent jurisdiction to authorise trustee remuneration (though it has no jurisdiction to alter beneficial interests).[155]

(2) The rule against perpetuities; so the remuneration clause is outside the scope of that rule.[156]

(3) All tax purposes[157]; no one has ever doubted that a trustee remuneration clause may be included in an IP trust and an A&M trust and does not infringe the conditions for such trusts. If the settlor receives remuneration, this is not a benefit, for the IHT reservation of benefits rules,[158] or, by parity of reasoning, for the income tax or CGT settlement provisions.

(4) Charity law: see paragraph 24.8 (Trustee remuneration clause in charities).

Reviewing this list it is obvious that the succession law cases are anomalous and explicable only for historic reasons. Thus for all other purposes it is submitted that a modern court should regard the remuneration clause as administrative.

153 See 18.1 (Administrative/dispositive/beneficial). If these matters had first come before the courts today, when trustees charging clauses are the norm, the matter would have been decided differently. But the law is now settled.

154 TA (NI) 2001, s 28(2). The old law still applies in relation to charging clauses for the benefit of lay trustees. It is a pity the Law Commission did not adopt the simpler solution of abrogating the old law entirely. The point does not arise in the precedents in this book, which do not authorise lay trustees to charge.

155 *Re Duke of Norfolk* [1982] Ch 61.

156 This is mentioned expressly in PA(NI) 1966, s 8: the drafter plainly had the authorities in mind and was aware that he needed to deal with this power expressly, as it would not otherwise have been clear whether the power was to be classified as an administrative power, outside the perpetuity rule, or as a dispositive power, within it.

157 IHTA 1984, s 90 (trustees, annuities) is an exception.

158 The Revenue rightly accept this: see the curiously named Inland Revenue Capital Taxes Advanced Instruction Manual D.75 (sensibly ignoring the old Australian estate duty decision to the contrary, *Oakes v Stamp Duties Comr of New South Wales* [1954] AC 57). The same applies to trustee/director remuneration clauses discussed below.

Can the settlor charge if he is a trustee but there is a settlor exclusion clause?

20.64

The reader will recall that a trust will generally contain a settlor exclusion clause:

> *... no power conferred by this Settlement shall be exercisable for the benefit of the Settlor or the spouse of the Settlor ...*

It is considered that the settlor exclusion clause does not prevent remuneration of a settlor or spouse. This is because (looking at the matter broadly) the settlor or spouse has gained no advantage: he has worked for his remuneration. The alternative basis for reaching this conclusion is that the payment is administrative and not dispositive. On any view, it is not necessary to say expressly that the settlor and spouse cannot charge remuneration.

Trustee/director remuneration

20.65

The form used in this book is as follows:

> The Trustees may make arrangements to remunerate themselves for work done for a company connected with the Trust Fund.

Where trustees hold a majority of shares in a company they cannot receive remuneration for work done for the company. Where trustees have a minority shareholding, it seems that they should use their trust votes to oppose their own remuneration. This rule would prevent trustees from working for companies connected with the trust; hardly desirable. The general rule must therefore be reversed by express provision in the trust.

How should this be done? It is said that the standard trustee remuneration clause does not itself allow trustees to charge a company for work done for that company.[159] A common form is:

> *The Trustees may enter into a contract with and be remunerated as a director or other officer or employee or as agent or adviser of any company at any time or in any way connected with the Trust Fund and retain as the Trustees' absolute property any remuneration received in that capacity notwithstanding that his*

[159] *Re Gee* [1948] Ch 284. The reasoning is unconvincing and perhaps the point may come to be reviewed by the courts.

> *office or employment may have been obtained in right or by means or by reason of his position as one of the Trustees or any shares, stock, property, rights or powers belonging to or connected with the Trust Fund.*

The more succinct form used in this book is derived from a precedent upheld in *Re Llewellin.*[160] The Judge observed that it was not necessary to state in express terms that the trustees 'are not to be liable to account to the trust for the remuneration derived from their office'; that followed as a matter of necessary implication.

160 [1949] Ch 225.

CHAPTER 21

Bare trusts

21.1

A bare trust is one where the trustees hold property on trust for one or more beneficiaries absolutely.

Why use bare trusts?

21.2

The main attraction of the bare trust is that it is possible to use the CGT annual allowance of the beneficiaries. This advantage scarcely justifies the administration of setting up a bare trust for a single beneficiary (unless perhaps the settlor is a professional who will deal with the paperwork himself). But where the settlor has a number of children or grandchildren, the tax advantage of a bare trust for them (in equal shares) becomes more substantial. The wretched reforms of the FA 1998 tax the gains of a small trust much more heavily than an individual of modest means. This often tips the balance of advantage from substantive to bare trusts. For other consequences of using a bare trust, see para 25.5 (Consequences of using a bare trust). Investment Managers offer standard forms for use with their own funds, which should be satisfactory as the drafting is straightforward.

A precedent

21.3

This settlement is made [date] between:

1 [Name of settlor] of [address] ('the Settlor') of the one part and

2 2.1 [Name of first trustee] of [address] and
2.2 [Name of second trustee] of [address]
('the Original Trustees') of the other part.

Whereas

(A) The Settlor has ten grandchildren now living ('the Grandchildren') namely

(1) [name] who was born on [date].

[*continue with each grandchild on a new line*]

(B) This Settlement shall be known as the [Name-of-Settlor Settlement 2000].

Now this deed witnesses as follows:

1 Definitions

In this settlement:

1.1 **'The Trustees'** means the Original Trustees or the trustees of the settlement for the time being.

1.2 **'The Trust Fund'** means:

1.2.1 property transferred to the Trustees to hold on the terms of this Settlement; and

1.2.2 all property from time to time representing the above.

1.3 **'Trust Property'** means any property comprised in the Trust Fund.

2 The Trust Fund shall be held on trust for the Grandchildren in equal shares absolutely.

3 Appointment of Trustees

The power of appointing trustees is exercisable by the Settlor during [his] life and by will.

4 Further Provisions

The provisions set out in the schedule below shall have effect.

The beneficiary of the bare trust should not be a party to the deed.[1]

1 See para 9.8 (Who should be parties?).

CHAPTER 22

Trusts of life insurance policies

22.1

This chapter considers straightforward life insurance policies, ie policies which pay a sum of money on death. Different considerations apply to:

(1) seven-year reducing policies to cover the risk of IHT on a PET. These should usually be given to the donee of the PET;

(2) policies to pay a sum on survival to a specified age or prior death. The complication here is that the policyholder may want to give away the death benefit but retain the other benefit. More bespoke drafting is needed;

(3) policies (often called bonds) which contain only a nominal element of life insurance. In substance these are simply investments wrapped up in a life insurance package, and they do not require any particular form of trust;

(4) pension schemes (which may of course confer death benefits): see the next chapter.

A life insurance policy should not normally[1] be kept by the life assured. For the proceeds of the policy (which *ex hypothesi* the life assured will not live to see) would be subject to IHT on his death. A policy could be given to the individual's children. It is often more appropriate to transfer it to a trust for the benefit of the individual's children and widow.

Insurance company standard form

22.2

The drafter of a trust for a life policy has an easy option; this is to adopt the standard form supplied free of charge[2] by the insurance company concerned. This is generally more or less adequate.[3] But even where all possible care is taken on

1 One exception is when the policy is to be security for a loan taken out by the life assured.

2 Because a charge would be an offence: see para 1.11 (Formal qualifications for the drafter).

3 This is the authors' experience. But there are (or at least have been) a few rotten eggs in this basket. It usually takes many years for the problem to emerge (which conveniently helps the company's limitation defence to any claim). For instance, *Pappadakis v Pappadakis* [2000] 1 WTLR 719, accessible at www.kessler.co.uk, discloses some shoddy practice in Abbey Life in the 1980s.

behalf of the insurance company, the forms suffer from a number of defects. First, they are standardised. The drafter had to devise a single form which was short, comprehensible, and which requires a minimum of subsequent attention. (This is by no means easy.) The form will provide for an interest in possession for children and a power of appointment. In practice a discretionary trust is usually more suited to the needs of beneficiaries if there is a family solicitor to keep an eye on the 10-year anniversaries. Secondly, the insurance company standard documentation is drafted to deal with one policy only, but where a client has a number of policies it is convenient to use a single trust (or possibly a series of similar trusts) but not to use separate trusts in different forms. The reader will not be surprised that the insurance company's forms come supplied with a stiff disclaimer so if problems do arise, an action against the insurance company would not be easy.[4]

How much more satisfactory to draft a proper trust drafted with the individual's circumstances in mind. If there is some other trust in the family, that may be a suitable trust to hold the life insurance policy, one should not multiply trusts unnecessarily.

Trusts created pursuant to contract of insurance

22.3

The contract with the insurance company (and the policy provided pursuant to that contract) may provide that the policy is from its inception to be held on trust.[5] It is necessary to check that this is not the case, so that the client owns his policy and can transfer it into a trust.

Trust created over existing policy

22.4

There are two methods to create a trust of a life insurance policy belonging to the client:

(1) *Declaration of trust by settlor:*
   (a) the settlor executes a declaration of trust, under which he declares that he holds the policy on trust;

4 Another short cut, mentioned here for completeness, is to express the life insurance to be 'effected for the benefit of the individual's wife and children.' This is a short form, which brings into effect a primitive trust for those objects: Married Women's Property Act 1882, s 11. The form of 1882 would not today be regarded as adequate. It would be better to use the life insurance company's standard form.

5 This is a convenient way of creating trusts in the life insurance company standard form. The question whether particular wording created a trust is discussed in a number of cases, summarised in *Re Foster* [1966] 1 WLR 222. A shameful, unnecessary case law because competent drafting should always make it plain whether or not a trust is intended. The absence of modern case law suggests this lesson may have been learned.

(b) it is then usual (not strictly essential but convenient) for the settlor to appoint one or more additional trustees to act with him.[6]

(2) *Transfer to trustees to hold on trust:*
   (a) the settlor (and trustees) execute a trust deed; and
   (b) the settlor assigns the policy to the trustees.[7]

The simplest course is that:
(1) the trust is not set out in the contract or the terms of the policy;
(2) the settlor and trustees execute the trust;[8] and
(3) in a separate deed, the settlor assigns the policy to the trustees.

IHT implications of using a discretionary trust

22.5

A discretionary trust is usually[9] the best form. When the policy is transferred to the trust it will normally have relatively little value. So a gift of the policy to the trust will not give rise to IHT, because of the annual exemption or the nil-rate band.[10] The payment of regular premiums for the life insurance policy will normally be an exempt transfer.[11]

The gift of the policy to the trust will not give rise to a gift with reservation provided that the owner of the policy is excluded from benefit under the trust.

6 This appointment may be:
(i) set out in the deed of declaration of trust; or
(ii) set out in a separate deed of appointment.
Either way, the appointment has the effect of an assignment of the policy to the new trustees: TA(NI) 1958, s 39. Notice should be given to the insurance company.

7 This assignment may be:
(1) set out in the trust deed, or
(2) set out in a separate deed.
Notice should be given to the insurance company.

8 Of course if the trust exists already and new policies are to be assigned to it, then a simple deed of assignment will be required.

9 The only exceptions are if the settlor has made a substantial chargeable transfer in the last seven years; or if the 'normal expenditure' IHT exemption will not apply on payment of the premiums.

10 This assumes that:
(1) the settlor has made no chargeable transfers in the seven years prior to creating the trust; and
(2) the settlor assigns the policy to the trust as soon as it is taken out; or if there is a delay, the settlor is not so ill or so old that he is likely to die soon (making the policy a valuable asset);
(3) the policy is paid out of annual premiums and not by a single substantial one-off payment.
If these assumptions were wrong there might be an IHT charge on the transfer of the policy to a discretionary trust. If so an IP trust or A&M trust might be used.

11 IHTA 1984, s 21 (normal expenditure out of income). It follows that IHTA 1984, s 67 (added property) will not apply in computing 10-year charges.

Likewise, the payment of premiums will not give rise to a gift with reservation for IHT purposes provided that the person who pays the premiums is excluded from benefit under the trust. Thus in a simple case where the settlor takes out the policy and pays the premiums, the settlor must be excluded from benefit. Strictly speaking, his spouse need not be excluded. The usual course is to exclude settlor and spouse, but not the widow of the settlor.

The position is different where a husband and wife (or an unmarried couple) take out a joint policy, payable on the death of the survivor of the two of them. In such cases the premiums will normally be paid by the husband and the wife jointly, and the policy would belong to them jointly. It is then necessary to exclude them both from the trust; see para 9.11 (Form where trust made by joint settlors).

Ten-year charges and exit charges during lifetime of settlor

22.6

While the trust is discretionary in form, it will be within the scope of Chapter III, Part III of the IHTA 1984, which imposes 10-year charges and exit charges.

The amount of the 10-year charge would normally[12] be nil if the value of the trust property (the policy) falls within the nil-rate band at that time. That will be the case if:

(1) the death benefit is within the nil-rate band; or
(2) the life assured is in good health on the 10-year anniversary.[13]

The trustees should therefore review the position shortly before each 10-year anniversary.[14] The amount of an exit charge before the first 10-year anniversary would be nil, so a 10-year charge can be avoided if necessary by an appropriate appointment. It would only be desirable to make some appointment at that stage if the settlor is old or in very poor health at that time and the policies have a value above the nil-rate band.

It is just possible that the settlor might die unexpectedly immediately before the 10-year anniversary. In that case there could be a charge on the 10-year anniversary. The maximum rate is 6% but normally the rate will be much less or nil. That risk is an acceptable price to pay for the significant advantage of flexibility offered by the discretionary trust.

12 Assuming the settlor had not made chargeable transfers in the last seven years.

13 Note for completeness that IHTA 1984, s 167 has specific rules on the valuation of life policies. However, in practice this section will not make a great deal of difference.

14 To avoid the necessity for this, insurance company standard forms usually confer interests in possession on the children of the settlor. This works passably well, but the flexibility of a discretionary trust will usually be slightly better.

Tax returns

22.7

No IHT return is normally[15] required on the creation of the trust. IHT returns would be required on:
(1) subsequent 10-year anniversaries; and
(2) on the occasion of the trust ceasing to be discretionary in form (exit charge).

If this was accidentally overlooked (which perhaps often happens when the trust fund is small and the charge nil) the maximum penalty is £100.[16] No other returns are required while the trust has no taxable income or gains.

Advantages of multiple discretionary trusts

22.8

A client who has created a discretionary trust over a life policy may wish to take out another policy to increase his life cover. The question arises whether he should use the same trust for both policies or create a new trust.

A single trust is all that is needed where the total death benefit of all policies in the trust is within the nil-rate band. The trust is in principle outside the scope of IHT because the exit and 10-year charges are nil.

The advantage of separate trusts is that each will have in effect its own nil-rate band, so 10-year charges and exit charges which would apply to a more substantial discretionary trust (above the nil-rate band) will be reduced or avoided. This assumes that the law remains broadly as it now is, but one can only plan on that assumption. The disadvantage is complexity and additional administration costs. Also, other trusts made by the same settlor will enjoy a smaller CGT annual exemption, though in practice this may not concern many settlors.

Everyone would prefer to use a single trust for all of a client's policies. But it depends on the circumstances and values involved. If the total death benefit of all policies is less than £300,000, say, then a single trust is certainly preferable. In such cases there need not normally be any significant 10-year or exit charge. As

15 This assumes that:
(1) the value transferred by any gift to the trust (together with all previous chargeable transfers within the 12 months) does not exceed £10,000; and
(2) the total chargeable transfers made during the 10 years preceding the transfer does not exceed £40,000.
For this purpose potentially exempt transfers may be ignored: they are not 'chargeable transfers'. See para 30.11 (Returns and other matters).

16 IHTA 1984, s 245. One hopes that the Revenue would charge no penalty in practice.

the values increase, the balance of advantage shifts to some extent towards separate trusts. If the death benefit exceeds £1m then multiple trusts would be better. For cases in between, the answer depends on how much trouble and expense one is prepared to take in order to optimise the tax position. The tax problem is not so much the 10-year charges during the lifetime of the client (which will usually be nil or manageable, as explained above). The advantage of multiple trusts is very long term: if one single trust is used, and has a very substantial trust fund, the trustees will be reluctant to keep the trust discretionary in form once the policies mature, after the death of the settlor. This is because the IHT cost of doing so (the 10-year charges) will make this unattractive.[17] If there are a number of separate trusts, the 10-year charges will be much reduced or nil, and this would allow the trustees to let the trusts remain discretionary in form.

A similar question arises if the client is taking out substantial life cover, say £1m. It would best from a tax point of view to create four separate trusts, each holding separate policies for £¼m rather than one single policy.

The question is whether the costs incurred will justify the long-term IHT saving. As a rule of thumb it is suggested that the balance of advantage favours the use of multiple separate trusts (each with a trust fund within the nil-rate band) only if the total sum insured exceeds £1m. In practice that will be rare. If there is to be more than one trust, care is needed in execution of the arrangements. The trusts should not be identical in form.[18] They should not commence on the same day.[19]

Some drafting points

22.9

Trusts of life insurance policies tend to be held in store and not reviewed for many years. Standard forms of life insurance companies often contain a 'missing trustee' form. This may help solve a problem which no doubt arises occasionally in practice:

17 At 2002/03 rates some sample computations of the IHT 10-year charge are as follows:

Value of trust fund on TYA	£300,000	£600,000	£1,000,000	£2,000,000
Tax rate	1.00%	3.5%	4.5%	5.25%
10-year charge	£3,000	£21,000	£45,000	£105,000

18 In *Rysaffe v IRC* [2002] EWHC 1114 (Ch), [2002] STC 872 five settlements identical in all except formal respects were held to be a separate settlement but 'it would have been clearer if there had been a few differences between them at the outset' (para 25). A Revenue argument based on associated operations was also rejected.

19 This aggregates the tax charge: see IHTA 1984, ss 62, 66(4)(c). A settlement commences when property first becomes comprised in it: IHTA 1984, s 60. In *Rysaffe v IRC* [2002] EWHC 1114 (Ch), [2002] STC 872 the settlor wrote a single cheque for £50 to his solicitors. The judge found, on the basis of evidence not set out in the judgment, that £10 became comprised in each settlement on separate days. It would have been clearer to write five separate cheques, banked on separate days.

> Where a trustee ('the Missing Trustee') cannot be found and the other trustees ('the Remaining Trustees') have made all reasonable efforts to trace him, the Remaining Trustees being not less than two in number may by deed discharge the Missing Trustee. A recital in that deed stating that the Missing Trustee cannot be found and that all reasonable efforts have been made to trace him shall be conclusive evidence in favour of any person dealing with the Trustees in good faith.

It would be sensible to appoint a professional trustee younger than the settlor, along with the settlor (if desired) and a friend or member of the family (if desired).

Some standard forms provide:

> No lien shall be created on the policy as a result of any payment of a premium by the Settlor.

This does no harm but is not necessary. The question of whether a payment of a policy premium (or any other sum for the trust) creates a right to reimbursement (by a lien) is not determined by the terms of the trust. It is determined by the intention of the payer at the time of the payment. In normal circumstances one would assume that the intention of the settlor paying a premium was to benefit the trust, and the settlor did not intend he should have a right of reimbursement.[20]

Precedent trust for life policy

22.10

The standard discretionary trust will be appropriate with modification of the accumulation period.

> This settlement is made [date] between:
> 1. [Name of settlor] of [address] ('the Settlor') of the one part and
> 2. 2.1 [Name of first trustee] of [address] and
>   2.2 [Name of second trustee] of [address]
>   ('the Original Trustees') of the other part.
>
> Whereas:
> 1. The Settlor has [two] children:
>   1.1 [Adam Smith] ('[Adam]') who was born on [date] and
>   1.2 [Mary Smith] ('[Mary]') who was born on [date].

[20] *Re Smith* [1937] Ch 636; *De Vigier v IRC* (1964) 42 TC 24 at 40 (lien intended); *Re Roberts* [1946] Ch 1 (no lien intended).

This Settlement shall be known as the [John Smith Discretionary Settlement 1998].

Now this deed witnesses as follows:

1. **Definitions**

In this settlement:

1.1 **'The Trustees'** means the Original Trustees or the trustees of the settlement for the time being.

1.2 **'The Trust Fund'** means:

1.2.1 property transferred to the Trustees to hold on the terms of this Settlement; and

1.2.2 all property from time to time representing the above.

1.3 **'Trust Property'** means any property comprised in the Trust Fund.

1.4 **'The Trust Period'** means the period of 80 years beginning with the date of this Settlement. That is the perpetuity period applicable to this Settlement under the rule against perpetuities.

1.5 **'The Beneficiaries'** means:

1.5.1 The children and descendants of the Settlor.

1.5.2 The spouses, widows and widowers (whether or not remarried) of 1.5.1 above.

1.5.3 The [widow] (whether or not remarried) of the Settlor.

1.5.4 Any Person or class of Persons nominated to the Trustees by:

1.5.4.1 the Settlor or

1.5.4.2 two Beneficiaries (after the death of the Settlor)

and whose nomination is accepted in writing by the Trustees.

1.5.5 At any time during which there are no Beneficiaries within 1.5.1 above:

1.5.5.1 [specify 'fall back' beneficiaries if desired, eg nieces and nephews and their families].

1.5.5.2 [any company, body or trust established for charitable purposes only].

1.6 **'Person'** includes a person anywhere in the world and includes a Trustee.

2. **Trust Income**

Subject to the Overriding Powers below:

2.1 The Trustees may accumulate the whole or part of the income of the Trust Fund during the Trust Period. That income shall be added to the Trust Fund.

2.2 The Trustees shall pay or apply the remainder of the income to or for the benefit of any Beneficiaries, as the Trustees think fit, during the Trust Period.

3. **Overriding Powers**

The Trustees shall have the following powers ('Overriding Powers'): [set out standard overriding powers]

4. **Default Clause**
Subject to that, the Trust Fund shall be held on trust for [Adam and Mary in equal shares – or specify default trusts as appropriate] absolutely.
5. Appointment of Trustees
(1) The power of appointing trustees is exercisable by the Settlor during [his] life and by will.
(2) [Set out provision concerning Missing Trustee: see para 22.9 (Some drafting points).]
6. Further Provisions
The provisions set out in the schedule below shall have effect.
[For a shorter form, omit the schedule and say instead of the above:
'The standard provisions of the Society of Trust and Estate Practitioners (1st Edition) shall apply with the deletion of paragraph 5. Section 11 Trusts of Land and Appointment of Trustees Act 1996 (consultation with beneficiaries) shall not apply.']
7. Stamp Duty Certificate
The Settlor certifies that this deed falls within category N of the Stamp Duty (Exempt Instruments) Regulations.
8. Exclusion of Settlor and Spouse
Notwithstanding anything else in this Settlement, no power conferred by this settlement shall be exercisable, and no provision shall operate so as to allow Trust Property or its income to become payable to or applicable for the benefit of the Settlor or the spouse of the Settlor in any circumstances whatsoever.

In witness, [etc]

THE SCHEDULE: FURTHER PROVISIONS

[Here set out the administrative provisions suitable to the discretionary settlement.]

CHAPTER 23

Trusts of pension death benefits

23.1

This chapter is concerned with death benefits under the following classes of pension schemes:

(1) approved personal pension arrangements within the meaning of ICTA 1988, Part XIV, ch IV (schemes made from 1 July 1988);
(2) schemes approved under ICTA 1988, ss 620 or 621 (Part XIV, ch III) (schemes made before 1 July 1988, formerly known as ICTA 1970, ss 226 and 226A policies 'Retirement Annuity Schemes');
(3) exempt Approved Schemes (generally known as occupational pension schemes or Retirement Benefit Schemes) within the meaning of ICTA 1988, Part XIV, ch I.

In this chapter 'pension death benefits' means:
(1) the member's fund or
(2) a payment under a life insurance contract
which may under the terms of the pension scheme be payable as a lump sum on the death of the member of the scheme.

A pension scheme is a more complex asset than a simple life insurance policy discussed in the last chapter. It will normally provide annuities as well as death benefits, and the member will neither wish nor have power to assign the annuities to a trust. But many of the considerations which apply are similar.

In what follows it is assumed in the first instance that the pension is governed by the Integrated Model Rules for Personal Pension Schemes 'IMR/PPS' (issued 2000)[1] but possible variations are also considered.

1 Available on the Inland Revenue website (www.inlandrevenue.gov.uk/pensionschemes/model_rules.htm).

Is it desirable (or possible) to transfer pension death benefits to a trust?[2]

23.2

Under the IMR/PPS slightly different rules apply to
(1) the payment of the Member's Fund (which may be paid out as a lump sum if the member dies before benefits start) and
(2) a Protected Rights Fund (which arises where the member has contracted out of SERPS)
(3) payment under a life insurance contract which may be made under the scheme.

The Member's Fund (if the member dies before benefits start)

23.3

The position is as follows:
(1) the member may have chosen[3] that the member's fund should be used to buy a 'survivor's pension', ie a pension for the widow, widower or dependants. In that case the fund is used to buy an annuity (the annuitant herself has certain options which need not be discussed here). It will not pass to a trust. In what follows it is assumed that the member has not made this choice;
(2) subject to (1), there may be specific provision regarding the payment of the member's fund under the contract applying to the scheme in question. However this is rare and is assumed here not to be the case.

Ignoring those two possibilities, the position is governed by IMR/PPS, rule 9.15 which provides:

> 9.15 **Non-Protected Rights Fund – lump sum.** Subject to Rule 13.5,[4] if a Member dies and no Survivor's pension has become payable under Rules 9.1 or 9.2,[5] then the Scheme Administrator may as soon as practicable and subject to Rule 9.16, pay out the Member's Fund (other than any Protected Rights Fund) as a lump sum:
> (1) [this applies if there is specific provision in the contract].
> (2) If (1) is not applicable and at the time of the Member's death the Scheme Administrator is satisfied that the contract[6] is subject to a valid trust

2 See Xenia Frostick, 'What happens when a member dies' Occupational Pensions, August 2000, accessible on www.kessler.co.uk.
3 Pursuant to IMR/PPS, rule 9.1
4 Rule 13 deals with transfer payments from other schemes.
5 See (1) above.
6 The context shows:
(1) that the reference to 'the contract' is a reference to the right to payment of the Member's Fund if the member dies before the benefit starts; which may not be a contractual right!
(2) The member has the power to assign this right to a trust which satisfies the necessary condition. *Quaere* whether this is an assignment or the exercise of a power of nomination.

[under which no beneficial interest in a benefit can be payable to the Member, the Member's estate or the Member's legal[7] personal representatives][8] to the trustees of the trust; or

(3) if (1) and (2) are not applicable, at the discretion of the Scheme Administrator, to or for the benefit of any one or more of the following in such proportions as the Scheme Administrator decides:-
   (a) any persons (including trustees) whose names the Member has notified to the Scheme Administrator in writing prior to the date of the member's death;
   (b) the Member's surviving spouse, children and remoter issue;
   (c) the Member's Dependants;
   (d) the individuals entitled under the Member's will to any interest in the Member's estate;
   (e) the Member's legal personal representatives.

9.16 **Lump sum payable by Scheme Administrator – time limit.** The Scheme Administrator will pay any lump sum within 2 years of the Member's death. If this is not practicable then, at the end of 2 years, it will be transferred to a separate account outside the Scheme until it can be paid.

It is suggested that the best choice for a member with substantial death benefits is to transfer the right to the death benefits to trustees. Trustees of his own choosing are likely to be more familiar with his wishes, and with the circumstances of the beneficiaries, than the Scheme Administrator. This also gives him the scope to draft an appropriate trust for their benefit.

An alternative would be to notify the Scheme Administrator of a suitable trust pursuant to rule 9.15(3)(a). The trust might be created for the purpose or an existing family trust. The difference between this and an assignment is that the Scheme Administrator would have to consider whether to exercise its discretion in favour of this trust, or whether to pay it to other beneficiaries named in rule 9.15(3). Unfortunately there is also some doubt as to what perpetuity period is allowed for a trust to which the pension provider transfers the death benefit. The safe period is 21 years from the death of the member.[9] For the time being this course is not the best solution.

If neither of these are taken then the Scheme Administrator will either distribute capital to the beneficiaries, or create trusts for them using the power of advancement in r 19.5(3).[10] This raises the same perpetuity problem so it is slightly less than ideal. In practice no serious problem should arise *provided* that the member does

7 It is traditional for pensions and life insurance documentation to refer to 'legal' personal representatives, whereas for everyone else the expression used is just 'personal representatives'.

8 Words in brackets added in the 1995 amendment to the 1992 version of IMR/PPS.

9 See *Thomas on Powers* (1st edn, 1998) Sweet & Maxwell, pp 162 ff. This problem will be solved in England if the Law Commission's recommendations become law: Law Commission Report No 251 (the Rules against Perpetuities and Excessive Accumulations).

10 See para 10.11 (Power of advancement used to create new trusts).

not have the right to the death benefits or a right of nomination. In particular there is no problem if the Pension Scheme rules follow the 2000 IMR/PRS or incorporates the 1995 amendments to the 1992 version of IMR/PPS.[11]

The rules allow the Scheme Administrator two years before making the payment, and a delay may offer the incidental advantage that funds grow tax free within the scheme for that additional period. This advantage is available whether or not the death benefit is transferred to an express trust.

Personal Pension Scheme: Payment under Life Insurance Contract

23.4

The relevant rules of IMR/PPS provide:-

> 4.15 **Using contributions to buy life insurance.** A Member may, if allowed to do so under the Scheme, choose for all ... or part of the contributions in respect of him or her (excluding Protected Payments as defined in Rule 5.1) to be used by the Scheme Administrator as premiums on a life insurance contract with an Insurer. The contract must provide a lump sum to be paid only if the Member dies before a specified age (not later than age 75). This lump sum shall be payable in accordance with Rule 10, provided that
>
> [4.15.1] rights to benefits under such a life insurance contract may not be assigned, and Rule 10.1(3) shall not apply unless this proviso is expressly deleted in the contract documentation in respect of specific Arrangements or parts of Arrangements.
>
> ...
>
> [paragraphing added for convenience]
>
> **10. Member dies before pension starts – life insurance**
>
> **Lump sum payable under life insurance contract.** 10. 1 If some of the contributions in respect of a Member have been used to pay premiums under a life insurance contract as described in Rule 4.15, the Scheme

[11] The Revenue argues, perhaps correctly, that where the pension rules takes the pre-1995 form, before benefits start the member has a general power to dispose of the fund, so the members fund is subject to IHT on his death: IHTA 1984, ss 5(2) and 151(4). So if a member is a member of an old scheme which uses the pre-1995 amendment wording, either a trust should be created (excluding the member) or the wording of the rule should be amended.

Administrator will, as soon as practicable and subject to Rule 9.16, pay the lump sum benefit from the contract:-

(1) in accordance with any specific provision regarding payment of such sums under the contract; or

(2) if (1) is not applicable and at the time of the Member's death the Scheme Administrator is satisfied that the contract is subject to a valid trust [under which no beneficial interest in a benefit can be payable to the Member, the Member's estate or the Member's legal personal representatives][12] to the trustees of the trust; or

(3) subject to the proviso to Rule 4.15, if (1) and (2) are not applicable and at the time of the Member's death the contract is vested in an assignee, other than the Member's estate or the Member's legal personal representatives, to the assignee;[13] or

(4) if (1), (2) and (3) are not applicable, at the discretion of the Scheme Administrator, to or for the benefit of any one or more of the following in such proportions as the Scheme Administrator decides:-

    (a) any persons (including trustees) whose names the Member has notified to the Scheme Administrator in writing prior to the date of the Member's death;

    (b) the Member's surviving spouse, children and remoter issue;

    (c) the Member's Dependants;

    (d) the individuals entitled under the Member's will to any interest in the Member's estate;

    (e) the Member's legal personal representatives.

The position here is similar as in relation to the Member's Fund, but slightly simpler as there is no option relating to a survivor's pension: see para 23.3 (The Member's Fund). In practice the life insurance benefit can be dealt with by the same trust as that which holds the right to the Member's Fund in the event of the member's death before benefits start.

Schemes not governed by IMR/PPS

23.5

In some cases the rules of the pension scheme may provide that the death benefit is payable at the discretion of the pension provider or employer either to individuals or to a trust for their benefit. In order to comply with the Inland Revenue requirements of approved schemes, the rules will require distribution within two years of the member's death.[14] In this case the member does not own the death

12 Words in brackets date back to the 1995 amendment to IMR/PPS.

13 In the context this must mean an assignee other than a trust within rule10.1(2). Odd drafting.

14 IR12 (Practice Notes on approval of occupational pension schemes) para 11.5; IR76 (Personal Pension Schemes) para 10.36.

benefit and has no power to transfer it into a trust. The death benefit is outside the scope of IHT.[15]

Before 6 April 1980, retirement annuity schemes under ss 226 and 226A of the Income and Corporation Taxes Act 1970 directed death benefits to be paid to the member's personal representatives. Old schemes may need amendment before the member has power to assign his right to the death benefit to a trust.

Accordingly it will be necessary to review each pension policy in some detail before creating a trust of the death benefit, because one cannot assume that the member either owns the death benefit or has power to assign it to a trust.

Drafting a trust of the pension death benefit

23.6

The drafter may have offered to him the pension provider's standard form: see 22.2 (Insurance company standard form).

There are again two methods to create a trust of a pension death benefit:
(1) *Declaration of trust:*
   (a) The settlor executes a declaration of trust, under which he declares that he holds the entire pension policy on trust. However, the trust will only deal with the death benefits, so that the annuities remain in the beneficial ownership of the settlor.
   (b) It is then usual (not strictly essential but convenient) to appoint one or more additional trustees to act with the settlor.[16]
(2) *Transfer to trustees:*
(a) the settlor (and trustees) execute a settlement; and
(b) the settlor assigns the pension death benefit to the trustees of the trust.[17]

The right to the death benefit is part of the single chose in action which is the pension policy,[18] and one cannot at law assign part of a chose in action.[19] However,

15 In particular, the pension scheme is outside the scope of 10-year and exit charges by virtue of IHTA 1984, s 58(1)(d).
16 This appointment may be:
(1) set out in the declaration of trust; or
(2) set out in a separate deed of appointment.
The appointment has the effect of an assignment of the policy to the new trustees: TA(NI) 1958, s 39. Notice should be given to the pension provider.
17 This assignment may be:
(i) set out in the trust deed, or
(ii) set out in a separate deed.
Notice should be given to the Pension Provider.
18 No authority is needed for the proposition that a policy is, in principle, a single chose in action, but for an example of this, see *Foskett v McKeown* [2001] 1 AC 102.
19 Judicature (NI) Act 1978, s 87(1).

the assignment is valid in equity and no difficulty should arise out of the use of an equitable assignment.

The simplest course is (2), using a separate deed of assignment, ie:
(1) the settlor and trustees execute the settlement; and
(2) in a separate deed, the settlor assigns the death benefits to the trustees.

Of course if the trust exists already and new death benefits are to be assigned to the trust then the separate deed of assignment will be required in any event.

IHT on the pension death benefit

23.7

Statement of Practice 10/86 provides:

> **'Death benefits under superannuation arrangements**
>
> The Board confirm that their previous practice of not charging capital transfer tax on death benefits that are payable from tax-approved occupational pension and retirement annuity schemes under discretionary trusts also applies to inheritance tax.
>
> The practice extends to tax under the gifts with reservation rules as well as to tax under the ordinary inheritance tax rules.'

The statement is not very helpful. There are a wide variety of circumstances in which death benefits might be charged to IHT and it is not made clear in this statement to which of them this practice of 'not charging IHT on death benefits' is meant to apply.

IHT on death of member

23.8

The Revenue has always made it plain that they do charge IHT on the death of the member, in accordance with the law if:
(1) the right to the death benefit is an asset of the estate of the member or
(2) the member has a general power of nomination.[20]

20 See Statement of 7/5/76, SP E3, and the notes reprinted in *Capital Taxes and Estate Planning Quarterly* 1988, No 2, pp 18–22.

Ten-year and exit charges

Discretionary trusts holding the right to a pension death benefit are not subject to 10-year charges and exit charges on the right to the death benefit, before the death of the member.[21]

What is the position after the death of the member and before the fund is paid to the trustees, a period which may last up to two years? It is considered that the right is still outside the scope of ten year and exit charges; and though the point could be argued both ways, a purposive (ie sensible) construction supports this view and the Revenue appears to accept it.

Once the death benefit is paid to the trustees, the proceeds fall strictly within the scope of IHT. In practice, by a sensible but unpublished concession,[22] the Revenue does not impose an exit charge or a ten-year charge on an appointment within two years of death. So the trustees should review the position promptly on the death of the settlor, and if appropriate make an appointment within two years.

IHT on creation of trust over death benefit

23.9

The declaration of trust over the death benefit will not normally give rise to a transfer of value for IHT because the benefit will have no significant value at that time.[23] There will be no reservation of benefit problem as the settlor will be excluded.

21 This is for two reasons (either of which would suffice):

(1) the right to the death benefit is excluded property under IHTA 1984, s 48(1) (reversionary interest). Section 48(1)(b) is not in point since (i) in an IMR/PPS form scheme the member has no right to the death benefit and (ii) the member is not a 'settlor' as defined;

(2) the right to a death benefit is not 'relevant property' by virtue of IHTA 1984, s 58(1)(d):

> 'Property which is part of *or held for the purposes of* [pension] fund or scheme.'

The right to the death benefit may not be part of the fund or scheme but it is held for the purposes of the scheme. It is submitted that s 58(2) does not withdraw this relief until after payment of the lump sum.

22 The concession is referred to in Richard Oerton, 'Trusts of Death Benefits' 1993 *Capital Tax Planning* 52, accessible on www.kessler.co.uk; Trust Discussion Forum V2 No 3 (Jan 2001).

23 If the pension is a new one, this is straightforward. Even if the pension is an existing one with a substantial member's fund, the death benefit will not be payable if the member survives to take his pension, and a death benefit consisting of the right to the Member's Fund is not payable if the member elects for a survivor's pension. So the death benefit has no real value.

IHT on payment of contributions

23.10

Payment of pension contributions under pension schemes will not give rise to a transfer of value for IHT,[24] or a gift with reservation of benefit.[25]

Should there be a separate discretionary trust for each pension policy death benefit?

23.11

A person will often have a number of pension policies. The advantage of separate trusts is that each will normally have its own nil-rate band, so the 10-year charges and exit charges will be reduced. The disadvantage is complexity and additional administration costs. It is a matter of balancing the two conflicting requirements and the issue is the same as for simple life insurance policies, discussed in the previous chapter.

Should one single trust hold simple life insurance policies and pension policy death benefits?

It has been suggested that one trust might hold: (1) pension policy death benefits; and (2) policies of life assurance. Although the pension death benefit is outside the scope of IHT during the life of the member, the simple insurance policies are not. So it will in due course become necessary to compute the 10-year charge and the exit charge on the life insurance policy. The value of the death benefits is strictly to be taken into account in making this computation. The value of the death benefits could theoretically have a significant effect on the amount of the charge on the life policy.[26] For this reason it would on balance be preferable to have two separate trusts, made on separate days, one dealing with death benefits under pension schemes and the other dealing with life policies. This is not unduly onerous in practice. In most cases the death benefits would never be payable since

24 For a variety of reasons (any one of which would suffice):
(1) IHTA 1984, s 12(1) (Dispositions allowable for income tax);
(2) IHTA 1984, s 21 (Normal expenditure out of income);
(3) the payment is not normally a transfer of value as it does not reduce the value of the estate of the payor (as it increases the value of his pension annuity).

25 Because the payment is not a disposal 'by way of gift'. SP10/86 seems to show that the Revenue accepts this. Consistent with this, the Revenue accepts that a pension scheme is not a 'settlement' within the income tax definition, since there is no 'bounty': CGT Manual 14596.

26 Even though the right to the death benefit is not relevant property; see IHTA 1984, ss 66(4)(b), 69(5)(a). But normally the death benefits have no or little value.

the member will survive to take his pension. If the member dies before taking the annuity, the two trusts can be combined later.

Precedent trust for death benefits under personal pension fund

23.12

This draft is a slight revision of the draft set out in para 22.11 (Precedent trust for life policy):

This trust *etc*

Now this deed witnesses as follows:

1. **Definitions**
   [Set out standard definitions of 'The Trustees', 'The Trust Fund', 'The Trust Period' and 'The Beneficiaries' and 'Person'. There are two non-standard definitions:
   1.1 **'Trust Property'** means all lump sum payments payable on or in respect of the death of the Settlor under [give details of Pension Scheme].
2. **Trust Income**
   Subject to the Overriding Powers below:
   2.1 The Trustees may accumulate the whole or part of the income of the Trust Fund during the Trust Period. That income shall be added to the Trust Fund.
   2.2 The Trustees shall pay or apply the remainder of the income to or for the benefit of any Beneficiaries, as the Trustees think fit, during the Trust Period.
3. **Overriding Powers**
   [set out standard overriding powers]
4. **Default Clause**
   Subject to that, the Trust Fund shall be held on trust for [specify default trusts as appropriate] absolutely.
5. **Appointment of Trustees**
   The power of appointing trustees is exercisable by the Settlor during [his] life and by will.
6. **Further Provisions**
   [Set out standard form]
7. **Stamp Duty Certificate**
   The Settlor certifies that this deed falls within category N of the Stamp Duty (Exempt Instruments) Regulations.
8. **Exclusion of Settlor and Spouse**
   Notwithstanding anything else in this settlement, no power conferred by this settlement shall be exercisable, and no provision shall operate so

as to allow Trust Property or its income to become payable to or applicable in any circumstances whatsoever for the benefit of:

(1) the Settlor
(2) the estate of the Settlor
(3) the legal personal representatives of the Settlor[27] or
(4) the spouse of the Settlor.

In witness, [etc]

THE SCHEDULE: FURTHER PROVISIONS

[Here set out the administrative provisions suitable to the discretionary settlement.]

27 The reference to the estate and the legal personal representatives is not strictly necessary, but is put in to echo the express requirement of IMR/PPS, rules 9.15 and 10.1(2).

CHAPTER 24

Charitable trusts[1]

Northern Ireland: a charities backwater

24.1

Administration of charities in Northern Ireland is, of course, fundamentally different to that in England.[2] Notwithstanding vociferous demands for a Charity Commissioner for Northern Ireland from many quarters,[3] the administration and regulation of charities remains in disarray. In the absence of any system of charities registration it is the Charity Title Section, Inland Revenue (Charities),[4] (previously known as FICO) which has effectively become the primary adjudicator of charitable status in Northern Ireland.[5] Those practitioners who have the unenviable task of navigating a professional course through the many uncertainties of charity practice in this jurisdiction generally rely heavily on the various reports, publications and model documentation produced by the English Charity Commission and rarely encounter difficulties with the Inland Revenue. A similar approach is adopted in this chapter.

Charities take a variety of forms and can be categorised in different ways. The authors would draw a distinction between:

(1) a charity set up by an individual as a vehicle for his personal charitable donations (here called a 'personal charity'); and
(2) a charity of a more specialist or independent nature.

1 On charity tax generally, see *Venables and Kessler on the Taxation of Charities* (4th edn, 2003) Key Haven Publications.
2 The definition of 'charity' is virtually identical in Northern Ireland and England.
3 Most recently by the report (July 2003) into the much publicised management dispute at the Northern Ireland Hospice. The case for a Commissioner is well set out in Modernisation of Charity Law in Northern Ireland (HMSO, 1984); Proposals for the Modernisation of Charity Law and its Administration (NICVA, 1984). See also the recommendations in Charity Law Matters (HMSO, 2001).
4 St John's House, Merton Road, Bootle, Merseyside, L69 9BB.
5 Support is also provided by the Northern Ireland Council for Voluntary Action and the Charities Branch of the Department of Social Development. The former maintains a database of Northern Ireland charities.

A personal charity is generally a fairly standard piece of drafting. Part II of this book contains a precedent.

The more independent types of charity vary widely and need more bespoke drafting. An unincorporated association or a company would often be a more suitable vehicle that a trust. The standard drafts of the English Charity Law Association[6] and of the Charity Commissioners[7] are a useful drafting resource for these.

Some general comments

24.2

The draft should normally confer a power to expend capital: permanent endowment is a terrible nuisance.

Some drafts contain a good deal of material implied by law, eg an express duty to prepare accounts.[8] That is perhaps useful for a charity with lay trustees who may not have access to legal advice and might mistake the legal position. It should not be necessary for a standard 'personal charity' with a solicitor acting as trustee.

Remember that fundraising literature is important – as donations may be held on the terms of that literature and not on the terms of the trust! An appalling prospect if drafted by fundraisers and not reviewed by a lawyer.

If a charitable trust is in a non-standard form, it is always advisable to confirm its status with the Inland Revenue before making substantial gifts to it.

Name

24.3

In England there is a statutory requirement to give a charitable trust a name, under which it will be registered: Charities Act 1993, s 3(3). In Northern Ireland a name is required to secure an Inland Revenue reference number.

It is important to ensure that the name is not already in use. In England, the Charity Commission will rightly object if an existing charity has the same name and discourage use of names of former charities.[9] With 180,000 registered charities

6 See www.charitylawassociation.org.uk.
7 Obtainable from www.charitycommission.gov.uk.
8 The statutory duty is found in Charities Act (NI) 1964, s 27.
9 See www.charitycommission.gov.uk/supportingcharities/OGS/G018A005.asp.

there is real possibility of duplication of names! So check on the Charity Commission website and with NICVA[10] before choosing a name.

Charities which are not personal charities do occasionally like to change their name. The Charity Commission has recommended the form:

> The name of the charity shall be ..... or such other name as the Trustees may from time to time decide *with the approval of the Charity Commissioners.*[11]

Obviously the italicised words are senseless in a Northern Ireland trust and should be omitted.[12]

Trustees

24.4

The Charity Commission states:

> 'It is for each organisation to decide what number of charity trustees best meets its needs. As a general guide, every charity usually has at least 3 charity trustees and most charities find that between 3 and 9 trustees is adequate.'[13]

It is prudent for a charity not to have a single trustee, or two related trustees (eg husband and wife).[14]

In the case of a personal charity, the settlor will want the power to appoint new trustees and no provisions are needed for trustees' meetings. Where the charity is more of an independent organisation, the trustees of the charity will usually appoint their successors. In England, it is recommended that there be a provision that:

> A trustee may be appointed or discharged by resolution of a meeting of the charity trustees.

This brings in the relatively informal method of appointment and retirement of trustees authorised by the Charities Act 1993, s 83. There is no equivalent to this provision in Northern Ireland but there is no harm done by including the clause. There should also be a power for charity trustees to resign:

10 See para 4.35.

11 'Information Sheet 2: Minimum requirements for governing document' (undated).

12 Even in England it is suggested that the italicised words be deleted. The Charity Commissioners have certain powers to require a new name (Charities Act 1993, s 6) but there is no point in spelling this out in the deed or in extending their powers so that no name change can take place without their approval. See Kessler *Drafting Trusts and Will Trusts* (6th edn, 2002).

13 CC22 Choosing & preparing a governing Document, February 2001, para 65.

14 In England, the Charity Commission could be expected to object to this.

> A Trustee may resign by giving notice in writing to the other Trustees. On receipt of such notice the retiring Trustee shall cease to be a Trustee provided that there shall be remaining at least two persons to act as Trustees or a Trust Corporation (within the meaning of article 9 of the Administration of Estates (NI) Order 1979).

Where there are more than three trustees, a quorum clause is desirable. The Charity Commission guidance on the point seems sensible: 'If there are 3, 4 or 5 charity trustees we would suggest that the quorum should be 2, but if there are 6 or more charity trustees, we would suggest that the quorum should be stated as '3, or one third of all the current charity trustees, whichever is more'.[15]

Table A articles offer precedents for a quorum clause and regulation of trustees' meetings.[16]

Exclusion of settlor and non charitable purposes

24.5

> Notwithstanding anything else in this deed, no power conferred by this Charitable Trust shall be exercisable, and no provision shall operate so as to allow Trust Property or its income:
> (1) to become payable to or applicable for the benefit of the Settlor or the spouse of the Settlor
> (2) to be applied for any purpose that is not Charitable.

This is a useful precaution. Contrast para 18.17 (Protection clauses). There is no need for a settlor exclusion clause[17] but one is generally included and it can do no harm. Certainly do not have an extended one!

Rule against accumulation

24.6

In Northern Ireland there is effectively no restriction on the time during which a charitable trust may accumulate income.

15 Information Sheet 2, Minimum Requirements for Governing Document (undated).

16 See Table A, arts 88 ff.

17 Normally, a payment to or for the benefit of the settlor would not be a charitable payment and so impossible; exceptionally, it might be possible (eg if the settlor becomes destitute) but such a payment would not breach ICTA 1988, s 660A.

Administrative provisions for charities

24.7

The administrative powers should be conservatively drawn. Starting with the standard form in this book, the following amendments are suggested.

- A statutory power of investment, without the provisions disapplying the obligation to diversify the Trust Fund or permitting speculative or hazardous investments;
- No power of joint investment;
- Limited powers relating to capital and income;
- No provisions about use of trust property;
- Only the statutory powers of nominees and custodians;
- No exemption for supervision of company;
- No provisions dealing with disclaimer or statutory apportionment;
- No power to change the proper law.[18] Express powers to appoint foreign trustees or to carry on the administration outside the UK are not generally appropriate to a charity. (The statutory power can be used to appoint a foreign trustee if this is actually appropriate to the circumstances of the charity.)

Remuneration of trustees

24.8

The remuneration of charitable trustees has become an increasingly contentious issue. It is suggested that charitable trusts should normally have a power to remunerate professional trustees. Even if there is no immediate intention to use the power, trustee remuneration may become appropriate in the future.

A trustee remuneration clause is consistent with charitable status: the clause does not prevent what would otherwise be a charitable trust from qualifying as a charity, for charity law or tax law purposes. In England this is now accepted by the Charity Commission. In their words:

> 'Where a charity is being set up the trusts may include a provision for the remuneration of the trustees. Provided that this provision is couched in terms which tie the nature and level of remuneration to the services undertaken by the trustee (even as trustee) we shall not object to its inclusion in the charity's trust deed.'[19]

18 A trust without a UK proper law could rarely (if ever) qualify as a charity for tax or charity law purposes: see *Venables and Kessler on the Taxation of Charities* (4th edn, 2003) Key Haven Publications.

19 Decisions of the Charity Commissioners, Vol 2, p 14 (April 1994). The same view is taken in the Trustee Remuneration Consultation Document, Charity Commission, September 1999 and booklet CC11 (Payment to Charity Trustees). This view is also supported by TA(NI) 2001, s 30.

The Charity Commission recommend that a charity charging clause should contain restrictions that:

(1) the majority of trustees should not be remunerated;
(2) a trustee must withdraw from a meeting where his remuneration is under discussion.

The restrictions are probably wise. There must be a risk of laxity (or worse) in the remuneration of charity trustees. These restrictions may help to avoid that. It is therefore suggested that the restrictions set out above should be included in the trustee remuneration clause in normal cases. The Charity Law Association model draft imposes further safeguards.

A charging clause in a charitable trust should expressly authorise charging for services capable of being provided by a lay trustee.[20] TA(NI) 2001, s 28(3) enacts a presumption that professional trustees of a charitable trust cannot charge for non professional work. This should be reversed in the wording of the charging clause.

Trustee/director remuneration. A charity may own a non-charitable subsidiary; either because a private company has been given to the charity, or in order to avoid income tax on trading income.[21] If the trustees are directors of that company, they will need express authorisation in the trust in order to be paid remuneration for work done for the company: see para 20.65 (Trustee/director remuneration). It is submitted that the law is the same as for direct trustee remuneration: the standard clause authorising retention of trustee remuneration is consistent with charitable status. Here, however, it is understood that the Charity Commission does not agree and may refuse to register a charity with such a clause. In practice the Charity Commission view tends to prevail.[22]

Insurance for claims against charity trustees

The law should distinguish between:

(1) insurance where the proceeds belong to the trust fund. This will be permitted under general trust law, or at least, under the general power of management used in this book;[23]

20 In the absence of such a clause the power for a charity trustee to charge for lay services is governed by the unnecessarily complex rules of TA(NI) 2001, s 28. For the position for non-charitable trusts see para 20.59 (Layman's work).

21 *Venables and Kessler on the Taxation of Charities* (4th edn, 2003) Key Haven Publications, ch 6 (Trading by Charities).

22 A practical solution may be to give non-voting shares to the charity so the charity does not have control over the remuneration of its subsidiary.

23 All insurance of this class may benefit trustees, in the sense that they are personally liable for claims (with an indemnity against the Trust Fund) and so concerned to ensure that the trust fund is sufficient to meet these claims, but that should not matter.

(2) insurance where the proceeds belong beneficially to the trustees. This is not permitted under general trust law except in special cases.[24]

It is suggested that the general law is satisfactory in the case of ordinary private trusts. However express provision is appropriate in active charitable trusts and pension trusts where the need for insurance may be greater. This form is not needed for a charity which holds assets and merely distributes funds on to other charities or for charitable purposes.

The following form is proposed:

> The Trustees may take out insurance which protects or indemnifies Trustees against the risk of personal liability arising from:
> (1) breach of trust by the Trustees;
> (2) the costs of a successful defence to a criminal prosecution brought against a trustee in his capacity as trustee of this trust.

The insurers shall not be liable to a trustee for loss arising from any act or omission which that trustee knew to be a breach of trust or which was committed by that trustee in reckless disregard of whether it was a breach of trust or not.[25]

Procedure after execution of charitable trust

24.9

The steps to be taken are set out in the IR Guidance Notes for Charities.[26]

Transfers to the charity are exempt from duty.[27]

24 The case law is thin but there have been two cases in category (2). A £525 missing beneficiary insurance policy was permitted in the case of *Re Evans* [1999] 2 All ER 777 in circumstances where an application to the court for directions would have given rise to far greater expense. By contrast, insurance was not permitted to cover: (i) far fetched claims of (non-fraudulent) breach of trust; and (ii) claims by overlooked beneficiaries which could be dealt with by a notice under TA 1925, s 27 (the equivalent of TA(NI) 1958, s 28): *Kemble v Hicks (No 2)* [1999] OPLR 1 [1999] Pens LR 287, accessible on www.kessler.co.uk.

25 A restriction on these lines is rightly required by the Charity Commission: see the Charity Commission Booklet CC49 (Charities and Insurance) para 21, accessible on www.charity-commission.gov.uk.

26 Sections 2.3–2.5, accessible on www.inlandrevenue.gov.uk/charities.

27 See *Venables and Kessler on the Taxation of Charities* (4th edn, 2003) Key Haven Publications, ch 5 (Stamp duty).

Charitable will trusts

24.10

It is possible to create a charitable trust by will or to make a gift by will to an existing charitable trust. It is good practice to create a lifetime trust (if need be a pilot trust with a nominal trust fund) and make a gift to it by will. The trust can then be registered with the Inland Revenue and its charitable status will not be in dispute when the will takes effect: this will simplify the administration of the estate and avoid the risk that the trust may fail. This should not be necessary if the trust is in an absolutely standard form.

CHAPTER 25

Trusts of damages

This chapter is concerned with trusts set up to hold damages sometimes called 'personal injuries trusts'. Different (though overlapping) considerations apply depending whether the claimant is (1) an adult with mental capacity (2) a child under 18 or (3) a person lacking mental capacity (adopting the terminology of the Mental Health (NI) Order 1986, 'a patient').

Benefit 'disregard' of trust of damages

25.1

Trusts of damages have welfare benefit advantages.[1] For the purposes of income support, one must disregard:

> Where the funds of a trust are derived from a payment made in consequence of any personal injury to the claimant, the value of the trust fund and the value of the right to receive any payment under that trust.[2]

This applies whether the claimant is an adult, child or patient. Any form of trust will satisfy this; even a bare trust.[3]

Trust of damages for adult with mental capacity

25.2

An adult with mental capacity can of course transfer his damages to a trust if he wants this advantage. He has a free choice what sort of trust to create.

1 On this topic see generally, D Coldrick *Personal Injury Trusts* (2002) Ark Publishing.

2 Income Support (General) Regulations (NI) 1987, Sch 9, para 46 and Sch 10, para 12. Similar exemption applies for other benefits.

3 This follows from the words of the regulation and no authority is needed. Some further support could be drawn from a curate's egg of a Social Security Commissioner's decision, CIS 368/1994 [1996] 3 JSSL D136, accessible on www.kessler.co.uk.

It is suggested that the most appropriate form for a fund producing income is normally a discretionary trust, of which the settlor is a beneficiary. The settlor may be one of the trustees.

The benefit 'disregard' does not apply for tax purposes. The income tax and CGT settlement provisions will apply to the trust, but for a client of modest means that will happily be a more satisfactory result than if they did not apply. The gift to the settlement is a chargeable transfer so the sum given should not exceed the nil-rate band. The gift will also be a gift with reservation for IHT, but this is not a problem if the entire estate of the settlor can be expected to fall within the nil-rate band.

For property not producing income, an IP trust for the settlor or a bare trust may be preferable.

For property in excess of the nil-rate band, an IP trust or bare trust would be preferable (if appropriate, investing the fund in non-income producing assets). An IHT disabled persons trust (where possible) may be better: see para 26.8 (IHT disabled person's trust).

Jurisdiction to transfer child's damages to bare trust

25.3

The problem for a child is how to create a trust, if one is desired, as the child lacks legal capacity to do so himself. RSC Ord 80 r 10 provides:

> (1) Where in any proceedings-
> (a) money is recovered by or on behalf of or for the benefit of a child or patient; or
> (b) money paid into court is accepted by or on behalf of a child or patient,
> the money shall be dealt with in accordance with directions given by the court under this rule and not otherwise.
> (2) Directions given under this rule may provide that the money shall be wholly or partly
> [a] paid into court and invested or
> [b] otherwise dealt with.
> (Paragraphing added)

It is submitted that this rule empowers the court to direct the payment of money to a bare trust, that is, a trust where the trustees hold property on trust for the minor beneficiary absolutely.[4] This rule does not empower the court to order the payment of the money to a substantive trust (ie a trust which is not a bare trust, for

4 A bare trust involves in a sense a delegation of the court's power to deal with the funds, but such delegation is a method of 'dealing with' the funds and so authorised.

instance, a trust under which the principal beneficiary is only entitled to the income of the fund during his life, with remainder to some other beneficiary after his death).[5]

A precedent bare trust for child

25.4

The following precedent is proposed:

This declaration of trust is made [date] by
(1) [Name of first trustee] of [Address] and
(2) [Name of second trustee] of [Address]
('the Original Trustees').

Whereas:
(A) [Name of Judge] ordered on [date] [set out terms of Order]
(B) This Trust shall be known as the [Peter Smith] Trust 2004.
Now this deed witnesses as follows:

1. **Definitions**
   In this settlement:
   (1) '**The Trustees**' means the Original Trustees or the trustees of the settlement for the time being.
   (2) '**The Trust Fund**' means:
      (a) Property transferred to the Trustees to hold on the terms of this Settlement; and
      (b) All property from time to time representing the above.
   (3) **'Trust Property'** means any property comprised in the Trust Fund.
   (4) **'[Peter]'** means [Peter Smith] of [address].
   (5) **'Person'** includes a person anywhere in the world and includes a Trustee.
2. **Trust Income and Capital**
   (1) The Trustees may pay or apply the income of the Trust Fund to or for the education, maintenance or benefit of [Peter] and shall hold the remaining income on Trust for [Peter] as an accretion to the Trust Fund absolutely.
   (2) The Trustees shall hold the capital of the Trust Fund on trust for [Peter] absolutely.

5 There are two reasons for reaching this conclusion:
(1) Rule 10 is an administrative (not dispositive) power. So 'otherwise dealt with' should be construed *ejusdem generis* so that only administrative matters can be dealt with. The payment to a bare trust is an administrative matter but payment to a substantive trust would be dispositive;
(2) *Allen v Distillers Co Ltd* [1974] QB 384 reached this conclusion in relation to identical wording in the English RSC Ord 80, r 12 (pre Civil Procedure Rules), stating as the general rule that the Court has no power to order a substantive settlement of a child's property.

3. **Power of Advancement**
   Section 33 of the Trustee Act (NI) 1958 shall apply with the deletion of proviso (1) (a).
4. **Appointment of Trustees**
   The power of appointing trustees is exercisable by the Trustees.
5. **Further Provisions**
   The provisions set out in the schedule below shall have effect.

In witness, [etc]

<u>The Schedule: Administrative Provisions</u>

[The administrative provisions should be conservatively drawn. Starting with the standard form in this book, the following amendments are proposed:

Use the first sentence of the standard form power of investment only.

The following administrative provisions should be deleted as inappropriate to a bare trust of this kind:

income & capital: sub clause (d); supervision of companies; appropriation; payment to charities; conflict of interest; power to appoint foreign trustees.]

Consequences of using bare trust

25.5

The consequences of using a bare trust are as follows:
(1) on the death of the child under the age of 18 the fund must pass under the intestacy rules, in principle, to his parents. After the age of 18 the fund will pass according to the will of the child. The Master of the Office of Care and Protection could of course make a will for an adult who does not have mental capacity to do so himself;
(2) for tax purposes the fund is treated as the child's, so that he is subject to tax on trust income and gains, and the funds form part of his estate for IHT;
(3) if the child attains 18, and has mental capacity, he can call for the fund to be transferred to him.

A bare trust satisfies the benefits 'disregard', and meets the administrative need of finding a manager for the funds during the minority of the beneficiary. The court would normally appoint solicitors to act as trustees.[6] The trust is not really

6 It would not normally be appropriate to appoint parents to act as trustees, because of the conflict of interest and risk of breach of trust, though there is no real objection to parents acting as trustees jointly with a solicitor. (Theoretically parents could seek to have the funds transferred to them by virtue of their powers over the children's property conferred by the

satisfactory for a fund of any size since it is not appropriate that the child should be given power over a large fund on attaining the age of 18.

Exercising the power of advancement to turn a bare trust into a substantive trust

The bare trust may contain a wide power of advancement. It is considered that this would authorise the trustees to transfer the funds to a new substantive trust if this is for the benefit of the beneficiary.[7] That is a matter which could be considered further (at any time after the creation of the trust and in particular before the beneficiary's 18th birthday) if there are good reasons why it would benefit the beneficiary to transfer the funds to a substantive trust under which he was the principal beneficiary.

Creation of a substantive trust of child's damages by compromise

25.6

If:
(1) the parties agree a compromise of the claim;
(2) the terms of the compromise include the transfer of funds to a substantive trust; and
(3) the compromise is for the benefit of the child
then the court can approve the terms of the compromise, even though the court has no power to order the creation of a substantive trust of its own initiative.

An appropriate form of trust would be somewhat narrower than the standard A&M trusts used elsewhere in this book. The following is suggested:[8]

(1) A&M trusts while the child is under the age of 25;
(2) a life interest to the child on attaining the age of 25;
(3) power of advancement in favour of the child;
(4) on the child's death the fund would be held;
  (a) on such terms as the child may appoint; subject to which
  (b) on the intestacy rules; subject to which
  (c) for such charities concerned with disabilities similar to those suffered by the child as the trustees shall select.

Children (NI) Order 1995, art 6(3). In such cases trustees should seek the guidance of the court, and it is suggested that the court would have a discretion whether or not to allow the parents control of the funds.)

7 See para 10.11 (Power of advancement used to create new trusts).

8 A draft along these lines was used for Thalidomide victims: *Allen v Distillers Co Ltd* [1974] QB 384.

The consequence of such a trust would be:

(1) on the death of the child over 25, for most practical purposes, the same as a bare trust;

(2) from the point of view of state benefits, the trust income and capital may not be regarded as the child's income and capital (except to the extent that the fund is used to pay income to the child);

(3) overall the tax position would not be very substantially better or worse than a bare trust:

   (a) for IHT, the usual rules of A&M trusts apply. There would in principle be a charge to tax on the death of the child over the age of 25;

   (b) for CGT and income tax the position would depend on whether the child would be regarded as 'settlor'. The authors inclines to the view that the child would not be a settlor;

(4) when the child attains 18 – even if he has mental capacity – he cannot call for the fund to be transferred to him because it is not 'his' fund.

Trusts for minors: commentary

25.7

Minors may be awarded damages of several million pounds. No donor would ever make a gift of such a sum on terms that the minor becomes absolutely entitled to it at the age of 18. At the very least, entitlement should be deferred to the age of 25. Fortunately this result can be achieved by indirect methods under the present law. It is suggested that the court ought to have jurisdiction to create appropriate trusts directly.[9]

Trusts of damages for patients

25.8

A patient lacks capacity to make his trust, so his position is similar to a child. However, in this case the court does have power to create a settlement for the patient.[10] The alternative of creating a settlement by compromise is also open, but needs the consent of the court.[11]

9 The court had some power to do this under the Infant Settlements Act 1855, until its repeal by the Age of Majority Act (NI) 1969. For damage limitation by trustees, see para 4.1 (Too much money).

10 Mental Health (NI) Order 1986, art 99(1)(d). It is considered that the patient is the 'settlor' of a settlement created under this power.

11 While no established practice has yet properly developed in NI, it would seem that the court will not be prepared to approve widely drawn, flexible trusts. It is likely that account would be taken of the Court of Protection Practice Note on the settlement of personal injury awards to patients, dated 15 November 1996, accessible on www.offsol.demon.co.uk/pract8fm.htm.

Award under the Criminal Injuries Compensation Scheme

25.9

There is jurisdiction for an award under the Criminal Injuries Compensation Scheme to be transferred to a settlement.[12]

12 Criminal Injuries (NI) Order 2002, art 5(2)(d).

CHAPTER 26

Trusts for disabled beneficiaries

Mentally handicapped beneficiaries

26.1

Trusts are the traditional means of providing for a mentally handicapped beneficiary. It is plainly inadvisable to transfer funds absolutely to a person who is not able enough to manage them. If a mentally handicapped person with assets in his own name is unable to manage his property or appoint an attorney, it would generally be necessary to appoint a controller to act for him. The appointment is made by the Master of the Office of Protection under the Mental Health (Northern Ireland) Order 1986. The appointment of a controller inevitably imposes formal procedures and may involve substantial costs (5% of the beneficiary's income) and should be avoided where possible.

Choosing provisions for disabled beneficiaries

26.2

For administrative provisions see para 20.52 (Administrative provisions for mentally handicapped beneficiaries). Drafting beneficial provisions for the benefit of the disabled is more difficult than normal because account must be taken of two additional considerations: welfare benefits and tax reliefs. (It is some comfort that an adviser need not always consider both sets of rules in relation to the same matter: a beneficiary on benefits will not be concerned about tax and a beneficiary concerned about tax may have escaped the poverty trap imposed by the benefit system. But the two can overlap.)

Welfare benefits

26.3

This is a daunting topic, nearly as large as income tax, and even more volatile. When advising on wills or lifetime gifts for persons qualifying for benefit the adviser must consider the impact on benefits. The authors do not propose to examine this topic in detail but two general propositions will be made:

(1) the benefit system discourages gifts of capital (beyond a small limit) to any person claiming means tested benefits;
(2) the benefit system penalises beneficiaries who receive trust income, withdrawing benefits pound for pound. Accordingly beneficiaries on means tested benefits should not be life tenants: the trusts should generally be discretionary in form.[1]

Tax reliefs for disabled beneficiaries[2]

26.4

In this area tax planning and trust drafting are so interwoven that it is not possible to discuss one without understanding the other. There are three tax reliefs which will govern the drafting:

(1) IHT relief on gifts for 'dependent relatives';
(2) enhanced CGT annual allowance for 'CGT Disabled Person's Trust';
(3) special IHT rules for 'IHT Disabled Person's Trust'.

IHT relief on gifts for 'dependent relatives'

26.5

Under the IHTA 1984, s 11, it is possible to make substantial gifts to trusts for the benefit of the disabled (including the mentally handicapped) without a transfer of value, so there is no inheritance tax liability if the donor dies within seven years of the gift. Of course, care is needed to satisfy the various conditions. A discussion is outside the scope of this book.[3] In the case of an elderly donor (or in any case where insurance against the IHT on death within seven years is expensive) this is a matter which would justify specialist advice.

1 The *possibility* of benefit under discretionary trusts does not at the present time affect means tested benefits. It has in the past and may again in the future. The risk is greater for IHT and CGT Disabled Person's Trusts. There is little the drafter can sensibly do to anticipate such changes in the law. The *provision* of benefits from a trust may or may not affect welfare benefits, depending on the circumstances.

2 For a full analysis of the rules relating to CGT and IHT Disabled Person's Trusts, see Richard Oerton, 'Trusts for the Disabled: An Augean Stable?' (1993) PCB 161, accessible on www.kessler.co.uk.

3 But see *Venables on IHT Planning* (3rd edn) D6.2.3 for a brief discussion.

CGT disabled person's trust[4]

26.6

All trusts qualify for a CGT annual allowance. Normally this is set at one half the amount of the individual's allowance; (2003/04 £7,900 ÷ 2 = £3,950). A CGT disabled person's trust enjoys the full and not the half allowance. This tax advantage is therefore worth about £1,000 in a year in which a trust realises capital gains. It is not a very significant tax relief.

The conditions are set out in TCGA 1992, Sch 1, para 1:

(1) the Beneficiary must be:
   (a) mentally disabled, ie incapable of administering his property or managing his affairs by reason of mental disorder; or
   (b) physically disabled, defined as those in receipt of certain attendance or disability living allowances;[5]
(2) the terms of the trust must provide that during the life of the beneficiary:
   (a) not less than half of the property which is applied is applied for the benefit of that beneficiary; and
   (b) (i) that person is entitled to not less than half of the income arising from that property, or
      (ii) no such income may be applied for the benefit of any other person.[6]

A trust loses the benefit of the relief if the beneficiary ceases to qualify as disabled, within the definition. It seems that a trust does not qualify for the relief unless it is known at the outset that the second condition will be satisfied *throughout* the life of the beneficiary.[7] Thus trust income must be: (i) (at least as to half) paid to or applied for the benefit of the beneficiary; or (ii) accumulated. In Northern Ireland the income may be accumulated for the entire trust period. This is much more beneficial than the position in England where after the accumulation period at least half of the trust income must be applied for the benefit of the beneficiary and so he must have an interest in possession.

Mixed trusts

26.7

The Revenue CGT Manual provides:

4 Authors' terminology for a trust which satisfies the conditions of the TCGA 1992, Sch 1. The statute does not provide a convenient label for this kind of trust, although ICTA 1988, s 715 (accrued income scheme) refers to the trusts as 'disabled person's trusts'. The discussion in the CGT Manual 18050 is essential reading before attempting the drafting.

5 The test is therefore somewhat stricter than that for the IHT dependent relative relief.

6 It is considered that income which is accumulated is not 'applied for the benefit of any person'. The Revenue accepts this: CGT Manual 18061.

7 The Revenue takes this view: CGT Manual 18061A.

'18067. Mixed settlements

It is possible that only part of a settlement may fulfil the qualifying conditions. For example, the trust may secure that during the lifetime of the disabled person the income and any capital applied of a specified fund is to be applied as described above. If the fund itself meets the conditions, then the trustees of the settlement are entitled to the main exemption. Paragraph 1 (1) refers to "settled property" and not to "all the settled property comprised in the settlement."

By way of contrast if the disabled beneficiary is entitled to an undivided share of the property, as in the example in CG18064, then the tests are to be applied to the whole of the settled property. So if there are three life tenants, each entitled to one-third of the income, and one is disabled, the conditions are not met.'

This is perhaps surprising but probably the correct construction of the statute. Accordingly the best way to draft a CGT disabled person's trust is to split the trust fund into two parts:

(1) a specified fund which is restricted to satisfy the conditions. It may be most convenient to provide that the disabled beneficiary is life tenant of this fund;
(2) the balance may be held on whatever trusts seem most appropriate.

IHT disabled person's trust

26.8

Special IHT rules apply to 'IHT disabled person's trusts'[8]:

(1) a gift to the trust is a PET;[9]
(2) the disabled beneficiary is treated as having an interest in possession.[10]

These rules are compulsory: it is not possible to disclaim them by making an election.

The first relief is unnecessary, since it would be easy to make gifts which are PETs in any event.[11] The second relief is in fact a mixed blessing. The settled

8 Authors' terminology for a trust which satisfies the conditions of IHTA 1984, s 89. The trusts are there called 'trusts for disabled persons'. The term 'disabled trust' is used in IHTA 1984, s 3A.

9 IHTA 1984, s 3A. If the disabled beneficiary makes the gift, it is not a transfer of value for IHT.

10 IHTA 1984, s 89.

11 The relief exists for historical reasons. In 1986 a gift to an interest in possession trust was a chargeable transfer; there was a need for a special relief for gifts for mentally disabled persons. (It is harder to see the case for a special relief for physically disabled persons; but no matter.) The relief has little role since the FA 1987 when gifts to interest in possession trusts became PETs.

property is not subject to the discretionary trust regime. This seems like an advantage. However, the property is subject to the interest in possession trust rules and suffers IHT on the death of the disabled beneficiary. If the beneficiary *actually* had an interest in possession in the trust property the IHT position is the same and it is better for CGT: the trust qualifies for the CGT tax-free uplift on the death of the beneficiary. But the IHT disabled person's trust allows the practical advantage of accumulating income.

26.9

The conditions are set out in the IHTA 1984, s 89:

(1) The beneficiary must be mentally or physically disabled. This condition is the same as that for the CGT disabled person's trust, except that the condition need only be satisfied at the time of the gift to the trust.

(2) The terms of the trust must provide that during the life of the beneficiary:
   (a) not less than half of the settled property which is applied is applied for the benefit of that beneficiary; this is again the same as the CGT condition;
   (b) no interest in possession exists during the life of the disabled person; this is different from the CGT condition.

Again, the second condition must be satisfied throughout the beneficiary's life. While this condition is incompatible with the condition for a CGT disabled person's trust, if the trust is governed by English law,[12] the more generous accumulation period in Northern Ireland allows a trust to satisfy the conditions for both the CGT and IHT disabled person's trust.

Disabled beneficiaries: conclusion

How then should one provide for disabled beneficiaries?

Small funds

26.10

The amounts involved may be too small to justify a trust. The best course then must be to seek a suitable individual who will take the funds and (without obligation) use them for the beneficiary.

If no suitable individual is found, a scheme operated by MENCAP[13] may be considered. Under this scheme an individual creates a discretionary trust in his

12 Unless accumulation is possible throughout the life of the disabled beneficiary: see para 26.6 (CGT disabled trust). That would be the case if: (1) a suitable foreign proper law is chosen: or (2) the disabled beneficiary is the settlor.

13 www.mencap.org.uk.

life, with a nominal trust fund, and bequeaths additional funds by will. A MENCAP company acts as trustee. MENCAP only administers trusts set up under its standard form and does not act with co-trustees. Charges are raised, but on a non-profit making basis. Administrative costs should therefore be less than for comparable private trusts.

Substantial funds: provision by will

26.11

The uncertainties are so great that the most sensible form of will must be a discretionary will trust: this course allows the important decisions to be deferred until after the death of the testator.

Substantial funds: lifetime provision

26.12

Where sums involved are within the IHT nil-rate band (or twice that amount, if husband and wife are making gifts) then the best course would be to make a gift to a discretionary trust.

Where sums involved are large, and means tested benefits not a consideration, the best course will generally be to create an interest in possession trust.

Should one use standard form IP, A&M or discretionary trusts; or make amendments in order to satisfy the conditions for a CGT disabled person's trust? The latter course would somewhat limit the trustees' flexibility but that drawback can and should be minimised by creating a trust with two separate funds, in accordance with para 26.7 (Mixed trusts). It is a question of how much trouble and expense one is prepared to take in order to optimise the tax position. For a trust which is expected to realise chargeable gains regularly, this is just about worthwhile.

It is possible to envisage circumstances where the IHT disabled person's trust is the most suitable form of trust, but in practice this is not often likely to be the case.

Where the settlor cannot expect to survive seven years, the gift should be made so as to qualify for dependent relative relief: see para 26.5 (IHT relief on gifts for dependent relatives).

Commentary

26.13

The taxation of trusts for the benefit of the disabled is a tax backwater, which is surprising considering the prominence that disabled rights have taken elsewhere. What is needed is a single, coherent set of rules for inheritance tax and capital gains tax. The case for reform seems unanswerable. It might, perhaps, be slipped in as part of the project to rewrite tax legislation in plain English (in the unlikely event that this ambitious project ever rewrites the IHT and CGT legislation).

CHAPTER 27

Governing law, place of administration and jurisdiction clauses

The governing law

27.1

A trust must have a 'governing law'[1] whose significance is as follows:

(1) the law governs the validity, construction, effect and administration of the trust.[2] But only occasionally will the many differences between trust jurisdictions matter in practice to a well drafted trust;

(2) it cannot be a breach of trust to comply with rules of the governing law relating to tax, a settlor's (or beneficiary's) right of recovery for tax, or exchange control. It may be a breach of trust to comply with other countries' rules on such matters;[3]

(3) the law is occasionally relevant for tax;[4]

1 A note on terminology. The terms 'applicable law' and 'governing law' and 'proper law' are synonymous. All of them have found favour with statutory drafters. 'Governing law' is the term used in modern offshore choice of law legislation: eg the Bahamian Trusts (Choice of Governing Law) Act 1989 . 'Applicable law' is the term used in the Hague Convention. 'Proper law' was used in FA 1949, s 22 (an estate duty provision). As noted in *Philipson-Stow v IRC* [1961] AC 727 the word 'proper' is somewhat inapt; and it is not necessary to use any particular epithet. 'Governing law' is used here as the most transparent term of the three.

2 Hague Convention on the Law Applicable to Trusts (hereafter 'the Hague Convention') implemented by the Recognition of Trusts Act 1987, s 8 explains the meaning of this phrase in some detail.

3 'It is difficult to see how the will trustees could possibly be in breach of trust in complying with the provisions of that system of law which the testator, by necessary implication, selected to regulate the rights of the parties under the trusts constituted by his will.' *Re Cable* [1977] 1 WLR 7 at 23. See also *Re Latham* [1962] Ch 616.

4 This is rare, which is not surprising, since the settlor has power to chose the governing law: However:

(1) some UK double tax treaties apply different rules depending on the governing law of the trust;

(2) the source of a life tenant's income (for UK tax purposes) will normally be the underlying assets. However, if the law (unlike the position in Northern Ireland or England) does not give the life tenant the right to the trust income as it arises, but only the right to a sum from the Trustees, then the 'source' will be the trust. This is significant for the remittance basis and 'source-ceasing' tax planning. See Kessler *Taxation of Foreign Domiciliaries* (2nd edn, 2003) Key Haven Publications, para 6.114.16 (Income from trusts: identifying the source).

(3) The governing law may be relevant for foreign law or tax purposes.

(4) the law is one factor (no more) in determining whether a Court has or will exercise jurisdiction over the trust;[5]
(5) the law is one factor (no more) in determining the *situs* of an equitable interest under the trust.[6]

Express selection of governing law

27.2

The settlor of a lifetime trust may in principle choose any governing law which recognises trusts.[7] The same applies to a trust created by will.[8]

If no express choice is made a trust is governed by the law with which it is most closely connected.[9] In England, James Kessler's *Drafting Trusts and Will Trusts* advises that in the usual case it is unnecessary for the drafter expressly to select the governing law. A trust with English settlor and beneficiaries, English trustees and trust property will, by clear implication, be governed by English law. It is only where there is a foreign element B for instance where the settlor and the trustees are not all domiciled and resident in the same place that it is recommended that the trust should expressly direct which governing law is to apply. Otherwise it may be difficult to identify the governing law.[10]

5
(1) The English court has jurisdiction to administer a trust with a foreign governing law: *Re Cable* [1977] 1 WLR 7;
(2) the English court has jurisdiction to vary a trust with a foreign governing law but 'where there are substantial foreign elements in the case ... the Court must consider carefully whether it is proper for it to exercise the jurisdiction;' *Re Paget* [1965] 1 WLR 1046;
(3) for the purposes of the Civil Jurisdiction and Judgments Act 1982 – which extends to NI – and the 1968 Brussels Convention, a Trust is 'domiciled' in Northern Ireland if NI Law 'is the system of law with which the trust has its closest and most real connection' (CJJA 1982, s 45(3)). The governing law chosen is an important factor (but not, it is submitted, a conclusive factor) in applying this test;
(4) a writ may be served outside NI on an action claim to execute trusts which 'ought to be executed according to Northern Ireland law' (RSC Ord 11, r 1(j)).

6 The *situs* of an equitable interest is not usually important, but it could matter, eg in ascertaining the jurisdiction whose rules govern dispositions of the equitable interest (matters such as formality, capacity, intestacy); or for tax (particularly stamp duty). The *situs* of a unit in a unit trust is an important question for tax (until unit trusts are entirely replaced by OEICs and similar corporate entities). On these questions see Kessler *Taxation of Foreign Domiciliaries* (2nd edn, 2003) Key Haven Publications, ch 31 (Situs of Assets).

7 Hague Convention, art 6; this was also broadly the position at common law: Dicey & Morris *Conflict of Laws* (13th edn, 2000) ch 29. There is a good discussion of the older cases in *Dymond's Death Duties* (15th edn, 1975) p 1286. For exceptions see below.

8 The law governing a trust created by the will must be distinguished from the law governing the administration of the testator's estate during the period of administration and other rules relating to succession rights. The latter raise different issues which are outside the scope of this book.

9 Hague Convention, art 7 (which further explains the concept of 'closely connected'). The same principle applies at common law: *Chellaram v Chellaram* [1985] Ch 409 at 431.

10 Dicey and Morris *The Conflict of Laws* (13th edn, 2000) para 29.008, assembles many authorities illustrating the courts' travails in determining the governing law in the absence of a choice of law clause; all unnecessary had the drafts specified the law.

While the same principles apply to Northern Ireland – a trust with Northern Ireland settlor, trustees and beneficiaries will clearly be governed by Northern Ireland law – the authors' preference is to include an express governing law clause. In particular, the Inland Revenue may raise time-consuming queries about the absence of the 21-year accumulation period if this is not done. A draft for a lifetime trust is:

> 'The law of Northern Ireland governs the validity of this Settlement, and its construction, effects and administration. The Courts of Northern Ireland have exclusive jurisdiction in any proceedings involving rights or obligations under this Settlement.'[11]

In a will the form 'This will takes effect in accordance with English law' was held to be sufficient in *Tod* v *Barton.*[12] But the authors would prefer to be more explicit and say:

> This will takes effect in accordance with the law of Northern Ireland. In particular, the law of Northern Ireland governs the validity of the settlement constituted by this Will, and its construction, effects and administration. The Courts of Northern Ireland have exclusive jurisdiction in any proceedings involving rights or obligations under that settlement.

It is obviously not correct to say: 'the law of the United Kingdom' although Northern Ireland practitioners are unlikely to make this mistake.

Selection of foreign governing law

27.3

A settlor may choose a foreign governing law. This opens an agreeable prospect: a free market in legal systems; where the settlor (or his advisers) may select whichever offers the most suitable rules and institutions for his purposes.

The selection of a foreign governing law (ie a non-UK law) might offer the following advantages:

Freedom from restrictive rules of trust law. This has less relevance to the Northern Ireland trust practitioner. In England the drafter of an A&M trust especially will find himself tempted to select a foreign jurisdiction to avoid the absurdities of the rule against accumulations (the famous *Vestey* trusts were governed by the law of Northern Ireland).

11 The wording of the first sentence is derived from art 8 of the Hague Convention; the second sentence is discussed below under 'Exclusive jurisdiction clause'.

12 [2002] WTLR 469.

Taxation. In practice tax advantages will be rare: see para 27.1 (The governing law).

Protection from expropriation. A foreign governing law would be a defence against enforcement (in foreign jurisdictions) of future UK confiscatory legislation. The possibility of such legislation seems remote.

Ease of administration. If foreign trustees are appointed, they may prefer their local law to govern their trust. The retention of Northern Ireland governing law is unlikely ever to be a serious handicap to trust administration.

These are somewhat tenuous advantages. There is also a drawback to the selection of a foreign governing law. A person dealing with the foreign-law trust may need to familiarise himself with the local law or seek local professional advice; or very likely, both. The choice of a foreign governing law may give rise to extra expense.

The freedom to select a foreign governing law is not absolute: The choice of a foreign governing law may be ineffective if 'manifestly incompatible with public policy.'[13] Would, for example, the English courts hold that the selection of a foreign governing law is contrary to public policy simply because the foreign law does not have the statutory rule against accumulations? The answer is plainly, no.[14]

In determining whether United Kingdom public policy requires the rejection of an express selection of a foreign governing law, some commentators suggest that a relevant factor would be whether the foreign governing law has any real connection with the trust. Thus they recommend that where a foreign governing law is selected, the initial trustees or trust property should be in the same jurisdiction. It is then harder still to question the governing law of the trust. While this might be adopted as a precaution it is not in the authors' view necessary.[15]

13 Hague Convention, art 18.

14 It is impossible to contend that avoidance of the rule against accumulations would be 'manifestly incompatible with public policy' because the Law Commission have recommended the abolition of the rule against accumulations (and indeed canvassed the case for abolition of the rule against perpetuities), the Government has accepted the recommendation, and many (if not most) jurisdictions – including NI – have never had, or have repealed the rule. Even though the rule was regarded as an important rule of public policy when introduced in 1800, notions of public policy change with the passage of time: contrast the attenuation of the law of maintenance: *Bevan Ashford v Yeandle* [1999] Ch 239. The Hague Convention has altered the common law rule under which the selection of a foreign governing law could not prevent the rule against accumulations applying to land in England, freehold or even leasehold: *Freke v Lord Carbery* (1873) LR 16 Eq 461.

15 Difficulties and absurdities arise if, say, (contrary to the authors' firm view) the English courts were to hold that a trust is governed by English law, notwithstanding an express selection of a foreign governing law. The foreign jurisdiction would almost certainly take the view that the same trust was governed by its law. (Some foreign trust laws state this expressly – eg Bahamian Trusts (Choice of Governing Law) Act 1989, s 4: 'A term of a trust expressly declaring that the laws of the Bahamas shall govern the trust is valid, effective and conclusive regardless of any other circumstance.' But the same conclusion would generally be reached at common law.) The resulting battle of jurisdictions might be determined by factors such as

It is in principle possible to arrange that the law of one jurisdiction should govern the validity of a trust, and the law of another jurisdiction should govern its administration.

The conclusion is that the drafter of a United Kingdom resident trust should not in normal circumstances select a foreign governing law.

Power to change the governing law[16]

27.4

A power to change the governing law of a trust is valid in Northern Ireland law.[17]

A change of governing law may significantly alter the effect of a trust. For example, a change of proper law may be used to do the following:

(1) override the restriction that the statutory power of advancement is limited to one half of the trust fund.[18] (This may be useful in the surprising number of trusts that include a power to change the governing law but do not extend the statutory power of advancement);

(2) extend the perpetuity period;[19]

(3) confer on the court power to vary the trust without the consent of the beneficiaries;[20]

---

residence of trustees and *situs* of trust assets. So if an Irish law trust more than 21 years old decided to invest in England land, the trustees would suddenly be unable to accumulate income and a beneficiary may acquire an interest in possession! These difficulties go to show that the Courts should hesitate to impose English trust law against the express declaration of the settlor.

16 On this topic, see Paul Matthews *Trusts: Migration and Change of Proper Law* (1997) Key Haven Publications.

17 Hague Convention, art 10 envisages such a power, subject to the public policy considerations of art 18. The power to change the governing law is a standard form, and the Courts have regard to the practice of conveyancing in deciding the law. This is also the view of Dicey and Morris *Conflict of Laws* (13th edn, 2000) para 29.020.

18 There is no such restriction in Trusts (Jersey) Law 1984, art 34(5).

19 For instance the Cayman Islands have a 150-year perpetuity period. From about 2070 there will be a stream of Jersey law trusts (which first became popular in the 1970s) approaching their 100th anniversary (which is their applicable trust period as the Jersey (Trusts) Law 1984 is retrospective). The authors predict that many of these will make such a change – unless (also predictable) Jersey law changes or Jersey lawyers devise some domestic solution.

20 Eg US Uniform Trust Code, s 412(a):

> 'The court may modify the administrative or dispositive terms of a trust or terminate the trust if, because of circumstances not anticipated by the settlor, modification or termination will further the purposes of the trust. To the extent practicable, the modification must be made in accordance with the settlor's probable intention.'

Also s 416:

> 'To achieve the settlor's tax objectives, the court may modify the terms of a trust in a manner that is not contrary to the settlor's probable intention. The court may provide that the modification has retroactive effect.'

(4) make an action for breach of trust harder to pursue;
(5) make a settlor's statutory indemnity for tax harder to enforce;[21]
(6) reverse the rule that references in the trust to 'children' include illegitimate and adopted children.[22]

Should trustees be given power to change the governing law? Practical applications for trusts governed by Northern Ireland law are relatively rare. However, the power is particularly useful for English law trusts once the trust is more than 21 years old, if the trustees wish to accumulate income. The following draft is proposed:

> The Trustees may during the Trust Period by deed with the consent of the Settlor during his life or of two Beneficiaries after his death declare that from the date of such declaration:
> (1) The law of any Qualifying Jurisdiction governs the validity of this Settlement, and its construction, effects and administration, or any severable aspect of this Settlement; and
> (2) The courts of any Qualifying Jurisdiction have exclusive jurisdiction in any proceedings involving rights or obligations under this Settlement.
> In this paragraph a 'Qualifying Jurisdiction' is one which recognises trusts (as defined in the Hague Convention on the Law Applicable to Trusts and on their Recognition).

The power to change the governing law should be subject to the safeguard that it should only be exercised with the consent of the protector, settlor or two beneficiaries.

Sometimes the trustees are given power to make alterations in the terms of the trust which are consequential to the change in the governing law, but this only duplicates the standard overriding powers.

Sometimes the power is made subject to the condition that no part of the trust should become unenforceable in the new jurisdiction; but this raises difficult questions as to what is meant by 'part of a trust' and 'unenforceable.' Sometimes the power is made subject to the condition that all (or substantially all) the terms of the trust should be capable of taking effect in the new jurisdiction. However, the purpose of changing the governing law may be precisely to alter the effect of the terms of the trust. It is suggested that the appropriate restriction should only be that the new governing law is one which recognises trusts (as defined in the Hague Convention on the Law Applicable to Trusts and on their Recognition).

21 There are too many such rights to compile a complete list, but the most important is TCGA 1992, Sch 5, para 6. The questions raised by such indemnities have become very important since the reforms of the FA 1998, but have not yet been explored in the courts.

22 See para 4.22 (Illegitimate beneficiaries); para 4.23 (Adopted beneficiaries).

Sometimes the power is made subject to the condition that the trust should not be revocable in the new jurisdiction. It is of course important that the power to change the governing law cannot be exercised to allow the settlor or his spouse to benefit from the settled property (assuming they are meant to be excluded from the trust, as will usually be the case); or to prevent the trust from qualifying as an A&M or interest in possession trust (if appropriate). However, the usual settlor exclusion clause and protection clause will ensure that this is the case and no additional wording is needed.[23]

Place of administration of trust

27.5

The form used in this book is as follows:

> The Trustees may carry on the administration of this Settlement anywhere they think fit.

The place of administration of the trust is important in ascertaining residence for certain tax purposes[24] and for some minor conflict of law issues.[25]

Trustees can as a matter of general principle carry on the administration of a trust wherever they think fit.[26] The clause is therefore strictly unnecessary. However, if

23 The Revenue lost an argument along these lines before the Special Commissioners: *IRC v Schroder* [1983] STC 480 at 489. There was, wisely, no appeal on this point.

24 'Place of administration' is one of a cluster of concepts expressed in slightly different ways, with slightly different nuances of meaning.

1 The place where 'the general administration of the trusts is ordinarily carried on' is relevant for trust residence for CGT: TCGA 1992, s 69. See Kessler *Taxation of Foreign Domiciliaries* (2nd edn, 2003) Key Haven Publications, ch 4 (residence of trustees).

2 The 'place of effective management' of a trust is relevant to determine trust residence for the purpose of double tax treaties using the Organisation for Economic Cooperation and Development Model. This concept is not quite the same as 'place of administration' as the emphasis is on 'top management'.

25 The place of administration does *not* determine the law applicable to matters of administration: *Chellaram v Chellaram* [1985] Ch 409; Hague Convention, art 8. (This needs stressing as the contrary view was once generally held, and still survives in some textbooks.) However:

1 'The place of administration of the trust designated by the Settlor' is relevant to ascertain the applicable law of the Trust, if no applicable law has been chosen expressly: Hague Convention, art 7;

2 the place of administration is relevant in applying the common law rules to decide whether a court has (or will exercise) jurisdiction over the trust: see *Chellaram v Chellaram*. In some foreign trust laws the point is made expressly: eg Trusts (Jersey) Law, art 5(d) ('the Court has jurisdiction where ... administration of any trust property of a foreign trust is carried on in Jersey.');

3 the place of administration may be relevant to a clause in a trust which refers to the place of administration (this book does not use that drafting technique.)

26 The authors cannot find authority for this proposition, but only since it has never been questioned. Of course in practice it would be normal for administration to be carried on where the trustees are resident.

it is desired to move the place of administration to a new jurisdiction, it is good practice to exercise this power by formal resolution.[27]

The choice of the place of administration does not significantly affect the beneficiary's rights. It is unnecessary to require a protector's consent to the exercise of the power or to restrict the power in any way.

Exclusive jurisdiction clause

27.6

A full discussion of jurisdiction over trusts is beyond the scope of this book. Happily, it is sufficient for the drafter to note art 17 of the Convention on Jurisdiction and the Enforcement of Judgments in Civil and Commercial Matters[28] which provides:

> 'The court or courts of a Contracting State on which a trust instrument has conferred jurisdiction shall have exclusive jurisdiction in any proceedings brought against a settlor, trustee or beneficiary, if relations between these persons or their rights or obligations under the trust are involved.'

The authors' practice is to include an exclusive jurisdiction clause where there is an express selection of governing law (as is recommended for Northern Ireland trusts), but not otherwise. The wording is based on the Convention:

> The Courts of Northern Ireland have exclusive jurisdiction in any proceedings involving rights or obligations under this Settlement.

'Forum of administration'

27.7

Old precedents used to specify a governing law and, separately, a 'forum of administration' of the settlement.[29] The purpose of the latter was:
(1) to specify the country whose courts had jurisdiction over administration;

[27] The resolution is no more than a step in the right direction. What matters is not where the trustees intend, or are required to carry on the administration, but where it is actually done. Contrast *Unit Construction Co Ltd v Bullock* [1960] AC 351, 38 TC 712.

[28] The Convention is Scheduled to the CJJA 1982.

[29] There was likewise power to alter the governing law and, separately, power to alter the forum of administration, eg the trust in *Chellaram v Chellaram* [1985] Ch 409: 'a power for the trustees by deed to declare that the settlement shall take effect in accordance with the law of some other place in any part of the world *and that the forum for the administration hereof shall thenceforth be the laws of that place.*'

(2) to specify the law governing matters of administration.

Now, however:

(1) the issue of jurisdiction is better dealt with in a form based on the Brussels Convention;

(2) the governing law governs matters of administration.[30]

Therefore it is not now appropriate or meaningful[31] for the drafter to specify a 'forum of administration' in addition to specifying a governing law and a place of exclusive jurisdiction.

30 The form goes back to the time when it was thought that:
(1) the governing law only governed issues of validity and construction; but
(2) the place of administration (or 'forum of administration') governed issues of administration.
Since 1987 at least it has been clear that the governing law in principle determines issues of administration along with everything else; see above.

31 The expression 'forum of administration' is often used in a way where it is unclear whether the meaning is: (i) courts with jurisdiction over administration; (ii) law governing administration; or (iii) place where administration is carried on. *Dymond's Death Duties* (15th edn, 1973) p 1299 states that in the older cases the term was used to refer to what is now called the proper law. The lack of clarity in the phrase is another reason to avoid the expression and an example of the imprecision which Latin sometimes hides when used in modern law.

CHAPTER 28

Restricting rights of beneficiaries

This chapter discusses techniques intended to restrict rights of beneficiaries. None of them are used in the precedents in this book.

Restrictions on disclosure of information

28.1

A client may wish to restrict rights of information in different ways and for different reasons:

(1) so that no individual beneficiary is entitled to find out what any other beneficiary inherits;

(2) so that younger beneficiaries do not find out about the trust assets until they reach a more mature age;

(3) so that distant 'fall back' beneficiaries who are not (in practice) likely to receive benefits do not receive any information.

There are two main ways in which a beneficiary might obtain information:

(1) in the case of a will, from the probate;

(2) in any case, from the right of a beneficiary to trust information.

A third method is by seeking disclosure in the course of litigation. The drafter cannot, however, restrict the Court's power to order disclosure in the course of litigation.

Probate of will

28.2

A will is of course a public document. However, one can avoid disclosure by using a secret trust.[1] Although the Will is a public document, the will itself will only

[1] An alternative to a secret trust is a 'half secret trust'. That is, a gift to the executors combined with a direction in the will that the executors are to hold the property on appropriate trusts.

show that there is a gift of the residuary estate to the executors. The reader of the will will guess that there is a secret trust, but he will not find out its terms from the will.

The value of the testator's estate will, however, be disclosed to the public. A beneficiary, knowing the value of his own share of the estate, and the value of the whole estate, may be able to draw some conclusions as to what other beneficiaries have obtained. If it is desired to avoid that problem then the client must create one or more trusts during his lifetime. This might be a trust under which the client has an interest in possession in this trust, with power to advance capital to him. The trust fund will not in principle form part of his free estate. So its value will not be included in the value of his free estate, which is the value that is made public. Of course, the tax consequences of this proposal would need consideration.

Beneficiaries' right to trust information[2]

The general law position

28.3

The law in Jersey has been explained in *Re Rabaiotti*[3] and it is considered that the English law is the same:

> A beneficiary is normally entitled to inspect trust documents such as the trust deed and documents which show the nature and value of the trust property, the trust income and how the trustees have been investing and distributing the trust property. However, there is a discretion in the Court to refuse disclosure to a beneficiary where it is satisfied that this would not be in the best interests of the beneficiaries as a whole.
>
> A beneficiary is not normally entitled to see a letter of wishes both because it is covered by the principles laid down in *Re Londonderry*[4] and because it is a document which is confidential to the trustees. However, there is a discretion in the Court to allow disclosure where it is satisfied that there is good reason to do so in any particular case.

The will itself will not say what the terms of these trusts are. Some commentators take the view that this type of trust rests on the principle of 'incorporation by reference'. If that is so then the underlying trust documentation should be publicly available with the will. To avoid this uncertain question a fully secret trust is preferable to a half secret trust.

2 See Disclosure of Information by Trustees, International Trust Laws, s B7 (Emily Campbell).

3 [2000] 2 ITELR 763, accessible on www.jerseylegalinfo.je.

4 [1965] Ch 918.

However, a letter of wishes will normally be disclosed as a matter of good administration and refusal to disclose might encourage disappointed beneficiaries to litigate.[5]

Can a trust exclude rights to information?

A clause which purports to remove or exclude the right to information entirely will be ignored as inconsistent with the true nature of a trust, or an attempt to oust the jurisdiction of the courts.[6]

The question of what restrictions can be imposed on the right to information is at present not at all clear. The courts would no doubt be inclined to give effect to a clause which imposes modest and sensible restrictions on the supply of information, for instance, a clause which prevents a person obtaining information if that person is merely a 'fall-back' discretionary beneficiary and is not likely to receive any benefits. But such a person would probably have no right to information anyway, applying general law principles.

One sometimes sees forms such as:

> *(i) Save as required by law[7] and subject to an order of any competent Court the Trustees shall not be bound to disclose to any person other than the Settlor any documents or other matter relating to this Trust.*

Since no one knows what rights to information are 'required by law', it is impossible to say what the position would be if this clause was valid. In practice, it is most likely that this sort of restriction on right to information would be held to be void.

Any attempt to withhold information is almost bound to lead to litigation, and the trustees' first step would then have to be to apply promptly to the court for guidance, in a *Beddoe* style application.

The settlor will not want his trust to be the test case in the future which decides some of these points. The best course is not to include any clause which purports to restrict beneficiaries' rights to information or forfeits their interests if they seek information.

5 *Scott v National Trust* [1998] 2 All ER 705.

6 See *Jones v Shipping Federation of British Columbia* (1963) 37 DLR (2d) 273, accessible on www.kessler.co.uk; Underhill & Hayton *The Law Relating to Trusts and Trustees* (16th edn, 2003) LexisNexis UK, p 681.

7 The words 'save as required by law' are not of course meant to preserve the usual right to information: they are meant to restrict it so far as the law allows.

Practical means of restricting rights of information

One viable route is to arrange that:

(1) each beneficiary has a settlement creating appropriate trusts for the benefit of that beneficiary and (say) his future family;[8]

(2) each settlement is a separate settlement for CGT and general trust law purposes;

(3) each beneficiary is not a beneficiary under the other settlements.

Since a beneficiary of one settlement is not a beneficiary under the other settlements, he cannot be entitled to information about the other settlements.

Where confidentiality of a statement of wishes is important it is suggested that the statement should be expressed to be confidential and give reasons for confidentiality (if not obvious). If appropriate the settlor might record two statements of wishes; one to be disclosed, the other expressed to be confidential, and setting out the further confidential material. This procedure places the maximum obstacles in the way of a beneficiary seeking disclosure.

Extension of powers of disclosure

28.4

The author has seen a form authorising disclosure to Government departments:

> *The Trustees may make such disclosures concerning this Trust or Trust Property (including disclosure of any direct or indirect beneficial interests therein and of any dealings therein) as may be properly required by any competent authority or person whether or not such disclosure may be enforced upon the Trustees.*

No one has ever doubted that the general law allows trustees to disclose information properly required; this form is only appropriate in foreign jurisdictions where the local law imposes greater secrecy requirements.

No named beneficiaries or unascertainable default beneficiary

28.5

Some drafters make it hard to ascertain who the default beneficiaries will be, so as to weaken the claims to information or to the trust fund. The furthest that the

8 Or, of course, if appropriate, a beneficiary may be given his share absolutely.

author would go down this road would be to provide that the default beneficiary should be 'such charities as the trustees shall determine'.

Sometimes the default beneficiary is expressed to be:

> *The persons who would have been entitled to the settlor's estate (and in the share or amounts and for the interest in and for which such persons respectively would have become so entitled thereto) under the law relating to the distribution of the moveable estate of a person dying intestate under the law in force in the jurisdiction of the proper law of the trust at the expiration of the trust period if the settlor had died on that date (but after the death of any other person dying on that date) wholly intestate and domiciled in the jurisdiction of the proper law of this trust without leaving any spouse him surviving and possessed only of an absolute beneficial interest in the net proceeds of sale and conversion of the trust fund.*

This form will often breach the rule against perpetuities.

Some tax lawyers have suggested that an appropriate default beneficiary might be the Chancellor of the Exchequer on the expiry of the trust period. Some academics propose the Warden of All Souls. But since there is (one may assume) no genuine intention to benefit the Chancellor or the Warden, this might be regarded by a hostile court as a sham.[9]

A variant of this idea is that there should be no beneficiaries named in the trust deed at all. The risk that a hostile court would regard this as a sham is greater than ever.

No challenge clauses

28.6

The following clause was held to be void:

> *[1] I declare that no beneficiary taking any share or interest under this my will whether absolutely contingently or in reversion shall whether during the lifetime of my family trustees or after their death challenge call into question or interfere with anything that my trustees may have done or which they may have omitted to do in the exercise of the very wide discretions given by me to my trustees by this my will in connection with my estate and*

9 It should not be held to be a sham, applying the well established case law test; but hostile courts have sometimes applied a looser test of sham. See Kessler, 'What is (and what is not) a Sham' (1999) The Offshore & International Taxation Review, vol 9, p 125, accessible on www.kessler.co.uk.

[2] I declare that in the event of any such challenge calling into question or interference then the benefit taken by any such person or persons or charity or charities under this my will shall be forfeited and in the event that such challenge calling into question or interference shall be made by any one or more of the ultimate charity trustees or charity beneficiaries interested in the ultimate gift under this my will then the interest taken by any such ultimate charity trustee or charity beneficiary who shall make such challenge call into question or interfere shall be forfeited and the capital and income representing such interest shall pass to the trustees for King Edward's Hospital Fund.

Re Levy [1960] Ch 346 at 366. It is recommended that no attempt should be made to use a clause along these lines.

Non-assignment clauses

28.7

No person interested under this trust may sell pledge assign or encumber his interest under this trust.

This provision is void in this jurisdiction, though some foreign trust laws permit it. A similar result can be achieved: see para 4.4 (A better solution).

CHAPTER 29

Stamp duty

29.1

The topic of stamp duty is frivolous and vexatious. It is frivolous because the duty is theoretically *five pounds* and in practice nil. It is vexatious because the rules are bizarre and obscure, and the maximum penalty for failing to pay the duty is £300. The FA 2003 reforms have generally removed the £5 charge but increased the vexation. This chapter sets out the law after the 'implementation date' for Stamp Duty Land Tax (SDLT) (1 December 2003).

A will is not subject to stamp duty. The following discussion applies to lifetime settlements only. It is assumed that there is no consideration for the transfer to the settlement. (Note the trap that the assumption of a mortgage is consideration for stamp duty purposes.)

The charges

29.2

Four categories of stamp duty charge are relevant:

(1) 'A transfer of property otherwise than on sale'.[1] This requires a £5 stamp.

(2) 'A declaration of any use[2] or trust of or concerning property unless the instrument constitutes a transfer on sale'. Another £5 stamp.[3]

(3) 'Any conveyance or transfer operating as a voluntary disposition *inter vivos*'.[4] This charge was abolished in 1985, but a document which would formerly have been subject to this charge has to be adjudicated and stamped 'with a

1 FA 1999, Sch 13, para. 16. 'Transfer' is widely defined to include 'every instrument, and every decree or order of a court or commissioners, by which any property is transferred to or vested in any person'.

2 The term 'use' is archaic, but the drafter has understandably retained the terminology used in the Stamp Act 1891.

3 FA 1999, Sch 13, para. 17.

4 An *inter vivos* disposition is a lifetime disposition (as opposed to a will).

particular stamp denoting that it is duly stamped or that it is not chargeable with any stamp duty'.[5] We refer to this as £0 stamp.
(4) 'Land transaction'. SDLT is not charged on a transfer of land for no consideration. However, if the land transaction is to be registered, there must be a certificate by the trustees that no land transaction return is required ('SDLT self certificate').[6]

Thus there is
(1) a £5 stamp on what we shall call:
  (a) a transfer of property; and
  (b) a declaration of trust.
(2) A £0 stamp on what we shall call a voluntary disposition, and a SDLT self certificate on land.

FA 2003 has reduced the scope of the two £5 charges: these now apply only on instruments relating to 'stock or marketable securities'.[7]

Category L exemption

29.3

The Stamp Duty (Exempt Instruments) Regulations 1987[8] provide that an instrument is exempt from £5 and £0 stamps if:
(1) it is 'of a kind specified in the Schedule'; and
(2) it is properly certified.

Only one of the 14 categories in the Schedule is relevant, Category L:

> The conveyance or transfer of property operating as a voluntary disposition inter vivos[9] for no consideration in money or money's worth nor any consideration referred to in section 57 of the Stamp Act 1891 (conveyance in consideration of a debt etc).

This regulation distinguishes between:
(1) a transfer of property (exempt if certified) and
(2) a declaration of trust (to which no exemption applies).

5 FA 1985, s 82.
6 See FA 2003, s 79 and Sch 11. This applies to land in the UK. References below to land are references to UK land and it is assumed that a transfer of legal title to land needs to be registered. The self-certificate form is obtainable from the Stamp Taxes Office.
7 FA 2003, s.125(1). 'Stock' and 'marketable securities' are elaborately defined in SA 1891, s 122. For convenience references to 'stock' in this chapter includes 'marketable securities'.
8 Amended by the Stamp Duty (Exempt Instruments) (Amendment) Regulations 1999.
9 The drafter has used as a precedent the former charge on voluntary dispositions. The reference to 'conveyance' is inappropriate after the 2003 reforms but that does not matter.

The context seems to show that a document which is a 'declaration of trust' is not to be regarded as a 'conveyance or transfer'.[10]

How the exemption applies

29.4

1. *S executes two documents which take effect* ***simultaneously:***
   (1) A transfer of property from S to T.
   (2) A trust deed (directing T to hold the property on certain trusts).

This is the most common way of creating a trust. The position is as follows:

(1) The transfer should receive a category L certificate.[11] If the transfer is of land, it also requires a SDLT self-certificate.

(2) The trust deed does not receive a category L certificate and is not stamped at all:

(a) The trust deed is not stamped £5 if the trust property is not stock because it cannot 'relate to stock'. It is considered that the trust deed is not a 'conveyance or transfer operating as a voluntary disposition'. So it is not stamped £0 either. Thus it is not stamped at all.

(b) If the trust deed is drawn so as to apply to all trust property transferred to the trustees, as in this book, it does not in our opinion 'relate to stock' (ie, relate specifically to stock), even if stock is actually transferred to the trustees. So then there is still neither £5 nor £0 stamp.[12]

The same applies if the transfer takes effect after the execution of the trust deed.

2. *(1) S executes a transfer of property to T. Immediately after the transfer, T holds the property as nominee for S.*
   (2) S ***subsequently*** *executes a trust deed directing T to hold the property on certain trusts.*

10 Almost every declaration of trust is in fact also a 'transfer' as defined in FA 1999, Sch 13, para. 16; but that definition is expressed to apply only for the purposes of para 16 and it is suggested that the context shows the definition does not apply for the purposes of the Stamp Duty (Exempt Instruments) Regulations.

11 If it does not receive a certificate, then:
(1) If the transfer is of stock, it requires a £5 stamp.
(2) If the transfer is not stock, it requires a £0 stamp.
Where the property transferred is stock, the certificate is conveniently set out on the back of the standard stock transfer form.

12 If that were wrong or if (exceptionally) the trust deed expressly referred to stock then the trust deed would be stamped £5 as a declaration of trust. It might be argued that the deed is also stamped as a 'transfer': almost every declaration of trust will be a 'transfer' as defined, since it will vest an equitable interest of some kind in some beneficiary. But the better view is that a straightforward declaration of trust in this example is to be regarded as a single instrument falling under more than one head of duty. The general rule is that an instrument chargeable under some specific head is not charged under some more general head so it is to be charged as a declaration of trust. See *Monroe and Nock on the Law of Stamp Duties*, looseleaf, para. 1-226 (Instruments answering more than one description). A full discussion (or any discussion) seems extravagantly disproportionate to the £5 duty at stake.

(1) The transfer should not receive a Category L certificate.[13]
   (a) If the transfer is of stock it requires a £5 stamp. If there are numerous transfer forms, perhaps one for each stock held by the transferor, each form will attract £5. However, if a single instrument is used to make the transfer, supplemented by a schedule of the stocks involved, instead of separate stock transfer forms, there is only one amount of £5 fixed duty. The Stamp Taxes Office accept this: see Stamp Taxes Manual at 9.75.
   (b) If the transfer is not stock, it is not stampable £5 or £0.
   (c) If the transfer is of land, it requires a SDLT self-certificate.
(2) The Trust Deed does not receive a Category L certificate.
   (a) The trust deed should be stamped £5 as a declaration of trust if the trust property is or includes stock. It does not fall within an exempt category.
   (b) If the trust property is not stock, the trust deed is not stamped £5. But it is a voluntary disposition and stamped £0.

3. *S executes a document declaring that he holds property (vested in S) on certain trusts.*

The document does not fall within an exempt category.
(1) If the property is stock, the document should be stamped £5 as a declaration of trust.
(2) If the property is not stock, the document should be stamped £0 as a voluntary disposition.

4. *S executes a single document which transfers property to T and directs T to hold the property on the trusts set out in the document.*

This document is (i) a transfer and (ii) a declaration of trust. The Stamp Taxes Office view is:

> A declaration of trust which establishes a trust **and** gifts[14] property is chargeable to £5 fixed duty as a declaration of trust **and** £5 as a gift but may be exempted from the £5 duty as a gift if it is certified as falling within Category L in the Schedule to the Stamp Duty (Exempt Instruments) Regulations 1987.[15]

(1) This is probably correct where the property is stock.[16]
(2) If the property is not stock, the document is stamped £0. If the property is land the document also requires a SDLT self certificate.

5. *A trust already exists. S transfers additional property to the trustees by a transfer which does not mention the trust, but it is understood that the property is to be treated as an addition to the trust fund.*

13 A transfer to a nominee is not within Category L as it does not operate as a voluntary disposition.
14 Ie a declaration of trust which is also a 'transfer' as defined.
15 Stamp Taxes Manual 9.6 (original emphasis.)
16 Though one could raise a decent argument that the principal object of the instrument is a transfer and so it is wholly exempt.

The document is a transfer. It should receive a Category L certificate.[17] If the transfer is of land, it also requires a SDLT self certificate.

6. *Property is held by nominees for S. S simultaneously executes two documents:*
   (1) A letter directing the nominees to hold to the order of T.
   (2) A trust deed directing T to hold the property on certain trusts.

(1) The letter is probably a transfer, but if it receives a category L certificate it is not subject to stamp duty. Without a certificate there would be £5 stamp (stock) or £0 stamp (not stock).
(2) The trust deed is dealt with as in example 1 above.

29.5

The current practice of the Stamp Office is not to supply blank sheets of paper pre-stamped at £5 or £0.[18]

Where possible a stamp duty certificate should be used, to avoid the fixed duty and the administrative chore of stamping. The requirements for a valid certificate are as follows[19]:

(1) The certificate must state the category in the schedule of the Regulations in which the instrument falls.
(2) The certificate must be signed by the settlor, or his solicitors.
(3) The certificate must either be included in the transfer, or indorsed upon it, or be physically attached *(ie* stapled or bound) to it.

A standard clause setting out a stamp duty certificate is the convenient course:

> The Settlor certifies that this transfer falls within category L of the Stamp Duty (Exempt Instruments) Regulations 1987.

The signature requirement is satisfied when the settlor signs the transfer in the usual way.

If a certificate is accidentally omitted it can be added at any subsequent time.[20] There is no penalty for an erroneous certificate, in the absence of an intent to defraud.

17 Without a certificate there would be £5 stamp (stock) or £0 stamp (not stock).
18 Though this was formerly the practice, and the Stamp Act 1891, s 3 expressly recognises that a document may be written on 'stamped material'.
19 Stamp Duty (Exempt Instruments) Regulations 1987, reg 3.
20 The Revenue accept this. Stamp Taxes Manual 2.24 provides:

> 'If it is clear that an uncertified document could have been given a valid certificate Stamp Taxes will give the customer the opportunity to add a certificate.'

Penalties for late stamping

29.6

The Stamp Taxes Manual states:

> The statutory rule is that the penalty due on late presentation of a document liable to duty of £5 is a maximum of £5 if it is up to 1 year late and a maximum of £300 if it is over 1 year late.[21]

This is correct but the Revenue have power to mitigate or remit the penalty.[22] The Manual continues:

> However, in practice we will mitigate the statutory penalty due to Nil if the document is presented up to 1 year late. No penalty will therefore be charged.

So far so good. The Manual continues:

> Over 1 year late but not more than 2 years late – £10 More than 2 years late – £25
>
> However the maximum penalty provide for by the 1999 Finance Act is £300. In cases where there appears to be a deliberate policy by the applicant or the person that they represent of failing to stamp fixed duty documents within the 30 day period allowed, consideration should be given to whether the full penalty should be imposed. In any case of this kind the papers should be referred to the Technical Group Adviser.

In practice since Stamp Duty (unlike SDLT) is an (almost) voluntary tax, it is unlikely that these penalties have been or ever will be paid.

Deeds of appointment

29.7

A deed of appointment exercising an overriding power is not subject to stamp duty.[23]

21 Stamp Taxes Manual 3.32.
22 Stamp Act 1891, s 15B. Interest is not payable on the £5 duty: Stamp Act 1891, s 15A(1)(a).
23 The fixed charge on 'Deed of any kind whatsoever' was abolished by FA 1985, s 85.

Commentary

29.8

All readers who have followed the text to this point will agree that these rules should be reviewed and (apart from the SDLT self certificate) abolished.

CHAPTER 30

Execution of wills and trust deeds

This chapter sets out the procedures to be carried out once a draft has reached its final form.

Review of draft

30.1

The counsel of perfection is as follows. Every document should be reviewed twice after it has reached its final form. The penultimate review should be made by the drafter, at least 24 hours after he last examined the document. This enables him to apply a fresh mind to his work. The final review should be made by a person other than the drafter. Where counsel has prepared the draft, this duty rests on his instructing solicitor. A draft produced in-house should be reviewed by another member of the firm. He should have the text of the document printed out in its final form ready for execution. It is no cynical asperity to observe that the existence of this peer review concentrates the mind of the drafter himself.

Bear in mind the text:

> '*Whoever thinks a faultless piece to see*
>
> *Thinks what ne'er was, nor is, nor ne'er shall be.*'

In the case of a female settlor or beneficiary, care needs to be taken to replace 'his' with 'her', and 'widower' for 'widow'. (Complete avoidance of personal pronouns may render this unnecessary, at the cost of clumsy phraseology.)

Special care needs to be taken where drafts have been amended or errors corrected. In such a case the drafter should review a mental checklist that:
(1) the revised clause fits properly into its context;
(2) the revision does not infringe the rule against perpetuities;
(3) the revision does not infringe the rule against accumulations;

(4) the clauses are renumbered as necessary, and references to clause numbers in the deed are systematically revised.

An omission of text is a remarkably difficult error to spot. This is an error as old as writing itself[1] but it still remains prevalent in the age of the word processor. A prime example from the authors' experience is a trust for a beneficiary 'if he shall attain the vesting age'; the vesting age not being defined.

Use and misuse of precedents

30.2

Standard drafts should be subjected to the same review procedure: they are not immune from error. Published precedents (this book included) should be reviewed with some suspicion: quite apart from the possibility of error, they may not be entirely suitable for the particular case. This advice is as old as precedent books themselves.[2]

Caution! Word processor at work

30.3

In England the Solicitors Indemnity Fund have issued this warning:[3]

> 'It is dangerous to place too much reliance upon equipment in the office. The fact that a document has been produced by a word processor does not obviate the need to check the document carefully, as shown in the two examples below.
>
> The indemnified law firm received instructions to prepare a lease of premises on behalf of a client. The client required the lease to contain an upwards only rent review. A draft lease was produced with commendable speed with the assistance of a word processor. The draft was not checked. It was taken for granted that the draft was correct. In fact a section of the rent review clause was omitted. No one knew why. The effect of the omission was to create an upwards and downwards rent review clause.

1 There is a well-known biblical example at 1 Samuel, 14.41.

2 'Here is good counsell and advice given, to set down in conveyances every thing in certaintie and particiularitie, for certaintie is the mother of quietnesse and repose, and incertaintie the cause of variance and contentions; and for obtaining of the one, and avoyding of the other, the best meane is, in all assurances, to take counsell of learned and well-experienced men, and not to trust only without advice to a precedent.' *Coke upon Littleton* 212a (1628).

3 *Law Society's Gazette*, 10 December 1997, Vol 94, p 34. Jokes about computerised errors were circulating at least two centuries ago; see Campbell's anecdote of Lord Eldon, accessible on www.kessler.co.uk.

The second example shows just how extreme the problem can be. A draft lease generated by the word processor was in fact patent nonsense. It contained every provision available in the precedent. The landlord was to maintain the structure, the tenant was to maintain the structure; the landlord was to insure, the tenant was to insure; the term was for five, ten, fifteen and twenty years. A cursory inspection would have revealed the problem.

To avoid this type of claim...

- Do not assume that a document generated by a word processor is correct.
- Always check the document both in draft form and when engrossed.
- Remember that it is the responsibility of the fee earner, not the secretary, to ensure the draft is correct.'

The Solicitors Indemnity Fund view is set out at length because the ad-men would have us think otherwise.[4] The reader must choose who to believe.

The clearer drafting style advocated in this book renders errors slightly less likely to occur, and slightly easier to spot; but (thankfully) it seems unlikely that the computer will render unnecessary a sharp eye and a clear mind on the part of the drafter.

Printing

30.4

The size of paper used was originally a vast and inconvenient desk size sheet. This gradually reduced to A3 and then to an elongated A4. Nowadays the standard A4 size is always used. The reason is probably that the office printers are set up for A4. Whatever the reason, it is a welcome change as standard A4 size is more convenient for the file.

Single or double spacing is a matter of style only.

A firm of solicitors traditionally puts its name and address on the backsheet or title page of a document, a sign of professional pride in authorship and a useful reference if, many years later, it becomes necessary to investigate the background.

As far as the written letters of the document are concerned, there are two concerns: natural decay and fraudulent alterations.

4 'Encyclopaedia of Forms & Precedents on CD-ROM has transformed the way we work. Previously time consuming tasks are now effortless ... drafts and re-drafts of documents are a thing of the past' (from advertising material).

Natural decay

30.5

Any trust may need to be examined for at least a century so the document must be durable.

With laser printers, the important factor is not the ink or toner, but the quality of paper. If the paper is not acid free, there is a danger of the letters falling off in course of time. Acid free paper must be used for the document itself and for the envelope or package in which it is stored. A paper supplier will advise.

Inkjet printed documents may be more susceptible to fading and some are said to have a life of 10 years or so. If this is true it is alarming. The authors have never encountered any difficulty in practice.

Fraudulent alterations

30.6

The possibility of fraudulent alteration of an existing will or trust seems remote. Quite apart from the practical difficulties inherent in such forgery, a comparison with other copies or drafts would be likely to reveal the fraud.

An old-fashioned protection against fraudulent alteration was the practice of lining in the space from the end of a sentence to the right-hand margin; this is thought to be unnecessary and is no longer standard practice.

Procedure on execution of a lifetime settlement

30.7

There are a number of further procedures to set in motion after the execution of a trust deed.

(1) Transfers of trust property to trustees

30.8

Trust property must be transferred to the trustees (or their nominees) or the trust will generally be ineffective. Each type of property must be transferred by the appropriate method.

Asset	**Method of transfer**
Cash	Transfer to bank account in name of trustees
Shares	Stock transfer form and entry on company register; consider need for consents from shareholders, directors or liquidator
Assets held by nominee	Written direction to nominee signed by beneficial owner
Registered land (unmortgaged)	Land Transfer form, and entry at Land Registry; restriction on the register;[5] consider need for landlord's consent (for a lease)
Unregistered land (unmortgaged)	Conveyance and application to register land; consider need for landlord's consent (for a lease)
Chattels	Deed of assignment
Life assurance policy	Deed of assignment and notice to Life Office
Equitable interest under an existing trust	Deed of assignment and notice to trustees of the existing trust

Transfer must be carried out without delay. Time for the purposes of the seven-year IHT period only begins to run when the trust property is transferred; and if the settlor died before the transfer the trust would not take effect.

(2) Statement of wishes

30.9

A statement of wishes is desirable where the trustees have a wide discretion. That applies to every precedent in this book. See 6.15 (Statement of wishes).

5 Land Registration Rules 1994 (NI SR 424). There are no unusual formalities in respect of such transfers by trustees. Since the trustees will be registered as full owners, it may be prudent to apply for registration under rule 105 of an inhibition protecting the rights of beneficiaries.

(3) Arrangements for payment of IHT on gift in case of death within seven years[6]

30.10

A gift to an IP trust or an A&M trust is a PET and so an IHT charge may arise if the donor does not survive seven years. This tax charge is primarily the liability of the trustees.[7] The possibilities are as follows:

(1) the donor may take out insurance against the risk of the IHT charge. He should give the policy to the donee (trustees);

(2) the donor may wish to provide in his will that tax should be paid out of his estate (rather than by the donee, as would otherwise have been the case);

(3) the donee may accept the risk of the IHT charge accruing if the settlor dies within seven years. Alternatively the donee may take out insurance.

6 See para 12.3 (Trustees to pay tax on gift to trust).

7 There is a lacuna in the statute here. IHTA 1984, ss 199 and 205 state that the settlor's personal representatives and the trustees (and for good measure some beneficiaries) are all liable against the Revenue to pay the IHT on a failed PET. The legislation does not spell out who - as between them - is primarily liable to pay the tax. Someone must bear the primary liability. It is inconceivable that the burden of tax will rest on whichever person the Revenue chooses to assess, so the question who bears the primary liability must be inferred as best one can from the provisions. The inference from IHTA 1984, ss 204(8) and 212 is that the trustees are primarily liable. Where the tax is paid by some other person, it is submitted that he has the right in equity to recover from the person who is primarily liable. See Emily Campbell, 'The Burden of Inheritance Tax on Lifetime Transfers' (1998) PCB 58, accessible on www.kessler.co.uk. However, this question is fairly academic. The curiously named CTO Advanced Instruction Manual, para U.27 provides:

> 'You should treat the following persons as primarily liable [to IHT on a failed PET]:
>
> - the transferee, or
> - where the property is settled by the transfer, the trustees.
>
> Where there are indications that there may be difficulties in collecting from the transferee or trustees (eg where the transferee has dealt with the property given, or is out of the jurisdiction, or the settlement has been wound up and the trust property distributed), you should consider whether, exceptionally, any other persons may be liable under IHTA 1984, s 199(1)(c) and (d) and, if so, take early action to collect from them ...
>
> The facility to have recourse to the transferor's personal representatives is not to be regarded as a soft option. We are to make all the attempts at recovering from the persons liable under IHTA 1984, s 199(1) that we would presently contemplate in a similar situation against any liable person.'

In circumstances where the Revenue chooses not to collect tax from the trustees, the unfortunate person who does pay the tax is likely to find his right of indemnity against the trustees hard to enforce.

Some commentators suggest that the donor should seek an express indemnity from the donee in respect of tax due on a failed PET. An express indemnity is not needed in ordinary circumstances. In particular, an express indemnity is never needed on a gift to a settlement with reputable trustees.

(4) Arrangements for loss of nil-rate band in case of death within seven years

30.11

If the donor dies within seven years of the gift, the donor's estate will, in principle, lose the benefit of the nil-rate band. This problem is quite distinct from (3) above (IHT payable on the gift itself). The tax burden falls on the donor's estate (or if the donor makes subsequent gifts, the tax burden falls on the subsequent donees). The amount of IHT in issue cannot be ascertained at the time of the gift, although one could make an educated guess.

Very occasionally the donee is required to give an indemnity in respect of this tax. This would require careful bespoke drafting to suit the circumstances. This problem would normally arise only when a parent needs to provide for children from different marriages.

(5) Returns and other matters

30.12

Once the trust has been completely constituted, a number of returns and other matters need attention:

(i) *Form 41G (Trust)*. This should be sent to the appropriate[8] Revenue Trust Tax Office to set up a trust record. This is not necessary if the trust will receive no income or gains for the long or medium term (eg a trust of a life insurance policy). It is also possible to complete form 41G but request that a dormant trust should not receive annual SA returns.

(ii) *IHT account.* An account (Form IHT 100) is needed when a gift is made to a discretionary trust.[9] The duty rests on the transferor and the trustees (so that each may be liable to penalties in the case of default). No account is required for a gift to an IP trust or an A&M trust but appropriate records should be kept in case of death within seven years. If the donor dies within seven years of his gift the PET is disclosed in the executor's account.

(iii) *Returns for non-resident trust.* Further returns are required for non-resident trusts.[10]

(iv) *CGT claims for hold-over relief or losses.* A claim may be needed for CGT hold-over relief. The election is made by the settlor alone: the trustees will

8 *The Revenue Trusts Settlements and Estates Manual*, para 1420 (The Correct Trust Office) explains how the work is shared around the trust offices.

9 IHTA 1984, s 216. The Inheritance Tax (Delivery of Accounts) (No 2) Regulations 1981 provide a *de minimis* exception which may apply in the case of a chargeable transfer of £10,000 or less, but that will not normally apply except for trusts of life insurance policies, or cases of 100% Business Property Relief.

10 IHTA 1984, s 218; TCGA 1992, Sch 5A.

not be parties to it. A further claim may be made under SP 8/92 to avoid a valuation.[11] A claim is also needed if an allowable loss arises on the disposal to the trust. These claims are usually dealt with in the settlor's tax return.

(v) *Stamp duty.* The trust deed may need to be presented to the Stamp Office for stamping.[12]

(vi) *Review will.* The donor should review his will as a matter of course following any substantial gift, to confirm that the terms of the will are still appropriate.

(vii) *Inform beneficiaries.* An adult beneficiary who has an interest in possession should be informed of his interest. This is particularly relevant if the fund does not produce income. Concealment may be taken as evidence of a sham.

(viii) *Diarise important deadlines.* For a discretionary trust, diarise the next 10-year anniversary. For an A&M trust, diarise the date that beneficiaries reach 25. If appropriate, diarise dates that beneficiaries become absolutely entitled. More precisely, diarise the date six months before the deadline, to allow time for action.

Procedure on execution of a will

30.13

To ensure that the formalities of execution are correctly followed, the proper course is that at least one of the witnesses of the will should be a solicitor.[13] The client may not wish to visit the solicitor's office, or to pay the cost of a solicitor visiting him. In such a case a letter should be sent to the client setting out the reasons why it is better to execute the will in the presence of a solicitor, with a recommendation to follow this course. If the client refuses to do so his refusal should be recorded in writing. Subsequently the client may be advised in writing of the formalities for execution of a will, and left to carry them out. The solicitor should check that the will appears on its face to have been properly executed if it is returned to him.[14]

The client should be advised to execute an Enduring Power of Attorney along with his will.

Earlier (revoked) wills should be retained but be marked as revoked by the new will.

The authors are grateful to John Hawes for the following sage advice:

11 'Capital Gains Tax: Hold-Over Relief and SP 8/92' (April 1997, Tax Bulletin 28).

12 Paragraph 29.1 (Stamp duty).

13 Since the enactment of TA(NI) 2001 a will may be witnessed by a partner of the firm, notwithstanding a charging clause in the firm's favour.

14 *Esterhuizen v Allied Dunbar Assurance plc* [1998] 2 FLR 668, accessible on www.kessler.co.uk.

'I have for many years now kept (or my secretary has) a perpetual diary in which the execution of every client's will is noted for review three years ahead. Every month during a quiet moment my secretary gets out the diary and prepares a standard letter saying, in effect, are you still alive and here's a copy of your will in case you want to change it. Please tick the appropriate box in the attached form and send it back in the SAE. At the same time, my secretary notes the diary for another three years ahead. This is good for the clients, it keeps my records straight if clients have moved and it is also good and cheap marketing as it reminds the clients that you are their solicitor.'[15]

Tax reviews after execution of trust

30.14

It is of course the general duty of the trustees to mitigate so far as possible the taxation of the trust. They should review the tax position at regular intervals.

In particular, the IHT position should be reviewed:
(1) if it seems likely that the settlor will not survive seven years from the time he creates the trust. It may be possible to mitigate the tax charge on his gift to the trust;
(2) on the death of a life tenant;
(3) shortly before the 25th birthday of an A&M beneficiary;
(4) shortly before a 10-year anniversary of a discretionary trust.

The CGT position should be reviewed:
(1) in good time before the trustees realise substantial gains;
(2) before a beneficiary becomes absolutely entitled to trust property.

Trustees who are not specialists in these matters may seek specialist advice.

15 Although it is important to frame the letter so that the client is not led to believe that a 'watching brief' is being kept over his tax affairs if there has been no express retainer for such. The Guidance published by the English Law Society's Standards and Guidance Committee (printed in the Society's *Probate Practitioner's Handbook*) includes the following statement: 'Without specific instructions from the client, a retainer for will preparation would not entail the solicitor in maintaining any such "watching brief"' but it is possible for a solicitor by his or her conduct to change a retainer so that a client comes to have a reasonable expectation that such a watching brief will be maintained. Solicitors would be well-advised to ensure that these matters are clear between themselves and their clients.' See eg *Hines* v *Willans* [1997] 5 CL 420, reported belatedly [2002] WTLR 299.

Precedents

Precedents for lifetime trusts

Interest in possession trust for adult beneficiary

This settlement is made [*date*] between:

1 [*Name of settlor*] of [*address*] ('the Settlor') of the one part and

2 2.1 [*Name of first trustee*] of [*address*] and

2.2 [*Name of second trustee*] of [*address*]

('the Original Trustees') of the other part.

Whereas this Settlement shall be known as the [*name-of-settlor Settlement 2004*].

Now this deed witnesses as follows:

1 Definitions

In this settlement:

1.1 **'The Trustees'** means the Original Trustees or the trustees of the settlement for the time being.

1.2 **'The Trust Fund'** means:

1.2.1 property transferred to the Trustees to hold on the terms of this Settlement; and

1.2.2 all property from time to time representing the above.

1.3 **'Trust Property'** means any property comprised in the Trust Fund.

1.4 **'The Trust Period'** means the period of 80 years beginning with the date of this Settlement. That is the perpetuity period applicable to this Settlement under the rule against perpetuities.

1.5 **'The Beneficiaries'** means:

1.5.1 The children and descendants of the Settlor.

1.5.2 The spouses, widows and widowers (whether or not remarried) of paragraph .1 of this sub-clause.
1.5.3 The [*widow*] (whether or not remarried) of the Settlor.
1.5.4 Any Person or class of Persons nominated to the Trustees by:
1.5.4.1 the Settlor or
1.5.4.2 two Beneficiaries (after the death of the Settlor)
and whose nomination is accepted in writing by the Trustees.
1.5.5 At any time during which there are no Beneficiaries within paragraph .1 of this sub-clause:
1.5.5.1 [*specify 'fall back' beneficiaries if desired, eg nieces and nephews and their families*];
1.5.5.2 [*any company, body or trust established for charitable purposes only*].
1.6 '[*Adam*]' means [*Adam Smith*] the [*son*] of the Settlor.
1.7 **'Person'** includes a person anywhere in the world and includes a Trustee.

2 Trust Income

Subject to the Overriding Powers below:
2.1 The Trustees shall pay the income of the Trust Fund to [*Adam*] during [*his*] life.
2.2 Subject to that, if [*Adam*] dies during the Trust Period, the Trustees shall pay the income of the Trust Fund to [*his widow*] during [*her*] life.
2.3 Subject to that, during the Trust Period, the Trustees shall pay or apply the income of the Trust Fund to or for the benefit of any Beneficiaries as the Trustees think fit.

3 Overriding Powers

The Trustees shall have the following powers ('Overriding Powers'):
3.1 Power of appointment
3.1.1 The Trustees may appoint that they shall hold the Trust Fund for the benefit of any Beneficiaries, on such terms as the Trustees think fit.
3.1.2 An appointment may create any provisions and in particular:
3.1.2.1 discretionary trusts;
3.1.2.2 dispositive or administrative powers;
exercisable by any Person.
3.1.3 An appointment shall be made by deed and may be revocable or irrevocable.
3.2 Transfer of Trust Property to other settlement
3.2.1 The Trustees may by deed declare that they hold any Trust Property on trust to transfer it to trustees of another settlement, wherever established, to hold on the terms of that settlement, freed and released from the terms of this Settlement.
3.2.2 The Trustees shall only exercise this power if:

3.2.2.1 every Person who may benefit is (or would if living be) a Beneficiary; or

3.2.2.2 with the consent in writing of

3.2.2.2.1 the Settlor, or

3.2.2.2.2 two Beneficiaries (after the death of the Settlor).

3.3 Power of advancement
The Trustees may pay or apply any Trust Property for the advancement or benefit of any Beneficiary.

3.4 The Overriding Powers shall be exercisable only:

3.4.1 during the Trust Period; and

3.4.2 at a time when there are at least two Trustees, or the Trustee is a company carrying on a business which consists of or includes the management of trusts.

4 Default Clause

Subject to that, the Trust Fund shall be held on trust for [*Adam or specify default trusts as appropriate*] absolutely.

5 Appointment of Trustees

The power of appointing trustees is exercisable:

5.1 by the Settlor during [*his*] life and by will, and after [*his*] death

5.2 by [*Adam*] after [*he*] has reached the age of 25 during his life and by will.

6 Further Provisions

The provisions set out in the schedule below shall have effect.

[*For a shorter form, say instead of the above:*

'The standard provisions of the Society of Trust and Estate Practitioners (Northern Ireland Version, 1st Edition) shall apply.'

And omit the schedule.]

[*Check the NI Standard Provisions have been finalised before using this form. This was not done at the time of going to print; updates available on www.kessler.co.uk*]

7 Exclusion of Settlor and Spouse

Notwithstanding anything else in this Settlement, no power conferred by this settlement shall be exercisable, and no provision shall operate so as to allow Trust

Property or its income to become payable to or applicable for the benefit of the Settlor or the spouse of the Settlor in any circumstances whatsoever.

8 Irrevocability

This Settlement is irrevocable.

9 Governing Law

The law of Northern Ireland governs the validity of this Settlement, and its construction, effects and administration. The Courts of Northern Ireland have exclusive jurisdiction in any proceedings involving rights or obligations under this Settlement.

In witness, [*etc*]

THE SCHEDULE: FURTHER PROVISIONS

Interest in possession trust for settlor

Note: This precedent is in small print since it is a relatively rare and specialised form.

This settlement is made [*date*] between:

1 [*Name of settlor*] of [*address*] ('the Settlor') of the one part and

2 2.1 [*Name of first trustee*] of [*address*] and

2.2 [*Name of second trustee*] of [*address*]

('the Original Trustees') of the other part.

Whereas this Settlement shall be known as the [*name-of-settlor Settlement 2004*].

Now this deed witnesses as follows:

1 Definitions

In this settlement:

1.1 **'The Trustees'** means the Original Trustees or the trustees of the settlement for the time being.

1.2 **'The Trust Fund'** means:

1.2.1 property transferred to the Trustees to hold on the terms of this Settlement; and

1.2.2 all property from time to time representing the above.

1.3 **'Trust Property'** means any property comprised in the Trust Fund.

1.4 **'The Trust Period'** means the period of 80 years beginning with the date of this Settlement. That is the perpetuity period applicable to this Settlement under the rule against perpetuities.

1.5 **'The Beneficiaries'** means:
  1.5.1 The Settlor and [*his*] children and descendants.
  1.5.2 The spouses, widows and widowers (whether or not remarried) of paragraph .1 of this sub-clause.
  1.5.3 Any Person or class of Persons nominated to the Trustees by:
    1.5.3.1 the Settlor or
    1.5.3.2 two Beneficiaries (after the death of the Settlor)
  and whose nomination is accepted in writing by the Trustees.
  1.5.4 At any time during which there are no Beneficiaries within paragraph .1 of this sub-clause:
    1.5.4.1 [*specify 'fall back' beneficiaries if desired, eg nieces and nephews and their families*];
    1.5.4.2 [*any company, body or trust established for charitable purposes only*].

1.6 **'Person'** includes a person anywhere in the world and includes a Trustee.

2 Trust Income

Subject to the Overriding Powers below:

2.1 The Trustees shall pay the income of the Trust Fund to the Settlor during [*his*] life.

2.2 Subject to that, if the Settlor dies during the Trust Period, the Trustees shall pay the income of the Trust Fund to [*his widow*] during [*her*] life.

2.3 Subject to that, during the Trust Period, the Trustees shall pay or apply the income of the Trust Fund to or for the benefit of any Beneficiaries as the Trustees think fit.

3 Overriding Powers

The Trustees shall have the following powers ('Overriding Powers'):

3.1 Power of appointment
  3.1.1 The Trustees may appoint that they shall hold the Trust Fund for the benefit of any Beneficiaries, on such terms as the Trustees think fit.
  3.1.2 An appointment may create any provisions and in particular:
    3.1.2.1 discretionary trusts;
    3.1.2.2 dispositive or administrative powers;
  exercisable by any Person.
  3.1.3 An appointment shall be made by deed and may be revocable or irrevocable.

3.2 Transfer of Trust Property to other settlement
  3.2.1 The Trustees may by deed declare that they hold any Trust Property on trust to transfer it to trustees of another settlement, wherever established, to hold on the terms of that settlement, freed and released from the terms of this Settlement.
  3.2.2 The Trustees shall only exercise this power if:

3.2.2.1 every Person who may benefit is (or would if living be) a Beneficiary; or

3.2.2.2 with the consent in writing of

3.2.2.2.1 the Settlor, or

3.2.2.2.2 two Beneficiaries (after the death of the Settlor).

3.3 Power of advancement
The Trustees may pay or apply any Trust Property for the advancement or benefit of any Beneficiary.

3.4 The Overriding Powers shall be exercisable only:

3.4.1 during the Trust Period; and

3.4.2 at a time when there are at least two Trustees, or the Trustee is a company carrying on a business which consists of or includes the management of trusts.

4 Default Clause

Subject to that, the Trust Fund shall be held on trust for [*the Settlor – or specify default trusts as appropriate*] absolutely.

5 Appointment of Trustees

The power of appointing trustees is exercisable by the Settlor during [*his*] life and by will.

6 Further Provisions

The provisions set out in the schedule below shall have effect.

[*For a shorter form, say instead of the above:*

'The standard provisions of the Society of Trust and Estate Practitioners (Northern Ireland Version, 1st Edition) shall apply.'

And omit the schedule.]

[*Check the NI Standard Provisions have been finalised before using this form. This was not done at the time of going to print; updates available on www.kessler.co.uk*]

7 Irrevocability

This Settlement is irrevocable.

8 Governing Law

The law of Northern Ireland governs the validity of this Settlement, and its construction, effects and administration. The Courts of Northern Ireland have exclusive jurisdiction in any proceedings involving rights or obligations under this Settlement.

In witness, [*etc*]

THE SCHEDULE: FURTHER PROVISIONS

[*Here set out the administrative provisions suitable to an IP trust: see below. This is set out in full on the CD.*]

Accumulation and maintenance trust for a single beneficiary

Note: This precedent is in small print since a settlement which includes future born beneficiaries is generally to be preferred. This form may be appropriate where:

* *The Settlor is confident that no siblings or cousins of the existing A&M Beneficiary will be born (who might also be desired to benefit along with that Beneficiary)*
* *In England this form is only suitable if the named A&M Beneficiary is at least 4 years old at the time the settlement is made, so the rule against accumulation will not apply. No such restriction applies in Northern Ireland and the form may be used whatever the age of the named A&M Beneficiary.*

This settlement is made [*date*] between:

1 [*Name of settlor*] of [*address*] ('the Settlor') of the one part and

2 2.1 [*Name of first trustee*] of [*address*] and

2.2 [*Name of second trustee*] of [*address*]

('the Original Trustees') of the other part.

Whereas:

1 [*Adam Smith*] the child of the Settlor, was born on [*date*].

2 This Settlement shall be known as the [*Adam Smith Settlement 2004*].

Now this deed witnesses as follows:

1 Definitions

In this settlement:

1.1 **'The Trustees'** means the Original Trustees or the trustees of the settlement for the time being.

1.2 **'The Trust Fund'** means:
 1.2.1 property transferred to the Trustees to hold on the terms of this Settlement; and
 1.2.2 all property from time to time representing the above.
1.3 **'Trust Property'** means any property comprised in the Trust Fund.
1.4 **'The Trust Period'** means the period of 80 years beginning with the date of this Settlement. That is the perpetuity period applicable to this Settlement under the rule against perpetuities.
1.5 **'The Beneficiaries'** means:
 1.5.1 The children and descendants of the Settlor.
 1.5.2 The spouses, widows and widowers (whether or not remarried) of paragraph .1 of this sub-clause.
 1.5.3 The [*widow*] (whether or not remarried) of the Settlor.
 1.5.4 Any Person or class of Persons nominated to the Trustees by:
  1.5.4.1 the Settlor or
  1.5.4.2 two Beneficiaries (after the death of the Settlor)
 and whose nomination is accepted in writing by the Trustees.
 1.5.5 At any time during which there are no Beneficiaries within paragraph .1 of this sub-clause:
  1.5.5.1 [*specify 'fall back' beneficiaries if desired, eg nieces and nephews and their families*];
  1.5.5.2 [*any company, body or trust established for charitable purposes only*].
1.6 **'Interest in Possession'** has the same meaning as in the Inheritance Tax Act 1984.
1.7 '[*Adam*] means [*Adam Smith*] the child of the Settlor.
1.8 **'Person'** includes a person anywhere in the world and includes a Trustee.

2 Trust Income

Subject to the Overriding Powers below:
2.1 While [*Adam*] is living and under the age of 25:
 2.1.1 The Trustees may apply the income of the Trust Fund for [*his*] maintenance, education or benefit.
 2.1.2 Subject to that, the Trustees shall accumulate the income of the Trust Fund.. That income shall be added to the Trust Fund.
2.2 Subject to that, the Trustees shall pay the income of the Trust Fund to [*Adam*] during [*his*] life.
2.3 Subject to that, if [*Adam*] dies during the Trust Period, the Trustees shall pay the income of the Trust Fund to [*his widow*] during [*her*] life.
2.4 Subject to that, during the Trust Period, the Trustees shall pay or apply the income of the Trust Fund to or for the benefit of any Beneficiaries, as the Trustees think fit.

3 Overriding Powers

Subject to the following clause the Trustees shall have the following powers ('Overriding Powers'):

3.1 *Power of appointment*

3.1.1 The Trustees may appoint that they shall hold the Trust Fund for the benefit of any Beneficiaries, on such terms as the Trustees think fit.

3.1.2 An appointment may create any provisions and in particular:

3.1.2.1 discretionary trusts;

3.1.2.2 dispositive or administrative powers;

exercisable by any Person.

3.1.3 An appointment shall be made by deed and may be revocable or irrevocable.

3.2 *Transfer of Trust Property to other settlement*

3.2.1 The Trustees may by deed declare that they hold any Trust Property on trust to transfer it to trustees of another settlement, wherever established, to hold on the terms of that settlement, freed and released from the terms of this Settlement.

3.2.2 The Trustees shall only exercise this power if:

3.2.2.1 every Person who may benefit is (or would if living be) a Beneficiary; or

3.2.2.2 with the consent in writing of

3.2.2.2.1 the Settlor, or

3.2.2.2.2 two Beneficiaries (after the death of the Settlor).

3.3 *Power of advancement*

The Trustees may pay or apply any Trust Property for the advancement or benefit of any Beneficiary.

3.4 The Overriding Powers shall be exercisable only:

3.4.1 during the Trust Period; and

3.4.2 at a time when there are at least two Trustees, or the Trustee is a company carrying on a business which consists of or includes the management of trusts.

4 Restrictions on Overriding Powers

The Overriding Powers may only be exercised over Trust Property in the following circumstances:

4.1 If [*Adam*] has or has had an Interest in Possession in the Property; or

4.2 If [*Adam*] has died; or

4.3 If, on the exercise of the power, [*Adam*] becomes beneficially entitled to the Property, or to an Interest in Possession in it.

5 Default Clause

Subject to that, the Trust Fund shall be held on trust for [*Adam – or specify default trusts as appropriate*] absolutely.

6 Appointment of Trustees

The power of appointing trustees is exercisable by the Settlor during [*his*] life and by will and after his death by [*Adam*] during his life if [*he*] is over the age of 25, and by will.

7 Further Provisions

The provisions set out in the schedule below shall have effect.

[*For a shorter form, say instead of the above:*

'The standard provisions of the Society of Trust and Estate Practitioners (Northern Ireland Version, 1st Edition) shall apply.

And omit the schedule.]

[*Check the NI Standard Provisions have been finalised before using this form. This was not done at the time of going to print; updates available on www.kessler.co.uk*]

8 Exclusion of Settlor and Spouse

Notwithstanding anything else in this Settlement, no power conferred by this settlement shall be exercisable, and no provision shall operate so as to allow Trust Property or its income to become payable to or applicable for the benefit of the Settlor or the spouse of the Settlor in any circumstances whatsoever.

9 Irrevocability

This Settlement is irrevocable.

10 Governing Law

The law of Northern Ireland governs the validity of this Settlement, and its construction, effects and administration. The Courts of Northern Ireland have exclusive jurisdiction in any proceedings involving rights or obligations under this Settlement.

In witness, [*etc*]

THE SCHEDULE: FURTHER PROVISIONS

[*Here set out the administrative provisions suitable to an A&M trust: see below. This is set out in full on the CD.*]

Accumulation and maintenance trust for a class of named beneficiaries

Note: This settlement is in small print since a settlement which includes future born beneficiaries is generally to be preferred. This form may be appropriate where:

1 The Settlor is confident that no siblings or cousins of the existing A&M Beneficiaries will be born (who might also be desired to benefit along with those Beneficiaries).

2 It is assumed that the named beneficiaries are children of the Settlor. The same form could be used (with trivial amendments) for named grandchildren of the settlor.

Note that in England this form is suitable only where the named A&M Beneficiaries are all at least four years old at the time the settlement is made. This is because of the Rule against Accumulations. No such restriction applies in Northern Ireland and subject to paragraphs 1 and 2 above this form is suitable whatever the age of the A&M Beneficiaries.

This settlement is made [*date*] between:

1 [*Name of settlor*] of [*address*] ('the Settlor') of the one part and

2 2.1 [*Name of first trustee*] of [*address*] and

2.2 [*Name of second trustee*] of [*address*]

('the Original Trustees') of the other part.

Whereas:

1 The Settlor has [three] children, namely:

1.1 [*Adam Smith ('Adam')*] who was born on [*date*].

1.2 [*Peter Smith ('Peter')*] who was born on [*date*].

1.3 [*Joanna Smith ('Joanna')*] who was born on [*date*].

2 This Settlement shall be known as the [*Name-of-settlor Children's Settlement 2004*].

Now this deed witnesses as follows:

1 Definitions

In this settlement:

1.1 **'The Trustees'** means the Original Trustees or the trustees of the settlement for the time being.

1.2 **'The Trust Fund'** means:

1.2.1 property transferred to the Trustees to hold on the terms of this Settlement; and

1.2.2 all property from time to time representing the above.

1.3 **'Trust Property'** means any property comprised in the Trust Fund.

1.4 **'The Trust Period'** means the period of 80 years beginning with the date of this Settlement. That is the perpetuity period applicable to this Settlement under the rule against perpetuities.

1.5 **'The Beneficiaries'** means:

1.5.1 The children and descendants of the Settlor.

1.5.2 The spouses, widows and widowers (whether or not remarried) of paragraph .1 of this sub-clause.

1.5.3 The [*widow*] (whether or not remarried) of the Settlor.

1.5.4 Any Person or class of Persons nominated to the Trustees by:

1.5.4.1 the Settlor or

1.5.4.2 two Beneficiaries (after the death of the Settlor)

and whose nomination is accepted in writing by the Trustees.

1.5.5 At any time during which there are no Beneficiaries within paragraph .1 of this sub-clause:

1.5.5.1 [*specify 'fall back' beneficiaries if desired, eg nieces and nephews and their families*];

1.5.5.2 [*any company, body or trust established for charitable purposes only*].

1.6 **'The Principal Beneficiaries'** means [*Adam, Peter and Joanna*].

1.7 **'Interest in Possession'** has the same meaning as in the Inheritance Tax Act 1984.

1.8 **'Person'** includes a person anywhere in the world and includes a Trustee.

2 Trust Income

Subject to the Overriding Powers below:

2.1 The Trust Fund shall be divided into equal shares ('the Shares') so that there shall be one Share for each Principal Beneficiary.

2.2 While a Principal Beneficiary is living and under the age of 25:

2.2.1 The Trustees may apply the income of his Share for the maintenance, education or benefit of any of the Principal Beneficiaries who are under the age of 25.

2.2.2 Subject to that, the Trustees shall accumulate the income of the Share. That income shall be added to the Trust Fund.

2.3 Subject to that, the Trustees shall pay the income of the Share to the Principal Beneficiary during his life.

2.4 Subject to that, if the Principal Beneficiary dies during the Trust Period, the Trustees shall pay the income of the Share to the widow of the Principal Beneficiary during her life.

2.5 Subject to that, during the Trust Period the Trustees shall pay or apply the income of the Share to or for the benefit of any Beneficiaries, as the Trustees think fit.

3 Overriding Powers

Subject to the following clause the Trustees shall have the following powers ('Overriding Powers'):

3.1 *Power of appointment*

3.1.1 The Trustees may appoint that they shall hold the Trust Fund for the benefit of any Beneficiaries, on such terms as the Trustees think fit.

3.1.2 An appointment may create any provisions and in particular:

3.1.2.1 discretionary trusts;

3.1.2.2 dispositive or administrative powers;

exercisable by any Person.

3.1.3 An appointment shall be made by deed and may be revocable or irrevocable.

3.2 *Transfer of Trust Property to other settlement*

3.2.1 The Trustees may by deed declare that they hold any Trust Property on trust to transfer it to trustees of another settlement, wherever established, to hold on the terms of that settlement, freed and released from the terms of this Settlement.

3.2.2 The Trustees shall only exercise this power if:

3.2.2.1 every Person who may benefit is (or would if living be) a Beneficiary; or

3.2.2.2 with the consent in writing of

3.2.2.2.1 the Settlor, or

3.2.2.2.2 two Beneficiaries (after the death of the Settlor).

3.3 *Power of advancement*

The Trustees may pay or apply any Trust Property for the advancement or benefit of any Beneficiary.

3.4 The Overriding Powers shall be exercisable only:

3.4.1 during the Trust Period; and

3.4.2 at a time when there are at least two Trustees, or the Trustee is a company carrying on a business which consists of or includes the management of trusts.

4 Restrictions on Overriding Powers

The Overriding Powers may only be exercised over Trust Property in the following circumstances:

4.1 If a Beneficiary has or has had an Interest in Possession in the Property; or

4.2 If there is no Principal Beneficiary under the age of 25; or

4.3 If, on the exercise of the power, a Principal Beneficiary under the age of 25 becomes beneficially entitled to the Property or to an Interest in Possession in it; or

4.4 If, after the exercise of the power:

4.4.1 one or more Qualifying Beneficiaries will on or before attaining a specified age not exceeding 25 become beneficially entitled to the Property or to an Interest in Possession in it; and

4.4.2 no Interest in Possession subsists in the Property and the income from it is to be accumulated so far as not applied for the maintenance, education or benefit of such Qualifying Beneficiaries.

'Qualifying Beneficiaries' here means:

4.4.2.1 the Principal Beneficiaries and future [*grand*]children of the settlor;

4.4.2.2 the children and widow of a Principal Beneficiary who dies before the age of 25.

5 Default Clause

Subject to that, the Trust Fund shall be held on trust for [*Adam, Peter and Joanna in equal shares – or specify default trusts as appropriate*] absolutely.

6 Appointment of Trustees

The power of appointing trustees is exercisable by the Settlor during [*his*] life and by will.

7 Further Provisions

The provisions set out in the schedule below shall have effect.

[*For a shorter form, say instead of the above:*

'The standard provisions of the Society of Trust and Estate Practitioners (Northern Ireland Version, 1st Edition) shall apply.'

And omit the schedule.]

[*Check the NI Standard Provisions have been finalised before using this form. This was not done at the time of going to print; updates available on www.kessler.co.uk*]

8 Exclusion of Settlor and Spouse

Notwithstanding anything else in this Settlement, no power conferred by this settlement shall be exercisable, and no provision shall operate so as to allow Trust Property or its income to become payable to or applicable for the benefit of the Settlor or the spouse of the Settlor in any circumstances whatsoever.

9 Irrevocability

This Settlement is irrevocable.

10 Governing Law

The law of Northern Ireland governs the validity of this Settlement, and its construction, effects and administration. The Courts of Northern Ireland have exclusive jurisdiction in any proceedings involving rights or obligations under this Settlement.

In witness, [*etc*]

THE SCHEDULE: FURTHER PROVISIONS

[*Here set out the administrative provisions suitable to an A&M trust: see below. This is set out in full on the CD.*]

Accumulation and maintenance trust for the children of settlor including unborn children

This settlement is made [*date*] between:

1 [*Name of settlor*] of [*address*] ('the Settlor') of the one part and

2 2.1 [*Name of first trustee*] of [*address*] and

2.2 [*Name of second trustee*] of [*address*]

('the Original Trustees') of the other part.

Whereas:

1 The Settlor has [*three*] children, namely:

1.1 [*Adam Smith ('Adam')*] who was born on [*date*].

1.2 [*Peter Smith ('Peter')*] who was born on [*date*].

1.3 [*Joanna Smith ('Joanna')*] who was born on [*date*].

2 This Settlement shall be known as the [*Name-of-settlor Settlement 2004*].

Now this deed witnesses as follows:

1 Definitions

In this settlement:

1.1 **'The Trustees'** means the Original Trustees or the trustees of the settlement for the time being.

1.2 **'The Trust Fund'** means:

1.2.1 property transferred to the Trustees to hold on the terms of this Settlement; and

1.2.2 all property from time to time representing the above.

1.3 **'Trust Property'** means any property comprised in the Trust Fund.

1.4 **'The Trust Period'** means the period of 80 years beginning with the date of this Settlement. That is the perpetuity period applicable to this Settlement under the rule against perpetuities.

1.5 **'The Beneficiaries'** means:

1.5.1 The children and descendants of the Settlor.

1.5.2 The spouses, widows and widowers (whether or not remarried) of paragraph .1 of this sub-clause.

1.5.3 The [*widow*] (whether or not remarried) of the Settlor.

1.5.4 Any Person or class of Persons nominated to the Trustees by:

1.5.4.1 the Settlor or

1.5.4.2 two Beneficiaries (after the death of the Settlor)

and whose nomination is accepted in writing by the Trustees.

1.5.5 At any time during which there are no Beneficiaries within paragraph .1 of this sub-clause:

1.5.5.1 [*specify 'fall back' beneficiaries if desired, eg nieces and nephews and their families*];

1.5.5.2 [*any company, body or trust established for charitable purposes only*].

1.6 **'Interest in Possession'** has the same meaning as in the Inheritance Tax Act 1984.

1.7 **'Person'** includes a person anywhere in the world and includes a Trustee

1.8 **'The Principal Beneficiaries'** means [*Adam, Peter and Joanna*] and any other child of the Settlor born:

1.8.1 at a time when a Principal Beneficiary is under the age of 25, and

1.8.2 during the Trust Period.

2 Trust Income

Subject to the Overriding Powers below:

2.1 The Trust Fund shall be divided into equal shares ('the Shares') so that there shall be one Share for each of the Principal Beneficiaries.

2.2 While a Principal Beneficiary is living and under the age of 25:

2.2.1 The Trustees may apply the income of his Share for the maintenance, education or benefit of any of the Principal Beneficiaries who are under the age of 25.

2.2.2 Subject to that, the Trustees shall accumulate the income of the Share. That income shall be added to the Trust Fund.

2.3 The Trustees shall pay the income of the Share to the Principal Beneficiary during his life if he attains the age of 25.

2.4 Subject to that, if the Principal Beneficiary dies during the Trust Period, the Trustees shall pay the income of the Share to the widow of the Principal Beneficiary during her life.

2.5 Subject to that, during the Trust Period the Trustees shall pay or apply the income of the Share to or for the benefit of any Beneficiaries, as the Trustees think fit.

3 Overriding Powers

Subject to the following clause the Trustees shall have the following powers ('Overriding Powers'):

3.1 *Power of appointment*

3.1.1 The Trustees may appoint that they shall hold the Trust Fund for the benefit of any Beneficiaries, on such terms as the Trustees think fit.

3.1.2 An appointment may create any provisions and in particular:

3.1.2.1 discretionary trusts;

3.1.2.2 dispositive or administrative powers;

exercisable by any Person.

3.1.3 An appointment shall be made by deed and may be revocable or irrevocable.

3.2 *Transfer of Trust Property to other settlement*

3.2.1 The Trustees may by deed declare that they hold any Trust Property on trust to transfer it to trustees of another settlement, wherever established, to hold on the terms of that settlement, freed and released from the terms of this Settlement.

3.2.2 The Trustees shall only exercise this power if:

3.2.2.1 every Person who may benefit is (or would if living be) a Beneficiary; or

3.2.2.2 with the consent in writing of

3.2.2.2.1 the Settlor, or

3.2.2.2.2 two Beneficiaries (after the death of the Settlor).

3.3 *Power of advancement*

The Trustees may pay or apply any Trust Property for the advancement or benefit of any Beneficiary.

3.4 The Overriding Powers shall be exercisable only:

3.4.1 during the Trust Period; and

3.4.2 at a time when there are at least two Trustees, or the Trustee is a company carrying on a business which consists of or includes the management of trusts.

4 Restrictions on Overriding Powers

The Overriding Powers may only be exercised over Trust Property in the following circumstances:

4.1 If a Beneficiary has or has had an Interest in Possession in the Property; or

4.2 If there is no Principal Beneficiary under the age of 25; or

4.3 If, on the exercise of the power, a Principal Beneficiary under the age of 25 becomes beneficially entitled to the Property or to an Interest in Possession in it; or

4.4 If, after the exercise of the power:

4.4.1 one or more Qualifying Beneficiaries will on or before attaining a specified age not exceeding 25 become beneficially entitled to the Property or to an Interest in Possession in it; and

4.4.2 no Interest in Possession subsists in the Property and the income from it is to be accumulated so far as not applied for the maintenance, education or benefit of such Qualifying Beneficiaries.

'Qualifying Beneficiaries' here means:

4.4.2.1 the Principal Beneficiaries; and

4.4.2.2 the children and widow of a Principal Beneficiary who dies before the age of 25.

5 Default Clause

Subject to that, the Trust Fund shall be held on trust for [*Adam, Peter and Joanna in equal shares – or specify default trusts as appropriate*] absolutely.

6 Appointment of Trustees

The power of appointing trustees is exercisable by the Settlor during [*his*] life and by will.

7 Further Provisions

The provisions set out in the schedule below shall have effect.

[*For a shorter form, say instead of the above:*

'The standard provisions of the Society of Trust and Estate Practitioners (Northern Ireland Version, 1st Edition) shall apply..'

And omit the schedule.]

[*Check the NI Standard Provisions have been finalised before using this form. This was not done at the time of going to print; updates available on www.kessler.co.uk*]

8 Exclusion of Settlor and Spouse

Notwithstanding anything else in this Settlement, no power conferred by this Settlement shall be exercisable, and no provision shall operate so as to allow Trust Property or its income to become payable to or applicable for the benefit of the Settlor or the spouse of the Settlor in any circumstances whatsoever.

9 Irrevocability

This Settlement is irrevocable.

10 Governing Law

The law of Northern Ireland governs the validity of this Settlement, and its construction, effects and administration. The Courts of Northern Ireland have exclusive jurisdiction in any proceedings involving rights or obligations under this Settlement.

In witness, [*etc*]

THE SCHEDULE: FURTHER PROVISIONS

[*Here set out the administrative provisions suitable to an A&M trust: see below. This is set out in full on the CD.*]

Accumulation and maintenance trust for the grandchildren of settlor including unborn grandchildren

This is only a slight variation of the children's settlement set out above.

This settlement is made [*date*] between:

1 [*Name of settlor*] of [*address*] ('the Settlor') of the one part and

2 2.1 [*Name of first trustee*] of [*address*] and

2.2 [*Name of second trustee*] of [*address*]

('the Original Trustees') of the other part.

Whereas:

1 The Settlor has [*three*] grandchildren, namely:

1.1 [*Adam Smith ('Adam')*] who was born on [*date*].

1.2 [*Peter Smith ('Peter')*] who was born on [*date*].

1.3 [*Joanna Smith ('Joanna')*] who was born on [*date*].

2 This Settlement shall be known as the [*Name-of-settlor Settlement 2004*].

Now this deed witnesses as follows:

1 Definitions

In this settlement:

1.1 **'The Trustees'** means the Original Trustees or the trustees of the settlement for the time being.

1.2 **'The Trust Fund'** means:

1.2.1 property transferred to the Trustees to hold on the terms of this Settlement; and

1.2.2 all property from time to time representing the above.

1.3 **'Trust Property'** means any property comprised in the Trust Fund.
1.4 **'The Trust Period'** means the period of 80 years beginning with the date of this Settlement. That is the perpetuity period applicable to this Settlement under the rule against perpetuities.
1.5 **'The Beneficiaries'** means:
 1.5.1 The children and descendants of the Settlor.
 1.5.2 The spouses, widows and widowers (whether or not remarried) of paragraph .1 of this sub-clause.
 1.5.3 The [*widow*] (whether or not remarried) of the Settlor.
 1.5.4 Any Person or class of Persons nominated to the Trustees by:
  1.5.4.1 the Settlor or
  1.5.4.2 two Beneficiaries (after the death of the Settlor)
 and whose nomination is accepted in writing by the Trustees.
 1.5.5 At any time during which there are no Beneficiaries within paragraph .1 of this sub-clause:
  1.5.5.1 [*specify 'fall back' beneficiaries if desired, eg nieces and nephews and their families*];
  1.5.5.2 [*any company, body or trust established for charitable purposes only*].
1.6 **'The Grandchildren'** means [*Adam, Peter and Joanna*] and any other grandchild of the Settlor born:
 1.6.1 at a time when a Grandchild is under the age of 25; and
 1.6.2 during the Trust Period.
1.7 **'Interest in Possession'** has the same meaning as in the Inheritance Tax Act 1984.
1.8 **'Person'** includes a person anywhere in the world and includes a Trustee.

2 Trust Income

Subject to the Overriding Powers below:
2.1 The Trust Fund shall be divided into equal shares ('the Shares') so that there shall be one Share for each Grandchild.
2.2 So long as a Grandchild is living and under the age of 25:
 2.2.1 The Trustees may apply the income of his Share for the maintenance, education or benefit of any of the Grandchildren who are under the age of 25.
 2.2.2 Subject to that, the Trustees shall accumulate the income of the Share. That income shall be added to the Trust Fund.
2.3 The Trustees shall pay the income of the Share to the Grandchild during his life if he attains the age of 25.
2.4 Subject to that, if the Grandchild dies during the Trust Period, the Trustees shall pay the income of the Share to the widow of the Grandchild during her life.
2.5 Subject to that, during the Trust Period the Trustees shall pay or apply the income of the Share to or for the benefit of any Beneficiaries, as the Trustees think fit.

3 Overriding Powers

Subject to the following clause the Trustees shall have the following powers ('Overriding Powers'):

3.1 Power of appointment

3.1.1 The Trustees may appoint that they shall hold the Trust Fund for the benefit of any Beneficiaries, on such terms as the Trustees think fit.

3.1.2 An appointment may create any provisions and in particular:

3.1.2.1 discretionary trusts;

3.1.2.2 dispositive or administrative powers

exercisable by any Person.

3.1.3 An appointment shall be made by deed and may be revocable or irrevocable.

3.2 Transfer of Trust Property to other settlement

3.2.1 The Trustees may by deed declare that they hold any Trust Property on trust to transfer it to trustees of another settlement, wherever established, to hold on the terms of that settlement, freed and released from the terms of this Settlement.

3.2.2 The Trustees shall only exercise this power if:

3.2.2.1 every Person who may benefit is (or would if living be) a Beneficiary; or

3.2.2.2 with the consent in writing of

3.2.2.2.1 the Settlor, or

3.2.2.2.2 two Beneficiaries (after the death of the Settlor).

3.3 Power of advancement

The Trustees may pay or apply any Trust Property for the advancement or benefit of any Beneficiary.

3.4 The Overriding Powers shall be exercisable only:

3.4.1 during the Trust Period; and

3.4.2 at a time when there are at least two Trustees, or the Trustee is a company carrying on a business which consists of or includes the management of trusts.

4 Restrictions on Overriding Powers

The Overriding Powers may only be exercised over Trust Property in the following circumstances:

4.1 If a Beneficiary has or has had an interest in Possession in the Property; or

4.2 If there is no Grandchild under the age of 25; or

4.3 If, on the exercise of the power, a Grandchild under the age of 25 becomes beneficially entitled to the Property or to an Interest in Possession in it; or

4.4 If, after the exercise of the power:

4.4.1 one or more Qualifying Beneficiaries will on or before attaining a specified age not exceeding 25 become beneficially entitled to the Property or to an Interest in Possession in it; and

4.4.2 no Interest in Possession subsists in the Property and the income from it is to be accumulated so far as not applied for the maintenance, education or benefit of such Qualifying Beneficiaries.

'Qualifying Beneficiaries' here means:

4.4.2.1 the Grandchildren; and

4.4.2.2 the children and widow of a Grandchild who dies before the age of 25.

5 Default Clause

Subject to that, the Trust Fund shall be held on trust for [*Adam, Peter and Joanna in equal shares – or specify default trusts as appropriate*] absolutely.

6 Appointment of Trustees

The power of appointing trustees is exercisable by the Settlor during [*his*] life and by will.

7 Further Provisions

The provisions set out in the schedule below shall have effect.

[*For a shorter form, say instead of the above:*

'The standard provisions of the Society of Trust and Estate Practitioners (Northern Ireland Version, 1st Edition) shall apply.'

And omit the schedule.]

[*Check the NI Standard Provisions have been finalised before using this form. This was not done at the time of going to print; updates available on www.kessler.co.uk*]

8 Exclusion of Settlor and Spouse

Notwithstanding anything else in this Settlement, no power conferred by this Settlement shall be exercisable, and no provision shall operate so as to allow Trust Property or its income to become payable to or applicable for the benefit of the Settlor or the spouse of the Settlor in any circumstances whatsoever.

9 Irrevocability

This Settlement is irrevocable.

10 Governing Law

The law of Northern Ireland governs the validity of this Settlement, and its construction, effects and administration. The Courts of Northern Ireland have exclusive jurisdiction in any proceedings involving rights or obligations under this Settlement.

In witness, [*etc*]

THE SCHEDULE: FURTHER PROVISIONS

[*Here set out the administrative provisions suitable to an A&M trust: see below. This is set out in full on the CD.*]

Discretionary trust

This settlement is made [*date*] between:

1 [*Name of settlor*] of [*address*] ('the Settlor') of the one part and

2 2.1 [*Name of first trustee*] of [*address*] and

2.2 [*Name of second trustee*] of [*address*]

('the Original Trustees') of the other part.

Whereas:

1 The Settlor has [*two*] children:

1.1 [*Adam Smith*] ('[*Adam*]') who was born on [*date*] and

1.2 [*Mary Smith*] ('[*Mary*]') who was born on [*date*].

2 This Settlement shall be known as the [*Name-of-settlor Settlement 2004*].

Now this deed witnesses as follows:

1 Definitions

In this settlement:

1.1 **'The Trustees'** means the Original Trustees or the trustees of the settlement for the time being.

1.2 'The Trust Fund' means:

1.2.1 property transferred to the Trustees to hold on the terms of this Settlement; and

1.2.2 all property from time to time representing the above.

1.3 **'Trust Property'** means any property comprised in the Trust Fund.

1.4 **'The Trust Period'** means the period of 80 years beginning with the date of this Settlement. That is the perpetuity period applicable to this Settlement under the rule against perpetuities.

1.5 'The Beneficiaries' means:

1.5.1 The children and descendants of the Settlor.

1.5.2 The spouses, widows and widowers (whether or not remarried) of paragraph .1 of this sub-clause.

1.5.3 The [*widow*] (whether or not remarried) of the Settlor.

1.5.4 Any Person or class of Persons nominated to the Trustees by:

1.5.4.1 the Settlor or

1.5.4.2 two Beneficiaries (after the death of the Settlor)

and whose nomination is accepted in writing by the Trustees.

1.5.5 At any time during which there are no Beneficiaries within paragraph .1 of this sub-clause:

1.5.5.1 [*specify 'fall back' beneficiaries if desired, eg nieces and nephews and their families*].

1.5.5.2 [*any company, body or trust established for charitable purposes only*].

1.6 **'Person'** includes a person anywhere in the world and includes a Trustee.

2 Trust Income

Subject to the Overriding Powers below:

2.1 The Trustees may accumulate the whole or part of the income of the Trust Fund during the Trust Period. That income shall be added to the Trust Fund.

2.2 The Trustees shall pay or apply the remainder of the income to or for the benefit of any Beneficiaries, as the Trustees think fit, during the Trust Period.

3 Overriding Powers

The Trustees shall have the following powers ('Overriding Powers'):

3.1 *Power of appointment*

3.1.1 The Trustees may appoint that they shall hold the Trust Fund for the benefit of any Beneficiaries, on such terms as the Trustees think fit.

3.1.2 An appointment may create any provisions and in particular:

3.1.2.1 discretionary trusts;

3.1.2.2 dispositive or administrative powers;

exercisable by any Person.

3.1.3 An appointment shall be made by deed and may be revocable or irrevocable.

3.2 *Transfer of Trust Property to other settlement*

3.2.1 The Trustees may by deed declare that they hold any Trust Property on trust to transfer it to trustees of another settlement, wherever established, to hold on the terms of that settlement, freed and released from the terms of this Settlement.

3.2.2 The Trustees shall only exercise this power if:

3.2.2.1 every Person who may benefit is (or would if living be) a Beneficiary; or

3.2.2.2 with the consent in writing of

3.2.2.2.1 the Settlor, or

3.2.2.2.2 two Beneficiaries (after the death of the Settlor).

3.3 *Power of advancement*

The Trustees may pay or apply any Trust Property for the advancement or benefit of any Beneficiary.

3.4 The Overriding Powers shall be exercisable only:

3.4.1 during the Trust Period; and

3.4.2 at a time when there are at least two Trustees, or the Trustee is a company carrying on a business which consists of or includes the management of trusts.

4 Default Clause

Subject to that, the Trust Fund shall be held on trust for [*Adam and Mary in equal shares – or specify default trusts as appropriate*] absolutely.

5 Appointment of Trustees

The power of appointing trustees is exercisable by the Settlor during [*his*] life and by will.

6 Further Provisions

The provisions set out in the schedule below shall have effect.

[*For a shorter form, say instead of the above:*

'The standard provisions of the Society of Trust and Estate Practitioners (Northern Ireland Version, 1st Edition) shall apply.'

And omit the schedule.]

[*Check the NI Standard Provisions have been finalised before using this form. This was not done at the time of going to print; updates available on www.kessler.co.uk*]

7 Exclusion of Settlor and Spouse

Notwithstanding anything else in this Settlement, no power conferred by this settlement shall be exercisable, and no provision shall operate so as to allow Trust

Property or its income to become payable to or applicable for the benefit of the Settlor or the spouse of the Settlor in any circumstances whatsoever.

8 Irrevocability

This Settlement is irrevocable.

9 Governing Law

The law of Northern Ireland governs the validity of this Settlement, and its construction, effects and administration. The Courts of Northern Ireland have exclusive jurisdiction in any proceedings involving rights or obligations under this Settlement.

In witness, [*etc*]

THE SCHEDULE: FURTHER PROVISIONS

[*Here set out the administrative provisions suitable to a discretionary trust: see below. This is set out in full on the CD.*]

Charitable trust

Note: The English Charity Commission have indicated that in principle they regard an equivalent version of this precedent (governed by English law) as a charity.

This Charitable Trust is made [*date*] between

1 [*Name*] of [*address*] ('the Settlor') of the one part and

2 2.1 [*Name*] of [*address*] and

2.2 [*Name*] of [*address*]

('the Original Trustees') of the other part.

Now this deed witnesses as follows:

1 Definitions

In this Deed:

1.1 **'The Trustees'** means the Original Trustees or the trustees of this Charitable Trust for the time being.

1.2 **'The Trust Fund'** means:

1.2.1 Property transferred to the Trustees to hold on the terms of this Charitable Trust and

1.2.2 Property from time to time representing the above.

1.3 **'Charitable'** means exclusively charitable according to the law of Northern Ireland.

1.4 **'Charity'** means any company, body or trust established for charitable purposes only.

1.5 **'Trust Property'** means any property comprised in the Trust Fund.

2 Name of Charitable Trust

This charitable trust shall be known as the [*name of settlor*] Charitable Trust or by such name as the Trustees shall determine.

3 Trust Income

3.1 Subject to the Powers over Capital below, the Trustees shall pay or apply the income of the Trust Fund to such Charities or for such Charitable purposes as the Trustees think fit.

3.2 The Trustees may accumulate any part of the income of the Trust Fund.

4 Powers over Capital

The Trustees shall have the following powers:

4.1 Power of appointment:

4.1.1 The Trustees may appoint that they shall hold the Trust Fund on such Charitable trusts as the Trustees think fit.

4.1.2 An appointment may create any provisions and in particular:

4.1.2.1 discretionary trusts

4.1.2.2 dispositive or administrative powers

exercisable by any person, but at all times this Charitable Trust shall remain a Charity.

4.1.3 An appointment shall be made by deed and may be revocable or irrevocable.

4.2 Power of advancement

The Trustees may pay or transfer any Trust Property to any Charity and may apply any Trust Property for any Charitable purposes.

5 Further Provisions

The provisions set out in the schedule below shall have effect in furtherance of the Charitable purposes of this Charitable Trust but not otherwise.

6 Exclusion of settlor and non-charitable purposes

Notwithstanding anything else in this deed, no power conferred by this Charitable Trust shall be exercisable, and no provision shall operate so as to allow Trust Property or its income:

6.1 to become payable to or applicable for the benefit of the Settlor or the spouse of the Settlor

6.2 to be applied for any purpose that is not Charitable.

7 New Trustees

The power of appointing trustees is exercisable by the Settlor during his life or by will.

8 Governing Law

The law of Northern Ireland governs the validity of this Settlement, and its construction, effects and administration. The Courts of Northern Ireland have exclusive jurisdiction in any proceedings involving rights or obligations under this Settlement.

IN WITNESS etc.

THE SCHEDULE

[*Here set out administrative provisions appropriate to a charity; see para 24.8 (Administrative provisions for charities). This is set out in full on the CD.*]

Precedents for Will Trusts

Will I
Discretionary will trust

I, [*Name of testator*] of [*address*] declare this to be my last Will.

1

I revoke all my earlier testamentary dispositions.

2 Appointment of Executors

I appoint:
2.1 [*Name*] of [*address*] and
2.2 [*Name*] of [*address*]
to be my executors and Trustees.

3 Personal Chattels

I give my personal chattels (as defined in section 45 of the Administration of Estates Act (Northern Ireland) 1955) to my [*wife*] absolutely.

4

[*Other legacies, appointment of guardians, etc, follow here.*]

5 Residuary Estate

5.1 My Executors shall:

5.1.1 pay my debts, funeral and testamentary expenses and Inheritance Tax on all property which vests in them; and

5.1.2 hold the remainder ('my Residuary Estate') as set out below.

5.2 Debts, funeral and testamentary expenses, legacies and Inheritance Tax shall be payable out of the capital of my estate (subject to the Trustees' administrative powers relating to capital and income).

6 Definitions

In this will:

6.1 **'The Trustees'** means my executors or the trustees for the time being.

6.2 **'The Trust Fund'** means:

6.2.1 my Residuary Estate and

6.2.2 all property from time to time representing the above.

6.3 **'Trust Property'** means any property comprised in the Trust Fund.

6.4 **'The Trust Period'** means the period of 80 years beginning with the date of my death. That period is the perpetuity period applicable to this Settlement under the rule against perpetuities.

6.5 **'The Beneficiaries'** means:

6.5.1 My children and descendants.

6.5.2 The spouses, widows and widowers (whether or not remarried) of paragraph .1 of this sub-clause.

6.5.3 My [*wife*].

[*This paragraph should be omitted if the beneficiary is unmarried.*]

6.5.4 Any Person or class of Persons nominated to the Trustees by two Beneficiaries and whose nomination is accepted in writing by the Trustees.

6.5.5 [*Any favoured charity*].

6.5.6 At any time during which there are no Beneficiaries within paragraph .1 of this sub-clause:

6.5.6.1 [*specify 'fall back' beneficiaries if desired, eg nieces and nephews and their families*]

6.5.6.2 [*any company, body or trust established for charitable purposes only*].

6.6 **'Person'** includes a person anywhere in the world and includes a Trustee.

7 Trust Income

Subject to the Overriding Powers below and during the Trust Period:

7.1 The Trustees may accumulate the whole or part of the income of the Trust Fund. That income shall be added to the Trust Fund.

7.2 The Trustees shall pay or apply the remainder of the income to or for the benefit of any Beneficiaries, as the Trustees think fit.

8 Overriding Powers

The Trustees shall have the following powers ('Overriding Powers'):

8.1 *Power of appointment*

8.1.1 The Trustees may appoint that they shall hold the Trust Fund for the benefit of any Beneficiaries, on such terms as the Trustees think fit.

8.1.2 An appointment may create any provisions and in particular:

8.1.2.1 discretionary trusts;

8.1.2.2 dispositive or administrative powers;

exercisable by any Person.

8.1.3 An appointment shall be made by deed and may be revocable or irrevocable.

8.2 *Transfer of Trust Property to another settlement*

8.2.1 The Trustees may by deed declare that they hold any Trust Property on trust to transfer it to trustees of another settlement, wherever established, to hold on the terms of that settlement, freed and released from the terms of this Settlement.

8.2.2 The Trustees shall only exercise this power if:

8.2.2.1 every Person who may benefit is (or would if living be) a Beneficiary; or

8.2.2.2 with the consent in writing of two Beneficiaries.

8.3 *Power of advancement*

The Trustees may pay or apply any Trust Property for the advancement or benefit of any Beneficiary.

8.4 The Overriding Powers shall be exercisable only:

8.4.1 during the Trust Period; and

8.4.2 at a time when there are at least two Trustees, or the Trustee is a company carrying on a business which consists of or includes the management of trusts, or when the power to appoint additional Trustees cannot be exercised.

9 Default Clause

Subject to that, the Trust Fund shall be held on trust for [*my children Adam and Mary in equal shares – or specify default beneficiaries as appropriate*] absolutely.

10 Standard Provisions

The Standard Provisions of the Society of Trust and Estate Practitioners (Northern Ireland Version, 1st Edition) shall apply.

[*Check the NI Standard Provisions have been finalised before using this form. This was not done at the time of going to print; updates available on www.kessler.co.uk*]

[*Alternatively say: 'The provisions set out in the Schedule below shall have effect' and set out the provisions in full in the schedule. The CD with this book has the form.*]

11 Governing Law

This Will takes effect in accordance with the law of Northern Ireland. In particular, the law of Northern Ireland governs the validity of the settlement constituted by this Will, and its construction, effects and administration. The Courts of Northern Ireland have exclusive jurisdiction in any proceedings involving rights or obligations under that settlement.

Signed by [*name of testator*] to give effect to this Will,

in the presence of two witnesses present at the same time,

who have each signed this Will in the presence of the Testator.

[*Signature of Testator*]

Date

1st Witness

Address

2nd Witness

Address

Will 2
Life interest for surviving spouse

I, [*Name of testator*] of [*address*] declare this to be my last Will.

1

I revoke all my earlier testamentary dispositions.

2 Appointment of Executors

I appoint:
2.1 [*Name*] of [*address*] and
2.2 [*Name*] of [*address*]
to be my executors and Trustees.

3 Personal Chattels

I give my personal chattels (as defined in section 45 of the Administration of Estates Act (Northern Ireland) 1955) to my [*wife*] absolutely.

[*Other legacies, appointment of guardians, etc, follow here.*]

4 Residuary Estate
4.1 My Executors shall:

4.1.1 pay my debts, funeral and testamentary expenses and Inheritance Tax on all property which vests in them; and

4.1.2 hold the remainder ('my Residuary Estate') as set out below.

4.2 Debts, funeral and testamentary expenses, legacies and inheritance tax shall be payable out of the capital of my estate (subject to the Trustees' administrative powers relating to capital and income).

5 Definitions

In this Will:

5.1 **'The Trustees'** means my executors or the trustees for the time being.

5.2 **'The Trust Fund'** means:

5.2.1 my Residuary Estate; and

5.2.2 all property from time to time representing the above.

5.3 **'Trust Property'** means any property comprised in the Trust Fund.

5.4 **'The Trust Period'** means the period of 80 years beginning with the date of my death. That period is the perpetuity period applicable to this Settlement under the rule against perpetuities.

5.5 **'The Beneficiaries'** means:

5.5.1 My children and descendants.

5.5.2 The spouses, widows and widowers (whether or not remarried) of paragraph .1 of this sub-clause.

5.5.3 My [*wife*].

5.5.4 Any Person or class of Persons nominated to the Trustees by two Beneficiaries and whose nomination is accepted in writing by the Trustees.

5.5.5 [*Any favoured charity*].

5.5.6 At any time during which there are no Beneficiaries within paragraph .1 of this sub-clause:

5.5.6.1 [*specify 'fall back' beneficiaries if desired, eg nieces and nephews and their families*]

5.5.6.2 [*any company, body or trust established for charitable purposes only*].

5.6 **'Person'** includes a person anywhere in the world and includes a Trustee.

6 Trust Income

Subject to the Overriding Powers below:

6.1 The Trustees shall pay the income of the Trust Fund to my [*wife*] during [*her*] life.

6.2 Subject to that, the Trustees may accumulate the whole or part of the income of the Trust Fund during the Trust Period. That income shall be added to the Trust Fund.

6.3 Subject to that, during the Trust Period, the Trustees shall pay or apply the income of the Trust Fund to or for the benefit of any Beneficiaries as the Trustees think fit.

7 Overriding Powers

The Trustees shall have the following powers ('Overriding Powers'):

7.1 *Power of appointment*

7.1.1 The Trustees may appoint that they shall hold the Trust Fund for the benefit of any Beneficiaries, on such terms as the Trustees think fit.

7.1.2 An appointment may create any provisions and in particular:

7.1.2.1 discretionary trusts;

7.1.2.2 dispositive or administrative powers;

exercisable by any Person.

7.1.3 An appointment shall be made by deed and may be revocable or irrevocable.

7.2 *Transfer of Trust Property to other settlement*

7.2.1 The Trustees may by deed declare that they hold any Trust Property on trust to transfer it to trustees of another settlement, wherever established, to hold on the terms of that settlement, freed and released from the terms of this Settlement.

7.2.2 The Trustees shall only exercise this power if:

7.2.2.1 every Person who may benefit is (or would if living be) a Beneficiary; or

7.2.2.2 with the consent in writing of two Beneficiaries.

7.3 *Power of advancement*

The Trustees may pay or apply any Trust Property for the advancement or benefit of any Beneficiary.

7.4 The Overriding Powers shall be exercisable only:

7.4.1 during the Trust Period; and

7.4.2 at a time when there are at least two Trustees, or the Trustee is a company carrying on a business which consists of or includes the management of trusts, or when the power to appoint additional Trustees cannot be exercised.

8 Default Clause

Subject to that, the Trust Fund shall be held on trust for [*my children Adam and Mary in equal shares – or specify default beneficiaries as appropriate*] absolutely.

9 Standard Provisions

The Standard Provisions of the Society of Trust and Estate Practitioners (Northern Ireland Version, 1st Edition) shall apply.

[*Check the NI Standard Provisions have been finalised before using this form. This was not done at the time of going to print; updates available on www.kessler.co.uk*]

[*Alternatively say: 'The provisions set out in the Schedule below shall have effect' and set out the provisions in full in the schedule. The CD with this book has the form.*]

Signed by [*name of testator*] to give effect to this Will,

in the presence of two witnesses present at the same time,

who have each signed this Will in the presence of the Testator.

10 Governing Law

This Will takes effect in accordance with the law of Northern Ireland. In particular, the law of Northern Ireland governs the validity of the settlement constituted by this Will and its construction, effects and administration. The Courts of Northern Ireland have exclusive jurisdiction in any proceedings involving rights or obligations under that settlement.

[*Signature of Testator*]

Date

1st Witness

Address

2nd Witness

Address

Will 3
Life interest for surviving spouse with absolute gift of nil rate sum

I, [*Name of testator*] of [*address*] declare this to be my last Will.

1

I revoke all my earlier testamentary dispositions.

2 Appointment of Executors

I appoint:
2.1 [*Name*] of [*address*] and
2.2 [*Name*] of [*address*]
to be my executors and Trustees.

3 Personal Chattels

I give my personal chattels (as defined in section 45 of the Administration of Estates Act (Northern Ireland) 1955) to my [*wife*] absolutely.

4 Gift of Nil Rate Sum

4.1 I give the Nil Rate Sum to [*my children in equal shares*] absolutely.

4.2 **'The Nil Rate Sum'** here means the maximum amount of cash which I can give on the terms of this clause without incurring any liability to Inheritance Tax on my death, but subject to the following clauses.

4.2.1 The Nil Rate Sum shall be nil if:

4.2.1.1 Inheritance Tax has been abolished at the time of my death; or

4.2.1.2 I am not married at the time of my death.

4.2.2 Any other legacy given by my will or any codicil shall be paid in priority to the Nil Rate Sum.

4.3 The Nil Rate Sum shall not exceed £500,000.

[*Since this is a simple absolute gift of the nil rate sum, this clause does not contain a £5,000 de minimis provision (intended to prevent a trust of a very small trust fund).*]

[*Other legacies, appointment of guardians, etc, follow here.*]

5 Residuary Estate

5.1 My Executors shall:

5.1.1 pay my debts, funeral and testamentary expenses and Inheritance Tax on all property which vests in them; and

5.1.2 hold the remainder ('my Residuary Estate') as set out below.

5.2 Debts, funeral and testamentary expenses, legacies and inheritance tax shall be payable out of the capital of my estate (subject to the Trustees= administrative powers relating to capital and income).

6 Definitions

In this Will:

6.1 **'The Trust Fund'** means:

6.1.1 my Residuary Estate; and

6.1.2 all property from time to time representing the above.

6.2 **'Trust Property'** means any part of the Trust Fund.

6.3 **'The Trustees'** means my executors or the trustees for the time being.

6.4 **'The Trust Period'** means the period of 80 years beginning with the date of my death. That period is the perpetuity period applicable to this Settlement under the rule against perpetuities.

6.5 **'The Beneficiaries'** means:

6.5.1 My children and descendants.

6.5.2 The spouses, widows and widowers (whether or not remarried) of paragraph .1 of this sub-clause.

6.5.3 My [*wife*].

6.5.4 Any Person or class of Persons nominated to the Trustees by two Beneficiaries and whose nomination is accepted in writing by the Trustees.

6.5.5 [*Any favoured charity*].

6.5.6 At any time during which there are no Beneficiaries within paragraph .1 of this sub-clause:

6.5.6.1 [*specify 'fall back' beneficiaries if desired, eg nieces and nephews and their families*]

6.5.6.2 [*any company, body or trust established for charitable purposes only*].

6.6 **'Person'** includes a person anywhere in the world and includes a Trustee.

7 Residuary Estate

Subject to the Overriding Powers below:

7.1 The Trustees shall pay the income of the Trust Fund to my [*wife*] during [*her*] life.

7.2 Subject to that, the Trustees may accumulate the whole or any part of the income of the Trust Fund during the Trust Period. That income shall be added to the Trust Fund.

7.3 Subject to that, during the Trust Period, the Trustees shall pay or apply the income of the Trust Fund to or for the benefit of any of the Beneficiaries as the Trustees think fit.

8 Overriding Powers

The Trustees shall have the following powers ('Overriding Powers'):

8.1 *Power of appointment*

8.1.1 The Trustees may appoint that they shall hold any Trust Property for the benefit of any Beneficiaries, on such terms as the Trustees think fit.

8.1.2 An appointment may create any provisions and in particular:

8.1.2.1 discretionary trusts;

8.1.2.2 dispositive or administrative powers;

exercisable by any Person.

8.1.3 An appointment shall be made by deed and may be revocable or irrevocable.

8.2 *Transfer of Trust Property to other settlement*

8.2.1 The Trustees may by deed declare that they hold any Trust Property on trust to transfer it to trustees of another settlement, wherever established, to hold on the terms of that settlement, freed and released from the terms of this Settlement.

8.2.2 The Trustees shall only exercise this power if:

8.2.2.1 every Person who may benefit is (or would if living be) a Beneficiary; or

8.2.2.2 with the consent in writing of two Beneficiaries.

8.3 *Power of advancement*

The Trustees may pay or apply any Trust Property for the advancement or benefit of any Beneficiary.

8.4 The Overriding Powers shall be exercisable only:

8.4.1 during the Trust Period; and

8.4.2 at a time when there are at least two Trustees, or the Trustee is a company carrying on a business which consists of or includes the management of trusts, or when the power to appoint additional Trustees cannot be exercised.

9 Default Clause

Subject to that, the Trust Fund shall be held on trust for [*my son Adam – or define the default beneficiary as appropriate*] absolutely.

10 Standard Provisions

The Standard Provisions of the Society of Trust and Estate Practitioners (Northern Ireland Version, 1st Edition) shall apply.

[*Check the NI Standard Provisions have been finalised before using this form. This was not done at the time of going to print; updates available on www.kessler.co.uk*]

[*Alternatively say: 'The provisions set out in the Schedule below shall have effect' and set out the provisions in full in the schedule. The CD with this book has the form.*]

11 Governing Law

This Will takes effect in accordance with the law of Northern Ireland. In particular, the law of Northern Ireland governs the validity of the settlement constituted by this Will, and its construction, effects and administration. The Courts of Northern Ireland have exclusive jurisdiction in any proceedings involving rights or obligations under that settlement.

Signed by [*name of testator*] to give effect to this Will,

in the presence of two witnesses present at the same time,

who have each signed this Will in the presence of the Testator.

[*Signature of Testator*]

Date

1st Witness

Address

2nd Witness

Address

Will 4
Life interest for surviving spouse with nil rate band discretionary trust

I, [*Name of testator*] of [*address*] declare this to be my last Will.

1

I revoke all my earlier testamentary dispositions.

2 Appointment of Executors

I appoint:
2.1 [*Name*] of [*address*] and
2.2 [*Name*] of [*address*]
to be my executors and Trustees.

3 Personal Chattels

I give my personal chattels (as defined in section 45 of the Administration of Estates Act (Northern Ireland) 1955) to my [*wife*] absolutely.

[*Other legacies, appointment of guardians, etc, follow here.*]

4 Residuary Estate

4.1 My Executors shall:

4.1.1 pay my debts, funeral and testamentary expenses and Inheritance Tax on all property which vests in them; and

4.1.2 hold the remainder as set out below.

4.2 Debts, funeral and testamentary expenses, legacies and inheritance tax shall be payable out of the capital of my estate (subject to the Trustees' administrative powers relating to capital and income).

5 Definitions

In this Will:

5.1 **'The Nil Rate Sum'** means the maximum amount of cash which I can give on the terms of the Nil Rate Fund without incurring any liability to Inheritance Tax on my death, but subject to the following clauses.

5.1.1 The Nil Rate Sum shall be nil if:

5.1.1.1 Inheritance Tax has been abolished at the time of my death; or

5.1.1.2 I am not married at the time of my death; or

5.1.1.3 The amount of the Nil Rate Sum would otherwise be less than £5,000.

5.1.2 Any other legacy given by my will or any codicil shall be paid in priority to the Nil Rate Sum.

5.2 **'The Nil Rate Fund'** means:

5.2.1 the Nil Rate Sum; and

5.2.2 all property from time to time representing the above.

5.3 **'The Trust Fund'** means:

5.3.1 the remainder of my estate after deducting the Nil Rate Fund and any other legacies; and

5.3.2 all property from time to time representing the above.

5.4 **'Trust Property'** includes any part of the Trust Fund and the Nil Rate Fund.

5.5 **'The Trustees'** means my executors or the trustees for the time being.

5.6 **'The Trust Period'** means the period of 80 years beginning with the date of my death. That period is the perpetuity period applicable to this Settlement under the rule against perpetuities.

5.7 **'The Beneficiaries'** means:

5.7.1 My children and descendants.

5.7.2 The spouses, widows and widowers (whether or not remarried) of paragraph .1 of this sub-clause.

5.7.3 My [*wife*].

5.7.4 Any Person or class of Persons nominated to the Trustees by two Beneficiaries and whose nomination is accepted in writing by the Trustees.

5.7.5 [*Any favoured charity*].

5.7.6 At any time during which there are no Beneficiaries within paragraph .1 of this sub-clause:

5.7.6.1 [*specify 'fall back' beneficiaries if desired, eg nieces and nephews and their families*]

5.7.6.2 [*any company, body or trust established for charitable purposes only*].

5.8 **'Person'** includes a person anywhere in the world and includes a Trustee.

6 Nil Rate Fund

During the lifetime of my [*wife*] and subject to the Overriding Powers below:

6.1 The Trustees may accumulate the whole or any part of the income of the Nil Rate Fund during the Trust Period. That income shall be added to the Nil Rate Fund.

6.2 Subject to that, during the Trust Period, the Trustees shall pay or apply the income of the Nil Rate Fund to or for the benefit of any of the Beneficiaries as the Trustees think fit.

6.3 Subject to that, the Trustees shall add the Nil Rate Fund to the Trust Fund.

7 The Trust Fund

Subject to the overriding powers below:

7.1 The Trustees shall pay the income of the Trust Fund to my [*wife*] during [*her*] life.

7.2 Subject to that, the Trustees may accumulate the whole or any part of the income of the Trust Fund during the Trust Period. That income shall be added to the Trust Fund.

7.3 Subject to that, during the Trust Period, the Trustees shall pay or apply the income of the Trust Fund to or for the benefit of any of the Beneficiaries as the Trustees think fit.

8 Overriding Powers

The Trustees shall have the following powers ('Overriding Powers'):

8.1 *Power of appointment*

8.1.1 The Trustees may appoint that they shall hold any Trust Property for the benefit of any Beneficiaries, on such terms as the Trustees think fit.

8.1.2 An appointment may create any provisions and in particular:

8.1.2.1 discretionary trusts;

8.1.2.2 dispositive or administrative powers;

exercisable by any Person.

8.1.3 An appointment shall be made by deed and may be revocable or irrevocable.

8.2 *Transfer of Trust Property to other settlement*

8.2.1 The Trustees may by deed declare that they hold any Trust Property on trust to transfer it to trustees of another settlement, wherever established, to hold on the terms of that settlement, freed and released from the terms of this Settlement.

8.2.2 The Trustees shall only exercise this power if:

8.2.2.1 every Person who may benefit is (or would if living be) a Beneficiary; or

8.2.2.2 with the consent in writing of two Beneficiaries.

8.3 *Power of advancement*

The Trustees may pay or apply any Trust Property for the advancement or benefit of any Beneficiary.

8.4 The Overriding Powers shall be exercisable only:

8.4.1 during the Trust Period; and

8.4.2 at a time when there are at least two Trustees, or the Trustee is a company carrying on a business which consists of or includes the management of trusts, or when the power to appoint additional Trustees cannot be exercised.

9 Default Clause

Subject to that, the Trust Fund shall be held on trust for [*my son Adam – or define the default beneficiary as appropriate*] absolutely.

10 Standard Provisions

The Standard Provisions of the Society of Trust and Estate Practitioners (Northern Ireland Version, 1st Edition) shall apply.

[*Check the NI Standard Provisions have been finalised before using this form. This was not done at the time of going to print; updates available on www.kessler.co.uk*]

[*Alternatively say: 'The provisions set out in the Schedule below shall have effect' and set out the provisions in full in the schedule. The CD with this book has the form.*]

11 Additional Provisions relating to Nil Rate Fund

Where during the lifetime of my [*wife*] there are separate sets of Trustees for the Nil Rate Fund and the Trust Fund:

11.1 The Trustees of the Nil Rate Fund may allow the payment of the Nil Rate Sum to be postponed for such period as they think fit and in such case no Trustee shall be personally liable for payment of the Nil Rate Sum except to the extent that he can recover such liability from the Trust Fund.

11.2 If payment is postponed beyond one year from my death, the Nil Rate Sum Legacy shall carry interest at the rate applicable to legacies (or shall be on such other terms as the trustees of the Trust Fund and the trustees of the Nil Rate Fund shall agree).

11.3 The Trustees of the Nil Rate Fund may waive payment of interest which has accrued and is payable before such interest is paid.

11.4 The Trustees of the Nil Rate Fund may waive the payment of the whole or any part of the Nil Rate Sum.

11.5 The provisions of this clause shall not be exercisable so as to prevent a Person from being entitled to an interest in possession in the Trust Fund

The provisions of this clause shall not be exercisable so as to give any Person an interest in possession in the Nil Rate Fund during the lifetime of my [*wife*].

12 Governing Law

This Will takes effect in accordance with the law of Northern Ireland. In particular, the law of Northern Ireland governs the validity of the settlement constituted by this Will, and its construction, effects and administration. The Courts of Northern Ireland have exclusive jurisdiction in any proceedings involving rights or obligations under that settlement.

Signed by [*name of testator*] to give effect to this Will,

in the presence of two witnesses present at the same time,

who have each signed this Will in the presence of the Testator.

[*Signature of Testator*]

Date

1st Witness

Address

2nd Witness

Address

Will 5
Nil rate band discretionary trust; residue to surviving spouse absolutely

Note: This precedent is intended for smaller estates. Where, after deduction of the nil rate band, there remains a substantial residue, it would generally be better to provide that the residue should be held on trust for the widow for life; not for the widow absolutely.

I, [*Name of testator*] of [*address*] declare this to be my last Will.

1

I revoke all my earlier testamentary dispositions.

2 Appointment of Executors

I appoint:
2.1 [*Name*] of [*address*] and
2.2 [*Name*] of [*address*]
to be my executors and Trustees.

[*Other legacies, appointment of guardians, etc, follow here.*]

3 Definitions

In this Will:

3.1

3.1.1 **'The Nil Rate Sum'** means the maximum amount of cash which I can give on the terms of the Nil Rate Fund without incurring any liability to Inheritance Tax on my death, but subject to the following clauses.

3.1.2 The Nil Rate Sum shall be nil if:

3.1.2.1 Inheritance Tax has been abolished at the time of my death; or

3.1.2.2 I am not married at the time of my death; or

3.1.2.3 The amount of the Nil Rate Sum would otherwise be less than £5,000.

3.1.3 Any other legacy given by my will or any codicil shall be paid in priority to the Nil Rate Sum.

3.2 **'The Nil Rate Fund'** means:

3.2.1 the Nil Rate Sum; and

3.2.2 all property from time to time representing the above.

3.3 **'Trust Property'** means any part of the Nil Rate Fund.

3.4 **'The Trustees'** means my executors or the trustees for the time being.

3.5 **'The Trust Period'** means the period of 80 years beginning with the date of my death. That is the perpetuity period applicable to this Will Trust under the rule against perpetuities.

3.6 **'The Beneficiaries'** means:

3.6.1 My children and descendants.

3.6.2 The spouses, widows and widowers (whether or not remarried) of paragraph .1 of this sub-clause.

3.6.3 My [*wife*].

3.6.4 Any Person or class of Persons nominated to the Trustees by two Beneficiaries and whose nomination is accepted in writing by the Trustees.

3.6.5 [*Any favoured charity*].

3.6.6 At any time during which there are no Beneficiaries within paragraph .1 of this sub-clause:

3.6.6.1 [*specify 'fall back' beneficiaries if desired, eg nieces and nephews and their families*]

3.6.6.2 [*any company, body or trust established for charitable purposes only*].

3.7 **'Person'** includes a person anywhere in the world and includes a Trustee.

4 Nil Rate Fund

Subject to the Overriding Powers below:

4.1 The Trustees may accumulate the whole or any part of the income of the Nil Rate Fund during the Trust Period. That income shall be added to the Nil Rate Fund.

4.2 Subject to that, during the Trust Period, the Trustees shall pay or apply the income of the Nil Rate Fund to or for the benefit of any of the Beneficiaries as the Trustees think fit.

4.3 Subject to that, the Nil Rate Fund shall be held on trust for [*my son Adam – or define the default beneficiary as appropriate*] absolutely.

5 Overriding Powers

The Trustees shall have the following powers ('Overriding Powers'):

5.1 Power of appointment

5.1.1 The Trustees may appoint that they shall hold any Trust Property for the benefit of any Beneficiaries, on such terms as the Trustees think fit.

5.1.2 An appointment may create any provisions and in particular:

5.1.2.1 discretionary trusts;

5.1.2.2 dispositive or administrative powers;

exercisable by any Person.

5.1.3 An appointment shall be made by deed and may be revocable or irrevocable.

5.2 Transfer of Trust Property to other settlement

5.2.1 The Trustees may by deed declare that they hold any Trust Property on trust to transfer it to trustees of another settlement, wherever established, to hold on the terms of that settlement, freed and released from the terms of this Settlement.

5.2.2 The Trustees shall only exercise this power if:

5.2.2.1 every Person who may benefit is (or would if living be) a Beneficiary; or

5.2.2.2 with the consent in writing of two Beneficiaries.

5.3 Power of advancement

The Trustees may pay or apply any Trust Property for the advancement or benefit of any Beneficiary.

5.4 The Overriding Powers shall be exercisable only

5.4.1 during the Trust Period; and

5.4.2 at a time when there are at least two Trustees, or the Trustee is a company carrying on a business which consists of or includes the management of trusts, or when the power to appoint additional Trustees cannot be exercised.

6 Residuary Estate

My Executors shall:

6.1 pay my debts, funeral and testamentary expenses and Inheritance Tax on all property which vests in them; and

6.2 hold the remainder on trust for my wife absolutely. [*It may be desired to provide for a simple gift over if the wife does not survive. Also see the next form.*]

6.3 Debts, funeral and testamentary expenses, legacies and inheritance tax shall be payable out of the capital of my estate (subject to the Trustees= administrative powers relating to capital and income).

7 Standard Provisions

The standard provisions of the Society of Trust and Estate Practitioners (Northern Ireland Version, 1st Edition).

[*Check the NI Standard Provisions have been finalised before using this form. This was not done at the time of going to print; updates available on www.kessler.co.uk*]

[*Alternatively say: 'The provisions set out in the Schedule below shall have effect' and set out the provisions in full in the schedule. The CD with this book has the form.*]

8 Additional Provisions relating to Nil Rate Fund

8.1 In this clause **'The Nil Rate Trustees'** means the trustees of the Nil Rate Fund.

Surviving spouse may undertake to pay nil rate sum personally

8.2

8.2.1 My executors may require the Nil Rate Trustees to accept a written undertaking from my spouse as a personal obligation binding on my spouse.

8.2.2 That undertaking shall be to pay the Nil Rate Sum or, if less, the value of my residuary estate at the time of the undertaking on demand to the Nil Rate Trustees. The undertaking may include any other terms and in particular:

8.2.2.1 fixed or floating security;

8.2.2.2 interest;

8.2.2.3 index linking the sum payable.

8.2.3 That undertaking will be in substitution for payment of the Nil Rate Sum by the executors to the Nil Rate Trustees. My executors shall be under no further liability in relation to the Nil Rate Sum.

Executors may charge residuary estate instead of paying Nil Rate Sum directly

8.3

8.3.1 My executors may charge all or part of my Residuary Estate with the payment of the Nil Rate Sum on demand of the Nil Rate Trustees.

8.3.2 That charge may be a fixed or floating charge. It may include any other terms and in particular:

8.3.2.1 interest;

8.3.2.2 index linking the sum payable.

8.3.3 To the extent of the value at my death of the property charged:

8.3.3.1 the charge will be in substitution for payment of the Nil Rate Sum by the executors to the Nil Rate Trustees; and

8.3.3.2 my executors shall be under no further liability in relation to the Nil Rate Sum.

8.3.4 My executors may transfer the property charged to my spouse who shall not thereby become personally liable for the sum charged.

Nil Rate Sum may be left outstanding

8.4 The Nil Rate Trustees may refrain from calling in the Nil Rate Sum (or exercising any rights in relation to the Nil Rate Sum) for as long as they think fit. They may waive the payment of any income or capital due in respect of the Nil Rate Sum. They shall not be liable if my spouse becomes unable to make any payment or if a security becomes inadequate or for any other loss which may occur through exercising any power given by this clause.

8.5 The powers given by this clause are exercisable even though my executors and the Nil Rate Trustees are the same persons.

8.6 My spouse shall not be the sole Nil Rate Trustee.

8.7 The provisions of this clause shall not be exercisable so as to give any Person an interest in possession in the Nil Rate Fund.

9 Governing Law

This Will takes effect in accordance with the law of Northern Ireland. In particular, the law of Northern Ireland governs the validity of the settlement constituted by this Will, and its construction, effects and administration. The Courts of Northern Ireland have exclusive jurisdiction in any proceedings involving rights or obligations under that settlement.

Signed by [*name of testator*] to give effect to this Will,

in the presence of two witnesses present at the same time,

who have each signed this Will in the presence of the Testator.

[*Signature of Testator*]

Date

1st Witness

Address

2nd Witness

Address

Will 6
Nil rate band discretionary trust
Residue to: (1) surviving spouse absolutely (2) discretionary trust (if no surviving spouse)

I, [*Name of testator*] of [*address*] declare this to be my last Will.

1

I revoke all my earlier testamentary dispositions.

2 Appointment of Executors

I appoint:
2.1 [*Name*] of [*address*] and
2.2 [*Name*] of [*address*]
to be my executors and Trustees.

[*Other legacies, appointment of guardians, etc, follow here.*]

3 Residuary Estate

3.1 My Executors shall:

3.1.1 pay my debts, funeral and testamentary expenses and Inheritance Tax on all property which vests in them; and

3.1.2 hold the remainder ('my Residuary Estate') as set out below.

3.2 Debts, funeral and testamentary expenses, legacies and inheritance tax shall be payable out of the capital of my estate (subject to the Trustees' administrative powers relating to capital and income).

4

My Executors shall hold my Residuary Estate on trust for my [*wife*] if [*she*] survives me absolutely.

5 Definitions

In this Will:

5.1 **'The Nil Rate Sum'** means the maximum amount of cash which I can give on the terms of the Trust Fund without incurring any liability to Inheritance Tax on my death, but subject to the following clauses.

5.1.1 The Nil Rate Sum shall be nil if:

5.1.1.1 Inheritance Tax has been abolished at the time of my death; or

5.1.1.2 I am not married at the time of my death; or

5.1.1.3 The amount of the Nil Rate Sum would otherwise be less than £5,000.

5.1.2 Any other legacy given by my will or any codicil shall be paid in priority to the Nil Rate Sum.

5.2 **'The Trust Fund'** means:

5.2.1 if my [*wife*] survives me, the Nil Rate Sum only; and

5.2.2 if my [*wife*] does not survive me, my Residuary Estate; and

5.2.3 all property from time to time representing the above.

5.3 **'Trust Property'** means any part of the Trust Fund.

5.4 **'The Trustees'** means my executors or the trustees for the time being.

5.5 **'The Trust Period'** means the period of 80 years beginning with the date of my death. That is the perpetuity period applicable to this Will Trust under the rule against perpetuities.

5.6 **'The Beneficiaries'** means:

5.6.1 My children and descendants.

5.6.2 The spouses, widows and widowers (whether or not remarried) of paragraph .1 of this sub-clause.

5.6.3 My [*wife*].

5.6.4 Any Person or class of Persons nominated to the Trustees by two Beneficiaries and whose nomination is accepted in writing by the Trustees.

5.6.5 [*Any favoured charity*].

5.6.6 At any time during which there are no Beneficiaries within paragraph .1 of this sub-clause:

5.6.6.1 [*specify 'fall back' beneficiaries if desired, eg nieces and nephews and their families*]

5.6.6.2 [*any company, body or trust established for charitable purposes only*].

5.7 **'Person'** includes a person anywhere in the world and includes a Trustee.

6 Trust Fund

Subject to the Overriding Powers below:

6.1 The Trustees may accumulate the whole or any part of the income of the Trust Fund during the Trust Period. That income shall be added to the Trust Fund.

6.2 Subject to that, during the Trust Period, the Trustees shall pay or apply the income of the Trust Fund to or for the benefit of any of the Beneficiaries as the Trustees think fit.

6.3 Subject to that, the Trust Fund shall be held on trust for [*my son Adam – or specify default beneficiary as appropriate*] absolutely.

7 Overriding Powers

The Trustees shall have the following powers ('Overriding Powers'):

7.1 *Power of appointment*

7.1.1 The Trustees may appoint that they shall hold any Trust Property for the benefit of any Beneficiaries, on such terms as the Trustees think fit.

7.1.2 An appointment may create any provisions and in particular:

7.1.2.1 discretionary trusts;

7.1.2.2 dispositive or administrative powers;

exercisable by any Person.

7.1.3 An appointment shall be made by deed and may be revocable or irrevocable.

7.2 *Transfer of Trust Property to other settlement*

7.2.1 The Trustees may by deed declare that they hold any Trust Property on trust to transfer it to trustees of another settlement, wherever established, to hold on the terms of that settlement, freed and released from the terms of this Settlement.

7.2.2 The Trustees shall only exercise this power if:

7.2.2.1 every Person who may benefit is (or would if living be) a Beneficiary; or

7.2.2.2 with the consent in writing of two Beneficiaries.

7.3 *Power of advancement*

The Trustees may pay or apply any Trust Property for the advancement or benefit of any Beneficiary.

7.4 The Overriding Powers shall be exercisable only:

7.4.1 during the Trust Period; and

7.4.2 at a time when there are at least two Trustees, or the Trustee is a company carrying on a business which consists of or includes the management of trusts, or when the power to appoint additional Trustees cannot be exercised.

8 Standard Provisions

The standard provisions of the Society of Trust and Estate Practitioners (Northern Ireland Version, 1st Edition) shall apply.

[*Check that the NI Standard Provisions have been finalised before using this form. This was not done at the time of going to print; updates available on www.kessler.co.uk*].

[*Alternatively say: 'The provisions set out in the Schedule below shall have effect' and set out the provisions in full in the schedule. The CD with this book has the form.*]

9 Additional Provisions relating to Nil Rate Sum

9.1 In this clause '**The Nil Rate Trustees**' means the trustees of the Nil Rate Sum.

Surviving spouse may undertake to pay nil rate sum personally

9.2

- 9.2.1 My executors may require the Nil Rate Trustees to accept in satisfaction of the Nil Rate Sum a promise by my [wife] to pay money on demand to the Nil Rate Trustees.
- 9.2.2 The promise may include such other terms as my executors think fit including:
  - 9.2.2.1 fixed or floating security;
  - 9.2.2.2 interest;
  - 9.2.2.3 index linking the sum payable.
- 9.2.3 My executors shall be under no further liability to see that the Nil Rate Trustees receive the Nil Rate Sum.

Executors may charge residuary estate instead of paying Nil Rate Sum directly

9.3

- 9.3.1 My executors may charge all or any part of my Residuary Estate with the payment of all or any part of the Nil Rate Sum on demand of the Nil Rate Trustees.
- 9.3.2 Such charge may be a fixed charge or a floating charge. It may include any terms my personal representatives think fit, including:
  - 9.3.2.1 fixed or floating security;
  - 9.3.2.2 interest;
  - 9.3.2.3 index linking the sum payable.
- 9.3.3 To the extent of the value at my death of the property charged, my executors shall be under no further liability to see that the Nil Rate Trustees receive the sum secured.
- 9.3.4 When my executors give an assent of the property charged, my [wife] shall not thereby become personally liable for the sum charged.

Nil Rate Sum may be left outstanding

9.4 The Nil Rate Trustees may refrain from calling in the Nil Rate Sum (or exercising any rights in relation to the Nil Rate Sum) for as long as they think fit. They may waive the payment of any income or capital due in respect of the Nil Rate Sum. They shall not be liable if my [*wife*] becomes unable to make any payment or if a security becomes inadequate or for any other loss which may occur through exercising any power given by this clause.

9.5 The powers given by this clause are exercisable even though my executors and the Nil Rate Trustees are the same persons.

9.6 My [*wife*] shall not be the sole Nil Rate Trustee.

9.7 The provisions of this clause shall not be exercisable so as to give any Person an interest in possession in the Nil Rate Sum.

10 Governing Law

This Will takes effect in accordance with the law of Northern Ireland. In particular, the law of Northern Ireland governs the validity of the settlement constituted by this Will, and its construction, effects and administration. The Courts of Northern Ireland have exclusive jurisdiction in any proceedings involving rights or obligations under that settlement.

Signed by [*name of testator*] to give effect to this Will,

in the presence of two witnesses present at the same time,

who have each signed this Will in the presence of the Testator.

[*Signature of Testator*]

Date

1st Witness

Address

2nd Witness

Address

Will 7
Nil rate band discretionary trust; residue to partner (not spouse) absolutely

Note: This precedent is intended for an unmarried testator. Where, after deduction of the nil rate band, there remains a substantial residue, it would generally be better to provide that the entire residue should be held on discretionary will trusts (form 1).

I, [*Name of testator*] of [*address*] declare this to be my last Will.

1

I revoke all my earlier testamentary dispositions.

2 Appointment of Executors

I appoint:
2.1 [*Name*] of [*address*] and
2.2 [*Name*] of [*address*]
to be my executors and Trustees.

[*Other legacies, appointment of guardians, etc, follow here.*]

3 Definitions

In this Will:
3.1
3.1.1 **'The Nil Rate Sum'** means A-B where:

3.1.1.1 A is the upper limit in Schedule 1 Inheritance Tax Act 1984 applicable to the chargeable transfer made on my death; and

3.1.1.2 B is the aggregate of the values transferred by any chargeable transfers made by me in the period of seven years ending with the day of my death, disregarding transfers made on that day;

but subject to the following clauses.

3.1.2 The Nil Rate Sum shall be nil if:

3.1.2.1 Inheritance Tax has been abolished at the time of my death; or

3.1.2.2 The amount of the Nil Rate Sum would otherwise be less than £5,000.

3.1.3 Any other legacy given by my will or any codicil shall be paid in priority to the Nil Rate Sum.

3.2 **'The Nil Rate Fund'** means:

3.2.1 the Nil Rate Sum; and

3.2.2 all property from time to time representing the above.

3.3 **'Trust Property'** means any part of the Nil Rate Fund.

3.4 **'The Trustees'** means my executors or the trustees for the time being.

3.5 **'The Trust Period'** means the period of 80 years beginning with the date of my death. That is the perpetuity period applicable to this Will Trust under the rule against perpetuities.

3.6 **"My Partner"** means [*specify name of partner*].

3.7 **'The Beneficiaries'** means:

3.7.1 My children and descendants.

3.7.2 The spouses, widows and widowers (whether or not remarried) of paragraph .1 of this sub-clause.

3.7.3 My Partner.

3.7.4 Any Person or class of Persons nominated to the Trustees by two Beneficiaries and whose nomination is accepted in writing by the Trustees.

3.7.5 [*Any favoured charity*].

3.7.6 At any time during which there are no Beneficiaries within paragraph .1 of this sub-clause:

3.7.6.1 [*specify 'fall back' beneficiaries if desired, eg nieces and nephews and their families*]

3.7.6.2 [*any company, body or trust established for charitable purposes only*].

3.8 **'Person'** includes a person anywhere in the world and includes a Trustee.

4 Nil Rate Fund

Subject to the Overriding Powers below:

4.1 The Trustees may accumulate the whole or any part of the income of the Nil Rate Fund during the Trust Period. That income shall be added to the Nil Rate Fund.

4.2 Subject to that, during the Trust Period, the Trustees shall pay or apply the income of the Nil Rate Fund to or for the benefit of any of the Beneficiaries as the Trustees think fit.

4.3 Subject to that, the Nil Rate Fund shall be held on trust for [*my son Adam – or define the default beneficiary as appropriate*] absolutely.

5 Overriding Powers

The Trustees shall have the following powers ('Overriding Powers'):

5.1 Power of appointment

5.1.1 The Trustees may appoint that they shall hold any Trust Property for the benefit of any Beneficiaries, on such terms as the Trustees think fit.

5.1.2 An appointment may create any provisions and in particular:

5.1.2.1 discretionary trusts;

5.1.2.2 dispositive or administrative powers;

exercisable by any Person.

5.1.3 An appointment shall be made by deed and may be revocable or irrevocable.

5.2 Transfer of Trust Property to other settlement

5.2.1 The Trustees may by deed declare that they hold any Trust Property on trust to transfer it to trustees of another settlement, wherever established, to hold on the terms of that settlement, freed and released from the terms of this Settlement.

5.2.2 The Trustees shall only exercise this power if:

5.2.2.1 every Person who may benefit is (or would if living be) a Beneficiary; or

5.2.2.2 with the consent in writing of two Beneficiaries.

5.3 Power of advancement

The Trustees may pay or apply any Trust Property for the advancement or benefit of any Beneficiary.

5.4 The Overriding Powers shall be exercisable only

5.4.1 during the Trust Period; and

5.4.2 at a time when there are at least two Trustees, or the Trustee is a company carrying on a business which consists of or includes the management of trusts, or when the power to appoint additional Trustees cannot be exercised.

6 Residuary Estate

My Executors shall:

6.1 pay my debts, funeral and testamentary expenses and Inheritance Tax on all property which vests in them; and

6.2 hold the remainder on trust for my Partner absolutely. [*It may be desired to provide for a simple gift over if the Partner does not survive.*]

6.3 Debts, funeral and testamentary expenses, legacies and inheritance tax shall be payable out of the capital of my estate (subject to the Trustees' administrative powers relating to capital and income).

7 Standard Provisions

The standard provisions of the Society of Trust and Estate Practitioners (Northern Ireland 1st Edition) shall apply.

[*Alternatively say: 'The provisions set out in the Schedule below shall have effect' and set out the provisions in full in the schedule. The CD with this book has the form.*]

8 Additional Provisions relating to Nil Rate Fund

8.1 In this clause **'The Nil Rate Trustees'** means the trustees of the Nil Rate Fund.

Surviving Partner may undertake to pay nil rate sum personally

8.2

8.2.1 My executors may require the Nil Rate Trustees to accept a written undertaking from my Partner as a personal obligation binding on my Partner.

8.2.2 That undertaking shall be to pay the Nil Rate Sum or, if less, the value of my residuary estate at the time of the undertaking on demand to the Nil Rate Trustees. The undertaking may include any other terms and in particular:

8.2.2.1 fixed or floating security;

8.2.2.2 interest;

8.2.2.3 index linking the sum payable.

8.2.3 That undertaking will be in substitution for payment of the Nil Rate Sum by the executors to the Nil Rate Trustees. My executors shall be under no further liability in relation to the Nil Rate Sum.

Executors may charge residuary estate instead of paying Nil Rate Sum directly

8.3

8.3.1 My executors may charge all or part of my Residuary Estate with the payment of the Nil Rate Sum on demand of the Nil Rate Trustees.

8.3.2 That charge may be a fixed or floating charge. It may include any other terms and in particular:

8.3.2.1 interest;

8.3.2.2 index linking the sum payable.

8.3.3 To the extent of the value at my death of the property charged:

8.3.3.1 the charge will be in substitution for payment of the Nil Rate Sum by the executors to the Nil Rate Trustees; and

8.3.3.2 my executors shall be under no further liability in relation to the Nil Rate Sum.

8.3.4 My executors may transfer the property charged to my Partner who shall not thereby become personally liable for the sum charged.

Nil Rate Sum may be left outstanding

8.4 The Nil Rate Trustees may refrain from calling in the Nil Rate Sum (or exercising any rights in relation to the Nil Rate Sum) for as long as they think fit. They may waive the payment of any income or capital due in respect of the Nil Rate Sum. They shall not be liable if my Partner becomes unable to make any payment or if a security becomes inadequate or for any other loss which may occur through exercising any power given by this clause.

8.5 The powers given by this clause are exercisable even though my executors and the Nil Rate Trustees are the same persons.

8.6 My Partner shall not be the sole Nil Rate Trustee.

8.7 The provisions of this clause shall not be exercisable so as to give any Person an interest in possession in the Nil Rate Fund.

9 Governing Law

This Will takes effect in accordance with the law of Northern Ireland. In particular, the law of Northern Ireland governs the validity of the settlement constituted by this Will, and its construction, effects and administration. The Courts of Northern Ireland have exclusive jurisdiction in any proceedings involving rights or obligations under that Settlement.

Signed by [*name of testator*] to give effect to this Will,

in the presence of two witnesses present at the same time,

who have each signed this Will in the presence of the Testator.

[*Signature of Testator*]

Date

1st Witness

Address

2nd Witness

Address

Precedents for Administrative Provisions

Precedents for Administrative Provisions

The following material is the basis for the schedule of administrative provisions when the STEP Standard Provisions are not used.

1 Additional powers

The Trustees have the following additional powers:

1.1 Investment

1.1.1 The Trustees may make any kind of investment that they could make if they were absolutely entitled to the Trust Fund. In particular the Trustees may invest in unsecured loans.

1.1.2 The Trustees are under no obligation to diversify the Trust Fund.

1.1.3 The Trustees may invest in speculative or hazardous investments but this power may only be exercised at the time when there are at least two Trustees, or the Trustee is a company carrying on a business which consists of or includes the management of trusts.

1.2 Joint property

The Trustees may acquire property jointly with any Person and may blend Trust Property with other property.

1.3 General power of management and disposition

The Trustees may effect any transaction relating to the management or disposition of Trust Property as if they were absolutely entitled to it.

1.4 Repair

The Trustees may repair and maintain Trust Property.

1.5 Improvement

The Trustees may develop or improve Trust Property in any way. None of the restrictions contained in sections 25–29 of the Settled Land Act 1882 or sections 13–15 of the Settled Land Act 1890 shall apply.

1.6 Income and capital

1.6.1 The Trustees may acquire:
  1.6.1.1 wasting assets and
  1.6.1.2 assets which yield little or no income
  for investment or any other purpose.

1.6.2 The Trustees are under no duty to procure distributions from a company in which they are interested.

1.6.3 The Trustees may pay taxes and other expenses out of income although they would otherwise be paid out of capital.

1.6.4 Generally, the Trustees are under no duty to hold a balance between conflicting interests of Beneficiaries.

1.6.5 The Trustees may (subject to the jurisdiction of the Court) determine whether receipts and liabilities are to be considered as capital or income, and whether expenses ought to be paid out of capital or income. The Trustees shall not be liable for any act done in pursuance of such determination (in the absence of fraud or negligence) even though it shall subsequently be held to have been wrongly made.

1.6.6 Income may be set aside and invested to answer any liabilities which in the opinion of the Trustees ought to be borne out of income or to meet depreciation of the capital value of any Trust Property. In particular, income may be applied for a leasehold sinking fund policy.

1.7 Application of trust capital as income

The Trustees may apply Trust Property as if it were income arising in the current year. In particular, the Trustees may pay such income to an Income Beneficiary as his income, for the purpose of augmenting his income.

[*Variant for lifetime Discretionary Settlement*

The above administrative provisions are suitable for any type of settlement. In a lifetime discretionary settlement they could be simplified by the following changes:
Clauses 1.6 and 1.7; the phrase 'income beneficiary' could be replaced by 'Beneficiary' and the definition of 'income beneficiary' may be deleted.

In a will creating a discretionary trust the same amendment could be made, but the authors would be inclined to retain the text unaltered.]

'Income Beneficiary' here means a Person to whom income of the Property is payable (as of right or at the discretion of the Trustees).

1.8 Use of trust property

1.8.1 The Trustees may acquire any interest in property anywhere in the world for occupation or use by an Income Beneficiary.

1.8.2 The Trustees may permit an Income Beneficiary to occupy or enjoy the use of Trust Property on such terms as they think fit.

1.8.3 The Trustees may lend trust money to an Income Beneficiary. The loan may be interest free and unsecured, or on such terms as the Trustees think fit. The Trustees may charge Trust Property as security for any debts or obligations of an Income Beneficiary.

1.8.4 **'Income Beneficiary'** here means a Person to whom income of the Property is payable (as of right or at the discretion of the Trustees).

[*For discretionary settlements, see cl 1.8 above.*]

1.9 Trade

The Trustees may carry on a trade, in any part of the world, alone or in partnership.

1.10 Borrowing

The Trustees may borrow money for investment or any other purpose. Money borrowed shall be treated as Trust Property.

1.11 Delegation

A Trustee or the Trustees jointly (or other Person in a fiduciary position) may authorise any person to exercise all or any functions on such terms as to remuneration and other matters as they think fit. A Trustee (or other Person in a fiduciary capacity) shall not be responsible for the default of that Person (even if the delegation was not strictly necessary or convenient) provided he took reasonable care in his selection and supervision. None of the restrictions on delegation in sections 12 to 15 Trustee Act (Northern Ireland) 2001 shall apply.

1.12 Nominees and custodians

1.12.1 The Trustees may appoint a person to act as their nominee in relation to such of the assets of the trust as they may determine. They may take such steps as are necessary to secure that those assets are vested in the nominee.

1.12.2 The Trustees may appoint a person to act as custodian in relation to such of the assets of the trust as they may determine. The Trustees may give the custodian custody of the assets and any documents or records concerning the assets. The Trustees are not obliged to appoint a custodian of securities payable to bearer.

1.12.3 The Trustees may appoint a person to act as nominee or custodian on such terms as to remuneration and other matters as they may think fit.

1.13 Offshore administration

The Trustees may carry on the administration of this Settlement anywhere they think fit.

1.14 Indemnities

The Trustees may indemnify any Person for any liability relating to the Settlement.

1.15 Security

The Trustees may mortgage or charge Trust Property as security for any liability incurred by them as Trustees (and may grant a floating charge so far as the law allows).

1.16 Supervision of company

The Trustees are under no duty to enquire into the conduct of a company in which they are interested, unless they have knowledge of circumstances which call for inquiry.

1.17 Appropriation

The Trustees may appropriate Trust Property to any Person or class of Persons in or towards the satisfaction of their interest in the Trust Fund.

1.18 Receipt by charities

Where Trust Property is to be paid or transferred to a charity, the receipt of the treasurer or appropriate officer of the charity shall be a complete discharge to the Trustees.

1.19 Release of powers

The Trustees (or other persons in a fiduciary position) may by deed release wholly or in part any of their rights or functions and (if applicable) so as to bind their successors.

1.20 Ancillary powers

The Trustees may do anything which is incidental or conducive to the exercise of their functions.

[*Variant for Discretionary Settlement*

In a discretionary settlement the trustees could be given the following additional powers: to be inserted at the end of clause 1, ie after clause 1.19:

1.20 Waiver

The Trustees may waive the payment of income before it becomes due.

1.21 Insurance Policies

The Trustees may pay premiums of any insurance policy out of income.]

2 Trust for Sale

The Trustees shall hold land on trust for sale with power to postpone the sale.

3 Minors

3.1 Where the Trustees may apply income for the benefit of a minor, they may do so by paying the income to the minor's parent or guardian on behalf of the minor, or to the minor if he has attained the age of 16. The Trustees are under no duty to inquire into the use of the income unless they have knowledge of circumstances which call for inquiry.

3.2 Where the Trustees may apply income for the benefit of a minor, they may do so by resolving that they hold that income on trust for the minor absolutely and:

- 3.2.1 The Trustees may apply that income for the benefit of the minor during his minority.
- 3.2.2 The Trustees shall transfer the residue of that income to the minor on attaining the age of 18.
- 3.2.3 For investment and other administrative purposes that income shall be treated as Trust Property.

4 Mentally handicapped beneficiary

Where income or capital is payable to a Beneficiary who does not have the mental capacity to appoint an attorney with an enduring general power, the Trustees may (subject to the directions of the Court or his Controller) apply that income or capital for his benefit.

5 Disclaimer

A Person may disclaim his interest in this Settlement wholly or in part.

6 Apportionment

Income and expenditure shall be treated as arising when payable, and not from day to day, so that no apportionment shall take place.

7 Conflicts of interest

7.1 In this paragraph:

7.1.1 **'A Fiduciary'** means a Person subject to fiduciary duties under the Settlement.

7.1.2 **'An Independent Trustee'**, in relation to a Person, means a Trustee who is not:

7.1.2.1 a brother, sister, ancestor, descendant or dependent of the Person;

7.1.2.2 a spouse of paragraph .1.2.1 above, or a spouse of the Person;

7.1.2.3 a company controlled by one or more of any of the above.

7.2 Subject to subparagraph .3 below a Fiduciary may:

7.2.1 enter into a transaction with the Trustees, or

7.2.2 be interested in an arrangement in which the Trustees are or might have been interested, or

7.2.3 act (or not act) in any other circumstances;

even though his fiduciary duty under the Settlement conflicts with other duties or with his personal interest;

7.3 Subparagraph .2 above only has effect if:

7.3.1 the Fiduciary first discloses to the Trustees the nature and extent of any material interest conflicting with his fiduciary duties, and

7.3.2 there is an Independent Trustee in respect of whom there is no conflict of interest, and he considers that the transaction arrangement or action is not contrary to the general interest of the Settlement.

7.4 The powers of the Trustees may be used to benefit a Trustee (to the same extent as if he were not a Trustee) provided that there is an Independent Trustee in respect of whom there is no conflict of interest.

8 Absolute discretion clause

8.1 The Powers of the Trustees may be exercised:

8.1.1 at their absolute discretion; and

8.1.2 from time to time as occasion requires.

8.2 The Trustees are not under any duty to consult with any Beneficiaries or to give effect to the wishes of any Beneficiaries.

9 Trustee remuneration

9.1 A Trustee acting in a professional capacity is entitled to receive reasonable remuneration out of the Trust Fund for any services that he provides to or on behalf of the Trust.

[*In the case of a will, add: 'in connection with my will or'.*]

9.2 For this purpose, a Trustee acts in a professional capacity if he acts in the course of a profession or business which consists of or includes the provision of services in connection with:

9.2.1 the management or administration of trusts generally or a particular kind of trust, or

9.2.2 any particular aspect of the management or administration of trusts generally or a particular kind of trust.

9.3 The Trustees may make arrangements to remunerate themselves for work done for a company connected with the Trust Fund.

10 Commissions and bank charges

10.1 A Person may retain any reasonable commission or profit in respect of any transaction relating to this Settlement even though that commission or profit was procured by an exercise of fiduciary powers (by that Person or some other Person) provided that:

10.1.1 The Person would in the normal course of business receive and retain the commission or profit on such transaction.

10.1.2 The receipt of the commission or profit shall be disclosed to the Trustees.

10.2 A bank may make loans to the Trustees and generally provide banking services upon its usual terms and shall not be liable to account for any profit so made even though the receipt of such profit was procured by an exercise of fiduciary powers (by the bank or some other Person).

11 Liability of trustees

11.1 The duty of reasonable care (set out in s 1, Trustee Act (Northern Ireland) 2001) applies to all the functions of the Trustees.

11.2 A Trustee shall not be liable for a loss to the Trust Fund unless that loss was caused by his own fraud or negligence.

11.3 A Trustee shall not be liable for acting in accordance with the advice of Counsel, of at least ten years' standing, with respect to the settlement. The Trustees may in particular conduct legal proceedings in accordance with such advice without obtaining a Court Order. A Trustee may recover from the Trust Fund any expenses where he has acted in accordance with such advice.

11.4 The above sub-paragraph does not apply:

11.4.1 if the Trustee knows or has reasonable cause to suspect that the advice was given in ignorance of material facts;

11.4.2 if proceedings are pending to obtain the decision of the court on the matter;

11.4.3 in relation to a Trustee who has a personal interest in the subject matter of the advice; or

11.4.4 in relation to a Trustee who has committed a breach of trust relating to the subject matter of the advice.

11.5 The Trustees may distribute Trust Property or income in accordance with this Settlement but without having ascertained that there is no Person who is or may be entitled to any interest therein by virtue of any illegitimate relationship. The Trustees shall not be liable to such a Person unless they have notice of his claim at the time of the distribution.

11.6 This paragraph does not prejudice any right of any Person to follow property or income into the hands of any Person, other than a purchaser, who may have received it.

12 Appointment and retirement of trustees

12.1 A Person may be appointed Trustee of the Settlement even though he has no connection with the United Kingdom.

12.2 A Trustee who has reached the age of 65 shall retire if:

12.2.1 he is requested to do so by his co-trustees, or by a Person interested in Trust Property; and

12.2.2 he is effectually indemnified against liabilities properly incurred as Trustee.

On that retirement a new Trustee shall be appointed if necessary to ensure that there will be at least two Trustees. This sub-paragraph does not apply to a Trustee who is the Settlor or the spouse or widow of the Settlor.

12.3 A Trustee may be discharged even though there is neither a trust corporation nor two Persons to act as trustees provided that there remains at least one trustee.

13 Governing law

This will takes effect in accordance with the law of Northern Ireland. In particular, the law of Northern Ireland governs the validity of the settlement constituted by this will, and its construction, effects and administration. The Courts of Northern Ireland have exclusive jurisdiction in any proceedings involving rights or obligations under that settlement.

13 Interest in possession and accumulation and maintenance protection clause

The provisions of this schedule shall not have effect:

13.1 so as to prevent a Person from being entitled to an interest in possession in Trust Property (within the meaning of the Inheritance Tax Act 1984);

13.2 so as to prevent the conditions of section 71(1) of the Inheritance Tax Act 1984 from applying to Trust Property.

[*The standard form may be used without alteration for the interest in possession settlement, and in the interests of standardisation it may be easiest to leave it as it is. However, it would be appropriate to delete 12.2; and alter the title to read: 'interest in possession protection clause'.*

This clause can be deleted for a discretionary settlement.

In a will trust the authors would be inclined to retain the text unaltered.]

Appendices

Standard Provisions of the Society of Trust and Estate Practitioners (Northern Ireland version)

Note: At the time of going to print the conditions have not been finalised but it is hoped that they will be final by the date of publication. For current details, see www.kessler.co.uk.

1. INTRODUCTORY

1(1) These Provisions may be called the standard provisions of the Society of Trust and Estate Practitioners (Northern Ireland version, 1st Edition).

1(2) These Provisions may be incorporated in a document by the words:-

The standard provisions of the Society of Trust and Estate Practitioners (Northern Ireland version, 1st Edition) shall apply

or in any manner indicating an intention to incorporate them.

2. INTERPRETATION

2(1) In these Provisions, unless the context otherwise requires:

(a) **'Income Beneficiary'**, in relation to Trust Property, means a Person to whom income of the Trust Property is payable (as of right or at the discretion of the Trustees).

(b) **'Person'** includes a person anywhere in the world and includes a Trustee.

(c) **'The Principal Document'** means the document in which these Provisions are incorporated.

(d) **'The Settlement'** means any settlement created by the Principal Document and an estate of a deceased Person to which the Principal Document relates.

(e) **'The Trustees'** means the personal representatives or trustees of the Settlement for the time being.

(f) **'The Trust Fund'** means the property comprised in the Settlement for the time being.
(g) **'Trust Property'** means any property comprised in the Trust Fund.
(h) **'A Professional Trustee'** means a Trustee who is or has been carrying on a business which consists of or includes the management of trusts or the administration of estates.

2(2) These Provisions have effect subject to the provisions of the Principal Document.

3. ADMINISTRATIVE POWERS

The Trustees shall have the following powers:

3(1) Investment
(a) The Trustees may invest Trust Property in any manner as if they were beneficial owners. In particular the Trustees may invest in unsecured loans.
(b) The Trustees may decide not to diversify the Trust Fund.

3(2) Management
The Trustees may effect any transaction relating to the management administration or disposition of Trust Property as if they were beneficial owners. In particular:
(a) The Trustees may repair and maintain Trust Property.
(b) The Trustees may develop or improve Trust Property.

3(3) Joint property
The Trustees may acquire property jointly with any Person.

3(4) Income and capital
The Trustees may pay taxes and other expenses out of income although they would otherwise be paid out of capital.

3(5) Accumulated income
The Trustees may apply accumulated income as if it were income arising in the current year.

3(6) Use of trust property
The Trustees may permit an Income Beneficiary to occupy or enjoy the use of Trust Property on such terms as they think fit. The Trustees may acquire any property for this purpose.

3(7) Application of trust capital
The Trustees may:
(a) lend money which is Trust Property to an Income Beneficiary without security, on such terms as they think fit,
(b) charge Trust Property as security for debts or obligations of an Income Beneficiary, or
(c) pay money which is Trust Property to an Income Beneficiary as his income, for the purpose of augmenting his income

provided that:
(i) the Trustees have power to transfer such Property to that Beneficiary absolutely; or

(ii) the Trustees have power to do so with the consent of another Person and the Trustees act with the written consent of that Person.

3(8) Trade

The Trustees may carry on a trade, in any part of the world, alone or in partnership.

3(9) Borrowing

The Trustees may borrow money for investment or any other purpose. Money borrowed shall be treated as Trust Property.

3(10) Delegation

A Trustee may delegate in writing any of his functions to any Person. A Trustee shall not be responsible for the default of that Person (even if the delegation was not strictly necessary or expedient) provided that he took reasonable care in his selection and supervision.

3(11) Deposit of documents

The Trustees may deposit documents relating to the Settlement (including bearer securities) with any Person.

3(12) Nominees

The Trustees may vest Trust Property in any Person as nominee, and may place Trust Property in the possession or control of any Person.

3(13) Offshore administration

The Trustees may carry on the administration of the trusts of the Settlement outside the United Kingdom.

3(14) Payment of tax

The Trustees may pay tax liabilities of the Settlement (and interest on such tax) even though such liabilities are not enforceable against the Trustees.

3(15) Indemnities

The Trustees may indemnify any Person for any liability properly chargeable against Trust Property.

3(16) Security

The Trustees may charge Trust Property as security for any liability properly incurred by them as Trustees.

3(17) Supervision of company

The Trustees are under no duty to enquire into the conduct of a company in which they are interested, unless they have knowledge of circumstances which call for enquiry.

3(18) Appropriation

The Trustees may appropriate Trust Property to any Person or class of Persons in or towards the satisfaction of their interest in the Trust Fund.

3(19) Receipt by charities

Where Trust Property is to be paid or transferred to a charity, the receipt of the treasurer or appropriate officer of the charity shall be a complete discharge to the Trustees.

3(20) Release of powers

The Trustees may by deed release any of their powers wholly or in part so as to bind future trustees.

3(21) Ancillary powers

The Trustees may do anything which is incidental or conducive to the exercise of their functions.

4. POWERS OF MAINTENANCE AND ADVANCEMENT

Sections 32 and 33 Trustee Act (Northern Ireland) 1958 shall apply with the following modifications:
(1) Section 32(2) shall be deleted.
(2) The words 'one-half' of in section 33(1)(a) shall be deleted.

5. TRUST FOR SALE

The Trustees shall hold land on trust for sale with power to postpone the sale.

6. MINORS

6(1) Where the Trustees may apply income for the benefit of a minor, they may do so by paying the income to the minor's parent or guardian on behalf of the minor, or to the minor if he has attained the age of 16. The Trustees are under no duty to enquire into the use of the income unless they have knowledge of circumstances which call for enquiry.

6(2) Where the Trustees may apply income for the benefit of a minor, they may do so by resolving that they hold that income on trust for the minor absolutely and:
- (a) The Trustees may apply that income for the benefit of the minor during his minority.
- (b) The Trustees shall transfer the residue of that income to the minor on attaining the age of 18.
- (c) For investment and other administrative purposes that income shall be treated as Trust Property.

7. DISCLAIMER

A Person may disclaim his interest under the Settlement wholly or in part.

8. APPORTIONMENT

Income and expenditure shall be treated as arising when payable, and not from day to day, so that no apportionment shall take place.

9. CONFLICTS OF INTEREST

9(1) In this paragraph:
- (a) **A Fiduciary** means a Person subject to fiduciary duties under the Settlement.
- (b) **An Independent Trustee,** in relation to a Person, means a Trustee who is not:

(i) a brother, sister, ancestor, descendant or dependent of the Person;
(ii) a spouse of the Person or of (i) above; or
(iii) a company controlled by one or more of any of the above.

9(2) A Fiduciary may:
(a) enter into a transaction with the Trustees, or
(b) be interested in an arrangement in which the Trustees are or might have been interested, or
(c) act (or not act) in any other circumstances

even though his fiduciary duty under the Settlement conflicts with other duties or with his personal interest;

Provided that:
(i) The Fiduciary first discloses to the Trustees the nature and extent of any material interest conflicting with his fiduciary duties, and
(ii) there is an Independent Trustee in respect of whom there is no conflict of interest, and he considers that the transaction arrangement or action is not contrary to the general interest of the Settlement.

9(3) The powers of the Trustees may be used to benefit a Trustee (to the same extent as if he were not a Trustee) provided that there is an Independent Trustee in respect of whom there is no conflict of interest.

10. POWERS OF TRUSTEES

The powers of the Trustees may be exercised:
(1) at their absolute discretion; and
(2) from time to time as occasion requires.

11. TRUSTEE REMUNERATION

11(1) A Trustee who is a solicitor or an accountant or who is engaged in a business may charge for work done by him or his firm in connection with the Settlement, including work not requiring professional assistance. This has priority to any disposition made in the Principal Document.

11(2) The Trustees may make arrangements to remunerate themselves for work done for a company connected with the Trust Fund.

12. LIABILITY OF TRUSTEES

12(1) A Trustee (other than a Professional Trustee) shall not be liable for a loss to the Trust Fund unless that loss was caused by his own fraud or negligence.

12(2) A Trustee shall not be liable for acting in accordance with the advice of Counsel of at least five years standing, with respect to the Settlement, unless, when he does so:
(a) he knows or has reasonable cause to suspect that the advice was given in ignorance of material facts; or

(b) proceedings are pending to obtain the decision of the court on the matter.

13. APPOINTMENT AND RETIREMENT OF TRUSTEES

13(1) A Person may be appointed trustee of the Settlement even though he has no connection with the United Kingdom.

13(2) A Professional Trustee who is an individual who has reached the age of 65 shall retire if:

(a) he is requested to do so by his co-trustees, or by a Person interested in Trust Property; and

(b) he is effectually indemnified against liabilities properly incurred as Trustee.

On that retirement a new Trustee shall be appointed if necessary to ensure that there will be two individuals or a Trust Corporation to act as Trustee. In this sub-paragraph Trust Corporation has the same meaning as in article 9 of the Administration of Estates (Northern Ireland) Order 1979.

This sub-paragraph does not apply to a Professional Trustee who is:

(a) a personal representative;

(b) the settlor of the Settlement; or

(c) a spouse or former spouse of the settlor or testator.

14. GOVERNING LAW

This Will takes effect in accordance with the law of Northern Ireland. In particular the law of Northern Ireland governs the validity of the settlement constituted by this Will, and its construction, effects and administration. The Courts of Northern Ireland have exclusive jurisdiction in any proceedings involving rights or obligations under that settlement.

15. PROTECTION FOR INTEREST IN POSSESSION AND ACCUMULATION AND MAINTENANCE SETTLEMENTS

These Provisions shall not have effect:

(a) so as to prevent a Person from being entitled to an interest in possession in Trust Property (within the meaning of the Inheritance Tax Act 1984);

(b) so as to prevent the conditions of section 71(1) Inheritance Tax Act 1984 from applying to Trust Property.

COMMENTARY ON THE STANDARD PROVISIONS[1]

How should the standard provisions be incorporated?

It would be possible to set the provisions out at length. However, the better course is to use a short form:

> **Standard provisions**
>
> The standard provisions of the Society of Trust and Estate Practitioners (Northern Ireland version, 1st Ed.) shall apply.

The Northern Ireland Standard Provisions (unlike the first edition of the English provisions) have been amended to take account of the TA(NI) 2001.

The substantive changes from the English provisions are as follows:

(1) the equivalent statutory provisions have been substituted in Clause 4 (Powers of Maintenance and Advancement);
(2) the Trust for Sale (Clause 5) has been retained – it is standard practice to delete this in England because it is unnecessary following the enactment of the TLATA 1996;
(3) the definition of Trust Corporation has been amended;
(4) the discretion not to hold a fair balance between income and capital has been removed, following comments that this was a wider power than some testators may want. (This will need to be inserted expressly if desired);
(5) there is an express choice of law clause.

When should the standard provisions be used?

The standard provisions are suitable for inclusion in any normal will or settlement.

In the case of a simple will, some of the provisions may be unnecessary. The drafter is recommended to incorporate the provisions by the short form. To pick and choose among the provisions loses many of the advantages of a standard form. It is a waste of professional time; and runs the risk of accidental omissions.

Are the standard provisions comprehensive?

The standard provisions form a comprehensive code of administrative provisions, and in the view of STEP it is not necessary to amend them.

[1] This commentary does not form part of the standard provisions.

What should one tell the client?

Many clients would probably not want a detailed explanation of the standard provisions. They would only wish to know that 'This is a standard way of providing the executors with a number of technical and routine provisions they need to administer the estate properly'.

Obtaining probate of a will including the standard provisions

A will including the STEP provisions is to be proved in the usual way. It is not necessary to prove the text of the provisions, or to refer to the provisions in the oath.

Duplication of the provisions

Practitioners may duplicate the standard provisions in any way. (Publishers should contact STEP for a formal licence agreement.)

APPENDIX 2

Annotated bibliography

General precedent works

Encyclopedia of Forms & Precedents LexisNexis UK covers a broad range of precedents, but includes detailed coverage of trusts and will trusts.

There are three heavy reference works which are now out-of-date. *Hallett's Conveyancing Precedents* (1965) Sweet & Maxwell, was used in its day for many discretionary trusts which still exist. *Key and Elphinstone's Precedents in Conveyancing* (15th edn, 1953) Sweet & Maxwell, and *Prideaux Precedents in Conveyancing* (25th edn, 1958) Stevens, are still useful if one wishes to search for old authorities.

Looseleaf trust precedents

Looseleaf is in the authors' view an unsuitable format for trust precedents,[1] but the following may be noted:

Potter & Monroe *Tax Planning* (Sweet & Maxwell). Principally a work of tax planning of a very high order, but also includes precedents.

Practical Trust Precedents (Longman).

Precedents for the Conveyancer (Sweet & Maxwell).

Will precedents

Among many are:

DT Davies *Will Precedents and Inheritance Tax* (4th ed, 1991) LexisNexis UK.

Wills, Probate & Administration Service (looseleaf) LexisNexis UK.

Parker's Modern Will Precedents (3rd edn, 1996) LexisNexis UK.

1 An abbreviated dyslogy. A user who wants to find what was said about a precedent he has used will in due course find the relevant looseleaf pages have been discarded. Trust precedent books need to remain available for later reference. Looseleaf books impose an immoderate burden on the author and an undue administrative burden in the office. They are expensive. One cannot comfortably open looseleaf works in the armchair. The CD-ROM will ultimately replace them.

Style

Legal drafting is by no means insulated from the broader issues of prose composition. Anyone interested in understanding our subject in this context should read first of all George Orwell's magnificent ground-breaking essay, 'Politics and the English Language' (1946; included in Penguin's *Essays of George Orwell*). Its influence on current thinking – eg, the Clinton Memorandum on plain English[2] – is readily apparent.

The movement for plain legal English is an international one, and legal drafting in England is also subject to international trends. The rewrite of tax legislation here was preceded by Australian and New Zealand rewrites. Appendix 3 offers some US and Canadian references.

There is good guidance to be found in Garner *A Dictionary of Modern Legal Usage* (2nd edn, 1995) OUP. This is on the model of *Fowler's Modern English Usage* addressed to legal drafting and legal writing generally and well worth having on the bookshelf.

Mellinkoff *The Language of the Law* (1963) Little, Brown & Co, is an excellent scholarly and historical study, also useful on the usage of particular words.

Drafting techniques

There are many books devoted to legal drafting in general. They are of limited practical use because most of a drafter's time is spent not with generalities, but with the specific rules of law affecting the subject matter of the draft. The interested reader is recommended to begin with Piesse *The Elements of Drafting* (9th edn, 1995) The Law Book Co. This is short and has a good bibliography.

General principles of construction

Trust law textbooks scarcely deal with construction, leaving the field to textbooks on wills which traditionally devote a short chapter to it. The condensed treatment tends to suggest a specious consistency of judicial attitude. Lord Denning *The Discipline of Law* (1st edn, 1979) LexisNexis UK (Part One, the Construction of Documents), good holiday reading, shows the opposite is the truth.

Hawkins on the Construction of Wills (5th edn, 2000) contains a fascinating chapter on general principles and does not fall into that trap. He is unusual in drawing into a legal textbook the philosophical distinction (used by Frege and later adopted

2 Accessible on www.kessler.co.uk.

by Russell and Wittgenstein) of *sense* and *reference*, which can be helpful.[3] Unfortunately this is spoilt by an over-emphasis on AJA 1982, s 21 (the English equivalent to WAP(NI)O 1994, art 25), which does not in our view represent 'a triumph of the intentional approach' (if it did, there would be a marked difference between wills and lifetime trusts, which has never been suggested).

The authors try first *Lewison's Interpretation of Contracts* (2nd edn, 1997) Sweet & Maxwell and are rarely disappointed.

Meaning of particular words and phrases

Hawkins and all the textbooks on wills offer chapters on gifts to classes of persons; words describing relationships; and the like. It is usually worth looking at more than one; each deals with aspects that the other does not. *Stroud's Judicial Dictionary* (6th edn, 2000) and Saunders *Words & Phrases Legally Defined* (3rd edn, 1988) might sometimes be useful.

Plain legal English guides

The movement for plain legal English has produced a considerable polemical literature.[4] This includes:

Mark Adler *Clarity for Lawyers* (1st edn, 1990) The Law Society.

Richard Windick *Plain English for Lawyers* (3rd edn, 1994) Carolina Academic Press.

Michele Asprey *Plain English for Lawyers* (2nd edn, 1996) Federation Press.

Peter Butt and Richard Castle *Modern Legal Drafting* (2001) CUP. This has an interesting chapter on the history of the Plain English movement.

3 Wilberforce J found the distinction (independently?) in *Fitch Lovell Ltd v IRC* [1962] 1 WLR 1325.

4 Those interested should join the worthwhile association 'Clarity', see www.adler.demon.co.uk/clarity.htm.

APPENDIX 3

Useful websites

UK sites

www.kessler.co.uk	James Kessler=s website. Includes free updates on the English version of this book and an archive of material referred to in this book. Please visit!
www.trustsdiscussionforum.co.uk	Includes an opportunity to subscribe to the Trusts Discussion Forum and archive of the Trusts Discussion Forum.
www.venables.co.uk	Delia Venables legal resources. Start here for UK legal links.
www.lawcom.gov.uk	The Law Commission website. Includes recent Law Commission reports including LC260 – Trustees= Powers and Duties and LC251 – The Rules Against Perpetuities and Excessive Accumulations.
www.charitycommission.gov.uk	The English Charity Commission=s website. The Register of Charities is online here, and this is useful for checking names and details of charities.
www.kcl.ac.uk/depsta/law/tlc	Trust Law Committee. Includes report on creditors of trustees and valuable consultation papers on capital/income, trustee exemption clauses and trustee indemnities.
www.jerseylegalinfo.je	Includes recent Jersey cases.

International sites

www.info.gov.hk/hkreform/lawlinks/contents.htm	Good starting point for non-UK legal links.

www.plainlanguage.gov	Website of the Plain Language Action Network. This is a US Government group working to improve communications from the federal government to the public. They believe better communications 'will increase trust in government, reduce government costs, and reduce the burden on the public'. Ambitious, but who is to say they are wrong? Take a look at their major guidance document *Writing User-Friendly Documents*.
www.nara.gov/fedred/ddhread.html	The (US) Federal Register=s *Document Drafting Handbook*.
www.ca-probate.com	Wills on the web. Includes *Will of an Extremely Distinguished Dog* (Eugene O'Neill) and actual wills of many celebrities and historical figures.
Http//home.att.net/~klearned/humor.htm	Legal jokes.

Index

[all references are to paragraph number]